USHER iBT TOEFL
INTERMEDIATE TEST
READING

(어셔 iBT 토플 인터미디어트 테스트 리딩)

어셔 어학 연구소

USHER iBT TOEFL INTERMEDIATE TEST
READING
어셔 iBT 토플 인터미디어트 테스트 리딩

초판 1쇄 발행 · 2016년 2월 1일
개정판 1쇄 발행 · 2018년 6월 1일
개정증보판 3쇄 발행 · 2024년 9월 1일

지은이 · 어셔 토플 연구소
펴낸곳 · (주) 어셔 어학 연구소
펴낸이 · 어셔 어학 연구소
주　소 · 서울시 서초구 반포대로 300 덕성빌딩 1층 어셔 어학연구소
전　화 · 02) 595-5679
홈페이지 · www.usher.co.kr
ISBN · 979-11-85317-07-6

정　가 · 24,000원

저작권자 · ⓒ2019, 어셔 어학연구소

이 책 및 mp3 내용의 저작권은 저자에게 있습니다.
서면에 의한 저자와 출판사의 허락없이 내용의 일부 혹은 전부를 인용하거나, 발췌하는 것을 금합니다.

COPYRIGHT© 2019 by Usher Language Research Institute
All rights reserved including the rights of reproduction In whole or part in any form Printed in Korea

PREFACE I

본 토플(TOEFL) 교재는 iBT토플을 공부하는 학생들의 다음과 같은 요청에서 제작 동기를 찾습니다.

☞ **급하게 토플(TOEFL)은 해야 하는데, 문제 유형조차 파악이 안 되는 경우**

- 토플 시험에 임박했는데, 토플 유형조차 파악이 안되었지만, 급하게 토플 유형파악 및 기초와 더불어 토플 실전 문제를 다뤄보고 싶은 학생들은 본 토플 교재의 문제지 부분만을 집중적으로 풀어보면 충분합니다.
- 총 **7회 분량**의 문제지가 들어 있으므로, 이 부분을 매일 1회씩 풀어보고, 문제에 대한 **유형과 난이도를 파악** 및 **시간 배분을** 연습한다면, **실전 시험 대비서**로서 확실한 몫을 담당해 줄 것입니다.

☞ **토플 기초일 경우,**

☞ **실제 토플 시험에 임박해서, 문제 풀이는 해야 하는데, 자세한 설명이 필요한 경우**

1. **기본적인 문장을 볼 줄 안다는 가정 하에** 본 토플 교재를 통해 부족한 부분을 채워 주시기 바랍니다.
2. 문제 풀이와 유형은 물론 **단어와 구문**부터 약하다면 지문의 모든 토플 **단어와 구문**을,
3. 문장의 **구조 파악**이 약하다면 **묶기** 부분을,
4. 문장의 단어, 구문, 문장 구조는 다 파악되지만 **매끄럽지 못하다면, 열 번 읽기**를 통해 확실한 마무리를 해 두시기 바랍니다.
   - 토플점수 올리는것은 실력 올리면 쉽게, 당연히 따라옵니다. 오랜 시간이 걸리는 일이 아닙니다. 확신을 갖고 열심히 해 주시기 바랍니다.

☞ **오답 패턴 정리가 필요한사람 / 위의 모든 것을 함과 더불어, 실전 iBT토플 경향 파악이 필요한 경우**

- 오답 패턴정리는 실상 시험문제 푸는데 별로 큰 어려움이 없습니다. 토플은 기본적으로 해석만 잘해도 기본점수 20점 이상은 나오고, 조금만 더 매끄럽다면 25점 확보는 기본으로 하고 들어가야 하는 시험입니다. 오답 패턴만을 생각 하시는 분들은, 문제 7회를 푼 뒤 각 설명 중에서 **답 근거와 문단 정리** 부분만을 확실히 해두신다면, 기본이 되는 오답 패턴 때문에 어려움을 느끼지는 않으시리라 생각합니다.

☞ **토플 독학해야 하는데, 문제유형뿐만 아니라, 자세한 문장 설명과 공부방법까지 필요한 경우**

☞ **토플 고득점을 위한 탄탄한 준비를 필요로 하는 경우**

- 토플 독학을 하는 분들, 토플 고득점을 위한 탄탄한 준비를 필요로 하는 분들도, 공부하는 과정 중에서 부족함이 느껴지신다면, 그 부분이 앞서 말한 부분 중 어디인지(1~4)를 우선 파악해주시고, 그리고 나서, 필요한 부분을 집중 정리 공략해 두시면, 큰 효용을 보실 수 있음을 확신합니다.

☞ **토플 고득점을 위한 토플 학원 추천 교재를 찾으시는 경우**

PREFACE II

학생들이 가장 많이 하는 질문을 서문에서 정리해 볼까 합니다.

질문 1 토플 시험 성적표를 보니, 독해, 듣기, 쓰기, 말하기 네 부분으로 되어 있던데 어떤 과목부터 해야 할까요?

유학생들의 현지에서의 학업을 위한 준비여부를 파악하기 위해 만들어진 시험인 토플에서의 독해부분은 수능 영어나, 비즈니스 영어인 토익 등과 비교해서 볼 때 어휘나, 문장의 복잡성 등이 아무래도 어려운 경향이 있습니다.

많은 학생들이 TOEFL LISTENING(토플 리스닝)을 먼저 걱정하곤 하는데, 이런 학생들에게 스크립트를 주고 문제를 풀어보라고 했을 때 파악되는 것은 결국 못 들어서가 아닌 기초적인 독해조차 안돼서 못하는 경우가 많습니다.

뿐만 아니라 TOEFL WRITING(토플 라이팅)에 대해서라면 무언가를 창작하고 싶다면 모방이 우선입니다. 글을 쓸 때도 마찬가지로 모방의 대상은 글을 읽는 것이기에 쓰기보다는 당연히 독해가 우선입니다.

나아가 천천히 생각하며 문장조차 만들어 내지 못하는 학생들이 짧은 순간 문장을 만드는 것은 물론 발음과 엑센트와 억양까지 신경 써 가며 해야 하는 TOEFL SPEAKING(토플 스피킹)은 더욱 더 설명하기 힘든 일입니다.

이런 점에서 이 iBT 토플 책을 보시는 여러분들은, 다음 순서를 꼭 기억해 주시기 바랍니다.

토플 단어암기 → 토플 문법 (문장보기) → 토플 독해 → 듣기, 쓰기, 말하기

혹시, 외국 생활이 먼저인 학생들은(중·고등학교 생활을 영어권 국가에서 한 학생들) 듣기, 쓰기, 말하기가 더 편할 수도 있을 것입니다. 하지만 만약 토플시험을 즉시 봐서 점수를 넘길 수 없는 학생이라면, 결국 외국 나가서 학교 다니며 기본 되는 영어실력을 충분히 쌓지 않아서 성적을 따지 못하는 경우라고 해도 틀린 말은 아닐 것입니다. 이런 경우 다른 과목에 비해서 귀찮은 토플 단어 암기와 독해, 특히 주로 문제로 나오는 어려운 문장을 보는 것에 취약할 것이고 이는 해외에서 살았었다는 이유만으로 어느 정도 해결되는 듣기나 말하기와는 달리 별도의 노력이 필요한 부분이므로 국내에서 새로이 공부하는 학생들과 크게 달라질 것 없이, 위의 순서대로 「토플 단어암기 → 토플 문법 (문장보기) → 토플 독해」 라는 순서는 따라야 할 것입니다.

이 토플 교재를 보시기 전의 여러분은 꼭 단어 암기는 기본으로 되어 있어야 하며 문장도 기본적인 틀은 잡혀있는 상태 이어야 할 것입니다. 꼭 이 순서를 기억해서 토플 공부를 해 주시기 바랍니다.

질문 2 문제 풀 때, 시간이 모자라요…….

TOEFL (토플) 시험 섹션 이름에서 알 수 있듯이, 토플 리딩과 리스닝은 정확히 (READING / LISTENING COMPREHENSION) 입니다. 묻고자 하는 것이 단순한 읽고 들을 수 있느냐 (READING / LISTENING) 가 아닌, 이해 (COMPREHENSION) 를 했느냐를 파악하는데 초점을 맞췄습니다.

단어와 문법이라는 기본이 닦여있다는 가정하에 독해력을 향상시키기 위해서는,
"빨리보다는 먼저 정확히" 에 초점을 맞춰 주시기 바랍니다. 점수는 이 두 가지가 잘되면 자연히 따라오게 됩니다. 많은 학생들이 얘기합니다. 시간이 모자라서 문제를 풀지 못한다고… 하지만, 이런 학생들에게 시간을 아무리 줘도 네 개의 선택지 중에서 두 개는 제끼더라도 결국 둘 중에 하나를 선택할 때는 여지없이 오답을 찍는 경우가 많습니다.

이유는 간단히 문장 해석이 정확히 되지 않으니 이런 어려움을 50년 동안 알고 있는 ETS가 낸 오답패턴을 결국 벗어나지 못해 답을 선택할 수 없는 것입니다.

그러므로 우선은 많은 문제를 풀지 못하더라도 푼 문제는 다 맞힌다는 생각으로 먼저 임해주시기 바랍니다. 만약 14문제 중 다 풀고도 시간이 모자라지 않지만 5문제 밖에 못 맞힌 학생과 시간이 없어 5문제 밖에 못 풀었지만 5문제를 다 맞힌 두 학생이 있다면 발전 가능성은 후자 쪽에 더 많습니다. 정확성을 키운 학생은 하던 방식대로 조금만 더 반복하면 시간은 자연히 줄지만 전자의 학생의 경우에는 실력 자체를 늘리는 일을 해야 하므로 문제 해결이 훨씬 어렵습니다.

그러므로, 꼭 「정확성 → 속도 → 그리고 토플 점수」를 기대하시기 바랍니다.

질문 3 본문 읽고, 문제 푸는 게 나을까요? vs 문제 풀며 본문을 읽는 게 나을까요?

두 방법 모두 장단점이 있습니다. 결론부터 실력을 기준으로 설명한다면, 대체로 전자는 실력이 있는 학생들이 푸는 방법이고, 후자는 실력이 약한 학생들이 쓰는 방법인 경우가 많습니다.

	본문 읽고 문제풀기	문제 풀며 본문 읽기(※44p 따라가며 풀기 참조)
실력 기준	실력있는 학생들이 할 수 있습니다.	실력이 약한 학생들이 점수를 내려 할 때 잘 쓰는 방법입니다.
장점	대체로 어려운 문제인 Summary, Infer, Purpose 를 잘 풀 수 있습니다.	대체로 쉬운 문제인 Fact 를 잘푸는 경향이 있습니다.
단점	덤벙대다 오히려 쉬운 문제인 Fact 문제를 잘 틀리는 경향이 있습니다.	실력이 되지 않아 어려운 문제인 Infer, Purpose, Summary 문제를 잘 풀지 못합니다.
보완 방법	문단정리 + 답근거 꼼꼼히 하는 연습을 많이 합니다.	문단정리 + 답근거 꼼꼼히 하는 것은 당연하고, 이러한 학생들의 문제는 실력이므로, 실력을 키워야 합니다. 많은 문제를 푸는 것보다 적은 지문이더라도 정확히 반복적으로 읽어서 읽는 실력 자체를 많이 늘릴 수 있도록 합니다.
공통점	* 외우지 않은 이상 단어 문제는 둘 다 어려울 수도, 쉬울 수도 있습니다. * 30점중 25점까지 맞는 것은 둘 다 할 수 있습니다. 하지만, 그 점수가 한계로 굳어지는 경향이 있습니다.	
결론	결국 25점을 넘어 30점으로 가기 위해서는 기초 실력 쌓는 것은 당연하고, 꼼꼼하게 풀어서 실수를 줄이는 것도 해야 하기에 두 가지를 합칠 수 있는 상황이 되어야 합니다. 즉, 문제를 다 풀고 5분 정도 남아서 미심쩍은 문제들은 다시 한 번 훑어볼 수 있도록 만들 수 있어야 합니다. (정확도 + 속도 둘 다 가질 것)	

토플은 어려운 시험이 아닙니다. 간단히 한글로 해석해 주고 풀어보라고 했는데도 못 풀만큼 내용이 어렵거나, 문제를 꼬아서 수험생을 힘들게 하는 시험이 아닙니다. **그저 해석이 되지 않고 이해가 되지 않아 힘들어한다고 해도 과언이 아닙니다.** 그러므로 토플 공부 순서는 문제를 많이 풀려고 하지 말고, **본문 이해를 정확히 하는 연습**을 우선하시기 바랍니다. 그림자를 잡아서 움직이려 하지 말고, 그림자를 만드는 몸을 움직이시기 바랍니다.

PREFACE II

> **질문 4** 토플 독해 공부할 때, 꼭 해야 하는 것은 무엇일까요?

긴장감있는 문제풀이 + (문제 푼 직후의 확실한 분석, 즉) 정확한 해석 + 문단정리 + 답근거는 필수사ㅎ 입니다.

문제를 풀 때, 정신 놓고 편안히 풀면 1시간이면 풀 세 지문을 두 시간이 넘게 풀고도 실수는 실수대로 많이 하곤 합니다. 게다가 실제 토플 시험을 준비하는 입장에서는 전혀 도움이 되지 않습니다. 아울러, 해설지는 그저 문제의 답을 적어 두고 해석만을 적어둔 것이 아닙니다. 여러분이 iBT 토플 공부하는 과정 중 꼭 해야 할 내용들을 체크해 놓은 것이므로 답근거와 문단정리를 한 후 해설지에서 꼭 두 가지를 비교해 보시기 바랍니다.

아직 스스로 생각할 때 실력이 모자라다고 생각되는 학생의 경우에는 위의 내용을 충분히 따른 후 그 외에 본문을 씹어 먹는다는 생각으로 분해 분석해야 합니다. 그러기 위해서는

틀린 문제를 왜 틀렸는지 분석 후, 단어 찾는 것은 당연하고 구문암기, 열 번 읽기 등을 통한 적용까지 마쳐야 합니다.

> **질문 5** 토플 시험이 얼마 안 남았어요. 가장 빨리 토플 독해 점수를 올릴 수 있는 방법은 무엇일까요?

토플 시험이 급박한 학생들이 가장 많이 하는 질문입니다. 이 질문은 두 가지로 나눠서 생각해봐야 합니다.
실력이 충분히 쌓은 경우와 그렇지 못한 경우.
실력이 충분치 못한 경우에는 답이 없습니다. 해석도, 내용 이해도 안되는 상태에서 이해를 묻는 시험문제를 풀 수 있다고 말할 수 없는 것은 당연할 것입니다. 하지만 실력은 기본이 된다는 가정하에서는 마무리 방법으로서 두가지를 해 볼만합니다.

1. 모니터 적응
대부분의 경우 학생들이 공부할 때는 종이로 공부를 하던 버릇이 있어서 모니터로, 시험을 보는 것이 특히나 모국어가 아닌 영어의 경우에는 더욱 더 문제가 될 경우가 적지 않습니다. 권하는 내용은 실제 시험을 보기 전, 모의고사를 두세 번 더 보는 것으로 실제 점수를 5점까지 끌어 올린 경우를 드물지 않게 보곤 합니다. 나름 자신이 있는 분들께 권해 드립니다.

2. 오답 정리
본인이 푼 문제지를 다 모아서 틀린 문제유형을 파악하고, 본인이 자주 낚이는 패턴을 분석해 보면, 본인만의 독특한 실수를 찾을 수 있습니다. 이것은 같은 반에서 공부했다고, 같은 수준이라고, 틀리는 문제가 같지는 않기 때문에 가르쳐 주는 선생님도 주변의 친구들도 심지어는 본인도 모르고 지나치는 경우가 많습니다. 하지만 당연히 풀어놓은 문제지가 없는 학생들의 경우에는 파악할 '재료' 가 없기 때문에 시도조차 기대할 수는 없습니다. 실제점수로 대략 3점 내지 5점 정도까지도 올릴 수 있습니다. 이때 주의할 것은 실수를 줄이도록 노력하는 것입니다. 더 나은 기술, 더 나은 실력보다는 내가 어이없이 한 실수만 줄여도 이 정도의 점수 향상 폭은 충분히 가능합니다.

3. 모의토플시험을 신청해서 본다.
실제토플 가격은 $220(약 28만원)입니다. 가격도 가격인 만큼, 실제 토플을 보기 전에 모의토플 보는 것을 추천합니다. 모의토플은 실제 토플과는 똑같은 시험 형식으로, 컴퓨터로 진행이 됩니다. 4과목을 다 응시 될 경우, full, 57,000원, reading, listening, 2과목을 응시할 경우 30,000원 정도 듭니다.

질문이 끝난후에 : 모니터 적응까지 마무리 지어야 합니다. 사설이 많이 길지만 장황한 문제지의 장점에 대한 설명보다는 당장 문제지를 선택해야 하는 학생들이 궁금해 할 내용들로 서문을 채웠습니다. 본 문제지는 이런 생각을 바탕으로 만들었기에 학생들에게 어떤 모습으로든 도움이 될 것이라 생각합니다. 하지만 그저 안다는 점과 아는 것을 행하는 점은 전혀 다른 문제입니다. 마지막으로 잘 해야 하는 점은 지금까지 설명한 것을 잘 실행하는 것입니다. 꼭 실행해서 좋은 결과를 이루시기 바랍니다.

질문 6 토플 독해 실력을 키울 때, 순서가 어떻게 되나요?

step 1 단어

일단, 단어가 안되면, 아무것도 안됩니다. 이건 독해라서가 아니라, **리딩, 리스닝, 스피킹 라이팅 모두에 해당**되는 내용이고, 그 중에서 특히, 독해 지문에서 모르는 단어가 지문당 10개가 넘어서면 위험 신호이고, 20개가 넘는다면, 판 끝났다고 생각하시면 됩니다.

step 2 구문 암기

단어가 마무리 되면, 그 단어만 가지고는 **단어 나열식 영어로만 때려 맞출 수 밖에** 없습니다. 그땐 단어끼리 같이 뭉치는 아이들의 **패턴을 파악해야 합니다.** 그래서 어셔어학원에서는 단어가 마무리 된 이후, 인터반(전체 5단계 중 3단계)부터 구문암기를 집중관리합니다. 이 부분이 진행되어야, 정확도가 확실히 늘어나기 시작합니다.

step 3 묶기

단어와 구문이 눈에 익힐때 쯤엔 문법파트에서 배운 대로 문장 구조는, 쉽게는 아니어도, 실수를 최소화 하면서 읽을 만큼은 되어야 합니다. 하지만, 학생들은 스스로 본인이 읽은 문장이 올바른지도 알지 못한 채, (특히, **절 처리와 분사처리**) 계속 진행하는 것은 도움되지 않습니다. 정확히 보는 것 쉽습니다. 그러니, **추측하지 말고 정확히 접근하는 버릇**만 잠시 들여 주시기 바랍니다. **답은 묶기입니다.** 영어로 된 모든 문장을 묶어두는 버릇이 생기면, 나중엔, 눈으로도 자연스레 처리되고, 정확도와 속도가 같이 늘 때 즈음엔 신경 쓰지 않아도 됩니다. 억지로 떼어내지 마시기 바랍니다. 너무 많이 해서 당연히 되었기 때문에 손을 떼어도 잘 될 때까지 (열심히 하면 두 달 내외면 됩니다) 모든 영어문장 (모든 과목)에서 해두시기 바랍니다.

step 4 열번 읽기

묶기까지 모두 되면 여러분들의 자신감은 상당히 늘어날 것입니다. 이 때만 되어도 20점은 무난히 넘길 수 있습니다. 하지만 아직 점수를 받은 것도, 끝난 것도 아니기에 점수 25점을 당연히 지나 30점이 될 때까지 긴장 풀지 말고, 앞의 세가지 단계를 지속적으로 반복해 두시기 바랍니다. 그 이후, "이건 내가 모를 수가 없다" 라는 생각이 들 때까지 **"열 번 읽기" 하시기 바랍니다.** 그리고 잘 되었는지 스스로 궁금하면, 초시계를 두고 지문을 읽어 보시기 바랍니다. 7분 내에 끊었나를 파악 바랍니다.

step 5 약간의 요령

25점이 넘어서면, 30점으로 가는데 약간의 요령이 필요합니다. 가령, insertion문제의 경우, 한국과는 다르게 두괄식을 선호하는 영어권 문화에 따라 해석으로도 안 풀리는 문제들은 따로 정리해두어야 할 내용들이 있습니다. 하지만 분명한 건 이런 내용들 **전부 설명하는데 30분도 걸리지 않습니다.** 이런 내용들을 몰라서 점수 25점 안 나오는 게 아니고 28점 안 나오는 게 아니므로, 이하 단계는 너무 신경 쓰지 마시기 바랍니다. 여기까지 오신 여러분들은 관성으로도 30점까지 갈 확률이 높습니다.

PREFACE II

step 6 실전연습

실전 연습이 마지막입니다. 이제 25점은 확실하고 28점도 종종 넘는 여러분들은 정말 **실전 연습**이 필요한 단계입니다. 시간이 문제된다고들 하는 경우가 가장 많은데, 의외의 내용은 25점 이하의 실력을 가진 학생들이 그런 얘기를 하는 경우가 많지 28점 이상들은 대체로 시간이 남습니다. (2지문 35분 줬을 때, 심하게는 17분만에 풀고 잤음에도 28점 나오는 학생도 있었습니다) 이 때의 문제는 꼼꼼함입니다.

어이없게 fact 문제에서 실수해서 한 두 개씩 틀리는 게 만점을 방해합니다. **꼼꼼해야** 합니다. 그리고 의외의 변수, 종이가 아닌 **모니터 적응**까지 마무리 지어야 합니다.

이상을 정리하면 다음과 같은 내용을 파악하실 수 있으리라 생각합니다.

〈독해 실력 향상 및 점수 향상의 필수단계〉

	step1	step2	step3	step4	step5	step6
	단어암기	구문	묶기	열번읽기	요령습득	실전연습
매일 과정 - 어셔에서 이뤄지는, 매일 시험으로, 확인해야 하는 내용입니다.	매일 200	묶기 시험	구문 시험	해석테스트	문제풀이및 시간조절	컴퓨터사용 모의시험
각 단계별 개념만 잡는 소요시간 (체화과정 제외)	2주	1일	1일	1일	30분	1일
체화과정 (적용과정) - 아는 것과 적용은 다릅니다.	2개월	1개월	2개월	1개월	1주	1주
어셔 과정 (어셔 커리큘럼과 연계 시)	완초1	완초2	인터	K1	K2	K1 이상
단계별 가능 점수 (30점 만점 중)	15	18	20	25	28	30

PREFACE III

반도에 흔한 고민 모음 (= 개념장착)

토플 리딩 노하우를 알려주세요. 리딩 문제 푸는 요령을 알려주세요.

먼저 묻습니다.
본문을 읽을 수나 있습니까?

예 vs 아니오
➡ "예" 라고 했다면 : 실력이 맞다면 현재 당신의 점수는 25점은 나왔어야 합니다.
➡ "아니오" 라고 했다면 : 다른 생각은 접어두시고, 본문부터 잘 읽으세요.

한글로 준다면?
- 문제 못 풀 수가 없습니다. 문제에 트릭도 없고, 너무 쉬운 문제입니다.

이렇게 쉬운 문제 푸는 요령?
- 묻습니다. 한글로 줬을 때, 다 푸는 당신에게 무엇을 가르쳐 줘야 하나요?
  '실수네요..' 인 당신에게 무엇을 가르쳐 줄까요?

반면, 그건 '한글이니까 그렇죠' 라고 말하는 당신에게 무엇을 가르쳐줄까요?
해석이 안되서 그러는 거라면,
'해석부터 하세요' 가 정답입니다.

결론 25점 이하는 다른 것에 신경 쓰지 마시고, 해석에만 집중하십시오.

시간이 문제인데요 ……

푼 곳까지 채점했을 때 25점이 나옵니까?

예 VS 아니오.
➡ "예" 라고 했다면 : 3일내로 시간 모자라지 않게 해줄 수 있습니다.
➡ "아니오" 라고 했다면 : 앞서 언급한 순서 무조건 따라 주시기 바랍니다.

속도로 고민할 만큼 정확도가 따라주지 않는 것입니다.
정확도 ➡ 속도

결론 정확도가 완성되면 속도는 전혀 문제 안됩니다.
정확도 올리는데 3개월이라면 (완초2~K1), 그래서 당신이 해냈다면, 속도는 3일내에 올려주겠습니다.

뭐가 됐든 25점 이상은 되야 합니다.

다 풀고 25점과, 다 못 풀고 25점 둘이 있다면,
다 못 풀고 25점이 훨씬 유리합니다.

PREFACE III

같은 반 애들이 오르는 것보다 너무 느려서 화가나요.

하지만 같은 반, 같은 교실에 앉아 있어도 변수는 다음과 같습니다.
1. 같은 반을 두 번이상 듣는 학생 (이미 암기는 해두었지만, 적용이 안 되는 상태입니다.)
2. 중고등학교 때, 수능공부 때, 때려 맞추는 감은 있는 학생 (뭐든 해둔 건 티가 납니다.)
3. 외국에서 살다가 온 학생(외국에서 몇 년 살고, 한국 와서 추천받아 토플학원 다니는 것 자체가 이미 이상한 겁니다. 그런 학생들은 화가 나도 됩니다. 그런 학생들처럼 외국 나가서도 살아보고 같이 못한 뒤에는 그런 생각 가져도 됩니다. 그런데 그 학생들이 외국 살다 온 덕에 잘하는 것에 대한 열등의식은 버려도 됩니다.)
4. 초·중고등학교 때, 열성 부모님 덕분에 미리 뭘 해둔 학생들(체계는 없는데, 완전 못하지는 않습니다. 그렇다고 점수가 확 나버릴 만큼도 아닌 어정쩡한 상태)
5. 외고, 특목고, 영문과, 영어 교육과 학생들(외국에서 산 것만큼이나, 외고 학생들이 같이 앉아있는 것 자체가 이상한 것입니다.)

위에 어느 것에도 해당되지 않아서, 힘들어 하는 학생들이 많습니다.
하지만 위의 경우에 해당하지 않아서, 없는 것을 자책한다고, 아쉬워한다고, 부모님 탓해봐야 달라지는 것 없고, 아쉬워할 일도, 자책할 일도, 탓할 일도 아닙니다. 맘먹고 덤비면, 오래 걸릴 일도 아니기 때문입니다.

단어부터 중고등학교 과정 마치는 데까지 3개월이면, 충분합니다. 읽기에 집중되어 있는 수능 정도의 수준은 아무것도 없는 상태에서, 제대로만 붙으면, 3개월이면 충분히 해볼 만하고, 예체능이라서, 정말 I my me mine도 모른다 해도, 한 두달만 더 붙이면 됩니다.

그런데, 되도 않게 토플 한 두 달에 마쳤다는 주변 얘기를 시작으로, (물론, 와서 해보니 그건 아니더라지만) 옆에 같은 반에서 시작했던 학생들에게마저 떨어진다는 느낌을 받는 순간, 그냥 여러분은 말린 겁니다.

결론부터 말하면 문제 푸는데 전혀 도움 안됩니다.

문제는 문제가 있는 곳에서 풀어야 하고, 하나하나 차근차근 잡아내고 골라내고, 다듬으면, 금방 좋아질 수 있는 내용인데, 인생에서 무슨 거대한 숙적을 만난 듯 몇 달째, 상담만....... 상담만 하지 말고, 담백하게 질문 바랍니다.

"(반배치 등의 상태가) 이런데, 뭐부터 해야 할까요?"
그러면, 답변도 담백하게 갑니다.

"단어부터 / 문법부터 / 구문부터 / 묶기부터 / 해태부터 / 통딕테부터 / 쉐도잉부터 / 노트테이킹부터 / 문제풀이부터 / 발음부터 / 타이핑부터 / 기본 표현부터 / brainstorming부터 / 시간 내 쓰는 연습부터 / 전체 모의고사 보면서 마무리 / 중에 하나를 하세요...." 라고.

위의 것 중에서 하나씩만 잡아나가면 됩니다.

전부 잡으면, 110점 이상 나옵니다.
이 글을 읽는 분들 중에서 다수가 80점이면 끝납니다.
높아 봐야 100점이고, 극상들만 110점 이상입니다.

위의 것 중에서, 반만 해도 80점은 나옵니다.

절대로 감정소모 하지 않아야 합니다.

시간이 없어요. 단어도 안 되는 것 같은데, 문법, 독해, 듣기도 해야 하고, 말하기 듣기는 답도 없어요. 근데 다 해야 해요.

꼭 기억 바랍니다.
적은, 한번에 많이 만들면 상황이 힘들어집니다.

나폴레옹과 히틀러 둘 다, 전 유럽을 다 삼켜놓고도 결국 패한 이유는
적을 동시에 많이 두어서 입니다.

답은 춘추 전국시대 때부터 있습니다.
중국에서 나라가 많을 때 동맹 성립과 깨짐이 반복적으로 생겼는데 이때 핵심은,

1. 나를 도와주는 상대냐 (아군이냐)
2. 나를 도와주지는 않더라도, 내게 해를 끼치면 안 되는 상대에게는 일단 화친을 맺었습니다.

즉, 동시에 적을 여럿 만들지 않는다는 것입니다.

나폴레옹과 히틀러 둘 다, 유럽 대륙 좌측엔 영국을, 우측엔 러시아를 적으로 두고 싸웠습니다. 문제는 화력을 한군데 모아야 하는데, 그걸 실행하지 못한 게 문제였습니다. (나폴레옹과 히틀러가 이기기를 바라는 건 아닙니다. ^^;)

동시에 싸움대상으로 놓아도 되는 경우는 하나입니다.
월등히 높은 실력 차.
그래서 동시 상대가 될 때.
스스로에게 물어봐 주시기 바랍니다.
위의 단계 중, 동시에 세 네 과목씩 동시 처리 가능한 게 어디까지인지. (동그라미 쳐보기)

PREFACE III

그럼에도, 수업 정도는 들어두면 좋은 이유

집에 부모님이 차를 운전하는 집 자녀들과, 그렇지 않은 집 자녀들 사이에서
운전 면허증 따기 쉬워하는 사람은 어렸을 때부터 당연하게, 봐온 사람입니다.
차 운전에 있어 기본 순서 정도는 그냥 압니다.
차에 타면, 일단, P에 기어가 들어가 있는지, (이것 모르고, 그냥 시동 키를 켜도 작동 않는다고 하는 사람 의외로 많습니다.)
차 시동을 켜는 스위치가 무엇인지 (키를 돌리는 것인지, 누르는 것인지)
이후에도, 비가 올땐 뭘 만져야 하는지,
어두울 땐 뭘 돌려야 하는지,
방향지시는 어떻게 하는지,
브레이크는 뭔지,
엑셀은 뭔지.
무엇 하나 가르쳐 주지 않아도 기본적으로 아는 사람과,
브레이크와 엑셀도 모르고 그냥 배우는 사람은 당연히 배우는 속도도, 숙지 속도도 다르게 된 이유는,
설명하지 않아도 명확할 것입니다.

미리 봐두시기 바랍니다.
옆에 사람들이 같은 실력이 아닌 것은 인정하더라도
배울 것은 배워두는 게 좋습니다.

노출은 잦을수록,
다면적 일수록 좋습니다.

옆에서 늘 같이 공부하던 사람들이,
어떤 점들을 해결하니, 어떤 결과가 나오는지,
어떤 단계에서 힘들어 하고,
그 단계를 지나는 사람들의 공통점이 무엇인지 찾아두면,
스스로 공부하며 방법에 대한 확신을 찾는 동안의 불안함과,
방법을 찾으며 소비하는 시간을 아껴둘 수 있습니다.
방법을 강사 샘에게 그냥 말로만, 전달받는 것과,
옆에 사람들이 하면서 해결하는 것을 본 뒤의 확신은
차원을 달리합니다.

많이 봐두시기 바랍니다. 그리고 긍정적 자극 받으시기 바랍니다.

부정적인 스트레스 받지 말고.

이하의 글은, 열심히 잘 따라주는 학생들의 성적 변화 패턴을 확인하여, 정리한 내용입니다.
잘 따라오는 학생들과 못 따라 오는 학생들로 나누겠습니다.

	빠른 학생의 패턴	느린 학생의 패턴	비고
	전제 - 한 지문 내에서 모르는 단어 10개 이상은 위험, 5개 이하로 떨어뜨릴 것. (어셔 단어장 암기 필수 - 중고등, 토플 단어 둘다 해두면 되는 양입니다.) - 항상 180개 이상일 것.	단어 안되면, 그냥 엉망이나 기대 버릴 것	-
1주차	구문 암기 시작	구문 암기 시작	-
2주차	구문 **반복 확인**(빠른 사람들)	구문 암기 진행	-
3주차	구문 암기 - **적용** 거의 같이됨	구문 **반복 확인** 시작	-
4주차	제대로 된 해태 시작 - 적용되면 **정확도** 늘기 시작 - 20점대 진입	구문 반복 확인만 되고 적용 안됨	-
5주차	문제풀이 시작 - 정확도(푼 건 거의 맞을 시) - **시간** 내 풀이 목표 시작 - 이미 25	구문 적용 시작	-
6주차	문풀 12-28 굳히기	구문 적용 진행	-
7주차	문풀 28 굳히기	구문 **적용**하고, 슬슬 정확도 오르기 시작	-
8주차	**시간 줄이기** - 15분내 - 30목표	**정확도** 자신감 생기기 시작 - 20점대 내외	리스닝 병행 시작(선택)
9주차	-	시간에 대한 욕심 내기 시작	-
10주차	-	**시간내** 풀이 가능 시작 - 25 진입	무조건 리스닝 병행 시작
11주차	-	문풀 12-28 굳히기	-
12주차	-	문풀 28 굳히기	-
13주차	-	**시간 줄이기** - 15분내 - 30목표	-

※ 다분히 개인차가 있지만, 단어 180개 전제 상태입니다. 단어 180개 이하는 더 늦어집니다.

<u>**수능 1등급은 토플 RC 23내외 나옵니다.**
6년 똑바로 공부해서 바로 나오던가, 두 달에 이 정도 나오면 짧은 거 아닐까요?</u>

PREFACE III

정확도를 올리고 싶으신가요?
리딩을 잘 하고 싶으신가요?
다음을 꼭 지켜주세요.

Reading

가장 중요
1. 동사가 나오기 전까지는 문장이 아무리 길어도 '은', '는', '이', '가'로 잡고 기다릴 것
2. 문장 속에서 '~ 이다.' 는 주절 동사 한번만 (등위접속사가 붙는 경우 제외)
   즉, 종속 접속사가 있으면, 그에 맞게, '~ 이지만', '~ 이므로' 등으로 해석
3. 해석은 앞에서부터 치고 나갈 것 (리스닝 대비도 가능)

위의 목록 완료 후,
4. 절 처리 / 분사 처리
5. 명사 처리 중요성 (전치사 뒤, 동사 뒤, 아무리 길어도 명사부터 볼 것)

→ 이에 대한 해결 방법-묶기
묶기 참고 (P.34)

+

Comprehension

되감기 (p.31)
문장 내 (단어 단위-구 단위-절 단위) → 문단 내 (문장 단위) → 지문 내 (문단 단위)
문장 내 중에서, 구 단위만 잘해도 20점
문단 내 중에서, 문장 단위만 잘해도 25점
지문 내 중에서, 문단 단위까지 잘하면 28점 이상!

느린 학생 패턴 (실력이 워낙 없어서 못하는 학생 말고)

자기 고집이 강한 학생 구체적으로,
단어 안 외우는 학생
구문 단어 안 외우는 학생
문법 안 되는 학생 (안되면서, 묶기도 안 하는 학생)
열 번 읽기 안 하는 학생

위의 패턴에 걸리는 학생은, 각 단계별 처방을 했음에도, 따라주지 않는다면, 시간이 지체될 수 밖에 없습니다.

TABLE OF CONTENTS

USHER iBT TOEFL INTERMEDIATE TEST READING
어셔 iBT 토플 인터미디어트 테스트 리딩

Introduction

Preface I. II. III. ★	3
Table of contents	15
1. 본 IBT 토플 교재의 특징 ★	16
2. 본 iBT 토플 교재의 구성	18
3. 계획표 짤 준비	22
4. 실력별 학습 계획	24
5. 토플 공부 방법 및 순서 ★	26
6. iBT TOEFL(iBT 토플) 소개	38
7. iBT TOEFL READING 소개	40
8. READING STRATEGIES ★	44

문제집

TEST 1 55
Comets 57
Darwin and Evolution Theory 61
잔소리 1 67

TEST 2 69
Determining the Ages of the Planets and the Universe 71
Early Research in Organic Chemistry 75
잔소리 2 81

TEST 3 83
El Niño 85
England's Sixteenth Century Economy 89
잔소리3 95

TEST 4 97
Environmental Impact of the Anasazi 99
Global Variations in Species Diversity 103
잔소리4 109

TEST 5 111
Documenting the Incas 113
Architectural Change in Eighth Century Japan 117
잔소리5 123

TEST 6 125
How Camels Survive in Arid Environments 127
Hunter-gatherers in Southwest Asia 131
잔소리 6 137

TEST 7 139
Life on Mars 141
Agriculture and Settlement around the Nile River 145

TEST 0.5 151
Sea Turtle Navigation 153

Vocabulary / 구문 정리	159
묶기	191
열번 읽기	223
부록	254

Practice Tests 7회

TEST 1 272
답안 & 문제 유형 분석표 273
TEST 1 해석 및 해설 274

TEST 2 290
답안 & 문제 유형 분석표 291
TEST 2 해석 및 해설 292

TEST 3 308
답안 & 문제 유형 분석표 309
TEST 3 해석 및 해설 310

TEST 4 326
답안 & 문제 유형 분석표 327
TEST 4 해석 및 해설 328

TEST 5 344
답안 & 문제 유형 분석표 345
TEST 5 해석 및 해설 346

TEST 6 362
답안 & 문제 유형 분석표 363
TEST 6 해석 및 해설 364

TEST 7 380
답안 & 문제 유형 분석표 381
TEST 7 해석 및 해설 382

TEST 0.5 398
답안 & 문제 유형 분석표 399
TEST 부록 해석 및 해설 400

부록(해석·해설) 408

별도 구매 서비스 소개

1. USHER 단어암기 프로그램 소개	437
2. 첨삭권 소개	440
3. 인강	442
4. 모의토플	444
5. 토플 Reading 공부방법	446
6. 토플 Listening 공부방법	449
7. 수강 후기	451

 본 iBT 토플 교재의 특징

USHER iBT TOEFL INTERMEDIATE TEST READING(어셔 iBT 토플 인터미디어트 테스트 리딩)

1 토플 리딩 실력을 늘리는 "공부 버릇" 안내

서문 강화
- 문제지 본문을 건드리기 전에 서문에 있는 개념 정리를 잘 봐두고, 잘 적용 바랍니다. 문제지에서만 얻어간다면, 이미 실력이 있는 학생들입니다. 약한 실력이 문제라면, 서문 내용과 각 단계별 주의 사항을 잘 따라 주시기 바랍니다.

2 실제 iBT 토플 시험과 가장 유사한 실전서

최신 바뀐 본문 반영
- 최신 출제 경향을 반영하여 학생들이 어려워하는 과학 주제는 물론 인문, 사회, 역사, 인물 등 지문의 다양화 및 상향된 난이도를 반영하였으며, 각 분야별 빈도를 참고하여 내용을 구성하였습니다.

최신 경향, 문제 반영
- 문제 역시 좀더 어려워진 최신 경향에 맞게 하였기에 효과적인 iBT토플 리딩 시험을 공략하기에 좋은 점을 모아두었습니다.

3 실력 향상을 위한 실전 문제 설명서

실전
- 중급이라해도, 실력 향상과 실제 시험 적용을 위해 실전 난이도 문제들로 구성하였습니다. 그리고 보다 자세히, 꼼꼼히 파고 들어 설명하였습니다.

유형별 제시전략
- 각 문제별 유형 전략을 제시하여 기본 실력을 전제로 가장 빠르고 효과적인 문제 접근을 가능케 하였습니다.

4 자세한 iBT 토플 공부방법 설명

공부 방법 설명
- 대부분의 여타 토플 교재들이 소홀히 하고 있는 해석에만 초점을 맞춘 것이 아닌 학생들이 공부하는 방법 자체를 설명해 두었습니다.

방법 활용
- 이를 잘 활용하기 위해 서문과 독해 학습방법, 독해 문제 풀이 전략(오답 패턴) 부분을 잘 활용해 주시기 바랍니다.

| 토플 공부도우미 | usherin.usher.co.kr

5 묶기

공부 과정 중에서 문제 풀이 방법에 대해 고민하지 말고, 본문 내용 파악 우선 바랍니다
- 그때 가장 우선 해야할 것이 문장구조 파악입니다.
  문장 구조를 파악할 때, 가장 도움 되는 방법으로 어셔에서 진행하는 것이 묶기입니다.
  문장 해석 안되면 일단 묶기부터 하시기 바랍니다.
  묶기가 다 되면, 해석의 탄탄한 기본이 닦입니다.

6 토플 독학하기 쉽게 설명된 해설서 (토플 학원 못다니는 학생들을 위한 추천서)

답근거 찾기
- 정확한 지문 해석은 물론, 해설 시에도 정답만을 짚어주는 기존의 해설서의 방식을 탈피하여, 답근거를 명확히 하는 연습을 할 수 있도록, 본문과 오답에 각각 답이 되는 이유와, 틀린 이유를 표시해 두었습니다. 토플 독학을 하는 학생들에게 큰 도움이 되도록 하였습니다.

해설서 활용법
- 꼭 먼저 문제를 풀고, 고민한 후, 정답지의 내용과 하나하나 비교하며 확인하시기 바랍니다.

7 체계적인 학습관리

일정표
- 스스로의 실력과 여건에 맞는 일정표를 작성하여 목표를 갖고 토플 공부에 임하여 더 좋은 결과를 가질 수 있도록 하였습니다.

리딩전략
- 모든 ETS문제는 정답과 오답을 만드는데 패턴이 있습니다. 이런 패턴들을 모아 정리하였습니다. 본인이 공부 중에 자꾸 틀리는 문제가 있다면, 그 문제의 오답 패턴 중 어떤 것 때문인지를 파악하여 빠른 효과를 기대할 수 있도록 하였습니다.

수준별 학습
- 학생 별로 공부를 해 본 학생과 해보지 않은 학생들간의 공부 법에 차이를 두어 본 토플책에 설명해 두었습니다. 목표를 어디까지 잡아야 할지를 잘 파악해서 무리한 계획을 세워, 중도 포기하는 일을 없도록 추천 계획표를 잘 이용 하시기 바랍니다.

8 잔소리

- 잔소리를 작성하여 각 TEST 사이에 적어두었습니다. 중복되는 내용이더라도, 한번 더 참고 및 적용 바랍니다. 하는 척만 하는 게 아닌, 해야 실력이 늡니다.

본 iBT 토플 교재의 구성

USHER iBT TOEFL INTERMEDIATE **TEST** READING(어셔 iBT 토플 인터미디어트 테스트 리딩)

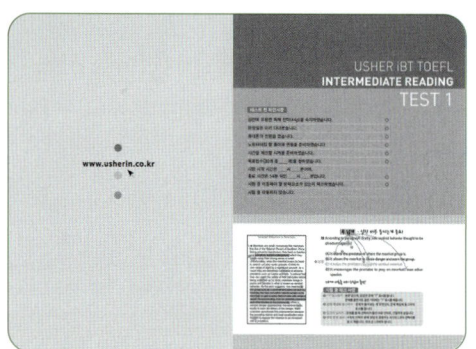

1. 시험 전 준비 사항

토플 시험 시작 전 시험칠 수 있는 환경인지 여부부터 파악하기 위해, 준비사항을 적어 놓았습니다. 토플 어학원에선 담당 매니저 선생님들이 챙겨주시지만, 혼자 공부할 때는 중간에 끊김이 생길 수 있으므로 특히 주의해서 지켜주시기 바랍니다.

2. Test

실전 감각유지 및 실제 iBT 토플 시험에서의 확실한 효과를 위해서 5회분의 문제를 구성하였습니다. 실제 시험과 같은 형식의 문제지로 주의해서 문제를 풀어주시기 바랍니다.

3. 시험 직후 체크 리스트 + 문제 유형 분석
(나의 취약점 분석)

iBT 토플 시험 직후 주의 사항과, 단순한 채점이 아닌, 스스로의 문제점을 점검할 수 있도록 유형 분석표를 만들어 놓았습니다. 답만 먼저 확인하지 말고, 어떤 유형에서 반복적으로 틀리는지, 어떤 유형이 어렵고 혼란스러운지 스스로 체크해 보면서 스스로 문제가 무엇인지 꼭 점검해 주시기 바랍니다. 서문에 있는 READING STRATEGIES(p.44)를 참고해 각각 유형별로 어떻게 접근해야 할지도 파악해 주시길 바랍니다.

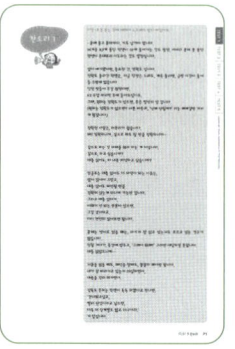

4. 잔소리

토플 리딩 뿐만 아니라 토플을 공부하면서 잊지 말아야 할 것들을 잔소리 형식으로 적어 놓았습니다. 누구나 잔소리를 듣기 싫어하지만, 항상 들어보면 틀린 말은 아닌, 나에게 이득이 되는 말들 뿐입니다. 아무리 알고 있다 해도 실천하는 것과는 다르기에, 계속 리마인드 시켜주고 실제로 실천하여 좋은 결과, 좋은 동기 부여가 되도록 꼭 다시 한번 참고하시기 바랍니다.

| 토플 공부도우미　usherin.usher.co.kr

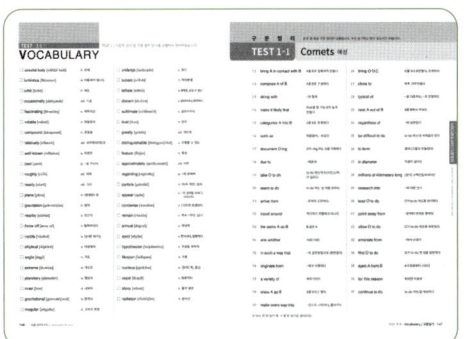

5. VOCABULARY + 구문정리
본문에 나온 토플 단어 정리와 구문을 각각 한페이지씩 정리해 두었습니다. 열번 읽기 위해서는 필히 단어와 구문암기를 먼저 한 후 넘어가시기 바랍니다.

6. 묶기
주어, 동사, 문장구조 파악을 정확하게 하기 위해 필수인 묶기를 지문 모든 문장에 적용시켰습니다. 스스로 1차적으로 묶기를 한 후, 처리가 안되는 부분을 참고하시기 바랍니다.

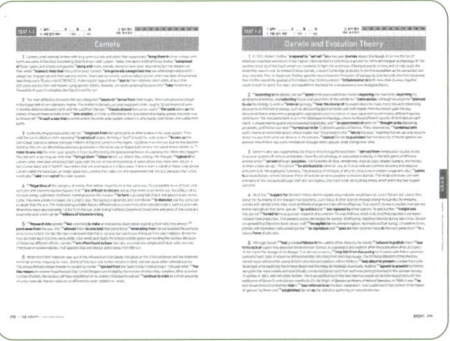

7. 열 번 읽기
문제지 맨 뒤에는 간단한 정답과 더불어, 각 본문만 주요 구문 표시만을 해두어 반복할 수 있도록 추가페이지를 만들었습니다. 그냥 버리지 말고, 꼭 들고 다니면서 반복적으로 읽어두시기 바랍니다

8. 정답 및 해석 + 해설
매회 문제를 푼 뒤, 이를 정확히 알기 위해 해석과 자세한 해설, 지문의 구조, 토플 단어 정리 뿐만 아니라, 토플 독학 하시는 분들을 위해 문제 초이스 내에 오답이유 표시 및 본문에 정답 근거 등의 공부 편의성을 위한 부가 내용을 넣었습니다.

2 본 iBT 토플교재의 구성

해석·해설 추가설명

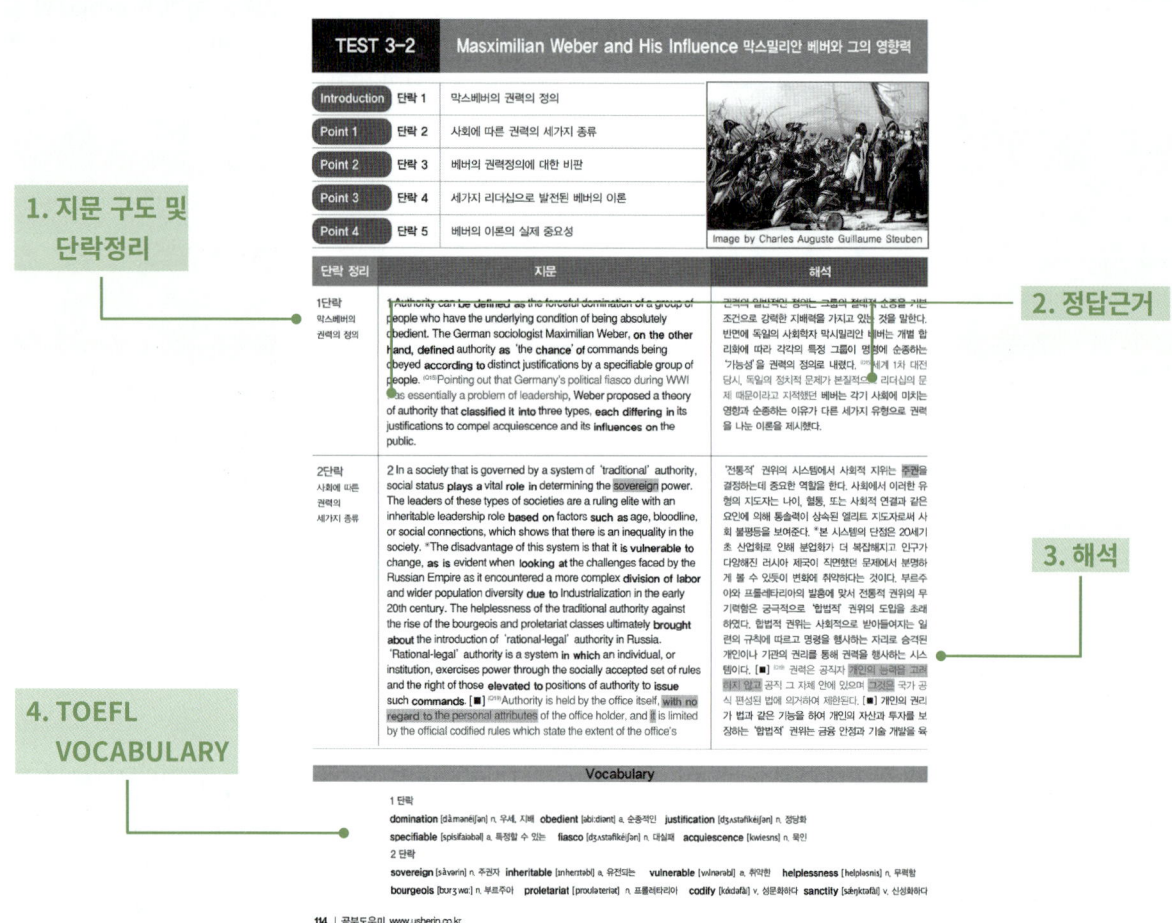

1. 지문 구조 및 단락정리

단락의 내용을 알아볼 수 있도록 도표화한 내용정리를 제공하였습니다. 내용정리와 더불어 제공한 사진을 보시면서 내용을 충분히 이해하시기 바랍니다.

2. 정답 근거

모든 문제는 정답근거가 없이는 문제를 만들지 않습니다. 꼭 정답 근거를 찾아가며 문제 푸는 버릇을 들이시기 바랍니다. 그냥 감으로 '어딘가에서..' 라는 식의 답 근거 제공은 ETS가 쉽게 엮어버리는 오답채택 확률을 높일 뿐입니다. 꼭, 본인이 답 근거라고 지목한 부분과, 답지의 부분이 맞는지 파악하는 습관을 들이시길 바랍니다.

3. 해석

지문 이해를 위해선 꼭 필요한 내용입니다. 하지만, 문장 해석에 급급해서 내용을 놓치는 일이 없도록 주의해서 '되감기'를 많이 해두시기 바랍니다. (p.31 참고)

4. TOEFL VOCABULARY (토플 단어)

독해할 때 사전 찾는 불편을 덜 수 있도록 지문에서 사용된 단어의 뜻과 발음을 제시하였습니다.

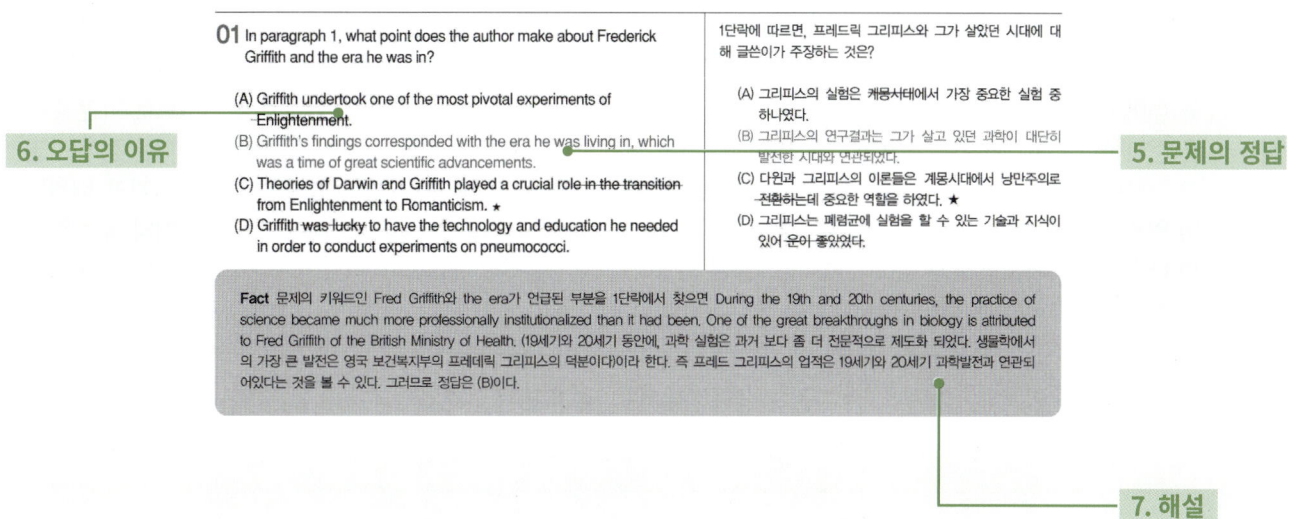

5. 문제의정답

문제의 정답에 색을 넣어 표시해 쉽게 알 수 있도록 하였고, 옆의 해석 부분과 가급적 찾기 쉽도록 위치를 맞추어 두었습니다.

6. 오답이유

일반 문제지들이 정답 근거만 제시하는 것에 반해, USHER iBT TOEFL INTERMEDIATE TEST READING (어셔 iBT 토플 인터미디어트 테스트 리딩) 에서는, 오답의 이유도 밝혀두어 혼자 공부하는 토플 독학생들에게 도움이 될 수 있도록 하였습니다.

7. 해설

답이 되는 이유와 오답 이유를 좀더 필요로 하는 학생들을 위해, 하나하나 풀어 더욱더 자세히 설명해 두었습니다. 하지만, 만약 정답 근거와 오답 표시를 보고 금방 이해가 간다면 굳이 다 읽으실 필요는 없습니다.

3 계획표 짤 준비

USHER iBT TOEFL INTERMEDIATE TEST READING(어셔 iBT 토플 인터미디어트 테스트 리딩)

1 난 왜 토플 공부 할까? = 토플 점수 따서 뭐할까? Know-why

많은 학생들이 주로 고민하는 것은 늘 know-how에 대한 연구입니다. 물론 효율적인 토플 공부방법 참 중요합니다. 하지만, 그보다 먼저 해야 할 것은 과연 내가 왜 이 짓(?!!!)을 하고 있는가를 분명히 하는 것입니다. 즉, 다른 말로 목적이 뚜렷해야 한다는 뜻입니다. 공부하는 다수의 학생들이 공부하면서 매우 지겨워 하는 이유는 간단히 아직 내가 왜 해야 하는지가 명확하지 않기 때문입니다. 당장 4개월 뒤 외국에 공부하러 나가야 한다거나, 외국으로 이민 수속을 준비하고 있고 2개월 뒤 비행기표를 끊어놓은 상황 또는 국내에서라면 과외자리를 얻기 위해선 보여줄 점수가 필요 하다면 당장 써먹어야 한다는 생각 때문에 하루하루를 정말 꽉꽉 채워서 공부할 수밖에 없습니다. 하지만, 배워봐야 언제 써먹을까 싶은 학생들에게, 특히나 공부의 목적이 단순히 점수를 위해서라면 대부분 공부할 때의 목적은 저 먼 나라의 이야기처럼 별 관심도 없습니다. (물론 중요하지 않다는 것은 아닙니다) 이런 상황이라면 공부하다가 도중에 그만두기 딱 입니다. 싫다면? 이유부터 생각해 봅시다.

< 나는 토플공부해서 ( )점 따면, ( ) 하겠다 >

2 위의 목표에서 ( ) 달 내에라는 말은 뺐습니다. 이유는 누구나 공부를 질질 끌면서 하기는 싫어합니다.

하지만, 그렇다고 내 능력은 생각지도 않고 시간 계획을 짜버리면 중간에 포기하기 쉽습니다.
남들은 1 ➔ 2 ➔ 3 ➔ 4 ➔ 5 단계를 가는 것이 정석이라고들 할 때, 왠지 나는 1 ➔ 3 ➔ 5로 갈 수 있을 것 같은 근거 없는 자신감? 이런 계획은 수시로 고칠 일만 더 만들 뿐 별로 도움 되진 않습니다.
지금은 시간을 생각하지 마십시오. 일단 샘플로 해보고 시간 계산해도 늦지 않습니다.
그리고 다음 단계도 생각하지 마십시오.
단어, 문법, 독해, 듣기, 쓰기, 말하기 어느 하나 다 안 중요한 것이 없다고 생각하는 순간,
무리한 계획을 세우게 되고, 그 후엔 스스로 질려 포기하기 쉽습니다.
하지만, 확실한 것은 지금 앞 단계를 확실히 끝내면 다음 단계로의 과정이 자연스레 이뤄진다는 점이고,
지금 확실치 않게 해두면,
두고두고 발목 잡는 일이 된다는 점입니다.

3 현재 나의 공부를 방해하는 요소 파악 - 뇌구조 놀이 (p.23)

다들 익숙한 놀이 이지만, 정말 잘 이용하는 것이 어려운 이유는 오직 한가지 솔직하지 못해서입니다.
솔직하게 적어보십시오.

| 토플 공부도우미 | usherin.usher.co.kr

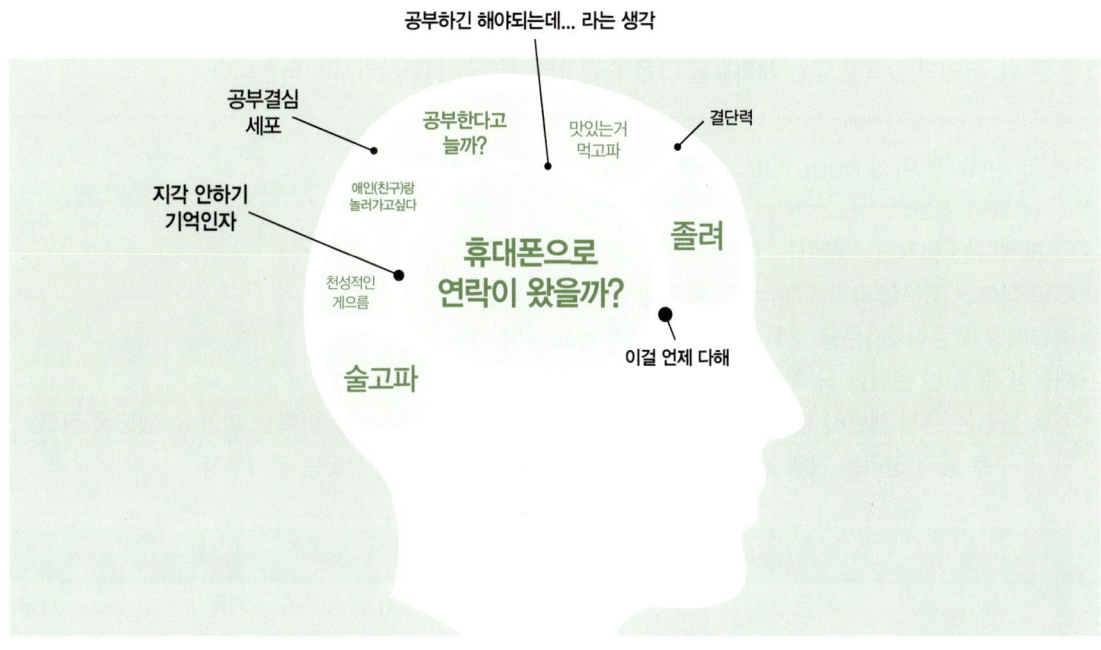

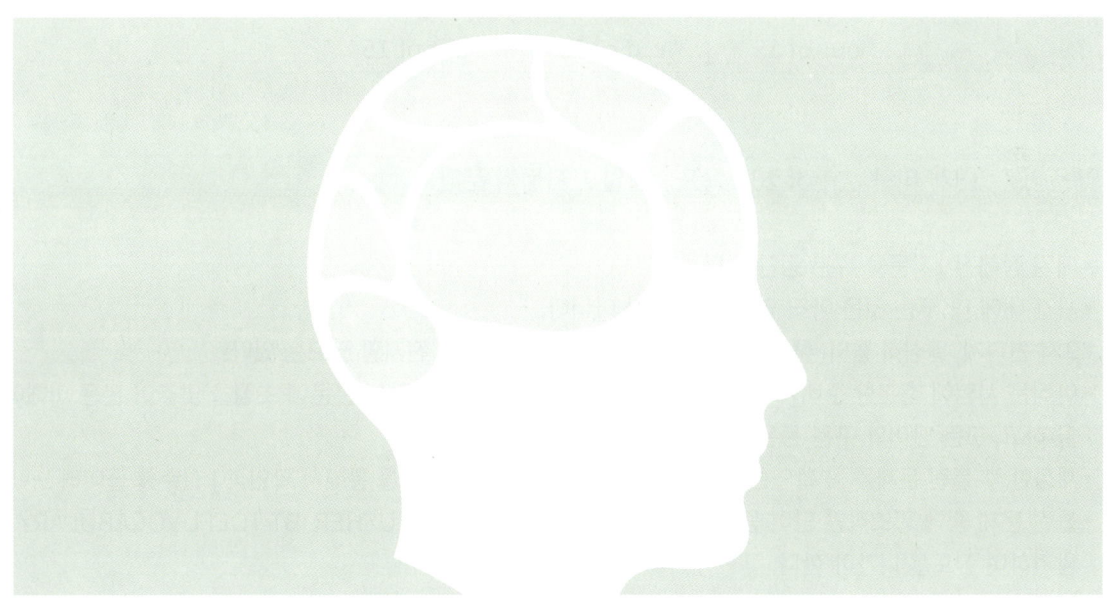

4 1번부터 3번까지의 내용들을 정리하고 나서 이제 본격적인 스스로의 공부방법을 짜보십시오.

# 실력별 학습 계획
USHER iBT TOEFL INTERMEDIATE TEST READING(어셔 iBT 토플 인터미디어트 테스트 리딩)

Test 1을 푼 뒤, 본인의 실력에 맞는 계획표를 다음을 참고해서 짜서 실행시키시기 바랍니다.

1 맞은 개수 18개 이상 out of 20 : **목표 - 매일 1회 (2지문씩 푼다)**

- 다 맞겠다는 생각으로 푼다.
- 매일 정해진 지문을 각각 17분씩 35분 동안 푼다.
- 매일매일 꾸준히 2지문을 소화하되, 꼭 확실히 짚고 넘어간다.
- 채점한 후 틀린 문제를 꼭 확인한 뒤, 실수를 줄이려 노력한다.
- 주로 틀리는 문제 패턴이 무엇인지 꼭 알아내서 다음 시험에선 같은 실수 반복을 피할 수 있도록 한다.
- 단어, 구문 등의 정리는 거의 끝났어야 하므로, 간단히 빠진 것 몇 개 정도는 챙겨두자.

	1일차	2일차	3일차	4일차	5일차
1주	지문 2 out of 15	지문 4 out of 15	지문 6 out of 15	지문 8 out of 15	지문 10 out of 15
	6일차	7일차	8일차		
2주	지문 12 out of 15	지문 14 out of 15	지문 15 out of 15		

2 맞은 개수 18개 미만 out of 20 : **목표 - 매일 1 지문씩 푼다**

- 매일 정해진 1지문을 17분 동안 푼다.
- 시간 내에 다 푸는 것은 아직 염두에 둘 때가 아니다.
  그저 편하게, 열심히 풀되, 풀었던 문제는 다 맞힌다는 생각으로 진지할 필요는 있다.
- 아직은 시험에 충분한 준비가 되어있지 않으므로, 반드시 문제보다는 본문에 초점을 맞추어 본문 이해에 노력을 하고, 모든 단어와 구문 등은 반드시 암기한다.
- 채점한 후 틀린 문제를 꼭 확인한 뒤, (스터디가 가능하다면, 스터디를 통해서 확인 후) 실수를 줄이려 노력한다.
- 틀린 문제 중에 기초적인 단어 등이 많이 포함되어 있다면, 무조건 USHER iBT TOEFL VOCABULARY 를 병행 암기하며 진도를 나가야 한다.
- 아직 시간계산 등의 어려움이 극복되지 않았을 것이고, 다 풀기도 빠듯할 것이지만, 시험 시간 동안 최선을 다하는 자세를 가져야 한다.

- 매일매일 꾸준히 1지문을 소화하되, 꼭 확실히 짚고 넘어간다.
- 아직 중간중간 처리되지 않는 문장, 단어, 구문 등은 필히 꼭 챙겨서 다음 시험에선 같은 실수 반복하지 않게 하여야 한다.
- 아직, 기본 실력 부분에서 밀리는 것이므로, 반복적으로 읽는 것을 게을리하지 않는다.
- 문제의 실수 여부보다는 실력 자체에 초점을 맞춰 노력한다.
- 아무리 시간이 많이 걸려도, 풀었던 문제지는 꼭 반복적으로 읽는 것을 많이 하여야 실력 향상을 이룰 수 있다.

	1일차	2일차	3일차	4일차	5일차
1주	지문 1 out of 15	지문 2 out of 15	지문 3 out of 15	지문 4 out of 15	지문 5 out of 15
	6일차	7일차	8일차	9일차	10일차
2주	지문 6 out of 15	지문 7 out of 15	지문 8 out of 15	지문 9 out of 15	지문 10 out of 15
	11일차	12일차	13일차	14일차	15일차
3주	지문 11 out of 15	지문 12 out of 15	지문 13 out of 15	지문 14 out of 15	지문 15 out of 15

5. 토플 공부 방법 및 순서

USHER iBT TOEFL INTERMEDIATE TEST READING(어셔 iBT 토플 인터미디어트 테스트 리딩)

복습

수업 중 얻은 내용을 다 이해한다는 생각으로 반드시 반복 복습해둔다.

i) 확실한 수업 내용 확인을 수업직후 이후 한번 더 적어보고(백지시험),
ii) 이 내용들에 포함된 모든 단어와 표현을 암기 후,
iii) 마지막으로는
  ㉠ 눈으로 읽다가,
  ㉡ 문장구조가 확실해지면, 입으로 내가 아나운서가 된것처럼 shadowing을 할 수 있을 만큼 반복적으로 읽는다. (10번)
iv) 많이 듣는 것은 이 과정들이 다 된 후 노래 듣듯이 편하게~^^

예습

수업준비 잘 할 것

= "잘" 이라 함은, 모든 수업내용을 모두 아는 것이 아닌, 수업시간에 내가 어디서 집중해야 하는가를 알 수 있게 "아는 것과 모르는 것을 구별" 해 두는 정도!

= (즉, 혼자 할 수 있는 것까지만 해두는 것!!! 모르는 단어 찾아 두는 것은 기본 중 기본)

수업직후!

수업 "끝나자마자" 바로 그 자리 에서 수업 내용을

i) 모두 같이 훑어보고
ii) 모든 내용 정리 후
iii) 모르는 것은 옆에 학생에게 물어서라도 알아둔다!
iv) 같이 스터디를 하는 학생들간에는 반드시 집에 가기 전에 정리한 암기사항들을 자체 시험을 통해 철저히 암기한다.

수업

예습 한 것을 근거로, 모르는 것을 집중적으로 확인한다.
(= 그럼으로써, 수업의 수준이 좌우된다)

다음 순서를 반드시 지켜 주시기 바랍니다. 순서는 다음과 같습니다.

예습

1. 시험 전 지시사항 체크
2. 시험 중 체크사항
3. 시험 직후 스터디
4. 개인 준비 시작 (단어 암기, 모르는 문장 표시, 묶기)

1. 시험 전 지시사항 체크

실전에 유용한 독해 전략(31p)을 숙지하였습니다. ○
화장실은 미리 다녀왔습니다. ○
휴대폰의 전원을 껐습니다. ○
노트테이킹 할 종이와 연필을 준비하였습니다. ○
시간을 체크할 시계를 준비하였습니다. ○
목표점수(20개 중 ___개)를 정하였습니다. ○
시험 시작 시간은 ___시 ___분이며, 종료 시간은 35분 뒤인 ___시 ___분입니다. ○
시험 중 이동해야 할 방해요소가 있는지 체크하였습니다. ○
시험 중 이동하지 않습니다. ○

2. 시험 중 체크사항

Sentinel Behavior in Meerkats

1.→ Meerkats are small, mongoose-like mammals that live in the Kalahari Desert of Southern Africa. Being primarily insectivores, they feed on beetles and scorpions buried underground, which they locate using their strong sense of smell. Unfortunately, when the meerkat lowers its head to search out prey under grasses, it limits its own range of sight by a significant amount. As a result they are extremely vulnerable to airborne predators such as hawks and owls. To ensure that they can reach the safety of their bolt-holes before being snatched up by birds, meerkats forage in packs and partake in what is known as sentinel behavior. As the term suggests, one meerkat in the group acts as a sentinel and does not look for food like the rest, but rather stands upright on its hind legs to gain a wider field of view with which it scans the surrounding area for possible predators and other threats to the community. When it senses danger approaching, the sentinel barks loudly to warn the others of the danger. Many scientists questioned this phenomenon because the revealing stance and loud vocalization were thought to expose the meerkat to an increased risk of predation.

폭 넓게 – 일단 버릇 들이는게 중요!

32 According to paragraph 1, why was sentinel behavior thought to be disadvantageous?

(A) It warns the predator of where the meerkat group is.
(B) It allows the meerkat to sense danger and warn the group.
(C) It helps the predators locate the sentinel meerkat.
(D) It encourages the predator to prey on meerkats over other species.

경쟁

스터디 자료들 미리 수집해 둘것!

2.1 "?" 표시하기

- 궁금한 걸 건드려야 실력이 늘어 납니다. 중요한 건, 시험 문제를 풀면서 다 기록을 남길 순 없으니 본문을 읽으며, 궁금한 곳에만 남겨 두는 겁니다. 표시 안 해두면, 나중에 기억도 안 납니다. 시간 없지만, 체크해 둬서 나중에 확인대상 정리라는 중요한 과정입니다.
- 문제에도 물음표 해둡니다. ? 결국 질문꺼리는 많을수록 실력 높이기 좋습니다. 귀중한 시간 투자해서 내가 모르는 것을 골라두는 작업은 절대 소홀히 하지 않습니다.

5 토플 공부 방법 및 순서

2.2 문제 핵심 단어에 동그라미
- 묻는 말에 대답합니다. 별거 아닌 것 같아도 중요합니다. 묻는 말에 대답합니다. 그래야 i) 읽어야 할 범위가 줄어들고, ii) 쓸데없이 고민하는 일 줄입니다.

2.3 답근거 날리기
- 멍하게 문제 푸는 학생들 참 많습니다. 생각하며 틀린 이유 단어로 날리다 보면, 재밌습니다. 그리고, 실력도 늡니다. 간결하게 날려야 합니다. 죽죽 그으면 안됩니다. 실력 키우는데 도움 안됩니다.

2.4 경쟁 문장 표시
- 경쟁 문장 체크 (모든 객관식 문제는 결국, 정답과 경쟁하는 것은, 1개입니다. 만약 4개 모두 모르겠으면 그냥 실력이 아닌 겁니다. 시험장 갈 정도라면, 마지막 하나와 결국 싸워야 맞는 겁니다).

3. 시험 직후 - 이견문제만 스터디 (답은 모른채 해야합니다.)

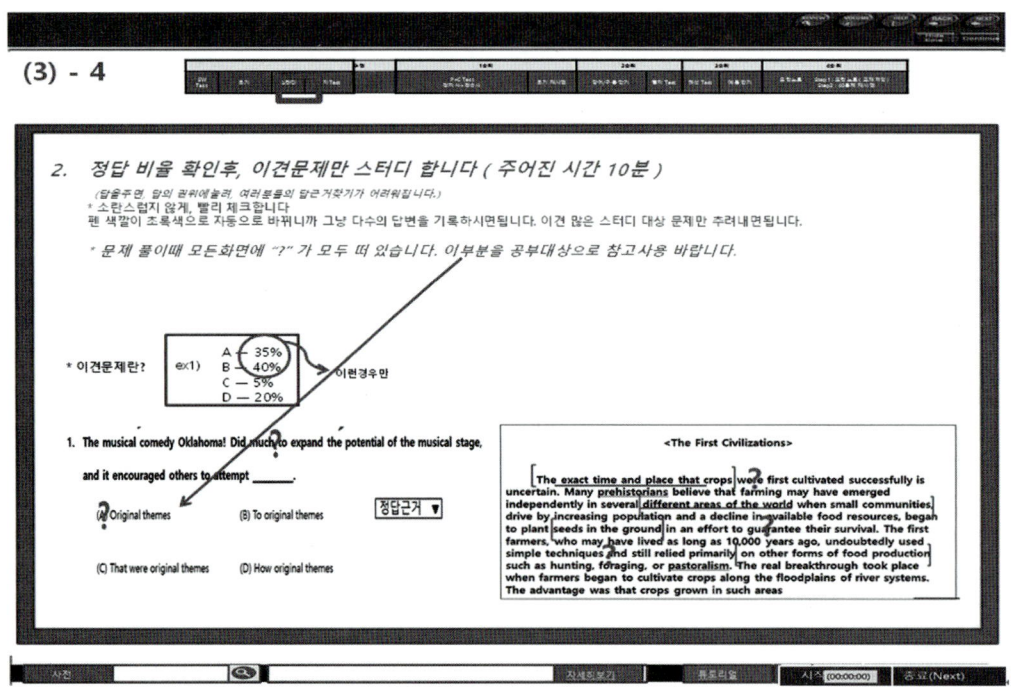

순서 :
i) (답 없이) 조원끼리 답 맞추고
ii) 이견문제 파악 후 (지문당 3-4문제! 넘으면 그 조 해산!), 스터디 (10분내)
iii) 답근거 (모두)
iv) ? 파악해서 서로 질문. 모르겠으면 형광펜 처리

4. 개별 공부 시작
모르는 단어 암기까지 / 모르는 문장 형광 표시 / 묶기 (할 수 있는 데까지)

수업 중

수업의 질은 철저하게 학생들이 예습을 얼마나 잘 해두었나에 달려있다 해도 과언이 아닙니다.
꼭 앞의 과정을 잘 정리해서 확실히 챙겨두시기 바랍니다.
특히, 궁금해서 밑줄 쳐 둔 부분 등은 집중해서 잘 처리해 주시기 바랍니다.

단, 우선 문장 해석 및 내용 정리 위주로 하되, 문제 푸는 나름의 요령은 어느 정도 실력에 신경 쓸 것!
세가지만 잘 지켜주시기 바랍니다.

1. 등 떼고
2. 펜 잡고
3. 멍 때리지 말고

세가지 안 하면, 할게 없습니다. 공부밖에.

수업 직후

수업시간에 적은 내용은 즉시 확인 + 정리해야 합니다.
보통 수업시간 50분 분량을 한번 훑어보는데 걸리는 시간은 많지 않습니다.
잘 집중했다면, 한번 다 보고, 화장실 다녀와도 될 만큼이니까, 꼭 해두시기 바랍니다. 한번 귀찮은 5분을 투자하면, 집에 가서 한 시간은 아낄 수 있고,
덤으로, 공부하는 것이 그렇게 어렵지만은 않다는 걸 알게 될 겁니다.

- 문제를 푼 곳까지 표시합니다. (잔소리1)
- 조원들과 수업시간 내용을 한번 확인합니다. 편의점으로, 화장실로 즉시 나가지 말고, 5분내로 잠시 검토하고 일어섭니다.

스터디 그룹 조원 중 한 명이 처음부터 중요내용이라고 짚어준 내용을 훑어 나갈 때, 나머지 조원들은 틀리거나 빠진 내용들을 채워주며 정리하면 됩니다. 시간은 5분 내외면 충분합니다.

** 학생들이 문장은 이해를 하되, 글 내용(문단)을 모르고 가는 경우가 많으므로, 반드시 간단히 문단 정리할 때, 내가 이해한 것 인지 꼭 스스로를 의심하며 읽어야 합니다. 가끔씩은 스터디 때, 또는 수업시간에 선생님이 정리해 준 내용을 스스로 이해한걸로 착각하고 넘어가는 학생들이 많습니다. (READING **COMPREHENSION**임을 명심!!)

5 토플 공부 방법 및 순서

복습

i) 단어 및 구문 암기 퀴즈 (스스로라도 해야 합니다 - 시험은 인간이 만든 가장 완벽한 시스템!!!) (***백지시험)
ii) 10번 읽기 (열 번 읽고, usherin.usher.co.kr > 난 오늘 흔적에 mp3 녹음해서 기록 남기기)
iii) mp3확인 (들으면서 다 알아 들어야 합니다. 이게 쉬운 것이 아니므로 안된다고 실망은 하지 말되, 되도록 노력해 보시기 바랍니다)

예습 - 수업 - 복습 중에서 **가장 중요한 것은 복습입니다.**
밥상 잘 차려놓고 먹지 않는 사람처럼, 예습 수업만 잘 준비하고 복습하지 않는 **"짓"** 은 하지 마시기 바랍니다.

1. 반드시 암기합니다.
　단어와 구문은 암기합니다. 이후, 꼭 시험으로 암기 여부 파악 합니다.

2. 암기와 적용은 다릅니다.
　묶기를 통해서, 문장을 바로 파악 하고 있는지 꼭 파악합니다.
　묶기의 중요성은, 다음 내용에서 확인 바랍니다.
　꼭 합니다. 실력을 올리는데 꼭 필요합니다.

■ 복습 부분에 대한 재강조

1. 백지시험 (반드시 암기 후 읽기!)

　누구나 시험 보는 것은 싫어합니다.
　하지만, 시험은 인간이 만든 가장 좋은 확인 방법입니다. 본인이 안다고 생각했던 내용들도 정작 확인 시에는 잘 모르고 있다는 점을 파악할 일이 있을 것입니다. 이런 경우, 스스로 문제점이 있다고 생각할 일이 아니고, 원래 공부과정 중 하나 로서 당연하게 받아들이되, 분발해서 모자란 부분을 잘 채워 나갈 수 있도록 하는 방법으로서 스스로 체크 하는 시험을 권해드립니다.

　＊시험 방법
　　각 지문 별로, 해석하다가 막히는 부분은 단어 아니면, 구문에서 막혔을 것입니다.
　　이런 경우, 혼자 공부할 경우에는, 시험지를 우선 작성해서 여러 장 복사해 놓거나, 여러 명이 같이 할 경우에는 한 명씩 돌아가면서 시험을 봐서 90% 이상 맞지 못하면,
　　통과시키지 않는 연습을 미리 해두면, 그날 부분은 확실한 복습을
　　하게 될 것입니다.

다시 한번!! 예습, 수업, 복습 중에서 **가장 중요한 것은 복습이라는 점**을 기억해 두시기 바랍니다. 그저 수업 시간에 앉아 있었다는 사실만으로, 노트에 적어놓았다는 사실만으로는 실력이 늘지 않습니다. 어떻게든, 그 내용들을 잘 정리해서 써 먹을 수 있을 만큼 만들어 두어야 진짜 본인 실력이 되는 것입니다.

2. 되감기
i) 문장 단위
ii) 문단 단위
iii) 글 단위

전체에서 두루 쓰이는 방법으로, 긴 문장일 경우에는 문장 내에서, 문단의 경우에는 문장과 문장 사이의 전개를, 글 전체라면, 각 문단별의 연결 관계를 생각하며 읽는 것을 말합니다.

되감기 방법

i) 문장
묶기 형식의 문장에서 문장을 완전히 파악하기 위해 주어, 동사, 구, 절 단위로 나누어 되감기를 합니다.

가장 중요한 건,

> 1. 동사가 나오기 전까지는 문장이 아무리 길어도 '은', '는', '이', '가' 로 잡고 기다려야 한다.
> 2. 문장 속에서 'rv이다' 는 주절 동사 한번만 나온다. (등위접속사가 붙는 경우 제외) 즉, 종속 접속사가 있으면, 그에 맞게, '~이지만', '~이므로' 등으로 해석한다.
> 3. 해석은 앞에서부터 치고 나가야 한다.

위에 것을 다 완료하면,

> 4. 절처리, 분사처리까지 신경써야 한다.
> 5. 전치사 뒤, 동사 뒤, 아무리 길어도 명사부터 보고 처리해야 한다.

Ex)

    1.   2.   3.   4.   5.   6.
A situation [(in which) an economic market is dominated (by a single seller) (of a product)] is known (as a monopoly)

1. **상황은**
2. 상황은, **이 상황내에서**
3. 상황은, 이 상황내에서 **경제시장이 지배되어지는 상황은**
4. 상황은, 이 상황내에서, 경제시장이 **하나의 상품이 하나의 판매자에 의해** 경제시장이 지배되어지는 상황은
5. 상황은, 이 상황내에서, 경제시장이 하나의 상품이 하나의 판매자에 의해 경제시장이 지배되어지는 상황은, **알려진다.**
6. 상황은, 이 상황내에서, 경제시장이 하나의 상품이 하나의 판매자에 의해 경제시장이 지배되어지는 상황은, 알려진다, **독점으로써**.
7. 경제 시장이 하나의 상품이 하나의 판매자에 의해 지배되어 지는 상황은 독점으로써 알려진다.

5 토플 공부 방법 및 순서

ii) 문단

문장 되감기 후, 문장이 모두 파악되면, 각 문단의 내용을 더욱 이해하기 위해 문단 안에 세부적인 내용을 나누어 되감기 합니다.

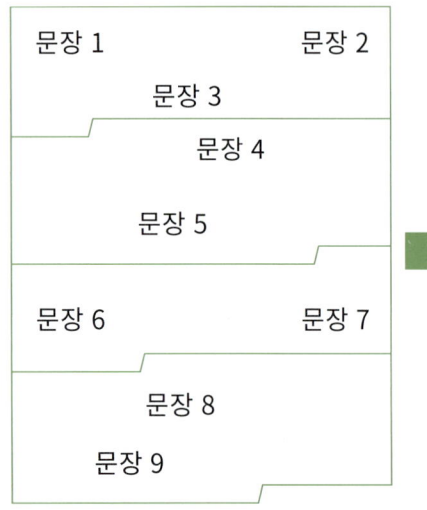

→ 1. Even before the Venetian Senate's act of 1474, isolated monopolies were granted in Europe. For example, in England the monarchs would grant letters patent, or "letters that lie open", to people in their graces, granting them a monopoly to produce or provide specific goods and services. This tradition of granting monopolies eventually led to the term 'patents' we use today. / 2. It was not, however, until the Venetian Act that the standardized process of granting patents occurred. Britain, influenced by this new concept, eventually implemented such a system as a kind of mercantilist instrument to attract emigrants with skills that could possibly aid Britain's industry with the guarantee of exclusive monopoly, after the significant economic drain caused by the War of the Roses. / 3. By the early 17th century, patents had become royal favors to subjects of loyalty or wealth, with monopolies being granted on products and services such as running ale-houses. This led to inefficiency and left room for the corruption that brought about the Statute of Monopolies of 1624, which required courts to outlaw all monopolies but those based on true inventive intentions. / 4. When the Industrial Revolution spurred an explosive number of new inventions, patents became an increasingly important component of the socioeconomic machine. This era marks a change in the perception of the role of patents in society, in that they were no longer given only for the introduction of a new finished product, but also for the introduction of technological know-how or processes. /

1. Venetian Senate 법령 이전에도 주어졌던 독점.
2. Venetian Senate 법령 이후 특허 수요의 표준화.
3. 특허의 비효율성과 부패를 막기 위해 생긴 Statute of Monopolies.
4. 산업화 이후, 특허의 역할 변화.

iii) 글

각각 문단 안에 내용까지 완전히 이해한 후, 전체적인 글의 흐름과 정리를 위해 글을 문단 별로 나누어 되감기 합니다.

TEST 2-1

1. 날짜: _____년 ___월 ___일
2. 구문 암기 여부: □ Yes / □ No
3. 읽기 횟수 (목표: 열 번 읽기) — 1회 2회 3회 4회 5회

The Effects of Light on Flowering

1 Plant growth and development are controlled by interactions between environmental factors and inner developmental processes. 1)**Amongst** the diverse environmental factors, light 2)**plays** the most essential **role**, affecting plants 3)**in** various **ways**, from their growth and 4)**ability to** 5)**produce** energy to their bloom time. For example, 6)**in the absence of** sufficient light, plants exhibit a unique growth pattern 7)**called** etiolation. These plants will produce thinner and longer stems with longer internodes to reach a faint light source or to find one, **in a** much more rapid **way** than those 8)**exposed to** adequate sunlight. A plant 9)**suffering from** etiolation will also produce fewer leaves.

2 Perhaps the most interesting influence light has on plants is on their flowering patterns. The blossoming of flowers in plants is an intricate and delicate process which has evolved to suit plants' different environments. To maximize the probability of their seeds being successfully dispersed, plants 10)**use** environmental factors **to determine** the current season. Some of these factors, like temperature and water availability, can fluctuate heavily. An unusually cool summer or unexpected rain outside the monsoon seasons would confuse the plants. Fortunately, plants can also 11)**use** the length of day **as** a cue. Length of day is perhaps the most reliable indicator of the season because it is controlled by the angle of Earth's rotation, which is unaltered by terrestrial events. Longer days always indicate springtime and the coming of summer while shorter days are only possible during autumn and winter.

3 12)**Depending on** their reaction to the length of the day, species of plants are traditionally categorized into three groups: the long-day, the short-day and day-neutral plants. A day-neutral plant produces flowers 13)**as soon as** it has sufficiently grown and developed, 14)**regardless of** the length of the day. The traditional names of long-day and short-day plants are, however, better 15)**described as** short-night and long-night plants since it is the duration of continuous darkness **rather than** the day length which controls flowering. Long-night plants produce flowers during times when there is more than a specified duration of continuous darkness. Conversely, short-night plants 16)**require** periods of darkness **to be** less than a specified period. The threshold for the length of darkness of both long-night and short-night plants differ by species. The duration of this **is called** the critical photoperiod. For example, spinach, a short-night plant, only produces flowers when **exposed to** less-than-eleven-hour intervals of darkness. Spinach's critical photoperiod is, therefore, eleven hours.

4 17)**Compared to** their flowering behavior, the actual method **used** by plants **to distinguish** daytime from nighttime is not well understood. 18)**So far**, botanists have discovered that plants utilize an internal clock and a light-detecting pigment **called** phytochrome 19)**in order to** measure the length of uninterrupted darkness. The internal biological clock **is used to measure** the length of time the plant has spent without light. It 20)**works as** a timer that starts ticking when the light goes out, and resets when it returns. This clock is found in almost all organisms, including humans, yet is poorly understood. There is, however, a better grasp of the phytochrome. Phytochrome is a pigment found in plants which has the **ability to detect** light and 21)**bring about** cellular change when it is present. One such cellular change is the resetting of the internal clock that measures the length of continuous darkness.

5 This mechanism is quite sensitive; many species of long-night plants that have their darkness interrupted for even a minute or two with 22)**either** sunlight **or** artificial light may not flower. This effect however does not occur with all types of light. It was found that red light 23)**shone on** a plant during the night is perceived by the plant and the plant resets its biological clock. But the same plant does not reset its clock when **exposed to** far-red light (light with a longer wavelength than red light), and therefore it produces flowers. This is 24)**not** because phytochrome cannot detect far-red light, **but** because it 25)**reacts to** the two types of light differently.

6 The discovery of what internal factors actually signal plants to flower **in response to** light has overarching potential in biology and agriculture, which 26)**makes** it an intriguing topic of study. Experiments conducted on cockleburs, a family of long-night plants that **require** more than eight hours of darkness **to flower**, revealed that despite their strong 27)**sensitivity to** light exposure, if even a single leaf of the cocklebur experiences a long night, while the rest of the plant is 28)**subjected to** short nights, it still produced flowers. This experiment suggested that a flowering factor 29)**is sent from** the leaves **to** the flower buds when the flowering conditions for the plants are met. **So far** scientists have not found this factor, but the most widely accepted notion is that interactions **among** multiple, as yet unidentified plant hormones or other compounds, 30)**referred to as** florigen, trigger flowering.

---

1. 식물의 성장에서 빛의 중요성
2. 개화가능성을 높이기 위한 식물의 적응
3. 낮의 길이에 대한 반응에 따른 식물의 3가지 분류
4. 식물들이 낮 시간과 밤 시간을 구별하는 방법
5. 어두움의 길이에 따른 다른 반응
6. 신호를 통한 개화

5 토플 공부 방법 및 순서

3. 묶기

근본적으로 크게 토플 성적을 올리거나, 실력을 올릴 때, 가장 필요한 것은, 누가 뭐래도 해석입니다.
하지만, 공부를 하고 싶은 맘은 누구나 있겠지만,
'어떻게' 를 궁금해 할 때,
잘하는 사람들은 '한번에 해석만 잘 하면 돼' 라고 말하는 것을
구분동작으로 나눌 필요가 있습니다.
이때, 당연히 필요한 것은 재료가 되는, 단어, 구문이고,
이 재료를 잘 엮어서 좋은 결과물을 만들어 내는 과정이 묶기라고 생각하시면 됩니다.
그런데, 대부분 단어 구문 암기 하는 것도 귀찮아 할 뿐만 아니라,
이렇게 암기해둔 내용조차 종종, 단어 나열식으로 대충 감으로만 처리하는 경우를 많이 봅니다.
절대 하면 안되는 행동입니다.
그렇다면, 이렇게 대충 감/으/로 누구는 해내고 누구는 못해낸다면, 그 부분을 미분할 필요가 있습니다.
대부분 타 학원에서는 / (슬래시) 만으로 대충 끊어 읽게 만드는 경우가 많은데,
어셔에서는 이것을 구체적으로 나눠놓았습니다.

---

01. Comets, small celestial bodies (with long luminous tails and orbits) [that occasionally bring them (in close contact) (with Earth)], are some (of the most fascinating objects) (in our solar system). Today, only about 4,900 (of these bodies) composed (of frozen gases and volatile compounds) (along with rocky metallic elements) have been discovered, but the distance (of their orbits) makes it likely [that many more exist]. Comets are generally categorized (into two orbit length dependent categories): long-period and short-period comets. Short-period comets, (such as Halley's Comet) [which has been documented appearing every 76 years (since 240 B.C.E.,)] make regular appearances (due to their relatively short orbits) (of less than 200 years) and are more well-known. Long-period comets, however, are rarely observed [because they take hundreds or thousands (of years) (to complete) one trip (around the sun)].

02. The main difference (between the two categories) seems (to arrive) (from their origins). Short-period comets begin (in the Kuiper belt) (of non-planetary matter). This field (of matter), just (past Neptune's orbit), roughly 50 50 astronomical units (1 AU=the distance between Earth and the sun) (from the sun), travels (around the sun) (on nearly the same plane) (as the planets). [If two (of these comets) strike one another], or [if one is affected (by the gravitation) (of a nearby planet)], the orbit may be thrown off (in such a way) [that a comet enters the inner solar system] [where it is affected (by solar forces) and visible (from Earth)].

1) 주어,동사
2) 절
3) 전치사구
4) 분사
5) to 부정사

★묶기 방법

1. 주어 동사 표시 - 밑줄로
☞ 특히 동사구는 전체 밑줄 (가운데 부사가 껴도 전체 밑줄!!!)
  예) would have done
☞ 동사 수동은 "화살표"를 "동사 위에" 뒤집어서 표시해 둘 것!!!
  예) was not normally cut away

2. [종속접속사 + 주어 + 동사] 절처리 예) [that are difficult (to discern)]

3. (p+n) 전치사구 예) (in close contact)

4. Ing/ed 분사 (항상 "박스로" 처리해 둘 것!) ※ 박스처리는 ing , ed , 형용사 만!
☞ 현재분사는 그냥 두고, 과거분사는 "화살표"를 "과거분사 위에" 뒤집어서 표시해 둘 것!
☞ 후치수식은 모두 후치수식 표시를 해둬야 합니다. 뒤에서 수식에 약한 한국 학생들에게는 필수입니다.
  ing 예) •[which has been documented appearing every 76 years.
  ed   예) •(by the matter) ejected (from the Swift-Tuttle comet)
  형용사 예) •undergo the changes typical (of all comets)

5. to 부정사는 (to do)만 묶을 것 = (전치사 + 동명사까지만)
  예) (to study) math = (by studying) math
  ☞ 만약 학생이 (전치사 + 동명사 + 명사)까지 묶으면 ➔ 이건, 동명사를 형용사로 해석한 경우이므로 잘못 해석됨.

6. 완초 1반은 n 기능까지 표시할 것

7. 채점 뒤, ❶ - 틀린 곳에 번호 적고, 고치고(형광펜으로)
  ❷ - 오른쪽 페이지에 이유 적을 것
  ❸ - ❷에 적힌 이유 중, 공통되는 것을 잡아낸 뒤
  ❹ - 다음 시험지에서 공통된 것이 또 잡히면, 긴장할 것

★만약, 묶기가 이해되지 않으면 문법기초가 약해서 입니다.
어셔 문법(Grammar)을 통해 꼭 기초를 다져 주시기 바랍니다.

5 토플 공부 방법 및 순서

4. 10번 읽기

다시 한번, 반드시 **암기 후 읽어야 합니다.** 읽다 보면 암기 되겠지… 란 생각은 통하지 않습니다.
앞선 백지 시험을 다 마쳤을 경우에서 멈추면, 외운 것을 적용할 수 있다고 장담할 수 있는 상황은 아닙니다.
결국, 자연스레 독해를 해둬야 문제가 해결될 수 있는데, 문제는 늘 같은 내용이 같은 문장 형태로 나오지 않는다는 사실입니다.
그렇다고, 막연히 그냥 어떻게 되겠지… 라는 생각으로 손을 놓으면 안되고, 꼭 수업 나간 지문을 반복적으로 읽으시기 바랍니다.
이때, 주의할 것은 그냥 소리 내서 읽으라는 말이 아닙니다.
꼭 내용을 이해하면서 해석하고, 문단문단마다 꼭 내용을 정리하면서 읽으셔야 합니다.
그냥 소리 내서 읽기만 하거나, 문장 해석만을 할 경우에는 많이 읽었더라도 이해 실력을 높이는 데는 도움이 되지 않습니다.
토플이 원하는 것은 READING이 아닌, COMPREHENSION입니다.!!!

10번 읽기 방법

4.1 어려운 문장만 확실해 질때 까지 열번 읽어서 랜덤하게 물어도 확실하게 답변할 수 있게 만들어야 합니다. 그리고 나머지 문장들을 4.2에 따라 진행합니다.

4.2 처음 읽을 때는 상당히 긴 시간이 걸릴 것입니다. 보통 iBT 지문 750자 내외를 기준으로 30분에서 한 시간 이상이 걸리기도 합니다. (단어를 다 외우고 구문을 다 외웠음에도) 하지만, 이건 본인의 실력이 나쁜 게 아닌 원래 정상적인 일입니다. 그리고 두 번째 읽을 때도 크게 차이가 나지는 않을 것입니다. 하지만, 세 번째 네 번째로 가면 갈수록 속도도 이해도도 높아지는 것을 느낄 수 있을 것입니다.

읽으면서 수시로 스스로에게 물어보시기 바랍니다. '이 지문을 2주 뒤 갑자기 읽어도 자신 있게 읽을 수 있을까?' 자신 있을 경우에만, 다음 공부로 넘어가시기 바랍니다.
바를 정(正)자를 지문 상단에 체크하면서 읽으시고, 소요되는 시간도 같이 체크해보시기 바랍니다.

항상 긴장하고 점검하며 공부해야 집중력도 유지됩니다. 보통 이렇게 되는 데는 최소 5번은 읽어야 자신감이 생길 것이고, 보수적으로 내용에 따라 열 번을 각오하고 읽으시는 것을 권해드립니다.

스스로 준비가 충분히 되어 있는지를 테스트 할 때는, 공부가 끝난 다음 날 문제지의 제일 뒤에 있는 지문만을 **모아놓은 '열번읽기' 를 펴고 읽었을 때,** 막힘없이 잘 이해가 될 만큼 읽히면 일차통과입니다.

이후, 주말마다 메모없는 책 뒤 부분만을 펴고 확인을 반복하시기 바랍니다. 확실히 굳히는 방법이기도 하며, 새로운 내용들이 보이기도 할 것입니다.

5. exam 프로그램 (어셔 재학생 대상)

묶기, 단어, 구문 시험을 exam 프로그램을 사용하여 매일 정기적으로 치루게 되면,
열흘 내에 각 항목의 반복 패턴을 파악할 수 있습니다.
그대로 열흘 내외를 더하면, 상당한 정도의 적용도를 기대할 수 있습니다.
잘 이용해서 좋은 결과 바랍니다.

▎구문단어

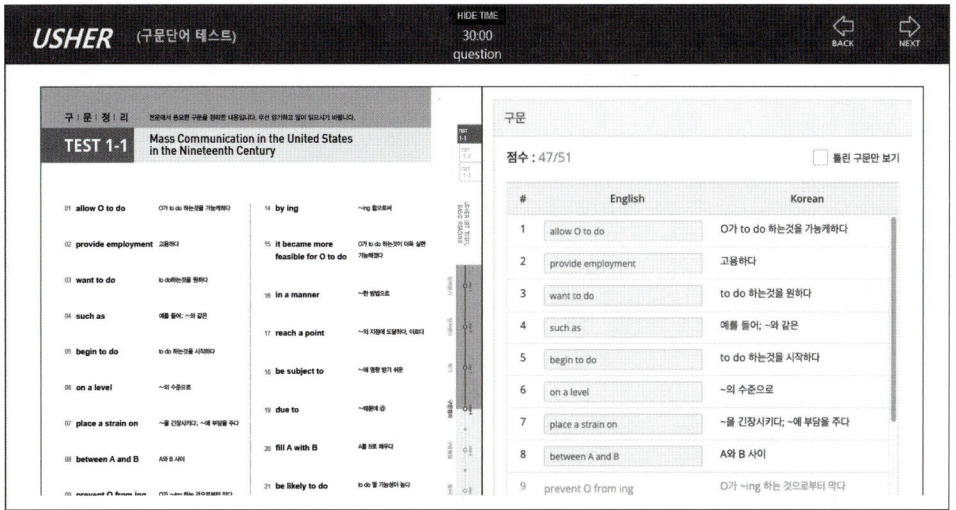

▎묶기

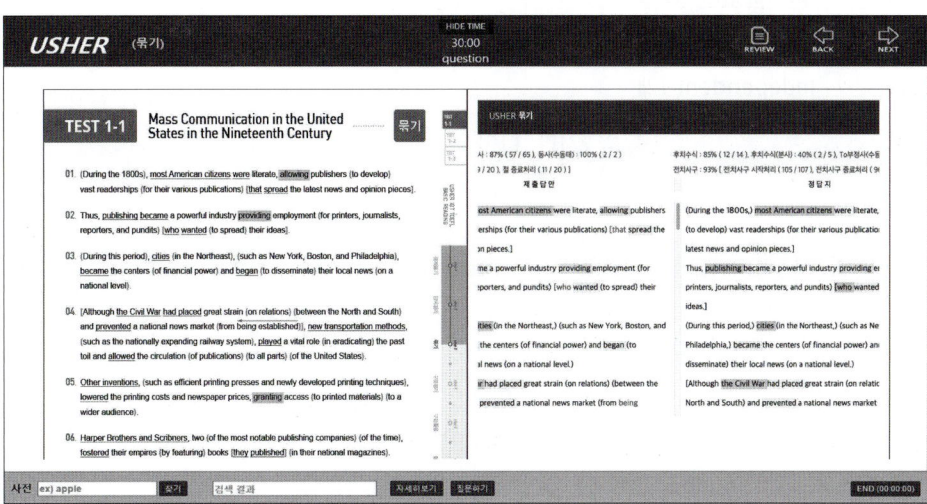

iBT TOEFL(iBT 토플) 소개

USHER iBT TOEFL INTERMEDIATE TEST READING(어셔 iBT 토플 인터미디어트 테스트 리딩)

iBT TOEFL (iBT 토플)이란?

TOEFL(Test of English as a Foreign Language)이란 주로 영어권 국가의 대학교에 진학하는 외국인 학생의 영어실력을 평가하기 위하여 만들어진 시험입니다. 현재 TOEFL (토플)은 iBT(internet-Based Test) TOEFL이라 불리며, PBT(Paper-Based Test) 와 CBT(Computer-Based Test)를 거쳐 채택된 3세대 시험방식입니다. 읽기, 듣기, 말하기, 쓰기의 다양한 분야의 영어실력을 보기 때문에 현재 세계적으로 가장 공신력 있는 영어시험으로 자리 잡았습니다.

iBT TOEFL (iBT 토플) 구성

시험순서	지문 개수	시간	세부사항	만점
Reading (상대평가)	Passage 2개 (700단어 X 2개)	35분	**Passage 당** 17분 30초 10문제	30점
Listening (상대평가)	Conversation 1개 Lecture 1개	36분	문제풀이시간 7분	30점
	Conversation 1개 Lecture 2개		문제풀이시간 10분	
Speaking (절대평가)	Independent 1개 Intergrated 3개	16분 내외	-	30점
Writing (절대평가)	Intergrated 1개 Independent 1개	29분	-	30점
	총 약 2시간 (116분)			총점 120점

꼭 알아두세요!

접수	시험일정이 나오면 접수 가능 * Late fee(응시 7일 전 시험 신청 시) 40$추가
비용	시험 - 미화 $ 220 (원화결제 가능) 취소한 성적 복원 - 미화 $ 20 성적 전송 - 미화 $ 20 (1개 기관당) 일자 변경 - 미화 $ 60 재채점 - 미화 $ 80 (1개 section당: 성적 불신시 speaking, writing만 가능)

시험	3일에 1번 수/토/일 가능
시험장소	전국 27개 도시에 있는 Test Center 및 세계 각국의 ETS Test Center (안양, 아산, 부천, 부산, 천안, 청주, 춘천, 대구, 대전, 고성, 고양, 군포, 광주, 경기, 경주, 경산, 화성, 인천, 제주, 전주, 진주, 오산, 포천, 성남, 서울, 울산, 용인 등 27개 도시 - 토플 시험장에 대한 자세한 정보는 usherin.usher.co.kr 참조)
준비물	토플 web site에 등록되어 있는 신분증 지참
성적 발표일	리딩 리스닝은 시험 직후, 스피킹 라이팅은 최소 6일 ~ 최대 14일
성적 유효기간	2년
토플 시험 등록 취소	시험 등록 후 7일 까지 : 전액환불 시험 등록 후 8일 이후 : 금액의 50% 환불 시험보기 4일전 : 금액의 50% 환불 콜센터에 전화하거나 홈페이지에서 취소 (e-mail로는 불가능)

시험장에서!

1. 시험절차   시험장에 도착하면 여권 확인 후, 성적표에 나올 사진을 찍고 감독관의 안내에 따라 순서대로 시험을 시작한다.

2. 필기도구   연필과 종이는 감독관이 나누어주므로 따로 필요가 없고, 부족하면 얼마든지 더 달라고 할 수 있다. 다만, Section 시작 전에 종이에 필기할 경우, 부정행위로 간주될 수 있으므로 각별히 주의하자.

3. 헤드폰 음량   시험 도중 언제든지 조절할 수 있다.

4. 마이크 음량   시험 시작 직후와 Speaking Section 직전에 조절할 수 있다.

5. 휴식시간   없음

6. 주의사항   각 응시자마다 시험 진행 시간이 다르기 때문에, 내가 Listening이나 Writing Section을 풀고 있을 때, 다른 사람의 목소리가 방해가 되는 경우가 많으니 염두해 두자.

 iBT TOEFL READING 소개

USHER iBT TOEFL INTERMEDIATE TEST READING(어셔 iBT 토플 인터미디어트 테스트 리딩)

iBT READING 영역에서는 유학을 나갔을 때, 학생들이 학교생활, 즉, 수업을 따라가는데 필요한 가장 기초적인 수준의 읽기 능력여부를 파악하는데 목적이 있습니다. 그러므로, 다양한 분야의 지문이 있지만, 꼭 배경 지식을 요구하지는 않으므로 시작부터 너무 겁먹을 필요는 없습니다. 하지만, 18분 이내에 1지문을 푸는 것을 대다수의 시험보는 학생들은 힘들어 하므로, 정확하고 빠른 독해 능력은 문제 푸는데 있어 핵심적인 부분이다. 여기서 중요한 것은 정확이 먼저이고 빠름은 다음순서라는 사실은 꼭 기억해야 합니다.

iBT READING 구성

총 지문 개수는 2개의 지문으로 구성되어 있습니다.
시험 시간도 35분으로 줄었습니다.

iBT READING 특징

- **NOTE TAKING**이 허용된다
- 지문에 제목이 주어진다.
- 전문용어 등은 뜻을 알려주는 **GLOSSARY**기능이 있다.

> **GLOSSARY**
> blood poisoning caused by pathogenic microorganisms and their toxic products in the bloodstream.

iBT READING 문제 유형 분석

난이도	문제 유형	문제 유형 설명	배점	지문당 문항 수
쉬움 (기본점수 약 50% 차지)	VOCABULARY	유의어 찾기	1점	1~2개
	FACT & NEGATIVE FACT	지문 내용과 맞거나, 틀린 내용 찾기	1점	3~5개
	REFERENCE	지시어가 가리키는 대상 찾기	1점	0~1개
어려움 (변별력 목적 약 50% 차지)	SENTENCE SIMPLICATION	문장 PARAPHRASE	1점	1개
	INSERTION	논리에 맞게 문장 끼워 넣기	1점	1개
	RHETORICAL PURPOSE	작가가 글속의 내용을 넣은 이유 찾기	1점	1~2개
	INFERENCE	제공된 정보로 내용 추론하기	1점	1~2개
	SUMMARY	문단 정리	2점	둘 중 선택적으로 하나만 나옴. 하지만, 주로 SUMMARY가 많이 나옴
	CATEGORY CHART	문단 속 정보를 알맞게 정렬하기	2~3점	

- 현재 풀고 있는 문제의 위치와, 시간확인 및 뒤로 돌아갈 수 있는 기능들이 우측 상단에 있다. (아래 그림 참조)

iBT READING 화면 구성

화면 상단 우측에 시험 진행 사항을 알려주는 부분이 있다. Question 14 of 20

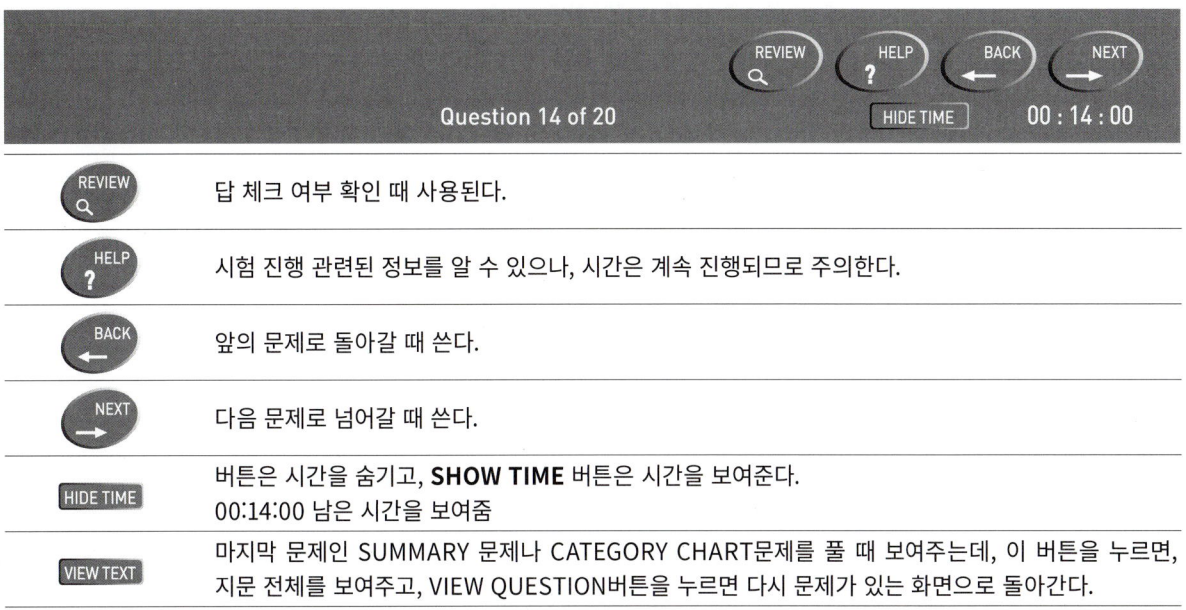

REVIEW	답 체크 여부 확인 때 사용된다.
HELP	시험 진행 관련된 정보를 알 수 있으나, 시간은 계속 진행되므로 주의한다.
BACK	앞의 문제로 돌아갈 때 쓴다.
NEXT	다음 문제로 넘어갈 때 쓴다.
HIDE TIME	버튼은 시간을 숨기고, **SHOW TIME** 버튼은 시간을 보여준다. 00:14:00 남은 시간을 보여줌
VIEW TEXT	마지막 문제인 SUMMARY 문제나 CATEGORY CHART문제를 풀 때 보여주는데, 이 버튼을 누르면, 지문 전체를 보여주고, VIEW QUESTION버튼을 누르면 다시 문제가 있는 화면으로 돌아간다.

READING DIRECTION 화면

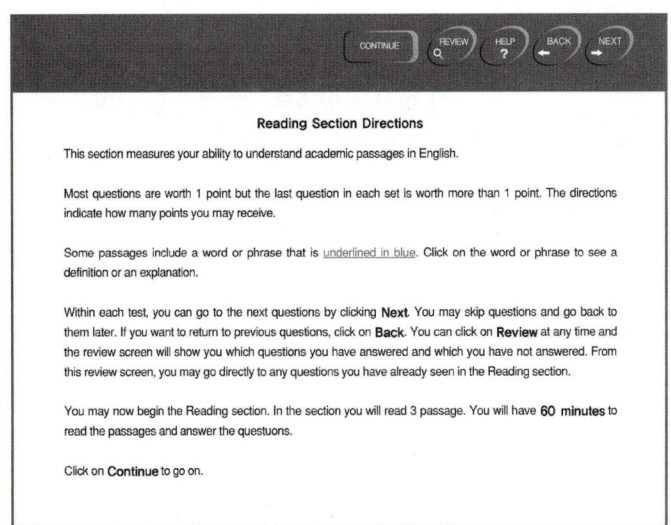

리딩 시험 진행방식을 설명해준다.

7 iBT TOEFL READING 소개

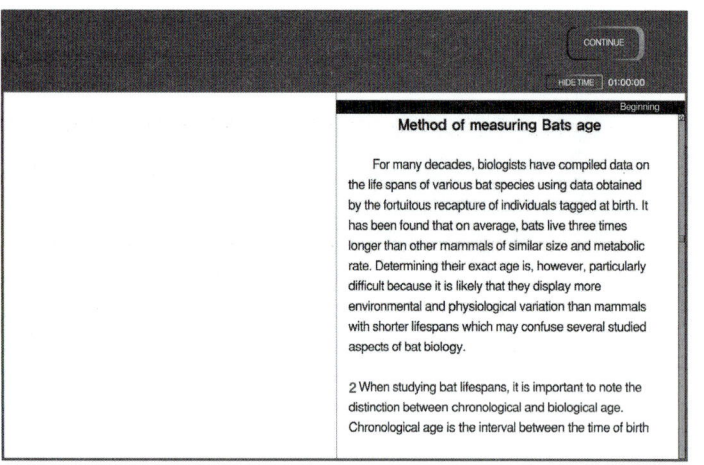

처음엔 문제없이 지문만 보여주는 화면이 있는데, 이때 스크롤을 내려 지문 전체를 봐야만 CONTINUE 버튼을 눌러 본 문제로 넘어갈 수 있다.

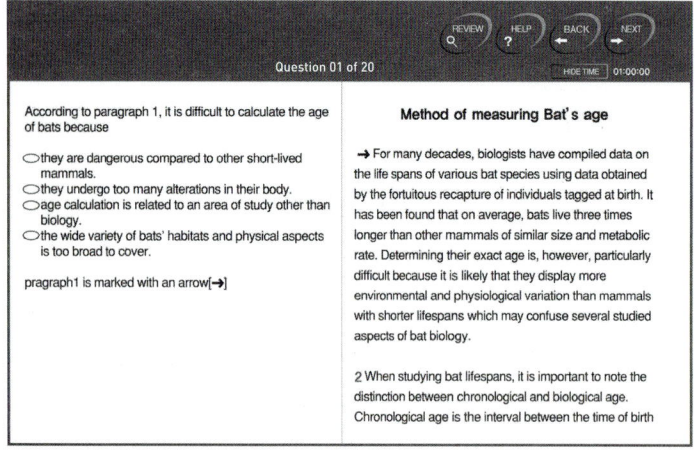

문제로 넘어가면, 문제는 왼쪽에, 지문은 오른쪽에 한 문제씩 보여지며, 우측 상단의 NEXT 버튼을 누르면 다음 문제로 넘어간다. 가끔 본문 속의 파란색 밑줄은 용어해설을 보여줄 때 쓰이며, 누르면 좌측 화면 하단에 나타난다.

SUMMARY 문제 화면

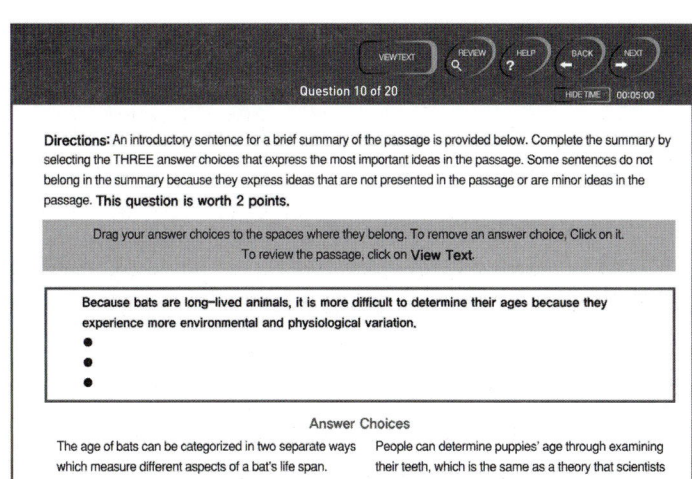

SUMMARY 문제가 나올 때는 화면 속엔 지문없이 문제만 전체 화면으로 보인다. 이때 상단의 VIEW TEXT버튼을 누르면 지문만 다시 보여주며, 다시 문제를 보고 싶을 땐, VIEW QUESTION버튼을 누르면 다시 돌아갈 수 있다. 답을 선택하는 방법은 초이스에 있는 보기를 박스 안에 드래그해서 놓으면 되고, 답을 바꿀 때는 보기를 한번 더 클릭하면 정답자리에서 없어진다.

CATEGORY 문제 화면

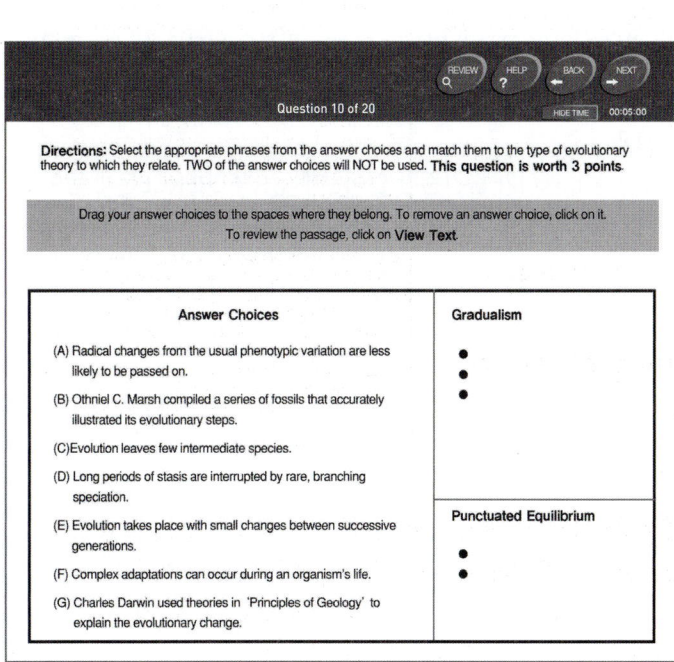

SUMMARY 문제와 같은 화면과 같은 답 선택 방법이 사용된다.

 READING STRATEGIES

USHER iBT TOEFL INTERMEDIATE TEST READING(어셔 iBT 토플 인터미디어트 테스트 리딩)

문제 유형을 확인하기 전에 우선, test 1을 풀어보고, 스스로에 대한 평가와 더불어 문제 유형 파악을 해주시기 바랍니다. 먼저 유형을 파악 해보는 것보다는, 일단, 풀어본 뒤 알아가는 것이 훨씬 빠르게 이해할 수 있기에, 각 문제 유형별 전략 뒤에는 test 1을 기준으로 확인 가능한 번호를 적어두었습니다.

쉬운 문제 유형	출제 비율
1. VOCABULARY 2. FACT & NEGATIVE FACT 3. REFERENCE	50%

어려운 문제 유형	출제 비율
4. SENTENCE SIMPLIFICATION 5. INSERTION 6. RHETORICAL PURPOSE 7. INFERENCE 8. SUMMARY 9. CATEGORY CHART	50%

시험이 임박한 학생들을 위한 독해 전략

* 서문에서 이미 학생들의 시간에 대한 수준별 대응책을 적어 놓았습니다. 하지만, 여기선, 대부분의 학생들이 시간이 모자라는 경우가 많으므로 이런 경우에 대해 우선적으로 다루었습니다.

1. 지문은 제목과 각 문단 첫 줄만 읽고, 곧바로 CONTINUE버튼을 눌러 문제로 넘어갑니다.
시간이 없는 경우가 많은데 지문을 다 읽고 넘어가는 경우 시간이 모자라 마지막 문제는 찍지도 못하고 끝나는 경우도 있기 때문에 미리 주의해야 합니다.

2. 문제 풀이하며 본문을 읽습니다. (시간이 없을 경우, 효과가 큼)
토플 문제 번호순서대로, 본문의 답 근거도 순서를 따릅니다. 게다가 중간중간 단어문제나 REFERENCE문제 등이 표시된 경우에는 그 문제보다 앞 문제라면 표시된 곳 앞에서, 뒷 문제라면 표시된 곳 뒤에서 답 근거를 찾으면 됩니다. (뒷 페이지 참조)

3. SKIMMING → SCANNING
대략 훑었어도, 답 근거가 어디쯤이라는 감이 오면, 그때부터는 집중해서 꼼꼼히 내용을 살펴야 합니다. 대부분 문제는 답은 둘 중에 하나로 좁혀지는데 이때 스캐닝 하지 않아 대충 읽고 답을 잡으면 오답에 낚일 확률이 높습니다. 문제 출제 기관인 ETS는 문제만 50년째 만들고 있는 기관입니다. 문제 푸는 여러분을 낚는 데는 상당한 노하우가 있습니다.

4. 문제를 풀며 수시로 내용을 파악해야 합니다.
마지막 SUMMARY문제는 문단 내용을 파악하지 못하면 풀지 못하게 만들어놨습니다. 그런데 문제는 한 문제 한 문제 푸는 데만 급급한 학생들의 경우에는 문단 정리를 하지 못하고, 마지막 SUMMARY문제를 만나는 경우인데, 이땐 대안이 없습니다. 수시로 내용을 정리하며 지나가야 마지막 문제를 잘 풀 수 있습니다. 그러므로 수시로 내용 파악을 해두어야 합니다.

5. 반드시 ① '**문제를 똑바로 읽고**' ② **핵심 단어**에 '**동그라미**'를 쳐서 묻는 내용을 명확히 한 후 ③ '**답 근거**'를 찾으시길 바랍니다.

*따라가면서 푼다는 말은....

1. **Fact**
2. **Infer**
3. **Purpose**
4. **Fact**
5. **Vocab**
6. **Sentence simplification**
7. **Negative fact**
8. **Vocab**
9. **Insert**
10. **Summary**

위의 ▢▢▢▢ 에 해당하는 문제들은 모두 힌트를 줄 수 있는 내용들입니다.

READING STRATEGIES

8 READING STRATEGIES

1 VOCABULARY - 유의어 찾기 문제

▶ 질문 형태

The word "_____" in the passage is closest in meaning to

The phrase "_____" in the passage is closet in meaning to

▶ 오답 패턴 (학생들이 잘 낚이는 경우 모음)
- 선택지 중 두 개의 단어가 모두 사전의 동의어에 있을 경우 (난이도 상)
- 선택지 중 어떤 단어도 사전의 동의어에 없을 경우 (난이도 상)
- 넣어봤을 때, 말은 되지만, 유의어는 아닌 경우
- 단어랑 스펠링이 비슷한 경우

▶ 핵심 전략
- 무조건 시험장 들어가기 전에 단어 책 한 권은 끝내고 들어가야 합니다. USHER iBT TOEFL VOCABULARY를 마친 후라면 **80%**는 처리가 가능합니다.

- **단어 문제는 무조건 시간을 벌어주는 문제유형입니다.**
  즉, 완전 쉬워서 딱 보고 답이 나왔기 때문에 시간을 벌어주거나, 완전 어렵게 나와서 고민해야 될 상황에서는 절대 고민하지 않고 그냥 콱 찍고 지나가야 합니다. 단어 문제가 어려울 때는 아무리 봐도 어차피 답을 정확히 잡을 수는 없습니다. 본인을 믿고 빨리 체크하고 다음 문제에서 승부를 거는 것이 더 낫습니다.
  그러므로 어려우나 쉬우나, 무조건 단어 문제에서는 시간을 벌어야 하고, 고민하지 않아야 합니다. 단, 아무리 쉬운 문제라도 꼭 문장에 넣어보고 대입 후 체크하도록 함을 잊어서는 안됩니다.

- 만약 단어 문제가 어렵게 난다면, 둘 중 하나입니다. 동의어가 선택지중에서 두 개가 있거나,
  동의어 전혀 없을 때
  이 땐, 문맥을 봐서 가장 알맞은 답을 찾아야 합니다.
  단어의 뉘앙스를 정확히 알고 있어야 알 수 있는 문제이므로 앞서 적은 대로 시간을 많이 들이지 않도록 합니다.

- **꼭 집어 넣어서 재확인을 해야 합니다.**
  아무리 동의어라도 문맥상 여러 개의 뜻 중에서 다른 의미로 사용될 수 있기 때문에 반드시 확인을 해봐야 합니다.

2 FACT & NEGATIVE FACT - 지문의 세부 정보를 맞게 적었거나 틀리게 적은 경우를 찾아내는 문제

▶ **질문 형태**
- Fact
  According to paragraph #, which of the following is true of (about) _____?
  According to paragraph #, _____?
  According to paragraph #, what / when / where / why / how _____?
- Negative fact
  According to paragraph #, all of the following are true of _____ EXCEPT
  According to paragraph #, all of the following statements about _____ EXCEPT
  According to paragraph #, which of the following is NOT true of _____?

▶ **오답 패턴 (학생들이 잘 낚이는 경우 모음)**
- 해석이 안될 경우 (난이도 상)
- 투 클릭(Two click) 문제 (정답 개수로 난이도 중)
- 단어만 사용하고 지문과 무관한 내용
- 언급 안된 내용이 그럴싸하게 적힌 경우
- "EXCEPT" 문제는 꼭 똑바로 묻는대로 대답할 것 (아닌 것 고르라는 얘기는 오답 세 개는 모두 본문에서 맞단 얘기! → 틀린 것 3개를 먼저 배제시켜서 잡는게 확실합니다)
- 상식으로 접근할 경우
- 반만 맞고 반은 틀린 경우 (특히 틀린 부분이 뒷부분일 경우, 학생들은 앞만 보고 답으로 선택하는 경우 주의할 것)
- 본문과 반대 내용을 적어둘 때 (은근히 혼동됨)

▶ **핵심 전략**
- 문제에서 **핵심 되는 단어**를 본문에서 빨리 찾습니다.
  모든 문제를 풀 때는 질문을 잘 읽어야 합니다. 알면서도 틀리는 경우가 많음은 한국어로 내는 시험이나 토플 시험이나 마찬가지입니다. 그러므로, 질문에서 묻는 내용 중 핵심이 되는 단어를 재빨리 지문에서 찾아야 답 근거를 정확히 찾을 수 있습니다. 평상시 문제 풀고 스터디 할 때 조원들과 답 근거 찾기를 열심히 해둔 학생이라면 절대 어렵게 푸는 문제는 아닙니다.
- 지문에서 찾은 내용을 PARAPHRASE한 것을 찾습니다.
  토플시험에는 이런 말이 있습니다. 듣기시험에선 들은 단어가 많은 선택지를 답으로 찍고, 독해시험에선 본문에서 본 단어가 많은 선택지는 피하십시오. 극단적이긴 하지만, 전혀 틀린 말은 아닙니다. 즉, 본문의 내용을 다른 단어로 바꿔서 정답을 내곤 하기 때문에 정보 전달은 올바로 하되, 표현은 모두 바뀌어져 있는 경우가 대부분입니다. 그리고 NEGATIVE FACT의 경우에는 지문과 내용이 다르거나, 언급되어 있지 않는 보기가 정답입니다.
- 너무 강한 표현은 주의해서 봅니다. (절대 답이 안되는 것은 아닙니다)
  예) never, only.

8 READING STRATEGIES

3 REFERENCE - 지문 속의 음영 표시된 지시어가 가리키는 단어가 무엇인지 찾는 문제

▶ **질문 형태**

The word " ▨▨▨▨ " in the passage refers to

The phrase " ▨▨▨▨ " in the passage refers to

▶ **오답 패턴 (학생들이 잘 낚이는 경우 모음)**
- 정답과 (단수 복수의) 수가 일치되는 주변의 명사를 미끼로 쓸 때
- 앞의 내용 중 혼동될만한 내용을 미리 던져두는 경우

▶ **핵심 전략 (앞문장의 주어나 목적어일 가능성이 크다)**
- 평상시 문장을 읽을 때, 인칭대명사 it, they, their나 지시대명사 this, that, those, 그리고 부정대명사 some, others가 무엇을 가리키는지를 늘 확인하며 표시하는 버릇이 필요합니다.
- 답은 앞 문장 또는 같은 문장 앞일 확률이 높습니다.
  지시어가 가리키는 단어는 문장의 뒤, 그리고 두 문장 이상 떨어진 앞 문장에선 찾지 않습니다.
- 답을 찾았다 싶어도 꼭 다시 바뀐 단어로 **집어넣어 보고** 확인합니다.
  자연스러운지 확인하지 않고 찍으면 틀릴 수 있습니다. 쉬운 문제유형이므로 실수하지 않도록 해야 합니다.

4. SENTENCE SIMPLIFICATION
- 본문에서 음영 표시된 한문장의 내용을 그대로 담고 있는 또 다른 문장을 찾아내는 문제

▶ 질문 형태

Which of the sentences below best expresses the essential information in the highlighted sentence in the passage? Incorrect choices change the meaning in important ways or leave out essential information.

▶ 오답 패턴 (학생들이 잘 낚이는 경우 모음)
- 일단, 어려운 문장구조이거나, 내용이 복잡하거나, 단어가 어려운 경우라는 것 자체
- 내용 중 일부를 생략하는 경우 (마이너로서 내용은 맞지만, 답이 안됨) (난이도 상)
- 내용은 그럴싸하나 순서나, 인과 등을 반대로 엮는 경우 (난이도 상)
- 논리적으로 비약하는 경우
- 상식으로 내용을 엮은 경우
- 일부는 맞고 일부는 틀린 경우

▶ 핵심 전략

- **평상시 문법부분이 강해야 합니다.**
  토플문제의 출제포인트는 뭐든 중간에 막히는 문장입니다. 쉽게 잘 해석되는 부분에서는 문제 출제를 않습니다. 특히나 Sentence Simplification 스타일의 문제는 작정하고 어려운 문장을 문제로 만든 것입니다. 그러므로, 평상시 대충 내용만 파악하는 독해 습관을 가진 학생들에겐 난감할 수 있는 유형입니다.

- **내용을 잘게 자릅니다. → 꼭 수렴시킵니다.**
  문장 속에서 다루고 있는 내용들을 잘게 자른 후, 그 내용들을 어떻게든 수렴시켜야 답이 됩니다. 문제 내용과 다르게 적는 오답 스타일은 쉽게 낸 것입니다. 이런 것은 당연히 오답처리 할 수 있어야 하고, 이보다 더 주의 할 것은 아무리 맞는 내용을 적었다 하더라도 생략된 것은 답이 아닙니다. 그러므로 꼭 잘게 자른 후, 그 내용들을 다 포함하였는지 꼼꼼히 따져봐야 합니다.

8 READING STRATEGIES

5 INSERTION - 지문에서 빠진 문장을 알맞은 위치에 넣는 유형

▶ **질문 형태**

Look at the four squares [■] that indicate where the following sentence could be added to the passage.

삽입문장

Where would the sentence best fit? Click on a square [■] to add the sentence to the passage.
(문제가 뜨면 지문에 4개의 ■가 뜨고 그 중에 하나를 찍으면 문장이 삽입이 됩니다)

▶ **오답 패턴 (학생들이 잘 낚이는 경우 모음)**
- **덩어리에서 작은 내용으로 넘어가는** 경우 (난이도 상)
- 답이 잘 보이지 않을 때는 끼워넣기 뒤의 문장에서 관련성 있는 단어가 있는지 찾아볼 것. (예 - test 4-13번)
- 중복되는 단어, 지시어 또는 연결어 없이 내용으로만 연결되는 문장 (난이도 상)
- 연결어로 연결되는 경우 (예 - however, moreover, thus) (이어지는 내용은 틀리지만 연결어 보고 단순 선택)
- 지시어나 중복되는 단어로 연결되는 경우 (예 - this, that, 중복단어)
- for example이 끼워넣을 문장에 나오면 앞에 내용보다 뒤에 내용이 훨씬 더 구체적입니다.

▶ **핵심 전략**

하
① • 일단 제시된 **끼워 넣을 문장을 읽습니다**.
② • 끼워 넣을 문장 중 IT, THIS, THAT 등 지시어가 나오면 쉬운 문제입니다.
   이런 문제는 지시어가 가리키는 단어를 앞 문장에서 찾을 수 있기만 하면 됩니다. 그러므로 쉽게 풀 수 있는 유형입니다.
   • in fact, indeed가 나오면 끼워넣기 문장은 앞의 문장의 반복입니다. 즉, 같은 내용을 포함한 (약간은 더 클 수 도 있는) 내용이 끼워넣을 문장앞에 와야 합니다.
③ • 끼워 넣을 문장 중, HOWEVER, MOREOVER, ALSO, THEREFORE 등 연결단어가 나오면 쉬운 문제입니다. **연결어** 역시, 내용을 매끄럽게 이어주기 위해 도움을 주는 단어이므로 이런 단어가 있을 땐 앞뒤 문장의 논리가 매끄러운 곳만 찾아내면 되기에 쉬운 문제입니다.

상
④ • 영어마인드로서 항상 **덩어리**를 먼저 얘기하고, 구체적인 예를 드는 스타일의 문제라면 어려운 문제입니다.
   원어민들은 항상 결론을 던지고 예를 드는 경우가 많습니다.
   하지만, 한글은 예를 들고 결론을 얘기해도 문제되지 않습니다. 예를 들면,
   I) 한국 학생들은 공부를 열심히 한다는 점을 알 수 있습니다.
      지하철에서도, 버스에서도, 도서관에서도, 복도에서도 늘 공부하는 학생들을 많이 만났기 때문입니다.
   II) 지하철에서도, 버스에서도, 도서관에서도, 복도에서도 늘 공부하는 한국 학생들을 많이 만났습니다.
   그렇기 때문에, 한국 학생들은 공부를 열심히 한다는 점을 알 수 있습니다. 답은 I)으로 해야 합니다. 이유는 한국어처럼, 두괄식, 미괄식, 병렬식, 수미 상관 등의 다양한 글 전개 방법을 취하는 것과 달리, **영어에서는 항상 결론을 먼저 던져놓는 두괄식 형태**의 글 전개가 많기 때문입니다. 한국 학생들에게, 위 두 가지에서 무엇이 맞냐고 묻는다면, 답하지 못하는 경우가 많습니다. 해석해 주고 풀라고 해도 헤매는 유일한 문제 스타일이 될 수 있는 유형이므로 꼭 전제를 먼저 인식해야 합니다.

"덩어리 → 구체적 내용"

극상
⑤ • 답을 체크하기 전에 꼭 문장에 **넣어보고** 확인합니다. 특히 끼워넣은 뒤, 뒤에 나오는 **지시어** it이나 this들을 설명 할 수 있어야 합니다.

6 RHETORICAL PURPOSE - 글쓴이가 글 속의 내용을 넣은 이유 찾기

▶ 질문 형태

The phrase "＿＿＿" in the passage refers to the explanation why
In paragraph #, what is the author's main purpose in the discussion of ＿＿＿＿＿＿＿?
Why does the author mention
In paragraph #, why does the author mention ＿＿＿＿?
Why does the author include a description of ＿＿＿＿＿＿＿＿?

▶ 오답 패턴 (학생들이 잘 낚이는 경우 모음)
- 문단 (paragraph) 전체가 큰 (passage) 전체에서 하는 기능을 물을 때 (난이도 상)
  (문단 정리가 있어야 함 = 서머리 문제)
- 가끔 어려운 문장을 섞은 부분에서 내는 경우 (난이도 상)
- 사실은 맞지만, 묻는 말에 대한 답이 아닌 경우 - 예) 결과를 묻는 질문에 과정은 오답 (난이도 상)
- 예의 특징으로서는 맞으나, 언급 이유는 아닌 경우 (난이도 상)
- 단어만 나열하고 딴소리 한 경우
- 상식으로 접근하는 경우
- 언급 없는 경우

▶ 핵심 전략

- **문제를 똑바로 읽습니다.**
  학생들이 가장 잘 하는 건 달을 보라고 가리켰건만, 달은 안보고 손가락만 보는 경우입니다.
  예를 들어, 국가의 기능이 약하면 국민들이 자구책을 찾습니다. 그 예로는 소말리아 해적과 같이 무정부 상태에서는 잔학하게 활동하는 해적무리들을 우리는 신문지상에서 종종 보곤 합니다. 라는 글에서 왜 해적을 언급했느냐 에 대해 보기에는, =
  A) 무정부 상태에서의 해적들은 잔학하게 활동 할 수도 있다는 점을 인식시키기 위하여
  B) 무정부 상태에서 국가의 기능이 약할 경우 일어날수 있는 예를 들기 위하여
  답은 당연히 B) 입니다. 하지만, A)를 찍는 경우는 해적이라는 단어의 임팩트와, 본문에서 분명히 해적들이 잔학 하게 활동한다는 내용이 있었기 때문입니다. 하지만, 절대 잊어서는 안 될 일이 질문이 묻는 말에 대답하는 것입니다. 왜 해적을 언급 했느냐 이지, 해적들에 대해 맞는 것을 고르라는 것이 아니므로, 주의해야 합니다

- 문제에서 언급한 부분만 읽지 말고 **앞부분(90%가 여기서 나옵니다.) 또는 뒷부분을 꼭 읽습니다.**
  문제에서 언급한 부분만 읽는 것은 앞서 예를든 것처럼, **예의 특징에 현혹되기 쉽기** 때문입니다.
  꼭 앞부분을 읽어서 흐름상 왜 그 얘기를 집어 넣었는지를 생각해봐야 합니다.

- 문제에 제시된 표현의 기능을 생각해봅니다.(**특히 argue와 explain의 차이를 분명히 구분합니다**)
  다음과 같은 말들이 주로 보기에 나옵니다.
  설명하기 위해서 / 예를 들기 위해서 / 비교, 대조하기 위해서 / 강조하기 위해서 / 주장하기 위해서 / 증명하기 위해서… 등

- 보기 내용을 끝까지 읽습니다.
  앞부분은 맞는 것 같지만, **뒤에서** 지문과 틀린 얘기로 **살짝 뒤트는** 경우가 있습니다.
  그러므로 마지막까지 다 읽고 지문과의 일치성을 꼭 파악하여야 합니다.

8 READING STRATEGIES

7 INFERENCE - 지문에서 콕 집어 얘기하지 않았지만, 충분히 추론할 수 있는 내용 찾기

▶ **질문 형태**

Which of the following can be inferred from paragraph # about _____?
It can be inferred from the discussion in paragraph # that _____
What can be inferred from paragraph # about _____?

▶ **오답 패턴 (학생들이 잘 낚이는 경우 모음)**
- 어려운 문장을 잘못 해석한 경우, 잘못 해석한 것이 꼭 선택지에 있음 (난이도 상)
- 비약 (난이도 상) * infer문제는 원래 본문에 fact문제처럼 직접적인 답 근거는 없지만, 그렇다고 비약해서는 안 됨
- 언급 없는 경우
- 상식으로 푼 경우
- 단어만 사용하고 딴소리 한 경우
- 반대 사실 언급
- 반은 맞고 반은 틀린 경우

▶ **핵심 전략**

- **문제의 키워드**를 본문에서 찾습니다.
  FACT 문제에서처럼 문제에서 묻는 핵심적인 키워드를 찾아야 한다는 공통점은 있으나, 대체로 FACT 문제보다 는 고민하게 만드는 문장에서 문제를 내는 경우가 많아, 많은 학생들이 어려워하는 문제 유형입니다. 기본 실력이 되어야 하므로, 문장을 읽다가 막힌다 싶으면 그곳이 INFERENCE 문제가 출제될 확률이 높은 곳입니다. 근본적으로 이해가 되지 않으면 풀리지 않으므로 기본 실력이 중요시 되는 유형입니다.

- **지문에서 근거**를 꼭 찾을 것
  문장을 근거로 하든, 문단을 근거로 하든, 결국 항상 본문에 근거를 두고 있으므로, 반드시 지문 내용 중 내용을 연결 지어 답을 찾아야 합니다.

- **상식이나 비약으로 문제를 풀지 않습니다.**
  꼭 주의해야 할 점은 상식이나 비약, 또는 혼자 소설을 써가며 문제를 푸는 경우입니다. 다시 한번, 꼭 본문에서 답 근거를 짚어낼 수 있어야 합니다.

8 SUMMARY - 지문 내용 중 문단 정리를 잘 한 것을 선택하는 문제

▶ 질문 형태

Directions: An introductory sentence for a brief summary of the passage is provided below. Complete the summary by selecting the THREE answer choices that express the most important ideas in the passage. Some sentences do not belong in the summary because they express ideas that are not presented in thepassage or are minor ideas in the passage. **This question is worth 2 points.**

Drag your answer choices to the spaces where they belong.
To remove an answer choice, click on it. To review the passage, click **View Text.**

Introductory sentence

-
-
-

(A)	(D)
(B)	(E)
(C)	(F)

▶ 오답 패턴 (학생들이 잘 낚이는 경우 모음)
- 너무 디테일한 내용은 맞아도 답이 아님, 단락급의 덩치가 있는 내용정리이어야 함(난이도 상)
- 상식으로 푼 경우
- 반만 맞고 반은 틀린 경우 (앞부분은 맞았다고 답으로 하면 안됨), 끝까지 다 잘 읽어보고 답을 고를 것
- 전혀 다른 말을 단어만 섞어서 하는 경우
- 완전히 틀린 내용

▶ 핵심 전략 (≒ Fact 문제 처럼)
- 오답부터 제낍니다. (정답 3개를 먼저 잡기가 더 어렵습니다)
- 박스 안의 INTRODUCTORY SENTENCE는 참고만 하고, 문단 급 내용을 고릅니다.
  답이라고 체크할 수 있기 위해선, 그 답이라고 생각한 문단이 과연 몇 문단을 아우를 수 있는지 꼭 생각해봐야 합니다. 즉, 정답들은 모두 몇 문단 내용이라고 짚을 수 있어야 합니다.
- 본문 내용과 맞아도 답이 아닐 수 있습니다.
  문단 급의 내용을 다뤄야 하므로, 비록 본문에서 언급한 맞는 내용이라 하더라도, 너무 디테일해서 틀릴 수도 있음을 주의해야 합니다. 즉, 맞아도(?) 맞지 않을 수(!!!) 있음을 주의해야 합니다.

8 READING STRATEGIES

9 CATEGORY CHART - CATEGORY화 시킬 수 있는 내용일 경우, 맞는 내용들을 짝지어 넣기

▶ 질문 형태

Directions: Complete the table below by selecting three answer choices that are characteristics of _____ and two answer choices that are characteristics of _____ . **This question is worth 3 points.**

Drag your answer choices to the spaces where they belong.
To remove an answer choice, click on it. To review the passage, click **View Text**.

Answer choice	Category 1
(A)	•
(B)	•
(C)	•
(D)	Category 2
(E)	•
(F)	•
(G)	•

▶ 오답 패턴 (학생들이 잘 낚이는 경우 모음)

FACT 문제를 지문 전반에서 짝짓기로 냈다고 생각하면 편합니다. 그러므로 FACT 문제와 오답 패턴도 상당히 유사합니다. 그러므로 성가시게 시간이 상당히 많이 걸립니다. (다행히 서머리 문제가 많이 나오고 이 유형의 문제는 드물게 나옵니다)

- 해석이 안될 경우 (난이도 상)
- 단어만 사용하고 지문과 무관한 내용
- 언급 안된 내용을 그럴싸하게 적힌 경우
- 상식으로 접근할 경우
- 반만 맞고 반은 틀린 경우 (특히 틀린 부분이 뒷부분일 경우, 학생들은 앞만 보고 답으로 선택하는 경우 주의할 것)
- 본문과 반대 내용을 적어둘 때 (은근히 혼동됨)

▶ 핵심 전략 (≒ 지문 전체 Fact)

- 우선 대부분의 마지막 문제는 SUMMARY가 나오므로 **이 유형의 문제는 많이 나오지 않습니다.**

- 하지만 만약 나온다면 시간을 많이 잡아먹는 유형입니다.
  그러므로 본문을 읽을 때 왠지 유형화 시킬 수 있는 본문 내용이라면 미리부터 지문에서 확인하기 쉽도록 비슷한 내용이라 생각되는 것들을 노트테이킹 해놓을 필요가 있습니다.

- 내용이 일치하는지를 꼭 재검토합니다.
  기억으로 문제를 풀면 틀리기 쉬운 문제유형입니다. 비록 시간은 많이 잡아 먹지만 FACT 문제처럼 꼼꼼히만 시간을 가지고 보면 어려운 문제만은 아닙니다. 하지만, 시간이 없어서 또는 귀찮아서라는 이유로 확인하지 않으면 틀릴 확률이 상당히 높은 문제유형입니다. 주의해야 합니다.

USHER iBT TOEFL
INTERMEDIATE READING
TEST 1

테스트 전 확인사항

실전에 유용한 독해 전략(44p)을 숙지하였습니다. ○

화장실은 미리 다녀왔습니다. ○

휴대폰의 전원을 껐습니다. ○

노트테이킹 할 종이와 연필을 준비하였습니다. ○

시간을 체크할 시계를 준비하였습니다. ○

목표점수(20개 중 ___개)를 정하였습니다. ○

시험 시작 시간은 ___시 ___분이며,
종료 시간은 35분 뒤인 ___시 ___분입니다. ○

시험 중 이동해야 할 방해요소가 있는지 체크하였습니다. ○

시험 중 이동하지 않습니다.

Sentinel Behavior in Meerkats

1. → Meerkats are small, mongoose-like mammals that live in the Kalahari Desert of Southern Africa. Being primarily insectivores, they feed on beetles and scorpions buried underground, which they locate using their strong sense of smell. Unfortunately, when the meerkat lowers its head to search out prey under grasses, it limits its own range of sight by a significant amount. As a result they are extremely vulnerable to airborne predators such as hawks and owls. To ensure that they can reach the safety of their bolt-holes before being snatched up by birds, meerkats forage in packs and partake in what is known as sentinel behavior. As the term suggests, one meerkat in the group acts as a sentinel and does not look for food like the rest, but rather stands upright on its hind legs to gain a wider field of view with which it scans the surrounding area for possible predators and other threats to the community. When it senses danger approaching, the sentinel barks loudly to warn the others of the danger. Many scientists questioned this phenomenon because the revealing stance and loud vocalization were thought to expose the meerkat to an increased risk of predation.

폭 넓게 - 일단 버릇 들이는게 중요!

32 According to paragraph 1, why was sentinel behavior thought to be disadvantageous?

(A) It warns the predator of where the meerkat group is.
(B) It allows the meerkat to sense danger and warn the group.
(C) It helps the predators locate the sentinel meerkat.
(D) It encourages the predator to prey on meerkats over other species.

스터디 자료들 미리 수집해 둘것!

시험 중 체크 사항

❶ "?"표시하기 : 본문 읽으며, 궁금한 곳에 "?" 표시를 합니다.
  문제를 풀면서도 질문 거리에는 "?" 표시를 해둡니다.
❷ 문제 핵심에 동그라미 : 문제가 물어보는 게 무엇인지, 문제 핵심에 동그라미 표시를 합니다.
❸ 답근거 날리기 : 문제를 풀 때 선택지가 틀린 이유 단어로, 간결하게 날립니다.
❹ 경쟁 문장 표시 : 4개의 선택지 중에 정답과 경쟁하는 마지막 1개의 선택지를 표시 해둡니다. 무조건 1개여야 합니다.

Reading Section Directions

This section measures your ability to understand academic passages in English.

Most questions are worth 1 point but the last question in each set is worth more than 1 point. The directions indicate how many points you may receive.

Some passages include a word or phrase that is underlined in blue. Click on the word or phrase to see a definition or an explanation.

Within each test, you can go to the next questions by clicking **Next**. You may skip questions and go back to them later. If you want to return to previous questions, click on **Back**. You can click on **Review** at any time and the review screen will show you which questions you have answered and which you have not answered. From this reviewscreen, you may go directly to any questions you have already seen in the Reading section.

You may now begin the Reading section. In the section you will read 2 passages. You will have **35 minutes** to read the passages and answer thequestions.

Click on **Continue** to go on.

Next 버튼을 이용하여 다음 문제로 이동하고 **Back** 버튼을 이용하여 이전문제로 이동할 수 있습니다. 문제에 답을 하지 않더라도 다음 문제로이동할 수 있으며, **Review** 버튼을 이용하여 각 문제별로 답을 체크했는지의 여부를 확인할 수 있습니다.
이번 테스트에서는 세 지문을 읽게 됩니다. **35분** 동안 지문을 읽고 문제에 답을 하세요.

Comets

01. Why does the author mention "Halley's Comet which has been documented appearing every 76 years"?

(A) To give the reader more information regarding the average duration of short-period comets
(B) To relate the concept of short-term comets to a comet that the reader is likely to know about already
(C) To introduce the idea that people have been studying comets and their orbits for thousands of years
(D) To differentiate short and long-period comets by giving an example of a comet with an irregularly long orbital duration

02. The term "relatively" in the passage is closest in meaning to:

(A) very
(B) surprisingly
(C) comparatively
(D) usually

03. What can be inferred from paragraph 1 about long and short-period comets?

(A) Long-period comets have a different composition than short-period comets, allowing them to embark on longer orbits.
(B) Many comets have remained undiscovered because they burn up before they are within a distance that makes them visible from Earth.
(C) Scientists are likely to know more about short-period comets than those with longer orbits because of their multiple observations.
(D) Halley's Comet probably deviated from its original orbit around the sun in the year 240 B.C.E.

1   Comets, small celestial bodies with long luminous tails and orbits that occasionally bring them in close contact with Earth, are some of the most fascinating objects in our solar system. Today, only about 4,900 of these bodies composed of frozen gases and volatile compounds along with rocky metallic elements have been discovered, but the distance of their orbits makes it likely that many more exist. Comets are generally categorized into two orbit-length-dependent categories: long-period and short-period comets. Short-period comets, such as Halley's Comet which has been documented appearing every 76 years since 240 B.C.E., make regular appearances due to their relatively short orbits of less than 200 years and are more well-known. Long-period comets, however, are rarely observed because they take hundreds or thousands of years to complete one trip around the sun.

2   The main difference between the two categories seems to arrive from their origins. Short-period comets begin in the Kuiper belt of non-planetary matter. The matter in the belt, just past Neptune's orbit, roughly 50 astronomical units (1 AU=the distance between Earth and the sun) from the sun, travels around the sun on nearly the same plane as the planets. If two of these comets strike one another, or if one is affected by the gravitation of a nearby planet, the orbit may be thrown off in such a way that a comet enters the inner solar system where it is affected by solar forces and visible from Earth.

3   Contrarily, long-period comets do not originate from the same plane as other bodies in the solar system. They orbit the sun in elliptical orbits spanning a variety of angles, forming a "shell" around the solar system known as the Oort Cloud. Scientists believe there are millions of inactive comets in this region, 10,000 AU from the sun. Due to this extreme distance they are not affected by

04. According to paragraph 2, which of the following is **NOT** true regarding the short period comets that orbit the sun?

(A) Short-period comets are believed to originate in the Kuiper belt beyond the orbit of the planets.
(B) Short-period comets seldom orbit around the sun on the same plane as the planets.
(C) Short-period comets differ from long-period comets mainly in where they originate from.
(D) Short-period comets can begin their unique revolutions around the sun after an external force dislodges them from their initial orbits.

05. What can be inferred about long-period comets from paragraph 3?

(A) The frequency with which long-period comets are spotted is less than that of short-period ones.
(B) Long-period comets are more visible than short-period comets because they originate farther from the sun and, therefore, contain more frozen matter.
(C) All long-period comets make just one revolution around the sun because they are expelled from the solar system after they pass by the sun.
(D) When they are sent on their usual orbit and get closer to the sun, they go through changes commonly seen among comets.

06. Which of the sentences below best expresses the essential information in the highlighted sentence in the passage? Incorrect choices change the meaning in important ways or leave out essential information.

(A) Whereas comets are inactive and frozen as they go around their orbit, when they approach the sun, the coma is formed with gases and dust that are given off as the sun's light heats the nucleus.
(B) The inactivity of the frozen masses during their orbit limits the ability to discern the luminosity of the gases and dust particles.
(C) The glowing gaseous coma develops when the comet gets closer to the sun and solar energy superheats the comet's frozen nucleus causing it to emit a bright ball of gas and dust.
(D) While comets remain frozen and dormant during most of their orbit, as they head for the sun, their nucleus is transformed into a coma, a glowing ball of dust and gases.

planetary gravitation in the same way as Kuiper belt comets. For one of these comets to make its way into the inner solar system it must be affected by the gravitational forces of a passing star. [■] When this happens they are sent on an irregular orbit that brings them closer to the sun where they undergo the changes typical of all comets. [■] After they have completed their pass near the sun, it may be thousands of years before they make their return. [■] There is even a subset of these long- period comets called the hyperbolic, or single-apparition, comets that make only one appearance near the sun, because their orbits eventually take them out of the solar system. [■]

4   Regardless of the category of comet, their telltale shape forms in the same way. They complete most of their orbit as frozen and relatively inactive masses that are difficult to discern, but as they come closer to the sun, the effects of its massive energy sublimate the frozen materials within this nucleus to form a glowing ball of dust and gases known as the coma. This coma greatly increases the comet's size. The nucleus is generally less than 60 km in diameter, but the coma can be larger than the sun. This most distinguishable feature differentiates comets from other celestial bodies, such as asteroids. When they reach approximately 1.5 AU from the sun, solar energy's effects become more extreme and parts of the coma are blown into a tail which can be millions of kilometers long.

5   Research into comets led scientists to make an interesting observation regarding their tails; they always point away from the sun. This allowed them to conclude that some force emanating from the sun pushed the particles in the coma to form the tail. We now understand that this is not one, but two forces. Pressure from solar radiation drives the dust particles back from the coma, while solar winds push back the ionized volatile gases surrounding the nucleus. Because of these two different

07. According to paragraph 5, which of the following is true regarding the tails of comets?

(A) Comets have tails that point away from the sun regardless of the direction in which the comet is travelling.
(B) In most comets two tails are visible because of the different directions from which they are approached by solar forces.
(C) Solar radiation burning up the dust particles in the coma makes one of the comet's tails appear to be blue.
(D) Pressure from solar radiation has a larger effect on forming the tails of comets than solar winds.

08. According to paragraph 6, which of the following can be inferred about comets that have completed the portion of their orbit that approaches the sun?

(A) When comets leave for the influence of the sun their tails quickly freeze which introduces another type of celestial body to the environment.
(B) Scientists disproved that the more orbits the comets make, the shorter their lifespans get.
(C) After all of the volatile gases have been used up, the rocky remnants will have no more influence in the solar system.
(D) Despite travelling along the same orbit, they are no longer as easily visible because without the coma and tail they are relatively small.

effects, comets are often found to have two tails, a curved one composed of dust and a second, composed of ionized volatiles, that appears blue and always points away from the sun.

6   When the comet makes its way out of the influence of solar power, the gases in the coma condense and the materials in the tail are lost, reducing its mass. Some of this dust and matter remains in orbit, and can cause other celestial events. The annual Perseid meteor shower is caused by matter ejected from the Swift-Tuttle comet during its 133-year orbit. For this reason, it has been hypothesized that comet lifespans are limited by the number of orbits they complete. After a certain number of orbits, the nucleus will have expelled all of its volatile components and will continue to orbit as a small grouping of stony materials that are relatively unaffected by solar radiation or winds.

09. Look at the four squares [■] that indicate where the following sentence could be added to the passage.

In fact, Comet West and C/1999 F1 have orbits that are estimated at 6 million years.

Where would the sentence best fit?

Click on a square [■] to add the sentence to the passage.

10. Directions: An introductory sentence for a brief summary of the passage is provided below. Complete the summary by selecting the THREE answer choices that express the most important ideas in the passage. Some sentences do not belong in the summary because they express ideas that are not presented in the passage or are minor ideas in the passage. **This question is worth 2 points.**

> **There are two types of comets which differ based on the duration of their orbits.**
> -
> -
> -

Answer Choices

(A) Short-period comets begin in the Kuiper Belt of the outer solar system and are dislodged by the effects of nearby planets, which puts them on a new relatively short orbit.

(B) Halley's Comet has been documented appearing every 76 years since 240B.C., making it the most famous short-period comet.

(C) The coma and tail that differentiate comets from asteroids and other solar bodies is caused by the frozen matter in the nucleus being turned into gas by the sun's forces.

(D) Comets dislodged from the Oort cloud by the effects of stars outside the solar system have orbits that last for longer than 200 years and may only appear once.

(E) Comets appear to have two distinct tails because the solar radiation and solar winds dissimilarly act on the same aspect of the coma.

(F) The comas of comets orbiting in the Oort Cloud do not last as long as those from the Kuiper belt because of their great distance from the sun.

Darwin and Evolution Theory

1 In 1831, Robert FitzRoy prepared to set sail on a two year journey aboard the Beagle to survey the South American coastlines and return three Yaghan tribe members it previously captured to Tierra del Fuego, an archipelago off the southernmost tip of the South American mainland. To fight the loneliness of being at sea for so long and to help study the lands they were to visit, he invited Charles Darwin, a recent Cambridge graduate, to join the expedition as his companion and ship naturalist. Prior to departure, FitzRoy gave his new companion *Principles of Geology* by Charles Lyell, who had requested that FitzRoy record the geological formations that he encountered. Unbeknownst to both men, their journey together would stretch to nearly five years and would form the basis for a revolutionary new biological theory.

2 According to his diaries, Darwin spent three years and three months exploring the new lands, recording his geographical findings, and collecting fossils and specimens of the wildlife he came across. Although he originally planned to use his findings to write a book on geology, over the course of his explorations he made many new and interesting discoveries in the field of biology, such as discovering giant armadillo and sloth fossils from the distant past. He also discovered that in areas with a geographic segregation, such as islands or seas separated by isthmuses, different species were found. This was particularly true in the Galapagos Archipelago, where he found different species of tortoises on each island, a unique marine iguana with a seaweed- based diet, and an assortment of birds he thought to be blackbirds, grosbeaks, and finches but later turned out to be 12 distinct species of finches. These discoveries, combined with Lyell's theory of uniformitarianism, which stated that "the present is the key to the past," meaning that we can only assume about the past from what we

---

11. According to paragraph 1, which of the following was NOT true about the Voyage of HMS Beagle?

(A) The journey lasted significantly longer than it was originally planned.
(B) The ship had previously travelled to South America.
(C) One of the main purposes of the trip was to survey the coastline of South America.
(D) Darwin and FitzRoy planned to research previously unknown biological theories during their extended voyage.

12. According to paragraph 1, which of the following can be inferred about Darwin's inclusion on the voyage of HMS Beagle?

(A) He was not essential for the completion of the mission upon which the Beagle was embarking.
(B) He was chosen because he had recently graduated from a prestigious university and could commit to the five year journey.
(C) He sought out a position on a boat where he could conduct research to help him prove his theory regarding species change.
(D) He was referred to the position by Charles Lyell who was interested in gaining information regarding the geology of South America.

13. According to paragraph 2, which of the following is true about Darwin's exploration of South America?

(A) He had relatively little time to explore the South American continent due to the long periods it took to travel between locations.
(B) The purpose of his explorations changed when he discovered many unique species and fossils.
(C) He discovered that areas like islands and the seas around isthmuses were capable of supporting many more species than other areas.
(D) His discoveries allowed him to prove the theory of uniformitarianism which stated that we can only assume about the past from what we observe in the present.

14. Which of the sentences below best expresses the essential information in the highlighted sentence in the passage? Incorrect choices change the meaning in important ways or leave out essential information.

   (A) The main idea of uniformitarianism, that things in the past happened in a similar way they do today, allowed Darwin to realize that the diversity he discovered was only possible if something was causing species to evolve over time.
   (B) Darwin and Lyell realized that uniformitarianism could explain the diversity of the species he found because if species are changing today they must have done so in the past because "the present is key to the past."
   (C) The main tenet of uniformitarianism, that we can only assume about the past what we can see in the present allowed Darwin to come up with the idea that animals changed over time because there are many different species in the world.
   (D) Upon the discovery of the diverse species, Charles Darwin developed the idea that something has caused changes in species over time, leading to the publication of Charles Lyell's uniformitarianism.

15. The term "induce" in the passage is closest in meaning to:

   (A) prevent
   (B) bring about
   (C) control
   (D) slow down

observe in the present, caused Darwin to postulate that the diversity of these species was possible only if there was some mechanism through which species could change over time.

3 [■] Darwin's idea was supported by the theory of homology Richard Owen derived from comparative studies of the structural systems of various vertebrates. [■] Owen found homology, or anatomical similarity, in the body parts of different animals which served different purposes. [■] This cannot be attributed to common use, so it must indicate common ancestry and adaptive evolution to fit the organisms' functions. [■] The presence of vestigial, or leftover, structures in modern organisms also points to an evolutionary system, because these structures serve no purpose in modern animals. The whale and snake are both examples of this, because although both are now legless, they have small vestigial leg bones, which point to a four-legged ancestor.

4 All of this support for Darwin's theory did not explain why evolution would have occurred. Darwin got a basic idea about this by looking at the changes that breeders could induce in their animals through animal husbandry. By breeding animals with certain traits they could artificially change the traits of the offspring. This couldn't, however, explain how species evolve naturally or how some species go extinct and are replaced by other species. To gain further insight into this, Darwin turned to the population research of economist Thomas Malthus, which indicated that population increases outpace food production. This overpopulation decreases the number of offspring reaching maturity during lean times. Darwin recognized that these two basic ideas could be applied to the animal kingdom. He theorized that during competitive times, animals with favorable traits would survive to reproduce and pass on their superior traits to the next generation in a natural form of selection.

16. What can be inferred from paragraph 4 about Darwin's conclusion regarding the reasons for species' change over time?

(A) The changes that breeders are able to produce in their livestock will eventually change the species as a whole.
(B) Human overpopulation and competition for food with the animal kingdom will cause a change in the species they hunt.
(C) During periods when the food supply runs low, the animals that survive will come to have superior traits.
(D) Organisms that mate and pass on their traits do so because they are more suited to the environment they are in.

17. What is the purpose of including information regarding Alfred Wallace in the passage?

(A) To disprove Darwin's ideas by offering a contrary view from another naturalist of the time
(B) To help understand that reproduction and species change was a popular field of study at the time
(C) To show that Darwin was unable to complete his theory until he got more information from another naturalist with similar ideas
(D) To introduce another researcher whose work in the field produced similar results and helped reinforce Darwin's theory

18. What can be inferred about the theories presented by Alfred Wallace from paragraph 5?

(A) They were overshadowed by Darwin's publication of his theories in *On the Origin of Species by Means of Natural Selection*.
(B) They were conducted in places different from those visited by Darwin, so they had little similarity with Darwin's theory.
(C) They were rejected by the Linnean Society of London because he presented them after Darwin's theories had already been accepted.
(D) They were largely ignored because he was not as socially or scientifically well-connected as Charles Darwin.

5   Although Darwin had great confidence in the validity of his theories, he initially refused to publish them due to his lack of supporting data and remained most famous as a geologist and explorer after the publication of his accounts of the trip in *The Voyage of the Beagle*. This did not, however, stop him from discussing his theories with fellow scientists Lyell and Owen, both of whom he befriended after returning from the long voyage. The formal publication of his theories did not occur until another young British naturalist and explorer, Alfred Wallace, was about to present a similar theory he developed while exploring the Amazon Basin and the Malay Archipelago. Eventually, Wallace agreed to present his theory alongside the more socially and scientifically connected Darwin and their work was jointly presented to the Linnean Society of London in 1858, with very little fanfare. The true significance of the new theories would not be fully recognized until the publication of Darwin's evolutionary manifesto, *On the Origin of Species by Means of Natural Selection*, in 1859. It was so well researched and presented that it was referred to as the best explanation "ever published of the manner of formation of species" by Owen and established Darwin as the definitive authority on natural selection.

19. Look at the four squares [■] that indicate where the following sentence could be added to the passage.

The forelimbs of most vertebrates, such as, bats, whales, humans, and horses, all share a basic design.

Where would the sentence best fit?

Click on a square [■] to add the sentence to the passage.

20. Directions: An introductory sentence for a brief summary of the passage is provided below. Complete the summary by selecting the THREE answer choices that express the most important ideas in the passage. Some sentences do not belong in the summary because they express ideas that are not presented in the passage or are minor ideas in the passage. **This question is worth 2 points.**

Discoveries made by Darwin during his voyage on HMS Beagle led him to develop a new theory regarding how species came about.

-
-
-

Answer Choices

(A) Darwin discovered many unique animal species and fossils which were geographically separate and had diverse traits that were possible only if there was some mechanism through which species could change over time.

(B) Absorbed in the study of biology, Darwin volunteered to be part of the HMS Beagle voyage and helped collect important information regarding species diversity.

(C) Upon the discovery of homology in the animals he observed, Darwin came to realize that different animals' body parts eventually come to perform similar functions.

(D) Darwin found support for his theory regarding the ability of species to change over time through the presence of anatomical similarities and vestigial structures in modern animals.

(E) The collaborative work on which Alfred Wallace and Charles Darwin published their theories has come to be known as On the Origin of Species by Means of Natural Selection today.

(F) The study of animal husbandry and research on human populations led Darwin to believe that the diverse animals he discovered were the result of competition allowing only animals with superior traits to reproduce and pass on these traits.

You have seen all of the questions in this part of the Reading section. You have time left to review.
As long as there is time remaining, you can check your work.

Click on **Return** to go back to the previous question.
Click on **Review** to see the review screen for this section.
Click on **Continue** to go on.
Once you leave this part of the Reading section, you WILL NOT be able to return to it.

이제 Reading Section이 끝났습니다.
Continue 버튼을 누르면 다시 문제를 검토할 수 없으므로 유의하세요.

시험보고 난 후 ... 체크 리스트 및 스터디 디렉션 | USHER iBT TOEFL INTERMEDIATE TEST READING

1. 내가 불안했던 문제만 재빨리 다시 보고, 불안하게 만든, 즉, 경쟁 초이스를 찾아서 왜 내가 헷갈려 했는지를 파악할 수 있는 메모를 해두시기 바랍니다. 시간이 지나거나, 다른 학생들과 스터디를 하면서는, 자신이 왜 낚였는지 이유조차 기억나지 않아 본인의 실수 패턴 파악이 힘들기 때문입니다.

2. 답지를 확인하지 않고 스터디를 하시기 바랍니다. (그래서, 답지를 문제지 뒤에 붙이지 않고, 본 설명만을 붙여 두었습니다.) 답지를 확인하지 않고 하는 이유는 답을 아는 순간, 답에 끼워 맞춰 설명하려 하고, 이런 태도는 본인 실력 향상에 도움이 되지 않기 때문입니다. 스터디 팀원들간에 대략적인 답을 맞춰보면, 대부분 답안의 윤곽이 나옵니다. 이럴 경우, 이견이 있는 문제만 집중적으로 다루고, 나머지는 개인별로 처리하시기 바랍니다.

3. 문제를 끝까지 다 풀었나요? 네 □ / 아니오 □
   다 못 풀었다면, 전체 20 문제 중 푼 문제는? _____ / 20
   시간 모자란 것에 대해서는 크게 신경 쓰지 않아도 됩니다. 무엇보다 중요한 것은 정확도 입니다.
   우선은 풀은 문제를 맞출 확률을 높이고, 그 다음 시간을 걱정해도 늦지 않습니다.

4. 어려웠다고 느껴지는 지문은? 과학 □ / 예술 □ / 인문 □ / 인물 □ / 사회 □
   과학지문이 현격히 다른 분야보다 많지만, 그래도, 공부하다 보면 자신만 어려워하는 분야는 모두 각각입니다. 그러므로, 혹시 배경지식 부분에서 필요한 것이 있다면, www.usherlN.co.kr 에 방문하셔서, 공부가 안될 때, 배경지식 부분을 쉬엄쉬엄 들러서 봐 두시길 바랍니다. 쉬엄쉬엄 입니다. 누가 뭐래도 실력있는 사람은 배경지식이 큰 영향을 끼치지는 않습니다.

5. (채점 후) 문제 풀 때 어렵다고 느낀 지문이 틀리는 개수와 쉬웠다고 느껴졌던 지문의 틀린 개수차이가 있나요? 예 □ / 아니오 □
   어느 순간 깨닫게 됩니다. 내가 잘 아는 내용이 나와서 자신 있게 푸나, 내가 모르는 지문이 나와서 겁먹고 푸나, 틀린 개수가 큰 차이가 나지 않는 것을…. 혹시 그걸 못 느끼신다면, 더욱더 열심히 하시기 바랍니다. ^^

6. 틀린 문제의 번호를 다음의 문제 유형 분석표와 비교해서 파악해 두시기 바랍니다.
   문제 유형을 파악해서 주의하는 것은, 누가 뭐래도 실력이 기본은 받쳐 줄 때 얘기입니다. 문제 푸는 스킬이나, 기타 문제 유형 파악 등은 기본적으로 본문 내용을 이해하고, 해석이 웬만큼 될 때 얘기입니다. 만약, 너무 힘들다면 너무 스트레스 받지 말고, 그냥 '아~ 그렇구나' 정도로 넘기셔도 됩니다. 단, 본문 이해는 절대 양보해서는 안됩니다.

| 문제 유형 분석표 | 40page 내용 중, 아래 표시되어 있는 문제 유형은 파악하기 쉬우나 나머지 문제들의 문제 유형 파악은 어려워 하는 경향이 있어 비워두었습니다. 문제유형 정답은 273page를 참조하세요. |

TEST 1-1

01
02 Vocabulary
03
04
05
06 Highlight
07
08
09 Insertion
10 Summary

TEST 1-2

11
12
13
14 Highlight
15 Vocabulary
16
17
18
19 Insertion
20 Summary

잔소리 1

시간 내 못 푸는 것에 대해서 스트레스 받지 마십시오.

- 문제 풀고 푼데까지, 기록 남겨야 합니다.
14개중 8,9개 풀던 학생이 12개 풀어가는 것도 발전, 서머리 문제 못 풀던 학생이 손대보려 시도하는 것도 발전입니다.

앞서 얘기했지만, 중요한 건, 정확도 입니다.
정확도 올라간 학생은, 지금 당장은 느려도, 계속 돌리면, 금방 시간이 줄어들 수밖에 없습니다.
당장 만들어 주길 원한다면,
K2 수업 마지막 주에 들어오십시오.
그때, 원하는 정확도가 있으면, 무슨 말인지 알 겁니다.
(원하는 정확도가 없으면? 나쁜 버릇과, '난왜 안될까?' 라는 패배감만 가지게 될겁니다.)

정확한 사람은, 마무리가 쉽습니다.
왜? 정확하니까, 감으로 해도 될 만큼 정확하니까…

감으로 하는 것 자체를 뭐라 하는 게 아닙니다.
감으로, 하고 싶습니까?
대충 읽어도, 다 내용 파악하고 싶습니까?

한글로는 대충 읽어도 다 파악이 되는 이유는,
많이 읽어서 그렇고,
대충 읽어도 파악될 만큼
정확히 읽는게 되니까 가능한 겁니다.
그리고 대충 읽다가,
이해가 안 되는 부분이 있으면,
그걸 감지하고,
다시 천천히 읽어보면 됩니다.

문제는 영어로 읽을 때는, 자기가 잘 읽고 있는지도 모르고 읽는 경우가 많습니다.
한참 가다가, 중간에 멈추고, '그래서 뭐래?' 그러면 대답하질 못합니다.
대충 읽었으니까…

지문을 읽을 때도, 해석을 할때도, 꼼꼼히 해야만 합니다.
내가 잘 따라가고 있는지 의심하면서,
내용을 정리 해가면서.

정독도 못하는 학생이 속독 하겠다고 한다면,
'건너뛰고싶고,
빨리 완성시키고 싶으면,
더욱 더 단계별로 밟고 지나가라.'
가 답입니다.

usherin.usher.co.kr

USHER iBT TOEFL
INTERMEDIATE READING
TEST 2

테스트 전 확인사항

실전에 유용한 독해 전략(44p)을 숙지하였습니다. ○
화장실은 미리 다녀왔습니다. ○
휴대폰의 전원을 껐습니다. ○
노트테이킹 할 종이와 연필을 준비하였습니다. ○
시간을 체크할 시계를 준비하였습니다. ○
목표점수(20개 중____개)를 정하였습니다. ○
시험 시작 시간은 ____시 ____분이며,
종료 시간은 35분 뒤인 ____시 ____분입니다. ○
시험 중 이동해야 할 방해요소가 있는지 체크하였습니다. ○
시험 중 이동하지 않습니다.

Sentinel Behavior in Meerkats

1. → Meerkats are small, mongoose-like mammals that live in the Kalahari Desert of Southern Africa. Being primarily insectivores, they feed on beetles and scorpions buried underground, which they locate using their strong sense of smell. Unfortunately, when the meerkat lowers its head to search out prey under grasses, it limits its own range of sight by a significant amount. As a result they are extremely vulnerable to airborne predators such as hawks and owls. To ensure that they can reach the safety of their bolt-holes before being snatched up by birds, meerkats forage in packs and partake in what is known as sentinel behavior. As the term suggests, one meerkat in the group acts as a sentinel and does not look for food like the rest, but rather stands upright on its hind legs to gain a wider field of view with which it scans the surrounding area for possible predators and other threats to the community. When it senses danger approaching, the sentinel barks loudly to warn the others of the danger. Many scientists questioned this phenomenon because the revealing stance and loud vocalization were thought to expose the meerkat to an increased risk of predation.

폭 넓게 - 일단 버릇 들이는게 중요!

32 According to paragraph 1, why was sentinel behavior thought to be disadvantageous?

(A) It warns the predator of where the meerkat group is.
(B) It allows the meerkat to sense danger and warn the group.
(C) It helps the predators locate the sentinel meerkat.
(D) It encourages the predator to prey on meerkats over other species.

스터디 자료들 미리 수집해 둘것!

시험 중 체크 사항

❶ "?"표시하기 : 본문 읽으며, 궁금한 곳에 "?" 표시를 합니다.
문제를 풀면서도 질문 거리에는 "?" 표시를 해둡니다.
❷ 문제 핵심에 동그라미 : 문제가 물어보는 게 무엇인지, 문제 핵심에 동그라미 표시를 합니다.
❸ 답근거 날리기 : 문제를 풀 때 선택지가 틀린 이유 단어로, 간결하게 날립니다.
❹ 경쟁 문장 표시 : 4개의 선택지 중에 정답과 경쟁하는 마지막 1개의 선택지를 표시 해둡니다. 무조건 1개여야 합니다.

Reading Section Directions

This section measures your ability to understand academic passages in English.

Most questions are worth 1 point but the last question in each set is worth more than 1 point. The directions indicate how many points you may receive.

Some passages include a word or phrase that is underlined in blue. Click on the word or phrase to see a definition or an explanation.

Within each test, you can go to the next questions by clicking **Next**. You may skip questions and go back to them later. If you want to return to previous questions, click on **Back**. You can click on **Review** at any time and the review screen will show you which questions you have answered and which you have not answered. From this reviewscreen, you may go directly to any questions you have already seen in the Reading section.

You may now begin the Reading section. In the section you will read 2 passages. You will have **35 minutes** to read the passages and answer thequestions.

Click on **Continue** to go on.

Next 버튼을 이용하여 다음 문제로 이동하고 **Back** 버튼을 이용하여 이전문제로 이동할 수 있습니다. 문제에 답을 하지 않더라도 다음 문제로이동할 수 있으며, **Review** 버튼을 이용하여 각 문제별로 답을 체크했는지의 여부를 확인할 수 있습니다.
이번 테스트에서는 세 지문을 읽게 됩니다. **35분** 동안 지문을 읽고 문제에 답을 하세요.

Determining the Ages of the Planets and the Universe

1 The orbits of planets and the majority of non-planetary objects in our solar system have a very interesting characteristic; despite their vast differences, they have astounding similarities. The most remarkable of these similarities is that nearly all of them orbit the sun in the same direction and on the same plane. Using this information, scientists determined that this likely occurred because the collapse of a gas cloud simultaneously formed the objects and sent them to orbit the sun. This fact has allowed us to learn more about the age of the Earth, the planets, and the universe itself.

2 It may seem that the easiest method of discerning Earth's age would be to simply sample materials we can extract from the crust, but this doesn't produce accurate results. Due to the life-supporting water that covers Earth's surface, terrestrial material is constantly exposed to the force of erosion. The constant changes erosion causes, compounded by volcanic activity and Earth's internal pressure and heat, make the discovery of rocks in Earth's crust that originate from the time of formation highly unlikely. For this reason, scientists must look for analogous objects in the solar system to help them answer this question. Luckily, the meteorites that have crashed into Earth's surface can provide them with this material. These masses began their existence as objects orbiting the sun, but Earth's gravitational pull forced them to enter its atmosphere and collide with the crust.

3 [■] The meteorites that have been discovered have varied in size, ranging from stony pebbles to massive planetoids called asteroids, and composition which has allowed scientists to draw conclusions about them and Earth's composition and origin. [■] From meteorite remnants found on Earth, the main three categories used to differentiate meteorites today are "stony meteorites," composed of rocky materials, "iron meteorites" composed

---

01. What does the word "they" refer to in the passage?

(A) orbits
(B) planets
(C) non-planetary objects
(D) characteristics

02. The term "discerning" in the passage is closest in meaning to:

(A) disproving
(B) determining
(C) disregarding
(D) deferring

03. Paragraph 2 mentions all of the following as facts related to attempts to come up with an accurate age for the Earth EXCEPT:

(A) The easiest method of discerning the Earth's age is to simply sample materials we can extract from the Earth's easily accessible crust.
(B) Over the course of time the rocks that formed in Earth's crust at its origin have been worn away by natural forces.
(C) Objects orbiting the sun can provide scientists with information about the age of the Earth.
(D) Meteorites that survived the plunge to Earth have given scientists more information on the formation of the Earth.

04. What can be inferred about using space objects to find the age of Earth from paragraph 3?

(A) The minerals found in the asteroids that have struck the earth are unique and have little similarity to those found on Earth.
(B) Although Earth and the meteorites that have been researched share a similar composition, they differ in their origin.
(C) The composition of the Earth's layers is similar to that of other space objects because they were all formed from the broken up space materials.
(D) The collection of minerals present in meteorites found on earth's surface allows scientists to determine how long they have been striking Earth and therefore its age.

05. According to paragraph 4, which of the following is NOT true about the age of Earth and certain space objects?

(A) The rocks on the surface of the moon are much older than those that are currently found in Earth's crust.
(B) The moon is relatively younger than the Earth and the meteorites which have struck it.
(C) Scientists have been able to prove their theory that most objects in the solar system originated concurrently.
(D) Radiometric testing on rocks from meteorites and the moon's surface yielded very similar results.

06. Which of the sentences below best expresses the essential information in the highlighted sentence in the passage? Incorrect choices change the meaning in important ways or leave out essential information.

(A) Rocks on the Earth's surface are affected by erosion and tectonic movements unlike meteors and moon rocks, so they could not be used to validate the notion that all matter in the solar system originated at the same time.
(B) Scientists affirmed the fact that all of the matter in the solar system came about simultaneously by comparing the age of meteorites with that of the rocks on the Moon's surface which are unaffected by erosion and crust movements.
(C) After conducting testing on moon rocks and meteorites, scientists determined that they were approximately the same age because they weren't exposed to water or the effects of erosion from movements in the crust.
(D) It was determined that all space materials originated at the same time when scientists discovered that meteorites and moon rocks were the same age.

mainly of iron with trace amounts of other elements, and "stony-iron meteorites" that consist of a mixture of the two. [■] Scientists believe that all three of these types of meteorites are the remnants of larger space bodies that broke apart due to collisions. [■] It is believed that the differences between the categories of meteorites are due to this violent break up of space materials with origins and, therefore, compositions similar to Earth's. The stony meteorites likely originated as the outer shells of these bodies and are analogous to Earth's mantle, while the iron meteorites that resemble Earth's core are probably fragments of the interior of the body and the stony-iron meteorites contain materials from both.

4 By studying these meteorites scientists have been able to determine their age. Using multiple radiometric methods of dating the materials, including the uranium-thorium, rubidium-strontium, and potassium-argon methods, showed a cluster of age data pointing to an origin around 4.6 billion years ago. Comparing this to the rocks from the moon's surface, which is free of the water that erodes rocks on Earth's surface and which displays little movement in its crust, yielded similar age data and allowed researchers to confirm their hypothesis that all of the materials in the solar system started at the same point in time.

5 While dating the elements of the solar system has been relatively straightforward, finding the age of the universe itself has been more complicated because there is no way to collect physical materials on which to conduct age testing. What has been learned has been gathered through theoretical analysis of the universe. One of the most important factors discovered is that all of the disk-shaped clusters of stars, called galaxies, are moving away from each other. Scientists conjecture that this occurs because the universe began with an explosion, known as the Big Bang, which sent all of the dense matter concentrated at the center of the explosion

07. In paragraph 5, the author mentions "glue coins to a balloon and inflate it" in order to

(A) help understand that the Big Bang concentrated all of the galaxies on the outside edge of the universe.
(B) give an idea of how the expansion of the universe is limited to a certain point then it will explode again.
(C) help understand how the expansion of the galaxies causes the universe to expand infinitely.
(D) give an example using everyday objects that will help visualize the expansion of the universe.

08. According to paragraph 6, which of the following can be inferred regarding the expansion of the universe?

(A) The expansion of the galaxies causes light to shift around them in a predictable manner that can be measured by astronomers.
(B) Scientists came up with the generalization that greater redshift will cause the light to travel farther.
(C) The redshift caused by the expanding intergalactic space occurs at a rate consistent enough to allow its use in determining the amount of time it has been travelling.
(D) Using the expansion of the universe allows astronomers to pinpoint why all of the matter in the system came into being.

hurtling across space. This process is akin to what would happen if one were to glue coins to a balloon and inflate it. The coins, like the galaxies, would remain the same size but the space between them would increase as the balloon got larger.

6   The expansion of the space between the galaxies is precisely what astronomers have used to estimate the universe's age. By measuring the wavelengths of light travelling through the universe they are able to measure a shift in the light's wavelength towards red end of the light spectrum. This redshift occurs because, as light travels in the space between the galaxies, the expansion of the space stretches out the light waves. Following this theory, the farther the light has traveled, the greater the redshift will be. Measuring the redshift in light from distant galaxies, astronomers have determined that all of the galaxies would have existed in one central location around 13.7 billion years ago. This, therefore, is the most likely the date and location of the Big Bang and the age of the universe.

09. Look at the four squares [■] that indicate where the following sentence could be added to the passage.

Some intact asteroids may have once struck the earth, but none have done so during recorded human history.

Where would the sentence best fit?

Click on a square [■] to add the sentence to the passage.

10. Directions: An introductory sentence for a brief summary of the passage is provided below. Complete the summary by selecting the THREE answer choices that express the most important ideas in the passage. Some sentences do not belong in the summary because they express ideas that are not presented in the passage or are minor ideas in the passage. **This question is worth 2 points.**

> Using physical and analytical methods, scientists have been able to determine the age of the solar system and the universe.
>
> -
> -
> -

Answer Choices

(A) The similar orbits of the planetary and nonplanetary objects in the solar system indicate that they were likely formed of similar materials at the same time.

(B) One of the types of meteorites found on Earth today comprises of rocky materials, which distinctly differentiate it from other types.

(C) Scientist determined that the earth was 4.6 billion years old due to radiometric dating done on meteorites with composition analogous to that of the Earth.

(D) Rocks in Earth's crust are older than those present on Moon's surface due to the presence of erosion on Earth.

(E) Scientists, lacking sufficient data to figure out the age of planets in the solar system, have determined it concurrent with the age of the universe obtained using redshift.

(F) The expansion of the intergalactic space and the presence of redshift indicate that the universe started with a centralized explosion 13.7 billion years ago.

Early Research in Organic Chemistry

1 The ancient practice of alchemy gave way to the early science of chemistry in the late 17th century. After hundreds of years of trying to turn base metals into gold, alchemists had developed a structure of theory, terminology, experimentation and basic laboratory techniques that were well-adapted for scientific study of Earth's elements. By the 18th century, chemists began to scientifically study the new elements they found and were able to identify many new ones that had never been studied before, such as cobalt, tungsten and various forms of carbon. The study of the last of these would eventually form one of the two modern divisions of the field of chemistry, organic chemistry.

2 The terms organic and inorganic chemistry were introduced in the early 1800s to more accurately differentiate between the different naturally occurring substances. Prior to this time scientists separated substances into three categories that matched the "Three Kingdoms of Nature": animal, vegetable and mineral. Of these, the animal and vegetable groups were reserved for substances that were produced by or related to life and were later incorporated into the study of organic (meaning from an organism) chemistry which covered all carbon-based compounds, while the inanimate mineral group gave way to the field of inorganic chemistry which covered all non-carbon compounds. Some scientists, such as Antoine Lavoisier, thought the organic field was a reasonable field of study, yet they were opposed by others who adhered to a theory of vitalism. Those that believed in vitalism felt that there was a "vital spark" or "force" in organic materials and that substances that contained it should not be experimented upon and that only inorganic materials were valid research subjects. Despite the eventual invalidation of the vitalist theory, by German chemist Friedrich Wohler's accidental synthesis of organic material in his laboratory, scientists involved in inorganic chemistry made much more rapid progress than those working on organic chemistry.

---

11. According to paragraph 1, which of the following was NOT true about the early science of chemistry?

(A) Early chemists were attempting to find a way to create gold from non-valuable base materials.
(B) Scientists were able to use the methodology developed in the field of alchemy to study the minerals that they found.
(C) The discovery of various forms of the element carbon would lead to the development of one of the two major fields of study in chemistry.
(D) During the 1700s scientists had begun to identify and study new elements in ways that they had not done before this time.

12. Which of the sentences below best expresses the essential information in the highlighted sentence in the passage? Incorrect choices change the meaning in important ways or leave out essential information.

(A) The term organic chemistry reorganized the earlier classification of living things to refer to the study of substances containing carbon, and the mineral group came under the field of inorganic chemistry.
(B) Scientists started using the term organic to refer to minerals derived from organisms, instead of "vegetable" and "animal," and used the term inorganic to refer to non-carbon based minerals.
(C) The primary difference between organic compounds and inorganic compounds is that organic compounds always contain carbon while most inorganic compounds do not contain it.
(D) After the animal and vegetable groups reserved for life-related substances were merged into the study of organic chemistry which covered carbon-based compounds, all other non-carbon compounds, such as minerals, formed the field of inorganic chemistry.

13. All of the following are mentioned in paragraph 2 about the field of organic chemistry EXCEPT: To receive credit, you must select TWO answer choices.

(A) Prior to the 1800s scientists used the terms vegetable and animal to describe living matter, but eventually began utilizing the term organic.
(B) Vitalism prohibited experimentation on organic materials because they contained a force that provided them life.
(C) The German chemist Friedrich Wohler, by purposefully synthesizing organic materials in his laboratory, disproved the theory of vitalism.
(D) Most scientists felt that it was impossible to study organic matter because they believed it contained a "vital spark."

14. What can be inferred from paragraph 3 about the main reason that organic chemistry lagged behind the field of inorganic chemistry?

   (A) Early scientists could not easily differentiate between organic and inorganic compounds in the natural world.
   (B) Scientists lacked the ability to discern the purest forms from the compounds seemingly similar to the pure ones.
   (C) The absence of organic compounds in Earth's crust made it difficult for scientists to find them when they were looking for research materials.
   (D) Access to inorganic compounds allowed early scientists many more opportunities to undertake experiments on them.

15. What is the purpose of including information regarding the mining of hydrogen from the air in paragraph 3?

   (A) To give an example of one of the easy ways in which an inorganic element can be attained in its pure form
   (B) To give more information about the type of element that is studied in the field of inorganic chemistry
   (C) To let the reader see that inorganic compounds are so prevalent that they can even be taken directly from the air
   (D) To show that some gases found in their pure form are found relatively easier than others in the atmosphere

16. In paragraphs 4 and 5, which of the following can be inferred using the process of distillation?

   (A) The standardization of the distillation process enabled scientists to overcome the problems in the analytical process.
   (B) Different vegetation types have variations in properties and amounts of liquid and gaseous substances in comparison to its solid state.
   (C) The standardization of the distillation process allowed scientists to derive more minerals from the blackened material created in the process.
   (D) Scientists found that the quantity of the remaining solid matter had little variations among different vegetable types.

3   This lag of organic chemistry occurred for various reasons, but perhaps the most obvious is the availability of elements and compounds on which scientists could experiment. In order for scientists to conduct experiments and determine the chemical forms of the elements, they need to obtain them in their purest forms. Inorganic compounds, on the whole, are more easily found in a reasonably pure state. Mineral deposits often hold lodes of compounds and elements such as oxides, pure metals and salts. Some gases, such as sulfur, can even be found in their pure elemental form on Earth, while others, like atmospheric gases, are easily broken down into their component parts. Hydrogen, for instance, can be mined from the air using a particular mineral acid on a metal plate.

4   Access to pure organic substances, on the other hand, is much more difficult. Extracting pure substances from plant or animal matter through the process of distillation, evaporating and condensing a substance to purify it, generally yields solid blackened debris along with liquid and gaseous discharges. Chemists studying the vegetable products found that the qualitative properties of the remaining solid matter varied little between different vegetable types, but quantitative and qualitative differences were found in the liquid and gaseous substances produced. They also found that altering the distillation process yielded significantly different results in these byproducts. By standardizing the distillation process they were able to make important advances in their ability to analyze organic matter.

5   Even after developing a standardized analytical process, organic chemists still faced challenges in their field. The most overwhelming of these was that the substances released during the distillation process were complex compounds of unknown purity, making it impossible to accurately determine the properties of any one element present in the substances. Another major problem was determining the source of the released

17. According to paragraph 5, which of the following is true about the more standardized analytical process that chemists developed?

(A) It provided them with all of the purified organic compounds they needed to conduct their experiments upon.
(B) It did not allow the scientists to know if they were creating the substances or if they were present in the original sample.
(C) It allowed scientists to distill the necessary components from the organic material without destroying it in the process.
(D) It greatly increased the purity of the organic material that the scientists were creating in the distillation process.

18. The term "crucial" in the passage is closest in meaning to:

(A) fatal
(B) relevant
(C) decisive
(D) unmistakable

materials. Were they present in the original sample, or were they produced through the process of distilling and destroying organic material? This uncertainty led organic chemists to search for ways to attain these substances without destroying the original matter. Many other less violent methods of distillation, such as using the lowest effective temperature to distill organic substances, were attempted, but did not fully overcome the problems that were inherent in the field.

6   This problem led organic chemists to consider substances such as blood, gelatin, and fat to be constituent elements in organisms as late as the 1830s. [■] Today we recognize that all of these substances are complex compounds composed of various molecules made of a great number of atoms of true elements. [■] Due to this, and similar, problems, understanding the actual chemical makeup of organic compounds was much more complex and challenging than it was in the field of inorganic, or mineral-based, chemistry. [■] The crucial breakthrough in organic chemistry came in 1858 when the concept of chemical structures in carbon atoms was simultaneously developed by Friedrich August Kekule' and Archibald Scott Couper. [■]

19. Look at the four squares [■] that indicate where the following sentence could be added to the passage.

This allowed chemists to more acutely understand the ability of carbon molecules to bond together in a carbon lattice through the observation and interpretation of chemical reactions.

Where would the sentence best fit?

Click on a square [■] to add the sentence to the passage.

20. Directions: An introductory sentence for a brief summary of the passage is provided below. Complete the summary by selecting the THREE answer choices that express the most important ideas in the passage. Some sentences do not belong in the summary because they express ideas that are not presented in the passage or are minor ideas in the passage. **This question is worth 2 points.**

> **The development of organic chemistry, which studies carbon based compounds, took much longer than the study of inorganic chemistry.**
>
> •
>
> •
>
> •

Answer Choices

(A) Eighteenth century scientists were able to identify many new elements that had never been previously studied, such as carbon, cobalt, and tungsten.

(B) The early division of organic and inorganic chemistry originated from the idea that living organisms, animals and vegetables, had a different chemical composition than non-living objects, such as rocks and soil.

(C) Whether in their pure form or in the atmosphere, gases are readily available for research purposes, making the study of organic chemistry simpler.

(D) The inability of early scientists to find pure sources of organic compounds and elements made their attempts to understand organic substances much more difficult than in the field of inorganic chemistry.

(E) The process of distillation produced liquid and gaseous organic substances that early organic chemists could experiment upon, but they had no way to determine where the substances originated or their purity.

(F) The substances, originally referred to as organic, derived from living organisms, such as blood, gelatin, and fat, later turned out to be inorganic elements.

You have seen all of the questions in this part of the Reading section. You have time left to review.
As long as there is time remaining, you can check your work.

Click on **Return** to go back to the previous question.
Click on **Review** to see the review screen for this section.
Click on **Continue** to go on.
Once you leave this part of the Reading section, you WILL NOT be able to return to it.

이제 Reading Section이 끝났습니다.
Continue 버튼을 누르면 다시 문제를 검토할 수 없으므로 유의하세요.

시험보고 난 후 ... 체크 리스트 및 스터디 디렉션

USHER iBT TOEFL INTERMEDIATE TEST READING

1. 내가 불안했던 문제만 재빨리 다시 보고, 불안하게 만든, 즉, 경쟁 초이스를 찾아서 왜 내가 헷갈려 했는지를 파악할 수 있는 메모를 해두시기 바랍니다. 시간이 지나거나, 다른 학생들과 스터디를 하면서는, 자신이 왜 낚였는지 이유조차 기억하지 않아 본인의 실수 패턴 파악이 힘들기 때문입니다.

2. 답지를 확인하지 않고 스터디를 하시기 바랍니다. (그래서, 답지를 문제지 뒤에 붙이지 않고, 본 설명만을 붙여 두었습니다.) 답지를 확인하지 않고 하는 이유는 답을 아는 순간, 답에 끼워 맞춰 설명하려 하고, 이런 태도는 본인 실력 향상에 도움이 되지 않기 때문입니다. 스터디 팀원들간에 대략적인 답을 맞춰보면, 대부분 답안의 윤곽이 나옵니다. 이럴 경우, 이견이 있는 문제만 집중적으로 다루고, 나머지는 개인별로 처리하시기 바랍니다.

3. 문제를 끝까지 다 풀었나요? 네 □ / 아니오 □
   다 못 풀었다면, 전체 20 문제 중 푼 문제는? _____ / 20
   시간 모자란 것에 대해서는 크게 신경 쓰지 않아도 됩니다. 무엇보다 중요한 것은 정확도 입니다.
   우선은 풀은 문제를 맞출 확률을 높이고, 그 다음 시간을 걱정해도 늦지 않습니다.

4. 어려웠다고 느껴지는 지문은? 과학 □ / 예술 □ / 인문 □ / 인물 □ / 사회 □
   과학지문이 현격히 다른 분야보다 많지만, 그래도, 공부하다 보면 자신만 어려워하는 분야는 모두 각각입니다. 그러므로, 혹시 배경지식 부분에서 필요한 것이 있다면, www.usherlN.co.kr 에 방문하셔서, 공부가 안될 때, 배경지식 부분을 쉬엄쉬엄 들러서 봐 두시길 바랍니다. 쉬엄쉬엄 입니다. 누가 뭐래도 실력있는 사람은 배경지식이 큰 영향을 끼치지는 않습니다.

5. (채점 후) 문제 풀 때 어렵다고 느낀 지문이 틀리는 개수와 쉬웠다고 느껴졌던 지문의 틀린 개수차이가 있나요? 예 □ / 아니오 □
   어느 순간 깨닫게 됩니다. 내가 잘 아는 내용이 나와서 자신 있게 푸나, 내가 모르는 지문이 나와서 겁먹고 푸나, 틀린 개수가 큰 차이가 나지 않는 것을…. 혹시 그걸 못 느끼신다면, 더욱더 열심히 하시기 바랍니다. ^^

6. 틀린 문제의 번호를 다음의 문제 유형 분석표와 비교해서 파악해 두시기 바랍니다.
   문제 유형을 파악해서 주의하는 것은, 누가 뭐래도 실력이 기본은 받쳐 줄 때 얘기입니다. 문제 푸는 스킬이나, 기타 문제 유형 파악 등은 기본적으로 본문 내용을 이해하고, 해석이 웬만큼 될 때 얘기입니다. 만약, 너무 힘들다면 너무 스트레스 받지 말고, 그냥 '아~ 그렇구나' 정도로 넘기셔도 됩니다. 단, 본문 이해는 절대 양보해서는 안됩니다.

문제 유형 분석표 40page 내용 중, 아래 표시되어 있는 문제 유형은 파악하기 쉬우나 나머지 문제들의 문제 유형 파악은 어려워 하는 경향이 있어 비워두었습니다. 문제유형 정답은 291page를 참조하세요.

TEST 2-1

01 Reference
02 Vocabulary
03
04
05
06 Highlight
07
08
09 Insertion
10 Summary

TEST 2-2

11
12 Highlight
13
14
15
16
17
18 Vocabulary
19 Insertion
20 Summary

잔소리 2

문제풀이 전 체크 사항

묶었나?
? 찍었나?
문제 동그라미 했나?
날렸나?

시험볼때무조건묶어야합니다.

이유 - 집중력 / 명확성
문제 풀기에 시간이 부족하다고 생각하는데,
절대 늦지 않습니다.
오히려, 묶고, 다 풀고도 시간이 남습니다.
묶다가 다 못 푼다고 하는 건, 묶는 과정이 들어가서가 아니라 실력부족인 겁니다.

어서 문법책을 보면,
묶기를 해야 하는 이유를 적어 뒀지만,
여기서는 다른 이유 하나를 더하려 합니다.
이유는 문법을 위해서가 아닌, 독해를 위해서니까…

누차 말하지만,
독해점수 25점 이하까지는 이유불문 무조건 묶어야 합니다.
25이상은?
시키지 않더라도 구조가 안보이는 문장은 묶어야 합니다.

이유는 간단합니다.
문장 보는 건 점수 터질 때까지도, 계속 발목을 잡는 이유가 되기 때문입니다. 나중에 25점을 넘어도, 단어, 구문, 묶기(문장구조파악)는 여전히 문제됩니다. 그런데, 정말 말 안듣는 학생들을 많이 봤습니다.

일찍 끝내고 싶으신가요? 그럼 더 하십시오.
싫은 만큼 더 하십시오.
연습이란 건,
하면 할수록 시간은 짧아지고,
나중엔 눈으로도 할 수있게 만들어줍니다.

이 상황은,
기어가지도 못하면서,
뛰는 게 부러워서,
걷는걸 생략하고,
뛰려고 노력하는 것과 다를 게 없습니다.

충분히 기어야 합니다.
그러다 보면, 일어설 것이고,
충분히 걸어야지만.
뛰게 됩니다.

되지도 않았으면서 뛰려 말고...
스스로 지나가다, 어떤 문장이든 안 묶고 그저 공부만 하려면 그냥
다른 책을 푸셔도 좋습니다.
도움이 되지 않는다면 절대 시키지 않습니다.
시간 투자를 하는 건,
다 이유가 있어서 입니다.

누구보다 빨리 마치게 해줄 자신 있습니다.
누구보다 정확하게 만들어줄 수 있습니다.
그러려면, 묶으십시오.
이것을 안 하면, 일반 책 푸는 것과 다른 효과를 낼 수 없습니다.

문제 풀이시간에, 감독하며 지나가다 안 묶는 것을 발견하고, 물으면
가장 잘 하는 대답은
"눈으로 푸는 것 연습 하려구요."
"시험장에선 손을 댈 수 없잖아요."
"버릇될 것 같아서요."

눈으로 풀게 만들어 줄려고 시키는 겁니다.
시험장에서 손 안대게 하려고 시키는 거고
버릇 안 들일려고 하는 겁니다.

시험장가서 같은 부분만 계속 읽고 또 읽고 앉아있기 싫으시다면,
무조건 묶으십시오.

USHER iBT TOEFL
INTERMEDIATE READING
TEST 3

테스트 전 확인사항

실전에 유용한 독해 전략(44p)을 숙지하였습니다.	○
화장실은 미리 다녀왔습니다.	○
휴대폰의 전원을 껐습니다.	○
노트테이킹 할 종이와 연필을 준비하였습니다.	○
시간을 체크할 시계를 준비하였습니다.	○
목표점수(20개 중____개)를 정하였습니다.	○
시험 시작 시간은 ____시 ____분이며, 종료 시간은 35분 뒤인 ____시 ____분입니다.	○
시험 중 이동해야 할 방해요소가 있는지 체크하였습니다.	○
시험 중 이동하지 않습니다.	

Sentinel Behavior in Meerkats

1.→ Meerkats are small, mongoose-like mammals that live in the Kalahari Desert of Southern Africa. Being primarily insectivores, they feed on beetles and scorpions buried underground, which they locate using their strong sense of smell. Unfortunately, when the meerkat lowers its head to search out prey under grasses, it limits its own range of sight by a significant amount. As a result they are extremely vulnerable to airborne predators such as hawks and owls. To ensure that they can reach the safety of their bolt-holes before being snatched up by birds, meerkats forage in packs and partake in what is known as sentinel behavior. As the term suggests, one meerkat in the group acts as a sentinel and does not look for food like the rest, but rather stands upright on its hind legs to gain a wider field of view with which it scans the surrounding area for possible predators and other threats to the community. When it senses danger approaching, the sentinel barks loudly to warn the others of the danger. Many scientists questioned this phenomenon because the revealing stance and loud vocalization were thought to expose the meerkat to an increased risk of predation.

폭 넓게 - 일단 버릇 들이는게 중요!

32 According to paragraph 1, why was sentinel behavior thought to be disadvantageous?

(A) It warns the predator of where the meerkat group is.
(B) It allows the meerkat to sense danger and warn the group.
(C) It helps the predators locate the sentinel meerkat.
(D) It encourages the predator to prey on meerkats over other species.

스터디 자료들 미리 수집해 둘것!

시험 중 체크 사항

❶ "?"표시하기 : 본문 읽으며, 궁금한 곳에 "?" 표시를 합니다.
　　　　　　　문제를 풀면서도 질문 거리에는 "?" 표시를 해둡니다.
❷ 문제 핵심에 동그라미 : 문제가 물어보는 게 무엇인지, 문제 핵심에 동그라미 표시를 합니다.
❸ 답근거 날리기 : 문제를 풀 때 선택지가 틀린 이유 단어로, 간결하게 날립니다.
❹ 경쟁 문장 표시 : 4개의 선택지 중에 정답과 경쟁하는 마지막 1개의 선택지를 표시 해둡니다. 무조건 1개여야 합니다.

Reading Section Directions

This section measures your ability to understand academic passages in English.

Most questions are worth 1 point but the last question in each set is worth more than 1 point. The directions indicate how many points you may receive.

Some passages include a word or phrase that is underlined in blue. Click on the word or phrase to see a definition or an explanation.

Within each test, you can go to the next questions by clicking **Next**. You may skip questions and go back to them later. If you want to return to previous questions, click on **Back**. You can click on **Review** at any time and the review screen will show you which questions you have answered and which you have not answered. From this reviewscreen, you may go directly to any questions you have already seen in the Reading section.

You may now begin the Reading section. In the section you will read 2 passages. You will have **35 minutes** to read the passages and answer thequestions.

Click on **Continue** to go on.

Next 버튼을 이용하여 다음 문제로 이동하고 **Back** 버튼을 이용하여 이전문제로 이동할 수 있습니다. 문제에 답을 하지 않더라도 다음 문제로이동할 수 있으며, **Review** 버튼을 이용하여 각 문제별로 답을 체크했는지의 여부를 확인할 수 있습니다.
이번 테스트에서는 세 지문을 읽게 됩니다. **35분** 동안 지문을 읽고 문제에 답을 하세요.

El Niño

1 The Humboldt Current carries cold water northward from the Antarctic along South America's western coast. [■] As it reaches the equator, the easterly trade winds blow the surface water westward and allow an upwelling of cold, nutrient-rich waters. [■] However, during December and January, the cold waters are replaced by a warmer countercurrent, greatly reducing the water's nutrient content and causing a lull in commercial fishing due to the lack of commercially viable fish, such as anchovies, in the warmer water. [■] Local residents termed this period "El Niño," or "the boy" in Spanish, due to its occurrence during the Christmas season, and use this downtime to tend to their equipment. [■]

2 Despite the traditionally short duration of El Niño, these warmer surface waters can linger and extend far into the equatorial Pacific. In fact, over the past six decades, climatologists have identified at least ten unusually long El Niño periods. ==In recent times, the traditional term for this period, El Niño, has become identified worldwide with these lengthy periods of warmer Pacific waters more than with the annual pattern, because of the great changes they can cause in weather patterns across the globe.==

3 Despite being known mainly as an eastern Pacific pattern, El Niño affects conditions across the vast waters of the Pacific. One of the first scientists to recognize this was early-20th century British physicist Gilbert Walker, who found an inverse correlation between atmospheric pressure at weather stations in the eastern and western Pacific. Walker noted that as the pressure of the eastern Pacific fell, that of the western Pacific rose, and vice versa in a see-saw-like pattern that he termed the Southern Oscillation. The relationship between this phenomenon and El Niño was later recognized as being so strong that they are often referred to collectively as the

---

01. What can be inferred from paragraph 1 about the waters off the western coast of South America?

(A) They are colder than the waters off the eastern coast of the continent due to the Humboldt Current.
(B) Their ability to support healthy populations of sea life is dependent upon the presence of winds blowing from the east.
(C) They provide the main source of nutrients for the agriculture of the western region of South America.
(D) Their temperature would have nothing to do with the Humboldt Current.

02. Which of the sentences below best expresses the essential information in the highlighted sentence in the passage? Incorrect choices change the meaning in important ways or leave out essential information.

(A) Scientists today use the term El Niño to identify the longer periods of warming in areas around the Pacific instead of the annual pattern because they greatly affect the weather patterns around the globe.
(B) El Niño has become the official name of the warming of the waters of the Pacific Ocean because of the great impact it has on the climates of regions across the globe.
(C) Because of the lengthier episodes of Pacific warming that occur today, the term El Niño is now used to identify the weather changes that occur worldwide.
(D) Now that the worldwide climatic effects of El Niño are better understood, the term is more closely associated with the extended warming periods than with the traditional warming period.

03. According to paragraph 1 and 2, which of the following is NOT true regarding El Niño?

(A) During the El Niño period, fishers tend to use their equipment in the downtime.
(B) The period of increased surface temperatures can last longer than the two months that were traditionally associated with El Niño.
(C) Scientists monitor the duration of the increased surface temperatures of the Pacific Ocean along the equator.
(D) The term "El Niño" is now used worldwide to refer to times when the warming of Pacific waters extends past the traditional period.

04. What does the word "it" refer to in the passage?

(A) southern Oscillation
(B) pressure increase
(C) disruption
(D) trade wind

05. According to paragraph 4, all of the following is true about the atmospheric pressure over the Pacific Ocean EXCEPT:

(A) Atmospheric pressure is usually higher over the Eastern Pacific than it is over the western region.
(B) The easterly trade winds are unusual in the southern equatorial region.
(C) When the pressure across the ocean becomes more equal, warmer surface temperatures creep eastward across the Pacific Ocean.
(D) The lowered atmospheric pressure gradient across the Pacific Ocean weakens the trade winds.

06. The term "severely" in the passage is closest in meaning to:

(A) easily
(B) regularly
(C) intensely
(D) abruptly

El Niño-Southern Oscillation.

4 Normally, the eastern Pacific's higher atmospheric pressure causes the easterly trade winds that typify the wind pattern of the southern equatorial region. These warm winds also cause the warm east-to-west surface current that moves across the Pacific Ocean along the equator. Eventually it causes an accumulation of warm surface water in the western Pacific, while the Humboldt Current's upwelling keeps surface temperatures in the eastern Pacific much lower. When the Southern Oscillation shifts and pressure rises in the west, the pressure gradient across the ocean is disrupted and the trade winds that were caused by it are severely weakened or reversed. With these no longer pushing westward on the warmer surface water it begins to creep eastward, marking the beginning of El Niño. As the warmer waters slide eastward, they further decrease the pressure and temperature gradients across the Pacific Ocean in a positive feedback loop. The pressure gradient that causes the winds is decreased as the eastern Pacific becomes warmer, which further decreases the pressure gradient and the winds.

5 Since this process was first theorized, scientists have attempted to trace it using historical records. By examining records of the daily surface temperature of the ocean, rainfall, atmospheric pressure, and fisheries data from South American inhabitants and Spanish colonists dating as far back as the 1400s, they have pieced together a detailed timeline of El Niño over the past six centuries. From this, it is clear that although El Niño occurred regularly throughout history its frequency is increasing. Comparing the records of the 16th century to modern ones shows that El Niño is now occurring nearly three times more often than it did then, occurring just over every 2 years now, but occurring in six year intervals historically. An even more alarming finding is that the temperature increase's severity is rising. This is troubling

07. Why does the author mention that "the entire United States suffered from more severe seasonal weather"?

(A) To illustrate that El Niño is responsible for the change of seasons in the United States
(B) To give more information regarding the droughts that are caused by the onset of an El Niño period
(C) To show that El Niño most severely affects countries found on the eastern side of the Pacific Ocean
(D) To emphasize the extent of the impact the El Niño had even on distant locations

08. According to paragraph 6, which of the following is true of the worldwide impact of El Niño?

(A) El Niño's climatic impact causes disruptions in the natural world that lead to major non-climatic issues for humans across the globe.
(B) It has been proven that a 1°C increase in the ocean's surface temperature yields a 20% increase in malaria-affected coastal regions of the tropical Pacific.
(C) All of the major conflicts that occurred during the 20th century began during an El Niño period.
(D) The El Niño that had an impact on the Northern Chinese Famine also triggered the French evolution.

because scientists now know that El Niño's effects are not limited to the southern Pacific, but also affect worldwide weather patterns. During the 1997-98 El Niño, for instance, the entire United States suffered from more severe seasonal weather.

6 Modern researchers have pointed to even more reasons to fear a stronger El Niño. It appears that El Niño also coincides with increased epidemics, especially those caused by mosquito-borne pathogens, civil conflict, and violence. One of the most well-researched aspects of this has been El Niño's effect on malaria. Scientists have proven that a 1°C increase in the ocean's surface temperature yields a 20% increase in malaria around the tropical Pacific's coasts. Others have noted that the risk of civil unrest and violence doubles to 6% during El Niño. They blame this on the widespread famine that occurs during these periods. They point to the Northern Chinese Famine of 1876 that killed 13 million and the El Niño effects of 1789-1793 that led to crop failures, which eventually sparked the French Revolution, as evidence of this. In modern times, it has been found that El Niño's effects have triggered 21% of conflicts worldwide since 1950.

09. Look at the four squares [■] that indicate where the following sentence could be added to the passage.

This rise of these nutritive waters provides the abundant food sources that are needed to sustain the nearly year-round commercial fishing industry off the coasts of Peru and Chile.

Where would the sentence best fit?

Click on a square [■] to add the sentence to the passage.

10. Directions: An introductory sentence for a brief summary of the passage is provided below. Complete the summary by selecting the THREE answer choices that express the most important ideas in the passage. Some sentences do not belong in the summary because they express ideas that are not presented in the passage or are minor ideas in the passage. **This question is worth 2 points.**

> The term "El Niño" refers to climatic changes related to disturbances in the normal pattern of temperature, pressure, and winds in the southern Pacific Ocean.
>
> •
>
> •
>
> •

Answer Choices

(A) The El Niño period has been experienced throughout history, but its incidence and intensity appear to have increased in modern times.

(B) The easterly trade winds blow the surface water westward and allow an upwelling of cold, nutrient-rich waters that travel along the Humboldt Current toward the equator.

(C) Historical records indicate that the collapse of the early South American civilization was due to the effects of El Niño.

(D) The changes in atmospheric pressure, surface temperature, and wind strength are linked in a positive feedback loop that extends all of their effects during El Niño periods.

(E) Gilbert Walker first recognized the relationship between the Southern Oscillation and the El Niño and further came up with the name of "El Niño - Southern Oscillation."

(F) Researchers have noted that the climatic changes of El Niño have coincided with many historical events not directly related to the weather, such as disease outbreaks and civil unrest.

11. According to paragraph 2, which of the following is true about agriculture in England during the Late Tudor Period?

(A) The increase in England's population during this period led many farmers to raise the prices of their goods because of the increased demand for food.
(B) Following the pattern of continental Europe, agriculture in England went through an "agricultural revolution" that increased the amount of food they could produce.
(C) Farmers reclaimed lands such as marshlands and woodlands to be used as pastures upon which they could graze their livestock.
(D) Crop output was greatly increased through the development of new farming practices that wouldn't occur in Europe for a few more centuries.

12. According to paragraph 3, which of the following is NOT true about the large family farms of the Elizabethan period?

(A) The great estates not divided into smaller parcels could produce much income.
(B) The possession of large farms was so important that many families arranged marriages for their children on the basis of increasing their landholdings.
(C) Under the practice of primogeniture inherited land could only be divided between the sons of a family, so daughters had no opportunity to gain large farms.
(D) During the Elizabethan period, large farms became more common as farmers looked for ways in which they could increase their agricultural output.

13. Why does the author mention "yeomen who had smaller landholdings" in paragraph 4?

(A) To give an example of the type of landowners who owned smaller landholdings
(B) To make the point that the maximization of profit from available land was not only reserved to the landed elite with large estates
(C) To give a better idea of the different names used to refer to wealthy landowners during the sixteenth century
(D) To contrast the amount of achievable profits between large and small landowners

England's Sixteenth Century Economy

1   Great changes occurred in England during the Late Tudor Period under the reign of Queen Elizabeth I In the latter half of the sixteenth and early seventeenth centuries. One of the most notable was the increase in the population to nearly that of the pre-Black Death period. In England and Wales, increased fertility and reduced mortality rates nearly doubled the population around this time, increasing from 2.5 million in the 1520s to 4.5 million by 1610. This dramatic increase, along with other factors led to vast changes in England's economy and allowed it to become Europe's largest, far surpassing those of the war and plague-ravaged continent.

2   One of the first direct effects of the population increase was a demand for more food. This caused an "agricultural revolution" in England 2-300 years before they occurred elsewhere in Europe. During this period, English farmers created farmlands from previously unsuitable areas, such as marshlands and woodlands, giving them more arable land on which to produce food. These farmers undertook a process of crop specialization that allowed them to be more efficient and market-driven, increasing their yields dramatically. For instance, they increased their grain production per acre by at least 30% between 1450 and 1650.

3   With the greater efficiency of the new farming methods, wealthy landowners increased their landholdings in order to increase their agricultural productivity. These landholdings were consolidated through the practice of primogeniture under which the eldest son inherited the entirety of his father's holdings, thus preventing the great estates from being divided up into smaller parcels which could not produce as much income. They also increased the size of their landholdings by marrying into other families with large estates. Marriages amongst the wealthiest Elizabethan families were arranged to ensure that both families maintained their social statuses. With their larger estates, these families could conduct more commercialized farming to meet the demand for

14. The term "tactics" in the passage is closest in meaning to:

(A) characteristics
(B) results
(C) developments
(D) strategies

15. According to paragraph 5, which of the following is true of the process of enclosure?

(A) It reduced the numbers of workers who were willing to tend the pastureland.
(B) Enclosure allowed land owners to use public lands to graze the animals they would sell to make a communal profit.
(C) The process of enclosure was started to allow farmers during the Tudor era to plant crops, since they were more valuable than grazing livestock.
(D) Enclosure allowed some farmers to become very wealthy while denying others the ability to farm.

16. What can be inferred about the influence of the guild system from paragraph 6?

(A) The guild system effectively protected industries in areas where competition had prevented rural manufactures from entering the market.
(B) The guilds in the cities were unaware of the goods manufactured in the countryside.
(C) The guilds in the cities made it more expensive to have products manufactured in the cities than in the countryside.
(D) The guilds put-out work to rural craftsman, further reinforcing their monopoly in the city.

agricultural products, which was driving prices higher.

4 These large landowners, and the yeomen who had smaller landholdings, maximized the profits they could draw from their property. To increase their profits, they planted crops which were in demand in the London markets. They also aggressively dealt with those to whom they rented their property. During this period, rents were increased and rental contracts were written to provide even more benefits to the landowners. One of the ways they did this was shortening the duration of their contracts to allow themselves more control over the land. Another way they maximized their profits was to charge potential tenants an "entry fee" before they would even consent to renting to them. Renters who could not, or would not, abide by the new contracts were simply evicted and replaced by those who could. Their tactics were quite one-sided, but they also encouraged their tenants to use farming practices that would increase their farming efficiency, such as crop rotation.

5 [■] Another method used to increase the profits of these large landholdings was to convert some of the farmland into pastureland upon which sheep could graze. [■] This conversion became possible because of the enclosure movement that occurred during the Tudor period. [■] In the process of enclosure, open fields that had previously been used for communal farming, grazing and hay production were fenced and their use became the sole right of the owner. [■] By converting their land into pastureland they could derive a higher profit while reducing the need for large numbers of workers to tend it.

6 Wool production led to even greater changes in the English economy of the time. While English wool had been exported since at least the 1200s, the in it was exported form began to change. Wool was traditionally exported in its raw form, but around this time the production and export of finished textiles overtook the English economy. This occurred through the cottage industry system under which a cloth manufacturer "put-out" work

17. Which of the sentences below best expresses the essential information in the highlighted sentence in the passage? Incorrect choices change the meaning in important ways or leave out essential information.

(A) The establishment of trade companies like the Muscovy and English East India Companies secured monopolies over trade routes to distant lands for English products like wool textiles, stirring an increase in international trade.

(B) Elizabethan England saw a great increase in the amount of international trade being done with companies such as the Muscovy Company and the English East India Company which had monopolies over selling woolen textiles made in Moscow and India.

(C) Companies like the Muscovy Company and the English East India Company were started to establish monopolistic trade routes with far-flung locales such as Moscow and India for products like English wool.

(D) During the sixteenth century, influenced by England's increased reputation in international trade, several privileged English companies developed monopolistic trade routes with distant locales such as Moscow and India.

18. What is the purpose of including paragraph 7 in the passage?

(A) To show how the increased trade networks for English goods during this period led to major changes such as the colonization of the Americas.

(B) To give an idea of how important Sir Thomas Gresham was in the international trade of wool textiles from England

(C) To point out the differences between the way trade of English wool textiles was conducted in Antwerp and in the Americas.

(D) To explain why companies such as the English East India Company and the Muscovy Company developed monopolistic trade routes.

to rural craftspeople who were provided with raw wool, which they carded, spun, and wove in their own homes. This reduced textile costs because it effectively cut out the guilds that controlled urban trade by creating monopolies and preventing competition between guild members.

7 During this period, the extent of England's international trade increased so markedly that companies, such as the Muscovy Company and the English East India Company, were chartered to develop monopolistic trade routes for English goods, such as wool textiles, with faraway places like Moscow and India. One of the major markets for these textiles was the Spanish-controlled city of Antwerp, where they were dyed and sold. Antwerp was so important a point that the English kept a representative stationed there permanently, Sir Thomas Gresham. Gresham increased England's reputation in Antwerp to the point that English merchants were able to operate on a credit-based system there, something very rare in the sixteenth century. He also championed the economic possibilities of the Americas, leading to England's early attempts to colonize the continents for commercial purposes.

19. Look at the four squares [■] that indicate where the following sentence could be added to the passage.

Seeing the growing demands for English wool internationally, landholders often considered rearing sheep as a more profitable way to utilize their land.

Where would the sentence best fit?

Click on a square [■] to add the sentence to the passage.

20. Directions: An introductory sentence for a brief summary of the passage is provided below. Complete the summary by selecting the THREE answer choices that express the most important ideas in the passage. Some sentences do not belong in the summary because they express ideas that are not presented in the passage or are minor ideas in the passage. **This question is worth 2 points.**

England's economy underwent many changes during the Elizabethan period.

-
-
-

Answer Choices

(A) Increased demand for English wool textiles led to many landowners converting their farmlands into pastureland on which sheep could graze and brought about the practice of enclosure across rural England.

(B) The dramatic increase in population during the sixteenth century raised the demand for food, thereby making farming, and consequently landownership, a very lucrative field and induced an agricultural revolution in England.

(C) In the sixteenth century, the introduction of a credit-based system in Antwerp contributed to England's increased reputation in the world.

(D) The export of wool textiles was very lucrative for the English government and it helped spur their further exploration and colonization of the Americas.

(E) The tradition of marriages among the wealthiest families allowed them to make the most profit from their landholdings.

(F) From the 16th to the 17th century, there was a great increase in the number of people in England and Wales because of hygienic improvements.

You have seen all of the questions in this part of the Reading section. You have time left to review.
As long as there is time remaining, you can check your work.

Click on **Return** to go back to the previous question.
Click on **Review** to see the review screen for this section.
Click on **Continue** to go on.
Once you leave this part of the Reading section, you WILL NOT be able to return to it.

이제 Reading Section이 끝났습니다.
Continue 버튼을 누르면 다시 문제를 검토할 수 없으므로 유의하세요.

시험보고 난 후 ... 체크 리스트 및 스터디 디렉션   USHER iBT TOEFL INTERMEDIATE TEST READI

1. 내가 불안했던 문제만 재빨리 다시 보고, 불안하게 만든, 즉, 경쟁 초이스를 찾아서 왜 내가 헷갈려 했는지를 파악할 수 있는 메모를 해두시기 바랍니다. 시간이 지나거나, 다른 학생들과 스터디를 하면서는, 자신이 왜 낚였는지 이유조차 기억하지 않아 본인의 실수 패턴 파악이 힘들기 때문입니다.

2. 답지를 확인하지 않고 스터디를 하시기 바랍니다. (그래서, 답지를 문제지 뒤에 붙이지 않고, 본 설명만을 붙여 두었습니다.) 답지를 확인하지 않고 하는 이유는 답을 아는 순간, 답에 끼워 맞춰 설명하려 하고, 이런 태도는 본인 실력 향상에 도움이 되지 않기 때문입니다. 스터디 팀원들간에 대략적인 답을 맞춰보면, 대부분 답안의 윤곽이 나옵니다. 이럴 경우, 이견이 있는 문제만 집중적으로 다루고, 나머지는 개인별로 처리하시기 바랍니다.

3. 문제를 끝까지 다 풀었나요? 네 □ / 아니오 □
   다 못 풀었다면, 전체 20 문제 중 푼 문제는? _____ / 20
   시간 모자란 것에 대해서는 크게 신경 쓰지 않아도 됩니다. 무엇보다 중요한 것은 정확도 입니다.
   우선은 푼 문제를 맞출 확률을 높이고, 그 다음 시간을 걱정해도 늦지 않습니다.

4. 어려웠다고 느껴지는 지문은? 과학 □ / 예술 □ / 인문 □ / 인물 □ / 사회 □
   과학지문이 현격히 다른 분야보다 많지만, 그래도, 공부하다 보면 자신만 어려워하는 분야는 모두 각각입니다. 그러므로, 혹시 배경지식 부분에서 필요한 것이 있다면, www.usherIN.co.kr 에 방문하셔서, 공부가 안될 때, 배경지식 부분을 쉬엄쉬엄 들러서 봐 두시길 바랍니다. 쉬엄쉬엄 입니다. 누가 뭐래도 실력있는 사람은 배경지식이 큰 영향을 끼치지는 않습니다.

5. (채점 후) 문제 풀 때 어렵다고 느낀 지문이 틀리는 개수와 쉬웠다고 느껴졌던 지문의 틀린 개수차이가 있나요? 예 □ / 아니오 □
   어느 순간 깨닫게 됩니다. 내가 잘 아는 내용이 나와서 자신 있게 푸나, 내가 모르는 지문이 나와서 겁먹고 푸나, 틀린 개수가 큰 차이가 나지 않는 것을…. 혹시 그걸 못 느끼신다면, 더욱더 열심히 하시기 바랍니다. ^^

6. 틀린 문제의 번호를 다음의 문제 유형 분석표와 비교해서 파악해 두시기 바랍니다.
   문제 유형을 파악해서 주의하는 것은, 누가 뭐래도 실력이 기본은 받쳐 줄 때 얘기입니다. 문제 푸는 스킬이나, 기타 문제 유형 파악 등은 기본적으로 본문 내용을 이해하고, 해석이 웬만큼 될 때 얘기입니다. 만약, 너무 힘들다면 너무 스트레스 받지 말고, 그냥 '아~ 그렇구나' 정도로 넘기셔도 됩니다. 단, 본문 이해는 절대 양보해서는 안됩니다.

문제 유형 분석표 40page 내용 중, 아래 표시되어 있는 문제 유형은 파악하기 쉬우나 나머지 문제들의 문제 유형 파악은 어려워 하는 경향이 있어 비워두었습니다. 문제유형 정답은 309page를 참조하세요.

TEST 3-1

01
02 Highlight
03
04 Reference
05
06 Vocabulary
07
08
09 Insertion
10 Summary

TEST 3-2

11
12
13
14 Vocabulary
15
16
17 Highlight
18
19 Insertion
20 Summary

잔소리 3

문제풀이 전 체크 사항

묶었나?
? 찍었나?
문제 동그라미 했나?
날렸나?

궁금한 것을 잘 이용하는게, 가장 재밌고 효율적으로 공부하는 방법입니다.

관심도 없으면, 질문도 없고, 궁금한 것도 없기 마련 입니다.

하지만 흥미로운 것은, 아무리 싫어하는 과목도, 중간고사 기말고사 때는, 시험이 끝난 뒤, 10분밖에 없는 쉬는 시간을 굳이 전 시간에 본 시험을 가채점 하면서 보내는 학생들이 있습니다.
왜그런지는 저도 모르지만 가끔 저도 그러긴 했습니다. 궁금해서..

그걸 잘 이용하면 됩니다.
궁금할 땐, 사전 한번 찾아보고, 옆 사람이랑 답이 왜 되는지 얘기만 해봐도 팍! 팍!! 머리 속에 박히게 됩니다.

이정도로 공부할 때 확실하고 효과적인 원동력도 없습니다.
정말 이것만 잘 이용해도 대박입니다.
하지만 문제는 이런 궁금점이 늘 있지 않다는 점,
아니, 늘 없다는 점이 문제입니다.

심지어 이렇게까지나 궁금했던 내용조차
오전 시험 다 끝나고, 점심시간 되면 별로 관심 없어집니다.
그냥 피곤할 뿐이고, 난 이미 시험 망친걸 알 뿐이고...
저녁이 되면? 시험때 뭘 본지 기억조차 안납니다.
다음날이면? 담당 선생님이 답지 들고 와서 가르쳐 준다 해도,
별로 관심 없습니다.
그렇게나 궁금해했던 내용인데도 말입니다.

그러니, 시험 즉시 가장 궁금해 할때, 그 때 즉시 건드려야 합니다.
시간은 오래일 필요 없습니다.
딱 서로 이견있는 문제만 골라낸 뒤,
그것만 집중적으로 얘기해보면 됩니다.
싸워도 됩니다. 우겨도 됩니다. 혼자 다굴 당해도 좋고,
그게 혼자만 맞아도 좋고, 혼자만 틀려도 좋습니다.

중요한 건, 자신의 답을 얘기할 때는 분명한 근거가 있어야 한다는 겁니다.
잘된 근거 제시라면, 실력이 늘어가는 과정이고,
잘못된 근거 제시라도, 실력을 올바르게 늘여가는데 어떤 도움보다 큰 도움이 될 것입니다.

꼭 자기 주장을 강하게 어필하면서,
내 주장이 맞는지를 꼭 확인 해봐야 합니다.

usherin.usher.co.kr

USHER iBT TOEFL
INTERMEDIATE READING
TEST 4

테스트 전 확인사항

실전에 유용한 독해 전략(44p)을 숙지하였습니다. ○

화장실은 미리 다녀왔습니다. ○

휴대폰의 전원을 껐습니다. ○

노트테이킹 할 종이와 연필을 준비하였습니다. ○

시간을 체크할 시계를 준비하였습니다. ○

목표점수(20개 중 ____개)를 정하였습니다. ○

시험 시작 시간은 ____시 ____분이며,
종료 시간은 35분 뒤인 ____시 ____분입니다. ○

시험 중 이동해야 할 방해요소가 있는지 체크하였습니다. ○

시험 중 이동하지 않습니다.

Sentinel Behavior in Meerkats

1. → Meerkats are small, mongoose-like mammals that live in the Kalahari Desert of Southern Africa. Being primarily insectivores, they feed on beetles and scorpions buried underground, which they locate using their strong sense of smell. Unfortunately, when the meerkat lowers its head to search out prey under grasses, it limits its own range of sight by a significant amount. As a result they are extremely vulnerable to airborne predators such as hawks and owls. To ensure that they can reach the safety of their bolt-holes before being snatched up by birds, meerkats forage in packs and partake in what is known as sentinel behavior. As the term suggests, one meerkat in the group acts as a sentinel and does not look for food like the rest, but rather stands upright on its hind legs to gain a wider field of view with which it scans the surrounding area for possible predators and other threats to the community. When it senses danger approaching, the sentinel barks loudly to warn the others of the danger. Many scientists questioned this phenomenon because the revealing stance and loud vocalization were thought to expose the meerkat to an increased risk of predation.

폭 넓게 - 일단 버릇 들이는게 중요!

32 According to paragraph 1, why was sentinel behavior thought to be disadvantageous?

(A) It warns the predator of where the meerkat group is.
(B) It allows the meerkat to sense danger and warn the group.
(C) It helps the predators locate the sentinel meerkat.
(D) It encourages the predator to prey on meerkats over other species.

스터디 자료들 미리 수집해 둘것!

시험 중 체크 사항

❶ "?"표시하기 : 본문 읽으며, 궁금한 곳에 "?" 표시를 합니다.
　　문제를 풀면서도 질문 거리에는 "?" 표시를 해둡니다.
❷ 문제 핵심에 동그라미 : 문제가 물어보는 게 무엇인지, 문제 핵심에 동그라미 표시를 합니다.
❸ 답근거 날리기 : 문제를 풀 때 선택지가 틀린 이유 단어로, 간결하게 날립니다.
❹ 경쟁 문장 표시 : 4개의 선택지 중에 정답과 경쟁하는 마지막 1개의 선택지를 표시 해둡니다. 무조건 1개여야 합니다.

Reading Section Directions

This section measures your ability to understand academic passages in English.

Most questions are worth 1 point but the last question in each set is worth more than 1 point. The directions indicate how many points you may receive.

Some passages include a word or phrase that is underlined in blue. Click on the word or phrase to see a definition or an explanation.

Within each test, you can go to the next questions by clicking **Next**. You may skip questions and go back to them later. If you want to return to previous questions, click on **Back**. You can click on **Review** at any time and the review screen will show you which questions you have answered and which you have not answered. From this reviewscreen, you may go directly to any questions you have already seen in the Reading section.

You may now begin the Reading section. In the section you will read 2 passages. You will have **35 minutes** to read the passages and answer thequestions.

Click on **Continue** to go on.

Next 버튼을 이용하여 다음 문제로 이동하고 **Back** 버튼을 이용하여 이전문제로 이동할 수 있습니다. 문제에 답을 하지 않더라도 다음 문제로이동할 수 있으며, **Review** 버튼을 이용하여 각 문제별로 답을 체크했는지의 여부를 확인할 수 있습니다.
이번 테스트에서는 세 지문을 읽게 됩니다. 35분 동안 지문을 읽고 문제에 답을 하세요.

Environmental Impact of the Anasazi

1   The Anasazi people, ancient Native Americans who resided in pit houses, pueblos, and cliff dwellings, flourished in America's present-day Four Corners region before suddenly abandoning their elaborate villages and palace complexes. Archeologists long thought that studies of the rings of the trees used in the structures found there indicated that these people had been driven from their villages and home region, due to a climatic event known as the "Great Drought." This, however, began to be called into question recently. Today, historians believe that the Anasazi evacuation had been an ongoing event before the "Great Drought" and that the drought was not an unprecedented event; villagers had likely survived others before it. This has left them researching what could have actually caused an entire civilization to abandon its home territory. Archeologist Tim Kohler has come up with one possible explanation, human interaction with the natural environment.

2   Kohler believes that the Anasazi's interactions with their surroundings eventually led to their downfall. To support his hypothesis, Kohler put forth a case study regarding the Anasazi living in southwestern Colorado's Dolores River basin around 600 A.D. Over a few hundred years, their population increased greatly and they built large villages complete with kivas and Great Houses, until around 900 A.D. when the area's abandonment began. Many archeologists believe that shortened growing seasons occurred during this era, which would have made it difficult to produce the main Anasazi staple, corn. ==Kohler takes exception to this theory, however, and points to problems that developed due to this growing population's settlement in villages, which caused a pressing need for increased agricultural output, forcing changes in the Anasazi's interactions with the environment, leading to deforestation, soil depletion, and their eventual abandonment of the area.==

---

01. What can be inferred from paragraph 2 about Tim Kohler's theory regarding the disappearance of the Anasazi?

(A) He believed that human activity was a more direct cause of the downfall of the Anasazi than weather patterns.
(B) He found it difficult to believe that corn was the main staple of the Anasazi population at the time.
(C) He chose to study the Dolores River basin villages because the "Great Drought" had not affected them as much as it had other tribes.
(D) He felt that the environment had nothing to do with the disappearance and that it was entirely caused by human beings.

02. Which of the sentences below best expresses the essential information in the highlighted sentence in the passage? Incorrect choices change the meaning in important ways or leave out essential information.

(A) Kohler believed that the radical farming practices the Anasazi employed to increase agricultural output made the land inarable and rather prohibited its population from growing further.
(B) Consenting to other archaeologists, he also believed that the need to increase food production led to environmental problems that eventually forced the Anasazi away.
(C) Kohler tried to convince other archeologists that the deforestation and soil depletion caused by the Anasazi settlements was a result of environmental changes that eventually caused the villagers to abandon their homes.
(D) Kohler disagreed with other archeologists and thought that the removal of trees, soil nutrients and the fleeing of the Anasazi were brought about by manmade environmental changes caused by the settlement in villages, which increased their need for food.

03. The term "replenish" in the passage is closest in meaning to:

(A) rearrange
(B) replace
(C) repair
(D) refill

04. According to paragraph 3, which of the following is true about the slash-and-burn technique?

(A) It is rarely a productive way of growing food because it leads to the total depletion of the nutrients in soil.
(B) It is a sustainable means of acquiring the food should the population be dense.
(C) If properly conducted, it can fulfill the food production needs of a small civilization.
(D) Although it destroys the environment, it is necessary for civilizations that have settled in one place to produce food.

05. Why does the author mention the Anasazi's use of "swidden, or slash-and-burn, technique." in paragraph 3?

(A) To make the point that humans have known how to convert forestland into arable meadowland for many generations
(B) To introduce one way that early farmers utilized the environment to produce the food they needed
(C) To explain how the Anasazi returned nutrients to the soil after they had overused it
(D) To show one of the farming methods that works well for a lifestyle after leaving its sedentary settlement

06. According to paragraph 4 which of the following is NOT one of the pieces of evidence that Kohler used to deduce that human-environmental interaction had caused the Anasazi disappearance?

(A) Changes in the type of wood used in the Anasazi villages over time were discovered.
(B) The Anasazi gathered seeds from the pinion pine trees to use as food.
(C) Anasazi food sources changed to species found on open ranges.
(D) The seeds of first colonizing species were found in excavations of later Anasazi villages.

3 [■] Prior to their settlement, the Anasazi population had been semi-nomadic in the Dolores River basin, farming the reasonably fertile, thin soils of the flat-topped mesas using the swidden, or slash-and-burn, technique for over 1,000 years. [■] Using this method, they burned down forests to plant the crops they needed and utilized the new farmland until it became unsuitable for producing crops, at which time they moved on to an adjacent area and repeated the process, allowing the previous area to lie fallow and replenish the nutrients necessary for its future use. [■] This may appear to be a destructive way of growing food that ruins the land, but with less dense populations and a schedule of movement that allows the land adequate time for replenishment between planting, swidden is a sustainable means of acquiring the food that societies need. [■]

4 Kohler found several types of evidence to show that changes in human-environmental interactions were more responsible for the Anasazi disappearance than climatic events. Surprisingly, his first source was the same as the one that had led archeologists astray, trees. Kohler noted a pattern in the types of wood found in charcoal deposits from different periods. It seemed that juniper and pinion pine were replaced by faster growing shrubbery and cottonwoods. He also discovered that the Anasazi switched from using pinion pines for construction to younger juniper trees, a less desirable wood source, but one that is more fire resistant and easier to propagate in open settings. This, likely, indicated that the pinion became scarcer around the village as the growing population's demand increased. This would have also affected their food supply as pinion seeds were also gathered as a food source. Additionally, their clearing of the surrounding areas would have had an impact on their hunting as well. As time progressed, the Anasazi apparently switched from hunting woodland rabbits and deer to jackrabbits and antelope, species native to open environments. Seeds excavated from the settlements provided Kohler's final piece of evidence. During excavation of later settlements, a marked increase in

07. According to paragraph 5, which of the following was NOT true about the Anasazi's settlement in villages?

(A) It was the result of their need to increase the population needed to gather more food.
(B) It made them less able to cope with environmental change because they required constant food sources.
(C) It wreaked havoc on the local farmlands and made them unsuitable for growing crops.
(D) It provided benefits to the tribe enabling them to produce more food for the growing population.

08. What can be inferred about the settlement of villages from paragraph 5?

(A) Civilizations that settle in villages are much more resistant to environmental changes that affect their ability to produce the food they need to support their populations.
(B) Villages that produce an abundance of food during the main growing season are immune from the effects of environmental changes.
(C) As time goes on, villagers implement novel ways to deal with the agricultural problems that arise due to a large stationary population.
(D) Even predictable climatic fluctuations, other than minor ones, brought about the abandonment of a civilization.

pioneer species seeds was found, indicating a disturbance in the natural environment.

5 Kohler postulates that the Anasazi aggregated in villages due to the organizational benefits they offered in the face of soil depletion during their early periods. These large settlements allowed them to share food, invest in group food processing units and pool their labor for longer distance hunting or trading trips. Settling in one area, however, brought about new problems, like soil depletion and increased distance to usable fields, which led to increased agricultural risk. This led to agricultural intensification using methods, such as developing mechanisms to better control water flow. These larger villages with more technical agricultural methods produced more food, but were more susceptible to a rapid collapse. The cooperative management of resources for the village meant that they were less flexible in response to environmental changes, so a weak growing season had a widespread impact on the village. For this reason, even a minor, predictable climate change could have led the Anasazi to abandon their settlements.

09. Look at the four squares [■] that indicate where the following sentence could be added to the passage.

> **Kohler's contention was that the permanent settlement of a large, growing population like the Dolores River basin Anasazi relying upon this method would lead to their eventual destruction.**

Where would the sentence best fit?

Click on a square [■] to add the sentence to the passage.

10. Directions: An introductory sentence for a brief summary of the passage is provided below. Complete the summary by selecting the THREE answer choices that express the most important ideas in the passage. Some sentences do not belong in the summary because they express ideas that are not presented in the passage or are minor ideas in the passage. **This question is worth 2 points.**

Human-environmental interaction led to the eventual abandonment of the Dolores River basin.

-
-
-

Answer Choices

(A) Villages with large, or increasing, populations need to undergo agricultural intensification to increase the amount of food they produce for their residents, but these changes can make the village more vulnerable to less extreme climate changes.

(B) When the increase in the Anasazi population in the Dolores River basin outpaced its food production level, it started making changes in its interactions with other villagers.

(C) In the end, archeologists attributed the abandonment of the Anasazi settlements in the Dolores River basin to a catastrophic change in the climate conditions called the "Great Drought."

(D) Early Anasazi groups were semi-nomadic farmers who utilized the process of swidden to clear forestland for the use as farmland before they settled in the Dolores River basin around 600 A.D.

(E) The cooperative management of resources in the Anasazi societies eased the burden with which the people had when they responded to environmental changes.

(F) Archeological exploration or settlements of different eras has shown that the settlement of the Anasazi in the Dolores River basin led to changes in the type of trees used, food sources and seeds found there.

11. What can be inferred from paragraph 1 about species diversity today?

   (A) The north and south poles are home to the lowest species diversity on Earth.
   (B) There are more plants in tropical regions, but more animals in northern regions.
   (C) The tropics now contain more species than have ever been recorded in history.
   (D) Elevation seems to play a large role in the difference in species diversity.

12. Select the TWO answer choices that are mentioned in paragraph 2 as being the effects of the temperature and light on species diversity. To receive credit, you must select TWO answers.

   (A) Their stability comes short of explaining the difference in the diversity gradient between areas of different latitude.
   (B) Temperature and the stability of light have no effect on the diversity of species in an ecosystem.
   (C) Freezing temperatures do not appear to be a limiting factor for the diversity of species in an ecosystem.
   (D) The polar seafloor does not have a diverse ecosystem because it is excluded from the effects of the sun's light.

13. What does the word "they" refer to in the passage?

   (A) feathers
   (B) carcasses
   (C) vultures
   (D) scraps

Global Variations in Species Diversity

1   A peculiar aspect of the world today is the presence of a gradient, or gradual change, in species diversity from the tropics to the polar areas. Species population surveys have shown that regions nearer the equator have the highest species diversity, and as one moves to higher latitudes, diversity drops off dramatically. This gradient can be seen across all species, both flora and fauna, and from higher-level mammals to lower order protozoans.

2   One of the first explanations for this was that temperature and light stability in tropical regions, when compared to the seasonal fluctuations of both in polar regions, allowed more species to develop; however, temperature and light do not seem to fully control species diversity. This can be seen by looking at the seas in polar regions, which remain at a nearly constant temperature year-round yet still have low species diversity. It may then seem logical that the northern seas' near-freezing temperatures preclude diversity levels as high as those of the tropics, but as one moves deeper to the seafloor, which remains in perpetual, frigid darkness with neither light nor warmth from the sun, there is relatively higher species diversity. Therefore, another important factor, such as the availability of food, must affect species diversity.

3   One aspect of the food supply that could affect the diversity of species is that in tropical regions, the food supply remains relatively stable year-round due to the uniform climate. Because of this, species can specialize in feeding on one food source without the risk of it not being available at various times of year. As they become more dependent on their food sources, species adapt more fully and become highly specialized. This allows multiple species to feed on one food source but only marginally compete with one another. This can be seen in the various carrion feeding vultures of the African plains. Although various species of vultures are present on the Serengeti, they have developed different niches.

14. What can be inferred about the food supply in tropical regions from paragraph 3?

(A) Species in tropical regions experience greater food diversity when they specialize on their food sources.
(B) Due to the immense competition rate among the species in tropical regions, they have set out to develop niche specializations.
(C) The limited food diversity in the tropical region forces animals to adapt to survive, which creates more species diversity.
(D) The year-round supply of food allows animals that reside in the tropics to be more specialized feeders than those of latitudes that are more northerly.

15. The term "marginally" in the passage is closest in meaning to:

(A) slightly
(B) jointly
(C) theoretically
(D) seasonally

16. Why does the author mention "freshwater pearl mussels"?

(A) To provide an example that shows that lifespans are shorter at lower latitudes
(B) To show that small animals tend to have longer lifespans than larger animals
(C) To emphasize the wide latitudinal ranges of some species
(D) To illustrate a species-diversifying factor by using an example of a species with a wide lifespan range.

For example, one species has a beak that can tear through leathery hides and a head devoid of feathers, which allows them to stick their heads into the carcass and not worry about becoming contaminated because the sun will bake the refuse from their baldheads. Another has adapted to feeding on the innards, while still others consume the bones and random scraps. Even though they are all eating from the same carcasses, they are all ensured a constant supply of food because their niche specializations effectively lower the competition rate.

4   Species that live in higher latitudes, on the other hand, face a constantly changing food supply. During the warmer season, tundra species have a plethora of food sources, such as plant life and newly hatched krill, which are fed on by animals such as caribou, seabirds, fish, and oceanic mammals. However, when the long, frigid winter sets in, the area is rather barren, leading many specialized feeders to migrate to other areas. There are, however, animals with a more generalist feeding style that remain in the tundra year-round, seasonally adapting their feeding patterns. The gray wolf, for example, switches from consuming small mammals and migratory birds during the warmer months to hunting weakened caribou during the winter. This assures the species of constant food supplies throughout the year. These distinct feeding patterns, therefore, do not limit species diversity, since they allow a variety of tundra species to coexist despite the relatively lower overall food supply.

5   Since the variability in light, temperature, and food supply does not necessarily reduce species diversity in an area, there must be another explanation for the great latitudinal difference. One new theory is that the evolutionary process itself caused this phenomenon. The theory of "effective evolutionary time" draws upon earlier research that showed that evolution occurs more quickly in smaller species that inhabit warmer temperatures. [■] This likely occurs due to the higher physiological rates of smaller species in tropical regions, which lead to shorter

17. According to paragraph 5, which of the following is true regarding the "effective evolutionary time" theory? To receive credit, you must select TWO answer choices.

(A) Proponents of the theory discovered that smaller animals evolve faster in warmer environments than they do in colder climates.
(B) The theory provides that species diversity has enabled species to fill unexploited niches, ultimately leading to their evolution.
(C) The theory suggests that new niches in tropical ecosystems would be filled much quicker than those in polar ecosystems.
(D) Scientists developed the theory after observing that animals such as the freshwater pearl mussel rarely mutated in northern climates.

18. Which of the sentences below best expresses the essential information in the highlighted sentence in the passage? Incorrect choices change the meaning in important ways or leave out essential information.

(A) While one may reasonably conclude that species diversity is lower in colder ecosystems, the chilly, lightless depths of the arctic oceans, which receive no solar heat or illumination, display some of the highest species diversity in the arctic region.
(B) Despite lacking light and heat, the ocean's seafloor displays a higher level of species diversity than either the tropical or the northern regions because of the constant temperatures found there.
(C) One can assume that the extremely cold temperature of the northern seas is what prevents them from having diversity levels as high as those of the tropical regions.
(D) Although there is relatively higher species diversity in the northern seafloors, it may not seem logical that the near-freezing temperatures of the arctic regions discourage the diversity levels from catching up with those of the tropics.

ligespans.[■] A rather striking example of this is the freshwater pearl mussel, which can inhabit freshwater streams in a variety of latitudes and whose maximum lifespan varies depending on latitude, from 29 years at 43°N to nearly 200 at 66°N. [■] While it may seem that the lifespan differences in a species would have little effect on overall diversity, it can be shown to have a great impact. [■] The shorter lifespans of species in warmer areas result in shorter generation lengths, thereby causing a higher mutation rate and speed of selection than in higher latitudes. This rapid mutation and selection enables distinct species to be produced much more quickly than in the colder northern regions. These new species then begin filling unexploited niches in the tropical ecosystem and become even more particularly adapted as more generations are produced.

19. Look at the four squares [■] that indicate where the following sentence could be added to the passage.

This can also be seen in plant species by comparing the relatively shorter lifespans and earlier reproduction rates of plants from tropical regions with those from northern latitudes, such as the giant redwood which has been recorded as living up to 3500 years.

Where would the sentence best fit?

Click on a square [■] to add the sentence to the passage.

20. Directions: An introductory sentence for a brief summary of the passage is provided below. Complete the summary by selecting the THREE answer choices that express the most important ideas in the passage. Some sentences do not belong in the summary because they express ideas that are not presented in the passage or are minor ideas in the passage. **This question is worth 2 points.**

> **A peculiar aspect of the world today is the presence of a gradient, or gradual change, in the diversity of species at different latitudes.**
>
> •
>
> •
>
> •

Answer Choices

(A) The higher temperatures and the abundance of light near the equator dehydrate species in tropical areas, shortening their lifespans.

(B) The stable food supply in tropical regions enables species to become specialized in feeding on one food source, lowering the competition rate.

(C) Although there are more stable food supplies in warmer regions, animals in northern climates have developed feeding strategies that allow them to ensure access to food year-round.

(D) When the stability of food supplies in higher latitudes fluctuates, it poses danger to both specialists and generalists inhabiting the regions.

(E) The increased physiological rates of species in warmer climates results in shorter lifespans that lead to more rapid mutations which in turn cause a larger number of species to exist in tropical regions.

(F) The adaptation of the freshwater pearl mussel illustrates the wide spectrum of ecosystems to which marine-animals can adapt.

You have seen all of the questions in this part of the Reading section. You have time left to review.
As long as there is time remaining, you can check your work.

Click on **Return** to go back to the previous question.
Click on **Review** to see the review screen for this section.
Click on **Continue** to go on.
Once you leave this part of the Reading section, you WILL NOT be able to return to it.

이제 Reading Section이 끝났습니다.
Continue 버튼을 누르면 다시 문제를 검토할 수 없으므로 유의하세요.

시험보고 난 후 ... 체크 리스트 및 스터디 디렉션

USHER iBT TOEFL INTERMEDIATE TEST READING

1. 내가 불안했던 문제만 재빨리 다시 보고, 불안하게 만든, 즉, 경쟁 초이스를 찾아서 왜 내가 헷갈려 했는지를 파악할 수 있는 메모를 해두시기 바랍니다. 시간이 지나거나, 다른 학생들과 스터디를 하면서는, 자신이 왜 낚였는지 이유조차 기억나지 않아 본인의 실수 패턴 파악이 힘들기 때문입니다.

2. 답지를 확인하지 않고 스터디를 하시기 바랍니다. (그래서, 답지를 문제지 뒤에 붙이지 않고, 본 설명만을 붙여 두었습니다.) 답지를 확인하지 않고 하는 이유는 답을 아는 순간, 답에 끼워 맞춰 설명하려 하고, 이런 태도는 본인 실력 향상에 도움이 되지 않기 때문입니다. 스터디 팀원들간에 대략적인 답을 맞춰보면, 대부분 답안의 윤곽이 나옵니다. 이럴 경우, 이견이 있는 문제만 집중적으로 다루고, 나머지는 개인별로 처리하시기 바랍니다.

3. 문제를 끝까지 다 풀었나요? 네 □ / 아니오 □
   다 못 풀었다면, 전체 20 문제 중 푼 문제는? _____ / 20
   시간 모자란 것에 대해서는 크게 신경 쓰지 않아도 됩니다. 무엇보다 중요한 것은 정확도 입니다.
   우선은 푼 문제를 맞출 확률을 높이고, 그 다음 시간을 걱정해도 늦지 않습니다.

4. 어려웠다고 느껴지는 지문은? 과학 □ / 예술 □ / 인문 □ / 인물 □ / 사회 □
   과학지문이 현격히 다른 분야보다 많지만, 그래도, 공부하다 보면 자신만 어려워하는 분야는 모두 각각입니다. 그러므로, 혹시 배경지식 부분에서 필요한 것이 있다면, www.usherlN.co.kr 에 방문하셔서, 공부가 안될 때, 배경지식 부분을 쉬엄쉬엄 들러서 봐 두시길 바랍니다. 쉬엄쉬엄 입니다. 누가 뭐래도 실력있는 사람은 배경지식이 큰 영향을 끼치지는 않습니다.

5. (채점 후) 문제 풀 때 어렵다고 느낀 지문이 틀리는 개수와 쉬웠다고 느껴졌던 지문의 틀린 개수차이가 있나요? 예 □ / 아니오 □
   어느 순간 깨닫게 됩니다. 내가 잘 아는 내용이 나와서 자신 있게 푸나, 내가 모르는 지문이 나와서 겁먹고 푸나, 틀린 개수가 큰 차이가 나지 않는 것을…. 혹시 그걸 못 느끼신다면, 더욱더 열심히 하시기 바랍니다. ^^

6. 틀린 문제의 번호를 다음의 문제 유형 분석표와 비교해서 파악해 두시기 바랍니다.
   문제 유형을 파악해서 주의하는 것은, 누가 뭐래도 실력이 기본은 받쳐 줄 때 얘기입니다. 문제 푸는 스킬이나, 기타 문제 유형 파악 등은 기본적으로 본문 내용을 이해하고, 해석이 웬만큼 될 때 얘기입니다. 만약, 너무 힘들다면 너무 스트레스 받지 말고, 그냥 '아~ 그렇구나' 정도로 넘기셔도 됩니다. 단, 본문 이해는 절대 양보해서는 안됩니다.

문제 유형 분석표 40page 내용 중, 아래 표시되어 있는 문제 유형은 파악하기 쉬우나 나머지 문제들의 문제 유형 파악은 어려워 하는 경향이 있어 비워두었습니다. 문제유형 정답은 327page를 참조하세요.

TEST 4-1

01
02 Highlight
03 Vocabulary
04
05
06
07
08
09 Insertion
10 Summary

TEST 4-2

11
12
13 Reference
14
15 Vocabulary
16
17
18 Highlight
19 Insertion
20 Summary

잔소리 4

결론부터!! 묻는 말에 대답해야 합니다.

심각하게는, 수업시간에 예, 아니오라는 답이 나올 수 없는 질문조차도, 이상하게 예, 아니오로 대답하는 경우가 많습니다.

질문을 정확히 파악하면 유리한 점.
1. 시간을 아낄 수 있다.
2. 정확도를 높일 수 있다.
3. 읽을 부분을 줄여도 된다.
4. 고민하지 않아도 될 내용은 과감히 생략이 가능하다.

이런 이유들이라면, 무조건 해야 하지 않을까요?

그런데도, 질문을 파악하지 않은 채 자기 고집대로 문제를 풀려 합니다.

물론 결과도 좋지 않습니다.
지나친 반복을 봐 왔고, 같은 실수를 안하셨으면 합니다.
이것을 피하는 방법은 간단합니다.
문제에 핵심단어에 동그라미만 치면 됩니다.
얘가 나한테 뭘 묻는지만 파악하면 된다는 겁니다.
어렵지도 않습니다.

꼭 동그라미 쳐둬야 합니다.

문제풀이 전 체크 사항

묶었나?
? 찍었나?
문제 동그라미 했나?
날렸나?

usherin.usher.co.kr

USHER iBT TOEFL
INTERMEDIATE READING
TEST 5

테스트 전 확인사항

실전에 유용한 독해 전략(44p)을 숙지하였습니다. ○

화장실은 미리 다녀왔습니다. ○

휴대폰의 전원을 껐습니다. ○

노트테이킹 할 종이와 연필을 준비하였습니다. ○

시간을 체크할 시계를 준비하였습니다. ○

목표점수(20개 중 ____개)를 정하였습니다. ○

시험 시작 시간은 ____시 ____분이며,
종료 시간은 35분 뒤인 ____시 ____분입니다. ○

시험 중 이동해야 할 방해요소가 있는지 체크하였습니다. ○

시험 중 이동하지 않습니다.

Sentinel Behavior in Meerkats

1. → Meerkats are small, mongoose-like mammals that live in the Kalahari Desert of Southern Africa. Being primarily insectivores, they feed on beetles and scorpions buried underground, which they locate using their strong sense of smell. Unfortunately, when the meerkat lowers its head to search out prey under grasses, it limits its own range of sight by a significant amount. As a result they are extremely vulnerable to airborne predators such as hawks and owls. To ensure that they can reach the safety of their bolt-holes before being snatched up by birds, meerkats forage in packs and partake in what is known as sentinel behavior. As the term suggests, one meerkat in the group acts as a sentinel and does not look for food like the rest, but rather stands upright on its hind legs to gain a wider field of view with which it scans the surrounding area for possible predators and other threats to the community. When it senses danger approaching, the sentinel barks loudly to warn the others of the danger. Many scientists questioned this phenomenon because the revealing stance and loud vocalization were thought to expose the meerkat to an increased risk of predation.

폭 넓게 - 일단 버릇 들이는게 중요!

32 According to paragraph 1, why was sentinel behavior thought to be disadvantageous?

(A) It warns the predator of where the meerkat group is.
(B) It allows the meerkat to sense danger and warn the group.
(C) It helps the predators locate the sentinel meerkat.
(D) It encourages the predator to prey on meerkats over other species.

스터디 자료들을 미리 수집해 둘것!

시험 중 체크 사항

❶ "?"표시하기 : 본문 읽으며, 궁금한 곳에 "?" 표시를 합니다.
　　　　　　문제를 풀면서도 질문 거리에는 "?" 표시를 해둡니다.
❷ 문제 핵심에 동그라미 : 문제가 물어보는 게 무엇인지, 문제 핵심에 동그라미 표시를 합니다.
❸ 답근거 날리기 : 문제를 풀 때 선택지가 틀린 이유 단어로, 간결하게 날립니다.
❹ 경쟁 문장 표시 : 4개의 선택지 중에 정답과 경쟁하는 마지막 1개의 선택지를 표시 해둡니다. 무조건 1개여야 합니다.

Reading Section Directions

This section measures your ability to understand academic passages in English.

Most questions are worth 1 point but the last question in each set is worth more than 1 point. The directions indicate how many points you may receive.

Some passages include a word or phrase that is underlined in blue. Click on the word or phrase to see a definition or an explanation.

Within each test, you can go to the next questions by clicking **Next**. You may skip questions and go back to them later. If you want to return to previous questions, click on **Back**. You can click on **Review** at any time and the review screen will show you which questions you have answered and which you have not answered. From this reviewscreen, you may go directly to any questions you have already seen in the Reading section.

You may now begin the Reading section. In the section you will read 2 passages. You will have **35 minutes** to read the passages and answer thequestions.

Click on **Continue** to go on.

Next 버튼을 이용하여 다음 문제로 이동하고 **Back** 버튼을 이용하여 이전문제로 이동할 수 있습니다. 문제에 답을 하지 않더라도 다음 문제로이동할 수 있으며, **Review** 버튼을 이용하여 각 문제별로 답을 체크했는지의 여부를 확인할 수 있습니다.
이번 테스트에서는 세 지문을 읽게 됩니다. **35분** 동안 지문을 읽고 문제에 답을 하세요.

01. According to paragraph 1, which of the following is NOT true about the Inca civilization that existed in South America?
   (A) They were unable to record their history until after their civilization had been conquered by outsiders.
   (B) They were military and organizationally superior to many of the cultures that surrounded their capital city.
   (C) They did not have their own record on their conquest of neighboring countries.
   (D) Their written language was too complex for most people to use, so they used Spanish to record their histories.

02. Why does the author mention 3,000 miles of coastline in paragraph 1?
   (A) To point out that the Incan Empire eventually overtook the entire western coast of South America
   (B) To give an example of the great distances that Incan warriors travelled in order to defend their civilization from invasion
   (C) To show the reader that the Inca could travel great distances even before the introduction of horses by the Spanish
   (D) To show the reader how far the Inca expanded their territory from its beginning in the city of Cusco

03. Why does the author mention that the Spanish "simply adapted the information to the Spanish style of governance" in paragraph 2?
   (A) To explain how the Spanish dealt with the information they were given about aspects of the Inca civilization that they didn't fully understand
   (B) To point out one of the ways that the Spanish directly influenced the way of life in the early Incan society
   (C) To reveal that the problems of the Inca ruling system could be solved by the Spanish system
   (D) To give an example of the Spanish conquistador's feelings of superiority over the Inca they found in Peru

Documenting the Incas

1 Beginning with the founding of the capital city of Cusco in the early 1200s, the Inca Empire expanded along the mountainous west coast of South America. Within 250 years, their conquests of neighboring societies allowed them to control over 3,000 miles of coastline and land covering parts of present day Peru, Bolivia, Ecuador, Chile and Argentina. The power of their army and their effective administration of this vast empire made them the greatest of the New World civilizations. This great empire would, however, collapse less than 100 years later when the Spanish conquistador Francisco Pizarro arrived and conquered the area for Spain in the 1530s. Since the Inca language did not have writing system, much of what is currently known about this magnificent civilization was recorded by these Spanish conquerors. This has led to many problems related to the veracity of the historical records of the early Inca Empire.

2 The first of these is that the ruling system used by the Inca was different from that of the Spanish Empire and may not have been fully understood by the early conquerors. In order to record the historical information, they gleaned from their Inca informants. Then, they simply adapted the information to the Spanish style of governance. [■] A good example of this is their list of Inca rulers. [■] The Inca told the early conquerors of thirteen kings who ruled over the empire, and the Spanish recorded them as thirteen sequential rulers, as that was how the monarchy worked in Spain; however, it isn't clear if these recorded names were individuals or titles. [■] If they were titles, they could have been held concurrently, and there may have been fewer than thirteen kings that ruled over the empire. [■] Since the empire only flourished under the last four kings, this isn't a major problem in understanding the Inca culture, but it points to how cultural bias and inaccuracies regarding the Inca could have begun with the earliest recorded histories of them.

04. What can be inferred about the rulers of the Inca Empire from the information presented in paragraph 2?

(A) Their names were very similar and this caused confusion for the Spanish writers who were recording their history.
(B) We now know that there were fewer than thirteen of them ruling concurrently over the empire.
(C) It is still unclear how many kings actually ruled over the Incas because of possible inaccuracies in the historical record.
(D) A Spanish cultural bias that placed more importance on the last four successful rulers caused inaccuracy in the accounts of the early rulers.

05. What role does paragraph 3 play in the passage?

(A) It shows that the conquistadors intentionally falsified the historical records they kept to show their superiority over the Inca.
(B) It is meant to emphasize that the intention of the Spanish conquest was to amass more gold.
(C) It introduces the possibility that the inaccuracies found in the historical record were not merely caused by misunderstandings.
(D) It helps understand how the conquered Incans lied to the Spanish conquistadors to secure themselves better positions.

06. What can be inferred from paragraph 6 about place names in the Incan empire?

(A) Scientists have mixed the various names by different Spanish writers up with the changes in the locations of the settlements.
(B) The Spanish writers purposefully used inaccurate place names to prevent other writers from knowing where they had been.
(C) In the 500 years since the Spanish invasion, the descendants of the Inca were enforced to change the names of their towns and provinces to confuse the conquerors.
(D) Modern researchers have had difficulty mapping out the areas once inhabited by the ancient Incas.

3   Another problem with the accounts compiled by the Spanish was that they may have been intentionally inaccurate. The Spanish wanted to downplay certain aspects of the Inca civilization, such as the extent of their wealth. If the conquistadors accurately recorded Incan gold production, they would have had to turn it all over to the Spanish Crown. By downplaying the extent of the Inca's wealth, the conquistadors were able to amass their own gold caches. The inaccuracies may have also been the fault of the Inca themselves. Since they were helping their new conquerors, the Inca may have misled them to make themselves look better or exaggerated their importance in society.

4   Relying on elite members of the Incan society to learn about their history caused another problem. Since they had no written language system, all of their historical information had been passed down through the oral tradition. Over time, many of these stories may have developed unintentional inaccuracies. A prime example of this would be the founding of Cusco, which was said to have happened after four brothers and four sisters emerged from a cave and led followers they found in another cave to the site of Cusco, where they founded the civilization. The origin of these early leaders and stories of their exploits were likely exaggerated to paint them in a more impressive light. Because of the nature of the oral tradition, it is probable that the more recent Incan stories were likely to be more accurate.

5   The Inca may have also whitewashed the accounts of their expansion and conquest of neighboring settlements, such as the Lupaca to their south. Because of their policy of dispersing uncooperative people and repopulating the area with people who they were able to deal with, the Incan leaders were the only sources of Spanish knowledge of their empire and were, therefore, able to control the description of their conquests and could portray themselves as righteous and invincible warriors. This makes it all but impossible to establish the accuracy of their narratives.

07. Which of the sentences below best expresses the essential information in the highlighted sentence in the passage? Incorrect choices change the meaning in important ways or leave out essential information.

(A) The Spanish learned the names and titles of the 13 consecutive rulers who reigned over the Incas before they arrived.
(B) The Spanish applied their system of consecutive monarchy when writing about the 13 Inca leaders they learned about; even though the names they were given may not have been actual people, but rather governmental positions.
(C) The Incas recounted the lives of their 13 sequential leaders using names and titles similar to those in the monarchy system in Spain so that the Spanish could easily understand their history.
(D) The list of Inca leaders may have been inaccurate because the Spanish did not realize that the names they were given were actually the titles of the positions held by the leaders, not their given names.

08. The term "chronology" in the passage is closest in meaning to:

(A) an ordering of past events according to how long they lasted
(B) an explanation of why past events happened when they did
(C) a study of past events
(D) a list that pairs events with dates

6   A final problem that calls the truthfulness of the Spanish-written histories into question is the incongruent uses of place names. It seems that different writers used various names to describe the areas, such as provinces and towns that they encountered in the Incan Empire. This, compounded with the great changes in the locations of settlements over the last five centuries, makes it difficult to verify any of the location information in accounts of the Incan Empire.

7   Despite the possibility of all of these inaccurate accounts creeping into the Spanish-written historical records of the Incan Empire, researchers still find them to be important source materials. By cross-referencing different accounts of the same events and using archeological research, scientists can verify some of the accounts to form an accurate chronology and picture of what actually went on during the Incan Empire.

09. Look at the four squares [■] that indicate where the following sentence could be added to the passage.

As time went on, these kinds of inaccuracies would have been compounded since most scholars would have used these recordings as primary sources for their later research.

Where would the sentence best fit?

Click on a square [■] to add the sentence to the passage.

10. Directions: An introductory sentence for a brief summary of the passage is provided below. Complete the summary by selecting the THREE answer choices that express the most important ideas in the passage. Some sentences do not belong in the summary because they express ideas that are not presented in the passage or are minor ideas in the passage. **This question is worth 2 points.**

> **Although it was once the most powerful empire in the New World, it is difficult to get accurate firsthand accounts of the Inca Civilization.**
>
> -
> -
> -

Answer Choices

(A) At the height of their Empire the Incas controlled most of the western coast of South America and their territory extended into five countries.

(B) Many of the early records written by the Spanish are inaccurate due to misunderstandings and inherent cultural biases.

(C) The Spanish and Inca may have both intentionally misrepresented the history of the Empire for their own personal gain and glorification.

(D) Conflicting accounts of the Incan conquests given by the adversaries and themselves further puzzled researchers.

(E) Movements and inaccurate record keeping have made it difficult to locate the settlements that existed during the height of the Inca Empire.

(F) Researchers still use firsthand accounts by the Inca Empire despite the inaccuracies they contain.

Architectural Change in Eighth Century Japan

1   Japanese architecture underwent dramatic changes as the Nara period began in the early 8th century. During this period, great political and societal changes, such as the establishment of the capital at Heijō-kyō(modern day Nara), made traditional architectural arrangements and styles less advantageous and necessitated a new system. On this quest for more adequate architectural styles, the Japanese were influenced by the architecture of continental Asian powers, such as China's Tang Dynasty.

2   One of the most glaring catalysts for the change in architectural styles was the shift in marriage practices of the Japanese elite. Prior to this period, Japanese rulers married members of one of the most powerful clans of the period, the Soga-lords' families, in politically motivated alliances, and established palaces at the bride's family home in addition to that of their own family headquarters. The royal court generally resided with the bride's family for the first years of their marriage and then moved between their multiple palaces throughout the marriage as children grew older and alliances shifted. This system was workable during this period because of the relatively small royal court and rudimentary architectural styles.

3   Prior to the Nara period, traditional Japanese structures, such as palaces, gate towers, fortresses, and shrines were built with wooden beams, dirt floors, and thatched roofs. Since these beams were in direct contact with the moist ground, they often rotted away in less than 20 years. The simple, temporary nature of these buildings meant that they could be moved or constructed in new areas without great labor or material expenditures and were easily rebuildable when damaged. This was important to Shinto adherents because replacing buildings allowed for a spiritual cleansing of the land. This taboo against unclean spirits also led to the continuous movement of the capital before the Nara period; new

---

11. What can be inferred about architecture in eighth century Japan from paragraph 1?
    (A) It lagged behind the far more sophisticated architectural styles that were found in continental Asia.
    (B) It only retrogressed due to the new system derived from the great changes in society.
    (C) Changes in Japanese architecture were brought about by societal and political changes that occurred in Tang China.
    (D) The founding of the city of Heijō-kyō was possible because of changes that occurred in the Japanese architectural style.

12. The term "alliances" in the passage is closest in meaning to:
    (A) conflicts
    (B) partnerships
    (C) transactions
    (D) communications

13. According to paragraph 3, all of the following are typical of Japanese construction prior to the Nara period EXCEPT:
    (A) Early Japanese buildings were constructed using wood and thatching that rotted easily when exposed to the elements.
    (B) The easy deterioration of the materials used in early Japanese construction meant that it was difficult to move the buildings without damaging them.
    (C) The materials used to build early Japanese buildings allowed them to be built in a multitude of locations with little difficulty or cost.
    (D) The Shinto religion prescribed that buildings should be constructed using materials and building techniques that made them easily replaceable.

14. According to paragraph 4, which of the following can be inferred regarding the royal court during the Nara period?

   (A) The work done by the government workers associated with the court could not proceed without proper housing.
   (B) The growth in the size of bureaucracy necessitated a corresponding need to make the court more mobile to find enough housing.
   (C) Emperors who ruled during the Nara period overlooked the importance of supervising an immense number of government personnel.
   (D) The court's settlement in Heijō-kyō was the result of it being the hometown of the largest portion of government workers at the time.

15. According to paragraph 5, which of the following is NOT true regarding new construction methods used during the Nara period?

   (A) Japanese Buddhists built temple styles taken after by the continental neighbors using tiled roofs and mortise joints.
   (B) The Japanese built a new capital city using more durable construction materials that allowed its buildings to be more permanent.
   (C) The construction techniques utilized during this period allowed the construction of some buildings that have lasted for a long time.
   (D) The Japanese borrowed extensively from their neighbors, including both the methods of construction and the basic design aspects of buildings and cities.

16. Which of the sentences below best expresses the essential information in the highlighted sentence in the passage? Incorrect choices change the meaning in important ways or leave out essential information.

   (A) Japanese architects adopted building designs and techniques from their neighbors that were durable to make other cities similar to their imperial city.
   (B) The Japanese new capital city with increased durability and enhanced design was constructed by architects from neighboring countries.
   (C) Japanese built more durable buildings with better construction design and techniques derived from their adjacent countries in order to establish their capital city.
   (D) The new construction techniques used in the Japanese imperial city, namely the stone foundations, mortise joints, and tiles roofs, were a model of urban design and construction techniques for their continental neighbors.

emperors moved the court to avoid contamination from the death of their predecessors.

4   Moving the capital became unfeasible during the Nara period due to the expansion of the bureaucracy involved in the court during the previous two centuries. By the time the Nara emperors rose to power, they were overseeing a staff of 10,000 workers and needed a location that provided adequate housing for them. The need to keep in contact with these people and to provide for them meant that palaces needed to be maintained in areas with abundant resources. Further, moving such a large court and reconstructing enough buildings to house them effectively killed the mobile capital tradition and led the emperors to settle in Heijō-kyō.

5   To construct this imperial city, Japanese architects looked to the urban design and construction techniques of their continental neighbors' geometrically situated capitals with their bulkier, more permanent buildings constructed using stone foundations, mortise joints, and tiled roofs which allowed them to stand for years. [■] The construction of a large, continental-style capital with these types of buildings required a tremendous amount of manpower and building materials, but it was attractive to emperors looking to legitimize their reigns in a manner directly comparable to the powerful Chinese dynasty. [■] The construction of these types of buildings was also heavily influenced by the widespread acceptance of Buddhism which had been introduced from the continental kingdoms two hundred years earlier. [■] During the Nara period, the Japanese Buddhists built temple complexes modeled after those found in continental nations, such as the Hōryū-ji, one of the oldest surviving wooden structures in the world. [■]

6   This shift in architecture during this period caused a series of conflicts across the Japanese royal court. Rulers wished to display their power through the construction of a grand capital rivaling that of the Tang

17. The term "reliance" in the passage is closest in meaning to:

(A) limit
(B) policy
(C) disagreement
(D) dependence

18. According to paragraph 6, which of the following is true about the conflicts that arose over construction techniques in Japan during the eighth century?

(A) The construction of a grand new capital to show off the power of the Japanese emperor led to a rivalry with the Tang Chinese.
(B) Japanese emperors were reluctant to give up their multitude of luxurious palaces to settle into the capital city.
(C) The Shinto and Buddhist stuck to a uniform construction style after having a religious conflict.
(D) Compromises in society made it possible for the rulers to maintain their grandiose court throughout the country.

Dynasty, but this was difficult at the time and required a great expenditure. In addition, while the opulent lifestyle of the new building styles would have been comfortable for the ruling class, they were hesitant to give up the multiple palaces they enjoyed under the mobile court system. Conflicts even arose between religions because of the Shinto belief in replacing buildings frequently and the Buddhists' desire for permanent religious buildings. Eventually, these conflicts were solved through a compromise in building methods. Shinto shrines, with their religious reliance on rebuilding and cleansing, and many residential buildings adhered to the traditional style that was more economical, mobile, and replaceable. Government buildings, city gates, and Buddhist temples, on the other hand, were constructed in the more permanent, grandiose continental style. Even the issues related to the immobility of the court were solved through an architectural compromise. Rulers, who were now in residence in the grand capital, constructed smaller palaces in remote areas where they could temporarily reside. This gave the court a bit of mobility and may have made it easier for them to oversee the parts of their populations which lived far away from the new capital city.

19. Look at the four squares [■] that indicate where the following sentence could be added to the passage.

After this, the Japanese officially adopted Buddhism, but conflicts with hostile believers in the Shinto Kami prevented them from building lasting Buddhist temples.

Where would the sentence best fit?

Click on a square [■] to add the sentence to the passage.

20. Directions: An introductory sentence for a brief summary of the passage is provided below. Complete the summary by selecting the THREE answer choices that express the most important ideas in the passage. Some sentences do not belong in the summary because they express ideas that are not presented in the passage or are minor ideas in the passage. **This question is worth 2 points.**

Changes in Japanese society during the 8th Century led to major architectural changes as well.

-
-
-

Answer Choices

(A) The construction of more durable buildings attracted Japanese rulers and was further influenced by the acceptance of Buddhism.

(B) Lacking enough manpower and building materials to build the continental-style capital, the Japanese rulers adhered to the system of moving across smaller palaces.

(C) The expanding bureaucracy of the Nara period increased the need to move around the capital from place to place to oversee their work more efficiently.

(D) With their rivalry with the Tang Dynasty, the Japanese strove to show off their architectural mightiness.

(E) During the Nara period the imperial court expanded to include over 10,000 workers who needed to be adequately housed in locations that made it easy for them to fulfill their obligations.

(F) A shift in the marriage customs of the Japanese elite during the Nara period made it less likely that the royal court would construct and reside in multiple palaces during their marriage.

You have seen all of the questions in this part of the Reading section. You have time left to review.
As long as there is time remaining, you can check your work.

Click on **Return** to go back to the previous question.
Click on **Review** to see the review screen for this section.
Click on **Continue** to go on.
Once you leave this part of the Reading section, you WILL NOT be able to return to it.

이제 Reading Section이 끝났습니다.
Continue 버튼을 누르면 다시 문제를 검토할 수 없으므로 유의하세요.

시험보고 난 후 ... 체크 리스트 및 스터디 디렉션
USHER iBT TOEFL INTERMEDIATE TEST READING

1. 내가 불안했던 문제만 재빨리 다시 보고, 불안하게 만든, 즉, 경쟁 초이스를 찾아서 왜 내가 헷갈려 했는지를 파악할 수 있는 메모를 해두시기 바랍니다. 시간이 지나거나, 다른 학생들과 스터디를 하면서는, 자신이 왜 낚였는지 이유조차 기억나지 않아 본인의 실수 패턴 파악이 힘들기 때문입니다.

2. 답지를 확인하지 않고 스터디를 하시기 바랍니다. (그래서, 답지를 문제지 뒤에 붙이지 않고, 본 설명만을 붙여 두었습니다.) 답지를 확인하지 않고 하는 이유는 답을 아는 순간, 답에 끼워 맞춰 설명하려 하고, 이런 태도는 본인 실력 향상에 도움이 되지 않기 때문입니다. 스터디 팀원들간에 대략적인 답을 맞춰보면, 대부분 답안의 윤곽이 나옵니다. 이럴 경우, 이견이 있는 문제만 집중적으로 다루고, 나머지는 개인별로 처리하시기 바랍니다.

3. 문제를 끝까지 다 풀었나요? 네 ☐ / 아니오 ☐
   다 못 풀었다면, 전체 20 문제 중 푼 문제는? _____ / 20
   시간 모자란 것에 대해서는 크게 신경 쓰지 않아도 됩니다. 무엇보다 중요한 것은 정확도 입니다.
   우선은 풀은 문제를 맞출 확률을 높이고, 그 다음 시간을 걱정해도 늦지 않습니다.

4. 어려웠다고 느껴지는 지문은? 과학 ☐ / 예술 ☐ / 인문 ☐ / 인물 ☐ / 사회 ☐
   과학지문이 현격히 다른 분야보다 많지만, 그래도, 공부하다 보면 자신만 어려워하는 분야는 모두 각각입니다. 그러므로, 혹시 배경지식 부분에서 필요한 것이 있다면, www.usherIN.co.kr 에 방문하셔서, 공부가 안될 때, 배경지식 부분을 쉬엄쉬엄 들러서 봐 두시길 바랍니다. 쉬엄쉬엄 입니다. 누가 뭐래도 실력있는 사람은 배경지식이 큰 영향을 끼치지는 않습니다.

5. (채점 후) 문제 풀 때 어렵다고 느낀 지문이 틀리는 개수와 쉬웠다고 느껴졌던 지문의 틀린 개수차이가 있나요? 예 ☐ / 아니오 ☐
   어느 순간 깨닫게 됩니다. 내가 잘 아는 내용이 나와서 자신 있게 푸나, 내가 모르는 지문이 나와서 겁먹고 푸나, 틀린 개수가 큰 차이가 나지 않는 것을…. 혹시 그걸 못 느끼신다면, 더욱더 열심히 하시기 바랍니다. ^^

6. 틀린 문제의 번호를 다음의 문제 유형 분석표와 비교해서 파악해 두시기 바랍니다.
   문제 유형을 파악해서 주의하는 것은, 누가 뭐래도 실력이 기본은 받쳐 줄 때 얘기입니다. 문제 푸는 스킬이나, 기타 문제 유형 파악 등은 기본적으로 본문 내용을 이해하고, 해석이 웬만큼 될 때 얘기입니다. 만약, 너무 힘들다면 너무 스트레스 받지 말고, 그냥 '아~ 그렇구나' 정도로 넘기셔도 됩니다. 단, 본문 이해는 절대 양보해서는 안됩니다.

문제 유형 분석표 40page 내용 중, 아래 표시되어 있는 문제 유형은 파악하기 쉬우나 나머지 문제들의 문제 유형 파악은 어려워 하는 경향이 있어 비워두었습니다. 문제유형 정답은 345page를 참조하세요.

TEST 5-1

01
02
03
04
05
06
07 Highlight
08 Vocabulary
09 Insertion
10 Summary

TEST 5-2

11
12 Vocabulary
13
14
15
16 Highlight
17 Vocabulary
18
19 Insertion
20 Summary

잔소리 5

본문에서 오답근거는 꼭 날려야 합니다.

학생들에게 문제를 풀면서, 답 근거를 찾으라고 그렇게도 많이 얘기 해왔습니다.
그럼에도, 정답 근거조차 잘 안 찾아옵니다.
하지만, 오답 근거까지 본문에서 날릴 것을 주문합니다.

왜?
그게 더 재밌고, 효과가 좋으니까..
두 가지 모두 좋은 건데 안할 이유가 있을까요?
그냥 멍하게 문제지만 보지 말고,
역시나, 묶고 – 모든 문장은 분명 묶어야 합니다.

문제풀이 전 체크 사항

묶었나?
? 찍었나?
문제 동그라미 했나?
날렸나?

묶다 보면, 문제에 나오는 한 단어 한 단어가 의미가 훨씬 세게 다가오고,
그 센 의미 중에서
"나 틀린 답! 나 틀린 답!!"
막 외치고 있는데도 틀리는 경우가 많습니다.
답 알려주면, 늘 같은 탄식, '아~'

체스, 바둑, 장기를 두다 보면, 가장 어이 없을 때가,
딱 상대가 두자마자 움직이려다 너무 쉽게 상대가 주는 게 의심스러워서, 잠시 생각해보면, 딱 함정인게 보입니다.
그리고 그걸 피하겠다고, 엄청 고민합니다. 노인장기의 시작인 거죠.
그리고는 결국?
딱 처음 그 첫번째, 가장 최악의 결정을 내리고 맙니다.
너무 당당하게, 자신 있게, 박력 있게.
그리곤 틀립니다.

내가 모른 것만 틀려도 숫자가 만만치 않습니다.
그러니 적어도 내가 아는 것에서는 절대 실수해서는 안됩니다.
실수를 줄이는 방법으로는 deletion 보다 좋은방법이 없고,
그 지우는 방법에선 "단어로 날리기" 만큼 좋은게 없습니다.

"짧게 쓸 시간이 없어서 길게 쓰겠습니다."
처음에 이 말을 듣고 '뭐래?' 싶었습니다.
결론부터 말하자면, 장황할 예정이라는 말입니다.

생각을 많이 하면, 말은 짧지만, 정수를 짚을 수 있습니다.
그러니, 생각을 많이 한 글은 정말 에센스만 남길 수 있기에 짧아질 수 있는 겁니다.
극과 극은 통한다고 하나요?

> **문제풀이 전 체크 사항**
>
> 묶었나?
> ? 찍었나?
> 문제 동그라미 했나?
> 날렸나?

그래서 짧게 던진 중요한 말은, 내가 처음 이 말을 들을 때처럼 '뭐래?' 라는 반응을 이끌어 내기도 합니다.
하지만, 반드시 기억해야 합니다.
정리 안된 사람들이 장황하다는 것을…

뭔가 상대방이 설명은 하는데 못 알아 듣겠으면,
뭔가 상대방에게 설명을 하는데, 정리가 잘 안되면,
그땐, 말하는 것과 듣는 것을 멈추고, 묻고 답해보면 됩니다.
수 차례 해보십시오.

그러면, 점점 쓸데없는 말들이 쳐나가질 것이고,
그러면, 문제 풀이에 큰 도움이될것입니다.

반드시 기억해야 합니다.
문제 풀이 요령은, 각 문제 스타일별로 오답을 피하는 노하우보다,
기본이 더 중요합니다.
문제 똑바로 읽기와, 단어로 날리기

이게 핵심입니다.
이것만 똑바로 해도 못 풀 문제는 없습니다.

USHER iBT TOEFL
INTERMEDIATE READING
TEST 6

테스트 전 확인사항

실전에 유용한 독해 전략(44p)을 숙지하였습니다. ○

화장실은 미리 다녀왔습니다. ○

휴대폰의 전원을 껐습니다. ○

노트테이킹 할 종이와 연필을 준비하였습니다. ○

시간을 체크할 시계를 준비하였습니다. ○

목표점수(20개 중____개)를 정하였습니다. ○

시험 시작 시간은 ____시 ____분이며,
종료 시간은 35분 뒤인 ____시 ____분입니다. ○

시험 중 이동해야 할 방해요소가 있는지 체크하였습니다. ○

시험 중 이동하지 않습니다.

Sentinel Behavior in Meerkats

1.→ Meerkats are small, mongoose-like mammals that live in the Kalahari Desert of Southern Africa. Being primarily insectivores, they feed on beetles and scorpions buried underground, which they locate using their strong sense of smell. Unfortunately, when the meerkat lowers its head to search out prey under grasses, it limits its own range of sight by a significant amount. As a result they are extremely vulnerable to airborne predators such as hawks and owls. To ensure that they can reach the safety of their bolt-holes before being snatched up by birds, meerkats forage in packs and partake in what is known as sentinel behavior. As the term suggests, one meerkat in the group acts as a sentinel and does not look for food like the rest, but rather stands upright on its hind legs to gain a wider field of view with which it scans the surrounding area for possible predators and other threats to the community. When it senses danger approaching, the sentinel barks loudly to warn the others of the danger. Many scientists questioned this phenomenon because the revealing stance and loud vocalization were thought to expose the meerkat to an increased risk of predation.

폭 넓게 - 일단 버릇 들이는게 중요!

32 According to paragraph 1, why was sentinel behavior thought to be disadvantageous?

(A) It warns the predator of where the meerkat group is.
(B) It allows the meerkat to sense danger and warn the group.
(C) It helps the predators locate the sentinel meerkat.
(D) It encourages the predator to prey on meerkats over other species.

스터디 자료들 미리 수집해 둘것!

시험 중 체크 사항

❶ "?"표시하기 : 본문 읽으며, 궁금한 곳에 "?" 표시를 합니다.
　　　　　　　 문제를 풀면서도 질문 거리에는 "?" 표시를 해둡니다.
❷ 문제 핵심에 동그라미 : 문제가 물어보는 게 무엇인지, 문제 핵심에 동그라미
　　　　　　　　　　　　표시를 합니다.
❸ 답근거 날리기 : 문제를 풀 때 선택지가 틀린 이유 단어로, 간결하게 날립니다.
❹ 경쟁 문장 표시 : 4개의 선택지 중에 정답과 경쟁하는 마지막 1개의 선택지를
　　　　　　　　　표시 해둡니다. 무조건 1개여야 합니다.

Reading Section Directions

This section measures your ability to understand academic passages in English.

Most questions are worth 1 point but the last question in each set is worth more than 1 point. The directions indicate how many points you may receive.

Some passages include a word or phrase that is underlined in blue. Click on the word or phrase to see a definition or an explanation.

Within each test, you can go to the next questions by clicking **Next**. You may skip questions and go back to them later. If you want to return to previous questions, click on **Back**. You can click on **Review** at any time and the review screen will show you which questions you have answered and which you have not answered. From this reviewscreen, you may go directly to any questions you have already seen in the Reading section.

You may now begin the Reading section. In the section you will read 2 passages. You will have **35 minutes** to read the passages and answer thequestions.

Click on **Continue** to go on.

Next 버튼을 이용하여 다음 문제로 이동하고 **Back** 버튼을 이용하여 이전문제로 이동할 수 있습니다. 문제에 답을 하지 않더라도 다음 문제로이동할 수 있으며, **Review** 버튼을 이용하여 각 문제별로 답을 체크했는지의 여부를 확인할 수 있습니다.
이번 테스트에서는 세 지문을 읽게 됩니다. 35분 동안 지문을 읽고 문제에 답을 하세요.

How Camels Survive in Arid Environments

1   Their ability to survive extreme temperatures and food or water deprivation has made camels invaluable in Asia, Africa, and the Middle East. These large animals come in two varieties, Central Asia's two-humped Bactrian and the single-humped desert dromedaries of Africa and the Middle East, which were independently domesticated 5,000 years ago. They have since acted as beasts of burden, desert transport, and sources of wool, leather, milk and meat because they, unlike other livestock, have specialized mechanisms for survival in desert environments.

2   Their first adaptation is their ability to go for long periods without water. Unlike most animals, the camel can go without water for two weeks without negative effects. This is possible because they can drink up to 200 liters of water at once. When they drink these great amounts, some of the water is rapidly transferred to their blood streams and carried throughout the body to hydrate the bodily tissues. This is unique because in most animals such a dilution of the bloodstream would cause a fatal rupturing of the red blood cells. However, camels' specially adapted red blood cells can survive this and have a unique ovoid shape, compared to the rounder red blood cells of most animals, which allows them to flow more freely during times of dehydration.

3   Camels also handle water loss better than most animals. In humans, for instance, a 2% water loss stresses the body and anything more than 12% is fatal, but camels can survive losing 25% of their bodies' water content. This is because of how their bodies lose water. Unlike most animals, camels metabolize the water between cells and in their guts, rather than the water in their cells. By protecting the cellular water content, their bodies are able to function properly even after dramatic water losses.

---

01. According to paragraph 1, which of the following can be inferred about camels?

(A) The people who domesticated the camels had few other animals which they could attempt to domesticate.
(B) Applications of camels are quite limited because their adaptations are specially adjusted for survival in desert environments.
(C) Camels are only raised in arid areas because they cannot survive in areas that get a great deal of rainfall.
(D) The two populations of camels, Bactrian and dromedary, were derived from a common ancestor around 5,000 years ago.

02. According to paragraph 2 and 3, which of the following is true about the role of the blood stream in camel's ability to go for long periods without water?

(A) Camels' red blood cells are a special shape that allows them to withstand the sudden influx of water into their bloodstreams.
(B) The water that enters the camels' blood stream after they drink is rapidly brought to hump where it is stored for use later.
(C) Camels can drink and store large amounts of water at once because some of the water is rapidly absorbed into their bloodstreams.
(D) Camels can survive long periods of dehydration because their blood is not as liquid as that of other animals.

03. The author provides the information of "a 2% water loss stresses the body" in paragraph 3 in order to

(A) illustrate the point at which water loss becomes severe in human beings.
(B) emphasize the camels' ability to function properly even in the case of massive water loss.
(C) show how susceptible human beings are to dehydration when they are in desert environments.
(D) explain that the way humans lose water is different that of camels.

04. According to paragraph 2 and 3, all of the following are true of the use and loss of water in camels EXCEPT:

(A) Camels can survive after a loss of water that is twice as much as a human could endure.
(B) Camels utilize water from their digestive systems and other areas before drawing water from within their cells.
(C) Camels reduce the amount of water in their cells and protect the cellular water content.
(D) Camels' method of water metabolization allows them to consume water much less often than most other animals.

05. According to paragraph 4, which of the following was NOT one of the ways that camels were specially adapted to reduce water loss?

(A) Despite being exposed to extremely high temperatures, camels do not perspire as much as other mammals.
(B) The camel digestive system has become very efficient, producing waste products that have very low water contents.
(C) Camel respiration has developed in a way that allows it to be much more efficient in terms of water loss than other animals.
(D) Camels' turbinates increase the inhaling capacity of the nasal cavity and thus enhance their sense of smell.

4   In addition to being able to cope with water loss, camels have special abilities and adaptations which prevent it. The most obvious of these is the fact that camels sweat very little. They also have efficient digestive systems which produce very dry, concentrated urine and feces. Camel feces is so dry that it can be lit and used as fuel for fires almost immediately after being deposited. Another way they conserve water is through their respiratory system. In most animals, a large amount of water is exhaled during respiration, giving the breath a relative humidity of nearly 100%. Camels, on the other hand, breathe relatively slowly, reducing the number of exhaled breaths and have specialized scrolled nasal bones called turbinates, which increase the nasal cavity surface area, to nearly 1000 sq. cm., and capture moisture from the exhaled air, reducing its relative humidity up to 25%, and hydrate the dry desert air which they breathe in. The network of capillaries in their cooler nasal cavities also keeps the brain cooler through heat diffusion.

5   There is, perhaps, no better known, or misunderstood, camel adaptation to heat and dehydration than the hump. Commonly thought to hold water, these humps are actually fat accumulations. Unlike other animals, which are covered by a layer of fat, camels store theirs in their humps. Fat cells hold in body heat, so by having most of their fat concentrated on their backs, camels can more easily dissipate heat, reducing their internal temperatures. Water is also produced when this fat is metabolized, but it is all used up in the process.

6   Camels also deal with heat rather uniquely. Most mammals maintain a stable internal temperature and utilize physical processes, such as panting, sweating, or exposing more skin to open air in shaded regions, to maintain their temperatures as close to the ideal as possible. These methods reduce the animal's temperature but also cause water loss. Camels, on the other hand, avoid this by having an internal temperature that varies more widely than other mammals. [■] The diurnal

06. Which of the sentences below best expresses the essential information in the highlighted sentence in the passage? Incorrect choices change the meaning in important ways or leave out essential information.

(A) The nasal cavity of camels has uniquely adapted bones called turbinates that reclaim moisture from the breath as the camel exhales and allow the camel to take it back in when inhaling.
(B) Since camels have specialized nasal bones called turbinates that increase the nasal surface area and capture moisture from the air they breathe in, they are able to breathe more slowly than most large mammals.
(C) Camel respiration occurs very slowly because of the specialized bones, called turbinates, in the camels' nasal passages that increase the nasal surface area to capture more moisture from the breaths and add it back to the dry inhaled air.
(D) Camels respire slowly through a nasal cavity with specially adapted bones called turbinates that greatly increase the nasal surface area and allow the harvesting of moisture from the breath before expelling it and adding the moisture back into the dry inhaled air.

07. What can be inferred about the changes in camels' internal temperature from paragraph 6?

(A) Camels' internal temperatures vary to match the external temperatures, so they are more active during the daytime when their core temperature is warmer.
(B) Without the ability to bear large fluctuations in their internal temperatures, camels would not be able to refrain from using up their own moisture.
(C) Camels are capable of maintaining a stable internal temperature without using any physical techniques, processes that cause water loss.
(D) The changes in camels' body temperature over the course of the day are seldom affected by fluctuations in ambient temperatures.

08. The term "altogether" in the passage is closest in meaning to:
(A) merely
(B) fully
(C) necessarily
(D) even

variation in a camels' temperature can be as high as 6°C. [■] This wide temperature fluctuation would mean major problems for most other species. [■] Scientists believe that this fluctuation reduces the need for sweating and panting, which saves camels as much as 5L of water per day. [■]

7   Their physical features and actions not only dissipate heat but also avoid gaining heat altogether. Their tall, spindly legs keep their cores aloft, where air temperatures are cooler, and their uninsulated nearly hairless underbellies dissipate heat quickly. Further, their thin, light-colored wool doesn't absorb much heat and protects the skin from the effects of the sun. The fat in their hump also absorbs heat before it reaches the core, where it would increase the internal temperature. This is compounded by their natural proclivity for standing facing the sun, which reduces the amount of surface area directly exposed to the sun's rays.

09. Look at the four squares [■] that indicate where the following sentence could be added to the passage.

In humans, for instance, an internal temperature increase of even half this much can cause brain damage and even death.

Where would the sentence best fit?

Click on a square [■] to add the sentence to the passage.

10. Directions: An introductory sentence for a brief summary of the passage is provided below. Complete the summary by selecting the THREE answer choices that express the most important ideas in the passage. Some sentences do not belong in the summary because they express ideas that are not presented in the passage or are minor ideas in the passage. **This question is worth 2 points.**

The Physiology of the camel makes it uniquely able to survive in desert regions.

-
-
-

Answer Choices

(A) Because they can tolerate dry desert climates better than other livestock, camels evolved into two species 5,000 years ago and have acted as beasts of burden.

(B) The water present in camels' humps acts as an insulation tool and plays a vital role in holding in body heat.

(C) The camel's ability to dissipate heat is hardly attributed to its physical characteristics, such as its tall legs and light-colored wool.

(D) The camel's unique ability to withstand swings in its internal temperatures allows them to withstand high temperatures without the need for cooling methods that deplete water from the body.

(E) The internal systems of camels are very efficient and reduce the amount of water their bodies lose during normal metabolic processes.

(F) Their ability to cope with and fully function after losing as much as 25% of their bodies' water content and their blood's ability to withstand both sudden inundations of water and near dehydration allow camels to go without water for long spans.

11. According to paragraph 1, all of the following are true of the early Kebaran culture that existed in Southwest Asia EXCEPT:

(A) They moved across various environments of uniform climate over the course of the year.
(B) They were a hunter-gatherer society that had to move around to follow their food sources.
(C) Their apparatus advancement and grain consumption left a significant remark on mankind.
(D) They adapted tools to the each different area in which they lived.

12. Why does the author mention that cereal grains "currently make up 50% and 56% of the world's protein and food energy consumption, respectively" in paragraph 1?

(A) To explain why cereal grains remain the staple of most diets in less developed civilizations.
(B) To emphasize that the importance of consuming cereal in the ancient time has yet to surpass that of today's society.
(C) To point out that the Kebaran Civilization's utilization of cereal grains was so influential that it still affects our diets today.
(D) To show that cereal grains were an excellent source of nourishment without which the Kebaran probably would not have survived.

13. What is the purpose of paragraph 2 in the passage?

(A) It introduces a new civilization in place of the Kebaran society whose characteristics are important in the rest of the passage.
(B) It shows that after the plants moved to more nutrient rich soil, Kebaran were eventually able to produce farming crops.
(C) It supports the ideas presented in the first paragraph explaining the importance of cereal grains and nuts to the Kebaran Civilization.
(D) It suggests the idea that the Kebaran society did not last forever regardless of the continuation of tools and grain consumption.

Hunter-gatherers in Southwest Asia

1   During the end of the last glacial period, the Kebaran Civilization flourished in the area of Southwest Asia now known as the Middle East. This population was to have a large influence on humanity, because of their early consumption of cereals and their tool development. Being a nomadic civilization, they moved across a multitude of climates over the course of the year, spending their summers in the cooler highlands and their winters in the rocky waterside caves. This migration required them to adapt tools to suit each location. These were likely used to hunt gazelle and harvest wild cereals. Human consumption of these cereals became so important that they currently make up 50% and 56% of the world's protein and food energy consumption, respectively.

2   Despite the dietary changes they caused, the Kebaran society did not remain forever. Around 13,000 BC, a warmer, wetter period saw the rise of the Natufian Culture. Their appearance coincided with the shift in plant life in the area. As temperatures rose, plants that required the warmer temperatures of lower altitudes spread to higher altitudes. The production of pistachios, oak, almonds, wild barley and wild emmer wheat flourished as they moved from the lower altitude's sandy soil to the richer, clay-based soil of higher altitudes; these increased harvests allowed the Natufian Culture to expand as well. Within 1,500 years, the culture had completely replaced the Kebaran and spread from the mountains to the Mediterranean.

3   This culture proved to be more sedentary than its predecessors. This is an interesting case in history, since they settled before the advent of farming, relying instead on harvesting wild nuts and grains. Their entire society adapted a new hunting and gathering technique based on larger settlements that could harvest more of the crops. [■] These new settlements featured semi- subterranean pit-houses and pits where the crops could

14. What can be inferred by the fact that Natufian settlement was considered "an interesting case in history"?

(A) They were the only society that researchers ever found in the area where they lived.
(B) Most civilizations that were not nomadic relied upon domestication of plants and animals to produce the food they needed.
(C) Since the Natufians preferred relying on wild nut and grain crops, they were hesitant to be more sedentary than their predecessors.
(D) Although they devised a new hunting and gathering technique, the Natufians were farmers.

15. Which of the following is implied by the settlement of the Natufian society from the excavated artifacts mentioned in paragraph 5?

(A) The Natufians developed new social classes that were more complex than those in nomadic societies.
(B) Although the differing number of grave adornments may reflect societal ranking, it is mainly believed that this is due to the availability of shells.
(C) The Natufians felt that if they buried food vessels with their dead relatives they could ensure they would have nourishment in the afterlife.
(D) The dentalium seashells found in the graves were meant to show the great love a family had for its children.

16. Which of the sentences below best expresses the essential information in the highlighted sentence in the passage? Incorrect choices change the meaning in important ways or leave out essential information.

(A) The burial sites of children contained normal household items which showed that they were seen as less important members of society.
(B) The inclusion of decorative items, like seashells, denoted a higher position in the society than did the everyday items buried with other members of society, like children.
(C) The dentalium seashells were symbolically buried with low ranking members of society who did not have elaborate furnishings with which they could be buried.
(D) Seashells and ordinary furnishings were buried with the children of only the most elite members of the society.

be stored. [■] Artifacts from these camps show that the Natufians greatly increased the sophistication of their tools and confirmed their dietary reliance on grains. [■] They were even found to have created processing tools, such as grinding stones, and harvesting tools, like the flint blade sickle. [■] While these tools could be useful on a multitude of plants, their use for cereal harvesting has been proven by the presence of "sickle gloss" on their blades. This is when a flint blade becomes shiny due to the build-up of silica particles from cereal grass stalks.

4   The village locations were also affected by the crops they relied upon. They were generally located along the boundary between the coastal grasslands and the higher altitudes where nuts and cereals prospered. They also seemed to settle in places where they could collect high quality stone for creating new tools. By settling in these places, they could harvest the cereal crops as they came into season during the spring and harvest nuts in the fall, providing year-round nourishment. In addition to using their stored crops in summer and winter, they also hunted the lowland animals. They would even cooperate with neighboring communities to perform massive game drives and ambushes on gazelles and other animals.

5   Year-round food sources led to a Natufian population boom. As the population increased, a new, highly complex social structure developed. This was discovered through excavation of Natufian cemeteries, where evidence was found that indicated differences in social standing between tribe members. Certain burial sites contained the symbolic dentalium seashell, while others, even those of children, were filled with common furnishings such as stone bowls, showing a clear difference in societal standing of the deceased. These rankings may have been the result of the food redistribution and efforts to maintain order that would have been required by such a large sedentary community. Some argue that the number of dentalium shells per burial may differ simply because certain cemeteries are located where the shells are

17. Why does the author mention the climate change that occurred around 11,000 BC in paragraph 6?

(A) To point out that Natufians failed to learn the life cycle of cereal plants after last two millennia of relying on them
(B) To explain why the Natufian society was forced to find new areas to ensure its survival
(C) To call attention to the suitability of the lifestyle the Natufians enjoyed after the climate had changed
(D) To show the reason that the Natufian society moved from being hunter-gatherers to a becoming the first true farming society

18. The term "declining" in the passage is closest in meaning to:

(A) first being formed
(B) weakening
(C) at its best
(D) rapidly expanding

more available. However, these cemeteries also contained limestone grave covers and mortar markers, which are thought to have served as ritualistic territorial markers for the landsheld by the Natufian's highly-respected elders after they passed.

6 Eventually, as their population expanded, the Natufians faced another dramatic lifestyle upheaval due to climate change. Around 11,000 BC, the climate around the Mediterranean began to dry out. This reduced the area, in which the wild grains and nuts grew, and increased the society's need to settle near a reliable water source. This could have spelled the end of the Natufian society very quickly had they not learned the life cycle of the cereal plants over the previous two millennia of living off of and with them. Instead, they were able to deliberately plant and control the cereal plants. Even the modest scale of this early farming helped the society supplement their declining wild wheat and barley harvests and thus ensured their survival. Within a short time, farming flourished in Southwest Asia, and full-scale farming societies appeared, leading to more civilized hunter-gatherer/ farming communities in the area, where the Natufians developed the world's first dedicated form of agriculture.

Questions 19 ~ 20 of 20

19. Look at the four squares [■] that indicate where the following sentence could be added to the passage.

These large settlements were also generally located near smaller satellite camps where they could collect and process their finds.

Where would the sentence best fit?

Click on a square [■] to add the sentence to the passage.

20. Directions: An introductory sentence for a brief summary of the passage is provided below. Complete the summary by selecting the THREE answer choices that express the most important ideas in the passage. Some sentences do not belong in the summary because they express ideas that are not presented in the passage or are minor ideas in the passage. **This question is worth 2 points.**

Changes in civilizations in Southwest Asia had major effects on humankind.

-
-
-

Answer Choices

(A) Since the Natufian culture still remained in its primitive state, it had been more or less an egalitarian society.

(B) Changes in the diets of the Kebaran civilization led to changes in humanity that altered both the way people live and the food they eat that have lasted for over 13,000 years.

(C) If it were not for their knowledge on the life cycle of the cereal plants they had obtained over the previous two millennia, the Natufians would have flourished as a farming community.

(D) The Natufian Culture derived from the earlier nomadic Kebaran Society and eventually became the first settled society because of the abundance of food sources in the area, even before the development of farming.

(E) Because of the accumulations of silica particles from cereal stalks, anthropologists have recognized that the Natufians' blades were used for cereal harvesting.

(F) After many centuries of living near their food sources the Natufians learned enough about them to understand how they grew and utilized this information to domesticate the crops.

You have seen all of the questions in this part of the Reading section. You have time left to review.

As long as there is time remaining, you can check your work.

Click on **Return** to go back to the previous question.

Click on **Review** to see the review screen for this section.

Click on **Continue** to go on.

Once you leave this part of the Reading section, you WILL NOT be able to return to it.

이제 Reading Section이 끝났습니다.
Continue 버튼을 누르면 다시 문제를 검토할 수 없으므로 유의하세요.

시험보고 난 후 ... 체크 리스트 및 스터디 디렉션 | USHER iBT TOEFL INTERMEDIATE TEST READING

1. 내가 불안했던 문제만 재빨리 다시 보고, 불안하게 만든, 즉, 경쟁 초이스를 찾아서 왜 내가 헷갈려 했는지를 파악할 수 있는 메모를 해두시기 바랍니다. 시간이 지나거나, 다른 학생들과 스터디를 하면서는, 자신이 왜 낚였는지 이유조차 기억나지 않아 본인의 실수 패턴 파악이 힘들기 때문입니다.

2. 답지를 확인하지 않고 스터디를 하시기 바랍니다. (그래서, 답지를 문제지 뒤에 붙이지 않고, 본 설명만을 붙여 두었습니다.) 답지를 확인하지 않고 하는 이유는 답을 아는 순간, 답에 끼워 맞춰 설명하려 하고, 이런 태도는 본인 실력 항상에 도움이 되지 않기 때문입니다. 스터디 팀원들간에 대략적인 답을 맞춰보면, 대부분 답안의 윤곽이 나옵니다. 이럴 경우, 이견이 있는 문제만 집중적으로 다루고, 나머지는 개인별로 처리하시기 바랍니다.

3. 문제를 끝까지 다 풀었나요? 네 □ / 아니오 □
   다 못 풀었다면, 전체 20 문제 중 푼 문제는? _____ / 20
   시간 모자란 것에 대해서는 크게 신경 쓰지 않아도 됩니다. 무엇보다 중요한 것은 정확도 입니다.
   우선은 풀 문제를 맞출 확률을 높이고, 그 다음 시간을 걱정해도 늦지 않습니다.

4. 어려웠다고 느껴지는 지문은? 과학 □ / 예술 □ / 인문 □ / 인물 □ / 사회 □
   과학지문이 현격히 다른 분야보다 많지만, 그래도, 공부하다 보면 자신만 어려워하는 분야는 모두 각각입니다. 그러므로, 혹시 배경지식 부분에서 필요한 것이 있다면, www.usherlN.co.kr 에 방문하셔서, 공부가 안될 때, 배경지식 부분을 쉬엄쉬엄 들러서 봐 두시길 바랍니다. 쉬엄쉬엄 입니다. 누가 뭐래도 실력있는 사람은 배경지식이 큰 영향을 끼치지는 않습니다.

5. (채점 후) 문제 풀 때 어렵다고 느낀 지문이 틀리는 개수와 쉬웠다고 느껴졌던 지문의 틀린 개수차이가 있나요? 예 □ / 아니오 □
   어느 순간 깨닫게 됩니다. 내가 잘 아는 내용이 나와서 자신 있게 푸나, 내가 모르는 지문이 나와서 겁먹고 푸나, 틀린 개수가 큰 차이가 나지 않는 것을…. 혹시 그걸 못 느끼신다면, 더욱더 열심히 하시기 바랍니다. ^^

6. 틀린 문제의 번호를 다음의 문제 유형 분석표와 비교해서 파악해 두시기 바랍니다.
   문제 유형을 파악해서 주의하는 것은, 누가 뭐래도 실력이 기본은 받쳐 줄 때 얘기입니다. 문제 푸는 스킬이나, 기타 문제 유형 파악 등은 기본적으로 본문 내용을 이해하고, 해석이 웬만큼 될 때 얘기입니다. 만약, 너무 힘들다면 너무 스트레스 받지 말고, 그냥 '아~ 그렇구나' 정도로 넘기셔도 됩니다. 단, 본문 이해는 절대 양보해서는 안됩니다.

문제 유형 분석표   40page 내용 중, 아래 표시되어 있는 문제 유형은 파악하기 쉬우나 나머지 문제들의 문제 유형 파악은 어려워 하는 경향이 있어 비워두었습니다. 문제유형 정답은 363page를 참조하세요.

TEST 6-1

01
02
03
04
05
06 Highlight
07
08 Vocabulary
09 Insertion
10 Summary

TEST 6-2

11
12
13
14
15
16 Highlight
17
18 Vocabulary
19 Insertion
20 Summary

잔소리 6

포기하지 마십시오, 버릇됩니다.

살면서 이런 저런 일이 많을 겁니다.
그런데, 지나온 시간들을 돌아 주변을 살펴보면,
되는 사람은 계속 되고,
안 되는 사람은 계속 안 됩니다.

이유를 살펴보면 간단합니다.
되는 사람은 되는 버릇을 가지고 있고,
안 되는 사람은 안 되는 버릇을 가지고 있기 때문입니다.

방법론을 얘기 하는게 아닙니다.
되는 사람은 될 때까지 포기를 안 했다는 공통점이 있고,
안 되는 사람은 안 되면 놓을 줄 안다는 점이 있습니다.

되고 안 되고의 가장 큰 차이는,
실력이나,
타고난 것이나,
물려받은 것이나,
주어진 환경보다,

그냥 스스로 놓느냐, 아니냐의 차이인 듯 합니다.
그냥 놓는 사람은 계속 놓기 마련이고,
안 놓는 사람은 그냥 될 때까지 안 놓습니다.

어셔에서의 시간이
될 이유를 만들어 보는 시간이었으면 좋겠습니다.

다 왔다고 긴장을 풀어버리지도 마십시오. 아직 끝나지 않았습니다.
딱 봐도 힘들어 보이는 학생이 안 된다고 놔버릴 때는, '그럴수도있겠다' 싶습니다.
이겨본 적도 많지 않고,
지금 상태도 좋은 건 아니니…

하지만,
가르치는 입장에서 가장 아쉬울 때는,
전혀 안될 이유도 없고,
지금 상태도 절대 나쁘지 않은데,
어떤 이유 때문인지,
그냥 일찍 놔버려서 결국 목표지점 앞에서 관성이 떨어져 주저 앉는 경우입니다.
여긴 우주가 아닙니다. 한번 생긴 관성이 계속 가게 만들어 주지 않습니다.

빗속에서 축구공을 차본 적이 있으십니까?
일단, 물먹어 잘 나가지도 않습니다.
공을 차다 보면, 내 발목도 조심해야 합니다.
공을 차도 공중으로 뜨지도 않습니다.
최악은, 드리블을 할 때, 공을 패스할 때,
공이 물 웅덩이에 빠지면,
그냥 서있습니다. 탁! 섭니다.
그렇게 자신의 점수를 탁 서게 만들 일이 없다고 믿지 마십시오.
마지막까지 몰고 가서, 딱 목표된 지점을 지나야지만 끝난 겁니다.

끝날 때까진 끝난 게 아닙니다.
마지막까지 긴장을 풀어선 안됩니다.

USHER iBT TOEFL
INTERMEDIATE READING
TEST 7

테스트 전 확인사항

실전에 유용한 독해 전략(44p)을 숙지하였습니다. ○
화장실은 미리 다녀왔습니다. ○
휴대폰의 전원을 껐습니다. ○
노트테이킹 할 종이와 연필을 준비하였습니다. ○
시간을 체크할 시계를 준비하였습니다. ○
목표점수(20개 중____개)를 정하였습니다. ○
시험 시작 시간은 ____시 ____분이며,
종료 시간은 35분 뒤인 ____시 ____분입니다. ○
시험 중 이동해야 할 방해요소가 있는지 체크하였습니다. ○
시험 중 이동하지 않습니다.

폭 넓게 - 일단 버릇 들이는게 중요!

Sentinel Behavior in Meerkats

1. → Meerkats are small, mongoose-like mammals that live in the Kalahari Desert of Southern Africa. Being primarily insectivores, they feed on beetles and scorpions buried underground, which they locate using their strong sense of smell. Unfortunately, when the meerkat lowers its head to search out prey under grasses, it limits its own range of sight by a significant amount. As a result they are extremely vulnerable to airborne predators such as hawks and owls. To ensure that they can reach the safety of their bolt-holes before being snatched up by birds, meerkats forage in packs and partake in what is known as sentinel behavior. As the term suggests, one meerkat in the group acts as a sentinel and does not look for food like the rest, but rather stands upright on its hind legs to gain a wider field of view with which it scans the surrounding area for possible predators and other threats to the community. When it senses danger approaching, the sentinel barks loudly to warn the others of the danger. Many scientists questioned this phenomenon because the revealing stance and loud vocalization were thought to expose the meerkat to an increased risk of predation.

32 According to paragraph 1, why was sentinel behavior thought to be disadvantageous?

(A) It warns the predator of where the meerkat group is.
(B) It allows the meerkat to sense danger and warn the group.
(C) It helps the predators locate the sentinel meerkat.
(D) It encourages the predator to prey on meerkats over other species.

스터디 자료들 미리 수집해 둘것!

시험 중 체크 사항

❶ "?"표시하기 : 본문 읽으며, 궁금한 곳에 "?" 표시를 합니다.
  문제를 풀면서도 질문 거리에는 "?" 표시를 해둡니다.
❷ 문제 핵심에 동그라미 : 문제가 물어보는 게 무엇인지, 문제 핵심에 동그라미 표시를 합니다.
❸ 답근거 날리기 : 문제를 풀 때 선택지가 틀린 이유 단어로, 간결하게 날립니다.
❹ 경쟁 문장 표시 : 4개의 선택지 중에 정답과 경쟁하는 마지막 1개의 선택지를 표시 해둡니다. 무조건 1개여야 합니다.

Reading Section Directions

This section measures your ability to understand academic passages in English.

Most questions are worth 1 point but the last question in each set is worth more than 1 point. The directions indicate how many points you may receive.

Some passages include a word or phrase that is underlined in blue. Click on the word or phrase to see a definition or an explanation.

Within each test, you can go to the next questions by clicking **Next**. You may skip questions and go back to them later. If you want to return to previous questions, click on **Back**. You can click on **Review** at any time and the review screen will show you which questions you have answered and which you have not answered. From this reviewscreen, you may go directly to any questions you have already seen in the Reading section.

You may now begin the Reading section. In the section you will read 2 passages. You will have **35 minutes** to read the passages and answer thequestions.

Click on **Continue** to go on.

Next 버튼을 이용하여 다음 문제로 이동하고 **Back** 버튼을 이용하여 이전문제로 이동할 수 있습니다. 문제에 답을 하지 않더라도 다음 문제로이동할 수 있으며, **Review** 버튼을 이용하여 각 문제별로 답을 체크했는지의 여부를 확인할 수 있습니다.
이번 테스트에서는 세 지문을 읽게 됩니다. **35분** 동안 지문을 읽고 문제에 답을 하세요.

01. Why does the author mention "over 40 million Earth-sized planets orbiting Sun-like stars in their habitable zones"?

(A) To indicate the number of planets that support some form of life on their surfaces in the Milky Way
(B) To illustrate the large number of planets on which life could theoretically exist in just our galaxy
(C) To emphasize the unique characteristics of Mars to be selected as the subject of study among that many planets
(D) To contradict a common misperception of the estimated number of Earth-like planets

02. What can be inferred from paragraph 1 about the existence of life in the universe?

(A) The Milky Way alone contains more Earth-sized planets orbiting Sun-like stars than all other galaxies' combined.
(B) The majority of planets that exist in the universe are concentrated in the hospitable zones.
(C) Scientists have concentrated their search for life on Mars because of its unique location in the habitable zone.
(D) The planetary-mass objects outside the habitable zones lack sufficient atmospheric pressure to support liquid water.

03. The term "inhospitable" in the passage is closest in meaning to:

(A) unjust
(B) unfavorable
(C) impossible
(D) unpredictable

Life on Mars

1 Since the beginning of time, humans have wondered if they were alone in the universe. In the modern times, cosmologists and astrophysicists, Stephen Hawking and Carl Sagan, have claimed that extraterrestrial life is not only possible but probable. They base their theories on the Mediocrity, or Copernican, Principle, which states that because life developed on Earth, it is likely to develop or has already developed on planets with similar molecular structures where the laws of physics work similarly. Astronomers believe that over 40 million Earth-sized planets orbiting Sun-like stars in their habitable zones, the regions where atmospheric pressures allow liquid surface water, may exist in the Milky Way alone. One in particular has inspired scientists to search for signs of life, Mars.

2 Contrary to popular belief, Mars and Earth are remarkably similar. Although Earth is much larger than Mars, they have nearly identical land surfaces. They also share similar atmospheric chemistry when compared to other planets in our solar system. Further, Mars is subject to seasonal temperature variations like Earth's due to its 25° axis tilt, which is only 1.5° different than Earth's 23.5° tilt. A more important similarity that could allow life on Mars is the fact that both planets orbit in the Sun's habitable zone, which could allow Martian surface water in addition to the water frozen in its polar ice caps.

3 Despite these similarities, Mars' conditions are currently very inhospitable. [■] The most glaring problem is that the current Martian atmosphere is deadly for Earth-based organisms. [■] The thin, carbon dioxide (CO_2)-heavy composition of the atmosphere, besides being toxic to oxygen-dependent organisms, does not retain solar heat when it is not directly exposed to the Sun; therefore, nighttime temperatures drop precipitously and the average surface temperature is a frigid -30°C. [■] In addition, Mars' minimal atmosphere does little to prevent deadly ultraviolet solar radiation from reaching its

Questions 04 ~ 05 of 20

04. According to paragraph 4, which of the following is NOT true about the existence of water on the Martian surface?

(A) At the current time, there is no liquid water flowing across the surface of Mars.
(B) Prior to the disappearance of water, meteoroids whose presence is noted in today's craters struck Mars.
(C) Scientists believe that liquid water could have existed on Mars in the past if the atmosphere were able to hold in heat from the Sun.
(D) The effects of running water, such as the presence of eroded rocks in some places, have been noted on the surface of Mars.

05. What can be inferred about life on Mars from paragraph 5?

(A) Given an ideal set of adaptations, life could exist on Mars today even with the inhospitable conditions that exist there.
(B) There are organisms found on Mars to have lived under the surface to reduce the effects of solar radiation.
(C) Rocks on the Martian surface have been found to contain a lot of liquid water.
(D) Microorganisms often found on Mars have developed an outer shell to avoid solar forces.

surface in the way that ozone gases in Earth's atmosphere do. [■]

4   Another major problem that prevents life on Mars is the dearth of liquid surface water. While the ice caps do contain a tremendous amount of water and CO_2, scientists have been unable to find liquid water on Mars' surface, but this does not mean it never existed. Scientists believe that Earth's surface water was the result of venting from early volcanoes and have no reason to believe that this couldn't have happened on Mars, since there are now extinct volcanoes scattered across its surface. In addition, if its atmosphere was once thicker, it may have trapped enough solar heat to allow the water locked up in polar ice caps to form the rivers and seas whose effects are currently seen on the Martian landscape. In fact, craters left by meteoroids that struck the eroded areas of the surface, where it is assumed water once ran, show that they must have struck after the water disappeared and have been dated to several hundred million, if not a billion, years old.

5   These factors, however, do not necessarily prohibit the presence of life on Mars. While most organisms require protection from solar forces and access to water and oxygen, it is not a universal need. Bacteria that require CO_2 instead of oxygen have been discovered, and some organisms may be able to draw enough water from the trace amounts found in surface rocks. Further, protection from solar radiation can occur through a mechanism as simple as developing an outer shell or living under the surface to reduce the effects of solar radiation.

6   Another theory allowing life on Mars is the possibility of Earth-like conditions in the past. Scientists have discovered signs of flowing surface water, but Mars could have been even more Earth-like at one time. A change could have occurred as CO_2 became trapped in rocks. Since Mars lacks the tectonic and volcanic activity that

06. Which of the sentences below best expresses the essential information in the highlighted sentence in the passage? Incorrect choices change the meaning in important ways or leave out essential information.

(A) On Earth, plate movement and volcanic eruptions recycle CO2 back into its gaseous form in the atmosphere where it causes the greenhouse effect that destabilizes the atmosphere and is responsible for the hole in the Ozone layer.
(B) In absence of the ability to recycle CO2 from the air to the ground, Mars lacks the greenhouse effect and has an unstable atmosphere that gets easily dispersed over time.
(C) As it lacks the Earth's geological features that recycle CO2 back into its gaseous form in the atmosphere, Mars has an unstable atmosphere that is easily blown away due to the lack of the CO2's insulating greenhouse effect.
(D) Volcanic and tectonic changes on the Earth caused a cycling of CO2 that resulted in the disappearance of gaseous CO2 from Mars and led to a reduction in the greenhouse effect, bringing about even further environmental destabilization.

07. What does the word "It" refer to in the passage?

(A) tectonic and volcanic activity
(B) atmosphere
(C) carbon dioxide
(D) greenhouse effect

08. According to paragraph 7, which of the following can be inferred regarding the findings made by the Viking Spacecraft?

(A) They could not determine the state of the soil because of the harsh solar radiation's interaction with minerals.
(B) They proved that despite the lack of life currently observable on Mars, organisms once populated the planet.
(C) The discovery of nitrogen and phosphorus is a tell-tale indication of organic matter on Mars.
(D) The detection of any signs of previous life on the surface of Mars is unlikely due to the harsh conditions that destroy organic materials there.

cycles CO2 in the Earth's atmosphere, the atmosphere could have been depleted of gaseous CO2, over time, which would have reduced the greenhouse effect and destabilized the atmosphere, allowing most of it to dissipate over time. This could have allowed a gradual disappearance of water from Mars' surface or its absorption below Mars' crust, where it may still exist, until life became unsustainable.

7   Unfortunately, the two Viking spacecraft found no traces of life, either current or past, on the Martian surface. It was, however, found that the surface soil was self-sterilizing because the harsh solar radiation on the surface reacts with its minerals and destroys all organic matter. Interestingly, though, they did discover elements which would be necessary to support life, namely nitrogen and phosphorous. From these tests, the most that can be hypothesized is that even though the current conditions on Mars cannot currently support life, it may have been possible at some point in the past.

09. Look at the four squares [■] that indicate where the following sentence could be added to the passage.

This is compounded by Mars' lack of the type of magnetic field that protects the Earth from the effects of solar flares that further destroy its environment.

Where would the sentence best fit?

Click on a square [■] to add the sentence to the passage.

10. Directions: An introductory sentence for a brief summary of the passage is provided below. Complete the summary by selecting the THREE answer choices that express the most important ideas in the passage. Some sentences do not belong in the summary because they express ideas that are not presented in the passage or are minor ideas in thepassage. **This question is worth 2 points.**

> **The current conditions on Mars do not allow it to support life, but it may have at one time.**
>
> •
>
> •
>
> •

Answer Choices

(A) Since the beginning of recorded human history, scientists such as Copernicus, Stephen Hawking, and Carl Sagan have been on a quest to find extraterrestrial life on Mars.

(B) Presently, the lack of a suitable atmosphere that regulates solar energy and the lack of liquid water on the Martian surface make it all but impossible for living organisms to be present on Mars.

(C) Due to the lack of ozone gases in the atmosphere, Mars experiences more severe fluctuations in seasonal temperature than Earth does.

(D) Scientists have noted that Mars' atmosphere is unstable because it is rich in carbon dioxide and sufficient in greenhouse gases.

(E) Mars' location in the sun's hospitable zone and the possibility of past conditions that more closely resembled those on Earth could have allowed it to support life before it underwent great atmospheric changes.

(F) The Viking spacecraft found nothing that pointed to the existence of life on the Martian surface, but also noted that current reactions between the soil and solar radiation would have effectively destroyed any organic matter that may have been present.

Agriculture and Settlement around the Nile River

1 The lush vegetation of the Nile River valley stands in marked contrast to the barren white sands of the nearby Sahara. Surprisingly, this contrast was the impetus for the development of settlements and domesticated agriculture across Africa. <mark>Researchers have concluded that the Sahara previously had ample water supplies and attracted inhabitants from the surrounding areas; however, as conditions declined and the region became more arid, these people were driven out and forced to find new, fertile places to settle.</mark> The Nile valley filled this role and allowed these people to support themselves while they waited for the Saharan conditions to improve again.

2 These changes reveal one surprising aspect of the shift to agriculture and dependence on food production in Egypt; it did not begin in the Nile valley as is commonly assumed. The process of moving from a nomadic culture into one with established villages using technology to domesticate and produce the livestock and plants required for such a lifestyle actually began further west in what is now the arid Sahara. [■] Prior to the last glacial period, the Sahara was <mark>conducive to</mark> inhabitation due to its abundant vegetation, grasslands and woodlands, all of which encouraged nomadic groups to remain along its lakes, where they were guaranteed sufficient water and food from the lake and its surrounding areas as they hunted and gathered. [■] The area's eventual desertification forced these people and nearly all of the local wildlife to flee to a more suitable area, such as the fertile Nile River valley. [■] Here, they were boxed in on the narrow floodplain by the hostile deserts, the river, and settlers that were living around them, all of which restricted their ability to wander and gather food. [■]

3 Another aspect of the Nile Valley's settlement was the tremendous change that the river went through. Today, most people know that the Nile is the longest river in the

---

11. Which of the sentences below best expresses the essential information in the highlighted sentence in the passage? Incorrect choices change the meaning in important ways or leave out essential information.

(A) Scientists now believe that the inhabitants of the regions around the Sahara left for more hospitable places when the vegetation began to die and their water supplies dwindled.
(B) Research suggests that long ago people from neighboring areas moved to the Sahara region but they were forced to seek out new, more productive, habitats when the water supply dried up.
(C) People believe that the Sahara desert was repopulated by a large human settlement that had abandoned the region when the climate became less suitable for human habitation.
(D) Researchers hypothesize that nomadic people dwelling in arid areas were attracted to the Sahara with an ample amount of water supplies.

12. What can be inferred from paragraph 1 about the inhabitation of the Nile River valley and the Sahara region?

(A) Before the desertification of the Sahara region, the land in the Nile River valley was uninhabitable.
(B) The movement of the settlers in the Nile River valley was caused by an increase in the infertility of the Sahara region.
(C) At one time, settlement was not concentrated in the Nile River valley because it was smaller in size compared to today.
(D) The roaming tribes that inhabited the Sahara came from the Nile River valley when the influx of new settlers caused the land to become infertile.

13. According to paragraph 2, which of the following is NOT true regarding the shift to agriculture and dependence on food production in early Egypt? To receive credit, you must select TWO answers.

(A) The process of shifting from a nomadic lifestyle to a more settled existence began in the Sahara region.
(B) Early nomadic groups became more settled along lakes because they provided both the food and water required to support the population.
(C) The major change in the Sahara region forced the inhabitants to move to an area where widespread hunting and gathering was possible.
(D) When the semi-settled groups moved to the Nile region they joined the populations that were already cultivating food in the area.

14. The term "conducive to" in the passage is closest in meaning to:

(A) expanded to
(B) a result of
(C) favorable to
(D) able to handle

15. What can be inferred about the major changes that occurred in the Nile River from paragraph 3?

(A) In ancient Egyptian times the Nile was a much smaller but longer river that constantly changed directions across the interconnected riverbeds.
(B) Over time, the once elongated Nile River has been curtailed to today's limited size due to the excessive accumulation of sediment.
(C) Without the buildup of the fertile sediment that the river carried, the region would have been much less habitable.
(D) The yearly floods that occurred during the inundation spread silt across the floodplain and drained it of its nutrients.

16. According to paragraph 4, all of the following are true of the crops that the early settlers grew in the Nile River valley EXCEPT:

(A) The crops had originally been domesticated in the region but were sent to areas of Southwest Asia where they flourished.
(B) The wheat, barley, peas and lentils that they grew became the main source of sustenance for the population for generations.
(C) These crops were such an important part of their diet that they continue to be an important part of the local diet even today.
(D) The cultivating methods of relatively new crops native to Southwest Asia were introduced farther south.

world, but at the time it was much smaller and slower, running through a series interconnected riverbeds across the floodplain, instead of today's massive river. Eventually the sediment and silt carried through these channels aggregated and built up the floodplain, raising the river's level considerably. This allowed lush vegetation to grow along the floodplain and turned the Nile valley into an oasis sandwiched between the inhospitable Sahara and Eastern deserts, stretching 800 km from the present day Sudan to Cairo. As time wore on, settlers in this area became dependent upon the river and separated their year into three sections based upon its actions: the inundation when the overflowing river spread silt across the floodplain, the growing season when they tended their crops in the sediment-filled fields, and harvest time when they collected the bounty provided by the nutrients the river had brought them.

4 In this valley, early settlers cultivated food crops that had been previously domesticated in Southwest Asia, namely wheat, barley, peas, and lentils. These crops' ability to flourish in the Nile valley sustained these early civilizations for generations, and they remain important components of the Egyptian diet even to this day. As time went by, these settlements grew and used the river for transportation. This allowed them to introduce these crops to settlements farther south, where people had relied upon the cultivation of plants native to the African environment.

5 This verdant area also provided for the settlers' other dietary needs. Since the strip of land was narrow, the number of large mammals that could establish territories in this area was limited. In fact, the remains of only three large species have been found, the Dorcas gazelle, aurochs-a type of wild cattle, and the hartebeest. Settlers, therefore, relied on other protein sources, such as birds and fish. While migratory birds, like ducks and geese, were regularly taken, fish were the primary protein source, especially catfish. In addition, the seasonal variety of plant in the area gave them access to an

17. Why does the author mention that the crops from Southwest Asia "remain important components of the Egyptian diet even to this day"?

(A) To help understand the long lasting importance of these crops
(B) To illustrate an idea of the changes that have occurred in the Egyptian diet over time
(C) To make the point that these crops have grown in Egypt for so long that they're now considered Egyptian foods
(D) To stress the ability of the crops to flourish in the Nile valley and to sustain early civilizations

18. According to paragraph 6, which of the following can be inferred regarding the system of agriculture that the settlers developed in the Nile River valley?

(A) In little regard to the predictable patterns of flooding of the Nile River valley, the farming techniques enabled the settlers to build an empire.
(B) The ancient Egyptians began to domesticate crops to use for nourishment when hunting did not provide enough food.
(C) The novel techniques used by the ancient Egyptians enabled the production not of food crops but of industrial and fabric crops, such as papyrus as a writing medium.
(D) Without the advanced farming and water control techniques developed by the settlers, ancient Egypt would not have become the first civilization to practice widespread agriculture.

abundance of carbohydrate-rich foods. More than twenty varieties of edible plants, seeds, fruit, and vegetables have been excavated from the ruins of these early settlements.

6 Eventually, the fertile soils and predictable flooding of the river allowed the settlers to develop an empire whose wealth was based on the great agricultural bounty it was able to reap. Today, Ancient Egyptians are regarded as one of the first civilizations to practice widespread agriculture. They developed advanced farming techniques such as basin irrigation, which put them in control of the river level and allowed them to utilize it in a way that best suited their needs. These new developments allowed them to grow not only food crops but also industrial and fabric crops for use in cooking, medicine, and construction. The most well-known of these was papyrus, parts of which were used as food, as a material for construction and as a medium for writing. These developments spread outside of the Nile valley and changed African and world civilizations forever.

19. Look at the four squares [■] that indicate where the following sentence could be added to the passage.

Once they arrived in the river valley, they had little choice but to settle in one place.

Where would the sentence best fit?

Click on a square [■] to add the sentence to the passage.

20. Directions: An introductory sentence for a brief summary of the passage is provided below. Complete the summary by selecting the THREE answer choices that express the most important ideas in the passage. Some sentences do not belong in the summary because they express ideas that are not presented in the passage or are minor ideas in the passage. **This question is worth 2 points.**

The Sahara and Nile River valley shaped the development of human settlement and agriculture.

-
-
-

Answer Choices

(A) The desertification of the Sahara region forced its human and animal inhabitants to move to areas like the Nile valley where they had little choice but to settle and cultivate food.

(B) After the last glacial period, the Sahara region turned into an inhabitable area open to a large human population with its ample food sources.

(C) Changes in the Nile valley due to the aggregation of sediment made it a more fruitful region than the surrounding areas and provided food sources for humans.

(D) As people began using the Nile River for transportation, they started trading with settlers farther south, from whom they imported crops native to the African environment.

(E) The large mammals that inhabited the narrow fertile strip or land alongside the Nile River provided settlers with the constant, ample supply of the protein necessary for human survival.

(F) New techniques developed by the ancient Egyptians allowed them to form a wealthy empire that pioneered agricultural methods that were adopted by societies around the world.

You have seen all of the questions in this part of the Reading section. You have time left to review.

As long as there is time remaining, you can check your work.

Click on **Return** to go back to the previous question.

Click on **Review** to see the review screen for this section.

Click on **Continue** to go on.

Once you leave this part of the Reading section, you WILL NOT be able to return to it.

이제 Reading Section이 끝났습니다.
Continue 버튼을 누르면 다시 문제를 검토할 수 없으므로 유의하세요.

시험보고 난 후 ... 체크 리스트 및 스터디 디렉션   USHER iBT TOEFL INTERMEDIATE TEST READING

1. 내가 불안했던 문제만 재빨리 다시 보고, 불안하게 만든, 즉, 경쟁 초이스를 찾아서 왜 내가 헷갈려 했는지를 파악할 수 있는 메모를 해두시기 바랍니다. 시간이 지나거나, 다른 학생들과 스터디를 하면서는, 자신이 왜 낚였는지 이유조차 기억나지 않아 본인의 실수 패턴 파악이 힘들기 때문입니다.

2. 답지를 확인하지 않고 스터디를 하시기 바랍니다. (그래서, 답지를 문제지 뒤에 붙이지 않고, 본 설명만을 붙여 두었습니다.) 답지를 확인하지 않고 하는 이유는 답을 아는 순간, 답에 끼워 맞춰 설명하려 하고, 이런 태도는 본인 실력 향상에 도움이 되지 않기 때문입니다. 스터디 팀원들간에 대략적인 답을 맞춰보면, 대부분 답안의 윤곽이 나옵니다. 이럴 경우, 이견이 있는 문제만 집중적으로 다루고, 나머지는 개인별로 처리하시기 바랍니다.

3. 문제를 끝까지 다 풀었나요? 네 □ / 아니오 □
   다 못 풀었다면, 전체 20 문제 중 푼 문제는? _____ / 20
   시간 모자란 것에 대해서는 크게 신경 쓰지 않아도 됩니다. 무엇보다 중요한 것은 정확도 입니다.
   우선은 풀은 문제를 맞출 확률을 높이고, 그 다음 시간을 걱정해도 늦지 않습니다.

4. 어려웠다고 느껴지는 지문은? 과학 □ / 예술 □ / 인문 □ / 인물 □ / 사회 □
   과학지문이 현격히 다른 분야보다 많지만, 그래도, 공부하다 보면 자신만 어려워하는 분야는 모두 각각입니다. 그러므로, 혹시 배경지식 부분에서 필요한 것이 있다면, www.usherlN.co.kr 에 방문하셔서, 공부가 안될 때, 배경지식 부분을 쉬엄쉬엄 들러서 봐 두시길 바랍니다. 쉬엄쉬엄 입니다. 누가 뭐래도 실력있는 사람은 배경지식이 큰 영향을 끼치지는 않습니다.

5. (채점 후) 문제 풀 때 어렵다고 느낀 지문이 틀리는 개수와 쉬웠다고 느껴졌던 지문의 틀린 개수차이가 있나요? 예 □ / 아니오 □
   어느 순간 깨닫게 됩니다. 내가 잘 아는 내용이 나와서 자신 있게 푸나, 내가 모르는 지문이 나와서 겁먹고 푸나, 틀린 개수가 큰 차이가 나지 않는 것을…. 혹시 그걸 못 느끼신다면, 더욱더 열심히 하시기 바랍니다. ^^

6. 틀린 문제의 번호를 다음의 문제 유형 분석표와 비교해서 파악해 두시기 바랍니다.
   문제 유형을 파악해서 주의하는 것은, 누가 뭐래도 실력이 기본은 받쳐 줄 때 얘기입니다. 문제 푸는 스킬이나, 기타 문제 유형 파악 등은 기본적으로 본문 내용을 이해하고, 해석이 웬만큼 될 때 얘기입니다. 만약, 너무 힘들다면 너무 스트레스 받지 말고, 그냥 '아~ 그렇구나' 정도로 넘기셔도 됩니다. 단, 본문 이해는 절대 양보해서는 안됩니다.

문제 유형 분석표 40page 내용 중, 아래 표시되어 있는 문제 유형은 파악하기 쉬우나 나머지 문제들의 문제 유형 파악은 어려워 하는 경향이 있어 비워두었습니다. 문제유형 정답은 381page를 참조하세요.

TEST 7-1

01
02
03 Vocabulary
04
05
06 Highlight
07 reference
08
09 Insertion
10 Summary

TEST 7-2

11 Highlight
12
13
14 Vocabulary
15
16
17
18
19 Insertion
20 Summary

USHER iBT TOEFL
INTERMEDIATE READING

TEST 0.5

다음 내용은, TEST 부록으로 보너스 문제입니다.

"문제는 많이 풀수록 좋다는거 아시죠?"

Reading Section Directions

This section measures your ability to understand academic passages in English.

Most questions are worth 1 point but the last question in each set is worth more than 1 point. The directions indicate how many points you may receive.

Some passages include a word or phrase that is underlined in blue. Click on the word or phrase to see a definition or an explanation.

Within each test, you can go to the next questions by clicking **Next**. You may skip questions and go back to them later. If you want to return to previous questions, click on **Back**. You can click on **Review** at any time and the review screen will show you which questions you have answered and which you have not answered. From this reviewscreen, you may go directly to any questions you have already seen in the Reading section.

You may now begin the Reading section. In the section you will read 2 passages. You will have **35 minutes** to read the passages and answer thequestions.

Click on **Continue** to go on.

Next 버튼을 이용하여 다음 문제로 이동하고 **Back** 버튼을 이용하여 이전문제로 이동할 수 있습니다. 문제에 답을 하지 않더라도 다음 문제로이동할 수 있으며, **Review** 버튼을 이용하여 각 문제별로 답을 체크했는지의 여부를 확인할 수 있습니다.
이번 테스트에서는 세 지문을 읽게 됩니다. **35분** 동안 지문을 읽고 문제에 답을 하세요.

Sea Turtle Navigation

1   For centuries, oceanic navigation has been one of the biggest challenges to seafarers around the world because navigation on the high seas is more difficult than on land. Yet, since the early cretaceous period, the sea turtle has successfully travelled across vast oceans moving between foraging sites and nesting areas. This amazing ability has justifiably intrigued scientists for years. Celestial navigation, based on observing the positions of the Sun, Moon, and stars, has not been accepted as a method employable by sea turtles due to their poor eyesight. Another theory suggests that dissolved traces of unique odors from the turtles' destinations guide them, but this has also not gained much support because dispersal of the odors in the ocean would create a convoluted path and could, therefore, not explain how sea turtles migrate in a more- or -less straight line to their destination. Furthermore, depending on ocean currents, the odor trails may be travelling in the same direction as the turtles, thus never reaching them.

2   One theory, however, has gained support from the scientific community. Studies have found small amounts of a magnetic compound called magnetite in the brains of a few species of sea turtles. This compound, which is also found in pigeons, honeybees, and a variety of other animals, is known to play a crucial role in navigation. It was shown that, sea turtle hatchlings, when placed inside a pool within a magnetic chamber, altered their course in response to changes in the chamber's magnetic field. What makes sea turtles' utilization of magnetite interesting is the fact that it is so precise that sea turtles in the vast ocean can measure not only the intensity of the magnetic pull but also the difference in the angle of the magnetic poles. Previously, scientists thought that magnetite could only be used as a compass, providing directional information, but this ability allows turtles to orient themselves within a more detailed magnetic map of Earth.

---

01. Why hasn't the idea that sea turtles navigate by using odor trails gained much support from scientists?

(A) The odor trails may not drift in the direction of the sea turtles.
(B) Some feeding and breeding locations do not give off odors that can be identified by sea turtles.
(C) Odors from the sea turtles' destinations may be too finely dissolved to be detectable.
(D) Odor trails form in a relatively straight path across the ocean, making it difficult for sea turtles to come across them.

02. What is the purpose of paragraph 2 in the passage?

(A) An experiment is conducted to find a similarity between navigating animals.
(B) A hypothesis is suggested but then partially rejected by evidence.
(C) A problem is introduced and then its solution is described.
(D) A specific example is used to support a proposed theory.

03. Why does the author mention the experiment performed on sea turtle hatchlings in paragraph 2?

(A) To illustrate how poorly sea turtles measure Earth's magnetic pull
(B) To provide evidence that sea turtles use Earth's magnetic field to guide themselves
(C) To explain that the sea turtles' ability to use magnetite increases with age
(D) To prove that even baby sea turtles can use the magnetite to navigate through the sea

04. According to paragraph 3, scientists believe that sea turtles must combine magnetic mapping with other navigation methods because

(A) The poor eyesight prevents the sea turtles from reaching their destination successfully.
(B) The function of the turtles' magnetite is devoid of drawbacks.
(C) The turtles had difficulty finding their ultimate destinations far away from their current location.
(D) The sea turtles successfully arrived at their destination when their magnetic field was disturbed.

05. The word "substantial" in the passage is closest in meaning to

(A) significant
(B) gradual
(C) appropriate
(D) apparent

06. Which of the sentences below best expresses the essential information in the highlighted sentence in the passage? Incorrect choices change the meaning in important ways or leave out essential information.

(A) In order to avoid their predators, sea turtle hatchlings must travel into the depths of the ocean.
(B) Juvenile sea turtles swim to the deep waters as soon as they are born to elude predators not on land but in coastal waters.
(C) Sea turtles move towards the deep ocean so that their predators do not prey on them while on land or in coastal waters.
(D) Sea turtle hatchlings learn to elude their predators on land and in coastal waters as soon as they reach the deep waters.

3   To study the role of magnetite in sea turtle navigation further, Floriano Papi and a team of biologists designed an experiment in the late 1990s, in which green sea turtles travelling from Ascension Island back to Brazil were fitted with strong magnets on their heads. [■] Surprisingly, however, the magnets made no difference to the migratory performance of the turtles. [■] The findings demonstrated that the magnetite theory is not devoid of shortcomings. [■] Substantial evidence both for and against magnetic navigation led to the theory that while magnetic positioning plays a vital role in the open sea, far away from the destination, sea turtles use several other methods to complement it when they are young or when they are close to land. [■]

4   When sea turtles are born, they must immediately make their way into deep waters to escape predators on land and in coastal waters. Scientists hypothesize that the hatchlings calculate the direction towards water by using light intensity as a cue. The juveniles are thought to instinctively head towards light because moonlight reflecting against the water means that the ocean is brighter than land. Unfortunately, hatchlings have been reported to be disoriented by artificial light coming from human-occupied islands, severely decreasing their chances for survival. In the shallow coastal waters, the juvenile turtles detect the direction, in which the waves push them, to calculate which direction they must swim to get to deep waters.

5   When the turtle is making its way to land either to forage or to lay eggs, it uses the magnetite along with auditory and olfactory cues. It is hypothesized that turtles use both the low-frequency sounds of waves hitting the beach and the smell coming from land to pinpoint the location of their destination.

07. According to paragraph 4, what can be inferred about navigation in sea turtle hatchlings?

(A) Sea turtles do not use magnetic navigation until they mature into adults.
(B) Hatchlings can distinguish moonlight from artificial light.
(C) Sea turtles that hatch at night have higher chances of reaching the water compared to turtles that hatch during the day.
(D) Hatchlings learn to calculate the direction towards water by using light intensity as a cue.

08. According to paragraph 6, how do scientists know that turtles return to the breeding locations in which they were born?

(A) Sea turtles of the same breeding site had genetic markers that were identical to each other.
(B) They discovered that sea turtles inherit mtDNA from not their biological but foster mother.
(C) It was found that hawksbill turtles were the sole sea turtle inhabitants of several islands in the Persian Gulf.
(D) Despite efforts, islands that have ideal conditions for green sea turtle breeding have not been recolonized.

6   The mysteries of sea turtle navigation do not end with their navigation methods, but also extend to navigation patterns, as can be seen in the mitochondrial DNA (mtDNA- genetic material that is inherited solely from the maternal parent and is, therefore, identical in close relatives) of hawksbill turtles in the Persian Gulf. Each hawksbill turtle tested in the nesting site had the same mtDNA, with only minimal variability, leading to the conclusion that most of the hawksbill turtles in the nesting site have emerged from the same nest. This explains why areas around the world that appear ideal for sea turtle foraging and nesting are not recolonized after human interference wipes out the native populations. For example, Grand Cayman Island was once home to one of the largest green sea turtle populations in the world, but after the turtles were driven off by humans, wildlife protection laws and habitat reconstruction have proven unsuccessful in bringing back the turtles.

09. Look at the four squares [■] that indicate where the following sentence could be added to the passage.

Papi believed that the magnet would inhibit the turtles' ability to calculate its position on Earth.

Where would the sentence best fit?

Click on a square [■] to add the sentence to the passage.

10. Directions: An introductory sentence for a brief summary of the passage is provided below. Complete the summary by selecting the THREE answer choices that express the most important ideas in the passage. Some sentences do not belong in the summary because they express ideas that are not presented in the passage or are minor ideas in the passage. **This question is worth 2 points.**

The navigational skills of the sea turtles have intrigued scientists for years.

-
-
-

Answer Choices

(A) Although not fully understood, the most widely accepted method believed to be used by turtles is magnetic positioning through magnetite.

(B) Despite continuous efforts, such as wildlife protection and habitat reconstruction, Grand Cayman has yet retrieved the green sea turtle population it used to have.

(C) Depending on the age, the species, and the presence of predator in the vicinity, sea turtles use different methods of navigation.

(D) It is now believed that sea turtles use neither the position of the stars nor the smell of their destination as cues for directional navigation.

(E) Studying the mtDNA of sea turtles has shown that sea turtles usually return to the nesting area in which they were born.

(F) Using scents, light, and sounds as cues, sea turtles augment their navigation as juveniles or when near land.

You have seen all of the questions in this part of the Reading section. You have time left to review.

As long as there is time remaining, you can check your work.

Click on **Return** to go back to the previous question.

Click on **Review** to see the review screen for this section.

Click on **Continue** to go on.

Once you leave this part of the Reading section, you WILL NOT be able to return to it.

이제 Reading Section이 끝났습니다.
Continue 버튼을 누르면 다시 문제를 검토할 수 없으므로 유의하세요.

시험보고 난 후 ... 체크 리스트 및 스터디 디렉션 | USHER iBT TOEFL INTERMEDIATE TEST READ

1. 내가 불안했던 문제만 재빨리 다시 보고, 불안하게 만든, 즉, 경쟁 초이스를 찾아서 왜 내가 헷갈려 했는지를 파악할 수 있는 메모를 해두시기 바랍니다. 시간이 지나거나, 다른 학생들과 스터디를 하면서는, 자신이 왜 낚였는지 이유조차 기억나지 않아 본인의 실수 패턴 파악이 힘들기 때문입니다.

2. 답지를 확인하지 않고 스터디를 하시기 바랍니다. (그래서, 답지를 문제지 뒤에 붙이지 않고, 본 설명만을 붙여 두었습니다.) 답지를 확인하지 않고 하는 이유는 답을 아는 순간, 답에 끼워 맞춰 설명하려 하고, 이런 태도는 본인 실력 향상에 도움이 되지 않기 때문입니다. 스터디 팀원들간에 대략적인 답을 맞춰보면, 대부분 답안의 윤곽이 나옵니다. 이럴 경우, 이견이 있는 문제만 집중적으로 다루고, 나머지는 개인별로 처리하시기 바랍니다.

3. 문제를 끝까지 다 풀었나요? 네 □ / 아니오 □
   다 못 풀었다면, 전체 10 문제 중 푼 문제는? _____ / 10
   시간 모자란 것에 대해서는 크게 신경 쓰지 않아도 됩니다. 무엇보다 중요한 것은 정확도 입니다.
   우선은 풀은 문제를 맞출 확률을 높이고, 그 다음 시간을 걱정해도 늦지 않습니다.

4. 어려웠다고 느껴지는 지문은? 과학 □ / 예술 □ / 인문 □ / 인물 □ / 사회 □
   과학지문이 현격히 다른 분야보다 많지만, 그래도, 공부하다 보면 자신만 어려워하는 분야는 모두 각각입니다. 그러므로, 혹시 배경지식 부분에서 필요한 것이 있다면, usherin.usher.co.kr 에 방문하셔서, 공부가 안될 때, 배경지식 부분을 쉬엄쉬엄 들러서 봐 두시길 바랍니다. 쉬엄쉬엄 입니다. 누가 뭐래도 실력있는 사람은 배경지식이 큰 영향을 끼치지는 않습니다.

5. (채점 후) 문제 풀 때 어렵다고 느낀 지문이 틀리는 개수와 쉬웠다고 느껴졌던 지문의 틀린 개수차이가 있나요? 예 □ / 아니오 □
   어느 순간 깨닫게 됩니다. 내가 잘 아는 내용이 나와서 자신 있게 푸나, 내가 모르는 지문이 나와서 겁먹고 푸나, 틀린 개수가 큰 차이가 나지 않는 것을…. 혹시 그걸 못 느끼신다면, 더욱더 열심히 하시기 바랍니다. ^^

6. 틀린 문제의 번호를 다음의 문제 유형 분석표와 비교해서 파악해 두시기 바랍니다.
   문제 유형을 파악해서 주의하는 것은, 누가 뭐래도 실력이 기본은 받쳐 줄 때 얘기입니다. 문제 푸는 스킬이나, 기타 문제 유형 파악 등은 기본적으로 본문 내용을 이해하고, 해석이 웬만큼 될 때 얘기입니다. 만약, 너무 힘들다면 너무 스트레스 받지 말고, 그냥 '아~ 그렇구나' 정도로 넘기셔도 됩니다. 단, 본문 이해는 절대 양보해서는 안됩니다.

| 문제 유형 분석표 | 40page 내용 중, 아래 표시되어 있는 문제 유형은 파악하기 쉬우나 나머지 문제들의 문제 유형 파악은 어려워 하는 경향이 있어 비워두었습니다. 문제유형 정답은 399page를 참조하세요. |

TEST 부록

01

02

03

04

05 Vocabulary

06 Highlight

07

08

09 Insertion

10 Summary

USHER iBT TOEFL
INTERMEDIATE READING
VOCABULARY
구문정리

TEST 1-1
VOCABULARY

TEST 1-1지문의 단어 중 토플 필수 단어를 선별하여 정리하였습니다.

- ☐ celestial body [silétʃəl bádi] — n. 천체
- ☐ luminous [lú:mənəs] — a. 어둠에서 빛나는
- ☐ orbit [ɔ́:rbit] — n. 궤도
- ☐ occasionally [əkéiʒənəli] — ad. 가끔
- ☐ fascinating [fǽsnéitiŋ] — a. 매력적인
- ☐ volatile [válətil] — a. 휘발성의
- ☐ compound [kámpaund] — n. 혼합물
- ☐ relatively [rélətivli] — ad. 상대적(비교적)으로
- ☐ well-known [wélnóun] — a. 유명한
- ☐ past [pæst] — p. ~을 지나서
- ☐ roughly [rʌ́fli] — ad. 대략
- ☐ nearly [níərli] — ad. 거의
- ☐ plane [plein] — n. (평평한) 면
- ☐ gravitation [grævətéiʃən] — n. 중력
- ☐ nearby [níərbài] — a. 인근의
- ☐ throw off [θrou ɔ:f] — v. 떨쳐버리다
- ☐ visible [vízəbəl] — a. (눈에) 보이는
- ☐ elliptical [ilíptikəl] — a. 타원형의
- ☐ angle [ǽŋgl] — n. 각도
- ☐ extreme [ikstrí:m] — a. 극도의
- ☐ planetary [plǽnətèri] — a. 행성의
- ☐ inner [ínər] — a. 내부의
- ☐ gravitational [grævətéiʃənal] — a. 중력의
- ☐ irregular [irègjələr] — a. 고르지 못한

- ☐ undergo [ʌndərgóu] — v. 겪다
- ☐ subset [sʌ́bsèt] — n. 하위분류
- ☐ telltale [téltèil] — a. 명확한, 숨길 수 없는
- ☐ discern [disə́:rn] — v. 알아차리다, 파악하다
- ☐ sublimate [sʌ́bləmèit] — v. 승화시키다
- ☐ dust [dʌst] — n. 먼지
- ☐ greatly [gréitli] — ad. 대단히
- ☐ distinguishable [distíŋgwiʃəbəl] — a. 구별할 수 있는
- ☐ feature [fí:tʃər] — n. 특징
- ☐ approximately [əpráksəmitli] — ad. 거의
- ☐ regarding [rigá:rdiŋ] — p. ~에 관하여
- ☐ particle [pá:rtikl] — n. (아주 작은) 입자
- ☐ appear [əpíər] — v. ~인 것처럼 보이다, 나타나다
- ☐ condense [kəndéns] — v. (기체가) 응결되다
- ☐ remain [riméin] — v. 계속 ~이다, 남다
- ☐ annual [ǽnjuəl] — a. 매년의
- ☐ eject [idʒékt] — v. 쫓아내다, 탈출하다
- ☐ hypothesize [haipáθəsàiz] — v. 가설을 세우다
- ☐ lifespan [laifspæn] — n. 수명
- ☐ nucleus [nju:kliəs] — n. (원자) 핵, 중심
- ☐ expel [ikspél] — v. 방출하다
- ☐ stony [stóuni] — a. 돌이 많은
- ☐ radiation [rèidiéiʃən] — n. 방사선

TEST 1-1 Comets 혜성

01	bring A in contact with B	A를 B와 접촉하게 만들다		20	bring O O.C	O를 O.C로만들다, 초래하다
02	compose A of B	A를 B로 구성하다		21	close to	아주 가까이에서
03	along with	~와 함께		22	typical of	~을 대표하는; ~의 전형적인
04	make it likely that	that절 일 가능성이 높게 만들다		23	take A out of B	A를 B에서 꺼내다
05	categorize A into B	A를 B로 분류하다		24	regardless of	~에 상관없이
06	such as	예를들어, ~와같은		25	be difficult to do	to do 하는데 어려움이 있다
07	document O ing	O가 ~ing 하는 것을 기록하다		26	to form	결과 (그결과 만들었다)
08	due to	~때문에		27	in diameter	직경이 얼마인
09	take O to do	to do 하는데 O(시간,노력)가 걸리다		28	millions of kilometers long	(길이) 수백만킬로미터인
10	seem to do	to do 하는 것 처럼 보이다		29	research into	~에 대한 연구
11	arrive from	~로부터 도착하다		30	lead O to do	O가 to do 하도록 야기하다
12	travel around	여기저기 여행하고 다니다		31	point away from	~로부터 반대로 향하다
13	the same A as B	B 같은 A		32	allow O to do	O가 to do 하도록 허락하다
14	one another	서로(서로)		33	emanate from	~에서 나오다
15	in such a way that	~와 같은방법으로 (원인결과)		34	find O to do	O가 to do 인 것을 발견하다
16	originate from	~에서 비롯되다		35	eject A from B	A가 B로부터 나오다
17	a variety of	여러가지의		36	for this reason	이러한 이유로
18	know A as B	A를 B라고 알다		37	continue to do	to do 하는걸 계속하다
19	make one's way into	~안으로 나아가다, 들어가다				

※ 다시 한 번 암기 후 → 열 번 읽기로 넘어가자!

TEST 1-2
VOCABULARY

TEST 1-2지문의 단어 중 토플 필수 단어를 선별하여 정리하였습니다.

- sail [seil] — n. 항해
- journey [dʒə́ːrni] — n. 여행
- survey [səːrvéi] — v. 살피다, 점검하다
- coastline [kóustlàin] — n. 해안 지대
- capture [kǽptʃər] — v. 포획하다, 마음을 사로잡다
- loneliness [lóunlinis] — n. 고독
- expedition [èkspədíʃn] — n. 탐험
- companion [kəmpǽnjən] — n. 동반자
- departure [dipáːrtʃər] — n. 떠남, 출발
- geological [dʒìːəládʒikəl] — a. 지질학의
- encounter [enkáuntər] — v. 맞닥뜨리다
- nearly [níərli] — ad. 거의
- geographical [dʒìːəgrǽfikəl] — ad. 지리학상의
- finding [fáindiŋ] — n. (조사, 연구 등의) 결과
- wildlife [wáildlàif] — n. 야생동물
- geology [dʒìːálədʒi] — n. 지질학
- exploration [èksploréiʃən] — n. 탐사
- distant [dístənt] — a. 먼, 떨어져 있는
- past [pæst] — n. 과거, 지난날
- segregation [sègrigéiʃən] — n. 분리, 차별
- particularly [pərtíkjələrli] — ad. 특히
- assortment [əsɔ́ːrtmənt] — n. 모음, 종합 = mixture
- assume [əsjúːm] — v. 추정하다
- postulate [pástʃəlèit] — v. (이론 등의 근거로 삼기위해) 상정하다

- homology [həmálədʒi] — n. 일치 관계 (동족관계)
- comparative [kəmpǽrətiv] — a. 비교의
- vertebrate [vɔ́ːrtəbrèit] — n. 척추동물
- anatomical [ænətámikəl] — a. 해부학상의
- ancestry [ǽnsestri] — n. 가계, 혈통
- vestigial [vestídʒiəl] — a. (흔적으로) 남아있는
- leftover [léftòuvər] — n. 잔재
- induce [indjúːs] — v. 야기하다
- animal husbandry [ǽnəməl hʌ́zbəndri] — n. 축산업
- trait [treit] — n. 특성
- artificially [àːrtəfíʃəli] — ad. 인위적으로
- offspring [ɔ́(ː)fspriŋ] — n. 자식
- evolve [iválv] — v. 발달(진전)하다
- extinct [ikstíŋkt] — a. 멸종된
- overpopulation [òuvərpápjuléiʃən] — n. 인구 과잉
- maturity [mətjúərəti] — n. 성숙함
- validity [vəlídəti] — n. 유효함
- initially [iníʃəlly] — ad. 처음에
- account [əkáunt] — n. 설명
- voyage [vɔ́iidʒ] — n. 항해, 여행
- jointly [dʒɔ́intli] — ad. 공동으로
- significance [signífikəns] — n. 중대성, 의미
- manner [mǽnər] — n. 방식, 관습
- definitive [difínətiv] — a. 최종적인, 확정적인

TEST 1-2 Darwin and Evolution Theory 다윈과 진화론

구문정리 — 본문 중 중요 구문 정리한 내용입니다. 우선 암기하고 많이 읽으시기 바랍니다.

01	prepare to do	to do 하는 것을 준비하다
02	set sail	출항하다
03	on a journey	여행중에, 여행길에
04	return A to B	A를 B에게 돌려주다
05	prior to	~에 앞서, 먼저
06	unbeknownst to	~가 모르는사이에
07	stretch to	~로 늘어나다
08	according to	~에 의하면; ~에 따르면
09	spend time ing	~ing 하는데 시간을 소비하다
10	come across	~을 우연히 마주치다, 발견하다
11	plan to do	to do 하는 것을 계획하다
12	book on	~에 관한 책
13	over the course of	~하는 동안에
14	such as	예를들어, ~와 같은
15	an assortment of	여러가지의
16	think O to do	O가 to do 한다고 생각하다
17	turn out to be	~인 것으로 밝혀지다
18	combine A with B	A를 B와 결합하다
19	key to	~에 대한 핵심
20	over time	시간에 경과함에 따라
21	cause O to do	O가 to do 하는 것을 야기 하다
22	derive A from B	A를 B로부터 얻다
23	serve a purpose	~한 목적을 수행하다
24	attribute A to B	A를 B의 탓으로 돌리다
25	point to	~를 가리키다, 암시하다
26	support for	~에 대한 지지
27	go extinct	멸종되다
28	replace A by B	A를 B로 바꾸다
29	insight into	~에 대한 통찰력, 이해
30	turn to	~에 의지하다
31	apply A to B	A를 B에 적용하다
32	to reproduce	결과 (그 결과 번식했다)
33	pass on A to B	A를 B에게 전하다
34	in a form	~의 형태로
35	have confidence in	~라는 점에서 자신감을 갖다
36	refuse to do	to do 하는 것을 거절하다
37	due to the lack of	~의 부족, 결핍 때문에
38	stop O from ing	O가 ~ing 하는것으로부터 막다
39	be about to do	막 to do 하려는 참이다
40	agree to do	to do 하는것에 동의(합의) 하다
41	present A to B	A를 B에게 제시하다
42	so ~ that	너무 ~해서 ~하다
43	refer to A as B	A를 B라고 여기다
44	establish A as B	A를 B로서의 지위를 확립 하다

※ 다시 한 번 암기 후 → 열 번 읽기로 넘어가자!

TEST 2-1
VOCABULARY

TEST 2-1지문의 단어 중 토플 필수 단어를 선별하여 정리하였습니다.

☐ orbit [ɔ́:rbit]	n. 궤도	☐ crust [krʌst]	n. 지각
☐ majority [mədʒɔ(:)rəti]	n. 다수	☐ massive [mǽsiv]	a. 거대한
☐ solar system [sóulər sístəm]	n. 태양계	☐ asteroid [ǽstərɔ̀id]	n. 소행성
☐ vast [væst]	a. 어마어마한	☐ composition [kàmpəzíʃən]	n. 구성
☐ astounding [əstáundiŋ]	a. 믿기 어려운	☐ remnant [rèmnənt]	n. 나머지
☐ remarkable [rimá:rkəbəl]	a. 놀라운, 주목할 만한	☐ fragment [frǽgmənt]	n. 조각, 파편
☐ similarity [sìməlǽrəti]	n. 유사성	☐ around [əràund]	ad. 약, ~쯤
☐ nearly [níərli]	ad. 거의	☐ yield [ji:ld]	v. 내다, 산출하다
☐ determine [ditə́:rmin]	v. 알아내다, 밝히다	☐ straightforward [stréitfɔ́:rwərd]	a. 명확한
☐ occur [əkə́:r]	v. 일어나다, 발생하다	☐ complicated [kámpləkèitid]	a. 복잡한
☐ collapse [kəlǽps]	n. 붕괴	☐ conduct [kándʌkt]	v. (특정 활동을) 하다
☐ simultaneously [sàiməltéinisli]	ad. 동시에	☐ theoretical [θì:ərétikəl]	a. 이론의
☐ extract [ikstrǽkt]	v. 뽑다, 추출하다	☐ cluster [klʌ́stər]	n. 무리
☐ accurate [ǽkjərit]	a. 정확한	☐ conjecture [kəndʒèktʃər]	v. 추측하다
☐ terrestrial [tərèstriəl]	a. 육상(지상)의	☐ explosion [iksplóuʒən]	n. 폭파
☐ constantly [kánstəntli]	ad. 끊임없이	☐ dense [dens]	a. 밀집한
☐ erosion [iróuʒən]	n. 부식	☐ glue [glu:]	v. (접착제로) 붙이다
☐ volcanic [valkǽnik]	a. 화산의	☐ inflate [infléit]	v. 부풀리다
☐ analogous [ənǽləgəs]	a. 유사한	☐ precisely [prisáisli]	ad. 정확히
☐ meteorite [mí:tiəràit]	n. 운석	☐ estimate [éstəmèit]	v. 추산(추정)하다
☐ existence [igzístəns]	n. 존재	☐ farther [fá:rðər]	ad. 더 멀리

구문정리

본문 중 중요 구문 정리한 내용입니다. 우선 암기하고 많이 읽으시기 바랍니다.

TEST 2-1 Determining the Ages of the Planets and the Universe
행성들과 우주의 나이의 정의

01	majority of	다수의
02	in the same direction	같은 방향으로
03	allow O to do	O가 to do 하도록 허락하다
04	seem that	that절 하는 것 처럼 보이다
05	extract A from B	A를 B에서 뽑아내다
06	due to	~때문에
07	expose A to B	A를 B에 노출시키다
08	be compounded by	~로 인해 악화되다
09	make O O.C	O를 O.C 상태로 만들다; 발견하다
10	originate from	~에서 비롯되다
11	for this reason	이러한 이유로
12	look for	~을 찾다, 기대하다
13	help O do	O가 to do 하는 것을 도와주다
14	answer question	질문을 회답하다
15	crash into	~와 충돌하다
16	provide A with B	A에게 B를 제공하다
17	force O to do	O가 to do 하는 것을 강요하다
18	collide with	~와 충돌하다
19	vary in	~라는 점에서 다양하다; ~이 여러가지이다
20	range from A to B	범위가 A에서 B까지 이르다
21	draw conclusion	결론을 이끌어내다
22	used to do	to do 하기 위해 사용된
23	compose A of B	A를 B로구성하다
24	trace amount of	극소량
25	consist of	~로 구성되다
26	break apart	부서지다; 나누어지다
27	break up	붕괴
28	similar to	~와 비슷한
29	be analogous to	~와 비슷하다
30	by ing	~ing함으로써
31	be able to do	~할 수 있다
32	point to	~를 가리키다; 암시하다
33	compare A to B	A를 B와 비교하다
34	be free of	~이 없다
35	at the same point	같은 시점에서
36	way to do	to do 하는 방법
37	conduct a testing on	~에 대한 실험을 하다
38	call A B	A를 B라고 부르다
39	move away from	~에서 이동하다
40	begin with	~으로 시작하다
41	know A as B	A를 B라고 알다
42	at the center of	~의 가운데에
43	akin to	~와 유사한
44	if be to	만약 ~해야 한다면
45	remain the same size	같은 크기로 남다
46	shift in	~점에서의 변화
47	travel in	~을 돌아다니다
48	stretch out	펼쳐지다; 뻗다
49	following this theory	이 이론에 따라
50	the farther the greater	멀수록 크다

※ 다시 한 번 암기 후 → 열 번 읽기로 넘어가자!

TEST 2-2
VOCABULARY

TEST 2-2지문의 단어 중 토플 필수 단어를 선별하여 정리하였습니다.

☐ ancient [éinʃənt]	a. 고대의	☐ determine [ditə́:rmin]	v. 알아내다
☐ alchemy [ǽlkəmi]	n. 연금술	☐ obtain [əbtéin]	v. 얻다
☐ chemistry [kémistri]	n. 화학	☐ pure [pjuər]	a. 순수한
☐ base [beis]	n. 기본재료, 기초	☐ plant [plænt]	n. 식물
☐ terminology [tə̀:rmənálədʒi]	n. (어떤 개념을 나타내는) 전문 용어	☐ distillation [dìstəléiʃən]	n. 증류(법)
☐ experimentation [ikspèrəmentéiʃən]	n. 실험	☐ purify [pjúərəfài]	v. 정화하다
☐ laboratory [lǽbərətɔ̀:ri]	n. 실험실	☐ yield [ji:ld]	v. 내다, 산출하다
☐ scientifically [sàiəntífikəli]	ad. 과학적으로	☐ liquid [líkwid]	n. a. 액체(의)
☐ identify [aidéntəfài]	v. 확인하다	☐ qualitative [kwálətèitiv]	a. 질적인
☐ eventually [ivéntʃuəli]	ad. 결국	☐ quantitative [kwántətèitiv]	a. 양적인
☐ division [divíʒən]	n. 분할, 분배	☐ significantly [signífikəntly]	ad. 상당히
☐ term [tə:rm]	n. 용어, 말	☐ byproduct [baiprádəkt]	n. 부산물
☐ accurately [ǽkjərətli]	ad. 정확히	☐ analyze [ǽnəlàiz]	v. (물리, 화학) 분석하다
☐ prior to [práiər tu:]	p. ~이전에	☐ standardized [stǽndərdàiz]	a. 표준화 한
☐ separate [sépərèit]	v. 나누다, 분리하다	☐ overwhelming [òuvərhwélmiŋ]	a. 압도적인
☐ inanimate [inǽnəmit]	a. 무생물의	☐ release [rilí:s]	v. 방출하다
☐ inorganic [ìnɔ:rgǽnik]	a. 무기물의	☐ uncertainty [ʌnsə́:rtənti]	n. 불확실성
☐ reasonable [rí:zənəbəl]	a. 타당한	☐ attain [ətéin]	v. 획득하다
☐ vital [váitl]	a. 필수적인	☐ violent [váiələnt]	a. 폭력적인, 난폭한
☐ substance [sʌ́bstəns]	n. 실체, 물질	☐ overcome [òuvərkʌ́m]	v. 극복하다
☐ contain [kəntéin]	v. 함유하다	☐ consider [kənsídər]	v. ~로 여기다, 고려하다
☐ valid [vǽlid]	a. 유효한	☐ constituent [kənstítʃuənt]	n. 구성 성분
☐ research [risə́:rtʃ]	n. 연구, 조사	☐ molecule [máləkjù:l]	n. 분자
☐ subject [sʌ́bdʒikt]	n. 연구대상, 주제	☐ atom [ǽtəm]	n. 원자
☐ rapid [rǽpid]	a. 빠른	☐ due to [dju: tu:]	~때문에
☐ progress [prágres]	n. 진전	☐ makeup [meikʌp]	n. 구성, 구조
☐ various [véəriəs]	a. 여러가지의	☐ crucial [krú:ʃəl]	a. 중대한
☐ perhaps [pərhǽps]	ad. 아마, 어쩌면	☐ breakthrough [bréikərù:]	n. 돌파구
☐ availability [əvèiləbíləti]	n. 유효성, 가능성		
☐ conduct [kándʌkt]	v. (특정 활동을) 하다, 행동하다		

TEST 2-2 Early Research in Organic Chemistry 유기화학의 초기연구

구 | 문 | 정 | 리 본문 중 중요 구문 정리한 내용입니다. 우선 암기하고 많이 읽으시기 바랍니다.

01	give way to	~로 바뀌다 [대체되다]
02	try to do	to do 하려고 시도(노력)하다
03	turn A into B	A를 B로 바꾸다
04	by	~(시간)까지
05	begin to do	to do 하는 것을 시작하다
06	be able to do	to do 할 수 있다
07	prior to	~이전에
08	separate A into B	A를 B로 분리하다
09	reserve A for B	A를 B를 위해 따로 두다
10	relate A to B	A를 B와 관련시키다
11	incorporate A into B	A를 B에 통합시키다
12	adhere to	~을 고수하다(지키다)
13	experiment upon	~을 실험하다
14	involved in	~에 관련된
15	in order to do	to do 하기 위해
16	need to do	to do 할 필요가 있다
17	in form	~한 형식으로
18	on the whole	대체로, 전반적으로
19	in state	~한 상태로
20	break A down into B	A를 B로 분해하다
21	for instance	예를 들어
22	mine A from B	A를 B로부터 캐다, 채굴하다
23	access to	~에의 접근
24	on the other hand	다른 한편으로는, 반면에
25	extract A from B	A를 B에서 뽑아내다
26	along with	~와 함께
27	result in	(결과적으로) ~을 야기하다
28	make advance in	~ 점에서 진보하다
29	ability to do	to do 할 수 있는 능력
30	make O O.C	O가 O.C하는 것을 가능케 하다
31	present in	~에 있는
32	lead O to do	O가 to do 하게 야기하다
33	search for	~을 탐색하다
34	inherent in	~에 고유한, 내재된
35	composed of	~로 구성된
36	in the field of	~분야에서

※ 다시 한 번 암기 후 → 열 번 읽기로 넘어가자!

TEST 3-1
VOCABULARY

TEST 3-1지문의 단어 중 토플 필수 단어를 선별하여 정리하였습니다.

- [ ] current [kɔ́:rənt] — n. 흐름
- [ ] antarctic [æntá:rktik] — a. 남극의
- [ ] reach [ri:tʃ] — v. ~에 이르다, 도달하다
- [ ] equator [ikwéitər] — n. (지구의) 적도
- [ ] nutrient [njú:triənt] — n. 영양소
- [ ] lull [lʌl] — n. (활동 사이의) 잠잠한 시기
- [ ] viable [váiəbəl] — a. (생물)독자 생존 가능한
- [ ] resident [rèzidənt] — n. 거주자
- [ ] downtime [dáuntàim] — n. 작동하지 않은 시간
- [ ] equipment [ikwípmənt] — n. 장비, 용품
- [ ] linger [líŋgər] — v. 남다
- [ ] extend [iksténd] — v. 늘리다, 펼치다
- [ ] identify [aidéntəfài] — v. 확인하다, 알아보다
- [ ] traditional term [trədíʃənəl tə:rm] — n. 전통용어
- [ ] worldwide [wə́:rldwáid] — a. 전세계적인
- [ ] lengthy [léŋθi] — a. 너무 긴
- [ ] annual [ǽnjuəl] — a. 매년의
- [ ] affect [əfékt] — v. 영향을 미치다
- [ ] vast [væst] — a. 어마어마한
- [ ] recognize [rékəgnàiz] — v. 알아보다
- [ ] inverse [invə́:rs] — a. 반대의
- [ ] correlation [kɔ̀:rəléiʃən] — n. 연관성
- [ ] atmospheric [ætməsférik] — a. 대기의
- [ ] pressure [préʃər] — n. (대기의) 기압
- [ ] weather station [wéðər stéiʃən] — n. 기상 관측소
- [ ] term [tə:rm] — v. (특정 이름, 용어로) 칭하다
- [ ] phenomenon [finámənàn] — n. 현상
- [ ] collectively [kəléktivli] — ad. 집합적으로
- [ ] typify [típəfài] — v. 상징하다
- [ ] region [rí:dʒən] — n. 지역
- [ ] accumulation [əkjù:mjəléiʃən] — n. 축적
- [ ] severely [səvíərli] — ad. 혹독하게
- [ ] weaken [wí:kən] — v. 약화시키다
- [ ] reverse [rivə́:rs] — v. 뒤바꾸다
- [ ] creep [kri:p] — v. 살금살금 움직이다
- [ ] positive [pázətiv] — a. 긍정적인
- [ ] trace [treis] — v. 추적하다
- [ ] examine [igzǽmin] — v. 조사하다
- [ ] regularly [régjələrli] — ad. 정기적으로
- [ ] frequency [frí:kwənsi] — n. 빈도
- [ ] nearly [níərli] — ad. 거의
- [ ] interval [íntərvəl] — n. 간격
- [ ] alarming [əláː rmiŋ] — a. 걱정스러운
- [ ] severity [səvérəti] — n. 격렬, 혹독, 괴로움
- [ ] suffer [sʌ́fər] — v. (질병, 고통 등) 시달리다
- [ ] fear [fiər] — v. ~을 두려워하다
- [ ] epidemic [èpədémik] — n. 전염병
- [ ] pathogen [pǽθədʒən] — n. 병원균
- [ ] civil [sívəl] — a. 시민의
- [ ] violence [váiələns] — n. 폭력
- [ ] yield [ji:ld] — v. (결과, 수익 등을) 내다
- [ ] tropical [trápikəl] — a. 열대의
- [ ] unrest [ʌnrést] — n. 불안
- [ ] famine [fǽmin] — n. 기근
- [ ] eventually [ivéntʃuəli] — ad. 결국
- [ ] spark [spa:rk] — v. 유발하다
- [ ] revolution [rèvəlú:ʃən] — n. 혁명
- [ ] evidence [évidəns] — n. 증거
- [ ] trigger [trígər] — v. 촉발시키다

구문정리

본문 중 중요 구문 정리한 내용입니다. 우선 암기하고 많이 읽으시기 바랍니다.

TEST 3-1 El Niño 엘니뇨 현상

01	replace A by B	A를 B로 바꾸다
02	due to the lack of	~의 부족 때문에
03	term O O.C	O를 O.C로 부르다, 칭하다
04	use O to do	O를 to do 하는데 사용하다
05	tend to	~을 돌보다
06	extend into	~까지 확장하다
07	over decades	수십년 동안에
08	at least	적어도, 최소한
09	identify A with B	A를 B라고 확인하다
10	known as	~라고 알려진
11	vice versa	거꾸로도 또한 같음
12	in pattern	~한 패턴으로
13	recognize A as B	A를 B로 인정(인지)하다
14	so~ that	너무~해서~하다
15	refer to A as B	A를 B라고 여기다
16	move across	~전체에 걸쳐서 이동하다
17	keep O O.C	O를 O.C로 유지하다
18	begin to do	to do 하는 것을 시작하다
19	attempt to do	to do 하는 것을 시도하다
20	piece together	~을 짜맞추다, 종합하다
21	it is clear that	that절은 명확하다
22	compare A to B	A를 B와 비교하다
23	limit A to B	A를 B로 국한(제한)하다
24	not (only), but also	A 뿐 만아니라 B 또한
25	for instance	예를 들어
26	suffer from	~로 고통받다
27	reason to do	to do 할 이유
28	it appears that	that절 인 것 같다
29	coincide with	~와 동시에 일어나다, 일치하다
30	blame A on B	A를 B에 책임으로 돌리다
31	point to A as B	A를 B로 가리키다
32	lead to	~하는 것을 초래하다

※ 다시 한 번 암기 후 → 열 번 읽기로 넘어가자!

TEST 3-2
VOCABULARY

TEST 3-2지문의 단어 중 토플 필수 단어를 선별하여 정리하였습니다.

- [ ] occur [əkə́:r] — v. 발생하다, 일어나다
- [ ] reign [rein] — n. (왕의) 통치 기간
- [ ] latter [lǽtər] — a. (기간, 시기의) 후반의
- [ ] notable [nóutəbəl] — a. 눈에 띄는
- [ ] fertility rate [fəːrtíləti reit] — n. 출생률
- [ ] mortality rate [mɔːrtǽləti reit] — n. 사망률
- [ ] around [əráund] — ad. 약, ~쯤
- [ ] dramatic [drəmǽtik] — a. 극적인
- [ ] vast [væst] — a. 어마어마한
- [ ] plague [pleig] — n. 전염병
- [ ] ravage [rǽvidʒ] — a. 파괴된
- [ ] demand [dimǽnd] — n. 요구
- [ ] unsuitable [ʌnsúːtəbəl] — a. 적합하지 않은
- [ ] arable [ǽrəbəl] — a. 곡식을 경작하는
- [ ] undertake [ʌ̀ndərtéik] — v. 착수하다
- [ ] specialization [spèʃəlizéiʃən] — n. 특수화
- [ ] consolidate [kənsálədèit] — v. 통합하다, 강화하다
- [ ] inherit [inhérit] — v. 상속받다, 물려받다
- [ ] estate [istéit] — n. 사유지
- [ ] parcel [páːrsəl] — n. (땅의) 구획
- [ ] landholding [lǽndhòuldiŋ] — n. 토지 소유
- [ ] insure [inʃúər] — v. 보험에 들다
- [ ] social status [sóuʃəl stéitəs] — n. 사회적 지위
- [ ] property [prápərti] — n. 재산, 소유물
- [ ] aggressive [əgrésiv] — a. 공격적인
- [ ] tenant [ténənt] — n. 세입자, 소작인
- [ ] consent [kənsént] — v. 동의하다
- [ ] evict [ivíkt] — v. 쫓아내다
- [ ] tactic [tǽktik] — n. 전략, 전술
- [ ] pastureland [pǽstʃərlənd] — n. 목초지
- [ ] graze [greiz] — v. (소, 양 등이) 풀을 뜯다
- [ ] enclosure [enklóuʒər] — n. 울타리
- [ ] communal [kəmjúːnl] — a. 공동의
- [ ] fence [fens] — v. 울타리를 치다
- [ ] derive [diráiv] — v. 얻다, 끌어내다
- [ ] cottage [kátidʒ] — n. 작은 집
- [ ] craftspeople [krǽftspíːpl] — n. 장인
- [ ] monopoly [mənápəli] — n. 독점
- [ ] representative [rèprizentèitiv] — a. 대표하는
- [ ] station [stéiʃən] — n. 지위
- [ ] permanently [pə́ːmənəntli] — ad. 영구히
- [ ] reputation [rèpjətéiʃən] — n. 평판, 명성
- [ ] champion [tʃǽmpiən] — v. ~을 옹호하다

구문정리

본문 중 중요 구문 정리한 내용입니다. 우선 암기하고 많이 읽으시기 바랍니다.

TEST 3-2 — England's Sixteenth Century Economy 16세기 영국의 경제

01	under the reign of	~의 통치하에
02	in the latter half of	~의 후반부에
03	increase in	~라는 점에서의 증가
04	that of	앞명사 반복 피할때 (단수)
05	increase from A to B	A부터 B까지 증가
06	along with	~와 함께
07	lead to	~을 초래하다, ~로 이어지다
08	change in	~라는 점에서의 변화
09	allow O to do	O가 to do 하는것을 가능케 하다
10	demand for	~에 대한 요구
11	such as	예를 들어, ~와 같은
12	give A B	A에게 B를 주다
13	for instance	예를 들어
14	per	~당(마다)
15	at least	적어도, 최소한
16	between A and B	A와 B 사이
17	in order to do	to do 하기 위해
18	prevent O from ~ing	O가 ~ing 하는것을 막다
19	divide up A into B	A를 B로 나누다
20	marry into	~으로 시집가다
21	meet the demand	수요를 충족시키다
22	drive O O.C	O를 O.C 상태로 만들다
23	draw A from B	A를 B로부터 얻다
24	be in demand	수요가 있다
25	deal with	~와 거래하다; ~를 처리하다
26	rent A to B	A를 B에게 세 놓다
27	provide A to B	A를 B에게 제공하다
28	control over	~에 대한 통제
29	allow A B	A에게 B를 주다
30	consent to	~에 동의하다
31	abide by	~을 준수하다, 따르다
32	replace A by B	A를 B로 대체하다
33	encourage O to do	O가 to do 하는것을 격려하다, 고무하다
34	use O to do	O를 to do 하기 위해 사용하다
35	convert A into B	A를 B로 바꾸다, 전환하다
36	graze upon	(소·양 등이) 풀을 뜯다
37	because of	~때문에
38	in the process of	~의 과정에서
39	use A for B	A를 B를 위해 사용하다
40	begin to do	to do 하는 것을 시작하다
41	in a form	~의 형태로
42	provide A with B	A에게 B를 제공하다
43	cut out	잘라내다, 단절시키다
44	by ing	~함으로써
45	so ~ that ~	너무 ~해서 ~하다
46	keep O O.C	O를 O.C 상태로 유지하다
47	to the point that	that절 한 정도로
48	be able to do	to do 할 수 있다
49	on credit	외상으로, 신용대출로
50	attempt to do	to do 하려는 시도
51	for the purpose	~의 목적으로

※ 다시 한 번 암기 후 → 열 번 읽기로 넘어가자!

TEST 4-1
VOCABULARY

TEST 4-1지문의 단어 중 토플 필수 단어를 선별하여 정리하였습니다.

- ☐ reside [riːsáid] — v. 살다, 거주하다
- ☐ dwelling [dwéliŋ] — n. 주거지, 주택
- ☐ flourish [fləˊːriʃ] — v. 번창하다
- ☐ complex [kəmpléks] — n. 복합 건물
- ☐ indicate [índikèit] — v. (사실, 존재함을) 나타내다
- ☐ evacuation [ivæ̀kjuéiʃən] — n. 대피
- ☐ ongoing [ángòuiŋ] — a. 계속 진행중인
- ☐ unprecedent [ʌ̀nprésədènt] — a. 전례없는
- ☐ abandon [əbǽndən] — v. 버리다, 떠나다, 저버리다
- ☐ downfall [dáunfɔ̀ːl] — n. 몰락
- ☐ regarding [rigáːrdiŋ] — p. ~에 관하여
- ☐ deforestation [diːfɔ(ː)ristéiʃən] — n. 산림 벌채
- ☐ depletion [diplíːʃən] — n. 고갈
- ☐ semi-nomadic [sémi-noumǽdik] — n. 반유목
- ☐ fertile [fəˊːrtl] — a. 비옥한
- ☐ unsuitable [ʌ̀nsúːtəbəl] — a. 적합하지 않은
- ☐ adjacent [ədʒéisənt] — a. 인접한
- ☐ previous [príːviəs] — a. 이전의
- ☐ replenish [riplétniʃ] — v. 보충하다
- ☐ destructive [distrʌ́ktiv] — a. 파괴적인

- ☐ ruin [rúːin] — v. 망치다
- ☐ adequate [ǽdikwit] — a. 충분한
- ☐ sustainable [səstéinəbl] — a. 지속 가능한
- ☐ archeologist [àːrtʃálədʒist] — n. 고고학자
- ☐ astray [əstréi] — a. 길잃은
- ☐ desirable [dizáiərəbəl] — a. 바람직한, 호감가는
- ☐ fire resistant [faiər rizístənt] — a. 내화성의
- ☐ propagate [prápəgèit] — v. (식물) 번식시키다
- ☐ scarce [skɛərz] — a. 부족한
- ☐ additionally [ədíʃənəlli] — ad. 게다가
- ☐ progress [prágres] — n. 진전
- ☐ excavate [ékskəvèit] — v. 발굴하다
- ☐ disturbance [distəˊːrbəns] — n. 방해
- ☐ postulate [pástʃəlèit] — v. (사실이라고) 상정하다
- ☐ aggregate [ǽgrigèit] — v. 모이다, 집합하다
- ☐ pool [puːl] — v. 모으다
- ☐ intensification [intènsəfikéiʃən] — n. 강화
- ☐ collapse [kəlǽps] — n. v. 붕괴(하다)
- ☐ flexible [fléksəbəl] — a. 신축성있는

구문정리

본문 중 중요 구문 정리한 내용입니다. 우선 암기하고 많이 읽으시기 바랍니다.

TEST 4-1 — Environmental Impact of the Anasazi 아나사지의 환경적인 영향

01	reside in	~에 있다, ~에 거주하다
02	due to	~때문에
03	known as	~으로 알려진
04	begin to do	to do 되기 시작하다
05	call into question	~에 의문을 제기하다
06	leave O ~ing	O가 ~ing 하도록 놔두다
07	could have done	추측, ~했을 수도 있을 것이다
08	cause O to do	O가 to do 하도록 야기하다
09	come up with	~를 생각해내다
10	interact with	~와 상호관계하다
11	lead to	~를 초래하다
12	put forth	제안하다
13	over	~에 걸쳐서(시간에)
14	complete with	~이 완비된
15	would have done	추측, 아마 ~했을 것이다
16	take exception	이의를 제기하다
17	point to	~를 지목하다
18	need for	~를 위한 필요
19	change in	~라는 점에서의 변화
20	prior to	~이전에
21	burn down	~을 태우다
22	unsuitable for	~에 부적당한
23	move on to	~로 이동하다
24	allow O to do	O가 to do 하는것을 허용하다
25	lie fallow	(토지가) 묵고있다
26	for use	사용을 위해
27	appear to do	to do 하는 것처럼 보이다
28	means of	~의 수단
29	responsible for	~에 책임이 있는
30	seem that	that절 인 것처럼 보이다
31	be replaced by	~에 의해 대체되다
32	switch from A to B	A에서 B로 전환되다
33	demand increase	수요가 증가하다
34	food supply	식량공급
35	as well	또한
36	as time progress	시간이 경과함에 따라
37	native to	~에 고유한, 토종의, 토착의
38	excavate A from B	A를 B로부터 발굴하다
39	increase in	~에 있어서 증가
40	in the face of	~에도 불구하고, ~에 직면하여
41	invest in	~에 투자하다
42	brought about	~를 유발하다
43	susceptible to	~에 취약한
44	in response to	~에 반응해서
45	have an impact on	~에 대해 영향력을 가지다
46	for reason	~의 이유로
47	lead O to do	O가 to do 하도록 이끌다

※ 다시 한 번 암기 후 → 열 번 읽기로 넘어가자!

TEST 4-2
VOCABULARY

TEST 4-2지문의 단어 중 토플 필수 단어를 선별하여 정리하였습니다.

- peculiar [pikjú:ljər] — a. 이상한
- aspect [ǽspekt] — n. 측면
- gradual [grǽdʒuəl] — a. 점진적인
- tropic [trápik] — n. 열대지방
- survey [sə:rvéi] — n. 조사
- equator [ikwéitər] — n. 적도
- latitude [lǽtətjù:d] — n. 위도
- across [əkrɔ́:s] — p. 전체에 걸쳐
- flora [flɔ́:rə] — n. 식물군
- fauna [fɔ́:nə] — n. 동물군
- mammal [mǽməl] — n. 포유류
- stability [stəbíləti] — n. 안정성
- fluctuation [flʌ̀ktʃuéiʃən] — n. 변동
- remain [riméin] — v. 계속 (여전히) ~이다
- constant [kánstənt] — a. 끊임없는
- diversity [divɔ́:rsəti] — n. 다양성
- logical [ládʒikəl] — a. 타당한
- preclude [priklú:d] — v. 배제하다
- perpetual [pərpétʃuəl] — a. 영구적인
- frigid [frídʒid] — a. 몹시 추운
- relatively [rélətivli] — ad. 비교적으로, 상대적으로
- availability [əvèiləbíləti] — n. 유효성
- affect [əfékt] — v. 영향을 미치다
- stable [stéibl] — a. 안정된
- year-round [jíərráund] — a. 연중 계속되는
- uniform [jú:nəfɔ̀:rm] — a. 획일적인, 균일한
- specialize [spéʃəlàiz] — v. 전공하다
- various [vɛ́əriəs] — a. 여러 가지의
- marginally [má:rdʒənəly] — ad. 아주 조금
- carrion [kǽriən] — n. 썩어 가는 고기
- vulture [vʌ́ltʃər] — n. 독수리

- niche [nitʃ] — n. 틈새
- beak [bi:k] — n. 부리
- tear [tɛər] — v. 찢다 *발음주의 [tɛər]
- leathery [léðəri] — a. 가죽 같은
- devoid [divɔ́id] — a. ~이 전혀 없는
- stick [stik] — v. 찔러넣다
- carcass [ká:rkəs] — n. 시체
- contaminate [kəntǽmənèit] — v. 오염시키다
- bake [beik] — v. 굽다
- refuse [rifjú:z] — n. 쓰레기
- consume [kənsú:m] — v. 소모하다, 먹다
- scrap [skræp] — n. 조각, 파편
- ensure [enʃúər] — v. 보장하다
- food supply [fu:d səplái] — n. 식량 공급
- barren [bǽrən] — a. 척박한
- migrate [máigreit] — v. 이동하다
- migratory [máigrətɔ̀:ri] — a. 이주하는
- weakened [wí:kən] — a. 쇠약한
- assure [əʃúər] — v. 장담하다
- distinct [distíŋkt] — a. 뚜렷한
- coexist [kòuigzíst] — v. 공존하다
- evolutionary [èvəlú:ʃənèri] — a. 진화의
- phenomenon [finámənàn] — n. 현상
- inhabit [inhǽbit] — v. 거주하다
- physiological [fìziəládʒikəl] — a. 생리학의
- lifespan [láifspæn] — n. 수명
- overall [óuvərɔ̀:l] — a. 전반적인
- mutation [mju:téiʃən] — n. 돌연변이
- rapid [rǽpid] — a. 빠른
- unexploited [ʌ̀nikspló itid] — a. 미개척의
- ecosystem [í:kousìstəm] — n. 생태계

TEST 4-2

Global Variations in Species Diversity 세계적으로 다른 종들의 다양성

#	표현	뜻
01	change in	~라는 점에서의 변화
02	from A to B	A에서 B까지
03	move to	~로 이동하다
04	drop off	줄어들다; 놓고가다
05	both A and B	A와 B 둘다
06	when compared to	~와 비교했을 때
07	allow O to do	O가 to do 하는것을 가능케하다
08	seem to do	to do 하는 것처럼 보이다
09	look at	~을 (자세히) 살피다
10	at a temperature	~한 온도에서
11	year-round	1년 내내 계속되는
12	those of	앞 명사 반복 피하기 (복수)
13	in darkness	어둠 속에서
14	neither A nor B	A도 아니고 B도 아니다
15	such as	예를 들어, ~와 같은
16	due to	~때문에
17	because of	~때문에
18	specialize in	~을 전문으로 하다
19	at various times	여러 경우에, 다양한 시간대에
20	dependent on	~에 의존하는
21	feed on	~을 먹고 살다
22	compete with	~와 겨루다
23	one another	서로(서로)
24	devoid of	~이 없는
25	stick A into B	A를 B에 찔러 넣다
26	worry about	~에 대해 걱정하다
27	adapt to	~에 적응하다
28	on the other hand	다른 한편으로는, 반면에
29	a plethora of	많은, 대량의
30	set in	비·험한 날씨·전염병 등이 (계속될 기세로) 시작하다[되다]
31	migrate to	~로 이주하다
32	switch from A to B	A에서 B로 전환 되다
33	assure A of B	A에게 B에 대해서 장담하다, 확신시키다, 보장하다
34	a variety of	여러가지의
35	draw upon	~에 의지하다
36	lead O to do	O가 to do 하도록 야기하다
37	depending on	~에 따라
38	difference in	~점에서의 차이
39	have little effect on	~에 영향을 거의 주지 않는다
40	show O to do	O가 to do 하다는 것을 증명하다, 보여주다
41	result in	(결과적으로) ~을 낳다, 야기하다
42	in a latitude	~한 위도에서
43	begin ~ing	~ing 하는것을 시작하다

※ 다시 한 번 암기 후 → 열 번 읽기로 넘어가자!

TEST 5-1
VOCABULARY

TEST 5-1지문의 단어 중 토플 필수 단어를 선별하여 정리하였습니다.

- ☐ capital city [kǽpitl síti]   n. 수도
- ☐ mountainous [máuntənəs]   a. 산이 많은, 산악의
- ☐ conquest [káŋkwest]   n. 정복
- ☐ administration [ædmìnəstréiʃən]   n. 행정(부)
- ☐ vast [væst]   a. 어마어마한, 방대한
- ☐ civilization [sìvəlizéiʃən]   n. 문명
- ☐ collapse [kəlǽps]   v. 붕괴되다
- ☐ conquer [káŋkər]   v. 정복하다
- ☐ magnificent [mægnífəsənt]   a. 훌륭한
- ☐ conqueror [káŋkərər]   n. 정복자
- ☐ veracity [vərǽsəti]   n. 진실성
- ☐ ruling system [rúːliŋ sístəm]   n. 지배 방식
- ☐ informant [infɔ́ːrmənt]   n. 정보원
- ☐ monarchy [mánərki]   n. 군주제
- ☐ title [táitl]   n. 직함, 왕위
- ☐ flourish [flə́ːriʃ]   v. 번창하다
- ☐ bias [báiəs]   n. 편견
- ☐ inaccuracy [inǽkjərəsi]   n. 부정확
- ☐ compile [kəmpáil]   v. 자료를 엮다, 편집하다
- ☐ inaccurate [inǽkjərit]   a. 부정확한
- ☐ downplay [dáunplèi]   v. 경시하다
- ☐ accurately [ǽkjərətli]   ad. 정확히, 정밀하게
- ☐ amass [əmǽs]   v. 모으다

- ☐ mislead [mislíːd]   v. 잘못 인도하다
- ☐ exaggerate [igzǽdʒərèit]   v. 과장하다
- ☐ historical [histɔ́(ː)rikəl]   a. 역사적
- ☐ oral [ɔ́ːrəl]   a. 구술의
- ☐ unintentional [ʌninténʃənəl]   a. 고의가 아닌
- ☐ accurate [ǽkjərit]   a. 정확한
- ☐ whitewash [hwáitwàʃ]   v. 눈가림하려 하다
- ☐ dispersing [dispə́ːrsiŋ]   n. 분산
- ☐ uncooperative [ʌnkouápərèitiv]   a. 비협조적인
- ☐ description [diskrípʃən]   n. 서술, 묘사
- ☐ righteous [ráitʃəs]   a. 옳은
- ☐ invincible [invínzəbəl]   a. 천하무적의
- ☐ all but [ɔːl bʌt]   ad. 거의
- ☐ establish [istǽbliʃ]   v. 설립하다
- ☐ narrative [nǽrətiv]   n. 묘사
- ☐ truthfulness [trúːθfəlnis]   n. 정직함
- ☐ incongruent [inkáŋgruːənt]   a. 부적당한
- ☐ province [právins]   n. (행전 단위인) 주, 지방
- ☐ verify [vérəfài]   v. 확인하다
- ☐ cross-referencing [krɔ́ːs-réfərənsiŋ]   n. 상호 참조
- ☐ account [əkáunt]   n. 설명, 해석
- ☐ archeological [àːrkiáládʒikəl]   a. 고고학의
- ☐ chronology [krənálədʒi]   n. 연대순, 연대표

구문정리

본문 중 중요 구문 정리한 내용입니다. 우선 암기하고 많이 읽으시기 바랍니다.

TEST 5-1 Documenting the Incas 잉카의 기록들

01	begin with	~으로 시작하다
02	conquest of	~의 정복
03	allow O to do	O가 to do 하는 것을 가능케하다
04	control over	~을 통제하다
05	make O O.C	O를 O.C상태로 만들다
06	less than	~이하의, ~미만의
07	lead O to do	O가 to do 하도록 이끌다
08	related to	~와 관계있는, ~와 관련된
09	be different from	~와 다르다
10	that of	앞 명사 반복 피하기
11	in order to do	to do 하기 위해
12	glean A from B	A를 B로부터 주워 모으다, 수집하다
13	adapt A to B	A를 B에 적응시키다
14	tell A of B	A에게 B에 대해 얘기하다
15	may have done	추측, 했을지도 모른다
16	rule over	~을 지배하다, 통치하다
17	point to	~를 가리키다, 암시하다
18	want to do	to do 하기를 원하다
19	such as	예를 들어, ~와 같은
20	would have done	추측, ~했을 것이다
21	have to do	to do 해야만 한다
22	turn over	~에게 양도하다; 넘겨주다 (=deliver)
23	be able to do	to do 할 수 있다
24	mislead O to do	O가 to do 하도록 잘못 인도하다
25	rely on	~에 의지, 의존하다
26	pass down	(흔히 수동태로) (후대에) ~을 물려주다, 전해주다
27	over time	시간에 걸쳐서
28	be said to do	to do 라고 한다, 알려져 있다
29	emerge from	~에서 나오다
30	in light	~한 관점에서
31	it is probable that	that절 할 것 같다
32	be likely to do	to do 할 가능성이 있다
33	deal with	~을 다루다; ~를 처리하다
34	portray A as B	A를 B로 묘사하다
35	all but	거의
36	call O into question	O에 의문을 제기하다
37	seem to do	to do 하는 것처럼 보이다
38	use O to do	O를 to do 하기 위해 사용하다
39	compounded with	~로 인해 악화된
40	change in	~라는 점에서의 변화
41	make it difficult to do	to do 하는 것을 어렵게 하다
42	find O to do	O가 to do 하는 것을 발견하다
43	go on	일어나다, (어떤 상황이) 계속되다

※ 다시 한 번 암기 후 → 열 번 읽기로 넘어가자!

TEST 5-2
VOCABULARY

TEST 5-2지문의 단어 중 토플 필수 단어를 선별하여 정리하였습니다.

☐ undergo [ʌ̀ndərgóu]	v. (변화, 특히 안좋은 일) 겪다
☐ dramatic [drəmǽtik]	a. 극적인
☐ establishment [istǽbliʃmənt]	n. 기관, 시설
☐ arrangement [əréindʒmənt]	n. 배치, 배열
☐ necessitate [nisésətèit]	v. ~을 필요하게 만들다
☐ quest [kwest]	n. 요청
☐ adequate [ǽdikwit]	a. 충분한
☐ continental [kàntənéntl]	a. 대륙의
☐ catalyst [kǽtəlist]	n. (변화의) 촉매제
☐ motivated [móutəvèit]	a. 자극받은, 동기가 부여된
☐ alliance [əláiəns]	n. 동맹, 연합
☐ establish [istǽbliʃ]	v. 설립하다
☐ headquarters [hédkwɔ̀ːrtərz]	n. 본사, 본부
☐ court [kɔːrt]	n. 궁중, 대궐
☐ workable [wə́ːrkəbəl]	a. 실행 가능한
☐ relatively [rélətivli]	ad. 상대적으로, 비교적으로
☐ rudimentary [rùːdəméntəri]	a. 가장 기본적인
☐ prior to [práiər tuː]	phr. ~이전에
☐ fortress [fɔ́ːrtris]	n. 요새
☐ shrine [ʃrain]	n. 사원, 성지
☐ beam [biːm]	n. 가로기둥, 서까래
☐ rot [rɑt]	v. 썩히다
☐ temporary [témpərèri]	a. 일시적인
☐ expenditure [ikspénditʃər]	n. 비용, 지출
☐ adherent [ædhíərənt]	n. 지지자

☐ taboo [təbúː]	n. 금기
☐ contamination [kəntæ̀mənéiʃən]	n. 오염, 타락
☐ predecessor [prédisèsər]	n. 전임자
☐ unfeasible [ʌnfíːzəbəl]	a. 실행할 수 없는
☐ bureaucracy [bjuərɑ́krəsi]	n. 관료(제)
☐ oversee [òuvərsíː]	v. 감독하다
☐ maintain [meintéin]	v. 유지하다
☐ abundant [əbʌ́ndənt]	a. 풍부한
☐ imperial [impíəriəl]	a. 황제의
☐ permanent [pə́ːrmənənt]	a. 영구적인
☐ foundation [faundéiʃən]	n. 토대, 기반
☐ joint [dʒɔint]	n. 연결 부위
☐ tremendous [triméndəs]	a. 엄청난
☐ manpower [mǽnpàuər]	n. 인력
☐ legitimize [lidʒítəmətàiz]	v. 정당화 하다
☐ reign [rein]	n. 통치(기간)
☐ dynasty [dáinəsti]	n. 왕조
☐ conflict [kɑ́nflikt]	n. 갈등
☐ opulent [ɑ́pjələnt]	a. 호화로운
☐ hesitant [hézətənt]	a. 망설이는, 주저하는
☐ give up [giv ʌp]	v. 포기하다
☐ compromise [kɑ́mprəmàiz]	n. 타협
☐ grandiose [grǽndiòus]	a. 거창한
☐ immobility [ìmoubíləti]	n. 부동성
☐ a bit of [ə bit ɑv]	소량의

구문정리

본문 중 중요 구문 정리한 내용입니다. 우선 암기하고 많이 읽으시기 바랍니다.

TEST 5-2 — Architectural Change in Eighth Century Japan
8세기 일본의 건축학적 변화

01	quest for	~에 대한 추구, 탐색
02	change in	~라는 점에서의 변화
03	shift in	~라는 점에서의 변화
04	prior to	~이전에; ~에 앞서
05	in addition to	~에 더하여; ~뿐만 아니라
06	that of	앞 명사 반복 피하기 (단수)
07	reside with	~에 속하다, 거주하다
08	for years	수년동안
09	build A with B	A를 B로 짓다
10	in contact with	~와 접촉하는
11	important to	~에게 중요한
12	allow for	~을 허락하다, 가능케하다
13	taboo against	~에 관한 금기
14	lead O to do	O가 to do 하는것을 야기하다; 초래하다
15	due to	~때문에
16	the expansion of	~의 확대
17	involve A in B	A를 B에 연루시키다; 관여시키다
18	by the time	~시기가 되었을때
19	rise to power	권세를 얻다
20	keep in contact with	~와 접촉, 연락을 유지하다
21	provide for	~에 대해 준비하다
22	need to do	to do 할 필요가 있다
23	enough to do	to do 할만큼 충분히; to do 할만큼 충분한
24	settle in	정착하다
25	look to	~를 주의하다, 개선점을 고려하다
26	attractive to	~에게 있어서 매력적인
27	look to do	to do 하기를 바라다
28	in a manner	어떤 방법으로
29	comparable to	~와 맞먹는(필적하는)
30	introduce A from B	A를 B로부터 도입하다
31	model A after B	A를 B를 본떠서 만들다
32	wish to do	to do 하기를 원하다
33	at the time	그 때에
34	would have done	추측, ~했을 것이다 Ⓦ
35	hesitant to do	to do 하는 것을 주저하다
36	under system	제도 하에서
37	belief in	~대한 믿음
38	desire for	~에 대한 열망(하다)
39	in method	~방법으로
40	reliance on	~에 대한 의존
41	adhere to	~을 고수하다
42	on the other hand	다른 한편으로는
43	in style	거창하게, 유행되는
44	relate A to B	A를 B와 연관짓다
45	in residence	머무르는, 상주/ 주재하는
46	made it easier for them to oversee	그들이 감독하는것을 쉽게 만들었다
47	far away from	~로부터 멀리 떨어진 곳에

※ 다시 한 번 암기 후 → 열 번 읽기로 넘어가자!

TEST 6-1
VOCABULARY

TEST 6-1지문의 단어 중 토플 필수 단어를 선별하여 정리하였습니다.

☐ ability [əbíləti]	n. 능력
☐ extreme [ikstríːm]	a. 극도의, 극심한
☐ deprivation [dèprəvéiʃən]	n. 부족
☐ invaluable [invǽljuəbəl]	a. 매우 귀중한
☐ beast of burden [biːst əv bə́ːrdn]	n. 짐을 나르는 짐승
☐ adaptation [æ̀dæptéiʃən]	n. 적응
☐ rapidly [rǽpidli]	ad. 급속히, 신속히
☐ tissue [tíʃuː]	n. 세포(조직)
☐ dilution [dilúːʃən]	n. 묽게 함, 희석
☐ fatal [féitl]	a. 죽음을 초래하는, 치명적인
☐ rupture [rʌ́ptʃər]	n. (인체 내부 장기의) 파열
☐ ovoid [óuvɔid]	a. 타원형의
☐ handle [hǽndl]	v. 다루다
☐ metabolize [mətǽbɔlàiz]	v. 대사 작용을 하다
☐ gut [gʌt]	n. 소화관
☐ cellular [séljələr]	a. 세포의
☐ function [fʌ́ŋʃən]	n/v. 기능(하다)
☐ sweat [swet]	n/v. 땀(을 흘리다)
☐ digestive [didʒéstiv]	a. 소화의
☐ immediately [imíːdiitli]	ad. 즉시

☐ conserve [kənsə́ːrv]	v. 아끼다
☐ exhale [ekshéil]	v. 내뿜다
☐ respiration [rèspəréiʃən]	n. 호흡
☐ humidity [hjuːmídəti]	n. 습도
☐ cavity [kǽvəti]	n. 구멍(빈 부분)
☐ diffusion [difjúːʒən]	n. 발산
☐ accumulation [əkjùːmjəléiʃən]	n. 축적
☐ store [stɔːr]	n. v. 저장(하다)
☐ dissipate [dísəpèit]	v. 소멸하다(시키다)
☐ maintain [meintéin]	v. 유지하다
☐ stable [stéibl]	a. 안정된
☐ diurnal [daiə́ːrnəl]	a. 낮의
☐ fluctuation [flʌ̀ktʃuéiʃən]	n. 변동
☐ panting [pǽntiŋ]	a. 헐떡거리는
☐ altogether [ɔ̀ːltəgéðər]	ad. 완전히
☐ spindly [spíndli]	a. 막대기 같은
☐ aloft [əlɔ́(ː)ft]	ad. 떠있는, (하늘높이)
☐ absorb [əbsɔ́ːrb]	v. 흡수하다
☐ proclivity [prouklívəti]	n. 성향

TEST 6-1

구문정리 — 본문 중 중요 구문 정리한 내용입니다. 우선 암기하고 많이 읽으시기 바랍니다.

How Camels Survive in Arid Environments
어떻게 낙타들은 건조한 환경들에서 살아남나

01	ability to do	to do 할 수 있는 능력
02	make O O.C	O를 O.C 상태로 만들다
03	come in	to be available or obtainable
04	act as	~으로서 역할을 하다
05	for long periods	장시간동안
06	up to	(특정한 수·정도 등)~까지
07	transfer A to B	A를 B로 옮기다
08	compare A to B	A를 B에 비교하다
09	allow O to do	O가 to do 하는것을 가능케 하다
10	for instance	예를 들어
11	rather than	~보다는[대신에 / ~하지 말고]
12	be able to do	to do 할 수 있다
13	in addition to	~에 더하여
14	cope with	~에 대처하다, 처리하다
15	so ~ that	너무 ~해서 ~하다
16	use A as B	A를 B로서 사용하다
17	immediately after	직후에
18	a large amount of	다량의
19	give A B	A에게 B를 주다
20	on the other hand	반면에
21	keep O O.C	O를 O.C 상태로 유지하다
22	adaptation to	~에 대한 적응
23	think O to do	O가 to do 한다고 여기다, 생각하다
24	hold in	to keep something inside
25	have O done	O가 done되도록 하다, 만들다
26	concentrate on	~에 집중하다
27	use up	~을 다 쓰다
28	in the process	~의 과정에서
29	deal with	~을 처리하다
30	expose A to B	A를 B에 노출 시키다
31	maintain O O.C	O를 O.C 상태로 유지하다
32	as ~ as possible	가능한 한
33	close to	~에 가까운, 근접한
34	need for	~의 필요
35	per day	하루에
36	not only A but also B	A뿐만 아니라 B또한
37	avoid ~ing	~ing 하는것을 피하다
38	protect A from B	A를 B로부터 지키다
39	be compounded by	~로 인해 악화되다
40	stand ~ing	~ing 하면서 서있다

※ 다시 한 번 암기 후 → 열 번 읽기로 넘어가자!

TEST 6-2
VOCABULARY

TEST 6-2지문의 단어 중 토플 필수 단어를 선별하여 정리하였습니다.

- flourish [flə́:riʃ] — v. 번창하다
- Middle East [mídl iːst] — n. 중동
- influence [ínfluəns] — n. 영향
- humanity [hjuːmǽnəti] — n. 인류
- consumption [kənsʌ́mpʃən] — n. 먹는 것, 소비
- nomadic [noumǽdik] — a. 유목의
- multitude [mʌ́ltitjùːd] — n. 다수
- migration [maigréiʃən] — n. 이주
- require [rikwáiər] — v. 요구하다
- adapt [ədǽpt] — v. (새로운 용도, 상황에) 맞추다
- suit [suːt] — v. 맞다, 어울리다
- harvest [háːrvist] — v. 수확하다
- protein [próutiːin] — n. 단백질
- respectively [rispéktivli] — ad. 각자
- dietary [dáiətèri] — n. 규정식, 식이요법
- coincide [kòuinsáid] — v. 동시에 일어나다
- altitude [ǽltətjùːd] — n. 고도
- sandy [sǽndi] — a. 모래로 뒤덮인
- completely [kəmplíːtli] — ad. 완전히
- mediterranean [mèdətəréiniən] — a. 지중해의
- sedentary [sédəntèri] — a. 주로 앉아서 지내는
- predecessor [prédisèsər] — n. 전임자
- settle [sétl] — v. 정착하다
- advent [ǽdvent] — n. 도래, 출현
- entire [intáiər] — a. 전체의
- hunting and gathering [hʌ́ntiŋ ænd gǽðəriŋ] — n. 수렵채집
- feature [fíːtʃər] — v. 특징으로 삼다
- pit [pit] — n. 구덩이
- store [stɔːr] — v. 저장하다
- sophistication [səfìstəkéiʃən] — n. 세련, 정교함
- confirm [kənfə́ːrm] — v. 사실임을 보여주다
- stalk [stɔːk] — n. (식물의) 줄기
- boundary [báundəri] — n. 경계선
- coastal [kóustəl] — a. 해안의
- prosper [práspər] — v. 번영하다
- collect [kəlèkt] — v. 모으다, 수집하다
- year-round [jíərráund] — a. 연중 계속되는
- nourishment [nə́ːriʃmənt] — n. 음식물, 영양
- game [geim] — n. 사냥감
- ambush [ǽmbuʃ] — n. 매복
- social structure [sóuʃl strʌ́ktʃər] — n. 사회구조
- cemetery [sémətèri] — n. 묘지
- symbolic [simbálik] — a. 상징적인
- common [kámən] — a. 흔한, 평범한
- furnishing [fə́ːrniʃiŋ] — n. 장식품
- standing [stǽndiŋ] — n. 지위
- the deceased [ðə disíːst] — n. 고인
- ranking [rǽŋkiŋ] — n. 서열(표)
- redistribution [rìːdistríbju(ː)ʃən] — n. 재분배
- grave [greiv] — n. 무덤
- ritualistic [rìtʃuəlístik] — a. 의식 절차상의
- dramatic [drəmǽtik] — a. 극적인
- upheaval [ʌphíːvəl] — n. 격변, 대변동
- dry out [drai aut] — v. 메말라지다
- reliable [riláiəbəl] — a. 믿을(의존할) 수 있는
- deliberately [dilíbəritli] — ad. 고의로, 의도적으로
- modest [mádist] — a. (크기, 가격, 중요성 등) 보통의
- supplement [sʌ́pləmənt] — n. 보충물
- dedicate [dédikèit] — v. 바치다, 헌신하다
- spell [spel] — n. 기간

TEST 6-2

Hunter-gatherers in Southwest Asia
서남 아시아의 수렵 채집인들

본문 중 중요 구문 정리한 내용입니다. 우선 암기하고 많이 읽으시기 바랍니다.

01	know A as B	A를 B라고 알다
02	have an influence on	~에 영향을 끼치다
03	move across	~를 가로질러 가다
04	a multitude of	다수의
05	over the course of	~동안
06	require O to do	O가 to do 하는 것을 요구하다
07	so ~ that	너무 ~해서 ~하다
08	make up	~을 이루다, 형성하다
09	coincide with	~와 동시에 일어나다
10	shift in	~라는 점에서의 변화
11	spread to	~로 퍼지다
12	move from A to B	A에서 B로 이동하다
13	allow O to do	O가 to do 하는 것을 가능케 하다
14	as well	~ 또한
15	prove to be	(분명해지다) ~라고 판명나다
16	base A on B	A를 B에 기반을 두다
17	reliance on	~에 대한 의존
18	find O to do	O가 to do 하는 것을 발견하다
19	use for	~을 위한 사용
20	rely upon	~에 의존하다
21	seem to do	to do 하는 것처럼 보이다
22	in places	곳곳에서
23	settle in	~에 정착하다, 적응하다
24	come into season	제철이 되다
25	in addition to	~에 더하여
26	cooperate with	~와 협력하다, ~에 협조하다
27	lead O to do	O가 to do 하도록 이끌다
28	difference in	~점에서의 차이
29	fill A with B	A를 B로 함께 채우다
30	the result of	~의 결과
31	effort to do	to do 하려는 노력
32	think O to do	O가 to do 한다고 생각하다, 여기다
33	serve as	~로서 역할을 하다
34	begin to do	to do 하는 것을 시작하다
35	need to do	to do 할 필요
36	live off	~에 의지해서 살다
37	be able to do	to do 할 수 있다
38	help O do	O가 do 하는 것을 도와주다
39	flourish in	~에서 번창하다

※ 다시 한 번 암기 후 → 열 번 읽기로 넘어가자!

TEST 7-1
VOCABULARY

TEST 7-1 지문의 단어 중 토플 필수 단어를 선별하여 정리하였습니다.

- ☐ wonder [wʌ́ndər] — v. 궁금해하다
- ☐ extraterrestrial [èkstrətiréstriəl] — a. 외계의
- ☐ probable [prábəbl] — a. 있을 것 같은
- ☐ molecular [moulékjulər] — a. 분자의
- ☐ astronomer [əstránəmər] — n. 천문학자
- ☐ orbit [ɔ́:rbit] — n. v. 궤도(를 돌다)
- ☐ habitable zone [hǽbətəbəl zoun] — n. 거주(서식) 가능 지역
- ☐ atmospheric [æ̀tməsférik] — a. 대기의
- ☐ pressure [préʃər] — n. (대기의) 기압
- ☐ liquid [líkwid] — a. 액체의
- ☐ particular [pərtíkjələr] — a. 특정한
- ☐ inspire [inspáiər] — v. (욕구, 자신감을 갖도록) 고무하다
- ☐ remarkably [rimá:rkəbli] — ad. 현저하게, 매우
- ☐ identical [aidéntikəl] — a. 동일한
- ☐ axis [ǽksis] — n. 축
- ☐ tilt [tilt] — n. 기울기
- ☐ frozen [fróuzən] — a. 얼어붙은
- ☐ inhospitable [inháspitəbəl] — a. (기후 조건이) 사람이 지내기 힘든
- ☐ glaring [gléəriŋ] — a. 확연한
- ☐ precipitously [prisípətəsli] — ad. 가파르게, 급하게
- ☐ ultraviolet [ʌ̀ltrəváiəlit] — n. 자외선
- ☐ radiation [rèidiéiʃən] — n. 방사선
- ☐ dearth [də:rθ] — n. (~의) 부족

- ☐ tremendous [triméndəs] — a. 엄청난
- ☐ vent [vent] — v. 뿜어내다
- ☐ scatter [skǽtər] — v. (흩)뿌리다, 흩어지다
- ☐ trap [træp] — v. 모아두다, 가두다
- ☐ crater [kréitər] — n. 분화구
- ☐ disappear [dìsəpíər] — v. 사라지다
- ☐ prohibit [prouhíbit] — v. 금하다, ~하지 못하게 하다
- ☐ presence [prézəns] — n. 존재
- ☐ outer [áutər] — a. 바깥 표면의
- ☐ shell [ʃel] — n. 껍데기
- ☐ tectonic [tektánik] — a. (지질) 구조상의
- ☐ deplete [diplí:t] — v. 감소시키다
- ☐ greenhouse effect [grí:nhàus ifékt] — n. 온실 효과
- ☐ destabilize [di:stéibəlàiz] — v. 불안정하게 만들다
- ☐ dissipate [dísəpèit] — v. 소멸하다
- ☐ gradual [grǽdʒuəl] — a. 점진적인
- ☐ absorption [əbsɔ́:rpʃən] — n. 흡수
- ☐ unsustainable [ʌ̀nsəstéinéibəl] — a. 지속 불가능한
- ☐ spacecraft [spéiskræft] — n. 우주선
- ☐ destroy [distrɔ́i] — v. 파괴하다
- ☐ namely [néimli] — ad. 즉, 다시 말해
- ☐ hypothesize [haipáθəsàiz] — v. 가설을 세우다

TEST 7-1 Life on Mars 화성의 생명체

구문정리 본문 중 중요 구문 정리한 내용입니다. 우선 암기하고 많이 읽으시기 바랍니다.

01	not only A but (also) B	A 뿐만 아니라 B 또한
02	base A on B	A를 B에 기반을 두다
03	be likely to do	to do 할 가능성이 있다
04	inspire O to do	O가 to do 하도록 고무시키다
05	search for	~(문제에 대한 답)을 찾다
06	the number of	~의 수
07	contrary to	~에 반하여, ~와 반대로
08	compare A to B	A를 B와 비교하다
09	subject to	~하는 경향이 있는, ~를 겪는, ~에 영향을 받기 쉬운
10	in addition to	~에 더하여, ~일 뿐 아니라
11	toxic to	~에 독성이 있는
12	expose A to B	A를 B에 노출시키다
13	do little to do	거의 to do 하지 않는다
14	in the way that	that절한 방법으로
15	dearth of	~의 부족, 결핍
16	be unable to do	to do 할 수 없다
17	reason to do	to do 할 이유
18	enough O to do	O가 to do 하기에 충분한
19	allow O to do	O가 to do 하도록 허락하다
20	lock up A in B	A를 B에 가두다
21	prior to	~에 앞서, 먼저
22	protection from	~로부터의 보호
23	access to	~에의 접근
24	instead of	~대신에
25	draw A from B	A를 B에서 끌어내다, 얻다
26	find O to do	O가 to do 하는 것을 발견하다, 알다
27	at one time	한때에(과거의)
28	would have done	추측, ~했을 것이다
29	over time	시간에 걸쳐서
30	react with	~에 반응을 보이다
31	necessary to do	to do 하는데 필요한
32	in the past	옛날, 이전에

※ 다시 한 번 암기 후 → 열 번 읽기로 넘어가자!

TEST 7-2
VOCABULARY

TEST 7-2지문의 단어 중 토플 필수 단어를 선별하여 정리하였습니다.

☐ lush [lʌʃ]	a. 무성한	☐ interconnected [ìntərkənékt]	a. 상호 연결된
☐ barren [bǽrən]	a. 척박한	☐ sediment [sédəmənt]	n. 침전물
☐ surprisingly [sərpráiziŋli]	ad. 의외로, 놀랍게도	☐ channel [tʃǽnl]	n. 수로
☐ contrast [kántræst]	n. 차이, 대조	☐ considerably [kənsídərəbli]	ad. 상당히
☐ impetus [ímpətəs]	n. 자극제, 추동력	☐ inhospitable [inháspitəbəl]	a. 사람이 지내기 힘든
☐ settlement [sétlmənt]	n. 정착(지)	☐ inundation [ínəndéiʃən]	n. 범람
☐ domesticate [dəméstikeit]	v. (동물을) 길들이다	☐ overflowing [òuvərflóuiŋ]	a. 넘쳐 흐르는
☐ across [əkrɔ́:s]	p. ~전체에 걸쳐서	☐ nutrient [njú:triənt]	n. 영양소
☐ previously [prí:viəsli]	ad. 이전에	☐ cultivate [kʌ́ltəvèit]	v. 경작하다, 재배하다
☐ ample [ǽmpl]	a. 충분한	☐ namely [néimli]	ad. 즉, 다시 말해
☐ inhabitant [inhǽbətənt]	n. 주민, 서식동물	☐ flourish [flɔ́:riʃ]	v. 번창하다
☐ surrounding [səráundiŋ]	a. 인근의	☐ sustain [səstéin]	v. 살아가게 하다
☐ decline [dikláin]	v. 감소하다	☐ civilization [sìvəlizéiʃən]	n. 문명
☐ fertile [fɔ́:rtl]	a. 비옥한	☐ component [kəmpóunənt]	n. (구성) 요소
☐ settle [sétl]	v. 정착하다	☐ transportation [trænspərtéiʃən]	n. 수송, 운송
☐ role [roul]	n. 역할	☐ verdant [vɔ́:rdənt]	a. 신록의, 파릇파릇한
☐ reveal [rivíːl]	v. 드러내다	☐ dietary [dáiətèri]	n. 규정식, 식이요법
☐ nomadic [noumǽdik]	a. 유목의	☐ narrow [nǽrou]	a. 좁은
☐ livestock [láivstàk]	n. 가축	☐ remain [rimèin]	n. (죽은 사람, 동물의) 유해
☐ lifestyle [laifstail]	n. 생활방식	☐ protein [próuti:in]	n. 단백질
☐ further [fɔ́:rðər]	ad. 더 멀리에	☐ migratory [máigrətɔ̀:ri]	a. 이주하는
☐ conducive [kəndjú:siv]	a. ~에 더 좋은	☐ regularly [régjələrli]	ad. 정기적으로
☐ due to [dju:tu:]	p. ~때문에	☐ edible [édəbəl]	a. 먹을 수 있는
☐ abundant [əbʌ́ndənt]	a. 풍부한	☐ ruin [rú:in]	n. (파괴된 건물의) 잔해, 유적
☐ sufficient [səfíʃənt]	a. 충분한	☐ predictable [prédikitéibəl]	a. 예측할 수 있는
☐ desertification [dizə̀:rtəfikéiʃən]	n. 사막화	☐ empire [émpaiər]	n. 제국
☐ wildlife [wáildlàif]	n. 야생동물	☐ bounty [báunti]	n. 풍부함
☐ flee [fli:]	v. 달아나다, 도망하다	☐ reap [ri:p]	v. 수확하다
☐ restrict [ristríkt]	v. 제한하다	☐ widespread [wáidspréd]	a. 광범위한
☐ wander [wándər]	v. 헤매다	☐ irrigation [ìrəgéiʃən]	n. 관개
☐ tremendous [triméndəs]	a. 엄청난	☐ industrial [indʌ́striəl]	a. 산업(공업)의
☐ run [rʌn]	v. (물 등이) 흐르다	☐ fabric [fǽbrik]	n. 직물

구문정리

본문 중 중요 구문 정리한 내용입니다. 우선 암기하고 많이 읽으시기 바랍니다.

TEST 7-2 — Agriculture and Settlement around the Nile River
농업과 나일강 부근의 정착

01	in contrast to	~와 대조하여
02	impetus for	~에 추진력, 원동력
03	conclude that	that절이라고 결론을 내리다
04	force O to do	O가 to do 하도록 강요하다
05	allow O to do	O가 to do 하는것을 가능케 하다
06	wait for	~을 기다리다
07	shift to	~로의 변화
08	dependence on	~에의 의존
09	as	(관계대명사)앞의 내용 통째로 받을때
10	move from A into B	A에서 B로의 이동
11	what is now	오늘날의 무엇; 오늘날 어디
12	prior to	~이전에, 앞서
13	conducive to	~에 도움이 되는
14	box A in B	A를 B에 꼼짝 못하게 하다, 못 움직이게 하다
15	go through	~을 겪다
16	at the time	그 때에, 당시에
17	instead of	~대신에
18	build up	쌓아 올리다
19	turn A into B	A를 B로 바꾸다
20	as time wear on	시간이 경과함에 따라
21	dependent upon	~에 의존하는
22	separate A into B	A를 B로 분리하다
23	spread A across B	A를 B전역에 퍼트리다
24	bring A B	A에게 B를 가져다 주다
25	ability to do	to do 할 수 있는 능력
26	to this day	지금(이날)까지도
27	use A for B	A를 B을 위해 사용하다
28	rely upon	~에 의존하다
29	native to	~에 토종인, 출신의
30	provide for	~을 공급하다; 부양하다
31	the number of	~의 수
32	in addition	게다가, ~에 덧붙여
33	the variety of	여러가지의
34	access to	~에의 접근
35	an abundance of	많은, 풍부한
36	excavate A from B	A를 B로부터 발굴하다
37	base A on B	A를 B에 기반을 두다
38	be able to do	to do 할 수 있다
39	regard A as B	A를 B로 여기다
40	put A in B	A를 B상태에 놓다
41	in control of	~을 관리하고 있는
42	in a way	~한 방법으로
43	not only A but also B	A뿐만 아니라 B또한
44	for use in	~에 사용하기 위한
45	use A as B	A를 B로서 사용하다
46	outside of	~의 바깥쪽에

※ 다시 한 번 암기 후 → 열 번 읽기로 넘어가자!

TEST 부록
VOCABULARY

TEST부록지문의 단어 중 토플 필수 단어를 선별하여 정리하였습니다.

☐ navigation [nævəgéiʃən]	n. 항해
☐ seafarer [síːfɛ̀ərər]	n. 선원
☐ vast [væst]	a. 어마어마한
☐ intrigue [intríːg]	v. 강한 흥미를 불러일으키다
☐ celestial [silésʧəl]	a. 천체의
☐ eyesight [áisàit]	n. 시력
☐ odor [óudər]	n. 냄새
☐ destination [dèstənéiʃən]	n. 목적지, 도착지
☐ dispersal [dispə́ːrsəl]	n. 확산
☐ convoluted [kánvəlùːtid]	a. 대단히 난해한
☐ migrate [máigreit]	v. 이동하다
☐ more or less [mɔːr ɔːr les]	거의
☐ furthermore [fə́ːrðəmɔ̀ːr]	ad. 더욱이
☐ current [kə́ːrənt]	n. 해류
☐ gain [gein]	v. (정보, 지지 등을) 얻다
☐ crucial [krúːʃəl]	a. 결정적인
☐ place [pleis]	v. 놓다, 두다 = put
☐ chamber [ʧéimbər]	n. (생명체) ,~실, 공간
☐ alter [ɔ́ːltər]	v. 바꾸다
☐ utilization [jùːtəlizèiʃən]	n. 이용, 활용
☐ precise [prisáis]	a. 정확한
☐ measure [méʒər]	v. 측정하다
☐ intensity [inténsəti]	n. 강렬함
☐ magnetic pole [mægnétik poul]	n. 전자극
☐ compass [kʌ́mpəs]	n. 나침반
☐ surprisingly [sərpráiziŋli]	ad. 의외로, 놀랍게도

☐ finding [fáindiŋ]	n. (조사, 연구 등의) 결과
☐ demonstrate [démənstrèit]	v. 입증하다
☐ devoid [divɔ́id]	a. ~이 전혀 없는
☐ shortcoming [ʃɔ́ːrtkʌ̀miŋ]	n. 결점
☐ substantial [səbstǽnʃəl]	a. 상당한
☐ vital [váitl]	a. 필수적인
☐ escape [iskéip]	v. 달아나다
☐ predator [prédətər]	n. 포식자
☐ hypothesize [haipáθəsàiz]	v. 가설을 세우다
☐ calculate [kǽlkjəlèit]	v. 계산하다
☐ cue [kjuː]	n. 신호
☐ juvenile [dʒúːvənəl]	n. 청소년
☐ instinctively [instíŋktivli]	ad. 본능적으로
☐ hatchling [hæʧiŋ]	n. 갓 부화한 동물
☐ disorient [disɔ́ːriənt]	v. 방향 감각을 혼란시키다
☐ artificial [àːrtəfíʃəl]	a. 인공의
☐ shallow [ʃǽlou]	a. 얕은
☐ detect [ditékt]	v. 발견하다, 감지하다
☐ forage [fɔ́ːridʒ]	v. 먹이를 찾다
☐ auditory [ɔ́ːditɔ̀ːri]	a. 청각의
☐ low-frequency [lou-fríːkwənsi]	a. 저주파의
☐ solely [sóulli]	ad. 오로지, 단지
☐ maternal [mətə́ːrnl]	a. 모성의
☐ ideal [aidíːəl]	a. 이상적인
☐ interference [ìntərfíərəns]	n. 간섭, 방해
☐ habitat [hǽbətæt]	n. 서식지

구문정리

본문 중 중요 구문 정리한 내용입니다. 우선 암기하고 많이 읽으시기 바랍니다.

TEST 부록 — Sea Turtle Navigation 바다 거북이의 길찾기

01	for centuries	수 세기 동안
02	a challenge to	~에의 도전
03	travel across	~을 횡단하다, 통과하다
04	base A on B	A를 B에 기반을 두다
05	accept A as B	A를 B로 받아들이다
06	due to	~때문에
07	gain support	~의 후원(지지)를 얻다
08	in a line	직선으로, 한 줄로
09	depending on	~에 따라
10	in the same direction	같은 방향으로
11	support from	~로 부터의 지지
12	an amount of	상당한
13	a species of	일종의
14	a variety of	여러가지의, 다양한
15	play a role in	~에서 역할을 하다
16	in response to	~에 응하여
17	change in	~라는 점에서의 변화
18	so~ that~	너무 ~해서 ~하다
19	not only A but also B	A뿐만 아니라 B또한
20	difference in	~라는 점에서의 차이
21	use A as B	A를 B로서 사용하다
22	allow O to do	O가 to do 하는 것을 가능케 하다
23	travel from A to B	A에서 B까지 여행하다
24	fit A with B	A에게 B를 갖추다, 장착시키다
25	devoid of	~이 없는
26	lead O to do	O가 to do 하도록 야기하다
27	far away from	~로부터 멀리 떨어진 곳에
28	methods to do	to do 하는 방법
29	close to	~에 가까운, 근접한
30	make one's way into	~로 나아가다, 진출하다
31	report O to do	O가 to do하다고 전하다, 알리다
32	come from	~에서 나오다, 비롯되다
33	chance for	~의 가능성
34	along with	~와 함께
35	end with	~으로 끝나다
36	extend to	~까지 미치다
37	as	(관계대명사)앞의 내용 통째로 받을때
38	inherit A from B	A를 B에서 물려받다
39	lead to the conclusion	결론에 도달하다
40	emerge from	~에서 나오다, 벗어나다
41	ideal for	~에 이상적인
42	home to	~의 고향
43	drive off	몰아내다
44	unsuccessful in ~ing	~ing을 하는데 실패한

※ 다시 한 번 암기 후 → 열 번 읽기로 넘어가자!

usherin.usher.co.kr

USHER iBT TOEFL
INTERMEDIATE READING
묶기

TEST 1-1 Comets   묶기

01. Comets, small celestial bodies (with long luminous tails and orbits) [that occasionally bring them (in close contact) (with Earth)], are some (of the most fascinating objects) (in our solar system). Today, only about 4,900 (of these bodies) composed (of frozen gases and volatile compounds) along (with rocky metallic elements) have been discovered, but the distance (of their orbits) makes it likely [that many more exist]. Comets are generally categorized (into two orbit length dependent categories): long-period and short-period comets. Short-period comets, (such as Halley's Comet) [which has been documented appearing every 76 years (since 240 B.C.E.,)] make regular appearances (due to their relatively short orbits) (of less than 200 years) and are more well-known. Long-period comets, however, are rarely observed [because they take hundreds or thousands (of years) (to complete) one trip (around the sun)].

02. The main difference (between the two categories) seems (to arrive) (from their origins). Short-period comets begin (in the Kuiper belt) (of non-planetary matter). The matter (in the belt), just (past Neptune's orbit), roughly 50 astronomical units (1 AU=the distance between Earth and the sun) (from the sun), travels (around the sun) (on nearly the same plane) (as the planets). [If two (of these comets) strike one another], or [if one is affected (by the gravitation) (of a nearby planet)], the orbit may be thrown off (in such a way) [that a comet enters the inner solar system [where it is affected (by solar forces) and visible (from Earth)]].

03. Contrarily, long-period comets do not originate (from the same plane) (as other bodies) (in the solar system). They orbit the sun (in elliptical orbits) spanning a variety (of angles), forming a "shell" (around the solar system) known (as the Oort Cloud). Scientists believe [there are millions (of inactive comets) (in this region), 10,000 AU (from the sun)]. (Due to this extreme distance) they are not affected (by planetary gravitation) (in the same way) (as Kuiper belt comets). (For one) (of these comets) (to make) its way (into the inner solar system) it must be affected (by the gravitational forces) (of a passing star). [When this happens] they are sent (on an irregular orbit) [that brings them closer (to the sun) [where they undergo the changes typical (of all comets)]]. [After they have completed their pass

(near the sun)], it may be thousands (of years) [before they make their return]. (In fact), Comet West and C/1999F1 have orbits [that are estimated (at 6 million years)]. There is even a subset (of these long-period comets) called the hyperbolic, or single-apparition, comets [that make only one appearance (near the sun), [because their orbits eventually take them (out of the solar system)]].

04. (Regardless of the category) (of comet), their telltale shape forms (in the same way). They complete most (of their orbit) (as frozen and relatively inactive masses) [that are difficult (to discern)], but [as they come closer (to the sun)], the effects (of its massive energy) sublimates the frozen materials (within this nucleus) (to form) a glowing ball (of dust and gases) known (as the coma). This coma greatly increases the comet's size. This coma is generally less (than 60 km) (in diameter), but the coma can be larger (than the sun). This most distinguishable feature differentiates comets (from other celestial bodies), (such as asteroids). [When they reach approximately 1.5 AU (from the sun)], solar energy's effects become more extreme and parts (of the coma) are blown (into a tail) [which can be millions (of kilometers) long].

05. Research (into comets) led scientists (to make) an interesting observation (regarding their tails); they always point away (from the sun). This allowed them (to conclude) [that some force emanating (from the sun) pushed the particles (in the coma) (to form) the tail]. We now understand [that this is not one, but two forces]. Pressure (from solar radiation) drives the dust particles back (from the coma), [while solar winds push back the ionized volatile gases surrounding the nucleus]. (Because of these two different effects), comets are often found (to have) two tails, a curved one composed (of dust) and a second, composed (of ionized volatiles), [that appears blue and always points away (from the sun)].

06. [When the comet makes its way (out of the influence) (of solar power)], the gases (in the coma) condense and the materials (in the tail) are lost, reducing its mass. Some (of this dust and matter) remains (in orbit), and can cause other celestial events. The annual Perseid meteor shower is caused (by matter) ejected (from the Swift-Tuttle comet) (during its 133-year orbit). (For this reason), it has been hypothesized [that comet lifespans are limited (by the number) (of orbits) [they complete]]. (After a certain number) (of orbits), the nucleus will have expelled all (of its volatile components) and will continue (to orbit) (as a small grouping) (of stony materials) [that are relatively unaffected (by solar radiation or winds)].

TEST 1-2   Darwin and Evolution Theory

01.　(In 1831), Robert FitzRoy prepared (to set) sail (on a two year journey) (aboard the Beagle) (to survey) the South American coastlines and return) three Yaghan tribe members [it previously captured] (to Tierra del Fuego), an archipelago (off the southernmost tip) (of the South American mainland). (To fight) the loneliness (of being) (at sea) (for so long) and (to help) study lands [they were (to visit)], he invited Charles Darwin, a recent Cambridge graduate, (to join) the expedition (as his companion and ship naturalist). (Prior to departure), FitzRoy gave his new companion Principles of Geology (by Charles Lyell), [who had requested [that FitzRoy record the geological formations [that he encountered]]]. Unbeknownst (to both men), their journey together would stretch (to nearly five years) and would form the basis (for a revolutionary new biological theory).

02.　(According to his diaries), Darwin spent three years and three months exploring the new lands, recording his geographical findings, and collecting fossils and specimens (of the wildlife) [he came across]. [Although he originally planned (to use) his findings (to write) a book (on geology)], (over the course) (of his explorations) he made many new and interesting discoveries (in the field) (of biology), (such as discovering) giant armadillo and sloth fossils (from the distant past). He also discovered [that (in areas) (with a geographic segregation), (such as islands or seas) separated (by isthmuses), different species were found] This was particularly true (in the Galapagos Archipelago), [where he found different species (of tortoises) (on each island), a unique marine iguana (with a seaweed-based diet), and an assortment (of birds) [he thought (to be) blackbirds, grosbeaks, and finches but later turned out (to be) 12 distinct species (of finches)]]. These discoveries, combined (with Lyell's theory) (of uniformitarianism), [which stated [that "the present is the key (to the past)]", meaning [that we can only assume (about the past) (from [what we observe (in the present))]]], caused Darwin (to postulate) [that the diversity (of these species) was possible only [if there was some mechanism [(through which) species could change (over time)]]].

03.　Darwin's idea was supported (by the theory) (of homology) [Richard Owen derived (from comparative studies) (of the structural systems) (of various vertebrates)]. Owen found homology, or anatomical similarity, (in the body parts) (of different animals) [which served different purposes]. The forelimbs (of most vertebrates), (such as, bats, whales, humans, and horses), all share a basic design.

This cannot be attributed (to common use), so it must indicate common ancestry and adaptive evolution (to fit) the organisms' functions. The presence (of vestigial, or leftover, structures) (in modern organisms) also points (to an evolutionary system), [because these structures serve no purpose (in modern animals)]. The whale and snake are both examples (of this), [because [although both are now legless], they have small vestigial leg bones, [which point (to a four-legged ancestor)]].

04. All (of this support) (for Darwin's theory) did not explain [why evolution would have occurred]. Darwin got a basic idea (about this) (by looking) (at the change) [that breeders could induce (in their animals) (through animal husbandry)]. (By breeding) animals (with certain traits) they could artificially change the traits (of the offspring). This couldn't, however, explain [how species evolve naturally] or [how some species go extinct and are replaced (by other species)]. (To gain) further insight (into this), Darwin turned (to the population research) (of economist) Thomas Malthus, [which indicated [that population increases outpace food production]]. This overpopulation decreases the number (of offspring) reaching maturity (during lean times). Darwin recognized [that these two basic ideas could be applied (to the animal kingdom)]. He theorized [that (during competitive times), animals (with favorable traits) would survive (to reproduce) and pass on their superior traits (to the next generation) (in a natural form) (of selection)].

05. [Although Darwin had great confidence (in the validity) (of his theories)], he initially refused (to publish) them (due to his lack) (of supporting data) and remained most famous (as a geologist and explorer) (after the publication) (of his accounts) (of the trip) (in The Voyage of the Beagle). This did not, however, stop him (from discussing) his theories (with fellow scientists) Lyell and Owen, [both (of whom) he befriended (after returning) (from the long voyage)]. The formal publication (of his theories) did not occur [until another young British naturalist and explorer, Alfred Wallace, was about (to present) a similar theory [he developed [while exploring the Amazon Basin and the Malay Archipelago]]]. Eventually, Wallace agreed (to present) his theory (alongside the more socially and scientifically connected Darwin) and their work was jointly presented (to the Linnean Society) (of London) (in 1858), (with very little fanfare). The true significance (of the new theories) would not be fully recognized (until the publication) (of Darwin's evolutionary manifesto), On the Origin of Species by Means of Natural Selection, (in 1859). It was so well researched and presented [that it was referred to (as the best explanation) "ever published (of the manner) (of formation) (of species)" (by Owen) and established Darwin (as the definitive authority) (on natural selection)].

TEST 2-1   Determining the Ages of the Planets and the Universe   묶기

01. The orbits (of planets and the majority) (of non-planetary objects) (in our solar system) have a very interesting characteristic; (despite their vast differences), they have astounding similarities. The most remarkable (of these similarities) is [that nearly all (of them) orbit the sun (in the same direction) and (on the same plane)]. Using this information, scientists determined [that this likely occurred [because the collapse (of a gas cloud) simultaneously formed the objects and sent them (to orbit) the sun]]. This fact has allowed us (to learn) more (about the age) (of the Earth, the planets, and the universe) itself.

02. It may seem [that the easiest method (of discerning) Earth's age would be (to simply sample) materials [we can extract (from the crust)]], but this doesn't produce accurate results. (Due to the life supporting water) [that covers Earth's surface], terrestrial material is constantly exposed (to the force) (of erosion). The constant changes [erosion causes], compounded (by volcanic activity and Earth's internal pressure and heat), make the discovery (of rocks) (in Earth's crust) [that originate (from the time) (of formation)] highly unlikely. (For this reason) scientists must look (for analogous objects) (in the solar system) (to help) them answer this question. Luckily, the meteorites [that have crashed (into Earth's surface)] can provide them (with this material). These masses began their existence (as meteors) orbiting the sun, but Earth's gravitational pull forced them (to enter) its atmosphere and collide) (with the crust).

03. The meteorites [that have been discovered] have varied (in size), ranging (from stony pebbles) (to massive planetoids) called asteroids, and composition) [which has allowed scientists (to draw) conclusions (about them and Earth's composition and origin)]. Some intact asteroids may have once struck the earth, but none have done so (during recorded human history). (From meteorite remnants) found (on Earth), the main three categories used (to differentiate) meteorites today are "stony meteorites," composed (of rocky materials), "iron meteorites" composed mainly (of iron) (with trace amounts) (of other elements), and "stony-iron meteorites" [that consist (of a mixture) (of the two)]. Scientists believe [that all three (of these types) (of meteorites) are the remnants (of larger space bodies) [that broke apart (due to collisions)]]. It is believed [that the differences (between the categories (of meteorites) are (due to this violent break up) (of space materials) (with origins and, therefore, compositions) similar (to Earth's)].

The stony meteorites likely originated (as the outer shells) (of these bodies) and are analogous (to Earth's mantle), [while the iron meteorites [that resemble Earth's core] are probably fragments (of the interior) (of the body) and the stony-iron meteorites contain materials (from both)].

04. (By studying) these meteorites scientists have been able (to determine) their age. Using multiple radiometric methods (of dating) the materials, including the uranium-thorium, rubidium-strontium, and potassium-argon methods, showed a cluster (of age data) pointing (to an origin) around 4.6 billion years ago. Comparing this (to the rocks) (from the moon's surface), [which is free (of the water) [that erodes rocks (on Earth's surface)]] and [which displays little movement (in its crust)], yielded similar age data and allowed researchers (to confirm) their hypothesis [that all (of the materials) (in the solar system) started (at the same point) (in time)].

05. [While dating the elements (of the solar system) has been relatively straightforward], finding the age (of the universe) itself has been more complicated [because there is no way (to collect) physical materials [(on which) (to conduct) age testing]]. [What has been learned] has been gathered (through theoretical analysis) (of the universe). One (of the most important factors) discovered is [that all (of diskshaped clusters) (of stars), called galaxies, are moving away (from each other)]. Scientists conjecture [that this occurs [because the universe began (with an explosion), known (as the Big Bang), [which sent all (of the dense matter) concentrated (at the center) (of the explosion) hurtling (across space)]]. This process is akin (to [what would happen [if one were (to glue) coins (to a balloon) and inflate) it]]). The coins, (like the galaxies), would remain the same size but the space (between them) would increase [as the balloon got larger].

06. The expansion (of the space) (between the galaxies) is precisely [what astronomers have used (to estimate) the universe's age]. (By measuring) the wavelengths (of light) travelling (through the universe) they are able (to measure) a shift (in the light's wavelength) (towards red end) (of the light spectrum). This redshift occurs [because, [as light travels (in the space) (between the galaxies)], the expansion (of the space) stretches out the light waves]. (Following this theory), the farther the light has traveled, the greater the redshift will be. Measuring the redshift (in light) (from distant galaxies), astronomers have determined [that all (of the galaxies) would have existed (in one central location) around 13.7 billion years ago]. This, therefore, is the most likely the date and location (of the Big Bang) and the age (of the universe).

TEST 2-2 Early Research in Organic Chemistry

01. The ancient practice (of alchemy) gave way (to the early science) (of chemistry) (in the late 17th century). (After hundreds) (of years) (of trying) (to turn) base metals (into gold), Alchemists had developed a structure (of theory, terminology, experimentation and basic laboratory techniques) [that were well-adapted (for scientific study) (of Earth's elements)]. (By the 18th century), chemists began (to scientifically study) the new elements [they found] and were able (to identify) many new ones [that had never been studied before, (such as cobalt, tungsten and various forms) (of carbon)]. The study (of the last) (of these) would eventually form one (of the two modern divisions) (of the field) (of chemistry), organic chemistry.

02. The terms organic and inorganic chemistry were introduced (in the early 1800s) (to more accurately differentiate) (between the different naturally occurring substances). (Prior to this time) scientists separated substances (into three categories) [that matched the "Three Kingdoms (of Nature)": animal, vegetable and mineral]. (Of these), the animal and vegetable groups were reserved (for substances) [that were produced (by or related (to life)] and were later incorporated (into the study) (of organic chemistry) [which covered all carbon-based compounds], [while the inanimate mineral group gave way (to the field) (of inorganic chemistry) [which covered all non-carbon compounds]]. Some scientists, (such as Antoine Lavoisier), thought [the organic field was a reasonable field (of study)], yet they were opposed (by others) [who adhered (to a theory) (of vitalism)]. Those [that believed (in vitalism)] felt [that there was a "vital spark" or "force" (in organic materials)] and [that substances [that contained it] should not be experimented upon] and [that only inorganic materials were valid research subjects]. (Despite the eventual invalidation) (of the vitalist theory), (by German chemist Friedrich Wohler's accidental synthesis) (of organic material) (in his laboratory), scientists involved (in inorganic chemistry) made much more rapid progress (than those) working (on organic chemistry).

03. This lag (of organic chemistry) occurred (for various reasons), but perhaps the most obvious is the availability (of elements and compounds) [(on which) scientists could experiment]. (In order (for scientists) to conduct) experiments and determine) the chemical forms (of the elements), they need (to obtain) them (in their purest forms). Inorganic compounds, (on the whole), are more easily found (in a reasonably pure state). Mineral deposits often hold lodes (of compounds and elements) (such as oxides, pure metals and salts). Some gases, (such as sulfur), can even be found (in their pure elemental form) (on

Earth), [while others, (like atmospheric gases), are easily broken down (into their component parts)]. Hydrogen, (for instance), can be mined (from the air) using a particular mineral acid (on a metal plate).

04. Access (to pure organic substances), (on the other hand), is much more difficult. Extracting pure substances (from plant or animal matter) (through the process) (of distillation), evaporating and condensing a substance (to purify) it, generally yields solid blackened debris along (with liquid and gaseous discharges). Chemists studying the vegetable products found [that the qualitative properties (of the remaining solid matter) varied little (between different vegetable types), but quantitative and qualitative differences were found (in the liquid and gaseous substances) produced]. They also found [that altering the distillation process yielded significantly different results (in these byproducts)]. (By standardizing) the distillation process they were able (to make) important advances (in their ability) (to analyze) organic matter.

05. Even (after developing) a standardized analytical process, organic chemists still faced challenges (in their field). The most overwhelming (of these) was [that the substances released (during the distillation process) were complex compounds (of unknown purity), making it impossible (to accurately determine) the properties (of any one element) present (in the substances)]. Another major problem was determining the source (of the released materials). Were they present (in the original sample), or were they produced (through the process) (of distilling and destroying) organic material? This uncertainty led organic chemists (to search) (for ways) (to attain) these substances (without destroying) the original matter. Many other less violent methods (of distillation), (such as using) the lowest effective temperature (to distill) organic substances, were attempted, but did not fully overcome the problems [that were inherent (in the field)].

06. This problem led organic chemists (to consider) substances (such as blood, gelatin, and fat) (to be) constituent elements (in organisms) as late (as the 1830s). Today we recognize [that all (of these substances) are complex compounds composed (of various molecules) made (of a great number) (of atoms) (of true elements)]. (Due to this, and similar, problems), understanding the actual chemical makeup (of organic compounds) was much more complex and challenging [than it was (in the field) (of inorganic, or mineral-based, chemistry)]. The crucial breakthrough (in organic chemistry) came (in 1858) [when the concept (of chemical structures) (in carbon atoms) was simultaneously developed (by Friedrich August Kekule and Archibald Scott Couper)]. This allowed chemists (to more accurately understand) the ability (of carbon molecules) (to bond) together (in a carbon lattice) (through the observation and interpretation) (of chemical reactions).

TEST 3-1   El Niño   묶기

01.   The Humboldt Current carries cold water northward (from the Antarctic) (along South America's western coast). [As it reaches the equator], the easterly trade winds blow the surface water westward and allow an upwelling (of cold, nutrient-rich waters). The rise (of these nutritive waters) provides the abundant food sources [that are needed (to sustain) the nearly year-round commercial fishing industry (off the coasts) (of Peru and Chile)]. However, (during December and January), the cold waters are replaced (by a warmer countercurrent), greatly reducing the water's nutrient content and causing a lull (in commercial fishing) (due to the lack) (of commercially viable fish), (such as anchovies), (in the warmer water). Local residents termed this period "El Niño," or "the boy" (in Spanish), (due to its occurrence) (during the Christmas season), and use this downtime (to tend) (to their equipment).

02.   (Despite the traditionally short duration) (of El Niño), these warmer surface waters can linger and extend far (into the equatorial Pacific). (In fact), (over the past six decades), climatologists have identified (at least) ten unusually long El Niño periods. (In recent times), the traditional term (for this period), El Niño, has become identified worldwide (with these lengthy periods) (of warmer Pacific waters) more than (with the annual pattern), (because of the great changes) [they can cause (in weather patterns) (across the globe)].

03.   (Despite being known) mainly (as an eastern Pacific pattern), El Niño affects conditions (across the vast waters) (of the Pacific). One (of the first scientists) (to recognize) this was early-20th century British physicist Gilbert Walker, [who found an inverse correlation (between atmospheric pressure) (at weather stations) (in the eastern and western Pacific)]. Walker noted [that [as the pressure (of the eastern Pacific) fell], that (of the western Pacific) rose, and vice versa (in a see-saw-like pattern) [that he termed the Southern Oscillation]]. The relationship (between this phenomenon and El Niño) was later recognized (as being) so strong [that they are often referred to collectively (as the El Niño-Southern Oscillation)].

04.   Normally, the eastern Pacific's higher atmospheric pressure causes the easterly trade winds [that typify the wind pattern (of the southern equatorial region)]. These warm winds also cause the warm east-to-west surface current [that moves (across the Pacific Ocean) (along the equator)]. Eventually it causes an accumulation (of warm surface water) (in the western Pacific), [while the Humboldt Current's upwelling keeps surface temperatures (in the eastern Pacific) much lower]. [When the Southern Oscillation shifts and pressure rises (in the west)], the pressure gradient (across the ocean) is disrupted and the trade winds [that were caused (by it)] are severely weakened or reversed. (With these) no longer pushing westward (on the warmer surface water) it begins (to creep) eastward, marking the beginning (of El Niño). [As the warmer waters slide eastward], they further decrease the pressure and temperature gradients (across the Pacific Ocean) (in a positive feedback loop). The pressure gradient [that causes the winds] is decreased [as the eastern Pacific becomes warmer], [which further decreases the pressure gradient and the winds].

05. [Since this process was first theorized], scientists have attempted (to trace) it using historical records. (By examining) records (of the daily surface temperature (of the ocean), rainfall, atmospheric pressure, and fisheries data) (from South American inhabitants and Spanish colonists) dating as far back (as the 1400s), they have pieced together a detailed timeline (of El Niño) (over the past six centuries). (From this), it is clear [that [although El Niño occurred regularly (throughout history)] its frequency is increasing]. Comparing the records (of the 16th century) (to modern ones) shows [that El Niño is now occurring nearly three times more often [than it did] then, occurring just (over every 2 years) now, but occurring (in six year intervals) historically]. An even more alarming finding is [that the temperature increase's severity is rising]. This is troubling [because scientists now know [that El Niño's effects are not limited (to the southern Pacific), but also affect worldwide weather patterns]]. (During the 1997-98 El Nino), (for instance), the entire United States suffered (from more severe seasonal weather).

06. Modern researchers have pointed (to even more reasons) (to fear) a stronger El Niño. It appears [that El Niño also coincides (with increased epidemics, especially those caused (by mosquito-borne pathogens), civil conflict, and violence)]. One (of the most well-researched aspects) (of this) has been El Nino's effect (on malaria). Scientists have proven [that a 1°C increase (in the ocean's surface temperature) yields a 20% increase (in malaria) (around the tropical Pacific's coasts)]. Others have noted [that the risk (of civil unrest and violence) doubles (to 6%) (during El Niño)]. They blame this (on the widespread famine) [that occurs (during these periods)]. They point (to the Northern Chinese Famine) (of 1876) [that killed 13 million] and the El Niño effects) (of 1789-1793) [that led (to crop failures), [which eventually sparked the French Revolution]], (as evidence) (of this). (In modern times), it has been found [that El Nino's effects have triggered 21% (of conflicts) worldwide (since 1950)].

TEST 3-2 England's Sixteenth Century Economy 묶기

01. Great changes occurred (in England) (during the Late Tudor Period) (under the reign) (of Queen Elizabeth I) (in the latter half) (of the sixteenth) and early seventeenth centuries). One (of the most notable) was the increase (in the population) (to nearly that) (of the pre-Black Death period). (In England and Wales), increased fertility and reduced mortality rates nearly doubled the population (around this time), increasing (from 2.5 million) (in the 1520s) (to 4.5 million) (by 1610). This dramatic increase, along (with other factors) led (to vast changes) (in England's economy) and allowed it (to become) Europe's largest, far surpassing those (of the war and plague-ravaged continent).

02. One (of the first direct effects) (of the population increase) was a demand (for more food). This caused an "agricultural revolution" (in England) 2-300 years [before they occurred elsewhere (in Europe)]. (During this period), English farmers created farmlands (from previously unsuitable areas), (such as marshlands and woodlands), giving them more arable land [(on which) (to produce) food]. These farmers undertook a process (of crop specialization) [that allowed them (to be) more efficient and market-driven, increasing their yields dramatically]. (For instance), they increased their grain production (per acre) (by at least 30%) (between 1450 and 1650).

03. (With the greater efficiency) (of the new farming methods), wealthy landowners increased their landholdings (in order to increase) their agricultural productivity. These landholdings were consolidated (through the practice) (of primogeniture) [(under which) the eldest son inherited the entirety (of his father's holdings), thus preventing the great estates (from being divided up) (into smaller parcels) [which could not produce as much income]. They also increased the size (of their landholdings) (by marrying) (into other families) (with large estates). Marriages (amongst the wealthiest Elizabethan families) were arranged (to ensure) [that both families maintained their social statuses]. (With their larger estates), these families could conduct more commercialized farming (to meet) the demand (for agricultural products), [which was driving prices higher].

04. These large landowners, and the yeomen [who had smaller landholdings], maximized the profits [they could draw (from their property)]. (To increase) their profits, they planted crops [which were (in demand) (in the London markets)]. They also aggressively dealt (with those) [(to whom) they rented their properties]. (During this period), rents were increased and rental contracts were written (to provide) even more benefits (to the landowners). One (of the ways) [they did this] was shortening the duration

(of their contracts) (to allow) themselves more control (over the land). Another way [they maximized their profits] was (to charge) potential tenants an "entry fee" [before they would even consent (to renting) (to them)]. Renters [who could not, or would not, abide (by the new contracts)] were simply evicted and replaced (by those) [who could]. Their tactics were quite one-sided, but they also encouraged their tenants (to use) farming practices [that would increase their farming efficiency, (such as crop rotation)].

05. Another method used (to increase) the profits (of these large landholdings) was (to convert) some (of the farmland) (into pastureland) [(upon which) sheep could graze]. This conversion became possible (because of the enclosure movement) [that occurred (during the Tudor period)]. (In the process) (of enclosure), open fields [that had previously been used (for communal farming, grazing and hay production)] were fenced and their use became the sole right (of the owner). (Seeing the growing demands) (for English wool) internationally, landholders often considered rearing sheep (as a more profitable way) (to utilize) their land. (By converting) their land (into pastureland) they could derive a higher profit [while reducing the need (for large numbers) (of workers) (to tend) it].

06. Wool production led (to even greater changes) (in the English economy) (of the time). [While English wool had been exported (since (at least) the 1200s)], the form [it was exported in] began (to change). Wool was traditionally exported (in its raw form), but (around this time) the production and export (of finished textiles) overtook the English economy. This occurred (through the cottage industry system) [(under which) a cloth manufacturer "put-out" work (to rural craftspeople) [who were provided (with raw wool), [which they carded, spun, and wove (in their own homes)]]]. This reduced textile costs [because it effectively cut out the guilds [that controlled urban trade (by creating) monopolies and preventing) competition (between guild members)]].

07. (During this period), the extent (of England's international trade) increased so markedly [that companies, (such as the Muscovy Company and the English East India Company), were chartered (to develop) monopolistic trade routes (for English goods), (such as wool textiles), (with faraway places) (like Moscow and India)]. One (of the major markets) (for these textiles) was the Spanish-controlled city (of Antwerp), [where they were dyed and sold]. Antwerp was so important a point [that the English kept a representative stationed there permanently, Sir Thomas Gresham]. Gresham increased England's reputation (in Antwerp) (to the point) [that English merchants were able (to operate) (on a credit-based system) there, something very rare (in the 16th century)]. He also championed the economic possibilities (of the Americas), leading (to England's early attempts) (to colonize) the continents (for commercial purposes).

TEST 4-1 Environmental Impact of the Anasazi

01. The Anasazi people, ancient Native Americans who resided in pit houses, pueblos, and cliff dwellings, flourished in America's present-day Four Corners region before suddenly abandoning their elaborate villages and palace complexes. Archeologists long thought that studies of the rings of the trees used in the structures found there indicated that these people had been driven from their villages and home region, due to a climatic event known as the "Great Drought". This, however, began to be called into question recently. Today, historians believe that the Anasazi evacuation had been an ongoing event before the "Great Drought" and that the drought was not an unprecedented event; villagers had likely survived others before it. This has left them researching what could have actually caused an entire civilization to abandon its home territory. Archeologist Tim Kohler has come up with one possible explanation, human interaction with the natural environment.

02. Kohler believes that the Anasazi's interactions with their surroundings eventually led to their downfall. To support his hypothesis, Kohler put forth a case study regarding the Anasazi living in southwestern Colorado's Dolores River basin around 600 A.D.. Over a few hundred years, their population increased greatly and they built large villages complete with kivas and Great Houses, until around 900 A.D. when the area's abandonment began. Many archeologists believe that shortened growing seasons occurred during this era, which would have made it difficult to produce the main Anasazi staple, corn. Kohler takes exception to this theory, however, and points to problems that developed due to this growing population's settlement in villages, which caused a pressing need for increased agricultural output, forcing changes in the Anasazi's interactions with the environment, leading to deforestation, soil depletion, and their eventual abandonment of the area.

03. Prior to their settlement, the Anasazi population had been semi-nomadic in the Dolores River basin, farming the reasonably fertile, thin soils of the flat-topped mesas using the swidden, or slash-and-burn, technique for over 1,000 years. Using this method, they burned down forests to plant the crops they needed and utilized the new farmland until it became unsuitable for producing crops, at which time they moved on to an adjacent area and repeated the process, allowing the previous area to lie fallow and replenish the nutrients necessary for its future use. This may appear to be a destructive way of growing food that ruins the land, but with less dense populations and a schedule of movement) [that allows the land adequate time (for replenishment) (between planting)], swidden is a sustainable means (of acquiring) the food [that societies need]. Kohler's contention was [that the permanent settlement (of a large, growing population) (like the Dolores River basin Anasazi) relying (upon this method) would lead (to their eventual destruction)].

04. Kohler found several types (of evidence) (to show) [that changes (in human-environmental interactions) were more responsible (for the Anasazi disappearance) (than climatic events)]. Surprisingly, his first source was the same (as the one) [that had led archeologists astray], trees. Kohler noted a pattern (in the types) (of wood) found (in charcoal deposits) (from different periods). It seemed [that juniper and pinion pine were replaced (by faster growing shrubbery and cottonwoods)]. He also discovered [that the Anasazi switched (from using) pinion pines (for construction) (to younger juniper trees), a less desirable wood source, but one [that is more fire resistant and easier (to propagate) (in open settings)]]. This, likely, indicated [that the pinion became scarcer (around the village) [as the growing population's demand increased]]. This would have also affected their food supply [as pinion seeds were also gathered (as a food source)]. Additionally, their clearing (of the surrounding areas) would have had an impact (on their hunting) (as well). [As time progressed], the Anasazi apparently switched (from hunting) woodland rabbits and deer (to jackrabbits and antelope), species native (to open environments). Seeds excavated (from the settlements) provided Kohler's final piece (of evidence). (During excavation) (of later settlements), a marked increase (in pioneer species seeds) was found, indicating a disturbance (in the natural environment).

05. Kohler postulates [that the Anasazi aggregated (in villages) (due to the organizational benefits) [they offered] (in the face) (of soil depletion) (during their early periods)]. These large settlements allowed them (to share) food, invest) (in group food processing units) and pool) their labor (for longer distance hunting or trading trips). Settling (in one area), however, brought about new problems, (like soil depletion and increased distance) (to usable fields), [which led (to increased agricultural risk)]. This led (to agricultural intensification) using methods, (such as developing) mechanisms (to better control) water flow. These larger villages (with more technical agricultural methods) produced more food, but were more susceptible (to a rapid collapse). The cooperative management (of resources) (for the village) meant [that they were less flexible (in response) (to environmental changes)], so a weak growing season had a widespread impact (on the village). (For this reason), even a minor, predictable climate change could have led the Anasazi (to abandon) their settlements.

TEST 4-2 Global Variations in Species Diversity

01. A peculiar aspect (of the world today) is the presence (of a gradient), or gradual change, (in species diversity) (from the tropics) (to the polar areas). Species population surveys have shown [that regions (nearer the equator) have the highest species diversity, and [as one moves (to higher latitudes)], diversity drops off dramatically]. This gradient can be seen (across all species), both flora and fauna, and (from higher-level mammals) (to lower order protozoans).

02. One (of the first explanations) (for this) was [that temperature and light stability (in tropical regions), [when compared (to the seasonal fluctuations) (of both) (in polar regions)], allowed more species (to develop)]; however, temperature and light do not seem (to fully control) species diversity. This can be seen (by looking) (at the seas) (in polar regions), [which remain (at a nearly constant temperature) year-round yet still have low species diversity]. It may then seem logical [that the northern seas' near-freezing temperatures preclude diversity levels as high (as those) (of the tropics)], but [as one moves deeper (to the seafloor)], [which remains (in perpetual, frigid darkness) (with neither light nor warmth) (from the sun)], there is relatively higher species diversity. Therefore, another important factor, (such as the availability) (of food), must affect species diversity.

03. One aspect (of the food supply) [that could affect the diversity (of species)] is [that (in tropical regions), the food supply remains relatively stable year-round (due to the uniform climate)]. (Because of this), species can specialize (in feeding) (on one food source) (without the risk) (of it) not being available (at various times) (of year). [As they become more dependent (on their food sources)], species adapt more fully and become highly specialized. This allows multiple species (to feed) (on one food source) but only marginally compete) (with one another). This can be seen (in the various carrion- feeding vultures) (of the African plains). [Although various species (of vultures) are present (on the Serengeti)], they have developed different niches. (For example), one species has a beak [that can tear (through leathery hides)] and a head devoid (of feathers), [which allows them (to stick) their heads (into the carcass) and not worry) (about becoming) contaminated [because the sun will bake the refuse (from their baldheads)]]. Another has adapted (to feeding) (on the innards), [while still others consume the bones and random scraps]. [Even though they are all eating (from the same carcasses)], they are all ensured a constant supply (of food) [because their niche specializations effectively lower the competition rate].

04. Species [that live (in higher latitudes)], (on the other hand), face a constantly changing food supply. (During the warmer season), tundra species have a plethora (of food sources), (such as plant life and newly hatched krill), [which are fed on (by animals) (such as caribou, seabirds, fish, and oceanic mammals)]. However, [when the long, frigid winter sets in], the area is rather barren, leading many specialized feeders (to migrate) (to other areas). There are, however, animals (with a more generalist feeding style) [that remain (in the tundra) year-round, seasonally adapting their feeding patterns]. The gray wolf, (for example), switches (from consuming) small mammals and migratory birds (during the warmer months) (to hunting) weakened caribou (during the winter). This assures them (of constant food supplies) (throughout the year). These distinct feeding patterns, therefore, do not limit species diversity, [since they allow a variety (of tundra species) (to coexist) (despite the relatively lower overall food supply)].

05. [Since the variability (in light, temperature, and food supply) does not necessarily reduce species diversity (in an area)], there must be another explanation (for the great latitudinal difference). One new theory is [that the evolutionary process itself caused this phenomenon]. The theory (of "effective evolutionary time") draws (upon earlier research) [that showed [that evolution occurs more quickly (in smaller species) [that inhabit warmer temperatures]]]. This likely occurs (due to the higher physiological rates) (of smaller species) (in tropical regions), [which lead (to shorter lifespans)]. A rather striking example (of this) is the freshwater pearl mussel, [which can inhabit freshwater streams (in a variety) (of latitudes)] and [whose maximum lifespan varies depending (on latitude), (from 29 years) (at 43°N) (to nearly 200) (at 66°N)]. This can also be seen (in plant species) (by comparing) the relatively shorter lifespans and earlier reproduction rates (of plants) (from tropical regions) (with those) (from northern latitudes), (such as the giant redwood) [which has been recorded (as living) (up to 3500 years)]. [While it may seem [that the lifespan differences (in a species) would have little effect (on overall diversity)]], it can be shown (to have) a great impact. The shorter lifespans (of species) (in warmer areas) result (in shorter generation lengths), thereby causing a higher mutation rate and speed (of selection) [than (in higher latitudes)]. This rapid mutation and selection enables distinct species (to be produced) much more quickly [than (in the colder northern regions)]. These new species then begin filling unexploited niches (in the tropical ecosystem) and become even more particularly adapted [as more generations are produced].

TEST 5-1 Documenting the Incas

01. Beginning with the founding of the capital city of Cusco in the early 1200s, the Inca Empire expanded along the mountainous west coast of South America. Within 250 years, their conquests of neighboring societies allowed them to control over 3,000 miles of coastline and land covering parts of present day Peru, Bolivia, Ecuador, Chile and Argentina. The power of their army and their effective administration of this vast empire made them the greatest of the New World civilizations. This great empire would, however, collapse less than 100 years later when the Spanish conquistador Francisco Pizarro arrived and conquered the area for Spain in the 1530s. Since the Inca language did not have writing system, much of what is currently known about this magnificent civilization was recorded by these Spanish conquerors. This has led to many problems related to the veracity of the historical records of the early Inca Empire.

02. The first of these is that the ruling system used by the Inca was different from that of the Spanish Empire and may not have been fully understood by the early conquerors. In order to record the historical information, they gleaned from their Inca informants. Then, they simply adapted the information to the Spanish style of governance. As time went on, these kinds of inaccuracies would have been compounded since most scholars would have used these recordings as primary sources for their later research. A good example of this is their list of Inca rulers. The Inca told the early conquerors of thirteen kings who ruled over the empire, and the Spanish recorded them as thirteen sequential rulers, as that was how the monarchy worked in Spain; however, it isn't clear if these recorded names were individuals or titles. If they were titles, they could have been held concurrently, and there may have been fewer than thirteen kings that ruled over the empire. Since the empire only flourished under the last four kings, this isn't a major problem in understanding the Inca culture, but it points to how cultural bias and inaccuracies regarding the Inca could have begun with the earliest recorded histories of them.

03. Another problem with the accounts compiled by the Spanish was that they may have been intentionally inaccurate. The Spanish wanted to downplay certain aspects of the Inca civilization, such as the extent of their wealth. If the conquistadors accurately recorded Incan gold production,

they would have had (to turn) it all over (to the Spanish Crown). (By downplaying) the extent (of the Inca's wealth), the conquistadors were able (to amass) their own gold caches. The inaccuracies may have also been the fault (of the Inca themselves). [Since they were helping their new conquerors], the Inca may have misled them (to make) themselves look better or exaggerated their importance (in society).

04. Relying (on elite members) (of the Incan society) (to learn) (about their history) caused another problem. [Since they had no written language system], all (of their historical information) had been passed down (through the oral tradition). (Over time), many (of these stories) may have developed unintentional inaccuracies. A prime example (of this) would be the founding (of Cusco), [which was said (to have happened) [after four brothers and four sisters emerged (from a cave) and led followers [they found (in another cave)] (to the site) (of Cusco) [where they founded their civilization]]]. The origin (of these early leaders and stories) (of their exploits) were likely exaggerated (to paint) them (in a more impressive light). (Because of the nature) (of the oral tradition), it is probable [that the more recent Incan stories were likely (to be) more accurate].

05. The Inca may have also whitewashed the accounts (of their expansion and conquest) (of neighboring settlements), (such as the Lupaca) (to their south). (Because of their policy) (of dispersing) uncooperative people and repopulating) the area (with people) [who they were able (to deal) with], the Incan leaders were the only sources (of Spanish knowledge) (of their empire) and were, therefore, able (to control) the description (of their conquests) and could portray themselves (as righteous and invincible warriors). This makes it all but impossible (to establish) the accuracy (of their narratives).

06. A final problem [that calls the truthfulness (of the Spanish-written histories) (into question)] is the incongruent uses (of place names). It seems [that different writers used various names (to describe) the areas, (such as provinces and towns) [that they encountered (in the Incan Empire)]]. This, compounded (with the great changes) (in the locations) (of settlements) (over the last five centuries), makes it difficult (to verify) any (of the location information) (in accounts) (of the Incan Empire).

07. (Despite the possibility) (of all) (of these inaccurate accounts) creeping (into the Spanish-written historical records) (of the Incan Empire), researchers still find them (to be) important source materials. (By cross-referencing) different accounts (of the same events) and using) archeological research, scientists can verify some (of the accounts) (to form) an accurate chronology and picture (of [what actually went on (during the Incan Empire)]).

TEST 5-2 Architectural Change in Eighth Century Japan

01. Japanese architecture underwent dramatic changes [as the Nara period began (in the early 8th century)]. (During this period), great political and societal changes, (such as the establishment) (of the capital) (at Heijo-kyo) (modern day Nara), made traditional architectural arrangements and styles less advantageous and necessitated a new system. (On this quest) (for more adequate architectural styles), the Japanese were influenced (by the architecture) (of continental Asian powers), (such as China's Tang Dynasty).

02. One (of the most glaring catalysts) (for the change) (in architectural styles) was the shift (in marriage practices) (of the Japanese elite). (Prior to this period), Japanese rulers married members (of one) (of the most powerful clans) (of the period), the Soga-lords' families, (in politically motivated alliances), and established palaces (at the bride's family home) (in addition to that) (of their own family headquarters). The royal court generally resided (with the bride's family) (for the first years) (of their marriage) and then moved (between their multiple palaces) (throughout the marriage) [as children grew older and alliances shifted]. This system was workable (during this period) (because of the relatively small royal court and rudimentary architectural styles).

03. (Prior to the Nara period), traditional Japanese structures, (such as palaces, gate towers, fortresses, and shrines) were built (with wooden beams, dirt floors, and thatched roofs). [Since these beams were (in direct contact) (with the moist ground)], they often rotted away (in less than 20 years). The simple, temporary nature (of these buildings) meant [that they could be moved or constructed (in new areas) (without great labor or material expenditures) and were easily rebuildable [when damaged]]. This was important (to Shinto adherents) [because replacing buildings allowed (for a spiritual cleansing) (of the land)]. This taboo (against unclean spirits) also led (to the continuous movement) (of the capital) (before the Nara period); new emperors moved the court (to avoid) contamination (from the death) (of their predecessors).

04. Moving the capital became unfeasible (during the Nara period) (due to the expansion) (of the bureaucracy) involved (in the court) (during the previous two centuries). [(By the time) the Nara emperors rose (to power)], they were overseeing a staff (of 10,000 workers) and needed a location [that provided adequate housing (for them)]. The need (to keep) (in contact) (with these people) and

(to provide) (for them) meant [that palaces needed (to be maintained) (in areas) (with abundant resources)]. Further, moving such a large court and reconstructing enough buildings (to house) them effectively killed the mobile capital tradition and led the emperors (to settle) (in Heijo-kyo).

05. (To construct) this imperial city, Japanese architects looked (to the urban design and construction techniques) (of their continental neighbors' geometrically situated capitals) (with their bulkier, more permanent buildings) constructed using stone foundations, mortise joints, and tiled roofs [which allowed them (to stand) (for years)]. The construction (of a large, continental-style capital) (with these types) (of buildings) required a tremendous amount (of manpower and building materials,) but it was attractive (to emperors) looking (to legitimize) their reigns (in a manner) directly comparable (to the powerful Chinese dynasty). The construction (of these types) (of buildings) was also heavily influenced (by the widespread acceptance) (of Buddhism) [which had been introduced (from the continental kingdoms) two hundred years earlier]. (After this) the Japanese officially adopted Buddhism, but conflicts (with hostile believers) (in the Shinto Kami) prevented them (from building) lasting Buddhist temples. (During the Nara period), the Japanese Buddhists built temple complexes modeled (after those) found (in continental nations), (such as the Horyu-ji,) one (of the oldest surviving wooden structures) (in the world).

06. This shift (in architecture) (during this period) caused a series (of conflicts) (across the Japanese royal court). Rulers wished (to display) their power (through the construction) (of a grand capital) rivaling that (of the Tang Dynasty), but this was difficult (at the time) and required a great expenditure. (In addition), [while the opulent lifestyle (of the new building styles) would have been comfortable (for the ruling class)], they were hesitant (to give up) the multiple palaces [they enjoyed (under the mobile court system)]. Conflicts even arose (between religions) (because of the Shinto belief) (in replacing) buildings frequently and the Buddhists' desire) (for permanent religious buildings). Eventually, these conflicts were solved (through a compromise) (in building methods). Shinto shrines, (with their religious reliance) (on rebuilding and cleansing), and many residential buildings adhered (to the traditional style) [that was more economical, mobile, and replaceable]. Government buildings, city gates, and Buddhist temples, (on the other hand), were constructed (in the more permanent, grandiose continental style). Even the issues related (to the immobility) (of the court) were solved (through an architectural compromise). Rulers, [who were now (in residence) (in the grand capital)], constructed smaller palaces (in remote areas) [where they could temporarily reside]. This gave the court a bit (of mobility) and may have made it easier (for them) (to oversee) the parts (of their populations) [which lived far away (from the new capital city)].

TEST 6-1   How Camels Survive in Arid Environments 묶기

01. Their ability (to survive) extreme temperatures and food or water deprivation has made camels invaluable (in Asia, Africa, and the Middle East). These large animals come (in two varieties), Central Asia's two-humped Bactrian and the single-humped desert dromedaries (of Africa and the Middle East), [which were independently domesticated 5,000 years ago]. They have since acted (as beasts of burden), desert transport, and sources) (of wool, leather, milk and meat) [because they, (unlike other livestock), have specialized mechanisms (for survival) (in desert environments)].

02. Their first adaptation is their ability (to go) (for long periods) (without water). (Unlike most animals), the camel can go (without water) (for two weeks) (without negative effects). This is possible [because they can drink up to 200 liters (of water) (at once)]. [When they drink these great amounts], some (of the water) is rapidly transferred (to their blood streams) and carried (throughout the body) (to hydrate) the bodily tissues. This is unique [because (in most animals) such a dilution (of the bloodstream) would cause a fatal rupturing (of the red blood cells)]. However, camels' specially adapted red blood cells can survive this and have a unique ovoid shape, compared (to the rounder red blood cells) (of most animals), [which allows them (to flow) more freely (during times) (of dehydration)].

03. Camels also handle water loss better (than most animals). (In humans), (for instance), a 2% water loss stresses the body and anything more (than 12%) is fatal, but camels can survive losing 25% (of their bodies' water content). This is (because of [how their bodies lose water]). (Unlike most animals), camels metabolize the water (between cells) and (in their guts), rather (than the water) (in their cells). (By protecting) the cellular water content, their bodies are able (to function) properly even (after dramatic water losses).

04. (In addition to being) able (to cope) (with water loss), camels have special abilities and adaptations [which prevent it]. The most obvious (of these) is the fact [that camels sweat very little]. They also have efficient digestive systems [which produce very dry, concentrated urine and feces]. Camel feces is so dry [that it can be lit and used (as fuel) (for fires) almost immediately (after being deposited)]. Another way [they conserve water] is (through their respiratory system). (In most animals), a large amount (of

water) is exhaled (during respiration), giving the breath a relative humidity (of nearly 100%). Camels, (on the other hand), breathe relatively slowly, reducing the number (of exhaled breaths) and have specialized scrolled nasal bones called turbinates, [which increase the nasal cavity surface area, (to nearly 1000 sq. cm.), and capture moisture (from the exhaled air), reducing its relative humidity (up to 25%), and hydrate the dry desert air [which they breathe in]]. The network (of capillaries) (in their cooler nasal cavities) also keeps the brain cooler (through heat diffusion).

05. There is, perhaps, no better known, or misunderstood, camel adaptation (to heat and dehydration) (than the hump). Commonly thought (to hold) water, these humps are actually fat accumulations. (Unlike other animals), [which are covered (by a layer) (of fat)], camels store theirs (in their humps). Fat cells hold (in body heat), so (by having) most (of their fat) concentrated (on their backs), camels can more easily dissipate heat, reducing their internal temperatures. Water is also produced [when this fat is metabolized], but it is all used up (in the process).

06. Camels also deal (with heat) rather uniquely. Most mammals maintain a stable internal temperature and utilize physical processes, (such as panting, sweating, or exposing) more skin (to open air) (in shaded regions), (to maintain) their temperatures as close (to the ideal) as possible. These methods reduce the animal's temperature but also cause water loss. Camels, (on the other hand), avoid this (by having) an internal temperature [that varies more widely (than other mammals)]. The diurnal variation (in a camels' temperature) can be as high (as 6°C). This wide temperature fluctuation would mean major problems (for most other species). (In humans), (for instance), an internal temperature increase (of even half this much) can cause brain damage and even death. Scientists believe [that this fluctuation reduces the need (for sweating and panting), [which saves camels as much (as 5L) (of water) (per day)]].

07. Their physical features and actions not only dissipate heat but also avoid gaining heat altogether. Their tall, spindly legs keep their cores aloft, [where air temperatures are cooler, and their uninsulated nearly hairless underbellies dissipate heat quickly]. Further, their thin, light-colored wool doesn't absorb much heat and protects the skin (from the effects) (of the sun). The fat (in their hump) also absorbs heat [before it reaches the core, [where it would increase the internal temperature]]. This is compounded (by their natural proclivity) (for standing) facing the sun, [which reduces the amount (of surface area) directly exposed (to the sun's rays)].

TEST 6-2 Hunter-gatherers in Southwest Asia

01. (During the end) (of the last glacial period), the Kebaran Civilization flourished (in the area) (of Southwest Asia) now known (as the Middle East). This population was (to have) a large influence (on humanity), (because of their early consumption) (of cereals) and their tool development). Being a nomadic civilization, they moved (across a multitude) (of climates) (over the course) (of the year), spending their summers (in the cooler highlands) and their winters (in the rocky waterside caves). This migration required them (to adapt) tools (to suit) each location. These were likely used (to hunt) gazelle and harvest) wild cereals. Human consumption (of these cereals) became so important [that they currently make up 50% and 56% (of the world's protein and food energy consumption), respectively].

02. (Despite the dietary changes) [they caused], the Kebaran society did not remain forever. Around 13,000 BC, a warmer, wetter period saw the rise (of the Natufian Culture). Their appearance coincided (with the shift) (in plant life) (in the area). [As temperatures rose], plants [that required the warmer temperatures (of lower altitudes)] spread (to higher altitudes). The production (of pistachios, oak, almonds, wild barley and wild emmer wheat) flourished [as they moved (from the lower altitude's sandy soil) (to the richer, clay-based soil) (of higher altitudes)]; these increased harvests allowed the Natufian Culture (to expand) (as well). (Within 1,500 years), the culture had completely replaced the Kebaran and spread (from the mountains) (to the Mediterranean).

03. This culture proved (to be) more sedentary (than its predecessors). This is an interesting case (in history), [since they settled (before the advent) (of farming), relying instead (on harvesting) wild nuts and grains]. Their entire society adapted a new hunting and gathering technique based (on larger settlements) [that could harvest more (of the crops)]. These new settlements featured semi-subterranean pit-houses and pits [where the crops could be stored]. These large settlements were also generally located (near smaller satellite camps) [where they could collect and process their finds]. Artifacts (from these camps) show [that the Natufians greatly increased the sophistication (of their tools) and confirmed their dietary reliance (on grains)]. They were even found (to have created) processing tools, (such as grinding stones), and harvesting tools, (like the flint blade sickle). [While these tools could be useful (on a multitude) (of plants)], their use (for cereal harvesting) has been proven (by the presence) (of "sickle gloss") (on their blades). This is [when a flint blade becomes shiny (due to the build-up) (of silica particles) (from cereal grass stalks)].

04. The village locations were also affected (by the crops) [they relied upon]. They were generally located (along the boundary) (between the coastal grasslands and the higher altitudes) [where nuts and cereals prospered]. They also seemed (to settle) (in places) [where they could collect high quality stone (for creating) new tools]. (By settling) (in these places), they could harvest the cereal crops [as they came (into season) (during the spring)] and harvest nuts (in the fall), providing year-round nourishment. (In addition to using) their stored crops (in summer and winter), they also hunted the lowland animals [that fed (on the nuts and cereals)]. They would even cooperate (with neighboring communities) (to perform) massive game drives and ambushes (on gazelles and other animals).

05. Year-round food sources led (to a Natufian population boom). [As the population increased], a new, highly complex social structure developed. This was discovered (through excavation) (of Natufian cemeteries), [where evidence was found [that indicated differences (in social standing) (between tribe members)]]. Certain burial sites contained the symbolic dentalium seashell, [while others, even those (of children), were filled (with elaborate furnishings) (such as stone bowls)], showing a clear difference (in societal standing) (of the deceased). These rankings may have been the result (of the food redistribution and efforts) (to maintain) order [that would have been required (by such a large sedentary community)]. These cemeteries also contained limestone grave covers and mortar markers, [which are thought (to have served) (as ritualistic territorial markers) (for the lands) held (by the Natufian's highlyrespected elders) [after they passed]].

06. Eventually, [as their population expanded], the Natufians faced another dramatic lifestyle upheaval (due to climate change). Around 11,000 BC, the climate (around the Mediterranean) began (to dry out). This reduced the area, [(in which) the wild grains and nuts grew], and increased the society's need (to settle) (near a reliable water source). This could have spelled the end (of the Natufian society) very quickly [had they not learned the life cycle (of the cereal plants) (over the previous two millennia) (of living off of and with them)]. Instead, they were able (to deliberately plant and control) the cereal plants. Even the modest scale (of this early farming) helped the society supplement their declining wild wheat and barley harvests and thus ensured their survival. (Within a short time), farming flourished (in Southwest Asia), and full-scale farming societies appeared, leading (to more civilized hunter-gatherer/ farming communities) (in the area), [where the Natufians developed the world's first dedicated form (of agriculture)].

TEST 7-1 Life on Mars

01. (Since the beginning) (of time), humans have wondered [if they were alone (in the universe)]. (In the modern times), cosmologists and astrophysicists, Stephen Hawking and Carl Sagan, have claimed [that extraterrestrial life is not only possible but probable]. They base their theories (on the Mediocrity, or Copernican, Principle), [which states [that [because life developed (on Earth)], it is likely (to develop) or has already developed (on planets) (with similar molecular structures) [where the laws (of physics) work similarly]]. Astronomers believe [that over 40 million Earth-sized planets orbiting Sun-like stars (in their habitable zones), the regions [where atmospheric pressures allow liquid surface water], may exist (in the Milky Way) alone]. One (in particular) has inspired scientists (to search) (for signs) (of life), Mars.

02. Contrary (to popular belief), Mars and Earth are remarkably similar. [Although Earth is much larger (than Mars)], they have nearly identical land surfaces. They also share similar atmospheric chemistry [when compared (to other planets) (in our solar system)]. Further, Mars is subject (to seasonal temperature variations) (like Earth's) (due to its 25° axis tilt), [which is only 1.5° different (than Earth's 23.5° tilt)]. A more important similarity [that could allow life (on Mars)] is the fact [that both planets orbit (in the Sun's habitable zone), [which could allow Martian surface water (in addition to the water) frozen (in its polar ice caps)]].

03. (Despite these similarities), Mars' conditions are currently very inhospitable. The most glaring problem is [that the current Martian atmosphere is deadly (for Earth-based organisms)]. The thin, carbon dioxide (CO_2)-heavy composition (of the atmosphere), (besides being) toxic (to oxygen-dependent organisms), does not retain solar heat [when it is not directly exposed (to the Sun)]; therefore, nighttime temperatures drop precipitously and the average surface temperature is a frigid -30°C. (In addition), Mars' minimal atmosphere does little (to prevent) deadly ultraviolet solar radiation (from reaching) its surface (in the way) [that ozone gases (in Earth's atmosphere) do]. This is compounded (by Mars' lack) (of the type) (of magnetic field) [that protects the Earth (from the effects) (of solar flares) [that further destroy its environment]].

04. Another major problem [that prevents life (on Mars)] is the dearth (of liquid surface water). [While the ice caps do contain a tremendous amount of water and CO_2], scientists have been unable to find liquid water on Mars' surface, but this does not mean it never existed. Scientists believe that Earth's surface water was the result of venting from early volcanoes and have no reason to believe that this couldn't have happened on Mars, since there are now extinct volcanoes scattered across its surface. In addition, if its atmosphere was once thicker, it may have trapped enough solar heat to allow the water locked up in polar ice caps to form the rivers and seas whose effects are currently seen on the Martian landscape. In fact, craters left by meteoroids that struck the eroded areas of the surface, where it is assumed water once ran, show that they must have struck after the water disappeared and have been dated to several hundred million, if not a billion, years old.

05. These factors, however, do not necessarily prohibit the presence of life on Mars. While most organisms require protection from solar forces and access to water and oxygen, it is not a universal need. Bacteria that require CO_2 instead of oxygen have been discovered, and some organisms may be able to draw enough water from the trace amounts found in surface rocks. Further, protection from solar radiation can occur through a mechanism as simple as developing an outer shell or living under the surface to reduce the effects of solar radiation.

06. Another theory allowing life on Mars is the possibility of Earthlike conditions in the past. Scientists have discovered signs of flowing surface water, but Mars could have been even more Earthlike at one time. A change could have occurred as CO_2 became trapped in rocks. Since Mars lacks the tectonic and volcanic activity that cycles CO_2 in the Earth's atmosphere, the atmosphere could have been depleted of gaseous CO_2, over time, which would have reduced the greenhouse effect and destabilized the atmosphere, allowing most of it to dissipate over time. This could have allowed a gradual disappearance of water from Mars' surface or its absorption below Mars' crust, where it may still exist, until life became unsustainable.

07. Unfortunately, the two Viking spacecraft found no traces of life, either current or past, on the Martian surface. It was, however, found that the surface soil was self-sterilizing because the harsh solar radiation on the surface reacts with its minerals and destroys all organic matter. Interestingly, though, they did discover elements which would be necessary to support life, namely nitrogen and phosphorous. From these tests, the most that can be hypothesized is that even though the current conditions on Mars cannot currently support life, it may have been possible at some point in the past.

TEST 7-2 Agriculture and Settlement around the Nile River 묶기

01. The lush vegetation of the Nile River valley stands in marked contrast to the barren white sands of the nearby Sahara. Surprisingly, this contrast was the impetus for the development of settlements and domesticated agriculture across Africa. Researchers have concluded that the Sahara previously had ample water supplies and attracted inhabitants from the surrounding areas; however, as conditions declined and the region became more arid, these people were driven out and forced to find new, fertile places to settle. The Nile valley filled this role and allowed these people to support themselves while they waited for the Saharan conditions to improve again.

02. These changes reveal one surprising aspect of the shift to agriculture and dependence on food production in Egypt; it did not begin in the Nile valley as is commonly assumed. The process of moving from a nomadic culture into one with established villages using technology to domesticate and produce the livestock and plants required for such a lifestyle actually began further west in what is now the arid Sahara. Prior to the last glacial period, the Sahara was conducive to inhabitation due to its abundant vegetation, grasslands and woodlands, all of which encouraged nomadic groups to remain along its lakes, where they were guaranteed sufficient water and food from the lake and its surrounding areas as they hunted and gathered. The area's eventual desertification forced these people and nearly all of the local wildlife to flee to a more suitable area, such as the fertile Nile River valley. Once they arrived in the river valley they had little choice but to settle in one place. Here, they were boxed in on the narrow floodplain by the hostile deserts, the river, and settlers that were living around them, all of which restricted their ability to wander and gather food.

03. Another aspect of the Nile Valley's settlement was the tremendous change that the river went through. Today, most people know that the Nile is the longest river in the world, but at the time it was much smaller and slower, running through a series interconnected riverbeds across the floodplain, instead of today's massive river. Eventually the sediment and silt carried through these channels aggregated and built up the floodplain, raising the river's level considerably. This allowed lush vegetation to grow along the floodplain and turned the Nile valley into an oasis sandwiched between the inhospitable Sahara and Eastern deserts, stretching 800 km from the present day Sudan to Cairo.

[As time wore on], settlers (in this area) became dependent (upon the river) and separated their year (into three sections) based (upon its actions): the inundation [when the overflowing river spread silt (across the floodplain)], the growing season [when they tended their crops (in the sediment-filled fields)], and harvest time [when they collected the bounty provided (by the nutrients) [the river had brought them]].

04. (In this valley), early settlers cultivated food crops [that had been previously domesticated (in Southwest Asia), namely wheat, barley, peas, and lentils. These crops' ability (to flourish) (in the Nile valley) sustained these early civilizations (for generations), and they remain important components (of the Egyptian diet) even (to this day). [As time went by], these settlements grew and used the river (for transportation). This allowed them (to introduce) these crops (to settlements farther south), [where people had relied (upon the cultivation) (of plants) native (to the African environment)].

05. This verdant area also provided (for the settlers' other dietary needs). [Since the strip (of land) was narrow], the number (of large mammals) [that could establish territories (in this area)] was limited. (In fact), the remains (of only three large species) have been found, the Dorcas gazelle, aurochs-a type of wild cattle, and the hartebeest. Settlers, therefore, relied (on other protein sources), (such as birds and fish). [While migratory birds, (like ducks and geese), were regularly taken], fish were the primary protein source, especially catfish. (In addition), the seasonal variety (of plant) (in the area) gave them access (to an abundance) (of carbohydrate-rich foods). More (than twenty varieties) (of edible plants, seeds, fruit, and vegetables) have been excavated (from the ruins) (of these early settlements).

06. Eventually, the fertile soils and predictable flooding (of the river) allowed the settlers (to develop) an empire [whose wealth was based (on the great agricultural bounty) [it was able (to reap)]]. Today, Ancient Egyptians are regarded (as one) (of the first civilizations) (to practice) widespread agriculture. They developed advanced farming techniques (such as basin irrigation), [which put them (in control) (of the river level) and allow them (to utilize) it (in a way) [that best suited their needs]. These new developments allowed them (to grow) not only food crops but also industrial and fabric crops (for use) (in cooking, medicine, and construction). The most well-known (of these) was papyrus, [parts (of which) were used (as food), (as a material) (for construction) and (as a medium) (for writing). These developments spread (outside of the Nile valley) and changed African and world civilizations forever.

Sea Turtle Navigation

01. (For centuries), oceanic navigation has been one (of the biggest challenges) (to seafarers) (around the world) [because navigation (on the high seas) is more difficult [than (on land)]]. Yet, (since the early cretaceous period), the sea turtle has successfully travelled (across vast oceans) moving (between foraging sites and nesting areas). This amazing ability has justifiably intrigued scientists (for years). Celestial navigation, based (on observing) the positions (of the Sun, Moon, and stars), has not been accepted (as a method) employable (by sea turtles) (due to their poor eyesight). Another theory suggests [that dissolved traces (of unique odors) (from the turtles' destinations) guide them], but this has also not gained much support [because dispersal (of the odors) (in the ocean) would create a convoluted path] and could, therefore, not explain [how sea turtles migrate (in a more-or-less straight line) (to their destination)]. Furthermore, depending (on ocean currents), the odor trails may be travelling (in the same direction) (as the turtles), thus never reaching them.

02. One theory, however, has gained support (from the scientific community). Studies have found small amounts (of a magnetic compound) called magnetite (in the brains) (of a few species) (of sea turtles). This compound, [which is also found (in pigeons, honeybees, and a variety (of other animals))], is known (to play) a crucial role (in navigation). It was shown [that, sea turtle hatchlings, [when placed (inside a pool) (within a magnetic chamber), altered their course (in response) (to changes) (in the chamber's magnetic field)]]. [What makes sea turtles' utilization (of magnetite) interesting] is the fact [that it is so precise [that sea turtles (in the vast ocean) can measure not only the intensity (of the magnetic pull) but also the difference (in the angle) (of the magnetic poles)]]. Previously, scientists thought [that magnetite could only be used (as a compass), providing directional information, but this ability allows turtles (to orient) themselves (within a more detailed magnetic map) (of Earth).

03. (To study) the role (of magnetite) (in sea turtle navigation further), Floriano Papi and a team (of biologists) designed an experiment (in the late 1990s), [(in which) green sea turtles travelling (from Ascension Island) back (to Brazil) were fitted (with strong magnets) (on their heads)]. Papi believed [that the magnet would inhibit the turtle's ability (to calculate) their position (on Earth). Surprisingly, however, the magnets made no difference (to the migratory performance) (of the turtles). The findings demonstrated [that the magnetite theory is not devoid (of shortcomings)]. Substantial evidence both (for and against magnetic navigation) led (to the theory) [that [while magnetic positioning plays a vital role (in the open sea)], far away (from the destination), sea turtles use several other methods (to complement) it [when they are young] or [when they are close (to land)]].

04. [When sea turtles are born], they must immediately make their way (into deep waters) (to escape) predators (on land) and (in coastal waters). Scientists hypothesize [that the hatchlings calculate the direction (towards water) (by using) light intensity (as a cue). The juveniles are thought (to instinctively head) (towards light) [because moonlight reflecting (against the water) means [that the ocean is brighter (than land)]]. Unfortunately, hatchlings have been reported (to be disoriented) (by artificial light) coming (from human-occupied islands), severely decreasing their chances (for survival). (In the shallow coastal waters), the juvenile turtles detect the direction, [(in which) the waves push them (to calculate) [which direction they must swim (to get) (to deep waters)]].

05. [When the turtle is making its way (to land) either (to forage) or (to lay) eggs], it uses the magnetite (along with auditory and olfactory cues). It is hypothesized [that turtles use both the low-frequency sounds (of waves) hitting the beach and the smell coming (from land) (to pinpoint) the location (of their destination)].

06. The mysteries (of sea turtle navigation) do not end (with their navigation methods), but also extend (to navigation patterns), [as can be seen (in the mitochondrial DNA) (mtDNA-genetic material [that is inherited solely (from the maternal parent)) and is, therefore, identical (in close relatives) (of hawksbill turtles) (in the Persian Gulf)]]. Each hawksbill turtle tested (in the nesting site) had the same mtDNA, (with only minimal variability), leading (to the conclusion) [that most (of the hawksbill turtles) (in the nesting site) have emerged (from the same nest)]. This explains [why areas (around the world) [that appear ideal (for sea turtle foraging and nesting)] are not recolonized [after human interference wipes out the native populations]]]. (For example), Grand Cayman Island was once home (to one) (of the largest green sea turtle populations) (in the world), but [after the turtles were driven off (by humans)], wildlife protection laws and habitat reconstruction have proven unsuccessful (in bringing back) the turtles.

usherin.usher.co.kr

USHER iBT TOEFL
INTERMEDIATE READING
구문 외우고 열번 읽기

단계별
1. 정확히 구문 암기!
2. 하나하나 철저히 적용!
3. 확실히 적용할 줄 알면 7분내 지문 읽기!

Comets

1 Comets, small celestial bodies with long luminous tails and orbits that occasionally **(1)bring them in** close contact with Earth, are some of the most fascinating objects in our solar system. Today, only about 4,900 of these bodies **(2)composed of** frozen gases and volatile compounds **(3)along with** rocky metallic elements have been discovered, but the distance of their orbits **(4)makes it likely that** many more exist. Comets **(5)are generally categorized into** two orbit length-dependent categories: long-period and short-period comets. Short-period comets, such as Halley's Comet which has been documented appearing every 76 years since 240 B.C.E., make regular appearances **(6)due to** their relatively short orbits of less than 200 years and are more well-known. Long-period comets, however, are rarely observed because they **(7)take** hundreds or thousands of years to complete one trip around the sun

2 The main difference between the two categories **(8)seems to** **(9)arrive from** their origins. Short-period comets begin in the Kuiper belt of non-planetary matter. The matter in the belt, just past Neptune's orbit, roughly 50 astronomical units (1 AU=the distance between Earth and the sun) from the sun, **(10)travels around** the sun on nearly **(11)the same** plane **as** the planets. If two of these comets strike **(12)one another**, or if one is affected by the gravitation of a nearby planet, the orbit may be thrown off **(13)in such a way that** a comet enters the inner solar system where it is affected by solar forces and visible from Earth.

3 Contrarily, long-period comets do not **(14)originate from** the same plane as other bodies in the solar system. They orbit the sun in elliptical orbits spanning **(15)a variety of** angles, forming a "shell" around the solar system **(16)known as** the Oort Cloud. Scientists believe there are millions of inactive comets in this region, 10,000 AU from the sun. Due to this extreme distance they are not affected by planetary gravitation in the same way as Kuiper belt comets. For one of these comets to **(17)make its way into** the inner solar system, it must be affected by the gravitational forces of a passing star. When this happens they are sent on an irregular orbit that **(18)brings them** **(19)closer to** the sun where they undergo the changes **(20)typical of** all comets. After they have completed their pass near the sun, it may be thousands of years before they make their return. In fact, Comet West and C/1999 F1 have orbits that are estimated at 6 million years. There is even a subset of these long-period comets called the hyperbolic, or single-apparition, comets that make only one appearance near the sun, because their orbits eventually **(21)take** them **out of** the solar system.

4 **(22)Regardless of** the category of comet, their telltale shape forms in the same way. They complete most of their orbit as frozen and relatively inactive masses that **(23)are difficult to discern**, but as they come closer to the sun, the effects of its massive energy sublimates the frozen materials within this nucleus **(24)to form** a glowing ball of dust and gases known as the coma. This coma greatly increases the comet's size. The nucleus is generally less than 60 km **(25)in diameter**, but the coma can be larger than the sun. This most distinguishable feature differentiates comets from other celestial bodies, such as asteroids. When they reach approximately 1.5 AU from the sun, solar energy's effects become more extreme and parts of the coma are blown into a tail which can be **(26)millions of kilometers long**.

5 **(27)Research into** comets **(28)led** scientists **to make** an interesting observation regarding their tails; they always **(29)point away from** the sun. This **(30)allowed** them **to conclude** that some force **(31)emanating from** the sun pushed the particles in the coma to form the tail. We now understand that this is not one, but two forces. Pressure from solar radiation drives the dust particles back from the coma, while solar winds push back the ionized volatile gases surrounding the nucleus. Because of these two different effects, comets **(32)are often found to have** two tails, a curved one composed of dust and a second, composed of ionized volatiles, that appears blue and always points away from the sun.

6 When the comet makes its way out of the influence of solar power, the gases in the coma condense and the materials in the tail are lost, reducing its mass. Some of this dust and matter remains in orbit, and can cause other celestial events. The annual Perseid meteor shower is caused by matter **(33)ejected from** the Swift-Tuttle comet during it 133-year orbit. **(34)For this reason**, it has been hypothesized that comet lifespans are limited by the number of orbits they complete. After a certain number of orbits, the nucleus will have expelled all of its volatile components and will **(35)continue to orbit** as a small grouping of stony materials that are relatively unaffected by solar radiation or winds.

Comets

1 Comets, small celestial bodies with long luminous tails and orbits that occasionally bring them in close contact with Earth, are some of the most fascinating objects in our solar system. Today, only about 4,900 of these bodies composed of frozen gases and volatile compounds along with rocky metallic elements have been discovered, but the distance of their orbits makes it likely that many more exist. Comets are generally categorized into two orbit length-dependent - categories: long-period and short-period comets. Short-period comets, such as Halley's Comet which has been documented appearing every 76 years since 240 B.C.E., make regular appearances due to their relatively short orbits of less than 200 years and are more well-known. Long-period comets, however, are rarely observed because they take hundreds or thousands of years to complete one trip around the sun

2 The main difference between the two categories seems to arrive from their origins. Short-period comets begin in the Kuiper belt of non-planetary matter. The matter in the belt, just past Neptune's orbit, roughly 50 astronomical units (1 AU=the distance between Earth and the sun) from the sun, travels around the sun on nearly the same plane as the planets. If two of these comets strike one another, or if one is affected by the gravitation of a nearby planet, the orbit may be thrown off in such a way that a comet enters the inner solar system where it is affected by solar forces and visible from Earth.

3 Contrarily, long-period comets do not originate from the same plane as other bodies in the solar system. They orbit the sun in elliptical orbits spanning a variety of angles, forming a "shell" around the solar system known as the Oort Cloud. Scientists believe there are millions of inactive comets in this region, 10,000 AU from the sun. Due to this extreme distance they are not affected by planetary gravitation in the same way as Kuiper belt comets. For one of these comets to make its way into the inner solar system, it must be affected by the gravitational forces of a passing star. When this happens they are sent on an irregular orbit that brings them closer to the sun where they undergo the changes typical of all comets. After they have completed their pass near the sun, it may be thousands of years before they make their return. In fact, Comet West and C/1999 F1 have orbits that are estimated at 6 million years. There is even a subset of these long-period comets called the hyperbolic, or single-apparition, comets that make only one appearance near the sun, because their orbits eventually take them out of the solar system.

4 Regardless of the category of comet, their telltale shape forms in the same way. They complete most of their orbit as frozen and relatively inactive masses that are difficult to discern, but as they come closer to the sun, the effects of its massive energy sublimates the frozen materials within this nucleus to form a glowing ball of dust and gases known as the coma. This coma greatly increases the comet's size. The nucleus is generally less than 60 km in diameter, but the coma can be larger than the sun. This most distinguishable feature differentiates comets from other celestial bodies, such as asteroids. When they reach approximately 1.5 AU from the sun, solar energy's effects become more extreme and parts of the coma are blown into a tail which can be millions of kilometers long.

5 Research into comets led scientists to make an interesting observation regarding their tails; they always point away from the sun. This allowed them to conclude that some force emanating from the sun pushed the particles in the coma to form the tail. We now understand that this is not one, but two forces. Pressure from solar radiation drives the dust particles back from the coma, while solar winds push back the ionized volatile gases surrounding the nucleus. Because of these two different effects, comets are often found to have two tails, a curved one composed of dust and a second, composed of ionized volatiles, that appears blue and always points away from the sun.

6 When the comet makes its way out of the influence of solar power, the gases in the coma condense and the materials in the tail are lost, reducing its mass . Some of this dust and matter remains in orbit, and can cause other celestial events. The annual Perseid meteor shower is caused by matter ejected from the Swift-Tuttle comet during it 133-year orbit. For this reason, it has been hypothesized that comet lifespans are limited by the number of orbits they complete. After a certain number of orbits, the nucleus will have expelled all of its volatile components and will continue to orbit as a small grouping of stony materials that are relatively unaffected by solar radiation or winds.

Darwin and Evolution Theory

1 In 1831, Robert FitzRoy (1)**prepared to** (2)**set sail** (3)**on** a two year **journey** aboard the Beagle to survey the South American coastlines and return three-Yaghan tribe members it previously captured to Tierra del Fuegoan archipelago off the southernmost tip of the South American mainland. To fight the loneliness of being at sea for so long and to help study the lands they were to visit, he invited Charles Darwin, a recent Cambridge graduate, to join the expedition as his companion and ship naturalist. Prior to departure, FitzRoy gave his new companion Principles of Geology by Charles Lyell, who had requested that FitzRoy record the geological formations that he encountered. (4)**Unbeknownst to** both men, their journey together would stretch to nearly five years and would form the basis for a revolutionary new biological theory.

2 (5)**According to** his diaries, Darwin (6)**spent** three years and three months **exploring** the new lands, **recording** his geographical findings, and **collecting** fossils and specimens of the wildlife he (7)**came across**. Although he originally (8)**planned to use** his findings to write a (9)**book on** geology, (10)**over the course of** his explorations he made many new and interesting discoveries in the field of biology, such as discovering giant armadillo and sloth fossils from the distant past. He also discovered that in areas with a geographic segregation, such as islands or seas separated by isthmuses, different species were found. This was particularly true in the Galapagos Archipelago, where he found different species of tortoises on each island, a unique marine iguana with a seaweed-based diet, and (11)**an assortment of** birds he (12)**thought to be** blackbirds, grosbeaks, and finches but later (13)**turned out to be** 12 distinct species of finches. These discoveries, (14)**combined with** Lyell's theory of uniformitarianism, which stated that "the present is the (15)**key to** the past," meaning that we can only assume about the past from what we observe in the present, (16)**caused** Darwin **to postulate** that the diversity of these species was possible only if there was some mechanism through which species could change over time.

3 Darwin's idea was supported by the theory of homology Richard Owen (17)**derived from** comparative studies of the structural systems of various vertebrates. Owen found homology, or anatomical similarity, in the body parts of different animals which (18)**served** different **purposes**. The forelimbs of most vertebrates, such as, bats, whales, humans, and horses, all share a basic design. This cannot (19)**be attributed to** common use, so it must indicate common ancestry and adaptive evolution to fit the organisms' functions. The presence of vestigial, or leftover, structures in modern organisms also (20)**points to** an evolutionary system, because these structures serve no purpose in modern animals. The whale and snake are both examples of this, because although both are now legless, they have small vestigial leg bones, which point to a four-legged ancestor.

4 All of this (21)**support for** Darwin's theory did not explain why evolution would have occurred. Darwin got a basic idea about this by looking at the changes that breeders could induce in their animals through animal husbandry. By breeding animals with certain traits they could artificially change the traits of the offspring. This couldn't, however, explain how species evolve naturally or how some species (22)**go extinct** and (23)**are replaced by** other species. To gain further (24)**insight into** this, Darwin (25)**turned to** the population research of economist Thomas Malthus, which indicated that population increases outpace food production. This overpopulation decreases the number of offspring reaching maturity during lean times. Darwin recognized that these two basic ideas could (26)**be applied to** the animal kingdom. He theorized that during competitive times, animals with favorable traits would survive (27)**to reproduce** and (28)**pass on** their superior traits **to** the next generation (29)**in a** natural **form** of selection.

5 Although Darwin (30)**had** great **confidence in** the validity of his theories, he initially (31)**refused to publish** them (32)**due to his lack of** supporting data and remained most famous as a geologist and explorer after the publication of his accounts of the trip in The Voyage of the Beagle. This did not, however, (33)**stop him from discussing** his theories with fellow scientists Lyell and Owen, both of whom he befriended after returning from the long voyage. The formal publication of his theories did not occur until another young British naturalist and explorer, Alfred Wallace, (34)**was about to present** a similar theory he developed while exploring the Amazon Basin and the Malay Archipelago. Eventually, Wallace (35)**agreed to present** his theory alongside the more socially and scientifically connected Darwin and their work was jointly presented to the Linnean Society of London in 1858, with very little fanfare. The true significance of the new theories would not be fully recognized until the publication of Darwin's evolutionary manifesto, On the Origin of Species by Means of Natural Selection, in 1859. It was (36)**so** well researched and presented **that** it (37)**was referred to as** the best explanation "ever published of the manner of formation of species" by Owen and (38)**established** Darwin **as** the definitive authority on natural selection

Darwin and Evolution Theory

1 In 1831, Robert FitzRoy prepared to set sail on a two year journey aboard the Beagle to survey the South American coastlines and return three-Yaghan tribe members it previously captured to Tierra del Fuegoan archipelago off the southernmost tip of the South American mainland. To fight the loneliness of being at sea for so long and to help study the lands they were to visit, he invited Charles Darwin, a recent Cambridge graduate, to join the expedition as his companion and ship naturalist. Prior to departure, FitzRoy gave his new companion Principles of Geology by Charles Lyell, who had requested that FitzRoy record the geological formations that he encountered. Unbeknownst to both men, their journey together would stretch to nearly five years and would form the basis for a revolutionary new biological theory.

2 According to his diaries, Darwin spent three years and three months exploring the new lands, recording his geographical findings, and collecting fossils and specimens of the wildlife he came across. Although he originally planned to use his findings to write a book on geology, over the course of his explorations he made many new and interesting discoveries in the field of biology, such as discovering giant armadillo and sloth fossils from the distant past. He also discovered that in areas with a geographic segregation, such as islands or seas separated by isthmuses, different species were found. This was particularly true in the Galapagos Archipelago, where he found different species of tortoises on each island, a unique marine iguana with a seaweed-based diet, and an assortment of birds he thought to be blackbirds, grosbeaks, and finches but later turned out to be 12 distinct species of finches. These discoveries, combined with Lyell's theory of uniformitarianism, which stated that "the present is the key to the past," meaning that we can only assume about the past from what we observe in the present, caused Darwin to postulate that the diversity of these species was possible only if there was some mechanism through which species could change over time.

3 Darwin's idea was supported by the theory of homology Richard Owen derived from comparative studies of the structural systems of various vertebrates. Owen found homology, or anatomical similarity, in the body parts of different animals which served different purposes. The forelimbs of most vertebrates, such as, bats, whales, humans, and horses, all share a basic design. This cannot be attributed to common use, so it must indicate common ancestry and adaptive evolution to fit the organisms' functions. The presence of vestigial, or leftover, structures in modern organisms also points to an evolutionary system, because these structures serve no purpose in modern animals. The whale and snake are both examples of this, because although both are now legless, they have small vestigial leg bones, which point to a four-legged ancestor.

4 All of this support for Darwin's theory did not explain why evolution would have occurred. Darwin got a basic idea about this by looking at the changes that breeders could induce in their animals through animal husbandry. By breeding animals with certain traits they could artificially change the traits of the offspring. This couldn't, however, explain how species evolve naturally or how some species go extinct and are replaced by other species. To gain further insight into this, Darwin turned to the population research of economist Thomas Malthus, which indicated that population increases outpace food production. This overpopulation decreases the number of offspring reaching maturity during lean times. Darwin recognized that these two basic ideas could be applied to the animal kingdom. He theorized that during competitive times, animals with favorable traits would survive to reproduce and pass on their superior traits to the next generation in a natural form of selection.

5 Although Darwin had great confidence in the validity of his theories, he initially refused to publish them due to his lack of supporting data and remained most famous as a geologist and explorer after the publication of his accounts of the trip in The Voyage of the Beagle. This did not, however, stop him from discussing his theories with fellow scientists Lyell and Owen, both of whom he befriended after returning from the long voyage. The formal publication of his theories did not occur until another young British naturalist and explorer, Alfred Wallace, was about to present a similar theory he developed while exploring the Amazon Basin and the Malay Archipelago. Eventually, Wallace agreed to present his theory alongside the more socially and scientifically connected Darwin and their work was jointly presented to the Linnean Society of London in 1858, with very little fanfare. The true significance of the new theories would not be fully recognized until the publication of Darwin's evolutionary manifesto, *On the Origin of Species by Means of Natural Selection*, in 1859. It was so well researched and presented that it was referred to as the best explanation "ever published of the manner of formation of species" by Owen and established Darwin as the definitive authority on natural selection

Determining the Ages of the Planets and the Universe

1 The orbits of planets and the (1)**majority of** non-planetary objects in our solar system have a very interesting characteristic; despite their vast differences, they have astounding similarities. The most remarkable of these similarities is that nearly all of them orbit the sun (2)**in the same direction** and on the same plane. Using this information, scientists determined that this likely occurred because the collapse of a gas cloud simultaneously formed the objects and sent them to orbit the sun. This fact has (3)**allowed us to learn** more about the age of the Earth, the planets, and the universe itself.

2 It may (4)**seem that** the easiest method of discerning Earth's age would be to simply sample materials we can (5)**extract from** the crust, but this doesn't produce accurate results. Due to the life-supporting water that covers Earth's surface, terrestrial material (6)**is** constantly **exposed to** the force of erosion. The constant changes erosion causes, compounded by volcanic activity and Earth's internal pressure and heat, (7)**make the discovery** of rocks in Earth's crust that (8)**originate from** the time of formation highly unlikely. (9)**For this reason** scientists must (10)**look for** analogous objects in the solar system to (11)**help them** (12)**answer** this **question**. Luckily, the meteorites that have (13)**crashed into** Earth's surface can (14)**provide** them **with** this material. These masses began their existence as meteors orbiting the sun, but Earth's gravitational pull (15)**forced** them **to enter** its atmosphere and (16)**collide with** the crust.

3 The meteorites that have been discovered have (17)**varied in size,** (18)**ranging from** stony pebbles **to** massive planetoids called asteroids, and composition which has allowed scientists to (19)**draw conclusions** about them and Earth's composition and origin. Some intact asteroids may have once struck the earth, but none have done so during recorded human history. From meteorite remnants found on Earth, the main three categories (20)**used to differentiate** meteorites today are "stony meteorites," (21)**composed of** rocky materials, "iron meteorites" composed mainly of iron with (22)**trace amounts of** other elements, and "stony-iron meteorites" that (23)**consist of** a mixture of the two. Scientists believe that all three of these types of meteorites are the remnants of larger space bodies that broke apart due to collisions. It is believed that the differences between the categories of meteorites are due to this violent (24)**break up** of space materials with origins and, therefore, compositions (25)**similar to** Earth's. The stony meteorites likely originated as the outer shells of these bodies and (26)**are analogous to** Earth's mantle, while the iron meteorites that resemble Earth's core are probably fragments of the interior of the body and the stony-iron meteorites contain materials from both.

4 By studying these meteorites scientists have (27)**been able to determine** their age. Using multiple radiometric methods of dating the materials, including the uranium-thorium, rubidium-strontium, and potassium-argon methods, showed a cluster of age data pointing to an origin around 4.6 billion years ago. (28)**Comparing** this **to** the rocks from the moon's surface, which (29)**is free of** the water that erodes rocks on Earth's surface and which displays little movement in its crust, yielded similar age data and allowed researchers to confirm their hypothesis that all of the materials in the solar system started (30)**at the same point** in time.

5 While dating the elements of the solar system has been relatively straightforward, finding the age of the universe itself has been more complicated because there is no way to collect physical materials on which to conduct age testing. What has been learned has been gathered through theoretical analysis of the universe. One of the most important factors discovered is that all of the disk-shaped clusters of stars, called galaxies, are (31)**moving away from** each other. Scientists conjecture that this occurs because the universe (32)**began with** an explosion, (33)**known as** the Big Bang, which sent all of the dense matter concentrated (34)**at the center of** the explosion hurtling across space. This process is (35)**akin to** what would happen if one were to glue coins to a balloon and inflate it. The coins, like the galaxies, would remain the same size but the space between them would increase as the balloon got larger.

6 The expansion of the space between the galaxies is precisely what astronomers have used to estimate the universe's age. By measuring the wavelengths of light travelling through the universe they are able to measure a (36)**shift in** the light's wavelength toward red end of the light spectrum. This redshift occurs because, as light (37)**travels in** the space between the galaxies, the expansion of the space stretches out the light waves. (38)**Following this theory,** (39)**the farther** the light has traveled, **the greate**r the redshift will be. Measuring the redshift in light from distant galaxies, astronomers have determined that all of the galaxies would have existed in one central location around 13.7 billion years ago. This, therefore, is the most likely the date and location of the Big Bang and the age of the universe.

Determining the Ages of the Planets and the Universe

1 The orbits of planets and the majority of non-planetary objects in our solar system have a very interesting characteristic; despite their vast differences, they have astounding similarities. The most remarkable of these similarities is that nearly all of them orbit the sun in the same direction and on the same plane. Using this information, scientists determined that this likely occurred because the collapse of a gas cloud simultaneously formed the objects and sent them to orbit the sun . This fact has allowed us to learn more about the age of the Earth, the planets, and the universe itself.

2 It may seem that the easiest method of discerning Earth's age would be to simply sample materials we can extract from the crust, but this doesn't produce accurate results. Due to the life-supporting water that covers Earth's surface, terrestrial material is constantly exposed to the force of erosion. The constant changes erosion causes, compounded by volcanic activity and Earth's internal pressure and heat, make the discovery of rocks in Earth's crust that originate from the time of formation highly unlikely. For this reason scientists must look for analogous objects in the solar system to help them answer this question. Luckily, the meteorites that have crashed into Earth's surface can provide them with this material. These masses began their existence as meteors orbiting the sun, but Earth's gravitational pull forced them to enter its atmosphere and collide with the crust.

3 The meteorites that have been discovered have varied in size, ranging from stony pebbles to massive planetoids called asteroids, and composition which has allowed scientists to draw conclusions about them and Earth's composition and origin. Some intact asteroids may have once struck the earth, but none have done so during recorded human history. From meteorite remnants found on Earth, the main three categories used to differentiate meteorites today are "stony meteorites," composed of rocky materials, "iron meteorites" composed mainly of iron with trace amounts of other elements, and "stony-iron meteorites" that consist of a mixture of the two. Scientists believe that all three of these types of meteorites are the remnants of larger space bodies that broke apart due to collisions. It is believed that the differences between the categories of meteorites are due to this violent break up of space materials with origins and, therefore, compositions similar to Earth's. The stony meteorites likely originated as the outer shells of these bodies and are analogous to Earth's mantle, while the iron meteorites that resemble Earth's core are probably fragments of the interior of the body and the stony-iron meteorites contain materials from both.

4 By studying these meteorites scientists have been able to determine their age. Using multiple radiometric methods of dating the materials, including the uranium-thorium, rubidium-strontium, and potassium-argon methods, showed a cluster of age data pointing to an origin around 4.6 billion years ago. Comparing this to the rocks from the moon's surface, which is free of the water that erodes rocks on Earth's surface and which displays little movement in its crust, yielded similar age data and allowed researchers to confirm their hypothesis that all of the materials in the solar system started at the same point in time.

5 While dating the elements of the solar system has been relatively straightforward, finding the age of the universe itself has been more complicated because there is no way to collect physical materials on which to conduct age testing. What has been learned has been gathered through theoretical analysis of the universe. One of the most important factors discovered is that all of the disk-shaped clusters of stars, called galaxies, are moving away from each other. Scientists conjecture that this occurs because the universe began with an explosion, known as the Big Bang, which sent all of the dense matter concentrated at the center of the explosion hurtling across space. This process is akin to what would happen if one were to glue coins to a balloon and inflate it. The coins, like the galaxies, would remain the same size but the space between them would increase as the balloon got larger.

6 The expansion of the space between the galaxies is precisely what astronomers have used to estimate the universe's age. By measuring the wavelengths of light travelling through the universe they are able to measure a shift in the light's wavelength toward red end of the light spectrum. This redshift occurs because, as light travels in the space between the galaxies, the expansion of the space stretches out the light waves. Following this theory, the farther the light has traveled, the greater the redshift will be. Measuring the redshift in light from distant galaxies, astronomers have determined that all of the galaxies would have existed in one central location around 13.7 billion years ago. This, therefore, is the most likely the date and location of the Big Bang and the age of the universe.

Early Research in Organic Chemistry

1 The ancient practice of alchemy [1]**gave way to** the early science of chemistry in the late 17th century. After hundreds of years of [2]**trying to** [3]**turn** base metals **into** gold, alchemy had developed a structure of theory, terminology, experimentation and basic laboratory techniques that were well-adapted for scientific study of Earth's elements. [4]**By the 18th century**, chemists [5]**began to** scientifically **study** the new elements they found and [6]**were able to identify** many new ones that had never been studied before, such as cobalt, tungsten and various forms of carbon. The study of the last of these would eventually form one of the two modern divisions of the field of chemistry, organic chemistry.

2 The terms organic and inorganic chemistry were introduced in the early 1800s to more accurately differentiate between the different naturally occurring substances. [7]**Prior to** this time scientists [8]**separated** substances **into** three categories that matched the "Three Kingdoms of Nature": animal, vegetable and mineral. Of these, the animal and vegetable groups [9]**were reserved for** substances that [10]**were** produced by or **related to** life and [11]**were** later **incorporated into** the study of organic (meaning from an organism) chemistry which covered all carbon-based compounds, while the inanimate mineral group gave way to the field of inorganic chemistry which covered all non-carbon compounds. Some scientists, such as Antoine Lavoisier, thought the organic field was a reasonable field of study, yet they were opposed by others who [12]**adhered to** a theory of vitalism. Those that believed in vitalism felt that there was a "vital spark" or "force" in organic materials and that substances that contained it should not be [13]**experimented upon** and that only inorganic materials were valid research subjects. Despite the eventual invalidation of the vitalist theory, by German chemist Friedrich Wöhler's accidental synthesis of organic material in his laboratory, scientists [14]**involved in** inorganic chemistry made much more rapid progress than those working on organic chemistry.

3 This lag of organic chemistry occurred for various reasons, but perhaps the most obvious is the availability of elements and compounds on which scientists could experiment. [15]**In order for scientists to conduct** experiments and determine the chemical forms of the elements, they [16]**need to obtain** them [17]**in their purest forms**. Inorganic compounds, [18]**on the whole**, are more easily found [19]**in a reasonably pure state**. Mineral deposits often hold lodes of compounds and elements such as oxides, pure metals and salts. Some gases, such as sulfur, can even be found in their pure elemental form on Earth, while others, like atmospheric gases, [20]**are** easily **broken down into** their component parts. Hydrogen, [21]**for instance**, can [22]**be mined from** the air using a particular mineral acid on a metal plate.

4 [23]**Access to** pure organic substances, [24]**on the other hand**, is much more difficult. [25]**Extracting** pure substances **from** plant or animal matter through the process of distillation, evaporating and condensing a substance to purify it, generally yields solid blackened debris [26]**along with** liquid and gaseous discharges. Chemists studying the vegetable products found that the qualitative properties of the remaining solid matter varied little between different vegetable types, but quantitative and qualitative differences were found in the liquid and gaseous substances produced. They also found that altering the distillation process yielded significantly different [27]**results in** these byproducts. By standardizing the distillation process they were able to [28]**make** important **advances in** their [29]**ability to analyze** organic matter.

5 Even after developing a standardized analytical process, organic chemists still faced challenges in their field. The most overwhelming of these was that the substances released during the distillation process were complex compounds of unknown purity, [30]**making it impossible to** accurately **determine** the properties of any one element [31]**present in** the substances. Another major problem was determining the source of the released materials. Were they present in the original sample, or were they produced through the process of distilling and destroying organic material? This uncertainty [32]**led** organic chemists **to** [33]**search for ways to attain** these substances without destroying the original matter. Many other less violent methods of distillation, such as using the lowest effective temperature to distill organic substances, were attempted, but did not fully overcome the problems that were [34]**in herent in** the field.

6 This problem led organic chemists to [35]**consider** substances such as blood, gelatin, and fat **to be** constituent elements in organisms as late as the 1830s. Today we recognize that all of these substances are complex compounds [36]**composed of** various molecules made of a great number of atoms of true elements. Due to this, and similar, problems, understanding the actual chemical makeup of organic compounds was much more complex and challenging than it was [37]**in the field of** inorganic, or mineral-based, chemistry. The crucial breakthrough in organic chemistry came in 1858 when the concept of chemical structures in carbon atoms was simultaneously developed by Friedrich August Kekulé and Archibald Scott Couper. This allowed chemists to more accurately understand the ability of carbon molecules to bond together in a carbon lattice through the observation and interpretation of chemical reactions.

Early Research in Organic Chemistry

1 The ancient practice of alchemy gave way to the early science of chemistry in the late 17th century. After hundreds of years of trying to turn base metals into gold, alchemy had developed a structure of theory, terminology, experimentation and basic laboratory techniques that were well-adapted for scientific study of Earth's elements. By the 18th century, chemists began to scientifically study the new elements they found and were able to identify many new ones that had never been studied before, such as cobalt, tungsten and various forms of carbon. The study of the last of these would eventually form one of the two modern divisions of the field of chemistry, organic chemistry.

2 The terms organic and inorganic chemistry were introduced in the early 1800s to more accurately differentiate between the different naturally occurring substances. Prior to this time scientists separated substances into three categories that matched the "Three Kingdoms of Nature": animal, vegetable and mineral. Of these, the animal and vegetable groups were reserved for substances that were produced by or related to life and were later incorporated into the study of organic (meaning from an organism) chemistry which covered all carbon-based compounds, while the inanimate mineral group gave way to the field of inorganic chemistry which covered all non-carbon compounds. Some scientists, such as Antoine Lavoisier, thought the organic field was a reasonable field of study, yet they were opposed by others who adhered to a theory of vitalism. Those that believed in vitalism felt that there was a "vital spark" or "force" in organic materials and that substances that contained it should not be experimented upon and that only inorganic materials were valid research subjects. Despite the eventual invalidation of the vitalist theory, by German chemist Friedrich Wöhler's accidental synthesis of organic material in his laboratory, scientists involved in inorganic chemistry made much more rapid progress than those working on organic chemistry.

3 This lag of organic chemistry occurred for various reasons, but perhaps the most obvious is the availability of elements and compounds on which scientists could experiment. In order for scientists to conduct experiments and determine the chemical forms of the elements, they need to obtain them in their purest forms. Inorganic compounds, on the whole, are more easily found in a reasonably pure state. Mineral deposits often hold lodes of compounds and elements such as oxides, pure metals and salts. Some gases, such as sulfur, can even be found in their pure elemental form on Earth, while others, like atmospheric gases, are easily broken down into their component parts. Hydrogen, for instance, can be mined from the air using a particular mineral acid on a metal plate.

4 Access to pure organic substances, on the other hand, is much more difficult. Extracting pure substances from plant or animal matter through the process of distillation, evaporating and condensing a substance to purify it, generally yields solid blackened debris along with liquid and gaseous discharges. Chemists studying the vegetable products found that the qualitative properties of the remaining solid matter varied little between different vegetable types, but quantitative and qualitative differences were found in the liquid and gaseous substances produced. They also found that altering the distillation process yielded significantly different results in these byproducts. By standardizing the distillation process they were able to make important advances in their ability to analyze organic matter.

5 Even after developing a standardized analytical process, organic chemists still faced challenges in their field. The most overwhelming of these was that the substances released during the distillation process were complex compounds of unknown purity, making it impossible to accurately determine the properties of any one element present in the substances. Another major problem was determining the source of the released materials. Were they present in the original sample, or were they produced through the process of distilling and destroying organic material? This uncertainty led organic chemists to search for ways to attain these substances without destroying the original matter. Many other less violent methods of distillation, such as using the lowest effective temperature to distill organic substances, were attempted, but did not fully overcome the problems that were in herent in the field.

6 This problem led organic chemists to consider substances such as blood, gelatin, and fat to be constituent elements in organisms as late as the 1830s. Today we recognize that all of these substances are complex compounds composed of various molecules made of a great number of atoms of true elements. Due to this, and similar, problems, understanding the actual chemical makeup of organic compounds was much more complex and challenging than it was in the field of inorganic, or mineral-based, chemistry. The crucial breakthrough in organic chemistry came in 1858 when the concept of chemical structures in carbon atoms was simultaneously developed by Friedrich August Kekulé and Archibald Scott Couper. This allowed chemists to more accurately understand the ability of carbon molecules to bond together in a carbon lattice through the observation and interpretation of chemical reactions.

El Niño

1 The Humboldt Current carries cold water northward from the Antarctic along South America's western coast. As it reaches the equator, the easterly trade winds blow the surface water westward and allow an upwelling of cold, nutrient-rich waters. This rise of these nutritive waters provides the abundant food sources that are needed to sustain the nearly year-round commercial fishing industry off the coasts of Peru and Chile. However, during December and January, the cold waters (1)**are replaced by** a warmer countercurrent, greatly reducing the water's nutrient content and causing a lull in commercial fishing (2)**due to the lack of** commercially viable fish, such as anchovies, in the warmer water. Local residents (3)**termed this period** "El Niño," or "the boy" in Spanish, due to its occurrence during the Christmas season, and (4)**use** this down time **to** (5)**tend to** their equipment.

2 Despite the traditionally short duration of El Niño, these warmer surface waters can linger and (6)**extend far into** the equatorial Pacific. In fact, (7)**over** the past six **decades**, climatologists have identified (8)**at least** ten unusually long El Niño periods. In recent times, the traditional term for this period, El Niño, has become (9)**identified** worldwide **with** these lengthy periods of warmer Pacific waters more than with the annual pattern, because of the great changes they can cause in weather patterns across the globe.

3 Despite being (10)**known** mainly **as** an eastern Pacific pattern, El Niño affects conditions across the vast waters of the Pacific. One of the first scientists to recognize this was early-20th century British physicist Gilbert Walker, who found an inverse correlation between atmospheric pressure at weather stations in the eastern and western Pacific. Walker noted that as the pressure of the eastern Pacific fell, that of the western Pacific rose, and (11)**vice versa** (12)**in** a see-saw-like **pattern** that he termed the Southern Oscillation. The relationship between this phenomenon and El Niño was later (13)**recognized as** being (14)**so strong that** they (15)**are often referred to** collectively **as** the El Niño-Southern Oscillation.

4 Normally, the eastern Pacific's higher atmospheric pressure causes the easterly trade winds that typify the wind pattern of the southern equatorial region. These warm winds also cause the warm east-to-west surface current that (16)**moves across** the Pacific Ocean along the equator. Eventually it causes an accumulation of warm surface water in the western Pacific, while the Humboldt Current's upwelling (17)**keeps surface temperatures** in the eastern Pacific much **lower**. When the Southern Oscillation shifts and pressure rises in the west, the pressure gradient across the ocean is disrupted and the trade winds that were caused by it are severely weakened or reversed. With these no longer pushing westward on the warmer surface water it (18)**begins to creep** eastward, marking the El Niño. As the warmer waters slide eastward, they further decrease the pressure and temperature gradients across the Pacific Ocean in a positive feedback loop. The pressure gradient that causes the winds is decreased as the eastern Pacific becomes warmer, which further decreases the pressure gradient and the winds.

5 Since this process was first theorized, scientists have (19)**attempted to trace** it using historical records. By examining records of the daily surface temperature of the ocean, rainfall, atmospheric pressure, and fisheries data from South American inhabitants and Spanish colonists dating as far back as the 1400s, they have (20)**pieced together** a detailed timeline of El Niño over the past six centuries. From this, (21)**it is clear that** although El Niño occurred regularly throughout history its frequency is increasing. (22)**Comparing** the records of the 16th century **to** modern ones shows that El Niño is now occurring nearly three times more often than it did then, occurring just over every 2 years now, but occurring in six year intervals historically. An even more alarming finding is that the temperature increase's severity is rising. This is troubling because scientists now know that El Niño's effects are (23)**not** (24)**limited to** the southern Pacific, **but also** affect worldwide weather patterns. During the 1997-98 El Niño, (25)**for instance**, the entire United States (26)**suffered from** more severe seasonal weather.

6 Modern researchers have pointed to even more (27)**reasons to fear** a stronger El Niño. (28)**It appears that** El Niño also (29)**coincides with** increased epidemics, especially those caused by mosquito-borne pathogens, civil conflict, and violence. One of the most well-researched aspects of this has been El Niño's effect on malaria. Scientists have proven that a 1°C increase in the ocean's surface temperature yields a 20% increase in malaria around the tropical Pacific's coasts. Others have noted that the risk of civil unrest and violence doubles to 6% during El Niño. They (30)**blame** this **on** the widespread famine that occurs during these periods. They (31)**point to** the Northern Chinese Famine of 1876 that killed 13 million and the El Niño effects of 1789-1793 that (32)**led to** crop failures, which eventually sparked the French Revolution, **as** evidence of this. In modern times, it has been found that El Niño's effects have triggered 21% of conflicts worldwide since 1950.

El Niño

1 The Humboldt Current carries cold water northward from the Antarctic along South America's western coast. As it reaches the equator, the easterly trade winds blow the surface water westward and allow an upwelling of cold, nutrient-rich waters. This rise of these nutritive waters provides the abundant food sources that are needed to sustain the nearly year-round commercial fishing industry off the coasts of Peru and Chile. However, during December and January, the cold waters are replaced by a warmer countercurrent, greatly reducing the water's nutrient content and causing a lull in commercial fishing due to the lack of commercially viable fish, such as anchovies, in the warmer water. Local residents termed this period "El Niño," or "the boy" in Spanish, due to its occurrence during the Christmas season, and use this down time to tend to their equipment.

2 Despite the traditionally short duration of El Niño, these warmer surface waters can linger and extend far into the equatorial Pacific. In fact, over the past six decades, climatologists have identified at least ten unusually long El Niño periods. In recent times, the traditional term for this period, El Niño, has become identified worldwide with these lengthy periods of warmer Pacific waters more than with the annual pattern, because of the great changes they can cause in weather patterns across the globe.

3 Despite being known mainly as an eastern Pacific pattern, El Niño affects conditions across the vast waters of the Pacific. One of the first scientists to recognize this was early-20th century British physicist Gilbert Walker, who found an inverse correlation between atmospheric pressure at weather stations in the eastern and western Pacific. Walker noted that as the pressure of the eastern Pacific fell, that of the western Pacific rose, and vice versa in a see-saw-like pattern that he termed the Southern Oscillation. The relationship between this phenomenon and El Niño was later recognized as being so strong that they are often referred to collectively as the El Niño-Southern Oscillation.

4 Normally, the eastern Pacific's higher atmospheric pressure causes the easterly trade winds that typify the wind pattern of the southern equatorial region. These warm winds also cause the warm east-to-west surface current that moves across the Pacific Ocean along the equator. Eventually it causes an accumulation of warm surface water in the western Pacific, while the Humboldt Current's upwelling keeps surface temperatures in the eastern Pacific much lower. When the Southern Oscillation shifts and pressure rises in the west, the pressure gradient across the ocean is disrupted and the trade winds that were caused by it are severely weakened or reversed. With these no longer pushing westward on the warmer surface water it begins to creep eastward, marking the El Niño. As the warmer waters slide eastward, they further decrease the pressure and temperature gradients across the Pacific Ocean in a positive feedback loop. The pressure gradient that causes the winds is decreased as the eastern Pacific becomes warmer, which further decreases the pressure gradient and the winds.

5 Since this process was first theorized, scientists have attempted to trace it using historical records. By examining records of the daily surface temperature of the ocean, rainfall, atmospheric pressure, and fisheries data from South American inhabitants and Spanish colonists dating as far back as the 1400s, they have pieced together a detailed timeline of El Niño over the past six centuries. From this, it is clear that although El Niño occurred regularly throughout history its frequency is increasing. Comparing the records of the 16th century to modern ones shows that El Niño is now occurring nearly three times more often than it did then, occurring just over every 2 years now, but occurring in six year intervals historically. An even more alarming finding is that the temperature increase's severity is rising. This is troubling because scientists now know that El Niño's effects are not limited to the southern Pacific, but also affect worldwide weather patterns. During the 1997-98 El Niño, for instance, the entire United States suffered from more severe seasonal weather.

6 Modern researchers have pointed to even more reasons to fear a stronger El Niño. It appears that El Niño also coincides with increased epidemics, especially those caused by mosquito-borne pathogens, civil conflict, and violence. One of the most well-researched aspects of this has been El Niño's effect on malaria. Scientists have proven that a 1°C increase in the ocean's surface temperature yields a 20% increase in malaria around the tropical Pacific's coasts. Others have noted that the risk of civil unrest and violence doubles to 6% during El Niño. They blame this on the widespread famine that occurs during these periods. They point to the Northern Chinese Famine of 1876 that killed 13 million and the El Niño effects of 1789-1793 that led to crop failures, which eventually sparked the French Revolution, as evidence of this. In modern times, it has been found that El Niño's effects have triggered 21% of conflicts worldwide since 1950.

England's Sixteenth Century Economy

1 Great changes occurred in England during the Late Tudor Period **(1)under the reign of** Queen Elizabeth I **(2)In the latter half of** the sixteenth and early seventeenth centuries. One of the most notable was the **(3)increase in** the population to nearly **(4)that of** the pre-Black Death period. In England and Wales, increased fertility and reduced mortality rates nearly doubled the population around this time, increasing from 2.5 million in the 1520s to 4.5 million by 1610. This dramatic increase, **(5)along with** other factors, **(6)lead to** vast changes in England's economy and **(7)allowed it to become** Europe's largest, far surpassing those of the war and plague-ravaged continent.

2 One of the first direct effects of the population increase was a **(8)demand for** more food. This caused an "agricultural revolution" in England 2-300 years before they occurred elsewhere in Europe. During this period, English farmers created farmlands from previously unsuitable areas, such as marshlands and woodlands, giving them more arable land on which to produce food. These farmers undertook a process of crop specialization that allowed them to be more efficient and market-driven, increasing their yields dramatically. For instance, they increased their grain production **(9)per acre** by **(10)at least** 30% between 1450 and 1650.

3 With the greater efficiency of the new farming methods, wealthy landowners increased their landholdings **(11)in order to increase** their agricultural productivity. These landholdings were consolidated through the practice of primogeniture under which the eldest son inherited the entirety of his father's holdings, thus **(12)preventing** the great estates **from being (13)divided up into** smaller parcels which could not produce as much income. They also increased the size of their landholdings by **(14)marrying into** other families with large estates. Marriages amongst the wealthiest Elizabethan families were arranged to ensure that both families maintained their social statuses. With their larger estates, these families could conduct more commercialized farming to **(15)meet the demand** for agricultural products which was driving prices higher.

4 These large landowners, and the yeomen who had smaller landholdings, maximized the profits they could **(16)draw from** their property. To increase their profits, they planted crops which were in demand in the London markets. They also aggressively **(17)dealt with** those to whom they rented their property. During this period, rents were increased and rental contracts were written to provide even more benefits to the landowners. One of the ways they did this was shortening the duration of their contracts to **(18)allow themselves more control** over the land. Another way they maximized their profits was to **(19)charge** potential tenants an "entry fee" before they would even **(20)consent to** renting to them. Renters who could not, or would not, **(21)abide by** the new contracts were simply evicted and replaced by those who could. Their tactics were quite one-sided, but they also **(22)encouraged** their tenants **to use** farming practices that would increase their farming efficiency, such as crop rotation.

5 Another method **(23)used to increase** the profits of these large landholdings was to **(24)convert** some of the farmland **into** pastureland upon which sheep could graze. This conversion became possible because of the enclosure movement that occurred during the Tudor period. In the process of enclosure, open fields that had previously been **(25)used for** communal farming, grazing and hay production were fenced and their use became the sole right of the owner. Seeing the growing demands for English wool internationally, landholders often considered rearing sheep as a more profitable way to utilize their land. By converting their land into pastureland they could derive a higher profit while reducing the need for large numbers of workers to tend it.

6 Wool production led to even greater **(26)changes in** the English economy of the time. While English wool had been exported since at least the 1200s, the in it was exported form **(27)began to change**. Wool was traditionally exported **(28)in its raw form**, but around this time the production and export of finished textiles overtook the English economy. This occurred through the cottage industry system under which a cloth manufacturer "put-out" work to rural craftspeople who were provided with raw wool which they carded, spun, and wove in their own homes. This reduced textile costs because it effectively cut out the guilds that controlled urban trade by creating monopolies and preventing competition between guild members.

7 During this period, the extent of England's international trade increased so markedly that companies, such as the Muscovy Company and the English East India Company, were chartered to develop monopolistic trade routes for English goods, such as wool textiles, with faraway places like Moscow and India. One of the major markets for these textiles was the Spanish-controlled city of Antwerp where they were dyed and sold. Antwerp was so important a point that the English **(29)kept a representative stationed** there permanently, Sir Thomas Gresham. Gresham increased England's reputation in Antwerp **(30)to the point that** English merchants were able to operate **(31)on a credit** based system there, something very rare in the sixteenth century. He also championed the economic possibilities of the Americas, leading to England's early **(32)attempts to colonize** the continents **(33)for** commercial **purposes**.

England's Sixteenth Century Economy

1 Great changes occurred in England during the Late Tudor Period under the reign of Queen Elizabeth I In the latter half of the sixteenth and early seventeenth centuries. One of the most notable was the increase in the population to nearly that of the pre-Black Death period. In England and Wales, increased fertility and reduced mortality rates nearly doubled the population around this time, increasing from 2.5 million in the 1520s to 4.5 million by 1610. This dramatic increase, along with other factors, lead to vast changes in England's economy and allowed it to become Europe's largest, far surpassing those of the war and plague-ravaged continent.

2 One of the first direct effects of the population increase was a demand for more food. This caused an "agricultural revolution" in England 2-300 years before they occurred elsewhere in Europe. During this period, English farmers created farmlands from previously unsuitable areas, such as marshlands and woodlands, giving them more arable land on which to produce food.These farmers undertook a process of crop specialization that allowed them to be more efficient and market-driven, increasing their yields dramatically. For instance, they increased their grain production per acre by at least 30% between 1450 and 1650.

3 With the greater efficiency of the new farming methods, wealthy landowners increased their landholdings in order to increase their agricultural productivity. These landholdings were consolidated through the practice of primogeniture under which the eldest son inherited the entirety of his father's holdings, thus preventing the great estates from being divided up into smaller parcels which could not produce as much income. They also increased the size of their landholdings by marrying into other families with large estates. Marriages amongst the wealthiest Elizabethan families were arranged to ensure that both families maintained their social statuses. With their larger estates, these families could conduct more commercialized farming to meet the demand for agricultural products which was driving prices higher.

4 These large landowners, and the yeomen who had smaller landholdings, maximized the profits they could draw from their property. To increase their profits, they planted crops which were in demand in the London markets. They also aggressively dealt with those to whom they rented their property. During this period, rents were increased and rental contracts were written to provide even more benefits to the landowners. One of the ways they did this was shortening the duration of their contracts to allow themselves more control over the land. Another way they maximized their profits was to charge potential tenants an "entry fee" before they would even consent to renting to them. Renters who could not, or would not, abide by the new contracts were simply evicted and replaced by those who could. Their tactics were quite one-sided, but they also encouraged their tenants to use farming practices that would increase their farming efficiency, such as crop rotation.

5 Another method used to increase the profits of these large landholdings was to convert some of the farmland into pastureland upon which sheep could graze. This conversion became possible because of the enclosure movement that occurred during the Tudor period. In the process of enclosure, open fields that had previously been used for communal farming, grazing and hay production were fenced and their use became the sole right of the owner. Seeing the growing demands for English wool internationally, landholders often considered rearing sheep as a more profitable way to utilize their land. By converting their land into pastureland they could derive a higher profit while reducing the need for large numbers of workers to tend it.

6 Wool production led to even greater changes in the English economy of the time. While English wool had been exported since at least the 1200s, the in it was exported form began to change. Wool was traditionally exported in its raw form, but around this time the production and export of finished textiles overtook the English economy. This occurred through the cottage industry system under which a cloth manufacturer "put-out" work to rural craftspeople who were provided with raw wool which they carded, spun, and wove in their own homes. This reduced textile costs because it effectively cut out the guilds that controlled urban trade by creating monopolies and preventing competition between guild members.

7 During this period, the extent of England's international trade increased so markedly that companies, such as the Muscovy Company and the English East India Company, were chartered to develop monopolistic trade routes for English goods, such as wool textiles, with faraway places like Moscow and India. One of the major markets for these textiles was the Spanish-controlled city of Antwerp where they were dyed and sold. Antwerp was so important a point that the English kept a representative stationed there permanently, Sir Thomas Gresham. Gresham increased England's reputation in Antwerp to the point that English merchants were able to operate on a credit based system there, something very rare in the sixteenth century. He also championed the economic possibilities of the Americas, leading to England's early attempts to colonize the continents for commercial purposes.

Environmental Impact of the Anasazi

1 The Anasazi people, ancient Native Americans who [1]**resided in** pit houses, pueblos, and cliff dwellings, flourished in America's present-day Four Corners region before suddenly abandoning their elaborate villages and palace complexes. Archeologists long thought that studies of the rings of the trees used in the structures found there indicated that these people had been driven from their villages and home region, [2]**due to** a climatic event [3]**known as** the "Great Drought." This, however, [4]**began to be** [5]**called into question** recently. Today, historians believe that the Anasazi evacuation had been an ongoing event before the "Great Drought" and that the drought was not an unprecedented event; villagers had likely survived others before it. This has [6]**left them researching** what [7]**could have actually** [8]**caused** an entire civilization **to abandon** its home territory. Archeologist Tim Kohler has [9]**come up with** one possible explanation, human [10]**interaction with** the natural environment.

2 Kohler believes that the Anasazi's interactions with their surroundings eventually [11]**led to** their downfall. To support his hypothesis, Kohler [12]**put forth** a case study regarding the Anasazi living in southwestern Colorado's Dolores River basin around 600 A.D. [13]**Over** a few hundred years, their population increased greatly and they built large villages [14]**complete with** kivas and Great Houses, until around 900 A.D. when the area's abandonment began. Many archeologists believe that shortened growing seasons occurred during this era, which [15]**would have made** it difficult to produce the main Anasazi staple, corn. Kohler [16]**takes exception** to this theory, however, and [17]**points to** problems that developed due to this growing population's settlement in villages, which caused a pressing [18]**need for** increased agricultural output, forcing [19]**changes in** the Anasazi's interactions with the environment, leading to deforestation, soil depletion, and their eventual abandonment of the area.

3 [20]**Prior to** their settlement, the Anasazi population had been semi-nomadic in the Dolores River basin, farming the reasonably fertile, thin soils of the flat-topped mesas using the swidden, or slash-and-burn, technique for over 1,000 years. Using this method, they [21]**burned down** forests to plant the crops they needed and utilized the new farmland until it became [22]**unsuitable for** producing crops, at which time they [23]**moved on to** an adjacent area and repeated the process, [24]**allowing** the previous area **to** [25]**lie fallow** and replenish the nutrients necessary [26]**for** its future **use**. This may [27]**appear to be** a destructive way of growing food that ruins the land, but with less dense populations and a schedule of movement that allows the land adequate time for replenishment between planting, swidden is a sustainable [28]**means of** acquiring the food that societies need. Kohler's contention was that the permanent settlement of a large, growing population like the Dolores River basin Anasazi relying upon this method would lead to their eventual destruction.

4 Kohler found several types of evidence to show that changes in human-environmental interactions were more [29]**responsible for** the Anasazi disappearance than climatic events. Surprisingly, his first source was the same as the one that had led archeologists astray, trees. Kohler noted a pattern in the types of wood found in charcoal deposits from different periods. It [30]**seemed that** juniper and pinion pine [31]**were replaced by** faster growing shrubbery and cottonwoods. He also discovered that the Anasazi [32]**switched from** using pinion pines for construction **to** younger juniper trees, a less desirable wood source, but one that is more fire resistant and easier to propagate in open settings. This, likely, indicated that the pinion became scarcer around the village as the growing population's [33]**demand increased**. This would have also affected their [34]**food supply** as pinion seeds were also gathered as a food source. Additionally, their clearing of the surrounding areas would have had an impact on their hunting [35]**as well**. [36]**As time progressed**, the Anasazi apparently switched from hunting woodland rabbits and deer to jackrabbits and antelope, species [37]**native to** open environments. Seeds [38]**excavated from** the settlements provided Kohler's final piece of evidence. During excavation of later settlements, a marked [39]**increase in** pioneer species seeds was found, indicating a disturbance in the natural environment.

5 Kohler postulates that the Anasazi aggregated in villages due to the organizational benefits they offered [40]**in the face of** soil depletion during their early periods. These large settlements allowed them to share food, [41]**invest in** group food processing units and pool their labor for longer distance hunting or trading trips. Settling in one area, however, [42]**brought about** new problems, like soil depletion and increased distance to usable fields, which led to increased agricultural risk. This led to agricultural intensification using methods, such as developing mechanisms to better control water flow. These larger villages with more technical agricultural methods produced more food, but were more [43]**susceptible to** a rapid collapse. The cooperative management of resources for the village meant that they were less flexible [44]**in response to** environmental changes, so a weak growing season [45]**had** a widespread **impact on** the village. [46]**For this reason**, even a minor, predictable climate change could have [47]**led** the Anasazi **to abandon** their settlements.

Environmental Impact of the Anasazi

1 The Anasazi people, ancient Native Americans who resided in pit houses, pueblos, and cliff dwellings, flourished in America's present-day Four Corners region before suddenly abandoning their elaborate villages and palace complexes. Archeologists long thought that studies of the rings of the trees used in the structures found there indicated that these people had been driven from their villages and home region, due to a climatic event known as the "Great Drought." This, however, began to be called into question recently. Today, historians believe that the Anasazi evacuation had been an ongoing event before the "Great Drought" and that the drought was not an unprecedented event; villagers had likely survived others before it. This has left them researching what could have actually caused an entire civilization to abandon its home territory. Archeologist Tim Kohler has come up with one possible explanation, human interaction with the natural environment.

2 Kohler believes that the Anasazi's interactions with their surroundings eventually led to their downfall. To support his hypothesis, Kohler put forth a case study regarding the Anasazi living in southwestern Colorado's Dolores River basin around 600 A.D. Over a few hundred years, their population increased greatly and they built large villages complete with kivas and Great Houses, until around 900 A.D. when the area's abandonment began. Many archeologists believe that shortened growing seasons occurred during this era, which would have made it difficult to produce the main Anasazi staple, corn. Kohler takes exception to this theory, however, and points to problems that developed due to this growing population's settlement in villages, which caused a pressing need for increased agricultural output, forcing changes in the Anasazi's interactions with the environment, leading to deforestation, soil depletion, and their eventual abandonment of the area.

3 Prior to their settlement, the Anasazi population had been semi-nomadic in the Dolores River basin, farming the reasonably fertile, thin soils of the flat-topped mesas using the swidden, or slash-and-burn, technique for over 1,000 years. Using this method, they burned down forests to plant the crops they needed and utilized the new farmland until it became unsuitable for producing crops, at which time they moved on to an adjacent area and repeated the process, allowing the previous area to lie fallow and replenish the nutrients necessary for its future use. This may appear to be a destructive way of growing food that ruins the land, but with less dense populations and a schedule of movement that allows the land adequate time for replenishment between planting, swidden is a sustainable means of acquiring the food that societies need. Kohler's contention was that the permanent settlement of a large, growing population like the Dolores River basin Anasazi relying upon this method would lead to their eventual destruction.

4 Kohler found several types of evidence to show that changes in human-environmental interactions were more responsible for the Anasazi disappearance than climatic events. Surprisingly, his first source was the same as the one that had led archeologists astray, trees. Kohler noted a pattern in the types of wood found in charcoal deposits from different periods. It seemed that juniper and pinion pine were replaced by faster growing shrubbery and cottonwoods. He also discovered that the Anasazi switched from using pinion pines for construction to younger juniper trees, a less desirable wood source, but one that is more fire resistant and easier to propagate in open settings. This, likely, indicated that the pinion became scarcer around the village as the growing population's demand increased. This would have also affected their food supply as pinion seeds were also gathered as a food source. Additionally, their clearing of the surrounding areas would have had an impact on their hunting as well. As time progressed, the Anasazi apparently switched from hunting woodland rabbits and deer to jackrabbits and antelope, species native to open environments. Seeds excavated from the settlements provided Kohler's final piece of evidence. During excavation of later settlements, a marked increase in pioneer species seeds was found, indicating a disturbance in the natural environment.

5 Kohler postulates that the Anasazi aggregated in villages due to the organizational benefits they offered in the face of soil depletion during their early periods. These large settlements allowed them to share food, invest in group food processing units and pool their labor for longer distance hunting or trading trips. Settling in one area, however, brought about new problems, like soil depletion and increased distance to usable fields, which led to increased agricultural risk. This led to agricultural intensification using methods, such as developing mechanisms to better control water flow. These larger villages with more technical agricultural methods produced more food, but were more susceptible to a rapid collapse. The cooperative management of resources for the village meant that they were less flexible in response to environmental changes, so a weak growing season had a widespread impact on the village. For this reason, even a minor, predictable climate change could have led the Anasazi to abandon their settlements.

Global Variations in Species Diversity

1 A peculiar aspect of the world today is the presence of a gradient, or gradual ⁽¹⁾**change, in** species diversity from the tropics to the polar areas. Species population surveys have shown that regions nearer the equator have the highest species diversity, and as one ⁽²⁾**moves to** higher latitudes, diversity ⁽³⁾**drops off** dramatically. This gradient can be seen across all species, both flora and fauna, and from higher-level mammals to lower order protozoans.

2 One of the first explanations for this was that temperature and light stability in tropical regions, ⁽⁴⁾**when compared to** the seasonal fluctuations of both in polar regions, ⁽⁵⁾**allowed** more species **to develop**; however, temperature and light do not ⁽⁶⁾**seem to fully control** species diversity. This can be seen by ⁽⁷⁾**looking at** the seas in polar regions, which remain ⁽⁸⁾**at** a near constant **temperature** year-round yet still have low species diversity. It may then seem logical that the northern seas' near-freezing temperatures preclude diversity levels as high as ⁽⁹⁾**those of** the tropics, but as one moves deeper to the seafloor, which remains ⁽¹⁰⁾**in** perpetual, frigid **darkness** with ⁽¹¹⁾**neither** light **nor** warmth from the sun, there is relatively higher species diversity. Therefore, another important factor, such as the availability of food, must affect species diversity.

3 One aspect of the food supply that could affect the diversity of species is that in tropical regions, the food supply remains relatively stable year-round ⁽¹²⁾**due to** the uniform climate. Because of this, species can ⁽¹³⁾**specialize in** feeding on one food source without the risk of it not being available ⁽¹⁴⁾**at various times** of year. As they become more ⁽¹⁵⁾**dependent on** their food sources, species adapt more fully and become highly specialized. This allows multiple species to ⁽¹⁶⁾**feed on** one food source but only marginally ⁽¹⁷⁾**compete with** ⁽¹⁸⁾**one another**. This can be seenin the various carrion feeding vultures of the African plains. Although various species of vultures are present on the Serengeti, they have developed different niches. For example, one species has a beak that can tear through leathery hides and a head ⁽¹⁹⁾**devoid of** feathers, which allows them to ⁽²⁰⁾**stick** their heads **into** the carcass and not ⁽²¹⁾**worry about** becoming contaminated because the sun will bake the refuse from their baldheads. Another has ⁽²²⁾**adapted to** feeding on the innards, while still others consume the bones and random scraps. Even though they are all eating from the same carcasses, they are all ensured a constant supply of food because their niche specializations effectively lower the competition rate.

4 Species that live in higher latitudes, on the other hand, face a constantly changing food supply. During the warmer season, tundra species have a plethora of food sources, such as plant life and newly hatched krill, which are fed on by animals such as caribou, seabirds, fish, and oceanic mammals. However, when the long, frigid winter ⁽²³⁾**sets in**, the area is rather barren, leading many specialized feeders to ⁽²⁴⁾**migrate to** other areas. There are, however, animals with a more generalist feeding style that remain in the tundra year-round, seasonally adapting their feeding patterns. The gray wolf, for example, ⁽²⁵⁾**switches from** consuming small mammals and migratory birds during the warmer months **to** hunting weakened caribou during the winter. This ⁽²⁶⁾**assures** the species **of** constant food supplies throughout the year. These distinct feeding patterns, therefore, do not limit species diversity, since they allow ⁽²⁷⁾**a variety of** tundra species to coexist despite the relatively lower overall food supply.

5 Since the variability in light, temperature, and food supply does not necessarily reduce species diversity in an area, there must be another explanation for the great latitudinal difference. One new theory is that the evolutionary process itself caused this phenomenon. The theory of "effective evolutionary time" ⁽²⁸⁾**draws upon** earlier research that showed that evolution occurs more quickly in smaller species that inhabit warmer temperatures. This likely occurs due to the higher physiological rates of smaller species in tropical regions, which ⁽²⁹⁾**lead to** shorter lifespans. A rather striking example of this is the fresh water pearl mussel, which can inhabit freshwater streams in a variety of latitudes and whose maximum lifespan varies ⁽³⁰⁾**depending on** latitude, from 29 years at 43°N to nearly 200 at 66°N. This can also be seen in plant species by comparing the relatively shorter lifespans and earlier reproduction rates of plants from tropical regions with those from northern latitudes, such as the giant redwood which has been recorded as living up to 3500 years. While it may seem that the lifespan ⁽³¹⁾**differences in** a species would ⁽³²⁾**have little effect on** overall diversity, it can ⁽³³⁾**be shown to have** a great impact. The shorter lifespans of species in warmer areas ⁽³⁴⁾**result in** shorter generation lengths, thereby causing a higher mutation rate and speed of selection than ⁽³⁵⁾**in** higher **latitudes**. This rapid mutation and selection enables distinct species to be produce much more quickly than in the colder northern regions. These new species then ⁽³⁶⁾**begin filling** unexploited niches in the tropical ecosystem and become even more particularly adapted as more generations are produced.

Global Variations in Species Diversity

1 A peculiar aspect of the world today is the presence of a gradient, or gradual change, in species diversity from the tropics to the polar areas. Species population surveys have shown that regions nearer the equator have the highest species diversity, and as one moves to higher latitudes, diversity drops off dramatically. This gradient can be seen across all species, both flora and fauna, and from higher-level mammals to lower order protozoans.

2 One of the first explanations for this was that temperature and light stability in tropical regions, when compared to the seasonal fluctuations of both in polar regions, allowed more species to develop; however, temperature and light do not seem to fully control species diversity. This can be seen by looking at the seas in polar regions, which remain at a near constant temperature year-round yet still have low species diversity. It may then seem logical that the northern seas' near-freezing temperatures preclude diversity levels as high as those of the tropics, but as one moves deeper to the seafloor, which remains in perpetual, frigid darkness with neither light nor warmth from the sun, there is relatively higher species diversity. Therefore, another important factor, such as the availability of food, must affect species diversity.

3 One aspect of the food supply that could affect the diversity of species is that in tropical regions, the food supply remains relatively stable year-round due to the uniform climate. Because of this, species can specialize in feeding on one food source without the risk of it not being available at various times of year. As they become more dependent on their food sources, species adapt more fully and become highly specialized. This allows multiple species to feed on one food source but only marginally compete with one another. This can be seen in the various carrion feeding vultures of the African plains. Although various species of vultures are present on the Serengeti, they have developed different niches. For example, one species has a beak that can tear through leathery hides and a head devoid of feathers, which allows them to stick their heads into the carcass and not worry about becoming contaminated because the sun will bake the refuse from their baldheads. Another has adapted to feeding on the innards, while still others consume the bones and random scraps. Even though they are all eating from the same carcasses, they are all ensured a constant supply of food because their niche specializations effectively lower the competition rate.

4 Species that live in higher latitudes, on the other hand, face a constantly changing food supply. During the warmer season, tundra species have a plethora of food sources, such as plant life and newly hatched krill, which are fed on by animals such as caribou, seabirds, fish, and oceanic mammals. However, when the long, frigid winter sets in, the area is rather barren, leading many specialized feeders to migrate to other areas. There are, however, animals with a more generalist feeding style that remain in the tundra year-round, seasonally adapting their feeding patterns. The gray wolf, for example, switches from consuming small mammals and migratory birds during the warmer months to hunting weakened caribou during the winter. This assures the species of constant food supplies throughout the year. These distinct feeding patterns, therefore, do not limit species diversity, since they allow a variety of tundra species to coexist despite the relatively lower overall food supply.

5 Since the variability in light, temperature, and food supply does not necessarily reduce species diversity in an area, there must be another explanation for the great latitudinal difference. One new theory is that the evolutionary process itself caused this phenomenon. The theory of "effective evolutionary time" draws upon earlier research that showed that evolution occurs more quickly in smaller species that inhabit warmer temperatures. This likely occurs due to the higher physiological rates of smaller species in tropical regions, which lead to shorter lifespans. A rather striking example of this is the fresh water pearl mussel, which can inhabit freshwater streams in a variety of latitudes and whose maximum lifespan varies depending on latitude, from 29 years at 43°N to nearly 200 at 66°N. This can also be seen in plant species by comparing the relatively shorter lifespans and earlier reproduction rates of plants from tropical regions with those from northern latitudes, such as the giant redwood which has been recorded as living up to 3500 years. While it may seem that the lifespan differences in a species would have little effect on overall diversity, it can be shown to have a great impact. The shorter lifespans of species in warmer areas result in shorter generation lengths, thereby causing a higher mutation rate and speed of selection than in higher latitudes. This rapid mutation and selection enables distinct species to be produce much more quickly than in the colder northern regions. These new species then begin filling unexploited niches in the tropical ecosystem and become even more particularly adapted as more generations are produced.

Documenting the Incas

1 (1)**Beginning with** the founding of the capital city of Cusco in the early 1200s, the Inca Empire expanded along the mountainous west coast of South America. Within 250 years, their (2)**conquests of** neighboring societies (3)**allowed them to** (4)**control over** 3,000 miles of coastline and land covering parts of present day Peru, Bolivia, Ecuador, Chile and Argentina. The power of their army and their effective administration of this vast empire (5)**made them the greatest** of the New World civilizations. This great empire would, however, collapse less than 100 years later when the Spanish conquistador Francisco Pizarro arrived and conquered the area for Spain in the 1530s. Since the Inca language did not have writing system, much of what is currently known about this magnificent civilization was recorded by these Spanish conquerors. This has (6)**led to** many problems (7)**related to** the veracity of the historical records of the early Inca Empire.

2 The first of these is that the ruling system used by the Inca was (8)**different from** (9)**that of** the Spanish Empire and may not have been fully understood by the early conquerors. (10)**In order to record** the historical information, they (11)**gleaned from** their Inca informants. Then, they simply (12)**adapted the information to** the Spanish style of governance. As time went on, these kinds of inaccuracies would have been compounded since most scholars would have used these recordings as primary sources for their later research. A good example of this is their list of Inca rulers. The Inca (13)**told** the early conquerors **of** thirteen kings who ruled over the empire, and the Spanish recorded them as thirteen sequential rulers, as that was how the monarchy worked in Spain; however, it isn't clear if these recorded names were individuals or titles. If they were titles, they could have been held concurrently, and there (14)**may have been** fewer than thirteen kings that (15)**ruled over** the empire. Since the empire only flourished under the last four kings, this isn't a major problem in understanding the Inca culture, but it (16)**points to** how cultural bias and inaccuracies (17)**regarding** the Inca could have begun with the earliest recorded histories of them.

3 Another problem with the accounts compiled by the Spanish was that they may have been intentionally inaccurate. The Spanish (18)**wanted to downplay** certain aspects of the Inca civilization, such as the extent of their wealth. If the conquistadors accurately recorded Incan gold production, they would have had to (19)**turn** it all **over** to the Spanish Crown. By downplaying the extent of the Inca's wealth, the conquistadors (20)**were able to amass** their own gold caches. The inaccuracies may have also been the fault of the Inca themselves. Since they were helping their new conquerors, the Inca may have (21)**misled them to make** themselves look better or exaggerated their importance in society.

4 (22)**Relying on** elite members of the Incan society to learn about their history caused another problem. Since they had no written language system, all of their historical information had been passed down through the oral tradition. (23)**Over** time, many of these stories may have developed unintentional inaccuracies. A prime example of this would be the founding of Cusco, which (24)**was said to have happened** after four brothers and four sisters (25)**emerged from** a cave and led followers they found in another cave to the site of Cusco, where they founded their civilization there. The origin of these early leaders and stories of their exploits were likely exaggerated to paint them (26)**in** a more impressive **light**. Because of the nature of the oral tradition, (27)**it is probable that** the more recent Incan stories (28)**were likely to be** more accurate.

5 The Inca may have also whitewashed the accounts of their expansion and conquest of neighboring settlements, such as the Lupaca to their south. Because of their policy of dispersing uncooperative people and repopulating the area with people who they (29)**were able to** (30)**deal with**, the Incan leaders were the only sources of Spanish knowledge of their empire and were, therefore, able to control the description of their conquests and could (31)**portray** themselves **as** righteous and invincible warriors. This makes it (32)**all but** impossible to establish the accuracy of their narratives.

6 A final problem that (33)**calls** the truthfulness of the Spanish-written histories **into question** is the incongruent uses of place names. It (34)**seems that** different writers (35)**used** various **names to describe** the areas, such as provinces and towns that they encountered in the Incan Empire. This, (36)**compounded with** the great (37)**changes in** the locations of settlements over the last five centuries, makes it difficult to verify any of the location information in accounts of the Incan Empire.

7 Despite the possibility of all of these inaccurate accounts creeping into the Spanish-written historical records of the Incan Empire, researchers still (38)**find them to be** important source materials. By cross-referencing different accounts of the same events and using archeological research, scientists can verify some of the accounts to form an accurate chronology and picture of what actually (39)**went on** during the Incan Empire.

Documenting the Incas

1 Beginning with the founding of the capital city of Cusco in the early 1200s, the Inca Empire expanded along the mountainous west coast of South America. Within 250 years, their conquests of neighboring societies allowed them to control over 3,000 miles of coastline and land covering parts of present day Peru, Bolivia, Ecuador, Chile and Argentina. The power of their army and their effective administration of this vast empire made them the greatest of the New World civilizations. This great empire would, however, collapse less than 100 years later when the Spanish conquistador Francisco Pizarro arrived and conquered the area for Spain in the 1530s. Since the Inca language did not have writing system, much of what is currently known about this magnificent civilization was recorded by these Spanish conquerors. This has led to many problems related to the veracity of the historical records of the early Inca Empire.

2 The first of these is that the ruling system used by the Inca was different from that of the Spanish Empire and may not have been fully understood by the early conquerors. In order to record the historical information, they gleaned from their Inca informants. Then, they simply adapted the information to the Spanish style of governance. As time went on, these kinds of inaccuracies would have been compounded since most scholars would have used these recordings as primary sources for their later research. A good example of this is their list of Inca rulers. The Inca told the early conquerors of thirteen kings who ruled over the empire, and the Spanish recorded them as thirteen sequential rulers, as that was how the monarchy worked in Spain; however, it isn't clear if these recorded names were individuals or titles. If they were titles, they could have been held concurrently, and there may have been fewer than thirteen kings that ruled over the empire. Since the empire only flourished under the last four kings, this isn't a major problem in understanding the Inca culture, but it points to how cultural bias and inaccuracies regarding the Inca could have begun with the earliest recorded histories of them.

3 Another problem with the accounts compiled by the Spanish was that they may have been intentionally inaccurate. The Spanish wanted to downplay certain aspects of the Inca civilization, such as the extent of their wealth. If the conquistadors accurately recorded Incan gold production, they would have had to turn it all over to the Spanish Crown. By downplaying the extent of the Inca's wealth, the conquistadors were able to amass their own gold caches. The inaccuracies may have also been the fault of the Inca themselves. Since they were helping their new conquerors, the Inca may have misled them to make themselves look better or exaggerated their importance in society.

4 Relying on elite members of the Incan society to learn about their history caused another problem. Since they had no written language system, all of their historical information had been passed down through the oral tradition. Over time, many of these stories may have developed unintentional inaccuracies. A prime example of this would be the founding of Cusco, which was said to have happened after four brothers and four sisters emerged from a cave and led followers they found in another cave to the site of Cusco, where they founded their civilization there. The origin of these early leaders and stories of their exploits were likely exaggerated to paint them in a more impressive light. Because of the nature of the oral tradition, it is probable that the more recent Incan stories were likely to be more accurate.

5 The Inca may have also whitewashed the accounts of their expansion and conquest of neighboring settlements, such as the Lupaca to their south. Because of their policy of dispersing uncooperative people and repopulating the area with people who they were able to deal with, the Incan leaders were the only sources of Spanish knowledge of their empire and were, therefore, able to control the description of their conquests and could portray themselves as righteous and invincible warriors. This makes it all but impossible to establish the accuracy of their narratives.

6 A final problem that calls the truthfulness of the Spanish-written histories into question is the incongruent uses of place names. It seems that different writers used various names to describe the areas, such as provinces and towns that they encountered in the Incan Empire. This, compounded with the great changes in the locations of settlements over the last five centuries, makes it difficult to verify any of the location information in accounts of the Incan Empire.

7 Despite the possibility of all of these inaccurate accounts creeping into the Spanish-written historical records of the Incan Empire, researchers still find them to be important source materials. By cross-referencing different accounts of the same events and using archeological research, scientists can verify some of the accounts to form an accurate chronology and picture of what actually went on during the Incan Empire.

Architectural Change in Eighth Century Japan

1 Japanese architecture underwent dramatic changes as the Nara period began in the early 8th century. During this period, great political and societal changes, such as the establishment of the capital at Heijō-kyō (modern day Nara), made traditional architectural arrangements and styles less advantageous and necessitated a new system. On this **quest for** more adequate architectural styles, the Japanese were influenced by the architecture of continental Asian powers, such as China's Tang Dynasty.

2 One of the most glaring catalysts for the **change in** architectural styles was the **shift in** marriage practices of the Japanese elite. **Prior to** this period, Japanese rulers married members of one of the most powerful clans of the period, the Soga-lords' families, in politically motivated alliances, and established palaces at the bride's family home **in addition to that of** their own family headquarters. The royal court generally **resided with** the bride's family **for the first years** of their marriage and then moved between their multiple palaces throughout the marriage as children grew older and alliances shifted. This system was workable during this period because of the relatively small royal court and rudimentary architectural styles.

3 Prior to the Nara period, traditional Japanese structures, such as palaces, gate towers, fortresses, and shrines **were built with** wooden beams, dirt floors, and thatched roofs. Since these beams were **in** direct **contact with** the moist ground, they often rotted away in less than 20 years. The simple, temporary nature of these buildings meant that they could be moved or constructed in new areas without great labor or material expenditures and were easily rebuild able when damaged. This was **important to** Shinto adherents because replacing buildings **allowed for** a spiritual cleansing of the land. This **taboo against** unclean spirits also **led to** the continuous movement of the capital before the Nara period; new emperors moved the court to avoid contamination from the death of their predecessors.

4 Moving the capital became unfeasible during the Nara period **due to the expansion of** the bureaucracy **involved in** the court during the previous two centuries. **By the time the Nara emperors rose to power**, they were overseeing a staff of 10,000 workers and needed a location that provided adequate housing for them. The need to **keep in contact with** these people and to **provide for** them meant that palaces **needed to be maintained** in areas with abundant resources. Further, moving such a large court and reconstructing **enough** buildings **to house** them effectively killed the mobile capital tradition and led the emperors to **settle in** Heijō-kyō.

5 To construct this imperial city, Japanese architects **looked to** the urban design and construction techniques of their continental neighbors' geometrically situated capitals with their bulkier, more permanent buildings constructed using stone foundations, mortise joints, and tiled roofs which allowed them to stand for years. The construction of a large, continental-style capital with these types of buildings required a tremendous amount of manpower and building materials, but it was **attractive to** emperors **looking to legitimize** their reigns **in a manner** directly **comparable to** the powerful Chinese dynasty. The construction of these types of buildings was also heavily influenced by the widespread acceptance of Buddhism which had **been introduced from** the continental kingdoms two hundred years earlier. After this, the Japanese officially adopted Buddhism, but conflicts with hostile believers in the Shinto Kami prevented them from building lasting Buddhist temples. During the Nara period, the Japanese Buddhists built temple complexes **modeled after** those found in continental nations, such as the Hōryō-ji, one of the oldest surviving wooden structures in the world.

6 This shift in architecture during this period caused a series of conflicts across the Japanese royal court. Rulers **wished to display** their power through the construction of a grand capital rivaling that of the Tang Dynasty, but this was difficult **at the time** and required a great expenditure. In addition, while the opulent lifestyle of the new building styles **would have been** comfortable for the ruling class, they **were hesitant to give up** the multiple palaces they enjoyed **under** the mobile court **system**. Conflicts even arose between religions because of the Shinto **belief in** replacing buildings frequently and the Buddhists' **desire for** permanent religious buildings. Eventually, these conflicts were solved through a compromise **in** building **methods**. Shinto shrines, with their religious **reliance on** rebuilding and cleansing, and many residential buildings **adhered to** the traditional style that was more economical, mobile, and replaceable. Government buildings, city gates, and Buddhist temples, **on the other hand**, were constructed **in** the more permanent, grandiose continental **style**. Even the issues **related to** the immobility of the court were solved through an architectural compromise. Rulers, who were now **in residence** in the grand capital, constructed smaller palaces in remote areas where they could temporarily reside. This gave the court a bit of mobility and may have **made it easier for them to oversee** the parts of their populations which lived **far away from** the new capital city.

Architectural Change in Eighth Century Japan

1 Japanese architecture underwent dramatic changes as the Nara period began in the early 8th century. During this period, great political and societal changes, such as the establishment of the capital at Heijō-kyō (modern day Nara), made traditional architectural arrangements and styles less advantageous and necessitated a new system. On this quest for more adequate architectural styles, the Japanese were influenced by the architecture of continental Asian powers, such as China's Tang Dynasty.

2 One of the most glaring catalysts for the change in architectural styles was the shift in marriage practices of the Japanese elite. Prior to this period, Japanese rulers married members of one of the most powerful clans of the period, the Soga-lords' families, in politically motivated alliances, and established palaces at the bride's family home in addition to that of their own family headquarters. The royal court generally resided with the bride's family for the first years of their marriage and then moved between their multiple palaces throughout the marriage as children grew older and alliances shifted. This system was workable during this period because of the relatively small royal court and rudimentary architectural styles.

3 Prior to the Nara period, traditional Japanese structures, such as palaces, gate towers, fortresses, and shrines were built with wooden beams, dirt floors, and thatched roofs. Since these beams were in direct contact with the moist ground, they often rotted away in less than 20 years. The simple, temporary nature of these buildings meant that they could be moved or constructed in new areas without great labor or material expenditures and were easily rebuild able when damaged. This was important to Shinto adherents because replacing buildings allowed for a spiritual cleansing of the land. This taboo against unclean spirits also led to the continuous movement of the capital before the Nara period; new emperors moved the court to avoid contamination from the death of their predecessors.

4 Moving the capital became unfeasible during the Nara period due to the expansion of the bureaucracy involved in the court during the previous two centuries. By the time the Nara emperors rose to power, they were overseeing a staff of 10,000 workers and needed a location that provided adequate housing for them. The need to keep in contact with these people and to provide for them meant that palaces needed to be maintained in areas with abundant resources. Further, moving such a large court and reconstructing enough buildings to house them effectively killed the mobile capital tradition and led the emperors to settle in Heijō-kyō.

5 To construct this imperial city, Japanese architects looked to the urban design and construction techniques of their continental neighbors' geometrically situated capitals with their bulkier, more permanent buildings constructed using stone foundations, mortise joints, and tiled roofs which allowed them to stand for years. The construction of a large, continental-style capital with these types of buildings required a tremendous amount of manpower and building materials, but it was attractive to emperors looking to legitimize their reigns in a manner directly comparable to the powerful Chinese dynasty. The construction of these types of buildings was also heavily influenced by the widespread acceptance of Buddhism which had been introduced from the continental kingdoms two hundred years earlier. After this, the Japanese officially adopted Buddhism, but conflicts with hostile believers in the Shinto Kami prevented them from building lasting Buddhist temples. During the Nara period, the Japanese Buddhists built temple complexes modeled after those found in continental nations, such as the Hōryō-ji, one of the oldest surviving wooden structures in the world.

6 This shift in architecture during this period caused a series of conflicts across the Japanese royal court. Rulers wished to display their power through the construction of a grand capital rivaling that of the Tang Dynasty, but this was difficult at the time and required a great expenditure. In addition, while the opulent lifestyle of the new building styles would have been comfortable for the ruling class, they were hesitant to give up the multiple palaces they enjoyed under the mobile court system. Conflicts even arose between religions because of the Shinto belief in replacing buildings frequently and the Buddhists' desire for permanent religious buildings. Eventually, these conflicts were solved through a compromise in building methods. Shinto shrines, with their religious reliance on rebuilding and cleansing, and many residential buildings adhered to the traditional style that was more economical, mobile, and replaceable. Government buildings, city gates, and Buddhist temples, on the other hand, were constructed in the more permanent, grandiose continental style. Even the issues related to the immobility of the court were solved through an architectural compromise. Rulers, who were now in residence in the grand capital, constructed smaller palaces in remote areas where they could temporarily reside. This gave the court a bit of mobility and may have made it easier for them to oversee the parts of their populations which lived far away from the new capital city.

How Camels Survive in Arid Environments

1 Their (1)**ability to survive** extreme temperatures and food or water deprivation has made camels invaluable in Asia, Africa, and the Middle East. These large animals (2)**come in** two varieties, Central Asia's two-humped Bactrian and the single-humped desert dromedaries of Africa and the Middle East, which were independently domesticated 5,000 years ago. They have since (3)**acted as** beasts of burden, desert transport, and sources of wool, leather, milk and meat because they, unlike other livestock, have specialized mechanisms for survival in desert environments.

2 Their first adaptation is their ability to go (4)**for long periods** without water. Unlike most animals, the camel can go without water for two weeks without negative effects. This is possible because they can drink up to 200 liters of water at once. When they drink these great amounts, some of the water (5)**is** rapidly **transferred to** their blood streams and carried throughout the body to hydrate the bodily tissues. This is unique because in most animals such a dilution of the bloodstream would cause a fatal rupturing of the red blood cells. However, camels' specially adapted red blood cells can survive this and have a unique ovoid shape, compared to the rounder red blood cells of most animals, which (6)**allows** them **to flow** more freely during times of dehydration.

3 Camels also handle water loss better than most animals. In humans, (7)**for instance**, a 2% water loss stresses the body and anything more than 12% is fatal, but camels can survive losing 25% of their bodies' water content. This is because of how their bodies lose water. Unlike most animals, camels metabolize the water between cells and in their guts, rather than the water in their cells. By protecting the cellular water content, their bodies (8)**are able to function** properly even after dramatic water losses.

4 (9)**In addition to** being able to (10)**cope with** water loss, camels have special abilities and adaptations which prevent it. The most obvious of these is the fact that camels sweat very little. They also have efficient digestive systems which produce very dry, concentrated urine and feces. Camel feces is (11)**so dry that** it can be lit and (12)**used as** fuel for fires almost (13)**immediately after** being deposited. Another way they conserve water is through their respiratory system. In most animals, (14)**a large amount of** water is exhaled during respiration, giving the breath a relative humidity of nearly 100%. Camels, (15)**on the other hand**, breathe relatively slowly, reducing the number of exhaled breaths and have specialized scrolled nasal bones called turbinates, which increase the nasal cavity surface area, to nearly 1000 sq. cm., and capture moisture from the exhaled air, reducing its relative humidity up to 25%, and hydrate the dry desert air which they breathe in. The network of capillaries in their cooler nasal cavities also (16)**keeps the brain cooler** through heat diffusion.

5 There is, perhaps, no better known, or misunderstood, camel adaptation to heat and dehydration than the hump. Commonly (17)**thought to hold** water, these humps are actually fat accumulations. Unlike other animals, which are covered by a layer of fat, camels store theirs in their humps. Fat cells hold in body heat, so by (18)**having most** of their fat (19)**concentrated on** their backs, camels can more easily dissipate heat, reducing their internal temperatures. Water is also produced when this fat is metabolized, but it is all (20)**used up** (21)**in the process**.

6 Camels also (22)**deal with** heat rather uniquely. Most mammals maintain a stable internal temperature and utilize physical processes, such as panting, sweating, or (23)**exposing** more skin **to** open air in shaded regions, to (24)**maintain** their **temperatures** (25)**as** (26)**close to** the ideal **as possible**. These methods reduce the animal's temperature but also cause water loss. Camels, on the other hand, avoid this by having an internal temperature that varies more widely than other mammals. The diurnal variation in a camels' temperature can be as high as 6°C. This wide temperature fluctuation would mean major problems for most other species. In humans, for instance, an internal temperature increase of even half this much can cause brain damage and even death. Scientists believe that this fluctuation reduces the (27)**need for** sweating and panting, which (28)**saves camels** as **much as** 5L of water (29)**per day**.

7 Their physical features and actions (30)**not only** dissipate heat **but also** (31)**avoid gaining** heat altogether. Their tall, spindly legs keep their cores aloft, where air temperatures are cooler, and their uninsulated nearly hairless underbellies dissipate heat quickly. Further, their thin, light-colored wool doesn't absorb much heat and (32)**protects the skin from** the effects of the sun. The fat in their hump also absorbs heat before it reaches the core, where it would increase the internal temperature. This is compounded by their natural proclivity for standing facing the sun, which reduces the amount of surface area directly exposed to the sun's rays.

How Camels Survive in Arid Environments

1 Their ability to survive extreme temperatures and food or water deprivation has made camels invaluable in Asia, Africa, and the Middle East. These large animals come in two varieties, Central Asia's two-humped Bactrian and the single-humped desert dromedaries of Africa and the Middle East, which were independently domesticated 5,000 years ago. They have since acted as beasts of burden, desert transport, and sources of wool, leather, milk and meat because they, unlike other livestock, have specialized mechanisms for survival in desert environments.

2 Their first adaptation is their ability to go for long periods without water. Unlike most animals, the camel can go without water for two weeks without negative effects. This is possible because they can drink up to 200 liters of water at once. When they drink these great amounts, some of the water is rapidly transferred to their blood streams and carried throughout the body to hydrate the bodily tissues. This is unique because in most animals such a dilution of the bloodstream would cause a fatal rupturing of the red blood cells. However, camels' specially adapted red blood cells can survive this and have a unique ovoid shape, compared to the rounder red blood cells of most animals, which allows them to flow more freely during times of dehydration.

3 Camels also handle water loss better than most animals. In humans, for instance, a 2% water loss stresses the body and anything more than 12% is fatal, but camels can survive losing 25% of their bodies' water content. This is because of how their bodies lose water. Unlike most animals, camels metabolize the water between cells and in their guts, rather than the water in their cells. By protecting the cellular water content, their bodies are able to function properly even after dramatic water losses.

4 In addition to being able to cope with water loss, camels have special abilities and adaptations which prevent it. The most obvious of these is the fact that camels sweat very little. They also have efficient digestive systems which produce very dry, concentrated urine and feces. Camel feces is so dry that it can be lit and used as fuel for fires almost immediately after being deposited. Another way they conserve water is through their respiratory system. In most animals, a large amount of water is exhaled during respiration, giving the breath a relative humidity of nearly 100%. Camels, on the other hand, breathe relatively slowly, reducing the number of exhaled breaths and have specialized scrolled nasal bones called turbinates, which increase the nasal cavity surface area, to nearly 1000 sq. cm., and capture moisture from the exhaled air, reducing its relative humidity up to 25%, and hydrate the dry desert air which they breathe in. The network of capillaries in their cooler nasal cavities also keeps the brain cooler through heat diffusion.

5 There is, perhaps, no better known, or misunderstood, camel adaptation to heat and dehydration than the hump. Commonly thought to hold water, these humps are actually fat accumulations. Unlike other animals, which are covered by a layer of fat, camels store theirs in their humps. Fat cells hold in body heat, so by having most of their fat concentrated on their backs, camels can more easily dissipate heat, reducing their internal temperatures. Water is also produced when this fat is metabolized, but it is all used up in the process.

6 Camels also deal with heat rather uniquely. Most mammals maintain a stable internal temperature and utilize physical processes, such as panting, sweating, or exposing more skin to open air in shaded regions, to maintain their temperatures as close to the ideal as possible. These methods reduce the animal's temperature but also cause water loss. Camels, on the other hand, avoid this by having an internal temperature that varies more widely than other mammals. The diurnal variation in a camels' temperature can be as high as 6°C. This wide temperature fluctuation would mean major problems for most other species. In humans, for instance, an internal temperature increase of even half this much can cause brain damage and even death. Scientists believe that this fluctuation reduces the need for sweating and panting, which saves camels as much as 5L of water per day.

7 Their physical features and actions not only dissipate heat but also avoid gaining heat altogether. Their tall, spindly legs keep their cores aloft, where air temperatures are cooler, and their uninsulated nearly hairless underbellies dissipate heat quickly. Further, their thin, light-colored wool doesn't absorb much heat and protects the skin from the effects of the sun. The fat in their hump also absorbs heat before it reaches the core, where it would increase the internal temperature. This is compounded by their natural proclivity for standing facing the sun, which reduces the amount of surface area directly exposed to the sun's rays.

Hunter-gatherers in Southwest Asia

1 During the end of the last glacial period, the Kebaran Civilization flourished in the area of Southwest Asia now (1)**known as** the Middle East. This population was to (2)**have** a large **influence on** humanity, because of their early consumption of cereals and their tool development. Being a nomadic civilization, they (3)**moved across** (4)**a multitude of** climates (5)**over the course of** the year, spending their summers in the cooler highlands and their winters in the rocky waterside caves. This migration (6)**required** them **to adapt** tools to suit each location. These were likely used to hunt gazelle and harvest wild cereals. Human consumption of these cereals became (7)**so** important **that** they currently (8)**make up** 50% and 56% of the world's protein and food energy consumption, (9)**respectively**.

2 Despite the dietary changes they caused, the Kebaran society did not remain forever. Around 13,000 BC, a warmer, wetter period saw the rise of the Natufian Culture. Their appearance (10)**coincided with** the (11)**shift in** plant life in the area. As temperatures rose, plants that required the warmer temperatures of lower altitudes (12)**spread to** higher altitudes. The production of pistachios, oak, almonds, wild barley and wild emmer wheat flourished as they (13)**moved from** the lower altitude's sandy soil to the richer, clay-based soil of higher altitudes; these increased harvests (14)**allowed** the Natufian Culture **to expand** (15)**as well**. Within 1,500 years, the culture had completely replaced the Kebaran and spread from the mountains to the Mediterranean.

3 This culture (16)**proved to be** more sedentary than its predecessors. This is an interesting case in history, since they settled before the advent of farming, relying instead on harvesting wild nuts and grains. Their entire society adapted a new hunting and gathering technique (17)**based on** larger settlements that could harvest more of the crops. These new settlements featured semi-subterranean pit-houses and pits where the crops could be stored. These large settlements were also generally located near smaller satellite camps where they could collect and process their finds. Artifacts from these camps show that the Natufians greatly increased the sophistication of their tools and confirmed their dietary (18)**reliance on** grains. They (19)**were even found to have created** processing tools, such as grinding stones, and harvesting tools, like the flint blade sickle. While these tools could be useful on a multitude of plants, their (20)**use for** cereal harvesting has been proven by the presence of "sickle gloss" on their blades. This is when a flint blade becomes shiny due to the build-up of silica particles from cereal grass stalks.

4 The village locations were also affected by the crops they (21)**relied upon**. They were generally located along the boundary between the coastal grasslands and the higher altitudes where nuts and cereals prospered. They also (22)**seemed to settle** (23)**in places** where they could collect high quality stone for creating new tools. By (24)**settling in** these places, they could harvest the cereal crops as they (25)**came into season** during the spring and harvest nuts in the fall, providing year-round nourishment. (26)**In addition to** using their stored crops in summer and winter, they also hunted the lowland animals. They would even (27)**cooperate with** neighboring communities to perform massive game drives and ambushes on gazelles and other animals.

5 Year-round food sources (28)**led to** a Natufian population boom. As the population increased, a new, highly complex social structure developed. This was discovered through excavation of Natufian cemeteries, where evidence was found that indicated (29)**differences in** social standing between tribe members. Certain burial sites contained the symbolic dentalium seashell, while others, even those of children, (30)**were filled with** common furnishings such as stone bowls, showing a clear difference in societal standing of the deceased. These rankings may have been (31)**the result of** the food redistribution and (32)**efforts to maintain** order that would have been required by such a large sedentary community. These cemeteries also contained limestone grave covers and mortar markers, which (33)**are thought to have** (34)**served as** ritualistic territorial markers for the lands held by the Natufian's highly-respected elders after they passed.

6 Eventually, as their population expanded, the Natufians faced another dramatic lifestyle upheaval due to climate change. Around 11,000 BC, the climate around the Mediterranean (35)**began to dry out**. This reduced the area, in which the wild grains and nuts grew, and increased the society's (36)**need to settle** near a reliable water source. This could have spelled the end of the Natufian society very quickly had they not learned the life cycle of the cereal plants over the previous two millennia of (37)**living off** of and with them. Instead, they (38)**were able to** deliberately **plant and control** the cereal plants. Even the modest scale of this early farming (39)**helped** the society **supplement** their declining wild wheat and barley harvests and thus ensured their survival. Within a short time, farming (40)**flourished in** Southwest Asia, and full-scale farming societies appeared, leading to more civilized hunter-gatherer/farming communities in the area, where the Natufians developed the world's first dedicated form of agriculture.

Hunter-gatherers in Southwest Asia

1 During the end of the last glacial period, the Kebaran Civilization flourished in the area of Southwest Asia now known as the Middle East. This population was to have a large influence on humanity, because of their early consumption of cereals and their tool development. Being a nomadic civilization, they moved across a multitude of climates over the course of the year, spending their summers in the cooler highlands and their winters in the rocky waterside caves. This migration required them to adapt tools to suit each location. These were likely used to hunt gazelle and harvest wild cereals. Human consumption of these cereals became so important that they currently make up 50% and 56% of the world's protein and food energy consumption, respectively.

2 Despite the dietary changes they caused, the Kebaran society did not remain forever. Around 13,000 BC, a warmer, wetter period saw the rise of the Natufian Culture. Their appearance coincided with the shift in plant life in the area. As temperatures rose, plants that required the warmer temperatures of lower altitudes spread to higher altitudes. The production of pistachios, oak, almonds, wild barley and wild emmer wheat flourished as they moved from the lower altitude's sandy soil to the richer, clay-based soil of higher altitudes; these increased harvests allowed the Natufian Culture to expand as well. Within 1,500 years, the culture had completely replaced the Kebaran and spread from the mountains to the Mediterranean.

3 This culture proved to be more sedentary than its predecessors. This is an interesting case in history, since they settled before the advent of farming, relying instead on harvesting wild nuts and grains. Their entire society adapted a new hunting and gathering technique based on larger settlements that could harvest more of the crops. These new settlements featured semi-subterranean pit-houses and pits where the crops could be stored. These large settlements were also generally located near smaller satellite camps where they could collect and process their finds. Artifacts from these camps show that the Natufians greatly increased the sophistication of their tools and confirmed their dietary reliance on grains. They were even found to have created processing tools, such as grinding stones, and harvesting tools, like the flint blade sickle. While these tools could be useful on a multitude of plants, their use for cereal harvesting has been proven by the presence of "sickle gloss" on their blades. This is when a flint blade becomes shiny due to the build-up of silica particles from cereal grass stalks.

4 The village locations were also affected by the crops they relied upon. They were generally located along the boundary between the coastal grasslands and the higher altitudes where nuts and cereals prospered. They also seemed to settle in places where they could collect high quality stone for creating new tools. By settling in these places, they could harvest the cereal crops as they came into season during the spring and harvest nuts in the fall, providing year-round nourishment. In addition to using their stored crops in summer and winter, they also hunted the lowland animals. They would even cooperate with neighboring communities to perform massive game drives and ambushes on gazelles and other animals.

5 Year-round food sources led to a Natufian population boom. As the population increased, a new, highly complex social structure developed. This was discovered through excavation of Natufian cemeteries, where evidence was found that indicated differences in social standing between tribe members. Certain burial sites contained the symbolic dentalium seashell, while others, even those of children, were filled with common furnishings such as stone bowls, showing a clear difference in societal standing of the deceased. These rankings may have been the result of the food redistribution and efforts to maintain order that would have been required by such a large sedentary community. These cemeteries also contained limestone grave covers and mortar markers, which are thought to have served as ritualistic territorial markers for the lands held by the Natufian's highly-respected elders after they passed.

6 Eventually, as their population expanded, the Natufians faced another dramatic lifestyle upheaval due to climate change. Around 11,000 BC, the climate around the Mediterranean began to dry out. This reduced the area, in which the wild grains and nuts grew, and increased the society's need to settle near a reliable water source. This could have spelled the end of the Natufian society very quickly had they not learned the life cycle of the cereal plants over the previous two millennia of living off of and with them. Instead, they were able to deliberately plant and control the cereal plants. Even the modest scale of this early farming helped the society supplement their declining wild wheat and barley harvests and thus ensured their survival. Within a short time, farming flourished in Southwest Asia, and full-scale farming societies appeared, leading to more civilized hunter-gatherer/farming communities in the area, where the Natufians developed the world's first dedicated form of agriculture.

Life on Mars

1 Since the beginning of time, humans have wondered if they were alone in the universe. In the modern times, cosmologists and astrophysicists, Stephen Hawking and Carl Sagan, have claimed that extraterrestrial life is (1)**not only** possible **but** probable. They (2)**base** their theories **on** the Mediocrity, or Copernican, Principle, which states that because life developed on Earth, it (3)**is likely to develop** or has already developed on planets with similar molecular structures where the laws of physics work similarly. Astronomers believe that over 40 million Earth-sized planets orbiting Sun-like stars in their habitable zones, the regions where atmospheric pressures allow liquid surface water, may exist in the Milky Way alone. One in particular has (4)**inspired** scientists **to** (5)**search for** signs of life, Mars.

2 (6)**Contrary to** popular belief, Mars and Earth are remarkably similar. Although Earth is much larger than Mars, they have nearly identical land surfaces. They also share similar atmospheric chemistry when (7)**compared to** other planets in our solar system. Further, Mars is (8)**subject to** seasonal temperature variations like Earth's due to its 25°axis tilt, which is only 1.5° different than Earth's 23.5° tilt. A more important similarity that could allow life on Mars is the fact that both planets orbit in the Sun's habitable zone, which could allow Martian surface water (9)**in addition to** the water frozen in its polar ice caps.

3 Despite these similarities, Mars' conditions are currently very inhospitable. The most glaring problem is that the current Martian atmosphere (10)**is deadly for** Earth-based organisms. The thin, carbon dioxide (CO_2)-heavy composition of the atmosphere, besides being (11)**toxic to** oxygen-dependent organisms, does not retain solar heat when it (12)**is not directly exposed to** the Sun; therefore, nighttime temperatures drop precipitously and the average surface temperature is a frigid - 30°C. In addition, Mars' minimal atmosphere (13)**does little to** (14)**prevent** deadly ultraviolet solar radiation **from reaching** its surface (15)**in the way that** ozone gases in Earth's atmosphere do. This is compounded by Mars' lack of the type of magnetic field that protects the Earth from the effects of solar flares that further destroy its environment.

4 Another major problem that prevents life on Mars is the (16)**dearth of** liquid surface water. While the ice caps do contain a tremendous amount of water and CO_2, scientists have been (17)**unable to find** liquid water on Mars' surface, but this does not mean it never existed. Scientists believe that Earth's surface water was the result of venting from early volcanoes and have no (18)**reason to believe** that this couldn't have happened on Mars, since there are now extinct volcanoes scattered across its surface. In addition, if its atmosphere was once thicker, it may have trapped (19)**enough** solar heat **to** (20)**allow** the water (21)**locked up** in polar ice caps **to form** the rivers and seas whose effects are currently seen on the Martian landscape. In fact, craters left by meteoroids that struck the eroded areas of the surface, where it is assumed water once ran, show that they must have struck after the water disappeared and have been dated to several hundred million, (22)**if not** a billion, years old.

5 These factors, however, do not necessarily prohibit the presence of life on Mars. While most organisms require (23)**protection from** solar forces and (24)**access to** water and oxygen, it is not a universal need. Bacteria that require CO_2 (25)**instead of** oxygen have been discovered, and some organisms may be able to draw enough water from the trace amounts found in surface rocks. Further, protection from solar radiation can occur through a mechanism as simple as developing an outer shell or living under the surface to reduce the effects of solar radiation.

6 Another theory allowing life on Mars is the possibility of Earthlike conditions in the past. Scientists have discovered signs of flowing surface water, but Mars could have been even more Earth-like (26)**at one time**. A change (27)**could have occurred** as CO_2 became (28)**trapped in** rocks. Since Mars lacks the tectonic and volcanic activity that cycles CO_2 in the Earth's atmosphere, the atmosphere could have (29)**been depleted of** gaseous CO_2, over time, which would have reduced the greenhouse effect and destabilized the atmosphere, allowing most of it to dissipate (30)**over time**. This could have allowed a gradual disappearance of water from Mars' surface or its absorption below Mars' crust, where it may still exist, until life became unsustainable.

7 Unfortunately, the two Viking spacecraft found no traces of life, either current or past, on the Martian surface. It was, however, found that the surface soil was self-sterilizing because the harsh solar radiation on the surface (31)**reacts with** its minerals and destroys all organic matter. Interestingly, though, they did discover elements which would be (32)**necessary to support** life, namely nitrogen and phosphorous. From these tests, the most that can be hypothesized is that even though the current conditions on Mars cannot currently support life, it may have been possible at some point (33)**in the past**.

Life on Mars

1 Since the beginning of time, humans have wondered if they were alone in the universe. In the modern times, cosmologists and astrophysicists, Stephen Hawking and Carl Sagan, have claimed that extraterrestrial life is not only possible but probable. They base their theories on the Mediocrity, or Copernican, Principle, which states that because life developed on Earth, it is likely to develop or has already developed on planets with similar molecular structures where the laws of physics work similarly. Astronomers believe that over 40 million Earth-sized planets orbiting Sun-like stars in their habitable zones, the regions where atmospheric pressures allow liquid surface water, may exist in the Milky Way alone. One in particular has inspired scientists to search for signs of life, Mars.

2 Contrary to popular belief, Mars and Earth are remarkably similar. Although Earth is much larger than Mars, they have nearly identical land surfaces. They also share similar atmospheric chemistry when compared to other planets in our solar system. Further, Mars is subject to seasonal temperature variations like Earth's due to its 25°axis tilt, which is only 1.5° different than Earth's 23.5° tilt. A more important similarity that could allow life on Mars is the fact that both planets orbit in the Sun's habitable zone, which could allow Martian surface water in addition to the water frozen in its polar ice caps.

3 Despite these similarities, Mars' conditions are currently very inhospitable. The most glaring problem is that the current Martian atmosphere is deadly for Earth-based organisms. The thin, carbon dioxide (CO_2)-heavy composition of the atmosphere, besides being toxic to oxygen-dependent organisms, does not retain solar heat when it is not directly exposed to the Sun; therefore, nighttime temperatures drop precipitously and the average surface temperature is a frigid - 30°C. In addition, Mars' minimal atmosphere does little to prevent deadly ultraviolet solar radiation from reaching its surface in the way that ozone gases in Earth's atmosphere do. This is compounded by Mars' lack of the type of magnetic field that protects the Earth from the effects of solar flares that further destroy its environment.

4 Another major problem that prevents life on Mars is the dearth of liquid surface water. While the ice caps do contain a tremendous amount of water and CO_2, scientists have been unable to find liquid water on Mars' surface, but this does not mean it never existed. Scientists believe that Earth's surface water was the result of venting from early volcanoes and have no reason to believe that this couldn't have happened on Mars, since there are now extinct volcanoes scattered across its surface. In addition, if its atmosphere was once thicker, it may have trapped enough solar heat to allow the water locked up in polar ice caps to form the rivers and seas whose effects are currently seen on the Martian landscape. In fact, craters left by meteoroids that struck the eroded areas of the surface, where it is assumed water once ran, show that they must have struck after the water disappeared and have been dated to several hundred million, if not a billion, years old.

5 These factors, however, do not necessarily prohibit the presence of life on Mars. While most organisms require protection from solar forces and access to water and oxygen, it is not a universal need. Bacteria that require CO_2 instead of oxygen have been discovered, and some organisms may be able to draw enough water from the trace amounts found in surface rocks. Further, protection from solar radiation can occur through a mechanism as simple as developing an outer shell or living under the surface to reduce the effects of solar radiation.

6 Another theory allowing life on Mars is the possibility of Earthlike conditions in the past. Scientists have discovered signs of flowing surface water, but Mars could have been even more Earth-like at one time. A change could have occurred as CO_2 became trapped in rocks. Since Mars lacks the tectonic and volcanic activity that cycles CO_2 in the Earth's atmosphere, the atmosphere could have been depleted of gaseous CO_2, over time, which would have reduced the greenhouse effect and destabilized the atmosphere, allowing most of it to dissipate over time. This could have allowed a gradual disappearance of water from Mars' surface or its absorption below Mars' crust, where it may still exist, until life became unsustainable.

7 Unfortunately, the two Viking spacecraft found no traces of life, either current or past, on the Martian surface. It was, however, found that the surface soil was self-sterilizing because the harsh solar radiation on the surface reacts with its minerals and destroys all organic matter. Interestingly, though, they did discover elements which would be necessary to support life, namely nitrogen and phosphorous. From these tests, the most that can be hypothesized is that even though the current conditions on Mars cannot currently support life, it may have been possible at some point in the past.

Agriculture and Settlement around the Nile River

1 The lush vegetation of the Nile River valley stands ⁽¹⁾**in marked contrast to** the barren white sands of the nearby Sahara. Surprisingly, this contrast was the ⁽²⁾**impetus for** the development of settlements and domesticated agriculture across Africa. Researchers have ⁽³⁾**concluded that** the Sahara previously had ample water supplies and attracted inhabitants from the surrounding areas; however, as conditions declined and the region became more arid, these people ⁽⁴⁾**were** driven out and **forced to find** new, fertile places to settle. The Nile valley filled this role and ⁽⁵⁾**allowed** these people **to support** themselves while they ⁽⁶⁾**waited for** the Saharan conditions to improve again.

2 These changes reveal one surprising aspect of the ⁽⁷⁾**shift to** agriculture and ⁽⁸⁾**dependence on** food production in Egypt; it did not begin in the Nile valley ⁽⁹⁾**as** is commonly assumed. The process of ⁽¹⁰⁾**moving from** a nomadic culture **into** one with established villages using technology to domesticate and produce the livestock and plants required for such a lifestyle actually began further west in ⁽¹¹⁾**what is now** the arid Sahara. ⁽¹²⁾**Prior to** the last glacial period, the Sahara was ⁽¹³⁾**conducive to** inhabitation due to its abundant vegetation, grasslands and woodlands, all of which encouraged nomadic groups to remain along its lakes, where they were guaranteed sufficient water and food from the lake and its surrounding areas as they hunted and gathered. The area's eventual desertification forced these people and nearly all of the local wildlife to flee to a more suitable area, such as the fertile Nile River valley. Once they arrived in the river valley they had little choice but to settle in one place. Here, they ⁽¹⁴⁾**were boxed in** on the narrow floodplain by the hostile deserts, the river, and settlers that were living around them, all of which restricted their ability to wander and gather food.

3 Another aspect of the Nile Valley's settlement was the tremendous change that the river ⁽¹⁵⁾**went through**. Today, most people know that the Nile is the longest river in the world, but ⁽¹⁶⁾**at the time** it was much smaller and slower, running through a series interconnected riverbeds across the floodplain, ⁽¹⁷⁾**instead of** today's massive river. Eventually the sediment and silt carried through these channels aggregated and ⁽¹⁸⁾**built up** the floodplain, raising the river's level considerably. This allowed lush vegetation to grow along the floodplain and ⁽¹⁹⁾**turned** the Nile valley **into** an oasis sandwiched between the inhospitable Sahara and Eastern deserts, stretching 800 km from the present day Sudan to Cairo. ⁽²⁰⁾**As time wore on**, settlers in this area became ⁽²¹⁾**dependent upon** the river and ⁽²²⁾**separated** their year **into** three sections based upon its actions: the inundation when the overflowing river ⁽²³⁾**spread** silt **across** the floodplain, the growing season when they tended their crops in the sediment-filled fields, and harvest time when they collected the bounty provided by the nutrients the river had ⁽²⁴⁾**brought them**.

4 In this valley, early settlers cultivated food crops that had been previously domesticated in Southwest Asia, namely wheat, barley, peas, and lentils. These crops' ⁽²⁵⁾**ability to flourish** in the Nile valley sustained these early civilizations for generations, and they remain important components of the Egyptian even diet ⁽²⁶⁾**to this day**. As time went by, these settlements grew and ⁽²⁷⁾**used** the river **for** transportation. This allowed them to introduce these crops to settlements farther south, where people had ⁽²⁸⁾**relied upon** the cultivation of plants ⁽²⁹⁾**native to** the African environment.

5 This verdant area also ⁽³⁰⁾**provided for** the settlers' other dietary needs. Since the strip of land was narrow, ⁽³¹⁾**the number of** large mammals that could establish territories in this area was limited. In fact, the remains of only three large species have been found, the Dorcas gazelle, aurochsa type of wild cattle, and the hartebeest. Settlers, therefore, relied on other protein sources, such as birds and fish. While migratory birds, like ducks and geese, were regularly taken, fish were the primary protein source, especially catfish. ⁽³²⁾**In addition**, the seasonal ⁽³³⁾**variety of** plant in the area gave them ⁽³⁴⁾**access to** ⁽³⁵⁾**an abundance of** carbohydrate-rich foods. More than twenty varieties of edible plants, seeds, fruit, and vegetables have ⁽³⁶⁾**been excavated from** the ruins of these early settlements.

6 Eventually, the fertile soils and predictable flooding of the river allowed the settlers to develop an empire whose wealth ⁽³⁷⁾**was based on** the great agricultural bounty it ⁽³⁸⁾**was able to reap**. Today, Ancient Egyptians are ⁽³⁹⁾**regarded as** one of the first civilizations to practice widespread agriculture. They developed advanced farming techniques such as basin irrigation, which ⁽⁴⁰⁾**put them** ⁽⁴¹⁾**in control of** the river level and allowed them to utilize it ⁽⁴²⁾**in a way** that best suited their needs. These new developments allowed them to grow ⁽⁴³⁾**not only** food crops **but also** industrial and fabric crops ⁽⁴⁴⁾**for use in** cooking, medicine, and construction. The most well-known of these was papyrus, parts of which were ⁽⁴⁵⁾**used as** food, as a material for construction and as a medium for writing. These developments spread ⁽⁴⁶⁾**outside of** the Nile valley and changed African and world civilizations forever.

Agriculture and Settlement around the Nile River

1 The lush vegetation of the Nile River valley stands in marked contrast to the barren white sands of the nearby Sahara. Surprisingly, this contrast was the impetus for the development of settlements and domesticated agriculture across Africa. Researchers have concluded that the Sahara previously had ample water supplies and attracted inhabitants from the surrounding areas; however, as conditions declined and the region became more arid, these people were driven out and forced to find new, fertile places to settle. The Nile valley filled this role and allowed these people to support themselves while they waited for the Saharan conditions to improve again.

2 These changes reveal one surprising aspect of the shift to agriculture and dependence on food production in Egypt; it did not begin in the Nile valley as is commonly assumed. The process of moving from a nomadic culture into one with established villages using technology to domesticate and produce the livestock and plants required for such a lifestyle actually began further west in what is now the arid Sahara. Prior to the last glacial period, the Sahara was conducive to inhabitation due to its abundant vegetation, grasslands and woodlands, all of which encouraged nomadic groups to remain along its lakes, where they were guaranteed sufficient water and food from the lake and its surrounding areas as they hunted and gathered. The area's eventual desertification forced these people and nearly all of the local wildlife to flee to a more suitable area, such as the fertile Nile River valley. Once they arrived in the river valley they had little choice but to settle in one place. Here, they were boxed in on the narrow floodplain by the hostile deserts, the river, and settlers that were living around them, all of which restricted their ability to wander and gather food.

3 Another aspect of the Nile Valley's settlement was the tremendous change that the river went through. Today, most people know that the Nile is the longest river in the world, but at the time it was much smaller and slower, running through a series interconnected riverbeds across the floodplain, instead of today's massive river. Eventually the sediment and silt carried through these channels aggregated and built up the floodplain, raising the river's level considerably. This allowed lush vegetation to grow along the floodplain and turned the Nile valley into an oasis sandwiched between the inhospitable Sahara and Eastern deserts, stretching 800 km from the present day Sudan to Cairo. As time wore on, settlers in this area became dependent upon the river and separated their year into three sections based upon its actions: the inundation when the overflowing river spread silt across the floodplain, the growing season when they tended their crops in the sediment-filled fields, and harvest time when they collected the bounty provided by the nutrients the river had brought them.

4 In this valley, early settlers cultivated food crops that had been previously domesticated in Southwest Asia, namely wheat, barley, peas, and lentils. These crops' ability to flourish in the Nile valley sustained these early civilizations for generations, and they remain important components of the Egyptian even diet to this day. As time went by, these settlements grew and used the river for transportation. This allowed them to introduce these crops to settlements farther south, where people had relied upon the cultivation of plants native to the African environment.

5 This verdant area also provided for the settlers' other dietary needs. Since the strip of land was narrow, the number of large mammals that could establish territories in this area was limited. In fact, the remains of only three large species have been found, the Dorcas gazelle, aurochs a type of wild cattle, and the hartebeest. Settlers, therefore, relied on other protein sources, such as birds and fish. While migratory birds, like ducks and geese, were regularly taken, fish were the primary protein source, especially catfish. In addition, the seasonal variety of plant in the area gave them access to an abundance of carbohydrate-rich foods. More than twenty varieties of edible plants, seeds, fruit, and vegetables have been excavated from the ruins of these early settlements.

6 Eventually, the fertile soils and predictable flooding of the river allowed the settlers to develop an empire whose wealth was based on the great agricultural bounty it was able to reap. Today, Ancient Egyptians are regarded as one of the first civilizations to practice widespread agriculture. They developed advanced farming techniques such as basin irrigation, which put them in control of the river level and allowed them to utilize it in a way that best suited their needs. These new developments allowed them to grow not only food crops but also industrial and fabric crops for use in cooking, medicine, and construction. The most well-known of these was papyrus, parts of which were used as food, as a material for construction and as a medium for writing. These developments spread outside of the Nile valley and changed African and world civilizations forever.

Sea Turtle Navigation

1 **⁽¹⁾For centuries**, oceanic navigation has been one of the biggest ⁽²⁾**challenges to** seafarers around the world because navigation on the high seas is more difficult than on land. Yet, since the early cretaceous period, the sea turtle has successfully ⁽³⁾**travelled across** vast oceans moving between foraging sites and nesting areas. This amazing ability has justifiably intrigued scientists for years. Celestial navigation, ⁽⁴⁾**based on** observing the positions of the Sun, Moon, and stars, has not been ⁽⁵⁾**accepted as** a method employable by sea turtles ⁽⁶⁾**due to** their poor eyesight. Another theory suggests that dissolved traces of unique odors from the turtles' destinations guide them, but this has also not ⁽⁷⁾**gained** much **support** because dispersal of the odors in the ocean would create a convoluted path and could, therefore, not explain how sea turtles migrate ⁽⁸⁾**in** a more-or-less straight **line** to their destination. Furthermore, ⁽⁹⁾**depending on** ocean currents, the odor trails may be travelling ⁽¹⁰⁾**in the same direction** as the turtles, thus never reaching them.

2 One theory, however, has ⁽¹¹⁾**gained support** from the scientific community. Studies have found small ⁽¹²⁾**amounts of** a magnetic compound called magnetite in the brains of ⁽¹³⁾**a few species of** sea turtles. This compound, which is also found in pigeons, honeybees, and ⁽¹⁴⁾**a variety of** other animals, is known to ⁽¹⁵⁾**play a crucial role in** navigation. It was shown that, sea turtle hatchlings, when placed inside a pool within a magnetic chamber, altered their course ⁽¹⁶⁾**in response to** ⁽¹⁷⁾**changes in** the chamber's magnetic field. What makes sea turtles' utilization of magnetite interesting is the fact that it is ⁽¹⁸⁾**so precise that** sea turtles in the vast ocean can measure ⁽¹⁹⁾**not only** the intensity of the magnetic pull **but also** the ⁽²⁰⁾**difference in** the angle of the magnetic poles. Previously, scientists thought that magnetite could only ⁽²¹⁾**be used as** a compass, providing directional information, but this ability ⁽²²⁾**allows** turtles **to orient** themselves within a more detailed magnetic map of Earth.

3 To study the role of magnetite in sea turtle navigation further, FlorianoPapi and a team of biologists designed an experiment in the late 1990s, in which green sea turtles ⁽²³⁾**travelling from** Ascension Island back **to** Brazil ⁽²⁴⁾**were fitted with** strong magnets on their heads. Papi believed that the magnet would inhibit the turtles' ability to calculate their position on Earth. Surprisingly, however, the magnets made no difference to the migratory performance of the turtles. The findings demonstrated that the magnetite theory is not ⁽²⁵⁾**devoid of** short comings. Substantial evidence both for and against magnetic navigation ⁽²⁶⁾**led to** the theory that while magnetic positioning plays a vital role in the open sea, ⁽²⁷⁾**far away from** the destination, sea turtles use several other ⁽²⁸⁾**methods to complement** it when they are young or when they are ⁽²⁹⁾**close to** land.

4 When sea turtles are born, they must immediately ⁽³⁰⁾**make their way into** deep waters to escape predators on land and in coastal waters. Scientists hypothesize that the hatchlings calculate the direction towards water by using light intensity as a cue. The juveniles are thought to instinctively head towards light because moonlight reflecting against the water means that the ocean is brighter than land. Unfortunately, hatchlings have ⁽³¹⁾**been reported to be disoriented** by artificial light ⁽³²⁾**coming from** human-occupied islands, severely decreasing their ⁽³³⁾**chances for** survival. In the shallow coastal waters, the juvenile turtles detect the direction, in which the waves push them to calculate which direction they must swim to get to deep waters.

5 When the turtle is making its way to land either to forage or to lay eggs, it uses the magnetite ⁽³⁴⁾**along with** auditory and olfactory cues. It is hypothesized that turtles use both the low-frequency sounds of waves hitting the beach and the smell coming from land to pinpoint the location of their destination.

6 The mysteries of sea turtle navigation do not ⁽³⁵⁾**end with** their navigation methods, but also ⁽³⁶⁾**extend to** navigation patterns, ⁽³⁷⁾**as** can be seen in the mitochondrial DNA (mtDNA-genetic material that is ⁽³⁸⁾**inherited** solely **from** the maternal parent and is, therefore, identical in close relatives) of hawksbill turtles in the Persian Gulf. Each hawksbill turtle tested in the nesting site had the same mtDNA, with only minimal variability, ⁽³⁹⁾**leading to the conclusion** that most of the hawksbill turtles in the nesting site have ⁽⁴⁰⁾**emerged from** the same nest. This explains why areas around the world that appear ⁽⁴¹⁾**ideal for** sea turtle foraging and nesting are not recolonized after human interference wipes out the native populations. For example, Grand Cayman Island was once ⁽⁴²⁾**home to** one of the largest green sea turtle populations in the world, but after the turtles ⁽⁴³⁾**were driven off** by humans, wildlife protection laws and habitat reconstruction have proven ⁽⁴⁴⁾**unsuccessful in bringing** back the turtles.

Sea Turtle Navigation

1 For centuries, oceanic navigation has been one of the biggest challenges to seafarers around the world because navigation on the high seas is more difficult than on land. Yet, since the early cretaceous period, the sea turtle has successfully travelled across vast oceans moving between foraging sites and nesting areas. This amazing ability has justifiably intrigued scientists for years. Celestial navigation, based on observing the positions of the Sun, Moon, and stars, has not been accepted as a method employable by sea turtles due to their poor eyesight. Another theory suggests that dissolved traces of unique odors from the turtles' destinations guide them, but this has also not gained much support because dispersal of the odors in the ocean would create a convoluted path and could, therefore, not explain how sea turtles migrate in a more-or-less straight line to their destination. Furthermore, depending on ocean currents, the odor trails may be travelling in the same direction as the turtles, thus never reaching them.

2 One theory, however, has gained support from the scientific community. Studies have found small amounts of a magnetic compound called magnetite in the brains of a few species of sea turtles. This compound, which is also found in pigeons, honeybees, and a variety of other animals, is known to play a crucial role in navigation. It was shown that, sea turtle hatchlings, when placed inside a pool within a magnetic chamber, altered their course in response to changes in the chamber's magnetic field. What makes sea turtles' utilization of magnetite interesting is the fact that it is so precise that sea turtles in the vast ocean can measure not only the intensity of the magnetic pull but also the difference in the angle of the magnetic poles. Previously, scientists thought that magnetite could only be used as a compass, providing directional information, but this ability allows turtles to orient themselves within a more detailed magnetic map of Earth.

3 To study the role of magnetite in sea turtle navigation further, FlorianoPapi and a team of biologists designed an experiment in the late 1990s, in which green sea turtles travelling from Ascension Island back to Brazil were fitted with strong magnets on their heads. Papi believed that the magnet would inhibit the turtles' ability to calculate their position on Earth. Surprisingly, however, the magnets made no difference to the migratory performance of the turtles. The findings demonstrated that the magnetite theory is not devoid of short comings. Substantial evidence both for and against magnetic navigation led to the theory that while magnetic positioning plays a vital role in the open sea, far away from the destination, sea turtles use several other methods to complement it when they are young or when they are close to land.

4 When sea turtles are born, they must immediately make their way into deep waters to escape predators on land and in coastal waters. Scientists hypothesize that the hatchlings calculate the direction towards water by using light intensity as a cue. The juveniles are thought to instinctively head towards light because moonlight reflecting against the water means that the ocean is brighter than land. Unfortunately, hatchlings have been reported to be disoriented by artificial light coming from human-occupied islands, severely decreasing their chances for survival. In the shallow coastal waters, the juvenile turtles detect the direction, in which the waves push them to calculate which direction they must swim to get to deep waters.

5 When the turtle is making its way to land either to forage or to lay eggs, it uses the magnetite along with auditory and olfactory cues. It is hypothesized that turtles use both the low-frequency sounds of waves hitting the beach and the smell coming from land to pinpoint the location of their destination.

6 The mysteries of sea turtle navigation do not end with their navigation methods, but also extend to navigation patterns, as can be seen in the mitochondrial DNA (mtDNA-genetic material that is inherited solely from the maternal parent and is, therefore, identical in close relatives) of hawksbill turtles in the Persian Gulf. Each hawksbill turtle tested in the nesting site had the same mtDNA, with only minimal variability, leading to the conclusion that most of the hawksbill turtles in the nesting site have emerged from the same nest. This explains why areas around the world that appear ideal for sea turtle foraging and nesting are not recolonized after human interference wipes out the native populations. For example, Grand Cayman Island was once home to one of the largest green sea turtle populations in the world, but after the turtles were driven off by humans, wildlife protection laws and habitat reconstruction have proven unsuccessful in bringing back the turtles.

USHER iBT TOEFL
INTERMEDIATE READING

부록

다음 내용은, 부록으로
앞선 지문들에 있는 내용으로 풀 수 있는 보너스 문제입니다.

"문제는 많이 풀수록 좋다는거 아시죠?"

TEST 1 - 1
Comets

▶ 57페이지 2문단을 참고하세요.

01 The term "roughly" in the passage is closest in meaning to:

(A) clearly
(B) typically
(C) frequently
(D) approximately

2   The main difference between the two categories seems to arrive from their origins. Short-period comets begin in the Kuiper belt of non-planetary matter. The matter in the belt, just past Neptune's orbit, roughly 50 astronomical units (1 AU=the distance between Earth and the sun) from the sun,

▶ 58페이지 3문단을 참고하세요.

02 The term "undergo" in the passage is closest in meaning to:

(A) allow
(B) experience
(C) prevent
(D) cause

forces of a passing star. [■] When this happens they are sent on an irregular orbit that brings them closer to the sun where they undergo the changes typical of all comets. [■] After they have completed their pass near the sun, it may be thousands of years before they make their return. [■]

▶ 58페이지 4문단을 참고하세요.

03 What does the word "its" refer to in the passage?

(A) comet's
(B) orbit's
(C) inactive mass's
(D) sun's

but as they come closer to the sun, the effects of its massive energy sublimate the frozen materials within this nucleus to form a glowing ball of dust and gases known as the coma.

▶ 58페이지 4문단을 참고하세요.

04 According to paragraph 4, all of the following is true about the coma that develops around the comet as it orbits the sun **EXECPT**:

(A) The coma is formed as volatile frozen material becomes gaseous and expands around the comet's nucleus.
(B) The coma of some comets can expand so much that they are larger than the diameter of the sun.
(C) The presence of a coma is used to easily distinguish comets from other celestial bodies such as asteroids.
(D) When a comet approaches close enough to the sun, the coma becomes the long tail.

4   Regardless of the category of comet, their telltale shape forms in the same way. They complete most of their orbit as frozen and relatively inactive masses that are difficult to discern, but as they come closer to the sun, the effects of its massive energy sublimate the frozen materials within this nucleus to form a glowing ball of dust and gases known as the coma. This coma greatly increases the comet's size. The nucleus is generally less than 60 km in diameter, but the coma can be larger than the sun. This most distinguishable feature differentiates comets from other celestial bodies, such as asteroids. When they reach approximately 1.5 AU from the sun, solar energy's effects become more extreme and parts of the coma are blown into a tail which can be millions of kilometers long.

TEST 1 - 2
Darwin and Evolution Theory

▶ 61페이지 2문단을 참고하세요.

01 The term "segregation" in the passage is closest in meaning to:

(A) separation
(B) uniqueness
(C) harshness
(D) unity

such as discovering giant armadillo and sloth fossils from the distant past. He also discovered that in areas with a geographic segregation, such as islands or seas separated by isthmuses, different species were found.

▶ 62페이지 3문단을 참고하세요.

02 The word "it" in the passage refers to?

(A) common use
(B) similarity
(C) common ancestry
(D) adaptive evolution

This cannot be attributed to common use, so it must indicate common ancestry and adaptive evolution to fit the organisms' functions. [■]

▶ 62페이지 3문단을 참고하세요.

03 According to paragraph 3, which of the following is NOT true about the homology and vestigial structures?

(A) Richard Owen found similarities between the structures in vertebrates which served different purposes.
(B) Vestigial structures, like the non-used leg bones in whales and snakes, indicate that at one time their ancestors had working legs.
(C) The presence of homology and vestigial structures in modern organisms helped prove Darwin's idea that species change over time.
(D) Homology occurs because animals use body parts in the same way, so they evolve in a similar manner.

3 [■] Darwin's idea was supported by the theory of homology Richard Owen derived from comparative studies of the structural systems of various vertebrates. [■] Owen found homology, or anatomical similarity, in the body parts of different animals which served different purposes. [■] This cannot be attributed to common use, so it must indicate common ancestry and adaptive evolution to fit the organisms' functions. [■] The presence of vestigial, or leftover, structures in modern organisms also points to an evolutionary system, because these structures serve no purpose in modern animals. The whale and snake are both examples of this, because although both are now legless, they have small vestigial leg bones, which point to a four-legged ancestor.

▶ 63페이지 5문단을 참고하세요.

04 The term "jointly" in the passage is closest in meaning to:

(A) simply
(B) rightfully
(C) together
(D) therefore

Eventually, Wallace agreed to present his theory alongside the more socially and scientifically connected Darwin and their work was jointly presented to the Linnean Society of London in 1858, with very little fanfare.

TEST 2 - 1
Determining the Ages of the Planets and the Universe

▶ 71페이지 1문단을 참고하세요.

01 The term "vast" in the passage is closest in meaning to:

(A) powerful
(B) extensive
(C) wealthy
(D) ancient

1 The orbits of planets and the majority of non-planetary objects in our solar system have a very interesting characteristic; despite their vast differences, they have astounding similarities.

▶ 71페이지 1문단을 참고하세요.

02 According to paragraph 1, which of the following is true of the planets and the non-planetary objects in the solar system?

(A) The planets orbit the sun at the same speed because the gas cloud that collapsed to form them exerted a uniform force on them all.
(B) The collapse of a gas cloud, long after forming planets, created the majority of other non-planetary objects.
(C) The extreme gravitational force exerted by the sun caused the collapse of the dust cloud which formed most of the objects found in the solar system.
(D) The orbits of some non-planetary bodies in the solar system follow a path that is dissimilar to those of the planets.

1 The orbits of planets and the majority of non-planetary objects in our solar system have a very interesting characteristic; despite their vast differences, they have astounding similarities. The most remarkable of these similarities is that nearly all of them orbit the sun in the same direction and on the same plane. Using this information, scientists determined that this likely occurred because the collapse of a gas cloud simultaneously formed the objects and sent them to orbit the sun. This fact has allowed us to learn more about the age of the Earth, the planets, and the universe itself.

▶ 72페이지 5문단을 참고하세요.

03 The term "dense" in the passage is closest in meaning to:

(A) new
(B) thick
(C) mature
(D) seasonal

One of the most important factors discovered is that all of the disk-shaped clusters of stars, called galaxies, are moving away from each other. Scientists conjecture that this occurs because the universe began with an explosion, known as the Big Bang, which sent all of the dense matter concentrated at the center of the explosion

▶ 72페이지 5문단을 참고하세요.

04 According to paragraph 5, which of the following is true regarding the expansion of the universe?

(A) Collecting physical materials on which to conduct the universe's age testing is complicated but not impossible.
(B) Scientists who studied the Big Bang theorized that it is the reason for the drifting apart of the galaxies.
(C) Scientists proved the existence of the Big Bang through empirical analysis.
(D) Scientists have been able to determine the timing of the Big Bang, but cannot correlate it to the age of the universe.

5 While dating the elements of the solar system has been relatively straightforward, finding the age of the universe itself has been more complicated because there is no way to collect physical materials on which to conduct age testing. What has been learned has been gathered through theoretical analysis of the universe. One of the most important factors discovered is that all of the disk-shaped clusters of stars, called galaxies, are moving away from each other. Scientists conjecture that this occurs because the universe began with an explosion, known as the Big Bang, which sent all of the dense matter concentrated at the center of the explosion hurtling across space.

TEST 2 - 2
Early Research in Organic Chemistry

▶ 75페이지 1문단을 참고하세요.

01 The term "eventually" in the passage is closest in meaning to:

(A) finally
(B) certainly
(C) quickly
(D) easily

The study of the last of these would eventually form one of the two modern divisions of the field of chemistry, organic chemistry.

▶ 75페이지 2문단을 참고하세요.

02 Which of the following is true of the theory of Vitalism from paragraph 2?

(A) The "vital spark" or "force" that early scientists studying organic compounds were looking for turned out to be the element carbon.
(B) Antoine Lavoisier was an early supporter of the theory of Vitalism until he was persuaded to believe that the "vital spark" was not found in plants.
(C) Scientists opposed to the theory of Vitalism felt that all living creatures were created by a natural process that gave them life, not a "vital spark."
(D) The ability of a scientist to produce organic materials in the laboratory convinced scientists that there was no "vital spark" that gave organisms life.

2 The terms organic and inorganic chemistry were introduced in the early 1800s to more accurately differentiate between the different naturally occurring substances. Prior to this time scientists separated substances into three categories that matched the "Three Kingdoms of Nature": animal, vegetable and mineral. Of these, the animal and vegetable groups were reserved for substances that were produced by or related to life and were later incorporated into the study of organic (meaning from an organism) chemistry which covered all carbon-based compounds, while the inanimate mineral group gave way to the field of inorganic chemistry which covered all non-carbon compounds.

▶ 76페이지 3문단을 참고하세요.

03 The term "component" in the passage is closest in meaning to:

(A) special
(B) developmental
(C) constituent
(D) eventual

Some gases, such as sulfur, can even be found in their pure elemental form on Earth, while others, like atmospheric gases, are easily broken down into their component parts. Hydrogen, for instance, can be mined from the air using a particular mineral acid on a metal plate.

▶ 77페이지 5문단을 참고하세요.

04 The term "attain" in the passage is closest in meaning to:

(A) achieve
(B) employ
(C) expect
(D) seek

This uncertainty led organic chemists to search for ways to attain these substances without destroying the original matter. Many other less violent methods of distillation, such as using the lowest effective temperature to distill organic substances, were attempted, but did not fully overcome the problems that were inherent in the field.

TEST 3 - 1
El Niño

▶ 85페이지 3문단을 참고하세요.

01 The term "affects" in the passage is closesest in meaning to:

(A) influences
(B) explains
(C) improves
(D) depends on

3 Despite being known mainly as an eastern Pacific pattern, El Niño affects conditions across the vast waters of the Pacific. One of the first scientists to recognize this was early-20th century British physicist Gilbert Walker, who found an inverse correlation between atmospheric pressure at weather stations in the eastern and western Pacific.

▶ 85페이지 3문단을 참고하세요.

02 What can be inferred about the Southern Oscillation from paragraph 3?

(A) It has been found to better function in the eastern Pacific Ocean than in its western portions.
(B) It first occurred in the early 20th century when it was discovered by British physicist and statistician Gilbert Walker.
(C) It functions only as a cause of the El Niño across the vast Pacific waters.
(D) The atmospheric pressures in the two horizontal ends of the Pacific had an asymmetrical relationship.

3 Despite being known mainly as an eastern Pacific pattern, El Niño affects conditions across the vast waters of the Pacific. One of the first scientists to recognize this was early-20th century British physicist Gilbert Walker, who found an inverse correlation between atmospheric pressure at weather stations in the eastern and western Pacific. Walker noted that as the pressure of the eastern Pacific fell, that of the western Pacific rose, and vice versa in a see-saw-like pattern that he termed the Southern Oscillation.

▶ 86페이지 4문단을 참고하세요.

03 The term "accumulation" in the passage is closest in meaning to:

(A) acceptance
(B) creation
(C) fine detail
(D) growing collection

These warm winds also cause the warm east-to-west surface current that moves across the Pacific Ocean along the equator. Eventually it causes an accumulation of warm surface water in the western Pacific, while the Humboldt Current's upwelling keeps surface temperatures in the eastern Pacific much lower.

▶ 86페이지 5문단을 참고하세요.

04 According to paragraph 5, which of the following is true regarding the historical incidence of El Niño?

(A) Researchers have been able to prove that the effects of El Niño now last three times longer than they did in the 1600s.
(B) Spanish colonists kept detailed records of the surface temperature of the Pacific Ocean that allowed modern researchers to determine the length of previous El Niño periods.
(C) It appears that the temperature of the ocean's surface increases more dramatically during modern El Niño periods than it did in the past.
(D) Scientists have noticed that El Niño's warming has done the most severe damage to the United States of America.

5 Since this process was first theorized, scientists have attempted to trace it using historical records. By examining records of the daily surface temperature of the ocean, rainfall, atmospheric pressure, and fisheries data from South American inhabitants and Spanish colonists dating as far back as the 1400s, they have pieced together a detailed timeline of El Niño over the past six centuries. From this, it is clear that although El Niño occurred regularly throughout history its frequency is increasing.

TEST 3 - 2
England's Sixteenth Century Economy

▶ 89페이지 1문단을 참고하세요.

01 What can be inferred from paragraph 1 about the population of England during the Late Tudor Period?

(A) Population rates decreased from their all-time high because of the numerous deaths that occurred during the spread of the "Black Death."
(B) The population increase that occurred during this time made England the most populous country in the European region at the time.
(C) England's population and economic conditions increased more rapidly than those of continental countries because it was not as affected by disease and war as they were.
(D) Improvements in England's economy led to decreases in the mortality rate and increases in the fertility rate, causing the population to nearly double in 100 years.

1 Great changes occurred in England during the Late Tudor Period under the reign of Queen Elizabeth I In the latter half of the sixteenth and early seventeenth centuries. One of the most notable was the increase in the population to nearly that of the pre-Black Death period. In England and Wales, increased fertility and reduced mortality rates nearly doubled the population around this time, increasing from 2.5 million in the 1520s to 4.5 million by 1610. This dramatic increase, along with other factors led to vast changes in England's economy and allowed it to become Europe's largest, far surpassing those of the war and plague-ravaged continent.

▶ 90페이지 4문단을 참고하세요.

02 According to paragraph 4, all of the following were ways that landowners attempted to maximize the profits from their property EXCEPT:

(A) Entry fees were paid to tenants to allow them to maximize their profits.
(B) Landowners shortened the contracts as they pleased.
(C) They planted crops that were the most favorable for the market.
(D) They advocated for more efficient farm practices, like crop rotation, to be utilized on their properties.

4 These large landowners, and the yeomen who had smaller landholdings, maximized the profits they could draw from their property. To increase their profits, they planted crops which were in demand in the London markets. They also aggressively dealt with those to whom they rented their property. During this period, rents were increased and rental contracts were written to provide even more benefits to the landowners. One of the ways they did this was shortening the duration of their contracts to allow themselves more control over the land.

▶ 90페이지 4문단을 참고하세요.

03 The term "potential" in the passage is closest in meaning to:

(A) serious
(B) possible
(C) related
(D) common

One of the ways they did this was shortening the duration of their contracts to allow themselves more control over the land. Another way they maximized their profits was to charge potential tenants an "entry fee" before they would even consent to renting to them.

▶ 91페이지 7문단을 참고하세요.

04 The term "operate" in the passage is closest in meaning to:

(A) dominate
(B) function
(C) originate
(D) fail

Gresham increased England's reputation in Antwerp to the point that English merchants were able to operate on a credit-based system there, something very rare in the sixteenth century. He also championed the economic possibilities of the Americas, leading to England's early attempts to colonize the continents for commercial purposes.

TEST 4 - 1
Environmental Impact of the Anasazi

▶ 99페이지 1문단을 참고하세요.

01 According to paragraph 1, which of the following is true of the theories related to the disappearance of the Anasazi?

(A) The tree ring studies by the Anasazi indicate that these ancient people had been driven from their villages due to the Great Drought.
(B) Although the Anasazi were able to survive other droughts, they started evacuating after the Great Drought.
(C) The indication of drought conditions by the tree rings studied was not sufficient to explain the civilizations abandonment of the area.
(D) Tim Kohler's theory that human-nature interaction caused the Anasazi to flee resulted in the revelation of the "Great Drought."

1 The Anasazi people, ancient Native Americans who resided in pit houses, pueblos, and cliff dwellings, flourished in America's present-day Four Corners region before suddenly abandoning their elaborate villages and palace complexes. Archeologists long thought that studies of the rings of the trees used in the structures found there indicated that these people had been driven from their villages and home region, due to a climatic event known as the "Great Drought." This, however, began to be called into question recently.

▶ 99페이지 1문단을 참고하세요.

02 The word "it" in the passage refers to?

(A) question
(B) an ongoing event
(C) Great Drought
(D) evacuation

This, however, began to be called into question recently. Today, historians believe that the Anasazi evacuation had been an ongoing event before the "Great Drought" and that the drought was not an unprecedented event; villagers had likely survived others before it.

▶ 100페이지 3문단을 참고하세요.

03 The term "adjacent" in the passage is closest in meaning to:

(A) cool
(B) deep
(C) large
(D) nearby

Using this method, they burned down forests to plant the crops they needed and utilized the new farmland until it became unsuitable for producing crops, at which time they moved on to an adjacent area and repeated the process, allowing the previous area to lie fallow and replenish the nutrients necessary for its future use.

▶ 101페이지 5문단을 참고하세요.

04 The term "susceptible to" in the passage is closest in meaning to:

(A) well-known for
(B) slow to replace losses from
(C) likely to be affected by
(D) unable to benefit from

These larger villages with more technical agricultural methods produced more food, but were more susceptible to a rapid collapse. The cooperative management of resources for the village meant that they were less flexible in response to environmental changes, so a weak growing season had a widespread impact on the village.

TEST 4 - 2
Global Variations in Species Diversity

01 The term "ensured" in the passage is closest in meaning to:

(A) contributed to
(B) predicted
(C) resulted in
(D) guaranteed

Another has adapted to feeding on the innards, while still others consume the bones and random scraps. Even though they are all eating from the same carcasses, they are all ensured a constant supply of food because their niche specializations effectively lower the competition rate.

02 According to paragraph 4, all of the followings are true of the food supply in higher latitudes EXCEPT:

(A) Regions with higher latitude have less steady food supplies than regions near the equator.
(B) The seasonal nature of the food supply forces many animals to move towards different regions in search of food supplies.
(C) When the colder winter season begins the food supplies decrease and animals must either hibernate or migrate.
(D) The relatively lower overall food supply does not limit species diversity.

4 Species that live in higher latitudes, on the other hand, face a constantly changing food supply. During the warmer season, tundra species have a plethora of food sources, such as plant life and newly hatched krill, which are fed on by animals such as caribou, seabirds, fish, and oceanic mammals. However, when the long, frigid winter sets in, the area is rather barren, leading many specialized feeders to migrate to other areas. There are, however, animals with a more generalist feeding style that remain in the tundra year-round, seasonally adapting their feeding patterns.

03 The term "frigid" in the passage is closest in meaning to:

(A) cold
(B) original
(C) giant
(D) moving

During the warmer season, tundra species have a plethora of food sources, such as plant life and newly hatched krill, which are fed on by animals such as caribou, seabirds, fish, and oceanic mammals. However, when the long, frigid winter sets in, the area is rather barren, leading many specialized feeders to migrate to other areas.

04 According to paragraph 5, which of the following is true regarding evolution and longevity in tropical regions?

(A) Species that exist in the tropics tend to be smaller than those found in northern latitudes because their lifespans are significantly shorter.
(B) Tropical species reproduce and die more quickly than species from other regions, therefore successive generations, with mutations, are produced more rapidly.
(C) Animals in tropical regions experience a higher mutation rate than those in higher latitudes, thereby increasing their longevity.
(D) The shorter generation lengths of smaller species living in tropical regions hinder their maturation and therefore reproduction.

5 Since the variability in light, temperature, and food supply does not necessarily reduce species diversity in an area, there must be another explanation for the great latitudinal difference. One new theory is that the evolutionary process itself caused this phenomenon. The theory of "effective evolutionary time" draws upon earlier research that showed that evolution occurs more quickly in smaller species that inhabit warmer temperatures. [■] This likely occurs due to the higher physiological rates of smaller species in tropical regions, which lead to shorter ligespans.

TEST 5 - 1
Documenting the Incas

▶ 114페이지 4문단을 참고하세요.

01 What can be inferred about stories passed down through the oral tradition from paragraph 4?

(A) Because people are still alive to verify the events that occurred in them, recent stories are more accurate than ancient ones.
(B) Inaccuracies develop in the stories over time as they are passed down from one generation to the next.
(C) Most early stories, like the one about the founding of Cusco, are meant to explain how civilizations came to be.
(D) Spanish elites passed down inaccurate stories orally to the next generation in order to make themselves seem more impressive.

▶ 114페이지 4문단을 참고하세요.

02 The term "prime" in the passage is closest in meaning to:

(A) high-quality
(B) unused
(C) easily accessible
(D) low-lying

▶ 114페이지 4문단을 참고하세요.

03 The term "accurate" in the passage is closest in meaning to:

(A) popular
(B) correct
(C) understandable
(D) academic

▶ 114페이지 4문단을 참고하세요.

04 According to paragraph 5, which of the following is true about the Incan conquests over other tribes?

(A) The Incan leaders generally only took over areas where the people were the friendliest to them.
(B) No one really knows what truly happened in them because of the lack of verifiable sources outside of the Incan community.
(C) They were misrepresented in the histories recorded by the Spanish in order to further weaken the Incan Empire.
(D) The vast expanse of the Inca empire was the result of its leaders' righteousness and strength.

4 Relying on elite members of the Incan society to learn about their history caused another problem. Since they had no written language system, all of their historical information had been passed down through the oral tradition. Over time, many of these stories may have developed unintentional inaccuracies. A prime example of this would be the founding of Cusco, which was said to have happened after four brothers and four sisters emerged from a cave and led followers they found in another cave to the site of Cusco, where they founded the civilization.

Over time, many of these stories may have developed unintentional inaccuracies. A prime example of this would be the founding of Cusco, which was said to have happened after four brothers and four sisters emerged from a cave and led followers they found in another cave to the site of Cusco, where they founded the civilization.

The origin of these early leaders and stories of their exploits were likely exaggerated to paint them in a more impressive light. Because of the nature of the oral tradition, it is probable that the more recent Incan stories were likely to be more accurate.

5 The Inca may have also whitewashed the accounts of their expansion and conquest of neighboring settlements, such as the Lupaca to their south. Because of their policy of dispersing uncooperative people and repopulating the area with people who they were able to deal with, the Incan leaders were the only sources of Spanish knowledge of their empire and were, therefore, able to control the description of their conquests and could portray themselves as righteous and invincible warriors. This makes it all but impossible to establish the accuracy of their narratives.

TEST 5 - 2
Architectural Change in Eighth Century Japan

▶ 117페이지 1문단을 참고하세요.

01 The term "dramatic" in the passage is closest in meaning to:

(A) remarkable
(B) apparent
(C) interesting
(D) gradual

1 Japanese architecture underwent dramatic changes as the Nara period began in the early 8th century. During this period, great political and societal changes, such as the establishment of the capital at Heijō-kyō(modern day Nara), made traditional architectural arrangements and styles less advantageous and necessitated a new system.

▶ 117페이지 2문단을 참고하세요.

02 What can be inferred from paragraph 2 about early Japanese marriage customs?

(A) Living with the bride's family allowed the imperial in-laws a greater influence over the royal court.
(B) They, needing more rudimentary architectural styles, provided a catalyst for changes in architectural structures.
(C) They were feasible in the contemporary period because they were needed to make the already big royal court system even bigger.
(D) The imperial family married into families with large landholdings so they could gain the property needed to build more palaces.

2 One of the most glaring catalysts for the change in architectural styles was the shift in marriage practices of the Japanese elite. Prior to this period, Japanese rulers married members of one of the most powerful clans of the period, the Soga-lords' families, in politically motivated alliances, and established palaces at the bride's family home in addition to that of their own family headquarters. The royal court generally resided with the bride's family for the first years of their marriage and then moved between their multiple palaces throughout the marriage as children grew older and alliances shifted.

▶ 118페이지 5문단을 참고하세요.

03 What does the word "them" refer to in the passage?

(A) stone foundations
(B) mortise joints
(C) roofs
(D) buildings

Japanese architects looked to the urban design and construction techniques of their continental neighbors' geometrically situated capitals with their bulkier, more permanent buildings constructed using stone foundations, mortise joints, and tiled roofs which allowed them to stand for years.

▶ 118페이지 5문단을 참고하세요.

04 10. Why does the author mention that Hōryū-ji the "one of the oldest surviving wooden structures in the world." in paragraph 5?

(A) To show that structures built in Japan during the Nara period were the most durable buildings that had ever been created
(B) To contrast the great permanence of a Buddhist structure from the Nara period with the short period of usefulness of previous Japanese construction projects
(C) To give an idea of the new type of building materials used to construct Buddhist temples in Japan during the Nara period
(D) To introduce the idea that even though the Buddhist structures were more durable, they were similar to earlier buildings constructed of wood

5 To construct this imperial city, Japanese architects looked to the urban design and construction techniques of their continental neighbors' geometrically situated capitals with their bulkier, more permanent buildings constructed using stone foundations, mortise joints, and tiled roofs which allowed them to stand for years. [■] The construction of a large, continental-style capital with these types of buildings required a tremendous amount of manpower and building materials, but it was attractive to emperors looking to legitimize their reigns in a manner directly comparable to the powerful Chinese dynasty.

TEST 6 - 1
How Camels Survive in Arid Environments

▶ 127페이지 1문단을 참고하세요.

01 The term "mechanisms for" in the passage is closest in meaning to:

(A) benefits of
(B) need for
(C) means of
(D) importance

They have since acted as beasts of burden, desert transport, and sources of wool, leather, milk and meat because they, unlike other livestock, have specialized mechanisms for survival in desert environments.

▶ 128페이지 4문단을 참고하세요.

02 The term "diffusion" in the passage is closest in meaning to:

(A) learning
(B) spread
(C) adoption
(D) teaching

The network of capillaries in their cooler nasal cavities also keeps the brain cooler through heat diffusion.

▶ 128페이지 5문단을 참고하세요.

03 What can be inferred from paragraph 5 about the importance of the hump for camels living in desert regions?

(A) The storage of fat in the hump effectively reduces the temperature of the camel in hot environments.
(B) The hump stores fat that the camel can metabolize to form water when it hasn't been able to find water for a long time.
(C) The hump assists in keeping the whole body warm at night with the heat retained during the day.
(D) Camels' humps are confirmed to hold water and misunderstood to dissipate heat more easily.

5 There is, perhaps, no better known, or misunderstood, camel adaptation to heat and dehydration than the hump. Commonly thought to hold water, these humps are actually fat accumulations. Unlike other animals, which are covered by a layer of fat, camels store theirs in their humps. Fat cells hold in body heat, so by having most of their fat concentrated on their backs, camels can more easily dissipate heat, reducing their internal temperatures. Water is also produced when this fat is metabolized, but it is all used up in the process.

▶ 129페이지 7문단을 참고하세요.

04 According to paragraph 7, which of the following is true of camels' way of avoiding dehydration and overheating?

(A) The camel is not only able to deal with high internal temperatures, but its body is also adapted to reduce the absorption of heat from its surroundings.
(B) Unlike heat gaining, the camels' physical attributes have relatively little relation to heat dissipation.
(C) Camels utilize not behavioral patterns but physiological and physical characteristics to avoid gaining heat.
(D) Despite the thin, light-colored wool's lack of skin protection from the harmful effects of the sun, it doesn't absorb much heat.

7 Their physical features and actions not only dissipate heat but also avoid gaining heat altogether. Their tall, spindly legs keep their cores aloft, where air temperatures are cooler, and their uninsulated nearly hairless underbellies dissipate heat quickly. Further, their thin, light-colored wool doesn't absorb much heat and protects the skin from the effects of the sun. The fat in their hump also absorbs heat before it reaches the core, where it would increase the internal temperature. This is compounded by their natural proclivity for standing facing the sun, which reduces the amount of surface area directly exposed to the sun's rays.

TEST 6 - 2
Hunter-gatherers in Southwest Asia

▶ 131페이지 2문단을 참고하세요.

01 According to paragraph 2, which of the following is true of the effects of climate change in the Southwest Asian region?

(A) It caused the introduction of new forms of plant life that had not previously existed to low lying areas.
(B) It depleted the soil in the higher grounds that had been previously rich in nutrients.
(C) It allowed plants to spread out and produce more edible food products that the inhabitants could rely upon for sustenance.
(D) It caused the demise of the Kebaran society which could no longer migrate across the area due to the wetter weather.

2 Despite the dietary changes they caused, the Kebaran society did not remain forever. Around 13,000 BC, a warmer, wetter period saw the rise of the Natufian Culture. Their appearance coincided with the shift in plant life in the area. As temperatures rose, plants that required the warmer temperatures of lower altitudes spread to higher altitudes. The production of pistachios, oak, almonds, wild barley and wild emmer wheat flourished as they moved from the lower altitude's sandy soil to the richer, clay-based soil of higher altitudes; these increased harvests allowed the Natufian Culture to expand as well.

▶ 132페이지 4문단을 참고하세요.

02 According to paragraph 4, which of the following is true about the settlements of the Natufian Civilization?

(A) They had a great impact on the types of crops that grew near them.
(B) They even performed massive game drives to complement their deficient nourishment.
(C) They were situated in places that would allow their inhabitants the best access to the supplies they needed to feed themselves.
(D) They were generally found in the higher altitudes because of the abundant nuts and grains that grew there.

4 The village locations were also affected by the crops they relied upon. They were generally located along the boundary between the coastal grasslands and the higher altitudes where nuts and cereals prospered. They also seemed to settle in places where they could collect high quality stone for creating new tools. By settling in these places, they could harvest the cereal crops as they came into season during the spring and harvest nuts in the fall, providing year-round nourishment. In addition to using their stored crops in summer and winter, they also hunted the lowland animals.

▶ 132페이지 4문단을 참고하세요.

03 The term "relied upon" in the passage is closest in meaning to:

(A) depended on
(B) predicted
(C) developed from
(D) were shaped by

4 The village locations were also affected by the crops they relied upon. They were generally located along the boundary between the coastal grasslands and the higher altitudes where nuts and cereals prospered.

▶ 133페이지 6문단을 참고하세요.

04 The term "scale" in the passage is closest in meaning to:

(A) duties
(B) importance
(C) size
(D) needs

Even the modest scale of this early farming helped the society supplement their declining wild wheat and barley harvests and thus ensured their survival.

TEST 7 - 1
Life on Mars

▶ 141페이지 2문단을 참고하세요.

01 According to paragraph 2, which of the following is NOT true regarding comparisons between the Earth and Mars?

(A) Mars and Earth are nearly the identical size, but Earth has slightly more land mass.
(B) Due to the slight margin between Earth's and Mars' axis, the two planets share similar climate patterns.
(C) The atmospheric composition of the planets is more similar to one another than it is to the other planets in the solar system.
(D) Mars revolves around the sun in the same habitable zone that allows the Earth to support life.

2 Contrary to popular belief, Mars and Earth are remarkably similar. Although Earth is much larger than Mars, they have nearly identical land surfaces. They also share similar atmospheric chemistry when compared to other planets in our solar system. Further, Mars is subject to seasonal temperature variations like Earth's due to its 25° axis tilt, which is only 1.5° different than Earth's 23.5° tilt. A more important similarity that could allow life on Mars is the fact that both planets orbit in the Sun's habitable zone, which could allow Martian surface water in addition to the water frozen in its polar ice caps.

▶ 141페이지 2문단을 참고하세요.

02 The term "remarkably" in the passage is closest in meaning to:

(A) very closely
(B) surprisingly
(C) usually
(D) predictably

2 Contrary to popular belief, Mars and Earth are remarkably similar. Although Earth is much larger than Mars, they have nearly identical land surfaces. They also share similar atmospheric chemistry when compared to other planets in our solar system.

▶ 141페이지 3문단을 참고하세요.

03 According to paragraph 3, which of the following is true regarding the possibility of life existing on Mars?

(A) The atmosphere of Mars is unable to support any life forms because all living organisms require oxygen to survive.
(B) Nighttime temperatures drop precipitously due to the planet's minimal atmosphere doing little to prevent deadly ultraviolet solar radiation from reaching its surface.
(C) Mars' thin atmosphere allows more solar radiation to reach the planet's surface than most currently known life forms can handle.
(D) The thin composition of Mars' atmosphere is toxic to every type of organism but oxygen-dependent organisms.

3 Despite these similarities, Mars' conditions are currently very inhospitable. [■] The most glaring problem is that the current Martian atmosphere is deadly for Earth-based organisms. [■] The thin, carbon dioxide (CO_2)-heavy composition of the atmosphere, besides being toxic to oxygen-dependent organisms, does not retain solar heat when it is not directly exposed to the Sun; therefore, nighttime temperatures drop precipitously and the average surface temperature is a frigid -30°C. [■]

▶ 142페이지 4문단을 참고하세요.

04 The term "tremendous" in the passage is closest in meaning to:

(A) calm
(B) huge
(C) actual
(D) beautiful

4 Another major problem that prevents life on Mars is the dearth of liquid surface water. While the ice caps do contain a tremendous amount of water and CO_2, scientists have been unable to find liquid water on Mars' surface, but this does not mean it never existed.

TEST 7 - 2
Agriculture and Settlement around the Nile River

▶ 146페이지 3문단을 참고하세요.

01 The term "considerably" in the passage is closest in meaning to:

(A) gradually
(B) surprisingly
(C) predictably
(D) significantly

Eventually the sediment and silt carried through these channels aggregated and built up the floodplain, raising the river's level considerably.

▶ 146페이지 5문단을 참고하세요.

02 According to paragraph 5, which of the following is true regarding the food sources found in the Nile River valley?

(A) The large mammals found in the area provided the settlers with most of the protein they needed in their diets.
(B) Settlers were able to find most of the nourishment they needed in the valley due to a wealth of carbohydrate-rich foods.
(C) Despite a large number of resident bird species, the settlers preferred to catch fish to provide themselves with nourishment.
(D) The plants, seeds, fruit, and vegetables found in the region were not nutritious, so the settlers replaced them with their imported crops.

5   This verdant area also provided for the settlers' other dietary needs. Since the strip of land was narrow, the number of large mammals that could establish territories in this area was limited. In fact, the remains of only three large species have been found, the Dorcas gazelle, aurochs-a type of wild cattle, and the hartebeest. Settlers, therefore, relied on other protein sources, such as birds and fish. While migratory birds, like ducks and geese, were regularly taken, fish were the primary protein source, especially catfish. In addition, the seasonal variety of plant in the area gave them access to an abundance of carbohydrate-rich foods.

▶ 147페이지 6문단을 참고하세요.

03 What does the word "it" refer to in the passage?

(A) flooding
(B) empire
(C) river
(D) wealth

6   Eventually, the fertile soils and predictable flooding of the river allowed the settlers to develop an empire whose wealth was based on the great agricultural bounty it was able to reap. Today, Ancient Egyptians are regarded as one of the first civilizations to practice widespread agriculture.

▶ 147페이지 6문단을 참고하세요.

04 The term "widespread" in the passage is closest in meaning to :

(A) important
(B) advantageous
(C) common
(D) complex

6   Eventually, the fertile soils and predictable flooding of the river allowed the settlers to develop an empire whose wealth was based on the great agricultural bounty it was able to reap. Today, Ancient Egyptians are regarded as one of the first civilizations to practice widespread agriculture.

TEST 부록
Sea Turtle Navigation

▶ 153페이지 1문단을 참고하세요.

01 The term "Futhermore" in the passage is closest in meaning to

(A) similarly
(B) however
(C) in addition
(D) in general

Furthermore, depending on ocean currents, the odor trails may be travelling in the same direction as the turtles, thus never reaching them.

▶ 153페이지 2문단을 참고하세요.

02 The word "precise" in the passage is closest in meaning to

(A) repeated
(B) fast
(C) unusual
(D) exact

What makes sea turtles' utilization of magnetite interesting is the fact that it is so precise that sea turtles in the vast ocean can measure not only the intensity of the magnetic pull but also the difference in the angle of the magnetic poles.

▶ 154페이지 3문단을 참고하세요.

03 The word "it" in the passage refers to

(A) evidence
(B) magnetic positioning
(C) sea turtle
(D) land

Substantial evidence both for and against magnetic navigation led to the theory that while magnetic positioning plays a vital role in the open sea, far away from the destination, sea turtles use several other methods to complement it when they are young or when they are close to land. [■]

▶ 155페이지 6문단을 참고하세요.

04 According to paragraph 6, which of the following statements is a characteristic of Grand Cayman Island?

(A) Hawksbill turtles from Grand Cayman Island have migrated to the Persian Gulf.
(B) The green sea turtle population of the island is yet to be recovered.
(C) It is now difficult for sea turtles to reach the island because of the ongoing habitat reconstruction.
(D) Grand Cayman Island is still home to the largest green sea turtle population due to a global decline in green sea turtle populations.

6   The mysteries of sea turtle navigation do not end with their navigation methods, but also extend to navigation patterns, as can be seen in the mitochondrial DNA (mtDNA-genetic material that is inherited solely from the maternal parent and is, therefore, identical in close relatives) of hawksbill turtles in the Persian Gulf. Each hawksbill turtle tested in the nesting site had the same mtDNA, with only minimal variability, leading to the conclusion that most of the hawksbill turtles in the nesting site have emerged from the same nest. This explains why areas around the world that appear ideal for sea turtle foraging and nesting are not recolonized after human interference wipes out the native populations. For example, Grand Cayman Island was once home to one of the largest green sea turtle populations in the world, but after the turtles were driven off by humans, wildlife protection laws and habitat reconstruction have proven unsuccessful in bringing back the turtles.

usherin.usher.co.kr

USHER iBT TOEFL
INTERMEDIATE READING
TEST 해설지

USHER iBT TOEFL
INTERMEDIATE READING

TEST 1
답안 및 취약 유형 분석표

해석 · 해설

답안 및 문제 유형 분석표

TEST 1-1

01 (B) Purpose

02 (C) Vocabulary

03 (C) Inference

04 (B) Fact

05 (A) Inference

06 (A) Highlight

07 (A) Fact

08 (D) Inference

09 3rd ■ Insertion

10 (A), (C), (D) Summary

TEST 1-2

11 (D) Fact

12 (A) Inference

13 (B) Fact

14 (A) Highlight

15 (B) Vocabulary

16 (D) Inference

17 (D) Purpose

18 (A) Inference

19 3rd ■ Insertion

20 (A), (D), (F) Summary

각 문제 유형별 맞춘 개수를 아래에 적어 보세요.

유형	맞춘 답의 개수	정답률	
단어 (Vocabulary)	/ 2	정답률:	%
사실 확인 문제 (Fact)	/ 4	정답률:	%
지시어 찾기 (Reference)	/ 0	정답률:	%
끼워 넣기 (Insertion)	/ 2	정답률:	%
문장 변환문제 (Highlight)	/ 2	정답률:	%
목적 (Purpose)	/ 2	정답률:	%
추론 (Inference)	/ 6	정답률:	%
단락 요약(Summary / Category Chart)	/ 2	정답률:	%
전체	/ 20	정답률:	%

※ 자신이 취약한 유형은 READING STRATEGIES를 통해 다시 한번 점검하시기 바랍니다. (p.44)

TEST 1-1　Comets 혜성

Introduction	단락 1	단주기와 장주기 혜성
Point	단락 2	카이퍼대(帶)로부터 온 단주기 혜성
Point	단락 3	오르트 성운에서 온 장주기 혜성
Point	단락 4	태양의 영향으로 인한 꼬리 형성
Point	단락 5	꼬리를 만든다고 알려진 두 가지 태양력(힘): 태양 방사와 태양풍
Point	단락 6	혜성의 생명력

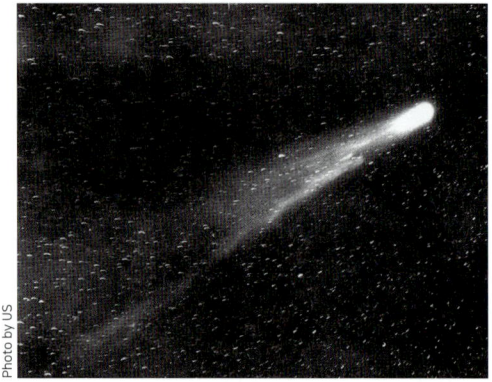

문단주제	본문내용	해석

단락 1
단주기와 정주기 행성

1 Comets, small celestial bodies with long luminous tails and orbits that occasionally **bring them** in close **contact with** Earth, are some of the most fascinating objects in our solar system. Today, only about 4,900 of these bodies **composed of** frozen gases and volatile compounds **along with** rocky metallic elements have been discovered, but the distance of their orbits **makes it likely that** many more exist. Comets **are generally categorized into** two orbit-length-dependent categories: long-period and short-period comets. [Q1-B], [Q3-C] Short-period comets, such as Halley's Comet which has been documented appearing every 76 years since 240 B.C.E. make regular appearances **due to** their relatively short orbits of less than 200 years and are more well-known. Long-period comets, however, are rarely observed because they **take** hundreds or thousands of years **to complete** one trip around the sun.

길고 빛나는 꼬리를 갖고 있고 때때로 지구에 가까이 오는 궤도를 갖고 있는 천체인 혜성들은 우리의 태양계에서 가장 흥미로운 것들 중 하나이다. 오늘날 금속성 암석과 함께 결빙가스 및 휘발성 혼합 물로 구성된 단지 4900여개의 혜성이 발견되었지만, 그들의 궤도의 거리가 (발견되지 않은) 더 많은 혜성의 존재를 가능하게 한다. 혜성들은 일반적으로 주기의 길이에 따라서 단주기, 장주기 두 가지 혜성으로 구분된다. [Q1-B], [Q3-C] 기원전 240년부터 76년마다 나타났다고 기록된 핼리혜성과 같은 단주기 혜성들은 200년 이하의 상대적으로 짧은 주기를 가지고 있기에 주기적으로 나타나고 더욱 잘 알려져 있다. 반면에 장주기 혜성들은 태양 주위를 도는 궤도를 완주하는데 수백 년 혹은 수천 년이 걸리기 때문에 드물게 목격된다.

단락 2
카이퍼대(帶)로부터 온 단주기 혜성

2 [Q4-C] The main difference between the two categories **seems to arrive from** their origin. [Q4-A] Short-period comets begin in the Kuiper belt of non-planetary matter. The matter in the belt, just past Neptune's orbit, roughly 50 astronomical units (1 AU = the distance between Earth and the sun) from the sun, **travels around** the sun on nearly **the same** plane

[Q4-C] 이 두 가지 분류의 가장 큰 차이점은 그것들의 기점으로부터 생긴다고 보여진다. [Q4-A]단주기 혜성들은 카이퍼대(帶)의 비(非) - 행성 물질로부터 시작된다. 이런 물질로 이루어진 해왕성의 궤도보다 아주 약간 벗어난 태양으로부터 대략 50AU 정도 떨어져 있는 지역은 행성들과 거의 같은 평면 위의 궤도를 돈다 (1AU는 지구와 태양 사이의

Vocabulary

1단락
luminous [lúːmənəs] a. 야광의, 빛나는
categorize [kǽtigəràiz] v. 분류하다 categorized a. 분류된
volatile [válətil] a. 변덕스러운
document [dákjəmənt] v. 문서로 기록하다 documented a. 문서로 기록된

2단락
origin [ɔ́rìdʒən] n. 기점
rotate [róuteit] v. 회전하다 rotating a. 회전하는
solar [sóulər] a. 태양의
astronomical [æ̀strənáːmikl] a. 천문학의
gravitation [græ̀vitéiʃn] n. 만유인력, 중력

단락 3
오르트 성운에서 온 장주기 혜성

단락 4
태양의 영향으로 인한 꼬리 형성

as the planets. If two of these comets strike **one another**, or if one is [Q4-D] affected by the gravitation of a nearby planet, the orbit may be thrown off **in such a way that** a comet enters the inner solar system where it is affected by solar forces and visible from Earth.

3   Contrarily, long-period comets do not **originate from** the same plane as other bodies in the solar system. They orbit the sun in elliptical orbits spanning **a variety of** angles, forming a "shell" around the solar system **known as** the Oort Cloud. Scientists believe there are millions of inactive comets in this region, 10,000 AU from the sun. Due to this extreme distance they are not affected by planetary gravitation in the same way as Kuiper belt comets. For one of these comets to **make its way into** the inner solar system it must be affected by the gravitational forces of a passing star. [■] When this happens they are sent on an irregular orbit that **brings them closer to** the sun where they undergo the changes **typical of** all comets. [■] [Q5-A] After they have completed their pass near the sun, it may be thousands of years before they make their return. [■] In fact, Comet West and C/1999 F1 have orbits that are estimated at 6 million years. [Q5-C] There is even a subset of these long-period comets called the hyperbolic, or single-apparition, comets that make only one appearance near the sun, because their orbits eventually **take** them **out of** the solar system. [■]

4   **Regardless of** the category of comet, their telltale shape forms in the same way. They complete most of their orbit as frozen and relatively inactive masses that **are difficult to discern**, but as they come closer to the sun, the effects of its massive energy sublimate the frozen materials within this nucleus to form a glowing ball of dust and gases known as the coma. This coma greatly increases the comet's size. The nucleus is generally less than 60 km **in diameter**, but the coma can be larger than the sun. This most distinguishable feature differentiates comets from other celestial bodies,

거리 이다). 만약 이 혜성들이 충돌하거나, 혹은 하나가 [Q4-D] 근처 행성의 중력에 의해서 영향을 받으면, 그 혜성은 아마 태양계 내부로 내던져지게 되고, 그곳에서 이 혜성은 태양의 영향을 받게 되고 지구에서 관측이 가능하다.

반면에 장주기 혜성은 태양계의 다른 천체들과 같은 평면 위에서 만들어지지 않는다. 그들은 태양 주위를 타원형 궤도를 따라서 넓은 폭의 각도를 가로지르며 돌고, 오르트 성운이라고 알려진 태양계 주변에 전자각(전자껍질)을 형성한다. 과학자들은 태양과 10,000AU 떨어진 이 층에 수백만 개의 활동하지 않는 혜성들이 있을거라고 믿고 있다. 이러한 엄청난 거리 때문에 이것들은 카이퍼대(帶) 혜성들과 같은 방법으로 거대 행성들의 중력에 의해서 영향을 받을 수 없다. 이러한 혜성들 중 하나가 태양계 내로 들어오려면, 지나가는 별의 중력에 의해서 영향을 받아야만 한다. [■] 이것이 발생하면 그들은 모든 혜성들의 특징이 되는 변화를 겪는 태양 가까이로 움직이는 불규칙한 궤도로 보내어지게 된다. [■] [Q5-A] 그들이 태양 가까이를 지난 후에는, 그들이 다시 돌아오기까지 수천 년이 걸릴 지도 모른다. [■] 사실, West와 C/1999 F1 혜성은 육백 만년 정도의 궤도를 갖는 것으로 예상된다. [Q5-C] 이 혜성들이 나타난 이후에 이것들의 궤도가 태양계 밖으로 나가기 때문에 태양 근처에 단 한번만 나타나기 때문에 쌍곡선(hyperbolic) 혹은 단독 출연(single-apparition) 혜성이라고 이름 붙여진 장주기 혜성들의 하위 부류도 있다. [■]

혜성의 종류와는 상관없이 혜성들의 감출 수 없는 모양은 같은 방법으로 만들어진다. 그들은 구분 하기 힘든 얼어있고 비교적 비활성된 질량으로 이루어져 있는 상태로 그들 궤도의 대부분을 움직이지만, 혜성들은 태양과 가까이 오면서, 이것의 거대한 에너지는 중심부의 얼어있는 물질을 기체화하고 코마라고 알려진 먼지와 기체로 이루어진 빛나는 공을 만들어 낸다. 이 코마는 혜성의 크기를 거대하게 증가시킨다. 중심부는 보통 지름이 60km이내 이지만 코마는 태양보다 클 수 있다. 이 가장 눈에 띄는 특징은 혜성을 소행성과 같은 다른 천체들로부터 구분시켜 준다. 이것들이 태양과

Vocabulary

3단락
elliptical [ilíptikl] a. 타원형의
inactive [inǽktiv] a. 활동하지 않는, 소극적인
apparition [æ̀pəríʃən] n. 나타남

span [spæn] n. (어떤 일이 지속되는) 기간, v. (얼마의 기간에) 걸치다
subset [sʌ́bsèt] n. 부분 집합, 일부분, 하위 부류
appear [əpíər] v. 나타나다, ~인 것 같다, 출현하다

hyperbolic [hàipərbálik] a. 태양의

4단락
telltale [téltèil] a. (어떤 것이 존재하거나 일이 있었음을 숨기려 해도) 숨길 수 없는
sublimate [sʌ́bləmèit] v. 승화시키다, 고체에서 기체로 가다

discern [disə́ːrn, -zə́ːrn] v. 알아차리다, 파악하다
distinguishable [distíŋgwiʃəbəl] a. 구별할 수 있는, 분간할 수 있는

such as asteroids. When they reach approximately 1. 5 AU from the sun, solar energy's effects become more extreme and parts of the coma are blown into a tail which can be **millions of kilometers long**.

단락 5
꼬리를 만든다고 알려진 두 가지 태양력(힘): 태양방사와 태양풍

5   Research into comets **led** scientists **to make** an interesting observation regarding their tails; [Q7-A] **they always point away from** the sun. This **allowed** them **to conclude** that some force **emanating from** the sun pushed the particles in the coma to form the tail. We now understand that this is not one, but two forces. Pressure from solar radiation drives the dust particles back from the coma, while solar winds push back the ionized volatile gases surrounding the nucleus. Because of these two different effects, comets **are often found to have** two tails, a curved one composed of dust and a second, composed of ionized volatiles, that appears blue and always points away from the sun.

대략 1.5AU만큼 가까워 질 때면, 태양 에너지의 영향은 더욱 극대화되고 코마의 어느 부분은 수백만 킬로미터까지 늘어날 수 있는 꼬리로 날라간다.

혜성에 관한 연구는 과학자들이 그것의 꼬리에 대해서 흥미로운 발견을 하게 했다; [Q7-A] 그들은 항상 태양과 반대 방향을 가리키고 있다는 것이다. 이것은 그들(과학자)이 태양으로부터 방출되는 힘이 코마속의 입자들에 압박을 가해 꼬리를 형성하게 한다는 결론에 다다르게 했다. 이제 우리는 이것이 한 가지가 아닌 두 가지의 힘이라는 것을 이해한다. 태양 방사로부터 생긴 압력은 먼지 입자들을 코마 로부터 밀어내고, 태양풍은 이온화된 중심부를 감 싸고 있는 휘발성 기체들을 밀어낸다는 것이다. 이러한 두 가지 영향 때문에 혜성들은 흔히 휘어진 모양을 가진 먼지의 자취로 이루어진 것과 태양과 반대 방향을 가리키는 파란색으로 나타나는 두 꼬리를 갖는다.

단락 6
혜성의 생명력

6   [Q8-D] When the comet makes its way out of the influence of solar power, the gases in the coma condense and the materials in the tail are lost, reducing its mass. Some of this dust and matter remains in orbit, and can cause other celestial events. The annual Perseid meteor shower is caused by matter **ejected from** the Swift-Tuttle comet during its 133-year orbit. **For this reason**, it has been hypothesized that comet lifespans are limited by the number of orbits they complete. [Q8-D] After a certain number of orbits, the nucleus will have expelled all of its volatile components and will **continue to orbit** as a small grouping of stony materials that are relatively unaffected by solar radiation or winds.

[Q8-D] 혜성이 태양의 영향에서 나올 때면, 코마 속의 기체는 압축하고 꼬리에 있는 물질들은 잃어 버리는데, 그렇기 때문에 혜성의 중심부의 질량은 줄어든다. 이러한 먼지와 물질은 궤도 내에 남게 되고, 다른 천체 행사를 만들기도 한다. 매년 일어나는 페르세우스 유성우는 스위프트-터틀(Swift-Turtle) 혜성의 133년짜리 궤도에서 분출된 잔재로부터 만들어졌다. 이러한 이유로 혜성의 수명은 궤도를 도는 수에 제한된다고 가정하게 되었다. [Q8-D] 일정 수만큼 태양의 주위를 돈 후에는 중심부는 휘발성의 물질들을 모두 배출했을 것이고, 태양 방사나 태양풍에 의해 영향을 거의 받지 않는 고체 물질들의 덩어리가 되어 계속 궤도를 따라 움직일 것이다.

Vocabulary

5단락 celestial [silést∫əl] a. 하늘의, 천체의
emanate [émənèit] v. (어떤 느낌, 특질 등을) 내뿜다
ionize [áiənàiz] v. 이온화하다

radiation [rèidiéi∫ən] n. 방사선, (열, 에너지 등의) 복사
surround [səráund] v. 둘러싸다, 에워싸다

6단락 condense [kəndéns] v. (기체가) 응결되다, 응결시키다
hypothesize [haipάθəsàiz] v. 가설을 세우다, 제기하다

eject [idʒékt] v. 쫓아내다, 내쫓다
lifespan [láifspæn] n. 수명   expel [ikspél] v. 배출하다

01

Why does the author mention "Halley's Comet which has been documented appearing every 76 years"?

(A) To give the reader more information regarding the average duration of short-period comets. ★
(B) To relate the concept of short-term comets to a comet that the reader is likely to know about already.
(C) To introduce the idea that people have been studying comets and their orbits for thousands of years.
(D) To differentiate short and long-period comets by giving an example of a comet with an irregularly long orbital duration.

글쓴이는 왜 매 76년마다 나타난다고 기록된 핼리혜성"을 언급하는가?

(A) 독자에게 단주기 혜성들이 평균적으로 지속되는 기간에 관한 더욱 많은 정보를 주기 위해서. ★
(B) 단주기 혜성의 개념을 독자들이 이미 알고 있을 만한 혜성과 연관 짓기 위해서.
(C) 사람들이 혜성들에 대해 수 천년 동안 공부해 왔다는 것을 알리기 위해서.
(D) 비정상적으로 긴 공전 주기의 예를 들어서 단주기 혜성과 장주기 혜성들을 구분 하기 위해서.

Purpose 지문에서 음영문구 Halley's Comet which has been documented appearing every 76 years (매 76년 마다 나타난다고 기록된 "핼리혜성")을 살펴보면 Short-period comets, such as Halley's Comet which has been documented appearing every 76 years since 240 B.C.E., make regular appearances due to their relatively short orbits of less than 200 years and are more well-known. (기원 전 240년부터 76년 마다 나타났다고 기록된 핼리혜성과 같은 단주기 혜성들은 200년 이하의 상대적으로 짧은 주기를 가지고 있기에 자주 나타나고 더욱 잘 알려져 있다)라고 말한다. 즉, 핼리혜성은 단주기 혜성들의 예로 언급된 것이며, 단주기 혜성들 중에서도 사람들에게 가장 잘 알려진 혜성이라는걸 알 수 있다. 따라서 정답은 (B)가 된다. (C)는 언급된 내용이 아니므로 오답이고, (D)는 핼리혜성은 단주기 혜성의 예로 언급된 것이기 때문에 오답이다. (A)는 핼리혜성의 주기가 단주기 혜성의 평균주기라는 내용이 언급되지 않으므로 오답이다.

02

The term "relatively" in the passage is closest in meaning to

(A) very [vèri]
(B) surprisingly [sərpráiziñli]
(C) comparatively [kəmpǽrətivli]
(D) usually [júːʒuəli, -ʒwəli] ★

지문의 단어 '상대적으로' 의 의미와 가장 유사한 것은?

(A) 매우
(B) 놀랍게도
(C) 비교적으로
(D) 대게 ★

Vocabulary 지문의 relatively(상대적으로)는 comparatively (비교적으로)와 동의어이므로 (C)가 정답이다.

03

What can be inferred from paragraph 1 about long and short-period comets?

(A) Long-period comets have a different composition than short-period comets, allowing them to embark on longer orbits.
(B) Many comets have remained undiscovered because they burn up before they are within a distance that makes them visible from Earth.
(C) Scientists are likely to know more about short-period comets than those with longer orbits because of their multiple observations.
(D) Halley's Comet probably deviated from its original orbit around the sun in the year 240 B.C.E.

단락 1로부터 장주기와 단주기 혜성들에 관해서 알 수 있는 것은?

(A) 장주기 혜성들은 단주기 혜성들보다 더욱 긴 궤도를 갖게 하는 다른 구성을 갖는다
(B) 많은 혜성들은 지구에서 보이게 되는 거리에 들어오기 전에 타버리기 때문에, 발견되지 않는다.
(C) 과학자들은 단주기 혜성들을 여러번 목격했기 때문에 장주기 혜성들보다 더욱 잘 알 확률이 높다.
(D) 핼리혜성은 기원 전 240년에 태양 주위를 도는 원래의 궤도에서 이탈했을 것이다. ★

Inference 질문의 키워드인 long and short-period comets가 언급된 부분을 살펴보면 Short-period comets make regular appearances due to their relatively short orbits of less than 200 years and are more well-known. (단주기 혜성들은 200년 이하의 상대적으로 짧은 주기를 가지고 있기에 자주 나타나고 더욱 잘 알려져 있다)라고 말한다. 즉, 장주기 혜성들 보다 단주기 혜성들이 더욱 자주 관측 된다는 걸 알 수 있고, 그러므로 단주기 혜성들에 관해서 과학자들이 비교적 더 잘 알고 있을 확률이 높다. 따라서 정답은 (C)가 된다. (A)는 두 가지의 혜성들이 다른 구성을 가지고 있다는 내용은 언급되지 않으므로 오답이고, (B)또한 언급되지 않는 내용이기 때문에 오답이다. (D)는 핼리혜성이 기원 전 240부터 기록되었다는 것이 핼리혜성이 원래의 궤도에서 튕겨져 나갔다는 뜻은 아니기 때문에 오답이다.

---

04 According to paragraph 2, which of the following is NOT true regarding the short period comets that orbit the sun?

(A) Short-period comets are believed to originate in the Kuiper belt beyond the orbit of the planets. ★
(B) Short-period comets ~~seldom~~ orbit around the sun on the same plane as the planets.
(C) Short-period comets differ from long-period comets mainly in where they originate from.
(D) Short-period comets can begin their unique revolutions around the sun after an external force dislodges them from their initial orbits.

단락 2에 의하면, 태양 주위를 도는 단주기 혜성들에 관해서 사실이 아닌 것은?

(A) 단주기 혜성들은 행성들의 궤도 넘어서 있는 카이퍼대 에서 만들어진다고 믿어진다. ★
(B) 단주기 행성들은 행성들과 동일한 평면에서 태양의 궤도를 거의 돌지 ~~않는다~~.
(C) 단주기 혜성들은 장주기 혜성들과 가장 큰 차이점은 그들의 기원이다.
(D) 단주기 혜성들은 외부의 힘에 의해서 그들의 첫번째 궤도에서 튕겨져 나간 후 태양을 중심으로 한 공전을 시작한다.

Fact 질문의 키워드인 short period comets that orbit the sun이 언급된 부분을 살펴보면 This field of matter, just past Neptune's orbit, roughly 50 astronomical units from the sun, travels around the sun on nearly the same plane as the planets. (이런 물질로 이루어진 해왕성의 궤도보다 아주 약간 벗어난 태양으로부터 대략 50AU 정도 떨어져 있는 지역은 행성들과 거의 같은 평면 위의 궤도를 돈다)라고 말한다. 즉, nearly the same plane이라는 단주기 혜성들이 태양 주위를 돌 때는 행돌들과 거의 같은 평면에서 돌기 때문에 정답은 (B)가 된다.

---

05 What can be inferred about long-period comets from paragraph 3?

(A) The frequency with which long-period comets are spotted is less than that of short-period ones.
(B) Long-period comets are ~~more visible~~ than short-period comets because they originate farther from the sun and, therefore, contain more frozen matter.
(C) All long-period comets make ~~just~~ one revolution around the sun because they are expelled from the solar system after they pass by the sun. ★
(D) When they are sent on their ~~usual~~ orbit and get closer to the sun, they go through changes commonly seen among comets.

단락 3에서 장주기 혜성들에 관해서 무엇을 추측할 수 있는가?

(A) 장주기 혜성들이 목격되는 빈도는 단주기 혜성들의 빈도보다 낮다.
(B) 장주기 혜성들은 태양과 멀리 떨어져 있는 곳에서 유래되기 때문에 얼어 있는 물질들을 더욱 많이 가지고 있고 그렇기 때문에 단주기 행성들보다 ~~더욱 잘 보인다~~.
(C) 모든 장주기 혜성들은 태양을 지난 후에 태양계에서 방출되기 때문에 ~~오직~~ 한 번의 공전을 한다. ★
(D) 장주기 혜성들은 ~~평상적~~ 궤도를 돌고 태양에 가까워질때 혜성들 사이에서 자주 목격되는 변화들을 겪는다.

Inference 질문의 키워드인 long-period comets가 언급된 부분을 살펴보면 After they have completed their pass near the sun, it may be thousands of years before they make their return. (그들이 태양 가까이를 지난 후에는, 그들이 다시 돌아오기까지 수천 년이 걸릴 지도 모른다)라고 말한다. 즉, 단주기 혜성들보다 장주기 혜성들이 목격되는 빈도가 낮다는 걸 유추할 수 있다. 따라서 정답은 (A)가 된다. (B)는 얼어붙은 물질들을 더 많이 갖고 있어서 더 잘 보인다는 내용은 언급되지 않으므로 오답이고, (C)는 항상 한번만 공전하는 것이 아니고, 그러는 경우도 항상 한 것을 얘기하는 것이기 때문에 오답이다. (D)는 usual한 궤도가 아니라 irregular orbit이기 때문에 오답이다.

06

Which of the sentences below best expresses the essential information in the highlighted sentence in the passage? Incorrect choices change the meaning in important ways or leave out essential information.

(A) i) Whereas comets are inactive and frozen as they go around their orbit, ii) when they approach the sun, iii) the coma is formed with gases and dust that are given off as the sun's light heats the nucleus.
(B) The inactivity of the masses during their orbit ~~limits~~ the ability to discern the luminosity of the gases and dust particles.
(C) iii) The glowing gaseous coma develops when ii) the comet gets closer to the sun and solar energy superheats the comet's frozen nucleus causing it to emit a bright ball of gas and dust. ★
(D) While comets remain frozen and dormant during most of their orbit, as they head for the sun, their nucleus is ~~transformed~~ into a coma, a glowing ball of dust and gases.

아래의 문장 중 지문 속의 음영 표시된 문장의 핵심 정보를 가장 잘 표현하고 있는 것은 무엇인가? 오답은 문장의 의미를 현저하게 바꾸거나 핵심 정보를 빠트리고 있다.

(A) i) 혜성들이 궤도를 돌 때 활동하고 있지 않고 얼어있는 반면에, ii) 태양에 가까워지면 태양열이 핵을 가열하면서 방출된 iii) 가스와 먼지는 코마를 형성한다.
(B) 혜성이 궤도를 도는 동안, 비활성은 먼지 입자와 가스의 밝음을 구별할 수 있는 능력을 ~~제한시킨다~~.
(C) iii) 기체로 된 빛을 발하는 코마는 ii) 혜성이 태양과 가까워지며 태양 에너지가 혜성의 얼어붙은 중심부를 아주 뜨겁게 가열시켜서 기체와 먼지로 이루어진 빛나는 덩어리를 내보낼 때 만들어진다. ★
(D) 대부분의 궤도를 냉동 휴면 상태를 유지하는 혜성은 태양을 향할 때 핵은 가스와 먼지가 타는 공 모양의 코마로 ~~바뀐다~~.

Highlight 문장을 살펴보자. i) They complete most of their orbit as frozen and relatively inactive masses that are difficult to discern, ii) but as they come closer to the sun, the effects of its massive energy sublimate the frozen materials within this nucleus to iii) form a glowing ball of dust and gases known as the coma. (i) 그들은 구분하기 힘든 얼어있고 비교적 비활성된 질량으로 이루어져 있는 상태로 그들 궤도의 대부분을 움직이지만, ii) 혜성들은 태양과 가까이 오면서, 이것의 거대한 에너지는 중심부의 얼어있는 물질을 기체화하고 iii) 코마 라고 알려진 먼지와 기체로 이루어진 빛나는 공을 만들어 낸다) 이 내용을 포함하고 있는 보기는 (A)이므로 (A)가 정답이다. (B)는 얼어붙은 혜성이 비 활동적일 땐 먼지 입자와 가스가 존재하지도 않기 때문에 오답이고, (D)는 핵이 코마로 변하는 것은 아니기 때문에 오답이다. (C)는 i)의 내용이 없으므로 오답이다.

07

According to paragraph 5, which of the following is true regarding the tails of comets?

(A) Comets have tails that point away from the sun regardless of the direction in which the comet is travelling.
(B) In most comets two tails are visible ~~because of~~ the different ~~directions~~ from which they are approached by solar forces. ★
(C) Solar ~~radiation~~ burning up the dust particles in the coma makes one of the comet's tails appear to be blue.
(D) Pressure from solar radiation has a ~~larger~~ effect on forming the tails of comets ~~than~~ solar winds.

단락 5에 의하면, 혜성의 꼬리에 관해서 옳은 것은?

(A) 혜성들의 꼬리는 혜성이 움직이고 있는 방향에 상관없이 태양의 반대 방향을 향한다.
(B) 대부분의 혜성들에서는 태양의 힘을 받는 ~~방향이~~ 다르기 ~~때문에~~ 두 개의 꼬리가 보인다. ★
(C) 태양 ~~방사~~가 코마에 존재하는 먼지 입자를 태우기 때문에 혜성의 꼬리가 ~~파란색으로~~ 나타난다.
(D) 태양 복사에너지의 압력은 태양 바람보다 혜성의 꼬리의 형성에 ~~더 큰~~ 영향을 끼친다.

Fact 질문의 키워드인 tails of comets가 언급된 부분을 살펴보면 they[tails] always point away from the sun. (그들은 [꼬리] 항상 태양과 반대 방향을 가리키고 있다)라고 말한다. 즉, 어떤 상황에서든 꼬리는 항상 태양의 반대 방향을 향하기 때문에 정답은 (A)가 된다. (B)는 다른 방향에서 태양에 의한 영향을 받은 것이 아니라 태양 압력과 태양 바람 두 가지 힘에 의하여 영향을 받은 것이기 때문에 오답이고, (C)는 태양 복사에너지 압력이 아니라 태양 바람이 꼬리를 파란색으로 보이게 하기 때문에 오답이다. (D)는 어느것이 더 큰 영향을 끼치는 것에 대한 내용은 언급되지 않으므로 오답이다.

08 According to paragraph 6, which of the following can be inferred about comets that have completed the portion of their orbit that approaches the sun?

(A) When comets leave ~~for~~ the influence of the sun, their tails quickly ~~freeze~~, which introduces another type of celestial body to the environment.
(B) Scientists ~~disproved~~ that the more orbits the comet make, the shorter their lifespans get.
(C) After all of the volatile gases have been used up, the rocky remnants will have ~~no more~~ influence in the solar system.
(D) Despite travelling along the same orbit, they are no longer as easily visible because without the coma and tail they are relatively small.

태양에 다가가는 궤도의 부분을 완주한 혜성들에 관하여 단락 6에서 추론할 수 있는 것은?

(A) 혜성이 태양의 영향력을 향할 때, 그들의 꼬리는 빠르게 얼고, 그것은 또다른 천체를 다른 환경에 소개한다
(B) 과학자들은 혜성이 궤도를 더 들수록 수명이 단축된다는 것을 ~~부정하였다~~.
(C) 휘발성의 기체들이 모두 소비된 후에는, 돌 투성이 파편은 ~~더 이상~~ 태양계에 영향을 끼치지 않는다.
(D) 그들은 비록 같은 궤도를 움직이지만 코마와 꼬리가 비교적 작기 때문에 더 이상 쉽게 보이지 않는다.

Inference 질문의 키워드인 comets that have completed the portion of their orbit that approaches the sun이 언급된 부분을 살펴보면 When the comet makes its way out of the influence of solar power, the gases in the coma condense and the materials in the tail are lost, reducing its mass. (혜성이 태양의 영향에서 나올때, 코마 속의 기체는 결합하고 꼬리에 있는 물질들은 잃어버리는데, 그렇기 때문에 혜성의 중심부의 질량은 줄어든다)라고 말한다. 즉, 혜성이 태양의 영향에서 나오게 되면 꼬리가 사라지고 크기가 작아지기 때문에 이전처럼 쉽게 보이지 않는다는 것이기 때문에 정답은 (D)가 된다. A)는, leave와 leave for를 구별해야하는데, leave는~를 떠나다이고, leave for~ 는 ~로 떠나다 이다. 지문 내용은, 태양으로 가면서 불타야 하는데, 태양의 영향력을 향하면서 freeze한다고 하였으므로, leave for 또는 freeze중 하나가 오답이고, (B)는 For this reason, it has been hypothesized that comet lifespans are limited by the number of orbits they complete. 증명한 것이 아니라 가정한 것이기 때문에 오답이다. (C)는 (A)와 같이 기체가 다 소비된 후에도 천체 행사를 만들기도 하기 때문에 오답이다.

09 Look at the four squares [■] that indicate where the following sentence could be added to the passage.

(In fact), Comet West and C/1999 F1 have orbits that are estimated at 6 million years.

Where would the sentence best fit? Click on a square [■] to add the sentence to the passage.

3rd

네 개의 네모[■]는 다음 문장이 삽입될 수 있는 부분을 나타내고 있다

사실, West와 C/1999 F1 혜성은 육 백 만년 정도의 궤도를 갖는 것으로 예상된다.

이 문장은 어느 자리에 들어가는 것이 가장 적절한가?

3번째

Insertion 삽입 문장의 단서는 6million years이다. 세 번째 네모 전 문장을 살펴보면 After they have completed their pass near the sun, it may be thousands of years before they make their return라고 말한다. 즉, 장주기 혜성들이 다시 돌아오기까지 수 백년 혹은 수 천년이 걸린다고 설명하고 이것에 대한 예를 들기 위해서 육백 만년의 궤도를 갖는 혜성들을 예로 언급한 것이므로 정답은 3번째 네모가 된다.

10

Directions: An introductory sentence for a brief summary of the passage is provided below. Complete the summary by selecting the THREE answer choices that express the most important ideas in the passage. Some sentences do not belong in the summary because they express ideas that are not presented in the passage or are minor ideas in the passage. **This question is worth 2 points**.

지시: 지문 요약을 위한 도입 문장이 아래에 주어져 있다. 지문의 가장 중요한 내용을 나타내는 보기 3개를 골라 요약을 완성하시오. 어떤 문장은 지문에 언급되지 않은 내용이나 사소한 정보를 담고 있으므로 요약에 포함되지 않는다. **이 문제는 2점이다.**

There are two types of comets which differ based on the duration of their orbits.

- (A) Short-period comets begin in the Kuiper Belt of the outer solar system and are dislodged by the effects of nearby planets, which puts them on a new relatively short orbit.
  - paragraph 2
- (C) The coma and tail that differentiate comets from asteroids and other solar bodies is caused by the frozen matter in the nucleus being turned into gas by the sun's forces.
  - paragraph 4
- (D) Comets dislodged from the Oort cloud by the effects of stars outside the solar system have orbits that last for longer than 200 years and may only appear once.
  - paragraph 3

궤도의 주기에 따라 다른 두 가지의 혜성이 있다.

- (A) 단주기 혜성들은 태양계 밖의 카이퍼대( )에서 시작해서 주변의 행성들의 영향을 받아 튕겨져 나가고, 새로운 비교적 짧은 궤도를 갖게 된다.
- (C) 혜성을 소행성과 다른 태양계의 천체들로부터 구분해 주는 코마와 꼬리는 중심부의 얼어붙은 물질들이 태양의 힘에 의해서 기체로 변하면서 생긴다.
- (D) 오르트 성운에서 튕겨져 나간 혜성들은, 태양계 밖의 별들의 영향을 받아서 태양계 안으로 튕겨 오고, 200년 이상 되는 주기를 갖게 되고 단 한번만 나타날 수도 있다.

(B) Halley's Comet has been documented appearing every 76 years since 240 B.C., making it the most famous shortperiod comet. - paragraph 2 detail

(E) Comets appear to have two distinct tails because the solar radiation and solar winds dissimilarly act on the ~~same~~ aspect of the ~~coma~~. - 틀린 정보

(F) The comas of comets orbiting in the Oort Cloud do not last ~~as long as~~ those from the Kuiper belt because of their great distance from the sun. - not mentioned

(B) 핼리혜성은 기원전 240년부터 매 76년마다 나타났다고 기록되어 온 가장 유명한 단주기 혜성이다.

(E) 혜성은 태양 방사와 태양풍이 코마가 같은 측면에 각각 다른 영향을 끼치므로 두 가지의 꼬리를 갖는다.

(F) 오르트 성운에서 궤도를 돌고 있는 혜성들의 코마는 태양과 멀리 떨어져 있기 때문에 카이퍼대(帶)의 것들만큼 오래 지속되지 않는다.

Summary 지문의 중심 내용은 혜성의 종류와 특징이다. (A)는 두 번째 단락의 중심내용인 카이퍼대로부터 온 단주기 혜성들의 특징을 요약한 것과 일치하고, (C)는 네 번째 단락의 중심내용인 꼬리의 형성과정과 일치하고, (D)는 세 번째 단락의 중심내용인 오르트 성운에서 온 장주기 혜성들의 내용과 일치한다. 따라서 답은 (A), (C), (D)이다.

TEST 1-2 Darwin and Evolution Theory 다윈과 진화론

Introduction	단락 1	다윈이 참여한 Beagle 항해의 배경 소개
Point	단락 2	균일론과 진화론의 발달
Point	단락 3	상동설이 진화론에 끼친 영향
Point	단락 4	적자생존의 개념 설명
Point	단락 5	다윈의 이론 출판의 과정과 사회적 인정

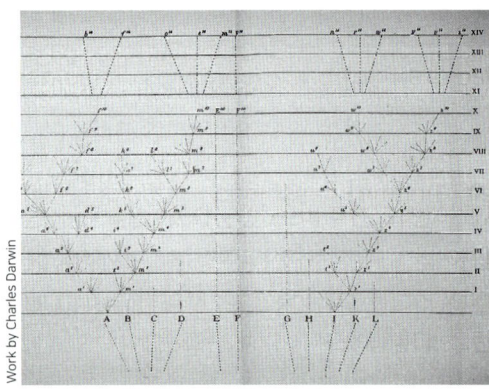
Work by Charles Darwin

문단주제	본문내용	해 석
단락 1 다윈이 참여한 Beaglr 항해의 배경 소개	**1** [Q11-C] In 1831, Robert FitzRoy **prepared to set sail on** a two year **journey** aboard the Beagle to survey the South American coastlines and [Q11-B] return three Yaghan tribe members it previously captured to Tierra del Fuego, an archipelago off the southernmost tip of the South American mainland. [Q12-A] To fight the loneliness of being at sea for so long and to help study the lands they were to visit, he invited Charles Darwin, a recent Cambridge graduate, to join the expedition [Q12-A] as his companion and ship naturalist. Prior to departure, FitzRoy gave his new companion *Principles of Geology* by Charles Lyell, who had requested that FitzRoy record the geological formations that he encountered. [Q11-A] **Unbeknownst to** both men, their journey together would stretch to nearly five years and would form the basis for a revolutionary new biological theory.	[Q11-C] 1831년에, 로버트 피쯔로이는 Beagle호를 타고 남아메리카의 해변가를 조사하고, [Q11-B] 이전에 포획된 야그한 부족원들을 남아메리카 대륙 남쪽 끝에 있는 군도인 티에라 델푸에고 섬으로 되돌려 주기 위해서 [Q15-C] 이 년짜리 항해를 떠날 준비를 했다. [Q12-A] 바다에 혼자 너무나 오래있을 외로움과 싸우고 그들이 방문할 지역에 대한 연구를 하는데 도움을 주기 위해서 그는 찰스 다윈이라는 캠브리지 졸업생을 [Q12-A] 그의 동료이자 배의 동식물 연구자로서 항해에 함께하도록 초대했다. 항해를 떠나기 전에, 피쯔로이 선장은 그에게 그가 발견할 지질학적 형성물을 기록해달라고 부탁한 찰스 리엘의 *지질학 원리*라는 책을 그의 새로운 동료에게 줬다. [Q11-A] 그 둘은 몰랐지만, 그들의 여행은 5년에 가깝게 길어지고 생물학 분야를 영원히 바꿀 새로운 생물학 이론의 기반을 이루게 된다.
단락 2 균일론과 진화론의 발달	**2** **According to** his diaries, Darwin **spent** three years and three months **exploring** the new lands, **recording** his geographical findings, and **collecting** fossils and specimens of the wildlife he **came across**. [Q13-B] Although he originally **planned to use** his findings to write a **book on** geology, **over the course of** his explorations he made many new, and interesting discoveries in the field of biology such as discovering giant armadillo and sloth fossils from the distant	그의 메모장에 따르면, 다윈은 삼년 삼 개월 동안을 새로운 지역들을 탐험하고, 새로운 지질학적 발견을 기록하고, 야생동물의 화석과 표본을 모으면서 보냈다. [Q13-B] 비록 원래 그는 그의 발견물을 지질학에 관한 책을 쓰는데 사용하려고 했지만, 그가 탐험을 하면서 먼 과거의 거대한 아르마딜로나 나무늘보의 화석과 같이 생물학의 분야에서 많은 새롭고 흥미로운 점들을 발견했다. 그는 또한 지형에 의해 분리된 바다와 섬 같은 지리적으로 격리된 지역에서는 가지각색의

Vocabulary

1단락
recent [ríːsənt] a. 최근의
departure [dipátʃər] n. 떠남, 출발
expedition [èkspədíʃən] n. 탐험, 원정
companion [kəmpǽnjən] n. 동반자, 동행

2단락
specimen [spésəmən] n. 견본, 샘플
assortment [əsɔ́ːetmənt] n. 모음, 종합
marine [məríːn] a. 바닷가, 해변의
distinct [distíŋkt] a. 뚜렷한, 분명한

past. He also discovered that in areas with a geographic segregation, such as islands or seas separated by isthmuses, different species were found. This was particularly true in the Galapagos Archipelago, where he found different species of tortoises on each island, a unique marine iguana with a seaweed-based diet, and **an assortment of** birds he **thought to be** blackbirds, grosbeaks, and finches but later **turned out to be** 12 distinct species of finches. These discoveries, **combined with** Lyell's theory of uniformitarianism, which stated that "the present is the **key to** the past," meaning that we can only assume about the past from what we observe in the present, **caused** Darwin **to postulate** that the diversity of these species was possible only if there was some mechanism through which species could change over time.

단락 3
상동설이 진화론에 끼친 영향

3   [■] Darwin's idea was supported by the theory of homology Richard Owen **derived from** comparative studies of the structural systems of various vertebrates. [■] Owen found homology, or anatomical similarity, in the body parts of different animals which **served** different **purposes**. [■] The forelimbs of most vertebrates, such as, bats, whales, humans, and horses, all share a basic design. This cannot **be attributed to** common use, so it must indicate common ancestry and adaptive evolution to fit the organisms' functions. [■] The presence of vestigial, or leftover, structures in modern organisms also **points to** an evolutionary system, because these structures serve no purpose in modern animals. The whale and snake are both examples of this, because although both are now legless, they have small vestigial leg bones, which point to a four-legged ancestor.

단락 4
적자생존의 개념 설명

4   All of this **support for** Darwin's theory did not explain why evolution would have occurred. Darwin got a basic idea about this by looking at the changes that breeders could induce in their animals through animal husbandry. By breeding animals with certain traits they could artificially change the traits of the offspring. This couldn't, however, explain how species evolve naturally or how some species **go extinct** and

Vocabulary

3단락   attribute [ətríbju:t] v. ~의 결과로 보다
ancestry [ǽnsestri] n. 가계, 혈통
vestigial [vestídʒiəl] a. (자취, 흔적으로) 남아 있는

4단락   induce [indjú:s] v. 설득하다, 유도하다
favorable [féivərəbəl] a. 호의적인, 찬성하는, 유리한
extinct [extinct] a. 멸종된

are replaced by other species. To gain further **insight into** this, Darwin **turned to** the population research of economist Thomas Malthus, which indicated that population increases outpace food production. This overpopulation decreases the number of offspring reaching maturity during lean times. Darwin recognized that these two basic ideas could **be applied to** the animal kingdom. [Q16-D] He theorized that during competitive times, animals with favorable traits would survive **to reproduce** and **pass on** their superior traits **to** the next generation **in** a natural **form** of selection.

단락 5
다윈의 이론 출판의 과정과 사회적 인정

5 Although Darwin **had** great **confidence in** the validity of his theories, he initially **refused to publish** them **due to his lack of** supporting data and remained most famous as a geologist and explorer after the publication of his accounts of the trip in The Voyage of the Beagle. This did not, however, **stop him from discussing** his theories with fellow scientists Lyell and Owen, both of whom he befriended after returning from the long voyage. The formal publication of his theories did not occur until another young British naturalist and explorer, Alfred Wallace, [Q17-D] **was about to present** a similar theory he developed while exploring the Amazon Basin and the Malay Archipelago. Eventually, Wallace **agreed to present** his theory alongside the more socially and scientifically connected Darwin and their work was jointly presented to the Linnean Society of London in 1858, with very little fanfare. [Q18-A] The true significance of the new theories would not be fully recognized until the publication of Darwin's evolutionary manifesto, *On the Origin of Species by Means of Natural Selection*, in 1859. It was **so** well researched and presented **that** it **was referred to as** the best explanation "ever published of the manner of formation of species" by Owen and **established** Darwin **as** the definitive authority on natural selection.

Vocabulary

5단락
- validity [vəlídəti] n. 타당성
- definitive [difínətiv] a. 최종적인, 확정적인
- befriend [bifrénd] v. 친구가 되어 준다
- authority [əɔ́ːriti] n. 권한, 재가, 권위
- manner [mǽnər] n. 일의 방식, 태도, 예의

11 According to paragraph 1, which of the following was **NOT** true about the Voyage of HMS Beagle?

(A) The journey lasted significantly longer than it was originally planned.
(B) The ship had previously travelled to South America. ★
(C) One of the main purposes of the trip was to survey the coastline of South America.
(D) Darwin and Fitzroy ~~planned~~ to research previously unknown biological theories during their extended voyage.

단락 1에 의하면, HMS Beagle의 항해에 관해서 사실이 아닌 것은?

(A) 그 여행은 원래 계획되었던것 보다 훨씬 더 오래 지속되었다.
(B) 그 배는 예전에 남 아메리카를 방문했었다. ★
(C) 이 여행의 주 목적 중 하나는 남아메리카의 해변을 조사하는 거였다.
(D) 다윈과 피츠로이는 그들의 연장된 여정 동안 기존에는 알려지지 않은 생물학적 이론들을 연구하기로 ~~계획하였다~~.

Fact 지문의 키워드인 Voyage of HMS Beagle이 언급된 부분을 살펴보면 Unbeknownst to both men, their journey together would stretch to nearly five years and would form the basis for a revolutionary new biological theory. (그 둘은 몰랐지만, 그들의 여행은 5년에 임박하게 길어지고 생물학 분야를 영원히 바꿀 새로운 생물학 이론의 기반을 이루게 된다)라고 말한다. 즉, 다윈과 피츠로이가 그들의 여정 동안 연구한 생물학적 이론들은 처음엔 계획된 게 아니었기 때문에 정답은 (D)가 된다.

12 According to paragraph 1, which of the following can be inferred about Darwin's inclusion on the voyage of HMS Beagle?

(A) He was not essential for the completion of the mission upon which the Beagle was embarking.
(B) He was chosen ~~because~~ he had recently graduated from a prestigious university and could commit to the five year journey.
(C) He ~~sought out~~ a position on a boat where he could conduct research to help him prove his theory regarding species change. ★
(D) He was referred to the position by ~~Charles Lyell~~ who was interested in gaining information regarding the geology of South America.

단락 1에 의하면 HMS Beagle에 다윈이 포함된 일에 관해서 추론될 수 있는 것은?

(A) 그는 Beagle이 완수하려는 임무에 필요하지 않았다.
(B) 그는 일류 대학에서 막 졸업했고, 5년 간의 여행을 떠날 수 ~~있었기에~~ 선택되었다.
(C) 그는 종들의 변화에 관한 그의 이론을 증명할 수 있게 도와줄 연구를 할 수 있는 배위에서의 자리를 ~~원했다~~. ★
(D) 그는 남아메리카의 지리학에 관한 정보를 얻는 것에 관심을 갖고 있던 ~~찰스 라엘~~에 의해 자리를 얻었다.

Inference 질문의 키워드인 Darwin's inclusion on the voyage of HMS Beagle이 언급된 부분을 살펴보면 To fight the loneliness of being at sea for so long and to help study the lands they were to visit (바다에 혼자 너무나 오래 있을 외로움과 싸우고 그들이 도착할 땅을 공부하는데 도움을 주기 위해서)라고 말한다. 즉, 다윈은 선장의 외로움을 달래주고 리엘의 임무를 완수하는 것을 도와주기 위해 포함되었다. Voyage of Beagle의 원래 목적은 남아메리카의 해변가를 수색하고 전에 포획된 부족원들을 되돌려주기 위함이므로, 다윈이 포함된 이유와는 상관이 없다는 것을 유추할 수 있다. 따라서 정답은 (A)가 된다. (B)는 다윈이 여정을 함께 하게 된 이유가 일류 대학에서 졸업했기 때문이라는 내용은 언급되지 않으며, 그들의 여행이 5년이나 걸릴 것은 둘 다 몰랐기 때문에 오답이다. (C)는 다윈은 초대 받은 사람이었기 때문에 오답이며, (D)는 다윈은 리엘이 아닌 피츠로이에 의해 초대받은 것이기 때문에 오답이다.

13 According to paragraph 2, which of the following is true about Darwin's exploration of South America?

(A) He had relatively ~~little time~~ to explore the South American continent due to the long periods it took to travel between locations.
(B) The purpose of his explorations changed when he discovered many unique species and fossils.
(C) He discovered that areas like islands and the ~~seas~~ around isthmuses were capable of supporting many more species than other areas. ★
(D) His discoveries allowed him to ~~prove~~ the theory of uniformitarianism which stated that we can only assume about the past from what we observe in the present.

단락 2에 의하면 다윈의 남아메리카 탐험에 관해서 사실인것은?

(A) 그는 목적지들 사이를 여행하는데 많은 ~~시간이~~ 들었기 때문에, 남아메리카를 탐험할 시간이 비교적 ~~적었다~~.
(B) 그의 탐험의 목적은 그가 많은 특이한 견본과 화석들을 찾았을 때 바뀌었다.
(C) 그는 다른 지역들~~보다 많은 수~~의 종들을 유지할 수 있는 지협들을 발견했다. ★
(D) 그의 발견들은 우리가 현재에 보는 것 만으로 과거를 추정할 수 밖에 없다고 말하는 균일론을 ~~증명하는~~ 것을 허락했다.

Fact 질문의 키워드인 Darwin's exploration of South America가 언급된 부분을 살펴보면 Although he was originally planning on using his findings to write a book on geology, over the course of his explorations he made many new and interesting discoveries in the field of biology (비록 원래 그는 그의 발견물을 지질학에 관한 책을 쓰는데 사용하려고 했지만, 그가 탐험을 하면서 생물학의 분야에서 많은 새롭고 흥미로운 점들을 발견했다)라고 말한다. 즉, 다윈의 본래의 목적과는 다르게 생물학 분야를 조사하게 되었기 때문에 정답은 (B)가 된다. (A)는 그들의 여정이 2년에서 5년으로 바뀌었다는 점을 보아, 그들의 시간이 제한되었다는 것은 옳지 않기 때문에 오답이다. (C)는 더 많은 종류들이 아니라 다른 종류들이기 때문에 오답이고, (D)는 다윈이 동일과정설을 참고한 것이지 증명한 것이 아니기 때문에 오답이다.

14

Which of the sentences below best expresses the essential information in the highlighted sentence in the passage? Incorrect choices change the meaning in important ways or leave out essential information.

(A) ii) The main idea of uniformitarianism, that things in the past happened in a similar way they do today, allowed Darwin to realize that i) the diversity he discovered iii) was only possible if something was causing species to evolve over time.

(B) Darwin and Lyell realized that uniformitarianism could explain the diversity of the species he found because if species are changing today they must have done so in the past because "the present is key to the past."

(C) ii) The main tenet of uniformitarianism, that we can only assume about the past what we can see in the present allowed iii) Darwin to come up with the idea that animals changed over time because there are many different species in the world. ★

(D) Upon the discovery of the diverse species, Charles Darwin developed the idea that something has caused changes in species over time, leading to the publication of Charles Lyell's uniformitarianism.

아래의 문장 중 지문 속의 음영 표시된 문장의 핵심 정보를 가장 잘 표현하고 있는 것은 무엇인가? 오답은 문장의 의미를 현저하게 바꾸거나 핵심 정보를 빠트리고 있다.

(A) ii) 과거에 일어난 일이 현재에도 똑같이 일어난다는 균일론의 중요한 개념은 다윈이 i) 그가 발견한 다양성은 iii) 오직 무엇인가가 종들을 시간의 흐름에 따라 진화하게 할 때에만 가능하다는 것을 깨닫게 했다.

(B) 다윈과 리엘은 만약 종들이 오늘날에도 바뀌고 있다면, "현재는 과거로의 열쇠" 이기 때문에 과거에도 그랬을 것이기 때문에 균일론이 종들의 다양성을 설명할 수 있다는 것을 깨달았다.

(C) 우리가 과거를 추정하는 방법은 현재를 관찰하는 방법 밖에 없다고 하는 ii) 균일론의 교리는 세계에 많은 종들이 존재한다는 이유로 iii) 다윈이 동물들이 시간에 따라서 변화한다는 개념을 생각하게 만들었다.★

(D) 다양한 종의 발견 직후, 찰스 다윈은 시간이 지남에 따라 무언가가 변화를 한다는 아이디어를 개발했고, 이는 찰스 리엘의 균일론의 출판을 야기시켰다.

Highlight 음영 표시된 문장은 i) These discoveries, ii) combined with Lyell's theory of uniformitarianism, which stated that "the present is the key to the past," meaning that we can only assume about the past from what we observe in the present, iii) caused Darwin to postulate that the diversity of these species was possible only if there was some mechanism through which species could change over time. (i) 이러한 발견들은 ii) 우리는 과거에 대해서 추론할 때 현재를 보는 방법밖에 없다는 뜻의 "현재는 과거로의 열쇠다" 라고 썼던 리엘의 동일과정설과 합쳐져서 iii) 다윈이 이러한 종들의 다양성은 종들이 시간에 걸쳐서 변화하는 메커니즘이 존재해야만 가능하다고 생각하게 했다) 이렇게 세가지 내용으로 나뉜다. 이 내용을 모두 포함한 (A)가 정답이 된다. (B)는 리엘은 동일과정설을 설립했을 뿐 다윈과 같은 생각을 가지고 있지는 않았기 때문에 오답이고, (C)는 i)의 내용을 포함하고 있지 않기 때문에 오답이다. (D)는 다윈이 발견한 다양한 종들에서 동일과정설을 발견한 것이 아니기 때문에, 그리고 그것 때문에 이론이 발달된 것이 아니기 때문에 오답이다.

15 The term "induce" in the passage is closest in meaning to

(A) prevent [privént]
(B) bring about [bring about]
(C) control [kəntróul] ★
(D) slow down [slou daun]

"유발하다"라는 단어가 이 글에서 뜻하는 가장 가까운 바는?

(A) 방지하다
(B) 초래하다
(C) 조절하다 ★
(D) 감속시키다

> **Vocabulary** 지문의 induce(유발하다)는 bring about(초래하다)과 동의어이므로 (B)가 정답이다.

16 What can be inferred from paragraph 4 about Darwin's conclusion regarding the reasons for species' change over time?

(A) The changes that breeders are able to produce in their livestock will eventually change the species as a whole.
(B) Human overpopulation and competition for food with the animal kingdom will cause a change in the species they hunt.
(C) During periods when the food supply runs low, the animals that survive will come to have superior traits. ★
(D) Organisms that mate and pass on their traits do so because they are more suited to the environment they are in.

단락 4에서 종들이 시간에 따라 변한 이유에 관한 다윈의 결론에 관해서 추론할 수 있는 것은?

(A) 사육자들이 그들의 가축들을 변화시킴으로써 나중에는 전체적인 종을 바꿀 수 있었다.
(B) 인구 과잉과 동물 왕국과의 음식 경쟁은 그들이 사냥하는 동물들의 종을 바꿀 것이다.
(C) 음식의 공급이 적어지는 기간에 살아남는 동물들은 우월한 특징을 가지게 될 것이다. ★
(D) 번식을 하고 그들의 특징을 물려 주는 생물들은 그들이 있는 환경에 더욱 잘 적응했기 때문에 그럴 수 있다.

> **Inference** 질문의 키워드인 reasons for species' change over time이 언급된 부분을 살펴보면 He theorized that during times of increased competition animals with more favorable traits would more likely survive to reproduce and pass on their superior traits to the next generation in a natural form of selection. (그는 경쟁적 시기에는 자연적인 형태의 선택으로 좋은 특성을 갖고 있는 동물들이 번식하기 위해 살아남아 그들의 우월한 특성들을 다음 세대에 물려줄 확률이 높다고 이론화했다)라고 말한다. 즉, 좋은 특성을 갖고 있는 동물들이 번식할 확률이 높으며, 그들의 우월한 특성들을 다음 세대에게 물려줄 수 있는 가능성이 높다는 뜻이기 때문에 정답은 (D)가 된다. (A)는 종 전체를 바꾼다는 내용은 언급되지 않으므로 오답이고, (B)는 인간사회가 동물왕국과 음식을 가지고 경쟁한다는 내용은 언급되지 않으므로 오답이다. (C)는 인과관계가 잘못잡혀 있는데, 우월한 특징을 가진 동물들이 살아남는 것이지, 살아남는 동물들이 우월한 특징을 가지게 된다는 것은 아니기 때문에 오답이다.

17 What is the purpose of including information regarding Alfred Wallace in the passage?

(A) To disprove Darwin's ideas by offering a contrary view from another naturalist of the time
(B) To help understand that reproduction and species change was a popular field of study at the time
(C) To show that Darwin was unable to complete his theory until he got more information from another naturalist with similar ideas ★
(D) To introduce another researcher whose work in the field produced similar results and helped reinforce Darwin's theory

알프레드 월러스에 관련된 정보가 글에 포함된 이유는?

(A) 다른 동시대의 박물학자들과 반대 의견을 제시하며 다윈의 아이디어가 틀렸음을 밝히기 위해서
(B) 번식과 종들의 변화가 당시에 인기있는 주제였다는 사실을 이해하는 것을 돕기 위해서.
(C) 다윈이 비슷한 생각을 가진 다른 박물학자로부터 더 많은 정보를 얻기 전까지는 그의 이론을 완성할 수 없었다는 것을 보이기 위해서. ★
(D) 같은 분야에서 비슷한 결과를 만들어내고 다윈의 이론을 지원해 준 업적을 갖고 있는 다른 연구원을 소개하기 위해서.

> **Purpose** 질문의 키워드인 Alfred Wallace가 언급된 부분을 살펴보면 Alfred Wallace was ready to present a similar theory he had developed while exploring the Amazon Basin and the Malay Archipelago. (알프레드 월러스가 아마존 호수와 말레이 제도를 다녀온 후에 만든 비슷한 이론을 발표할 준비가 되었다)라고 말한다. 즉, 그도 비슷한 결과를 갖고 있었고 다윈과 협력했기 때문에 정답은 (D)가 된다. (A)는 월러스는 다윈과 비슷한 주장을 하였기 때문에 오답이고, (B)는 번식과 종들의 변화가 당시에 인기있는 주제였다는 내용은 언급되지 않기 때문에 오답이다. (C)는 다윈이 충분한 근거가 없어서 발표를 못하고 있었던 것은 맞으나, 다른 학자로부터 더 많은 정보를 얻었다는 내용은 언급되지 않으므로 오답이다.

18

What can be inferred about the theories presented by Alfred Wallace from paragraph 5?

(A) They were overshadowed by Darwin's publication of his theories in *On the Origin of Species by Means of Natural Selection*.
(B) They were conducted in places different from those visited by Darwin, so they had ~~little~~ similarity with Darwin's theory. ★
(C) They were rejected by the Linnean Society of London because he presented them ~~after~~ Darwin's theories had already been accepted.
(D) They were largely ignored ~~because~~ he was not as socially or scientifically well-connected as Charles Darwin.

단락 5에서 알프레드 월러스에 의해서 발표된 이론들에 관해서 추론할 수 있는 것은?

(A) 그들은 다윈의 "종의 기원" 에 있는 이론들에 의해서 묻혔다.
(B) 그 이론들은 다윈이 찾아간 곳들과 다른 장소에서 진행되었기 때문에 다윈의 이론과 비슷한 점이 ~~적었~~다. ★
(C) 그들은 다윈의 이론들이 이미 받아들여진 ~~이후에~~ 발표 되었기 때문에 런던의 리넨 사회에서 거부당했다.
(D) 그 이론들은 알프레드 월러스가 다윈에 비해서 사회적으로나 과학적으로 적은 인맥을 갖고 있었기 ~~때문~~에 대부분 무시당했다.

> **Inference** 질문의 키워드인 theories presented by Alfred Wallace가 언급된 부분을 살펴보면 The true significance of the new theories would not be fully recognized until Darwin's publication of his evolutionary manifesto, On the Origin of Species by Means of Natural Selection, in 1859. (이 새로운 이론들의 진정한 중요성은 다윈이 진화론적 선언문 종의 기원을 1859년도에 출판할 때까지 인지되지 못했다)라고 말한다. 즉, 진정한 중요성은 다윈의 종의 기원 이 발표되기 전까지는 인지되지 못했다는 것을 의미하기 때문에 정답은 (A)가 된다. (B)는 두 이론은 비슷했기 때문에 오답이고, (C)는 둘이 같이 발표했기 때문에 오답이다. (D)는 알프레드 월러스가 다윈에 비해 사회적으로나 과학적으로 적은 인맥을 갖고 있던 건 사실이나, 그 이유 때문에 그들의 이론이 무시당한 건 아니므로 오답이다.

19

Look at the four squares [■] that indicate where the following sentence could be added to the passage.

The forelimbs of most vertebrates, such as, bats, whales, humans, and horses, all share a basic design.

Where would the sentence best fit? Click on a square [■] to add the sentence to the passage.

3rd

네 개의 네모[■]는 다음 문장이 삽입될 수 있는 부분을 나타내고 있다.

박쥐들, 고래들, 사람들, 말들과 같은 대부분의 척추동물의 앞다리는 모두 기본적인 디자인을 공통적으로 갖고 있다.

이 문장은 어느 자리에 들어가는 것이 가장 적절한가?

3번째

> **Insertion** 삽입 문장의 단서는 vertebrates와 share이다. 세 번째 네모 전 문장에 Owen found homology, or anatomical similarity, in the body parts of different animals which served different purposes라고 설명을 해 주는데, anatomical similarity는 share과, different animals 는 vertebrates로 해석될 수 있다. 즉, 삽입 문장은 다른 동물들(박쥐, 고래, 사람) 신체 부위의 유사점의 예로 쓰일 수 있기 때문에 정답은 3번째 네모이다.

20 **Directions:** An introductory sentence for a brief summary of the passage is provided below. Complete the summary by selecting the THREE answer choices that express the most important ideas in the passage. Some sentences do not belong in the summary because they express ideas that are not presented in the passage or are minor ideas in the passage. **This question is worth 2 points**

지시: 지문 요약을 위한 도입 문장이 아래에 주어져 있다. 지문의 가장 중요한 내용을 나타내는 보기 3개를 골라 요약을 완성하시오. 어떤 문장은 지문에 언급되지 않은 내용이나 사소한 정보를 담고 있으므로 요약에 포함되지 않는다. **이 문제는 2점이다.**

Discoveries made by Darwin during his voyage on HMS Beagle led him to develop a new theory regarding how species came about

- (A) Darwin discovered many unique animal species and fossils which were geographically separate and had diverse traits that were possible only if there was some mechanism through which species could change over time. - paragraph 2
- (D) Darwin found support for his theory regarding the ability of species to change over time through the presence of anatomical similarities and vestigial structures in modern animals. - paragraph 3
- (F) The study of animal husbandry and research on human populations led Darwin to believe that the diverse animals he discovered were the result of competition allowing only animals with superior traits to reproduce and pass on these traits. - paragraph 4

다윈이 HMS Beagle 위에서 항해한 도중 발견했던 것들은 그가 종들이 어떻게 만들어졌는지에 대한 이론을 개발하도록 했다.

- (A) 다윈은 지리학적으로 분리되고 오직 종들이 어떤 메커니즘을 통해 시간이 흐름에 따라서 변하지 않았다면 불가능했을 다양한 특징들을 갖고 있던 많은 특이한 동물 종들과 화석들을 발견했다.
- (D) 다윈은 종들이 시간이 흐르면서 변화할 수 있는 능력에 관한 그의 이론을 뒷받침해줄 증거들을 현대 동물들에게 존재하는 해부학적 유사성과 잔여 구조들에게서 찾았다.
- (F) 축산업에 관한 연구와 인구수에 관한 연구는 그가 발견한 다양한 동물들이 오직 우월한 특성을 가진 동물들만이 번식을 하고 그들의 특성을 물려줄 수 있게 하는 경쟁의 결과라는 것을 믿게 만들었다.

(B) Absorbed in the study of ~~biology~~, Darwin volunteered to be part of the HMS Beagle voyage and helped collect important information regarding species diversity. - 틀린정보

(C) Upon the discovery of homology in the animals he observed, Darwin came to realize that different animals' body parts eventually come to perform ~~similar~~ functions. - 틀린정보

(E) The collaborative work on which Alfred Wallace and Charles Darwin published their theories has come to be known as ~~On the Origin of Species by Means of Natural Selection today~~. - 틀린정보

(B) ~~생물학~~에 빠진 다윈은 비글호 탑승에 지원했고 많은 중요 정보들을 얻는 것에 도움을 주었다.

(C) 다윈은 자신이 관찰한 동물에서 상동을 발견했을 때, 그는 다른 동물들의 신체 부위가 결국에는 ~~유사한~~ 기능을 수행하게 된다는 것을 알게 되었다.

(E) 알프레드 월러스와 찰스 다윈이 자신들의 이론들을 공동으로 발표한 작업은 오늘날에 "~~종의 기원~~"으로 알려져있다.

Summary 지문의 중심 내용은 다윈의 진화론 발달 과정이다. (A)는 두 번째 단락의 중심내용인 다윈의 진화론 탄생 배경과 일치하고, (D)는 세 번째 단락의 중심내용인 리차드 오웬의 상동설이 진화론에 끼친 영향과 일치하고, (F)는 네 번째 단락의 중심내용인 적자생존과 일치한다. 따라서 답은 (A), (D), (F)이다.

USHER iBT TOEFL
INTERMEDIATE READING

TEST 2
답안 및 취약 유형 분석표

해석·해설

답안 및 문제 유형 분석표

TEST 2-1

01 (A) Reference
02 (B) Vocabulary
03 (A) Fact
04 (C) Inference
05 (B) Fact
06 (B) Highlight
07 (D) Purpose
08 (C) Fact
09 2nd ■ Insertion
10 (A), (C), (F) Summary

TEST 2-2

11 (A) Fact
12 (A) Highlight
13 (C), (D) Fact
14 (D) Inference
15 (A) Purpose
16 (B) Inference
17 (B) Fact
18 (C) Vocabulary
19 4th ■ Insertion
20 (B), (D), (E) Summary

각 문제 유형별 맞춘 개수를 아래에 적어 보세요.

유형	맞춘 답의 개수	정답률	
단어 (Vocabulary)	/ 2	정답률:	%
사실 확인 문제 (Fact)	/ 6	정답률:	%
지시어 찾기 (Reference)	/ 1	정답률:	%
끼워 넣기 (Insertion)	/ 2	정답률:	%
문장 변환문제 (Highlight)	/ 2	정답률:	%
목적 (Purpose)	/ 2	정답률:	%
추론 (Inference)	/ 3	정답률:	%
단락 요약(Summary / Category Chart)	/ 2	정답률:	%
전체	/ 20	정답률:	%

※ 자신이 취약한 유형은 READING STRATEGIES를 통해 다시 한번 점검하시기 바랍니다. (p.44)

TEST 2-1   Determining the Ages of the Planets and the Universe
행성들과 우주의 나이의 정의

Introduction	단락 1	태양 주변의 행성들의 주기와 행성들의 궤도와 구성물의 유사성
Point	단락 2	물에 의한 침식에 노출된 지구, 이에 따른 지구 밖의 행성물체 관찰의 필요성
Point	단락 3	여러 가지 종류들의 운석
Point	단락 4	운석들과 달의 나이를 알아내기 위한 방사성 연대 결정법
Point	단락 5	우주의 팽창으로 인한 우주의 나이의 정의의 어려움
Point	단락 6	적색편이를 이용한 우주 나이의 정의

Image by NASA

문단주제	본문내용	해석
단락 1 태양 주변의 행성들의 주기와 행성들의 궤도와 구성물의 유사성	**1** The orbits of planets and the majority of non-planetary objects in our solar system have a very interesting characteristic; despite their vast differences, they have astounding similarities. The most remarkable of these similarities is that nearly all of them orbit the sun **in the same direction** and on the same plane. Using this information, scientists determined that this likely occurred because the collapse of a gas cloud simultaneously formed the objects and sent them to orbit the sun. This fact has **allowed** us **to learn** more about the age of the Earth, the planets, and the universe itself.	행성들의 궤도와 태양계 안의 대부분의 비행성 물체들은 아주 흥미로운 특징을 가지고 있다; 그들의 다양한 차이점에도 불구하고 그것들은 믿기 어려운 유사성을 가지고 있다. 그 유사성들 중에서 가장 두드러진 것은 그것들 중의 거의 대부분은 태양 주위를 같은 방향과 같은 평면 위에서 궤도를 돈다는 것이다. 이 정보를 이용하여 과학자들은 이것이 동시에 물체들을 만들고 물체들을 태양 주변을 돌도록 보낸 가스 구름의 붕괴때문에 일어 났을 것이라고 정의를 내렸다. 이 사실은 우리로 하여금 지구, 그 행성들, 또한 우주 자체의 나이에 대해서 조금 더 배울 수 있도록 가능하게 해주었다.
단락 2 물에 의한 침식에 노출된 지구, 이에 따른 지구 밖의 행성물체 관찰의 필요성	**2** It may **seem that** the easiest method of discerning Earth's age would be to simply sample materials we can **extract from** the crust, but this doesn't produce accurate results. [Q23-B] Due to the life-supporting water that covers Earth's surface, terrestrial material **is** constantly **exposed to the force of erosion**. The constant changes erosion causes, compounded by volcanic activity and Earth's internal pressure and heat, **make the discovery** of rocks in Earth's crust that **originate from** the time of formation highly unlikely. [Q23-C] **For this reason**, scientists must **look for** analogous objects in the solar system to **help them answer** this **question**.	지구의 나이를 밝혀내는 방법 중에 가장 쉬운 방법은 간단히 지각에서 물체를 추출하는 것처럼 보일 것이다. 하지만 이 방법은 정확한 결과를 제공하지 않는다. [Q23-B] 지구의 표면을 덮고 있는 생명을 유지시키는 물 때문에, 육지의 물체들은 침식의 힘에 꾸준히 노출되어 있다. 침식이 야기시키는 그 꾸준한 변화와 화산 활동, 지구의 내부 압력과 열은 지구의 지각 안에서 행성들의 형성 시기 때에 만들어진 돌의 발견을 매우 가능성이 없게 만든다. [Q23-C] 이 이유 때문에 과학자들은 이 질문에 답하기 위해 서 반드시 태양계 안에서 유사한 물체를 찾아야만 한다. [Q23-D] 운이 좋게도 지구의 표면으로 추락된 운석들은 그들에게 이러한 자료를 제공해 줄 수

Vocabulary

1단락
- orbit [ɔ́ːrbit] n. 궤도, v. 궤도를 돌다
- remarkable [rimάːrkəbəl] a. 놀라운
- collapse [kəlǽps] n. 붕괴, v. 붕괴하다
- astounding [əstáundiŋ] a. 경악스러운, 믿기 어려운
- determine [ditə́ːrmin] v. 결정하다, 파악하다
- plane [plein] n. 평면, 차원
- similarity [sìməlǽrətiː] n. 유사점

2단락
- extract [ikstrǽkt] v. 추출하다
- seem [siːm] v. ~처럼 보이다
- terrestrial [təréstriəl] a. 육생의, 지구의
- discern [disə́ːrn] v. 분별하다
- gravitational pull n. 중력
- erosion [iróuʒən] n. 침식
- existence [igzístəns] n. 존재

	[Q23-D] Luckily, the meteorites that have **crashed into** Earth's surface can **provide** them **with** this material. These masses began their existence as objects orbiting the sun, but Earth's gravitational pull forced them to enter its atmosphere and collide with the crust.	있다. 이러한 덩어리들은 태양을 도는 유성으로서 처음에는 존재했다. 하지만 지구의 중력은 유성들을 지구의 대기로 진입하게 하고, 지각과 충돌하도록 만들었다.
단락 3 여러 가지 종류들의 운석	**3** [■] The meteorites that have been discovered have **varied in** size, **ranging from** stony pebbles **to** massive planetoids called asteroids, and composition which has allowed scientists to **draw conclusions** about them and Earth's composition and origin. [■] Some intact asteroids may have once struck the earth, but none have done so during recorded human history. From meteorite remnants found on Earth, the main three categories **used to differentiate** meteorites today are "stony meteorites," **composed of** rocky materials, "iron meteorites" composed mainly of iron with **trace amounts of** other elements, and "stony-iron meteorites" that **consist of** a mixture of the two. [■] Scientists believe that all three of these types of meteorites are the remnants of larger space bodies that broke apart due to collisions. [■] [Q24-C] It is believed that the differences between the categories of meteorites are due to this violent **break up** of space materials with origins and, therefore, compositions **similar to** Earth's. The stony meteorites likely originated as the outer shells of these bodies and **are analogous to** Earth's mantle, while the iron meteorites that resemble Earth's core are probably fragments of the interior of the body and the stony-iron meteorites contain materials from both.	[■] 지금까지 발견되어 왔던 운석들은 암석 자갈 크기부터 소행성 크기까지 크기가 다양하고 과학자들로 하여금 그것들과 지구의 구성과 기원에 대해서 결론을 내릴 수 있도록 해준 구성 성분도 다양하다. [■] 몇몇의 멀쩡한 소행성들은 아마도 지구에 충돌했을 것이다 그러나 기록된 인류역사 동안에는 그런 일이 발생하지 않았다. 지구에서 발견된 운석 조각으로부터, 운석들을 구분하기 위해서 오늘날에 사용되고 있는 기준들은, 암석 물질들로 이루어진 "암석 운석", 주로 철 성분과 적은 돌 성분으로 구성되어진 "철 운석", 그리고 이 두 가지 성분이 혼합되어 있는 "암석-철 운석" 이다. [■] 과학자들은 운석들의 이 세 가지 종류는 충격때문에 부숴진 더 큰 우주 물체의 파편이라고 믿는다. [■] [Q24-C] 운석들의 종류 사이의 차이점은 우주 물체의 붕괴때문 이어서 지구와 기원과 성분이 유사하다고 믿어진다. 그 암석 운석들은 지구의 맨틀과 유사 한 이러한 물체들의 외부 껍질로써 만들어 졌을 것이다. 반면에 지구의 핵과 유사한 철 운석들은 아마도 그 물체의 내부 파편일 것이고 암석-철 운석은 그 두 개로부터의 물질을 포함한다.
단락 4 운석들과 달의 나이를 알아내기 위한 방사성 연대 결정법	**4** By studying these meteorites scientists have **been able to determine** their age. [Q25-D] Using multiple radiometric methods of dating the materials, including the uraniumthorium, rubidium-strontium, and potassium-argon methods, showed a cluster of age data pointing to an origin around 4.6 billion years ago. [Q25-A] **Comparing** this **to the** rocks from the moon's surface, which **is free of** the water that erodes rocks on Earth's surface and which displays little	이러한 운석들을 연구함으로써 과학자들은 그것들의 나이를 밝힐 수 있었다. 우라늄-토리늄, 루비듐-스트론튬, 그리고 포테슘-아르곤 방법을 포함하는 [Q25-D] 여러 가지 방사성 연대 측정법을 사용하면서, 기원을 나타내는 46억년으로 군집된 정보들을 보여주었다. [Q25-A] 이 정보를 지구의 표면 위의 돌을 침식하는 물이 없고 지각변동이 거의 없는 달표면으로부터의 돌과 비교해 보았을 때에, 비슷한 연대 정보를 제공했고 연구자들로 하여금 [Q25-C] 태양계 안의 모든 물체들은 같은

Vocabulary

3단락
- planetoid [plǽnətɔ̀id] n. 미행성
- pebble [pébəl] n. 자갈
- collision [kəlíʒən] n. 충돌
- meteorite [míːtiəràit] n. 운석
- composition [kàmpəzíʃən] n. 구성
- category [kǽtəgɔ̀ːri] n. 항목
- analogous to phr. ~와 비슷한
- differentiate [dìfərénʃièit] v. ~을 구별하다

4단락
- determine [ditə́ːrmin] v. 측정하다
- cluster [klʌ́stər] n. 집속
- radiometric [rèidiámétrik] a. 방사성 탄소 연대 측정의
- display [displéi] v. 나타내다
- yield [jiːld] v. 생산하다
- method [méθəd] n. 방법
- hypothesis [haipáθəsis] n. 가설

movement in its crust, yielded similar age data and allowed researchers to confirm their hypothesis that [Q25-C] all of the materials in the solar system started **at the same point** in time.

시기에 시작되었다는 가설을 정립할 수 있도록 하였다.

단락 5
우주의 팽창으로 인한 우주의 나이의 정의의 어려움

5   While dating the elements of the solar system has been relatively straightforward, finding the age of the universe itself has been more complicated because there is no way to collect physical materials on which to conduct age testing. What has been learned has been gathered through theoretical analysis of the universe. One of the most important factors discovered is that all of the disk-shaped clusters of stars, called galaxies, are **moving away from** each other. Scientists conjecture that this occurs because the universe **began with** an explosion, **known as** the Big Bang, which sent all of the dense matter concentrated **at the center** of the explosion hurling across space. This process is **akin to** what would happen if one were to glue coins to a balloon and inflate it. The coins, like the galaxies, would remain the same size but the space between them would increase as the balloon got larger.

태양계 물체의 나이를 측정하는 것이 상대적으로 간단한 반면에, 우주 자체의 나이를 알아 내는 것은 조금 더 복잡하다. 나이를 측정하기 위한 물리적인 물체를 수집하는 방법이 없기 때문이다. 배워진 것들은 우주의 가설적인 분석을 통해서 얻어졌다. 발견된 요인들 중에 가장 중요한 것 중의 하나는 은하라 불리 지는 수많은, 원반모양의 별들의 군집은 서로 떨어지고 있다는 것이다. 과학자들은 이 현상은 밀도가 높은 물체들을 폭발의 중심에 집중시켜 놓고 우주에 걸쳐서 던져 버린 빅뱅이라고 알려진 폭발 때문에 일어난다고 추측한다. 이 과정은 동전들을 풍선에 접착시키고 풍선을 팽창시켰을 때 발생하는 현상과 비슷하다. 그 동전들은, 은하수와 같이, 풍선이 커지면 커질수록 동전의 크기는 그대로 이지만 동전들 간의 거리는 늘어날 것이다.

단락 6
적색편이를 이용한 우주 나이의 정의

6   [Q28C] The expansion of the space between the galaxies is precisely what astronomers have used to estimate the universe's age. By measuring the wavelengths of light travelling through the universe they are able to measure a **shift in** the light's wavelength towards red end of the light spectrum. This redshift occurs because, as light **travels in** the space between the galaxies, [Q28-A] the expansion of the space stretches out the light waves. [Q28-C] **Following this theory**, **the farther** the light has traveled, **the greater** the redshift will be. Measuring the redshift in light from distant galaxies, astronomers have determined that all of the galaxies would have existed in one central location around 13.7 billion years ago. This, therefore, is the most likely the date and location of the Big Bang and the age of the universe.

[Q28-C] 천문학자들이 우주의 나이를 측정하기 위해 사용해온 것은 바로 은하들 사이 공간의 팽창이다. 그들은 우주를 돌아다니는 빛의 파장을 측정함으로써, 빛 띠의 빨간 끝을 향한 빛의 파장의 이동을 측정할 수 있다. 빛이 은하 사이에 공간을 돌아다닐 때, [Q28-A] 공간의 팽창이 빛의 파장을 늘리기 때문에 이런 적색편이는 발생한다. [Q28-C] 이 이론을 따르면, 빛이 멀리 이동할수록, 적색편이는 더 커질 것이다. 빛의 적색편이를 멀리 떨어진 은하 로부터 측정함으로써, 천문학자들은 약 137억년전 즈음 모든 은하들은 하나의 중심 위치에 존재했었을 것이라고 밝혀냈다. 이것은, 그러므로, 가장 가능성 있는 빅뱅의 위치와 나이, 그리고 우주의 나이일 것이다.

Vocabulary

5단락   element [éləmèit] n. 요소   relatively [rélətivli] ad. 상대적으로   complicate [kámpləkèit] v. 복잡하게 하다
analysis [əiənàiz] n. 분석   explosion [iksplóuʒən] n. 폭발   hurl [həːrl] v. 던지다   cluster [klʌ́stər] n. 무리
straightforward [stréitfɔ́ːrwərd] a. 간단한, 복잡하지 않은, 솔직한   conjecture [kəndʒéktʃər] n. 추측한 내용, v. 추측하다

6단락   expansion [ikspǽnʃən] n. 확장, 팽창   wavelength [wéivlèŋkθ] n. 파장   redshift [rèdʃift] n. 적색편이
determine [ditə́ːrmin] v. 알아내다, 결정하다   precisely [prisáisli] ad. 정확히   galaxy [gǽləksi] n. 은하

01

What does the word "they" refer to in the passage?

(A) orbits
(B) planets ★
(C) non-planetary objects
(D) characteristics

지문에서 "그것들"이 나타내는 것은?

(A) 궤도
(B) 행성들 ★
(C) 비 행성 물체들
(D) 특징들

Reference they가 언급된 부분을 살펴보면 despite their vast differences, they have astounding similarities. (그것들은 믿기 어려운 유사점을 가지고 있다)라고 말한다. 앞 문장에선 행성들과 대부분의 비행성 물체들의 궤도를 주어로 두고 있는 것을 보아, they가 나타내고 있는 것은 궤도이다. 따라서 (A)가 답이 된다.

02

The term "discerning" in the passage is closest in meaning to

(A) disproving [disprúːv] ★
(B) determining [ditə́ːrminiŋ]
(C) disregarding [dìsrigáːrd]
(D) deferring [difə́ːr]

지문의 단어 "파악하는"의 의미와 가장 유사한 것은?

(A) 틀렸음을 입증하는 ★
(B) 정하는
(C) 무시하는
(D) 미루는

Vocabulary 지문의 discerning(파악하는)과 동의어인 determining(정하는)이 정답이 된다.

03

Paragraph 2 mentions all of the following as facts related to attempts to come up with an accurate age for the earth EXCEPT:

(A) The ~~easiest~~ method of discerning the Earth's age is to ~~simply sample~~ materials we ~~can~~ extract from the Earth's easily accessible crust.
(B) Over the course of time the rocks that formed in Earth's crust at its origin have been worn away by natural forces.
(C) Objects orbiting the sun can provide scientists with information about the age of the Earth. ★
(D) Meteorites that survived the plunge to Earth have given scientists more information on the formation of the Earth.

2단락에 따르면, 지구의 정확한 나이를 알아내기 위한 시도에 대한 사실이 아닌 것은?

(A) 지구의 나이를 파악하는 ~~가장 쉬운~~ 방법은 지구의 접근하기 쉬운 지각으로부터 자료를 채집하는 것이다.
(B) 시간이 지남에 따라 지구의 지각안에 형성된 돌들은 자연적인 힘에 의해 풍화 되어서 없어 졌다.
(C) 태양을 공전하는 물체는 학자들에게 지구의 나이에 대한 정보를 줄 수 있다. ★
(D) 땅과의 충돌(던져짐)에서 살아남은 운석은 학자들에게 지구의 형성에 대한 더 많은 정보를 제공해왔다.

Fact 질문의 키워드인 accurate age for the earth가 언급된 부분을 살펴보면 It may seem that the easiest method of discerning Earth's age would be to simply sample materials we can extract from the crust, but this doesn't produce accurate results. (지구의 나이를 밝혀내는 방법 중에 가장 쉬운 방법은 간단히 지각에서 물체를 수집하는 것처럼 보일 것이다)라고 말한다. 즉, 지각으로부터 자료를 채집하는 방법이 가장 쉬운 방법인 것 같지만, 정확한 결과를 제공해주지 못함으로 정답은 (A)가 된다.

04

What can be inferred about using space objects to find the age of Earth from paragraph 3?

(A) The minerals found in the asteroids that have struck the earth are unique and have ~~little~~ similarity to those found on Earth.
(B) Although Earth and the meteorites that have been researched share a similar composition, they ~~differ~~ in their origin.
(C) The composition of the Earth's layers is similar to that of other space objects because they were all formed from the broken up space materials.
(D) The collection of minerals present in meteorites found on earth's surface allows scientists to determine ~~how long~~ they have been striking Earth and therefore its age. ★

단락 3에서 우주 물체를 사용하여 지구의 나이를 알아내는 것에 대해 어떤 것이 추론될 수 있는가?

(A) 지구에 충돌한 소행성 안에서 발견된 금속들은 희귀하고 지구에서 발견된 것들과는 거의 같지 ~~않다~~.
(B) 지구와 연구된 운석들은 비슷한 구성을 가지고 있지만 기원은 ~~다르다~~.
(C) 지구와 다른 우주 물체들은 둘 다 부서진 우주 물질들에 의해 만들어졌기 때문에 지구 층의 구성은 다른 우주 물체들의 층 구성과 비슷하다.
(D) 지구의 표면에서 발견된 운석 안에 존재하는 미네랄들의 수집물들은 과학자들로 하여금 운석들이 ~~얼마나 오랫동안~~ 지구에 부딪혀 왔는지 알게 함으로써 지구의 나이를 파악할 수 있도록 해주었다. ★

Inference 질문의 키워드인 space objects가 언급된 부분을 살펴보면 (It is believed that the differences between the categories of meteorites are due to this violent break up of space materials with origins and, therefore, compositions similar to Earth's. (운석들의 종류 사이의 차이점은 우주 물체의 붕괴 때문이어서 지구와 기원과 성분이 유사하다고 믿어진다)라고 말한다. 즉, 실험에서 사용되는 우주 물체들은 지구와 유사한 기원과 성분을 가지고 있다는 것이다. 따라서 정답은 (C)가 된다. (A)는 우주 물체들과 지구는 큰 유사점을 가지고 있기 때문에 오답이고, (B)는 지구와 운석들이 비슷한 구성과 기원을 가지고 있으므로 오답이다. 마지막으로 실험의 목적은 운석들이 얼마나 오랫동안 지구에 부딪혀 왔는지를 알아내는 것이 아니라 지구의 나이를 알아내는 것이기 때문에 (D)는 오답이다.

05

According to paragraph 4, which of the following is **NOT** true about the age of Earth and certain space objects?

(A) The rocks on the surface of the moon are much older than those that are currently found in Earth's crust. ★
(B) The moon is relatively ~~younger than~~ the Earth and the meteorites which have struck it.
(C) Scientists have been able to prove their theory that most objects in the solar system originated concurrently.
(D) Radiometric testing on rocks from meteorites and the moon's surface yielded very similar results.

단락 4에 따르면, 지구와 특정 우주 물체의 나이에 대해 틀린 내용은?

(A) 달의 표면에 있는 돌은 현재 지구의 지각에서 발견되는 돌보다 훨씬 오래되었다. ★
(B) 달은 지구와 지구와 충돌한 운석보다는 상대적으로 ~~어리다~~.
(C) 과학자들은 태양계의 대부분의 물체는 동시에 생성되었다는 이론을 증명할 수 있었다.
(D) 운석과 달의 표면에 대한 방사성 연대 측정법은 비슷한 결과를 주었다.

Fact 질문의 키워드인 age of Earth and certain space objects가 언급된 부분을 살펴보면 Comparing this to the rocks from the moon's surface, which is free of the water that erodes rocks on Earth's surface and which displays little movement in its crust (이 정보를 지구의 표면 위의 돌을 침식하는 물이 없고 지각변동이 거의 없는 달 표면으로부터의 돌과 비교해 보았을 때)라고 말한다. 즉, 달엔 침식이 없고 지질 학적 움직임이 적기 때문에 표면에 있는 돌들이 비교적 잘 보존된다는 것이다. 다시 말해, 달 표면에서 발견되는 돌들이 지구표면에서 발견되는 돌들보다 오래됐다는 뜻이다. 따라서 (A)는 옳은 말이고, (B)는 달이 지구보다 어리다는 내용은 언급되지 않으므로 정답이 된다.

06

Which of the sentences below best expresses the essential information in the highlighted sentence in the passage? Incorrect choices change the meaning in important ways or leave out essential information.

(A) Rocks on the Earth's surface are affected by erosion and tectonic movements unlike meteors and moon rocks, so they ~~could not be~~ used to validate the notion that all matter in the solar system originated at the same time.

(B) i) Scientists affirmed the fact that all of the matter in the solar system came about simultaneously ii) by comparing the age of meteorites with that of the rocks on the Moon's surface which are unaffected by erosion and crust movements.

(C) After conducting testing on moon rocks and meteorites scientists determined that they were approximately the same age ~~because~~ they weren't exposed to water or the effects of erosion from movements in the crust.

(D) ii) It was determined that all space materials originated at the same time when scientists discovered that meteorites and moon rocks were the same age. ★

아래의 문장 중 지문 속의 음영 표시된 문장의 핵심 정보를 가장 잘 표현하고 있는 것은 무엇인가? 오답은 문장의 의미를 현저하게 바꾸거나 핵심 정보를 빠트리고 있다.

(A) 지구의 표면 위의 돌은 유성과 달의 돌들과는 달리 침식과 지각 판 운동에 의해 영향을 받아서, 그것들은 태양계 안의 모든 물체가 같은 시간에 만들어졌다는 사실을 증명하는 데에 ~~이용될 수가 없다.~~

(B) i) 과학자들은 운석들의 나이를 침식과 지각 운동에 영향을 받지 않은 달의 표면 위의 돌과 비교 함으로써 ii) 태양계 안의 모든 물체들은 동시대에 만들어졌다고 단언했다.

(C) 달의 돌들과 운석에 대해 시험을 해본 뒤에 과학자들은 그것들이 물이나 지각운동으로부터의 침식에 노출이 되어지지 않았기 ~~때문에~~ 나이가 비슷하다는 것을 파악하였다.

(D) ii) 과학자들이 운석들과 달의 돌들이 같은 나이라는 것을 발견한 뒤에 모든 우주 물체는 같은 시기에 만들어졌다고 파악되었다. ★

Highlight 음영 표시된 문장은 i) Comparing this to the rocks from the moon's surface, which is free of the water that erodes rocks on the Earth's surface and which displays little movement in its crust, ii) yielded similar age data and allowed researchers to confirm their hypothesis that all of the materials in the solar system started at the same point in time. (i) 이 정보를 지구의 표면 위의 돌을 침식하는 물이 없고 지각변동이 거의 없는 달 표면으로부터의 돌과 비교해 보았을 때, ii) 비슷한 연대 정보를 제공했고 연구자들로 하여금 태양계 안의 모든 물체들은 같은 시기에 시작되었다는 가설을 정립할 수 있도록 해 주었다) 이렇게 두 가지 내용으로 나뉜다. 이 내용을 모두 포함한 (B)가 정답이 된다. (A)와 (D)는 각각 ii)와 i)에 해당하는 내용이 없기 때문에 오답이고, (C)는 인과관계가 잘못 잡혀 있어 오답이다.

07

In paragraph 5, the author mentions "glue coins to a balloon and inflate it" in order to

(A) help understand that the Big Bang ~~concentrated~~ all of the galaxies on the outside edge of the universe.
(B) give an idea of how the expansion of the universe is ~~limited~~ to a certain point then it will explode again.
(C) help understand how the expansion of ~~the galaxies~~ causes the universe to expand infinitely. ★
(D) give an example using everyday objects that will help visualize the expansion of the universe.

글쓴이가 "팽창하는 풍선 위에 붙여 놓은 동전"을 말한 의도는?

(A) 빅뱅 이론이 모든 은하들을 우주 밖에 ~~집중시켰다~~는 것을 이해하는 것을 도와주기 위해서.
(B) 어떻게 지구의 팽창이 특정한 때에 ~~제한~~되어 있고 언제 다시 폭발할지에 대한 개념을 주기 위해서.
(C) 어떻게 ~~은하들의 팽창~~이 우주가 무한적으로 팽창하도록 하는지에 대한 이해를 돕기 위해서. ★
(D) 우주의 팽창을 평소의 물체를 이용함으로써 이해를 도와주기 위해서.

Purpose 음영 표시된 부분을 살펴보면 The coins, like the galaxies, would remain the same size but the space between them would increase as the balloon got larger. (은하와 같은 동전은 같은 크기를 유지할 것이지만 풍선이 커지면서 동전 사이의 거리는 증가할 것이다)라고 말한다. 즉, 우주의 팽창을 좀 더 이해하기 쉽도록 전달하기 위해 동전에 빗대어 설명하는 것이다. 따라서 정답은 (D)가 된다. (A)는 빅뱅은 중심에 집중되어 있던 물질들을 분산시켰기 때문에 오답이고, (B)는 우주의 팽창이 제한되어 있다고 한 내용은 언급되지 않으므로 오답이다. (C)는 은하들이 팽창하는 것이 아니라 우주가 팽창함으로써 은하들 사이에 공간이 넓어지는 것이므로 오답이다.

08

According to paragraph 6, which of the following can be inferred regarding the expansion of the universe?

(A) The expansion of the ~~galaxies~~ causes light to shift around them in a predictable manner that can be measured by astronomers. ★
(B) Scientists came up with the generalization that greater redshift will ~~cause~~ the light to travel farther.
(C) The redshift caused by the expanding intergalactic space occurs at a rate consistent enough to allow its use in determining the amount of time it has been travelling.
(D) Using the expansion of the universe allows astronomers to pinpoint ~~why~~ all of the matter in the solar system came into being.

단락 6에 따르면 우주의 팽창에 대해서 추론될 수 있는 내용은?

(A) 은하들의 팽창은 빛이 천문학자들에 의해 측정될 수 있는 예측 가능한 방법으로 전환시키도록 한다. ★
(B) 과학자들은 더 큰 적색편이가 빛을 더 멀리 가게할 것이라고 일반화했다.
(C) 은하들 사이간의 팽창에 의해 야기되는 적색편이는 이것이 얼마동안 돌아다녔는지 파악하기에 충분할 만큼 꾸준한 속도로 일어난다.
(D) 우주의 팽창을 이용하는 것은 천문학자들로 하여금 왜 모든 태양계 안의 물체들이 만들어졌는지 알 수 있게 해준다.

Fact   질문의 키워드인 expansion of the universe가 언급된 부분을 살펴보면 Following this theory, the farther the light has traveled, the greater the redshift will be.(이 이론에 따르면, 빛이 멀리 갈수록, 적색편이는 커질 것이다)라고 말한다. 즉, 적색편이를 통해서 우주의 나이를 측정 할 수 있었기 때문에 은하들 사이의 팽창에 의해 야기되는 적색편이는 꾸준한 속도로 일어났다는 뜻이다. 따라서, 정답은 (C)가 된다. (A)는 은하들의 팽창이 아닌 은하 사이 공간의 팽창이기 때문에 오답이고, (B)는 인과관계가 바뀌어서 오답이다. (D)는 왜 모든 물체들이 생성되었는지를 지적하게 해준 것이 아니라 언제와 어디에서 그것들이 한곳에 모여 있었는지를 알게 해 준 것이기 때문에 오답이다.

09

Look at the four squares [■] that indicate where the following sentence could be added to the passage.

Some intact asteroids may have once struck the earth, but none have done so during recorded human history.

Where would the sentence best fit? Click on a square [■] to add the sentence to the passage.

2nd

네 개의 네모 [■]는 다음 문장이 삽입될 수 있는 부분을 나타내고 있다.

몇몇의 멀쩡한 소행성들은 아마도 지구에 충돌했을 것이다, 하지만 인류의 역사 중에 그런 기록은 없었다.

이 문장은 어느 자리에 들어가는 것이 가장 적절한가?

2번째

Insertion   삽입 문장의 단서는 intact asteroids이다. 두 번째 네모 다음 문장의 From meteorite remnants found on Earth부분은 지구에서 발견된 운석 조각들을 이용해야만 연구가 가능하였기에 운석들을 3가지로 분류했다는 걸 의미한다. 즉, 소행성이 지구에 손상 없이 충돌했을지도 모른다는 내용의 삽입 문장은 운석에 대해 소개하고 있는 첫 번째 박스와 인간의 기록엔 없지만 자연에서 보존된 운석을 이용해 연구를 진행했다는 내용을 담은 세 번째 박스 사이인 두 번째 박스가 가장 적절하다.

10

Directions: An introductory sentence for a brief summary of the passage is provided below. Complete the summary by selecting the THREE answer choices that express the most important ideas in the passage. Some sentences do not belong in the summary because they express ideas that are not presented in the passage or are minor ideas in the passage. **This question is worth 2 points.**

지시: 지문 요약을 위한 도입 문장이 아래에 주어져 있다. 지문의 가장 중요한 내용을 나타내는 보기 3개를 골라 요약을 완성하시오. 어떤 문장은 지문에 언급되지 않은 내용이나 사소한 정보를 담고 있으므로 요약에 포함되지 않는다. **이 문제는 2점이다.**

Using physical and analytical methods, scientists have been able to determine the age of the solar system and the universe.

(A) The similar orbits of the planetary and non-planetary objects in the solar system indicate that they were likely formed of similar materials at the same time.
　　　　　　　　　　　　　　　　　　　　- paragraph 1, 3

(C) Scientist determined that the earth was 4.6 billion years old due to radiometric dating done on meteorites with composition analogous to that of the Earth.
　　　　　　　　　　　　　　　　　　　　- paragraph 4

(F) The expansion of the intergalactic space and the presence of redshift indicate that the universe started with a centralized explosion 13.7 billion years ago.
　　　　　　　　　　　　　　　　　　　　- paragraph 6

물리적인 방법과 분석적인 방법을 사용 하면서, 과학자들은 태양계와 우주의 나이를 파악할 수 있었다.

(A) 태양계의 행성 물체와 비 행성 물체의 비슷한 궤도는 그것들이 같은 물질로 같은 시기에 만들어 졌다고 나타내 준다.

(C) 과학자들은 지구의 성질과 비슷한 운석에 방사성 연대 측정을 해본 결과 지구가 46억년 정도 되었다고 파악했다.

(F) 은하의 팽창과 적색편이의 존재는 우주가 137억년전에 하나의 폭발로부터 시작되었다고 나타냈다.

(B) One of the types of meteorites found on Earth today comprises of rocky materials, which distinctly differentiate it from other types. - paragraph 3 detail

(D) Rocks in Earth's crust are ~~older~~ than those present on Moon's surface due to the presence of erosion on Earth. - 반/반

(E) Scientists, ~~lacking~~ sufficient data to figure out the age of planets in the solar system, have ~~determined~~ it ~~concurrent~~ with the age of the universe obtained using redshift. - 틀린 정보

(B) 오늘날 지구에서 발견된 운석의 종류 중 하나는 다른 종류와 뚜렷하게 구별되게 바위 물질로 구성되어 있다.

(D) 지구 지각 안의 돌은 지구에서 일어나는 침식 때문에 달 위의 돌보다 오래 되었다.

(E) 태양계에 있는 행성들의 나이를 파악하기에 충분 한 데이터가 없는 과학자들은 적색편이를 이용하여 얻은 우주의 나이와 행성들의 나이가 같다고 확정하였다.

Summary 　지문의 중심 내용은 지구와 우주의 나이를 측정하는 원리이다. (A)는 첫 번째 단락의 행성들과 비 행성들의 유사성을 요약한 내용과 일치하고, (C)는 네 번째 단락의 중심내용인 운석들과 달의 나이를 알아내기 위한 방사성 연대 결정법과 일치하고, (F)는 여섯 번째 단락의 중심내용인 적색편이를 이용한 우주 나이의 정의와 일치한다. 따라서 답은 (A), (C), (F)이다.

TEST 2-2 Early Research in Organic Chemistry 유기화학의 초기연구

Introduction	단락 1	화학의 역사 소개와 종류간의 분화
Point	단락 2	동물, 식물과 광물로 분류하던 것에서 현대의 유기, 무기 화학과 생기론으로의 변화
Point	단락 3	유기화학이 뒤떨어진 이유와 무기화학물질의 분리가 쉬운 것
Point	단락 4	유기물질들을 증류하려는 시도들
Point	단락 5	증류 후의 유기화합물이 가진 문제점들
Point	단락 6	잘못된 초기 발견들과 유기화학의 발전을 허락한 돌파구

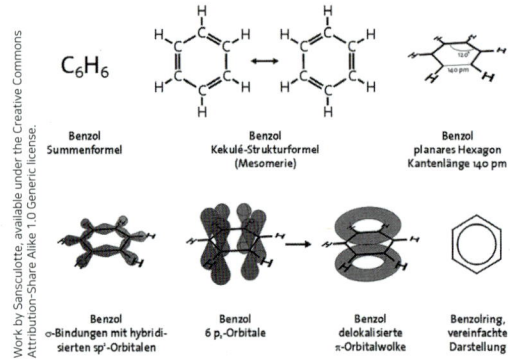

Work by Sansculotte, available under the Creative Commons Attribution-Share Alike 1.0 Generic license.

문단 주제	본문 내용	해 석
단락 1 화학역사 소개와 종류간의 분화	**1** The ancient practice of alchemy **gave way to** the early science of chemistry in the late 17th century. After hundreds of years of **trying to turn** base metals **into** gold, [Q1-B] alchemists had developed a structure of theory, terminology, experimentation and basic laboratory techniques that were well-adapted for scientific study of Earth's elements. [Q1-D] By the 18th **century**, chemists **began to** scientifically **study** the new elements they found and **were able to identify** many new ones that had never been studied before, such as cobalt, tungsten and various forms of carbon. [Q1-C] The study of the last of these would eventually form one of the two modern divisions of the field of chemistry, organic chemistry.	고대의 연금술 연습은 17세기 후반에 초기 화학으로 바뀌었다. 비금속을 금으로 바꾸려는 몇백년 동안의 시도 후에, [Q1-B] 연금술사들은 이론, 전문 용어, 실험 그리고 지구물질의 과학적인 연구에 아주 적당한 기초적인 실험 기술들을 발전시켰다. [Q1-D] 18세기에 화학자들은 그들이 발견한 새로운 원소들을 과학적으로 연구하기 시작했고 그들이 여태 연구한적 없었던 코발트, 텅스텐 그리고 다양한 탄소 물질과 같은 원소들도 찾을 수 있었다. [Q1-C] 탄소 물질의 연구는 결국 유기화학이라는 두 개의 근대 화학분야 중 하나를 형성하게 되었다.
단락 2 동물, 식물과 광물로 분류하던 것에서 현대의 유기, 무기 화학과 생기론으로의 변화	**2** The terms organic and inorganic chemistry were introduced in the early 1800s to more accurately differentiate between the different naturally occurring substances. **Prior to** this time scientists **separated** substances **into** three categories that matched the "Three Kingdoms of Nature": animal, vegetable and mineral. [Q3-A] Of these, the animal and vegetable groups **were reserved for** substances that **were produced by** or **related to** life and **were** later **incorporated into** the study of organic (meaning from an organism) chemistry which covered all carbon-based compounds, while the inanimate mineral group gave way to the field of inorganic	유기화학과 무기화학이라는 용어는 자연 발생적인 물질들을 더 정확하게 구분하기 위해서 1800년대에 도입되었다. 이 시기 이전에 과학자들은 물질을 '자연의 세가지 계'에 맞추어 세 분야로 나눴다: 동물계, 식물계, 그리고 무기물계. [Q3-A] 이들 중에서, 동물과 식물그룹은 생물로부터 생기거나 관련된 물질들을 위해 따로 두어졌고 모든 탄소기반 물질을 포함하는 유기(유기체에서 따온)화학연구로 포함되었으며, 반면에 무생물의 무기물 그룹은 모든 비탄소 물질들을 포함하는 무기화학으로 나아갔다. 앙투안 라부아지에와 같은 일부 학자들은 유기분야가 타당한 연구분야라고 생각했지만, 생기론을 지지하는 다른 학자들의 저항을

Vocabulary

1단락 terminology [tə̀ːrmənάlədʒi] n. 전문 용어
laboratory [lǽbərətɔ̀ːri] n. 연구실

give way to phr. 굴복하다, 양보하다
eventually [ivéntʃuəli] ad. 결국

experimentation [ikspèrəmentéiʃən] n. 실험

2단락 inorganic [ìnɔːrgǽnik] a. 무생물의
compound [kάmpaund] a. 합성의 n. 합성물
synthesis [sínθəsis] n. 종합, 통합

accurately [ǽkjərətli] ad. 정확하게
inanimate [inǽnəmit] a. 무생물의, 죽은
reasonable [ríːzənəbəl] a. 이치에 맞는

substance [sʌ́bstəns] n. 물질
invalidation [invæ̀dʒənéiʃən] n. 무
adhere [ædhíər] v. 부착하다

chemistry which covered all non-carbon compounds. Some scientists, such as Antoine Lavoisier thought the organic field was a reasonable field of study, yet they were opposed by others who **adhered to** a theory of vitalism. [Q3-B] Those that believed in vitalism felt that there was a "vital spark" or "force" in organic materials and that substances that contained it should not be **experimented upon** and that only inorganic materials were valid research subjects. Despite the eventual invalidation of the vitalist theory, by German chemist Friedrich Wohler's accidental synthesis of organic material in his laboratory, scientists **involved in** inorganic chemistry made much more rapid progress than those working on organic chemistry.

받았다. [Q3-B] 생기론을 믿는 사람들은 유기물에 "생명력"이나 "힘" 따위가 있다고 느꼈으며 이러한 것을 포함하고 있는 물질들은 실험되지 말아야 하며 오직 무기물들만이 합당한 연구 주제라고 여겼다. 독일의 화학자인 프레드릭 뵐러의 실험실에서 우발적인 유기물 합성에 의해 결국 생기론이 틀렸음이 밝혀졌지만, 무기 화학에 관여한 과학자들은 유기화학에 노력을 들인 사람보다 더 빠르게 전진을 보였다.

단락 3
유기화학이 뒤떨어진 이유와 무기화학물질의 분리가 쉬운 것

3 This lag of organic chemistry occurred for various reasons, but perhaps the most obvious is the availability of elements and compounds on which scientists could experiment. **In order** for scientists **to conduct** experiments and determine the chemical forms of the elements, they **need to obtain** them **in** their purest **forms**. [Q4-D] Inorganic compounds, **on the whole**, are more easily found **in** a reasonably pure **state**. Mineral deposits often hold lodes of compounds and elements such as oxides, pure metals and salts. Some gases, such as sulfur, can even be found in their pure elemental form on Earth, [Q5-A] while others, like atmospheric gases, **are** easily **broken down into** their component parts. Hydrogen, **for instance**, can **be mined from** the air using a particular mineral acid on a metal plate.

유기화학의 지연은 다양한 이유로 일어났지만, 그러나 아마도 가장 명백한 이유는 과학자들이 실험 가능한 원소와 화합물의 사용가능성 때문이다. 과학자들이 실험을 진행하고 원소들의 화학 형태를 밝히기 위해서는, 그들은 원소들의 가장 순수한 형태의 원천을 얻을 수 있어야 한다. [Q4-D] 무기화합물들은, 대체로, 적당히 순수한 상태로 더 쉽게 발견되었다. 무기퇴적물들은 종종 산화물, 순금속이나 소금과 같은 풍부한 화합물과 원소들을 지니고 있다. 황과 같은 몇몇 가스들은 지구 상에서 순수한 형태로 발견 되는 [Q5-A] 반면에, 대기 가스와 같은 다른 가스들은 그들의 구성 요소로 쉽게 분해되었다. 수소는, 예를 들면, 특정 무기산을 철판에 사용하여 공기로부터 캐내질 수 있다.

단락 4
유기물질들을 증류하려는 시도

4 **Access to** pure organic substances, **on the other hand**, is much more difficult. **Extracting** pure substances **from** plant or animal matter through the process of distillation, evaporating and condensing a substance to purify it, generally yields solid blackened debris **along with** liquid and gaseous discharges. [Q6-D] Chemists studying the vegetable products found that the qualitative properties of the remaining solid matter varied little between different vegetable types, but [Q6-B] quantitative and qualitative differences were found in the liquid and gaseous substances produced. They also found that

유기 분야에서 순수 물질로의 접근은, 반면에, 훨씬 더 어려웠다. 물질을 정제하기 위해 증류, 증발 그리고 응축 과정을 거쳐 동식물 물질로부터 순수한 물질을 추출하는 것은 대체적으로 액체와 기체의 배출물과 함께 그을린 고체 잔해를 생산하였다. [Q6-D] 채소생산물을 연구하는 화학자들은 남아 있는 고체 물질의 질적인 속성은 다른 식물들 간에서 적게 차이가 나지만 [Q6-B] 액체와 기체물질에서는 질과 양적인 차이가 발견된다는 것을 알아냈다. 그들은 또한 증류 과정을 바꾸는 게 부산물에서 다른 결과를 만든다는 것을 발견했다.

Vocabulary

3단락
- vitalism [váitəlìzəm] n. 생기론
- lodes of phr. 풍부한
- determine [ditə́:rmin] v. 결심하다 결정하다
- valid [vælid] a. 유효한, 정당한 근거가 있는
- various [véəriəs] a. 다양한
- on the whole phr. 전반적으로
- perhaps [pərhǽps] ad. 아마도
- availability [əvèiləbíləti] n. 유용성
- atmospheric [ætməsférik] a. 대기의

4단락
- distillation [dìstəlèiʃən] n. 증류
- purify [pjúərəfài] v. 정화하다, 정화되다
- byproduct [báprádəkt] n. 부산물
- qualitative [kwálətèitiv] a. 질적인
- evaporate [ivǽpərèit] v. 증발하다, 증발시키다
- quantitative [kwántətèitiv] a. 분량의

altering the distillation process yielded significantly different **results in** these byproducts. By standardizing the distillation process they were able to **make** important **advances in** their **ability to analyze** organic matter.

단락 5
증류 후의
유기화합물이
가진 문제점들

5 [Q6-A] Even after developing a standardized analytical process, organic chemists still faced challenges in their field. The most overwhelming of these was that the substances released during the distillation process were complex compounds of unknown purity, **making it impossible to** accurately **determine** the properties of any one element **present in** the substances. Another major problem was determining the source of the released materials. [Q7-B] Were they present in the original sample, or were they produced through the process of distilling and destroying organic material? This uncertainty **led** organic chemists **to search for ways to attain** these substances without destroying the original matter. Many other less violent methods of distillation, such as using the lowest effective temperature to distill organic substances, were attempted, but did not fully overcome the problems that were **inherent in** the field.

[Q6-A] 표준화된 분석 과정을 발전시키 이후에도, 유기 화학자들은 여전히 그들 분야에서 도전들에 직면하게 되었다. 이들 중 가장 압도적인 것은 증류 과정 동안 방출된 물질들이 미지의 순수성을 가진 착화합물이여서 물질에 있는 어떤 원소의 요소를 정확하게 알아내는 것을 불가능하게 만들었다는 것이다. 다른 주요한 문제는 방출된 물질의 원천을 알아내는 것이다. [Q7-B] 그것들은 기존 표본에서 그들이 존재하고 있던 것인가, 또는 증류와 유기물질을 파괴하는 과정에서 생산된 것인가? 이런 불확실성은 유기화학자들을 기존 물질을 파괴하지 않으면서 이러한 물질을 획득하는 방법을 탐구하도록 이끌었다. 유기물질을 증류하기 위해 가장 낮은 끓는 점을 사용하는것 같은 다른 덜 강렬한 증류 방법들이 시도되었지만, 고유한 문제들을 완전히 극복하지 못했다.

단락 6
잘못된
초기 발견들과
유기화학의
발전을 허락한
돌파구

6 This problem led organic chemists to consider substances such as blood, gelatin, and fat to be constituent elements in organisms as late as the 1830s. [■] Today we recognize that all of these substances are complex compounds **composed of** various molecules made of a great number of atoms of true elements. [■] Due to this, and similar, problems, understanding the actual chemical makeup of organic compounds was much more complex and challenging than it was **in the field of** inorganic, or mineral-based, chemistry. [■] The crucial breakthrough in organic chemistry came in 1858 when the concept of chemical structures in carbon atoms was simultaneously developed by Friedrich August Kekule and Archibald Scott Couper. [■] This allowed chemists to more accurately understand the ability of carbon molecules to bond together in a carbon lattice through the observation and interpretation of chemical reactions.

이 문제는 유기 화학자들이 최대 1830년대까지 피, 젤라틴, 그리고 지방과 같은 물질들을 유기체의 구성 분자로써 간주하도록 이끌었다. [■] 오늘날 우리는 이런 모든 물질들이 엄청난 수의 원소의 원자들로 만들어진 다양한 분자들로 구성된 착화합물 이라는 것을 인식한다. [■] 이런 문제 때문에, 그리고 유사하게, 유기화합물의 화학적 실제 구성을 이해하는 것은 무기물, 또는 광물 기반의 화학에서보다 훨씬 더 복잡하고 어렵다. [■] 유기화학에서 중요한 돌파구는 탄소원자의 화학적 구성에 대한 개념이 프레드리히 아우구스트 케큘러와 아치볼드 스콧 쿠우퍼가 동시에 개발하면서 1858년에 나타났다. [■] 이것은 화학자들이 관측과 화학 반응의 해석을 통해 탄소 격자 속에서 탄소 분자를 묶는 탄소의 능력을 더 정확하게 이해하게 도와주었다.

Vocabulary

5단락
- property [prápərti] n. 재산
- analytical [æNəlítikəl] a. 분석적인
- uncertainty [ʌnsə́:rtənti] n. 불확실성
- yield [ji:ld] v. 산출하다, 양도하다
- overwhelming [òuvərhwélmiŋ] a. 압도적인
- attain [ətéin] v. 달성하다, 이르다
- complex [kəmpléks] a. 복합의 n. 복합체
- inherent [inhíərənt] a. 고유의

6단락
- constituent [kənstítʃuənt] a. 구성하는 n. 구성
- consider [kənsídər] v. 숙고하다, 고려하다
- breakthrough [bréikθrù:] n. 획기적 발전, 돌파
- simultaneously [sàiməltéiniəsli] ad. 일제히
- crucial [krú:ʃəl] a. 결정적인
- structure [strʌ́ktʃər] n. 구조

11 According to paragraph 1, which of the following was NOT true about the early science of chemistry?

(A) Early ~~chemists~~ were attempting to find a way to create gold from non-valuable base materials.
(B) Scientists were able to use the methodology developed in the field of alchemy to study the minerals that they found.
(C) The discovery of various forms of the element carbon would lead to the development of one of the two major fields of study in chemistry.
(D) During the 1700s scientists had begun to identify and study new elements in ways that they had not done before this time. ★

단락 1에 따르면, 초기 화학에 대한 사실이 아닌 것은?

(A) 초기 화학자들은 가치없는 기초 물질로부터 금을 창조하기 위한 방법을 찾기 위해 노력했다.
(B) 과학자들은 그들이 찾은 무기물들은 연구하기 위해 연금술분야에서 개발된 방법론을 사용할 수 있었다.
(C) 탄소 원소의 다양한 형태의 발견은 두 개의 주요한 화학 연구 중 하나를 형성하는 것을 이끌었다.
(D) 1700년대 동안 과학자들은 그들이 이전에 하지 않았던 방법으로 새로운 원소들을 찾아내고 연구하기 시작했다. ★

Fact 문제의 키워드인 early science of chemistry가 언급된 부분을 살펴보면 After hundreds of years of trying to turn base metals into gold (비금속을 금으로 바꾸려는 몇 백년 동안의 시도 후에)라고 말한다. 즉, 비금속을 금으로 바꾸려는 시도했던 사람은 연금술사가 아니라 화학자들 이었기 때문에 (A)는 옳지 않은 내용이다.

12 Which of the sentences below best expresses the essential information in the highlighted sentence in the passage? Incorrect choices change the meaning in important ways or leave out essential information.

(A) i) The term organic chemistry reorganized the earlier classification of living things to refer to the study of substances containing carbon, and ii) the mineral group came under the field of inorganic chemistry.
(B) Scientists started using the term organic to refer to ~~minerals~~ derived from organisms, instead of "vegetable" and "animal," and used the term inorganic to refer to non-carbon based minerals.
(C) The primary difference between organic compounds and inorganic compounds is that organic compounds always contain carbon while most inorganic compounds do not contain it.
(D) ~~After~~ the animal and vegetable groups reserved for life-related substances were merged into the study of organic chemistry which covered carbon-based compounds, all other non-carbon compounds, such as minerals, formed the field of inorganic chemistry. ★

아래의 문장 중 지문 속의 음영 표시된 문장의 핵심 정보를 가장 잘 표현하고 있는 것은 무엇인가? 오답은 문장의 의미를 현저하게 바꾸거나 핵심 정보를 빠트리고 있다.

(A) i) 탄소를 포함하고 있는 물질의 연구를 나타내는 유기 화학이라는 용어는 살아있는 것들의 분류를 재편성하였고 ii) 무기물 그룹은 무기화학으로 포함되었다.
(B) 과학자들은 동물과 식물 대신에 유기물이라는 용어를 생물체로부터 파생된 무커물을 나타내기 위해서 사용하기 시작했고 무기물이라는 용어를 탄소 기반이 아닌 무기물을 나타내기 위해 사용했다.
(C) 유기화학과 무기화학의 주요 차이점은 대부분의 무기화합물은 탄소를 포함하고 있지 않는 반면, 유기화합물은 항상 탄소를 포함한다는 것이다.
(D) 생명과 관련된 물질로 지정된 동물과 식물 그룹이 탄소를 기반으로 하는 화합물을 포함하는 유기화학과 합쳐진 후 광물과 같은 비탄소 화합물들은 무기화학의 영역을 형성하였다. ★

Highlight 음영 표시된 문장은 i) Of these, the animal and vegetable groups were reserved for substances that were produced by or related to life and were incorporated into the study of organic(meaning from an organism) chemistry which covered all carbon-based compounds, ii) while the inanimate mineral group gave way to the field of inorganic chemistry which covered all non-carbon compounds. (i) 이들 중에서, 동물과 식물그룹은 생물로부터 생기거나 관련된 물질들을 위해 따로 두어졌고 유기(유기체에서 따온) 화학연구로 포함되었으며, ii) 반면에 무생물의 무기물 그룹은 모든 비탄소 물질들을 포함하는 무기화학으로 나아갔다) 이렇게 두 가지 내용으로 나뉜다. 이 내용을 모두 포함한 (A)가 정답이 된다. (B)가 틀린 이유는 organic은 무기물이 아닌 동물과 식물을 유기화학에 포함시켰기 때문에 오답이고, (D)는 유기화학과 무기화학중 누가 먼저 형성되었는지는 언급되지 않아 오답이다. (C)는 음영 표시된 문장의 주요 내용인 유기화학이 동물과 식물을, 그리고 무기화학이 무생물을 포함하고 있는 점을 담고 있지 않기 때문에 오답이다.

13

All of the following are mentioned in paragraph 2 about the field of organic chemistry EXCEPT: **To receive credit, you must select TWO answer choices.**

(A) Prior to the 1800s scientists used the terms vegetable and animal to describe living matter, but eventually began utilizing the term organic.
(B) Vitalism prohibited experimentation on organic materials because they contained a force that provided them life. ★
(C) The German chemist Friedrich Wohler, by ~~purposefully~~ synthesizing organic materials in his laboratory, disproved the theory of vitalism.
(D) Most scientists felt that it was ~~impossible~~ to study organic matter because they believed it contained a "vital spark."

단락 2에 따르면, 유기화학 분야에 대한 사실이 아닌 것은?

A) 1800년대 이전에 과학자들은 생물을 묘사하기 위해 식물과 동물이라는 용어를 사용했지만, 결국 유기물이라는 용어를 사용하기 시작했다.
(B) 유기물들이 생명 제공하는 힘을 포함하고 있었기 때문에 생기론은 유기물에 대한 실험을 금지하였다. ★
(C) 독일 화학자 프레데릭 벨러는 그의 연구실에서 ~~의도적으로~~ 유기물들을 합성함을 통해서 생기론을 반증하였다.
(D) 많은 과학자들이 유기물질이 그들에게 생명을 부여한 '생기'를 가지고 있다고 믿었기 때문에 유기물질을 연구하기 불가능하다고 느꼈다.

> **Fact** 문제의 키워드인 field of organic chemistry가 언급된 부분을 살펴보면 German chemist Friedrich wöhler's accidental synthesis of organic material in his laboratory.(독일 화학자인 프레드릭 벨러의 실험실에서의 우발적인 유기물 합성 덕에)라고 말한다. 즉, 프레드릭 벨러는 고의적으로 유기물을 합성한 것이 아니기 때문에 (C)는 오답이다. 또, substances that contained it should not be experimented upon("생기"를 포함하고 있는 물질들은 실험되지 말아야 함)라고 말하기 때문에, 과학자들이 유기물에 대해 연구를 하는 것이 불가능했던 것이 아니라 부적당했다는 것이다. 따라서 (D)는 오답이다.

14

What can be inferred from paragraph 3 about the main reason that organic chemistry lagged behind the field of inorganic chemistry?

(A) Early scientists could not easily ~~differentiate~~ between organic and inorganic compounds in the natural world.
(B) Scientists ~~lacked~~ the ability to ~~discern~~ the purest forms from the compounds seemingly similar to the pure ones. ★
(C) The ~~absence~~ of organic compounds in Earth's ~~crust~~ made it difficult for scientists to find them when they were looking for research materials.
(D) Access to inorganic compounds allowed early scientists many more opportunities to undertake experiments on them.

단락 3에서 무기화학에 비해 유기화학이 뒤쳐진 주된 이유에 대해 추론할 수 있는 것은?

(A) 초기 과학자들은 자연 상태에서 유기화합물과 무기화합물을 쉽게 ~~구분~~할 수 없었다.
(B) 과학자들은 순수한 것과 외관상 순수한 것들과 유사한 화합물로부터 순수한 형태의 이들을 ~~식별~~할 수 있는 능력이 ~~부족~~했다. ★
(C) 지구의 ~~지각~~에서 유기화합물이 ~~없는~~ 사실은 과학자들이 연구 주제를 찾을 때 유기화합물들을 찾기 어렵게 하였다.
(D) 무기화합물로의 접근은 초기 과학자들이 무기화합물에 실험을 행할 많은 기회를 허락하였다.

> **Inference** 문제의 키워드인 organic chemistry lagged가 언급된 부분을 살펴보면 Inorganic compounds, on the whole, are more easily found in a reasonably pure state.(무기화합물들은, 대체로, 합리적으로 순수한 상태로 더 쉽게 발견되었다)라고 한다. 즉, 유기화학이 무기화학보다 늦쳐진 이유는 순수한 상태의 유기화합물들을 찾기 힘들었기 때문이다. 따라서 (D)가 답이 된다. (A)와 (B)는 언급되지 않는 내용이기 때문에 오답이고, (C)는 지구에 유기화합물이 존재했으나 순수한 형태의 유기화합물을 찾는게 힘들었던 것이기 때문에 오답이다.

15

What is the purpose of including information regarding the mining of hydrogen from the air in paragraph 3?

(A) To give an example of one of the easy ways in which an inorganic element can be attained in its pure form
(B) To give more information about ~~the type of element~~ that is studied in the field of inorganic chemistry
(C) To let the reader see that inorganic compounds are so ~~prevalent~~ that they can even be taken directly from the air
(D) To show that some gases found in their pure form are found relatively ~~easier~~ than others in the atmosphere ★

단락 3에서 공기에서부터 수소를 캐내는 것과 관련된 정보를 포함한 목적은 무엇인가?

(A) 무기 원소를 그것의 순수한 형태로 얻을 수 있는 쉬운 방법 중 하나로써의 예시를 주기 위해서
(B) 무기화학 분야에서 연구되고 있는 ~~원소와 종류~~와 관련된 정보를 더 주기 위해서
(C) 독자로 하여금 무기 화합물이 너무 ~~흔해서~~ 심지어는 공기에서부터 직접적으로 추출되어질 수 있다는 것을 이해시키기 위해서
(D) 순수형태로 발견되는 일부 가스가 대기 안에 있는 다른 가스보다 ~~쉽게~~ 발견된다는 것을 보여주기 위해서 ★

Purpose 문제의 키워드인 hydrogen이 언급된 부분을 살펴보면 while others, like atmospheric gases, are easily broken down into their component parts (대기 가스와 같은 다른 가스들은 그들의 구성 부품으로 쉽게 분해되었다)라고 말한다. 즉, 순수한 형태의 수소를 쉽게 캐낼 수 있었다는 것을 알 수 있다. 따라서 (A)가 답이 된다. (C)는 무기화합물들이 흔하다는 것은 언급되지 않아 오답이고, (D)는 순수한 형태의 가스가 대기 가스보다 쉽게 발견된 게 아니라, 둘 다 동등하게 쉽게 발견된 것이기 때문에 오답이다.

16

In paragraphs 4 and 5, which of the following can be inferred using the process of distillation?

(A) The standardization of the distillation process enabled scientists to ~~overcome~~ the problems in the analytical process.
(B) Different vegetation types have variations in properties and amounts of liquid and gaseous substances in comparison to its solid state.
(C) The standardization of the distillation process allowed scientists to derive ~~more minerals~~ from the blackened material created in the process.
(D) Scientists found that the ~~quantity~~ of the remaining solid matter had little variations among different vegetable types. ★

단락 4와 5에서 증류 과정을 사용하는 것에 대하여 추론할 수 있는 것은?

(A) 증류 과정의 획일화는 과학자들이 분석 과정의 문제점들을 모두 ~~극복하게~~ 해주었다.
(B) 다른 식물 종류들은 고체 상태일 때에 비해 액체 및 기체 물질일 때 특성과 양에 변화가 있다.
(C) 증류 과정의 획일화는 과학자들이 과정에서 그을린 물질로부터 ~~더 많은 무기물~~을 얻을 수 있는 걸 허락했다.
(D) 과학자들은 남아있는 고체 물질의 ~~양이~~ 식물 종류들 사이에서 적은 차이가 난다는 것을 찾았다. ★

Inference 문제의 키워드인 process of distillation이 언급된 부분을 살펴보면 quantitative and qualitative differences were found in the liquid and gaseous substances produced. (액체 및 기체물질에서는 질과 양적인 차이가 발견된다는 것을 알아냈다)라고 말한다. 즉, 액체와 기체물질에서는 질(properties)과 양(amounts) 차이가 있기 때문에 정답은 (B)가 된다. (A)는 유기화학에만 쓰일 수 있다는 내용이 없기 때문에 오답이고, (C)는 더 많은 무기물을 생산하도록 도와준 것은 아니기 때문에 오답이다. (D)는 남아있는 물질의 양 차이가 아닌 질적 차이를 말하는 것이기 때문에 오답이다.

17 According to paragraph 5, which of the following is true about the more standardized analytical process that chemists developed?

(A) It ~~provided~~ them with all of the purified organic compounds they needed to conduct their experiments upon.
(B) It did not enable the scientists to know if they were creating the substances or if they were present in the original sample.
(C) It allowed scientists to distill the necessary components from the organic material ~~without destroying~~ it in the process. ★
(D) It greatly ~~increased~~ the purity of the organic material that the scientists were creating in the distillation process.

단락 5에 따르면, 화학자들이 개발한 더 획일화된 분석 과정에 대해 사실인 것은?

(A) 그것은 화학자들에게 그들의 실험을 진행하기 위해 필요한 모든 정제된 유기 화합물들을 ~~제공했다~~.
(B) 그것은 과학자들을 만약 그들이 물질을 창조해낸 것인지 또는 그들이 기본 표본에서 존재하고 있던 것인지 알도록 허락하지 않았다.
(C) 이것은 과학자들이 과정 중에 물질을 ~~파괴하지 않으~~면서 필요한 부분들을 유기 물질로부터 증류하도록 허락했다. ★
(D) 이것은 과학자들이 증류 과정 속에서 창조하던 유기물질의 순수성을 크게 ~~증가시켰다~~.

> **Fact** 문제의 키워드인 standardized analytical process가 언급된 부분을 살펴보면 Were they present in the original sample, or were they produced through the process of distilling and destroying organic material? (그것들은 기존 표본에서 그들이 존재하고 있던 것인가, 또는 증류와 유기물질을 파괴하는 과정에서 생산된 것인가?)라고 말한다. 즉, 물질이 이미 존재했는지 존재하지 않았는지에 대한 여부가 확실치 않으므로 답은 (B)가 된다. (C)는 distillation 과정에서 유기화합물을 완전히 보존할 수 있는 방법은 찾지 못했기 때문에 오답이다.

18 The term "crucial" in the passage is closest in meaning to

(A) fatal [féitl]
(B) relevant [réləvənt]
(C) decisive [disáisiv]
(D) unmistakable [ʌ̀nmistéikəbəl] ★

지문의 단어 "중요한"의 의미와 가장 유사한 것은?

(A) 치명적인
(B) 관련있는
(C) 결정적인
(D) 명백한 ★

> **Vocabulary** 지문의 crucial(중요한)은 decisive(결정적인)과 동의어이므로 정답은 (C)이다.

19 Look at the four squares [■] that indicate where the following sentence could be added to the passage.

> This allowed chemists to more accurately understand the ability of carbon molecules to bond together in a carbon lattice through the observation and interpretation of chemical reactions.

Where would the sentence best fit? Click on a square [■] to add the sentence to the passage.

4th

네 개의 네모[■]는 다음 문장이 삽입될 수 있는 부분을 나타내고 있다

> 이것은 화학자들이 관측과 화학 반응의 해석을 통해 탄소 격자 속에서 탄소 분자를 묶는 탄소의 능력을 더 정확하게 이해하는 것을 허락했다.

이 문장은 어느 자리에 들어가는 것이 가장 적절한가?

4번째

> **Insertion** 삽입문장에서의 "this"가 과학자들이 탄소의 능력에 대한 이해도를 높일 수 있도록 해주었다고 한다. 네 번째 네모의 앞 문장에서 돌파구에 대한 내용이 언급되며, 이 돌파구 덕분에 더 정확한 연구가 가능해졌다는 것이니 네 번째 네모에 예제를 넣는 것이 가장 타당함으로 답은 네 번째 네모이다.

20

Directions: An introductory sentence for a brief summary of the passage is provided below. Complete the summary by selecting the THREE answer choices that express the most important ideas in the passage. Some sentences do not belong in the summary because they express ideas that are not presented in the passage or are minor ideas in the passage. **This question is worth 2 points**

지시: 지문 요약을 위한 도입 문장이 아래에 주어져 있다. 지문의 가장 중요한 내용을 나타내는 보기 3개를 골라 요약을 완성 하시오. 어떤 문장은 지문에 언급되지 않은 내용이나 사소한 정보를 담고 있으므로 요약에 포함되지 않는다. **이 문제는 2점이다.**

The development of organic chemistry, which studies carbon based compounds, took much longer than the study of inorganic chemistry.

(B) The early division of organic and inorganic chemistry originated from the idea that living organisms, animals and vegetables, had a different chemical composition than non-living objects, such as rocks and soil. - paragraph 2

(D) The inability of early scientists to find pure sources of organic compounds and elements made their attempts to understand organic substances much more difficult than in the field of inorganic chemistry. - paragraph 3

(E) The process of distillation produced liquid and gaseous organic substances that early organic chemists could experiment upon, but they had no way to determine where the substances originated or their purity. - paragraph 5

탄소 기반의 화합물을 연구하는 유기화학의 발전은 무기화학의 연구보다 더 오래 걸렸다.

(B) 유기화학과 무기화학의 초기 구분은 동물이나 식물과 같은 살아 있는 유기체들은 돌이나 흙과 같은 살아 있지 않은 물체들과 다른 화학적 구성을 가지고 있다는 생각으로부터 유래하였다.

(D) 초기과학자들이 유기화합물과 원소의 순수한 원천을 찾지 못했던 것은 유기 물질들을 이해하려는 그들의 노력을 무기화합물 분야보다 훨씬 더 어렵게 만들었다.

(E) 증류 과정은 초기 유기 화학자들이 실험할 수 있던 액체와 기체 상태의 유기 물질을 생산했지만 그들은 물질들이 어디서 유래했는지 또는 순수한 지 판단할 방법이 없었다.

(A) Eighteenth century scientists were able to identify many new elements that had never been previously studied, such as carbon, cobalt, and tungsten. - paragraph 1 detail

(C) Whether in their pure form or in the atmosphere, gases are readily available for research purposes, ~~making~~ the study of ~~organic chemistry simpler.~~ - 틀린 정보

(F) The substances, originally referred to as ~~organic~~, derived from living organisms, such as blood, gelatin, and fat, later ~~turned out~~ to be ~~inorganic~~ elements. - 틀린 정보

(A) 18세기 과학자들은 이전에 연구되지 않던 탄소, 코발트, 텅스텐과 같은 새로운 원소들을 확인 할 수 있었다.

(C) 순수 형태이든 대기에 있는, 가스는 연구 목적으로 쉽게 사용 가능해서 ~~유기화학을 쉽게 연구할 수 있게 한다.~~

(F) 피, 젤라틴, 지방과 같이 원래 ~~유기화합물~~로 여겨 졌던 물질들이 나중에 ~~무기화합물~~ 이라고 밝혀졌다.

Summary   (B)는 유기화학과 무기화학의 분류 기준의 내용을 포함하고 있는 2단락을 요약한 것이고, (D)는 유기화학이 뒤떨어진 이유를 설명하는 3단락의 중심내용이며, (E)는 5단락에서 다루는 증류 후의 유기화합물이 가진 문제점들의 중심내용이다.

USHER iBT TOEFL
INTERMEDIATE READING

TEST 3
답안 및 취약 유형 분석표

해석 · 해설

답안 및 문제 유형 분석표

TEST 3-1

01 (B) Inference

02 (A) Highlight

03 (A) Fact

04 (C) Reference

05 (B) Fact

06 (C) Vocabulary

07 (D) Purpose

08 (A) Fact

09 2nd ■ Insertion

10 (A), (D), (F) Summary

TEST 3-2

11 (D) Fact

12 (C) Fact

13 (B) Purpose

14 (D) Vocabulary

15 (D) Inference

16 (C) Inference

17 (D) Highlight

18 (A) Purpose

19 4th ■ Insertion

20 (A), (B), (D) Summary

각 문제 유형별 맞춘 개수를 아래에 적어 보세요.

유형	맞춘 답의 개수	정답률
단어 (Vocabulary)	/ 2	정답률: %
사실 확인 문제 (Fact)	/ 5	정답률: %
지시어 찾기 (Reference)	/ 1	정답률: %
끼워 넣기 (Insertion)	/ 2	정답률: %
문장 변환문제 (Highlight)	/ 2	정답률: %
목적 (Purpose)	/ 3	정답률: %
추론 (Inference)	/ 3	정답률: %
단락 요약(Summary / Category Chart)	/ 2	정답률: %
전체	/ 20	정답률: %

※ 자신이 취약한 유형은 READING STRATEGIES를 통해 다시 한번 점검하시기 바랍니다. (p.44)

TEST 3-1   El Niño 엘니뇨 현상

Introduction	단락 1	엘니뇨 현상에 대한 소개와 배경
Point	단락 2	엘니뇨 현상의 확장된 의미
Point	단락 3	남방진동의 원리와 이것이 엘니뇨에 미치는 영향
Point	단락 4	엘니뇨 원리에 대한 이론 소개
Point	단락 5	엘니뇨 현상의 발생가능성과 심각성
Point	단락 6	엘니뇨 현상의 부수적인 피해

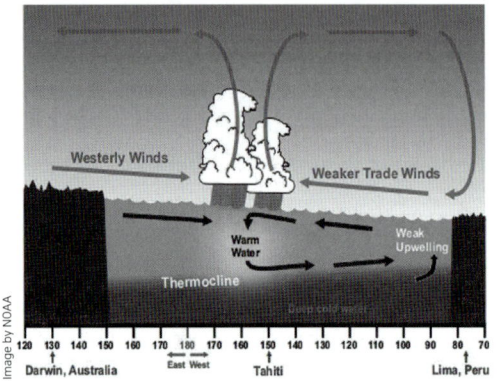

문단주제	본문내용	해석
단락 1 엘니뇨 현상에 대한 소개와 배경	**1** The Humboldt Current carries cold water northward from the Antarctic along South America's western coast. [■] [Q11-B] As it reaches the equator, the easterly trade winds blow the surface water westward and allow an upwelling of cold, nutrient-rich waters. [■] This rise of these nutritive waters provides the abundant food sources that are needed to sustain the nearly year-round commercial fishing industry off the coasts of Peru and Chile. However, during December and January, the cold waters **are replaced by** a warmer countercurrent, greatly reducing the water's nutrient content and causing a lull in commercial fishing **due to the lack of** commercially viable fish, such as anchovies, in the warmer water. [■] [Q13-A] Local residents **termed this period "El Niño,"** or "the boy" in Spanish, due to its occurrence during the Christmas season, and **use** this downtime **to tend to** their equipment. [■]	훔볼트 해류는 남극 지역에서 남아메리카 서해안을 따라 차가운 물을 끌어온다. [■] [Q11-B] 이 물들이 적도를 도달할때 동쪽 무역풍이 표층수를 서쪽으로 밀어내 차갑고 영양분이 풍부한 물의 용승을 불러일으킨다. [■] 이런 영양분이 많은 물들의 상승은 페루와 칠레의 해안에 위치한 연중 계속되는 상업적 어업을 유지하는데 필요한 풍부한 음식을 제공한다. 그러나, 12월과 1월의 차가운 물은 따뜻한 역해류로 대체되어, 해수의 영양분이 급격히 감소하고 따뜻한 해수속에 멸치와 같은 사업적 가치가 있는 어족이 부족해져 일시적인 어업을 불경기를 초래한다. [■] [Q13-A] 지역 주민들은 이 기간을 크리스마스 기간에 일어나기 때문에 "El Niño" 혹은 스페인어로 "그 남자" 라고 칭하고 이 시간을 자신들의 장비를 손질할 수 있는 시간으로 사용한다. [■]
단락 2 엘니뇨 현상의 확장된 의미	**2** Despite the traditionally short duration of El Niño, these [Q13-B] warmer surface waters can linger and **extend** far **into** the equatorial Pacific. In fact, **over** the past six **decades**, [Q13-C] climatologists have identified **at least** ten unusually long El Niño periods. In recent times, the traditional term for this period, [Q13-D] El Niño, has become **identified** worldwide with	역사적으로 엘니뇨의 발생기간은 짧지만, 이로 인해 발생한[Q13-B] 따뜻한 해면 표층수는 오랫동안 지속되고 태평양의 적도까지 확산된다. 사실 지난 60년 동안[Q13-C] 기후학자들은 엘니뇨 현상이 유별나게 길었던 기간이 적어도 10번 있었다고 밝혔다. 최근에 엘니뇨라는 전통적 용어가 전 세계 기후 패턴의 큰 변화를 일으킬 수 있기 때문에[Q13-D] 이들이 매년 일어나는 패턴보다는

Vocabulary

1단락
- equator [ikwéitər] n. 적도
- nutrient [njú:triənt] n. 영양소
- upwelling [ʌpwéliŋ] n. 용승
- anchovy [æntʃouvi] n. 멸치
- countercurrent [káuntərkə̀:rənt] n. 역류, 반류
- resident [rézədnt] n. 거주자

2단락
- extend [iksténd] v. 연장하다, 더 길게 만들다
- annual [ǽnjuəl] a. 매년의
- climatologist [klàimətálədʒist] n. 기후학자
- equatorial [ì:kwətɔ́:riəl] a. 적도의

these lengthy periods of warmer Pacific waters more than with the annual pattern, because of the great changes they can cause in weather patterns across the globe.

3   Despite being **known** mainly **as** an eastern Pacific pattern, El Niño **affects** conditions across the vast waters of the Pacific. One of the first scientists to recognize this was early-20th century British physicist Gilbert Walker, who found an inverse correlation between atmospheric pressure at weather stations in the eastern and western Pacific. Walker noted that as the pressure of the eastern Pacific fell, that of the western Pacific rose, and **vice versa in** a see-saw-like **pattern** that he termed the Southern Oscillation. The relationship between this phenomenon and El Ni no was later **recognized as** being **so** strong **that** they **are often referred to** collectively **as** the El Niño-Southern Oscillation.

4   [Q15-A] Normally, the eastern Pacific's higher atmospheric pressure causes [Q15-B] the easterly trade winds that typify the wind pattern of the southern equatorial region. These warm winds also cause the warm east-to-west surface current that **moves across** the Pacific Ocean along the equator. Eventually it causes an accumulation of warm surface waters in the western Pacific, while the Humboldt Current's upwelling **keeps surface temperatures** in the eastern Pacific much **lower**. When the Southern Oscillation shifts and pressure rises in the west, the pressure gradient across the ocean is disrupted and the trade winds that were caused by it are severely weakened or reversed. [Q15-C] With these no longer pushing westward on the warmer surface water it **begins to creep** eastward, marking the beginning of El Niño. As the warmer waters slide eastward, they further decrease the pressure and temperature gradients across the Pacific Ocean in a positive feedback loop. [Q15-D] The pressure gradient that causes the winds is decreased as the eastern Pacific becomes warmer, which further decreases the pressure gradient and the winds.

Vocabulary

3단락
inverse [invə́ːrs] a. 역, 반대의
atmospheric [æ̀tməsférik] a. 대기의

4단락
accumulation [əkjùːmjəléiʃən] n. 축적, 누적
hemisphere [hémisfìər] n. 반구

5단락
frequency [fríːkwənsi] n. 빈도

correlation [kɔ̀ːrəléiʃən] n. 연관성, 상관관계
oscillation [àsəléiʃən] n. 진동

gradient [gréidiənt] n. 경도
pressure [préʃər] n. 압력

severe [sivíər] a. 극심한

typify [típəfài] v. 전형적이다
creep [kriːp] v. 살금살금 움직이다

examine [igzǽmin] v. 조사하다

단락 5
엘니뇨 현상의
역사와 심각성

5   Since this process was first theorized, scientists have **attempted to trace** it using historical records. By examining records of the daily surface temperature of the ocean, rainfall, atmospheric pressure, and fisheries data from South American inhabitants and Spanish colonists dating as far back as the 1400s, they have **pieced together** a detailed timeline of El Niño over the past six centuries. From this, **it is clear that** although El Niño occurred regularly throughout history its frequency is increasing. **Comparing** the records of the 16th century **to** modern ones shows that El Niño is now occurring nearly three times more often than it did then, occurring just over every 2 years now, but occurring in six year intervals historically. An even more alarming finding is that the temperature increase's severity is rising. [Q17-D] This is troubling because scientists now know that El Niño's effects are **not limited to** the southern Pacific, **but also** affect worldwide weather patterns. During the 1997-98 El Niño, **for instance**, the entire United States **suffered from** more severe seasonal weather.

이 과정이 처음 이론화가 된 이후에 과학자들은 역사 기록을 통해 이를 추적하려고 노력했다. 1400년대부터 남아메리카 주민들과 스페인 식민지 주민들의 표층수, 강수량, 기압 그리고 어업 기록들을 분석하면서 지난 600년 동안의 엘니뇨 현상의 나름 상세한 타임라인을 짜맞추었다. 이것에 의하면 엘니뇨 현상을 역사 동안 주기적으로 일어났지만 이의 빈도는 증가하고 있다. 16세기의 기록과 현대시대의 기록을 비교하면 엘니뇨 현상이 거의 세 배 더 자주 일어나는 것을 알 수 있다. 역사적으로 6년 주기로 일어났지만 현재 2년마다 일어나게 된다. 이보다 더 걱정스러운 발견은 온도 상승의 심각성이 증가하고 있다는 것이다. [Q17-D] 이것은 과학자들이 엘니뇨가 그저 남태평양에 한정된 것이 아니라 전 세계 기후 패턴에 영향을 주는 것을 알게 되었기 때문에 문제가 된다. 예를 들어 1997-1998 엘니뇨 때 미국은 더 극한 계절적 기후에 시달렸다.

단락 6
엘니뇨 현상의
부수적인 피해

6   Modern researchers have pointed to even more **reasons to fear** a stronger El Niño. [Q18-A] **It appears that** El Niño also **coincides with** increased epidemics, especially those caused by mosquito-borne pathogens, civil conflict, and violence. One of the most well-researched aspects of this has been El Niño's effect on malaria. Scientists have proven that a 1°C increase in the ocean's surface temperature yields a 20% increase in malaria around the tropical Pacific's coasts. Others have noted that the risk of civil unrest and violence doubles to 6% during El Niño. They **blame** this **on** the widespread famine that occurs during these periods. They **point to** the Northern Chinese Famine of 1876 that killed 13 million and the El Niño effects of 1789-1793 that **led to** crop failures, which eventually sparked the French Revolution, **as** evidence of this. In modern times, it has been found that El Niño's effects have triggered 21% of conflicts worldwide since 1950.

현대 연구자들은 강력한 엘니뇨를 두려워할 이유들을 지적했다. [Q18-A] 엘니뇨가 모기 관련 병원균에 의한 유행병, 민족 분쟁 그리고 폭력의 증가와 동시에 일어난다는 것이다. 이 중 가장 잘 연구된 부분들이 말라리아 발생에 엘니뇨의 현상이다. 과학자들은 해수면 온도가 1°C 상승할 때 열대 태평양 해안 주변의 말라리아가 20% 증가한다는 것을 입증하였다. 어떤 이들은 민족 불안 그리고 폭력이 엘니뇨 기간 동안 6%로 두 배 늘어난다고 한다. 이런 과학자들은 이 기간 동안 일어나는 널리 퍼지는 기근을 탓한다. 이들은 천삼백만명을 죽인 1876년 북중국 기근과 1789-1793년의 엘니뇨 현상이 흉작을 야기했고, 이것은 결국 프랑스 혁명에 불을 지폈다고 지적했다. 현대 시기에 엘니뇨 현상의 영향이 1950년 이후 21%의 분쟁을 일으켰다고 한다.

Vocabulary

inhabitant [inhǽbətənt] n. 주민

6단락   epidemic [èpədémik] n. 유행병
aspect [ǽspekt] n. 측면

interval [íntərvəl] n. 간격
unrest [ʌnrést] n. 불안, 불만
tropical [trápikəl] a. 열대 지방의

limited [límitid] a. 제한된

widespread [wáidspréd] a. 광범위한

01

What can be inferred from paragraph 1 about the waters off the western coast of South America?

(A) They are ~~colder~~ than the waters off the ~~eastern coast~~ of the continent due to the Humboldt Current.
(B) Their ability to support healthy populations of sea life is dependent upon the presence of winds blowing from the east.
(C) They provide the ~~main source~~ of nutrients for the ~~agriculture~~ of the western region of South America.
(D) Their temperature would ~~have nothing to do with~~ the Humboldt Current. ★

단락 1에서 남아메리카 서해안 해상에 대해 어떤 것이 추론될 수 있는가?

(A) 이는 험볼트 해류에 의해 대륙 동쪽 물보다 ~~차갑다~~
(B) 이들이 해상 생물의 건강한 인구를 유지할 수 있는 능력은 동쪽에서 불어오는 바람의 존재에 의존한다.
(C) 이는 남아메리카 서쪽 지역의 ~~농업의~~ 영양분의 주 ~~재료~~ 들을 제공한다.
(D) 온도는 험볼트 해류와 아무런 ~~관련성이 없다~~. ★

Inference 키워드인 waters이 나오는 부분을 살펴보면, As they reach the equator, the easterly trade winds blow the surface water back and allow an upwelling of cold, nutrient-rich waters. (이 물들이 적도를 도달하자 동쪽 무역풍이 표층수를 밀어내 차갑고 영양분이 풍부한 물의 용승을 불러일으킨다)라고 말한다. 즉, 서해안 해상이 건강한 인구를 유지할 수 있도록 해주는 풍부한 영양분은 동쪽 무역풍에서 온다는 것이다. 그러므로 답은 (B)이다. (A)는 더 차갑다는 내용이 없으므로 오답이고, (C)는 어업상업에 영향을 끼친다는 언급은 있지만 농업의 영양분을 제공해준다는 내용이 없으므로 오답이다. (D)는 험볼트 해류와 동풍이 없으면 온도가 증가했을 것이기 때문에 오답이다.

02

Which of the sentences below best expresses the essential information in the highlighted sentence in the passage? Incorrect choices change the meaning in important ways or leave out essential information.

(A) Scientists today use the term El Niño to identify the longer periods of warming in areas around the Pacific instead of the annual pattern because they greatly affect the weather patterns around the globe.
(B) El Niño ~~has become the official name of~~ the warming of the waters of the Pacific Ocean ii) because of the great impact it has on the climates of regions across the globe.
(C) ~~Because of~~ the lengthier episodes of Pacific warming that occur today, the term El Niño is now used to identify the weather changes that occur worldwide. ★
(D) Now that the worldwide climatic effects of El Niño are ~~better understood~~, the term is more closely associated with the extended warming periods than with the traditional warming period.

아래의 문장 중 지문 속의 음영 표시된 문장의 핵심 정보를 가장 잘 표현하고 있는 것은 무엇인가? 오답은 문장의 의미를 현저하게 바꾸거나 핵심 정보를 빠뜨리고 있다.

(A) 현재 과학자들은 기상 패턴에 큰 영향을 끼치기 때문에 엘니뇨라는 용어를 매년 일어나는 패턴 대신에 태평양 주변의 지역에 따뜻함이 있는 긴 시간들을 말하는데 더 많이 사용한다.
(B) 엘니뇨는 ii) 전 세계 지역 기후에 미치는 큰 영향 때문에 태평양 물이 따뜻해지는 현상의 ~~공식 이름으로 되었다~~.
(C) 태평양 물의 따뜻해지는 일들이 길어졌기 ~~때문에~~ 엘니뇨라는 현상은 매년 일어나는 따뜻해지는 현상보다 전 세계적으로 일어나는 기후변화를 칭하는데 사용하고 있다. ★
(D) 엘니뇨 현상의 전 세계적 기후 영향이 ~~더욱 잘 이해가 되자~~ 이 용어는 이전의 따뜻한 기간보다 연장된 따뜻한 기간과 관련 있다.

Highlight 문장을 살펴보자. i) In recent times, the traditional term for this period, El Niño, has become identified worldwide with these lengthy periods of warmer Pacific waters more than with the annual pattern, ii) because of the great changes they can cause in weather patterns across the globe.(ii 최근에 엘니뇨라는 전통적 용어가 전세계 기후패턴의 큰 변화를 일으킬 수 있기 때문에 i) 이들이 매년 일어나는 패턴보다는 태평양의 따뜻한 물이 있는 긴 기간들을 말하는데 사용한다) 이 내용을 포함하고 있는 보기는 (A)이므로 (A)가 정답이다. (B)는 i)내용이 빠져있기 때문에 오답이며, (D)는 원인이 날씨 영향이 이해가 잘 되어서가 아니라 기후 패턴에 많은 영향을 끼치기 때문에 오답이다. (C)는 장기간의 따뜻해지는 현상 때문에 기후변화를 칭하는데 엘니뇨를 사용하고 있는게 아니라, 기후변화 때문에 장기간의 따뜻해지는 현상을 칭하려고 엘니뇨를 사용하고 있는 것이기 때문에 오답이다.

03 In paragraphs 1 and 2, which of the following is **NOT** true regarding El Niño?

(A) During the El Niño period, fishers ~~tend to use~~ their equipment in the downtime.
(B) The period of increased surface temperatures can last longer than the two months that were traditionally associated with El Niño. ★
(C) Scientists monitor the duration of the increased surface temperatures of the Pacific Ocean along the equator.
(D) The term "El Niño" is now used worldwide to refer to times when the warming of Pacific waters extends past the traditional period.

단락 1과 2에서, 엘니뇨에 대한 사실이 아닌 것은?

(A) 엘니뇨 기간 동안, 어부들은 그들의 장비를 비가동시간 동안 ~~사용하는 경향~~ 이 있다.
(B) 증가된 표층수 온도의 기간은 보통 엘니뇨와 연관 있었던 두 달보다 더 오래 지속된다. ★
(C) 과학자들이 적도 근처 태평양의 증가된 표층수 온도의 지속 기간을 감시한다
(D) 엘니뇨라는 용어는 현재 보통의 기간을 넘어가는 태평양의 따뜻한 물이 있는 시기를 칭하는데 사용되고 있다.

Fact (B)는 지문에서 Despite the traditionally short duration of El Niño, these warmer surface waters can linger and extend far into the equatorial Pacific. (엘니뇨는 역사적으로 일시적 기간으로 생각해왔지만, 이 같은 따뜻한 표층수는 오랫동안 남아있고 적도 태평양으로 갈 수가 있다)라고 주장하기 때문에 옳은 말이며, (C)는 In fact, over the past six decades, climatologists have identified at least ten unusually long El Niño periods. (사실 지난 60년 동안 기후학자들은 엘니뇨 현상이 유별나게 길었던 기간이 적어도 10번 있었다고 밝혔다)라고 하기 때문에 옳은 말이다. 마지막으로, (D)는 In recent times, the traditional term for this period, El Niño, has become identified worldwide with these lengthy periods of warmer Pacific waters more than with the annual pattern. (최근에 엘니뇨라는 전통적 용어가 전 세계 기후 패턴의 큰 변화를 일으킬 수 있기 때문에 이들이 매년 일어나는 패턴보다는 태평양의 따뜻한 물이 있는 긴 기간들을 말하는데 사용한다)라고 뒷받침되어 옳은 말이다. (A)는 Local residents termed this period "El Niño," or "the boy" in Spanish, due to its occurrence during the Christmas season, and use this downtime to tend to their equipment 에서 농부들이 그들의 장비를 사용하는 경향이 있는 것이 아니라 그들의 장비를 정비하는 것이기 때문에 오답이다.

04 What does the word "it" refer to in the passage?

(A) southern Oscillation ★
(B) pressure increase
(C) disruption
(D) trade wind

지문에서 "이것"이 의미하는 것은?

(A) 남방진동 ★
(B) 압력 증가
(C) 방해
(D) 무역풍

Reference it 이 언급된 부분을 살펴보면 When the Southern Oscillation shifts and pressure rises in the west, the pressure gradient across the ocean is disrupted and the trade winds that were caused by it are severely weakened or reversed 에서 무역풍은 기압경도가 방해된 것에 의해서 일어났기 때문에 정답은 (C)가 된다.

05 According to paragraph 4, all of the following is true about the atmospheric pressure over the Pacific Ocean EXCEPT:

(A) Atmospheric pressure is usually higher over the Eastern Pacific than it is over the western region.
(B) The easterly trade winds are ~~unusual~~ in the southern equatorial region.
(C) When the pressure across the ocean becomes more equal, warmer surface temperatures creep eastward across the Pacific Ocean.
(D) The lowered atmospheric pressure gradient across the Pacific Ocean weakens the trade winds. ★

단락 4에 따르면, 다음 중 태평양 상공의 대기압에 관한 것이 아닌 것은?

(A) 기압은 보통 서태평양보다 동태평양에서 더 높다.
(B) 동쪽 무역풍은 남반구 적도 지역에서 ~~흔하지 않다~~.
(C) 바다의 압력이 균등해질 때 따뜻한 수면 온도가 태평양 동쪽으로 흐르게 된다.
(D) 태평양의 낮아진 기압 경도는 무역풍을 약화시킨다. ★

Fact (A)는 Normally, the eastern Pacific's higher atmospheric pressure (보통 동태평양의 높은 기압은)에서 동태평양의 기압이 더 높다고 주장하기 때문에 옳은 말이며, (C)는 With these no longer pushing westward on the warmer surface water it begins to creep eastward, marking the beginning of El Niño. (이런 바람들이 더 이상 따뜻한 표층수를 서쪽으로 밀지 않자 이 따뜻한 표층수는 동쪽으로 서서히 움직이면 엘니뇨의 시작을 가리킨다)에서 따뜻한 표층수는 동쪽으로 서서히 움직인다 하여 옳은 말이다. (D)는 The pressure gradient that causes the winds is decreased as the eastern Pacific becomes warmer, which further decreases the pressure gradient and the winds. (바람을 일으키는 기압 경도는 감소하고 동태평양은 따뜻해지면서 기압 경도와 바람을 더더욱 감소시킨다) 즉, 결과적으로 기압 경도와 온도 경도 둘 다 낮아 진다는 뜻이므로 옳은 말이다. (B)는 The easterly trade winds are unusual in the southern equatorial region(동쪽 무역풍은 남반구 적도 지역에서 흔하지 않다). 동쪽 무역풍은 남반구 적도 지역에서 흔하다고 볼 수 있다. 따라서 정답은 (B)이다.

06 The term "severely" in the passage is closest in meaning to

(A) easily [íːzəli]
(B) regularly [régjələrli]
(C) intensely [inténsli]
(D) abruptly [əbrʌ́ptli] ★

지문의 단어 "심하게"의 의미와 가장 유사한 것은?

(A) 쉽게
(B) 주기적으로
(C) 강렬하게
(D) 급작스럽게 ★

Vocabulary 지문의 severely(심하게)와 동의어인 intensely(강렬하게)가 정답이 된다. Abruptly(급작스럽게)는 정도보다는 속도와 더 적합한 단어 이므로 오답이다.

07 Why does the author mention that "the entire United States suffered from more severe seasonal weather"?

(A) To illustrate that El Niño is responsible for the change of seasons in the United States ★
(B) To give more information regarding the droughts that are caused by the onset of an El Niño period
(C) To show that El Niño most severely affects countries found on the eastern side of the Pacific Ocean
(D) To emphasize the extent of the impact the El Niño had even on distant locations

작가는 왜 "1997-1998 엘니뇨 때 미국은 더 극한 계절적 기후에 시달렸다"라는 말을 언급하는가?

(A) 독자가 엘니뇨에 의해 미국의 계절의 변화가 일어났다는 것을 알리기 위해서 ★
(B) 엘니뇨 기간에 의해 생긴 가뭄에 관한 정보를 더 제공하기 위해서
(C) 엘니뇨가 태평양의 동쪽에 위치한 나라들을 가장 심하게 영향을 준다는 것을 보여주기 위해서
(D) 긴 엘니뇨 기간에 의해 영향을 받은 남태평양과 떨어진 지역의 예를 주기 위해서

Purpose 지문에서 음영문구 the entire United States suffered from more severe seasonal weather (미국은 더 극한 계절적 기후에 시달렸다)를 살펴보면 This is troubling because scientists now know that El Niños effects are not limited to the southern Pacific, but also affect worldwide weather patterns. (이것은 과학자들이 엘니뇨가 그저 남태평양에 한정된 것이 아니라 전세계 기후패턴에 영향을 주기 때문에 문제가 된다)라고 언급했다. 즉, the entire United States suffered from more severe seasonal weather (미국은 더 극한 계절적 기후에 시달렸다)는 남태평양과 멀리 떨어졌음에도 불구하고 영향을 받은 지역의 예를 주기 위함이다. (A)는 계절의 변화가 아니라 기후의 변화여서 오답이고, (B)는 가뭄은 언급된 내용이 아니라 오답이다. (C)는 동태평양 주변의 나라들에 가장 심한 영향을 주었다 라는 내용이 없어 오답이다.

08

According to paragraph 6, which of the following is true of the worldwide impact of El Niño?

(A) El Niño's climatic impact causes disruptions in the natural world that lead to major non-climatic issues for humans across the globe.
(B) It has been proven that a 1℃ increase in the ocean's surface temperature yields a 20% increase in malaria-affected coastal ~~regions~~ of the tropical Pacific. ★
(C) ~~All~~ of the major conflicts that occurred during the 20th century began during an El Niño period.
(D) The El Niño that had an impact on the Northern Chinese Famine ~~also~~ triggered the French Revolution.

단락 6에 따르면, 엘니뇨 현상의 전 세계적 영향에 대해서 사실인 것은 무엇인가?

(A) 엘니뇨의 기후 영향은 자연 세계에서 방해를 일으켜 이는 전 세계사람들에게 큰 비기후적 일들로 이어진다.
(B) 바다의 표면 온도가 1도 올라갈수록 말라리아의 영향을 받은 열대 태평양의 ~~지역은~~ 20% 증가 한다는 사실은 증명이 되었다. ★
(C) 20세기에 일어난 ~~모든~~ 중요한 분쟁들은 엘니뇨 기간에 일어났다.
(D) 북 중국 가뭄에 영향을 끼친 엘니뇨는 프랑스 혁명 ~~또한~~ 유발하였다.

Fact 6단락을 살펴보면 In modern times, it has been found that El Niños effects have triggered 21% of conflicts worldwide since 1950. (현대 시기에 엘니뇨 현상의 영향이 1950 이후 21%의 분쟁을 일으켰다고 한다). 즉, 엘니뇨는 기후적 영향뿐만 아니라 비기후적 일들에도 영향을 미친다는걸 알 수 있다. 따라서 답은 (A)가 된다. (C)는 20세기의 모든 분쟁들이 엘니뇨 기간에 발생했다는 내용은 언급되지 않으므로 오답이고, (D)는 프랑스 혁명을 유발시킨 엘니뇨와 중국에게 영향을 준 엘니뇨는 전혀 다른 것이다. (B)는 말라리아 영향을 받은 지역이 증가한게 아니라 지문에선 말라리아 그 자체의 증가를 의미하는 것이기 때문에 오답이다.

09

Look at the four squares [■] that indicate where the following sentence could be added to the passage.

This rise of these nutritive waters provides the abundant food sources that are needed to sustain the nearly year-round commercial fishing industry off the coasts of Peru and Chile.

Where would the sentence best fit? Click on a square [■] to add the sentence to the passage.

2nd

네 개의 네모 [■]는 다음 문장이 삽입될 수 있는 부분을 나타내고 있다.

이런 영양분이 많은 물들의 상승은 페루와 칠레의 해안에 위치한 연중 계속 되는 상업적 어업을 유지 하는데 필요한 풍부한 음식을 제공한다.

이 문장은 어느 자리에 들어가는 것이 가장 적절한가?

2번째

Insertion 삽입 문장의 단서는 nutrient 이다. 2번째 네모의 전 문장에 As they reach the equator, the easterly trade winds blow the surface water back and allow an upwelling of cold, nutrient-rich waters. (이 물들이 적도를 도달하자 동쪽 무역풍이 표층수를 밀어내 차갑고 영양분이 풍부한 물의 용승을 불러일으킨다)가 나오며 풍부한 영양분을 가진 물에 대해 논한다. 또한 2번째 네모 다음 문장은 계절의 변화와 함께 영양분이 줄어든다는 내용이 나오니 정답은 2번째 네모가 된다.

10

Directions: An introductory sentence for a brief summary of the passage is provided below. Complete the summary by selecting the THREE answer choices that express the most important ideas in the passage. Some sentences do not belong in the summary because they express ideas that are not presented in the passage or are minor ideas in the passage. **This question is worth 2 points**

지시: 지문 요약을 위한 도입 문장이 아래에 주어져 있다. 지문의 가장 중요한 내용을 나타내는 보기 3개를 골라 요약을 완성 하시오. 어떤 문장은 지문에 언급되지 않은 내용이나 사소한 정보를 담고 있으므로 요약에 포함되지 않는다. **이 문제는 2점이다.**

> The term "El Niño" refers to climatic changes related to disturbances in the normal pattern of temperature, pressure, and winds in the southern Pacific Ocean.
>
> (A) The El Niño period has been experienced throughout history, but its incidence and intensity appear to have increased in modern times. - paragraph 5
> (D) The changes in atmospheric pressure, surface temperature, and wind strength are linked in a positive feedback loop that extends all of their effects during El Niño periods. - paragraph 4
> (F) Researchers have noted that the climatic changes of El Niño have coincided with many historical events not directly related to the weather, such as disease outbreaks and civil unrest. - paragraph 6

> 엘니뇨라는 용어는 남태평양의 온도, 압력 그리고 바람의 정상적 패턴이 방해받는 기후 변화와 관련된 것을 말한다.
>
> (A) 엘니뇨 기간은 과거 동안 계속 이어졌지만 이의 발생과 결렬함은 현대 시대에 증가했다.
> (D) 기압, 수면 온도 그리고 바람 강도의 변화는 엘니뇨 기간 동안 모든 효과들을 연장시키는 피드백 루프와 연결되었다.
> (F) 연구자들은 엘니뇨의 기후 변화가 병 발생과 시민들의 불안과 같이 기후와 직접적으로 연관없는 역사적 사건들과 동시에 일어났다는 점을 알아냈다.

(B) The easterly trade winds blow the surface water westward and allow an upwelling of cold, nutrient-rich waters that travel along the Humboldt Current toward the equator. - paragraph 1 minor
(C) Historical records indicate that the collapse of the early ~~South American civilization~~ was due to the effects of El Niño.- 언급안됨
(E) Gilbert Walker first recognized the relationship between the Southern Oscillation and the El Niño and ~~further came up with~~ the name of "El Niño-Southern Oscillation."- 반/반

(B) 동 무역풍은 표층수를 서쪽으로 밀면서 험볼트 해류를 통해 적도로 이동하는 차갑고 영양분이 풍부한 물의 용승을 일으킨다.
(C) 역사적 기록들이 초기 ~~남마문명의 붕괴는~~ 붕괴는 엘니뇨 현상에 의한 것임을 나타낸다.
(E) 길버트는 남방진동과 엘니뇨 사이의 상관관계를 처음으로 알아냈고 ~~남방진동 엘니뇨라고 이름도 지었다.~~

Summary 지문의 중심 내용은 엘니뇨 현상의 원리와 이의 영향력이다. (A)는 다섯 번째 단락의 중심내용인 엘니뇨 현상의 발생가능성과 심각성의 향상을 요약한 것과 일치하고, (D)는 네 번째 단락의 중심내용인 엘니뇨 요소들의 피드백 루프를 형성하는 상관관계와 일치하고,(F)는 여섯 번째 단락의 중심내용인 엘니뇨 현상의 부수적인 피해와 일치한다. 따라서 답은 (A), (D), (F)이다.

TEST 3-2 England's Sixteenth Century Economy
16세기 영국의 경제

Introduction	단락 1	엘리자베스 시대 영국 경제 개혁의 근본적인 배경 소개
Point	단락 2	인구 증가가 농업에 끼친 영향
Point	단락 3	부동산 소유 증가의 방법과 그에 대한 이유
Point	단락 4	지주들의 이윤창출 전략
Point	단락 5	농지에서 목초지로의 변화와 울타리 체계
Point	단락 6	양모생산과 가내 공업의 영향
Point	단락 7	영국 국제무역의 영향력과 식민지화

Painting by Hendrick Cornelisz Vroom

문단주제 / 본문내용 / 해석

단락 1
엘리자베스 시대 영국 경제 개혁의 근본적인 배경 소개

1 Great changes occurred in England during the Late Tudor Period **under the reign of** Queen Elizabeth I **in the latter half of** the sixteenth and early seventeenth centuries. One of the most notable was the **increase in** the population to nearly **that of** the pre-Black Death period. In England and Wales, increased fertility and reduced mortality rates nearly doubled the population around this time, increasing from 2.5 million in the 1520s to 4.5 million by 1610. This dramatic increase, **along with** other factors, **led to** vast changes in England's economy and **allowed it to become** Europe's largest, far surpassing those of the war and plague-ravaged continent.

16세기 후반부과 초기 17세기 엘리자베스 1세 통치하의 늦은 Tudor 시기의 영국에는 많은 변화가 발생했다. 이 중 가장 주목할 만한 변화는 인구가 흑사병 시기 전의 수로 증가한 것이다. 영국과 웨일스에는 출산율의 증가와 사망률의 감소로 인해 1520년대의 250만명에서 1610년의 450만명으로 거의 두 배 가까이 증가했다. 이런 극적인 증가는 다른 요소들과 함께 영국 경제에 큰 변화를 일으켰고, 영국 경제는 전염병과 전쟁으로 황폐화된 다른 지역들의 경제를 능가할 정도로 유럽에서 가장 커졌다.

단락 2
인구 증가가 농업에 끼친 영향

2 One of the first direct effects of the population increase was a **demand for** more food. [Q21-D] This caused an "agricultural revolution" in England 2-300 years before they occurred elsewhere in Europe. During this period, English farmers created farmlands from previously unsuitable areas, such as marshlands and woodlands, giving them more arable land on which to produce food. These farmers undertook a process of crop specialization that allowed them to be more efficient and market-driven, increasing their yields dramatically. For instance, they increased their grain production **per acre** by **at least** 30% between 1450 and 1650.

인구 증가의 첫째로 직접적인 영향이 끼친 것은 식량에 대한 수요였다. [Q21-D] 이것은 다른 유럽지역에서 발생하기 2~300년 전에 영국에서 "농업 혁명"을 일으켰다. 이 기간 동안, 영국의 농부들은 전에는 농사에 적합하지 않은 습지대나 삼림지대에서 농사를 짓기 시작했고 이것은 그들에게 식량을 기를 수 있는 더 넓은 땅을 제공했다. 이러한 농부들은 더 효율적이고 시장 주도적으로 생산하게 되었고 그들의 수확 량도 극적으로 증가시킨 경작 전문화 과정을 취했다. 예를 들어 그들은 에이커 당 곡물 생산량을 1450년과 1650년대 사이에 최소 30% 증가시킬 수 있었다.

Vocabulary

1단락
- reign [rein] v. 통치하다
- mortality rate [mɔːrtǽləti reit] n. 사망률
- notable [nóutəbəl] a. 주목할 만한
- plague [pleig] n. 흑사병
- fertility rate [fəːrtíləti reit] n. 출산율
- ravage [rǽvidʒ] v. 약탈하다

2단락
- revolution [rèvəlúːʃən] n. 혁명
- unsuitable [ʌ̀nsúːtəbəl] a. 부적당한
- yield [jiːld] v. 결실을 거두다
- marshland [maːrʃlænd] n. 습지대
- arable [ǽrəbəl] a. 경작 가능한
- acre [éikər] n. 에이커
- woodland [wúdlənd] n. 삼림지대
- specialization [spèʃəlizéiʃən] n. 전문화

단락 3
부동산 소유 증가의 방법과 그에 대한 이유

3   With the greater efficiency of the new farming methods, [Q22-D] **wealthy landowners increased their landholdings in order to increase** their agricultural productivity. These landholdings were consolidated through the practice of primogeniture under which the eldest son inherited the entirety of his father's holdings, [Q22-A] **thus preventing the great estates from being divided up into** smaller parcels which could not produce as much income. They also increased the size of their landholdings by **marrying into** other families with large estates. [Q22-B] Marriages amongst the wealthiest Elizabethan families were arranged to ensure that both families maintained their social statuses. With their larger estates, these families could conduct more commercialized farming to **meet the demand** for agricultural products, which was driving prices higher.

단락 4
지주들의 이윤창출 전략

4   These large landowners, and the yeomen who had smaller landholdings, maximized the profits they could **draw from** their property. To increase their profits, they planted crops which were in demand in the London markets. They also aggressively **dealt with** those to whom they rented their property. During this period, rents were increased and rental contracts were written to provide even more benefits to the landowners. One of the ways they did this was shortening the duration of their contracts to **allow themselves more control over** the land. Another way they maximized their profits was to charge potential tenants an "entry fee" before they would even **consent to** renting to them. Renters who could not, or would not, **abide by** the new contracts were simply evicted and replaced by those who could. Their tactics were quite one-sided, but they also **encouraged** their tenants **to use** farming practices that would increase their farming efficiency, such as crop rotation.

단락 5
농지에서 목초지로의 변화와 울타리 체계

5   Another method **used to increase** the profits of these large landholdings was to **convert** some of the farmland **into** pastureland upon which sheep could graze. [■] This conversion became possible because of the enclosure movement that occurred during the Tudor period. [■] [Q25-D] In the process of enclosure, open fields that had previously been

Vocabulary

3단락
- productivity [pròudʌktívəti] n. 생산성
- parcel [páːsəl] n. 일부분
- consolidate [kənsálədèiti] v. 강화하다
- commercialized [kəmə́ːrʃəlàiz] v. 상업화 하다
- inherit [inhérit] v. 상속받다
- primogeniture [pràimoudʒénətʃər] n. 장자의 신분

4단락
- aggressively [əgrésivly] a. 공격적으로
- evicte [ivíkt] v. 쫓아내다
- tenant [ténənt] n. 세입자
- tactic [tǽktik] n. 전술
- abide [əbáid] v. 머무르다
- efficiency [ifíʃənsi] n. 능률

5단락
- convert [kənvə́ːrt] v. 전환하다
- graze [greiz] v. 방목하다
- communal [kəmjúːnl] a. 공동의

used for communal farming, grazing and hay production were fenced and their use became the sole right of the owner. [■] Seeing the growing demands for English wool internationally, landholders often considered rearing sheep as a more profitable way to utilize their land. By converting their land into pastureland they could derive a higher profit while reducing the need for large numbers of workers to tend it.

단락 6
양모생산과 가내
공업의 영향

6   Wool production led to even greater **changes in** the English economy of the time. While English wool had exported since at least the 1200s, the form it was exported in **began to change**. Wool was traditionally exported **in** its raw **form**, but around this time the production and export of finished textiles overtook the English economy. This occurred through the cottage industry system under which a cloth manufacturer "put-out" work to rural craftspeople who were provided with raw wool, which they carded, spun, and wove in their own homes. This reduced textile costs because it effectively cut out the [Q26-C] guilds that controlled urban trade by creating monopolies and preventing competition between guild members.

단락 7
영국 국제무역의
영향력과
식민지화

7   During this period, the extent of England's international trade increased so markedly that companies, such as the Muscovy Company and the English East India Company, were chartered to develop monopolistic trade routes for English goods, such as wool textiles, with faraway places like Moscow and India. One of the major markets for these woolen textiles was the Spanish-controlled city of Antwerp where they were dyed and sold. Antwerp was so important a point that the English **kept a representative stationed** there permanently, Sir Thomas Gresham. Gresham increased England's reputation in Antwerp **to the point that** English merchants were able to **operate** on a **credit**-based system there, something very rare in the sixteenth century. [Q28-A] He also championed the economic possibilities of the Americas, leading to England's early **attempts to colonize** the continents **for** commercial **purposes**.

Vocabulary

pastureland [pǽstʃərlənd] n. 목초지
tend [tend] v. 돌보다

6단락
export [ikspɔ́:rt] v. 수출하다
card [ka:rd] v. 방모하다
finished [fíniʃt] a. 완성된
guild [gild] n. 길드
craftspeople [krǽftpì:pl] n. 장인
monopoly [mənápəli] n. 독과점

7단락
faraway [fá:rəwèi] a. 먼
chartered [tʃá:rtərd] a. 공인된
station [stéiʃən] v. 주둔하다
reputation [rèpjətéiʃən] n. 평판
credit [krédit] n. 신용
merchant [mə́:rtʃənt] n. 상인

11 According to paragraph 2, which of the following is true about agriculture in England during Late Tudor Period?

(A) The increase in England's population during this period led many farmers to ~~raise the prices~~ of their goods because of the increased demand for food.
(B) ~~Following~~ the pattern of continental Europe, agriculture in England went through an "agricultural revolution" that increased the amount of food they could produce. ★
(C) Farmers reclaimed lands such as marshlands and woodlands to be used as ~~pastures~~ upon which they could graze their livestock.
(D) Crop output was greatly increased through the development of new farming practices that wouldn't occur in Europe for a few more centuries.

단락 2에 의하면, 영국의 늦은 Tudor 시대의 농업에 대해 옳은 것은?

(A) 이 시대의 영국 인구의 증가는 식량의 수요 증가 때문에 농부들이 그들의 상품의 가격을 높아게 만들었다.
(B) 유럽 대륙의 방식에 따라, 영국의 농업은 농업 혁신을 겪었고 이것은 그들이 생산할 수 있는 식량을 증가시켰다. ★
(C) 농부들은 습지대와 삼림지대를 목초지로 변환시켜 가축들을 방목하기 위해 사용될 수 있게 했다.
(D) 곡물의 생산은 몇 세기 동안 등장하지 않을 새로운 농작 방법으로 인해 크게 증가했다.

> **Fact** 문제의 키워드인 agriculture in England during Late Tudor Period가 언급된 부분을 살펴보면 This caused an "agricultural revolution" in England 2~300 years before they occurred elsewhere in Europe. (이것은 영국에 다른 유럽지역에 2~300년 동안 등장하지 않 "농업의 혁명"을 일으켰다)라고 한다. 즉, 영국이 유럽보다 몇 세기에 앞서 새로운 농작 방법을 통해 곡물 생산을 크게 증가시켰다는 것이다. 따라서 답은 (D)가 된다. (A)는 농부들이 인구 증가 때문에 상품 가격을 높였다 라는 내용은 언급되지 않기 때문에 오답이고, (B)는 유럽 전체에 산업 혁명이 일어나기 전에 영국에서 가장 먼저 일어났기 때문에 오답이다. (C)는 농부들이 땅을 목초지가 아니라 농지로 변환시켰기 때문에 오답이다.

12 According to paragraph 3, which of the following is **NOT** true about the large family farms of the Elizabethan period?

(A) The great estates not divided into smaller parcels could produce much income.
(B) The possession of large farms was so important that many families arranged marriages for their children on the basis of increasing their landholdings.
(C) Under the practice of primogeniture inherited land could only be ~~divided~~ between the ~~sons~~ of a family, so daughters had no opportunity to gain large farms.
(D) During the Elizabethan period, large farms became more common as farmers looked for ways in which they could increase their agricultural output.

단락 3에 의하면, 엘리자베스 시대의 큰 가족단위 농지에 대해 옳지 않은 것은 무엇인가?

(A) 작은 부분들로 나누어지지 않은 거대한 사유지들은 많은 수익을 얻을 수 있었다.
(B) 큰 농지를 소유하는 것은 가족들이 자식들이 그들의 소유할 수 있는 토지를 넓히기 위함으로 결혼을 할만큼 중요했다.
(C) 상속제도에 따라 물려받은 토지는 가족의 ~~아들들~~ 사이 에서만 ~~분배~~가 가능했기 때문에 딸들은 큰 농지를 소유할 기회가 없었다.
(D) 엘리자베스 시대에 농부들이 그들의 농업적 생산량을 증가시킬 수 있는 방법을 찾았고 이것은 큰 농지를 더욱 일반적이게 만들었다.

> **Fact** 문제의 키워드인 large family farms of the Elizabethan period가 언급된 부분을 살펴보면 These landholdings were consolidated through the practice of primogeniture under which the eldest son inherited the entirety of his father's holdings. (이러한 토지는 장남을 통한 상속으로 통합되었다)라고 한다. 즉, 상속을 받을 수 있었던 유일한 사람은 장남이었기 때문에 (C)가 옳지 않은 내용이다. 따라서 정답은 (C)가 된다.

13 Why does the author mention "yeomen who had smaller landholdings" in paragraph 4?

(A) To give an example of the type of landowners who owned smaller landholdings ★
(B) To make the point that the maximization of profit from available land was not only reserved to the landed elite with large estates.
(C) To give a better idea of the different names used to refer to wealthy landowners during the sixteenth century.
(D) To contrast the amount of achievable profits between large and small landowners

저자가 단락 4에서 "작은 땅을 소유하고 있는 소작농들"을 언급한 이유는 무엇인가?

(A) 작은 땅을 가진 지주들의 유형에 대한 예를 들기 위해서 ★
(B) 농작 가능한 땅으로부터의 수익의 최대화는 반드시 많은 땅을 소유하고 있는 엘리트들만 가능한 것이 아닌것을 알려주기 위해서
(C) 16세기에 부유한 지주들에게 다른 명칭이 사용되었다는 것에 대한 더 좋은 아이디어를 주기 위해서
(D) 크고 작은 토지 소유자 사이에 달성할 수 있는 이익의 양을 대조하기 위해서

Purpose 음영 문구인 yeomen who had smaller landholdings이 언급된 부분을 살펴보면 These large landowners, and the yeomen who had smaller landholdings, maximized the profits they could draw from their property. (이러한 넓은 땅을 소유한 사람들과 작은 땅을 소유하고 있는 자작농들은 그들의 소유지에서 얻을 수 있는 최대한의 수익을 내었다)라고 말한다. 즉, 큰 땅을 소유하고 있던 엘리트가 아니라 소작농 농민들도 땅을 통해 이윤을 극대했다는 것이다. 따라서, 답은 (B)가 된다. (A)는 지주들 중에 작은 땅을 가진 사람들이 있다는 것은 사실이나, 언급한 이유는 아니기 때문에 오답이고, (C)는 소작농은 상류층의 또 다른 이름으로 언급되지 않기 때문에 오답이다. (D)는 지주들 사이에 누가 더 큰 이윤을 얻을 수 있었는지 대조하는 내용은 언급되지 않았으므로 오답이다.

14 The term "tactics" in the passage is closest in meaning to

(A) characteristics [kæriktərístik] ★
(B) results [rizʌ́lts]
(C) developments [divéləpmənt]
(D) strategies [strǽtədʒi]

지문의 단어 "전략"의 의미와 가장 유사한 것은?

(A) 특징 ★
(B) 결과
(C) 발전
(D) 계획

Vocabulary 지문의 tactics(전략)은 strategies(계획)와 동의어이므로 정답은 (D)이다.

15 According to paragraph 5, which of the following can be inferred about the process of enclosure?

(A) It reduced the numbers of workers who were willing to tend the pastureland. ★
(B) Enclosure allowed land owners to use public lands to graze the animals they would sell to make a communal profit.
(C) The process of enclosure was started to allow farmers during the Tudor era to plant crops, since they were more valuable than grazing livestock.
(D) Enclosure allowed some farmers to become very wealthy while denying others the ability to farm.

단락 5에서, 울타리를 치는 과정으로부터 무엇을 추론할 수 있는가?

(A) 목초지에서 일할 의사가 있는 노동자들의 숫자를 감소시켰다. ★
(B) 울타리 방법은 지주들이 공공의 토지를 공동의 수익을 위해 동물을 방목시켜 판매하여 수익을 내게끔 했다.
(C) 울타리 방법은 양들보다 곡물이 더 귀중했기 때문에 농부들이 튜더 시대 때 곡식을 심을 수 있게 하기 위해 시작되었다.
(D) 울타리 방법은 몇몇의 농부들이 다른 사람들이 그 땅에 농작하는 것을 거부하며 아주 부유해질 수 있도록 해주었다.

Inference   지문의 키워드인 process of enclosure가 언급된 부분을 살펴보면 In the process of enclosure, open fields that had previously been used for communal farming, grazing and hay production were fenced and their use became the sole right of the owner. (울타리 체계의 과정으로 이전에는 공동으로 농사를 짓던 개방된 땅에 울타리를 쳐 방목과 건초 생산이 가능하게끔 만든 후 이 땅은 한 명의 지주에게 넘겨졌다)라고 한다. 즉, 땅에 대해 권리를 가지지 못한 농부들은 그 땅에서 농사를 지을 수 없었다는 것이다. 따라서 답은 (D)가 된다. (A)는 일할 의사가 있는 노동자들이 아니라 농장에서 필요로 하는 노동자들의 숫자가 감소한 것이기 때문에 오답이고, (B)는 공동의 이익이 아니라 개인 이익을 만들려고 한 것이므로 오답이다. (C)는 곡식을 심으려고 울타리 방법이 시작된 것이 아니라 동물들을 방목하기 위해서 시작된 것이므로 오답이다.

---

16   What can be inferred about the influence of the guild system from paragraph 6?

(A) The guild system ~~effectively protected~~ industries in areas where competition ~~had prevented~~ rural manufactures from entering the market.
(B) The guilds in the cities were ~~unaware~~ of the goods manufactured in the countryside. ★
(C) The guilds in the cities made it more expensive to have products manufactured in the cities than in the countryside.
(D) The ~~guilds~~ put-out work to rural craftsman, further reinforcing their monopoly in the city.

단락 6에서 길드 시스템으로부터 추론할 수 있는 것은 무엇인가?

(A) 길드 시스템은 경쟁이 외곽지 제조업자들이 시장에 들어오는 ~~것을 막아왔던~~ 지역에서의 산업을 효과적으로 ~~보호해 왔다.~~
(B) 도시에 있는 길드들은 시골에서 생산된 상품들이 존재하는지 ~~몰랐다.~~ ★
(C) 도시에 있는 길드들은 시골에서 생산되는 것보다 도시에서 생산하는 것을 더욱 비싸게 만들었다.
(D) ~~길드는~~ 외부 장인들에게 일을 분배해서 도시 내에서의 그들의 독점을 더 강화했다.

Inference   문제의 키워드인 influence of the guild system이 언급된 부분을 살펴보면 the guilds that controlled urban trade by creating monopolies and preventing competition between guild members (독과점을 형성하고 멤버들 사이의 경쟁을 방지하며 도시 무역을 통제하였던 길드)라고 한다. 즉, 도시의 길드 멤버들은 효과적으로 경쟁을 제거시킴으로써 도시에서 상품을 생산하는 것을 더 어렵고 비싸게 만들었다는걸 유추 할 수 있다. (A)길드 시스템은, 외부 제조업자들이 시장을 들어오는 것을 효과적으로 막지 못하였고, 도심지의 산업도 효과적으로 보호하지도 못하였으므로 오답이고, (D)는 길드가 아닌 새로운 옷 제조업자가 주체여야 하는데, 주체가 짝이 잘못되어 오답이다. (B)는 도시 길드 멤버들이 시골에서 생산되는 상품들의 존재여부를 몰랐다 라는 내용은 언급되지 않으므로 오답이다.

---

17   Which of the sentences below best expresses the essential information in the highlighted sentence in the passage? Incorrect choices change the meaning in important ways or leave out essential information.

(A) The establishment of trade companies like the Muscovy and English East India Companies secured monopolies over trade routes to distant lands for English products like wool textiles, ~~stirring~~ an increase in international trade.
(B) Elizabethan England saw a great increase in the amount of international trade being ~~done~~ by companies such as the Muscovy Company and the English East India Company which had monopolies over selling woolen textiles made in Moscow and India. ★
(C) ii) Companies like the Muscovy Company and the English East India Company were started to establish monopolistic trade routes with far-flung locales such as Moscow and India for products like English wool.
(D) i) During the sixteenth century, influenced by England's increased reputation in international trade, ii) several privileged English companies developed monopolistic trade routes with distant locales such as Moscow and India.

아래의 문장 중 지문 속의 음영 표시된 문장의 핵심 정보를 가장 잘 표현하고 있는 것은 무엇인가? 오답은 문장의 의미를 현저하게 바꾸거나 핵심 정보를 빠트리고 있다.

(A) Muscovy Company와 영국 동인도 회사와 같은 무역 회사의 창립은 양털 옷감과 같은 영국 상품을 위한 먼 지역까지의 무역로의 독점을 확보하였고 이것은 국제교류의 증가를 ~~커져왔다.~~
(B) 엘리자베스 시대의 영국은 모스크바와 인도~~에서 만들어진~~ 양털의 옷감을 판매하는 독점을 갖고 있었던 Muscovy Company와 영국 동인도 회사와 같은 회사와 국제교류의 규모의 증가를 봤다. ★
(C) ii) Muscovy Company와 영국 동인도 회사와 같은 회사들은 모스크바와 인도와 같은 먼 곳에 있는 독점의 무역로를 영국산 양털을 위해 설립하기 위해 시작했다.
(D) i) 16세기 때 국제무역에서 높아진 영국의 명성에 영향을 받아, ii) 여러 특권을 가진 영국 회사들이 모스크바와 인도와 같은 먼 장소들과 독점 무역 노선을 개발하였다.

Highlight 음영 표시된 문장은 i) During this period, the extent of England's international trade increased so markedly that ii) companies, such as the Muscovy Company and the English East India Company, were chartered to develop monopolistic trade routes for English goods, such as wool textiles, with faraway places like Moscow and India. (i) 이 기간 중, 영국 국제교류의 규모는 크게 급증하여 ii) Muscovy Company와 영국 동인도 회사와 같은 회사들은 모스크바와 인도로부터 양털 옷감과 같은 영국 상품에 대한 무역로를 독점하기 위해 창립되었다) 이렇게 두 가지 내용으로 나뉜다. 이 내용을 모두 포함한 (D)가 정답이 된다. (A)가 틀린 이유는 회사의 창립과 무역로가 생긴 것에 대한 인과관계가 반대로 되어있기 때문이다. (B)는 Muscovy Company와 동인도 회사는 영국이 무역을 한 회사가 아니라 영국의 회사이기 때문에 오답이고, (C)는 i)를 포함하고 있지 않기 때문에 오답이다.

18

What is the purpose of including paragraph 7 in the passage?

(A) To show how the increased trade networks for English goods during this period led to major changes such as the colonization of the Americas
(B) To give an idea of how important ~~Sir Thomas Gresham~~ was in the international trade of wool textiles from England
(C) To point out ~~differences~~ in the way trade was conducted in Antwerp and in the Americas
(D) To explain ~~why~~ companies such as the English East India Company and the Muscovy Company developed monopolistic trade routes ★

단락 7을 지문에 넣은 이유는 무엇인가?

(A) 이 시대에 영국의 증가된 무역로가 어떻게 아메리카 대륙으로의 식민지화로 이어졌는지 보여주기 위해서
(B) ~~Sir Thomas Gresham~~ 경이 영국 양모섬유 국제무역에서 얼마나 중요한 역할을 했는지 알려주기 위해서
(C) Antwerp와 아메리카 대륙에서 거래된 방법의 ~~차이~~를 나타내기 위해서
(D) 영국 동인도 회사와 Muscovy Company가 ~~왜~~ 독과점적인 무역로를 개발했는지 설명하기 위해서 ★

Purpose 단락 7의 마지막 부분인 He also championed the economic possibilities of the Americas, leading to England's early attempts to colonize the continents for commercial purposes. (또한 그는 미국대륙에서의 경제적 가능성을 도모하였고 이것은 영국이 초기에 상업적인 목적으로 식민지화를 시도한 일을 초래했다)를 보면 경제적 성장이 영국이 초기에 상업적인 목적으로 식민지화를 시도한 일을 초래했다는걸 알 수 있다. 즉, 단락 7의 목적은 아메리카 대륙의 식민지화의 이유를 알려주기 위함이다. (B)는 Sir Thomas Gresham의 중요성은 양모섬유 국제 무역이 아니라 국제무역 확장과 경제 성장에 기여했다는 점에서 두각을 나타냈기 때문에 오답이고, (C)는 두 지역의 거래방법의 차이점은 언급되지 않아서 오답이다. (D)는 이 두 회사가 왜 독과점적인 무역로를 개발했는지에 대한 내용은 언급되지 않아 오답이다.

19

Look at the four squares [■] that indicate where the following sentence could be added to the passage.

Seeing the growing demands for English wool internationally, landholders often considered rearing sheep as a more profitable way to utilize their land.

Where would the sentence best fit? Click on a square [■] to add the sentence to the passage.

4th

네 개의 네모 [■]는 다음 문장이 삽입될 수 있는 부분을 나타내고 있다.

영국 양털의 국제적으로 늘어나는 수요를 본 지주들은 자신들의 땅으로 양을 기르는데 사용하는 것이 더 많은 수익을 낼 것이라고 생각했다.

이 문장은 어느 자리에 들어가는 것이 가장 적절한가?

4번째

Insertion 삽입문장은 왜 지주들이 땅을 목초지로 만들었는지에 대한 이유를 설명해준다. 네 번째 박스 다음 문장에선 땅을 목초지로 전환하면서 더 높은 수익성을 얻을 수 있었다고 주장한다. 즉, 두 번째 네모 앞 목초지 전환, 세 번째 네모 앞 Enclosure Movement 소개, 네 번째 네모 앞 Enclosure Movement의 설명, 그리고 Insert 문장은 Enclosure Movement를 적극적으로 사용하게 된 이유. 따라서 정답은 네 번째 네모이다.

20

Directions: An introductory sentence for a brief summary of the passage is provided below. Complete the summary by selecting the THREE answer choices that express the most important ideas in the passage. Some sentences do not belong in the summary because they express ideas that are not presented in the passage or are minor ideas in the passage. **This question is worth 2 points.**

지시: 지문 요약을 위한 도입 문장이 아래에 주어져 있다. 지문의 가장 중요한 내용을 나타내는 보기 3개를 골라 요약을 완성 하시오. 어떤 문장은 지문에 언급되지 않은 내용이나 사소한 정보를 담고 있으므로 요약에 포함되지 않는다. **이 문제는 2점이다.**

England's economy underwent many changes during the Elizabethan period.

(A) Increased demand for English wool textiles led to many landowners converting their farmlands into pastureland on which sheep could graze and brought about the practice of enclosure across rural England.
　　　　　　　　　　　　　　　　　　　　　- paragraph 5

(B) The dramatic increase in population during the sixteenth century raised the demand for food, thereby making farming, and consequently landownership, a very lucrative field and induced an agricultural revolution in England.
　　　　　　　　　　　　　　　　　　　　- paragraph 2, 3, 4

(D) The export of wool textiles was very lucrative for the English government and it helped spur their further exploration and colonization of the Americas.
　　　　　　　　　　　　　　　　　　　　　- paragraph 7

영국의 경제는 엘리자베스 시대 때 많은 변화를 겪었다.

(A) 영국산 양털 옷감의 늘어나는 수요는 많은 지주들이 그들의 땅을 농작용으로부터 양을 방목할 수 있는 목초지로 바꾸게 하였고 이것은 영국 시골에 서의 울타리 방식을 야기시켰다.

(B) 16세기의 극적인 인구 증가는 식량에 대한 수요를 높였고 결국 농업 그리고 더 나아가 토지를 소유 하는 것을 돈벌이가 되는 업으로 만들었고 이것은 농업 혁신을 유도했다.

(D) 양털 옷감의 수출은 큰 돈벌이가 될 수 있었고 영국 정부는 이것으로 아메리카 대륙의 식민지화에 박차를 가했다.

(C) In the sixteenth century, the introduction of a credit-based system in Antwerp ~~contributed~~ to England's increased reputation in the world. - 틀린 정보

(E) The tradition of marriages among the wealthiest families allowed them to make the most profit from their landholdings. - paragraph 3 detail

(F) From the 16th to the 17th century, there was a great increase in the number of people in England and Wales because of ~~hygienic improvements~~. - 틀린 정보

(C) 16세기에 신용 시스템의 소개는 전 세계에서 영국의 명성을 높이는데 ~~기여했다~~.

(E) 부유층 간의 결혼 관습은 양가가 그들의 소유지로 부터 최대의 수익을 낼 수 있도록 하였다.

(F) 16세기와 17세기 사이에, ~~위생적인 발전덕분에~~ 잉글랜드 인구 수가 증가했다.

Summary　　지문의 중심 내용은 영국경제의 개혁이다. (A)는 다섯 번째 단락의 중심내용인 농지에서 목초지로의 변화와 일치하기 때문에 정답이고, (B)는 첫 번째와 두 번째 단락의 중심내용인 인구 증가가 농업에 끼친 영향과 일치하여 정답이고, (D)는 일곱 번째 단락의 영국 국제무역의 영향력과 식민지화와 일치하기 때문에 정답이다. (E), (F)는 각각 일곱 번째, 세 번째, 첫 번째 단락에 언급되는 내용이지만 모두 미미한 내용을 설명했으므로 오답이다. (C)는 틀린 정보이므로 오답이다.

USHER iBT TOEFL
INTERMEDIATE READING

TEST 4
답안 및 취약 유형 분석표

해석·해설

답안 및 문제 유형 분석표

TEST 4-1

01 (A) Inference

02 (D) Highlight

03 (D) Vocabulary

04 (C) Fact

05 (B) Purpose

06 (B) Fact

07 (A) Fact

08 (C) Inference

09 4th ■ Insertion

10 (A), (D), (F) Summary

TEST 4-2

11 (A) Inference

12 (A), (C) Fact

13 (C) Reference

14 (D) Inference

15 (A) Vocabulary

16 (D) Purpose

17 (A), (C) Inference

18 (A) Highlight

19 3rd ■ Insertion

20 (B), (C), (E) Summary

각 문제 유형별 맞춘 개수를 아래에 적어 보세요.

유형	맞춘 답의 개수	정답률	
단어 (Vocabulary)	/ 2	정답률:	%
사실 확인 문제 (Fact)	/ 4	정답률:	%
지시어 찾기 (Reference)	/ 1	정답률:	%
끼워 넣기 (Insertion)	/ 2	정답률:	%
문장 변환문제 (Highlight)	/ 2	정답률:	%
목적 (Purpose)	/ 2	정답률:	%
추론 (Inference)	/ 5	정답률:	%
단락 요약(Summary / Category Chart)	/ 2	정답률:	%
전체	/20	정답률:	%

※ 자신이 취약한 유형은 READING STRATEGIES를 통해 다시 한번 점검하시기 바랍니다. (p.44)

TEST 4-1 Environmental Impact of the Anasazi 아나사지의 환경적인 영향

Introduction	단락 1	아나사지, 이전에 유행했던 떠남의 이론, 그리고 콜러의 새 이론에 대한 소개
Point	단락 2	언제 정착했는지와 떠남의 추정된 이유
Point	단락 3	큰 마을로 정착하기 이전의 아나사지의 삶
Point	단락 4	인간과 자연 사이의 교류의 변화에 따른 증거
Point	단락 5	마을을 세운 이유와 그것이 야기한 문제들이 떠남을 불러일으킨 방법

Photo by Tadam, available under the Creative Commons Attribution-Share Alike 4.0 International, 3.0 Unported, 2.5 Generic, 2.0 Generic and 1.0 Generic license.

문단주제	본문내용	해석
단락 1 아나사지, 이전에 유행했던 떠남의 이론, 그리고 콜러의 새 이론에 대한 소개	**1** The Anasazi people, ancient Native Americans who **resided in** pit houses, pueblos, and cliff dwellings, flourished in America's present-day Four Corners region before suddenly abandoning their elaborate villages and palace complexes. Archeologists long thought that studies of the rings of the trees used in the structures found there indicated that these people had been driven from their villages and home region, **due to** a climatic event **known as** the "Great Drought." This, however, **began to be called into question** recently. Today, historians believe that the Anasazi evacuation had been occurring before the "Great Drought" and that the drought was not an unprecedented event; villagers had likely survived others before it. This has **left them researching** what **could have actually caused** an entire civilization **to abandon** its home territory. Archeologist Tim Kohler has **come up with** one possible explanation, human **interaction with** the natural environment.	옛날 북미 원주민이었던 아나사지 민족은 오늘날 미국의 포코너 지역에서 구덩이 집, 읍, 그리고 절벽 집에 살았었는데, 갑자기 그들의 화려한 마을과 궁궐들을 버리고 떠났다. 고고학자들은 그곳에서 발견된 건물들에 쓰인 나무의 나이테를 이용한 조사를 통해 그들이 기후와 관련된 사건인 "Great Drought"(거대한 가뭄) 때문에 자기 마을과 주거 지역에서 쫓겨났다고 오랫동안 생각해왔다. 하지만 최근에는 이것에 대하여 의문점이 제기되고 있다. 오늘날 역사가들은 아나사지 마을들의 대피가 "Great Draught" 이전에도 진행되고 있었다고 믿고 이 가뭄은 유례없는 가뭄이 아니었으며 이것 전의 가뭄들도 아나사지 마을사람들은 견뎌냈다고 믿는다. 이 사실은 역사가들이 무엇이 진짜로 이 문명을 주거지를 버리고 떠나게 했는지에 대해 조사 하게 만들었다. 고고학자 팀 콜러는 가능할지도 모르는 한가지 설명을 제기했으며 이것은 자연과 인간간의 상호 작용이다.
단락 2 언제 정착했는지와 떠남의 추정된 이유	**2** Kohler believes that the Anasazi's interactions with their surroundings eventually **led to** their downfall. To support his hypothesis, Kohler **put forth** a case study regarding the Anasazi living in southwestern Colorado's Dolores River basin around 600 A.D. **Over** a few hundred years, their population increased greatly and they built large villages **complete**	콜러는 아나사지와 주변과의 교류가 결국 자기들이 망하게 되는 원인이었다고 생각한다. 이 가설을 뒷받치기 위해서 콜러는 600AD쯤에 남서 콜로라도에 있는 돌로레스 강가 유역에 살던 아나사지 사람들에 대한 사례 연구를 제기했다. 그들이 그 지역을 버리고 떠나기 시작한 900 A.D.경까지, 몇 백년에 걸쳐 그들의 인구는 급격히 증가하였고

Vocabulary

1단락 pueblo [pwéblou] n. 읍 archaeologist [à:rkiáládʒist] n. 고고학자 tree ring [trí: riŋ] n. 나이테
drought [draut] n. 가뭄 interaction [ìntərǽkʃən] n. 상호 관계

2단락 hypothesis [haipάθəsis] n. 가설 basin [béisən] n. 유역 kiva [kivé] n. 키바 (종교 의식이나 회의에 쓰인 큰 방)
agricultural [ǽgrikʌ́ltʃərəl] a. 농업의 deforestation [di:fɔ́:risʃən] n. 삼림 벌채 depletion [diplí:ʃən] n. 고갈

with kivas and Great Houses, until around 900 A.D. when the area's abandonment began. Many archeologists believe that shortened growing seasons occurred during this era, which **would have made** it difficult to produce the main Anasazi staple, corn. Kohler **takes exception** to this theory, however, and **points to** [Q1-A] problems that developed due to this growing population's settlement in villages, which caused a pressing **need for** increased agricultural output, forcing **changes in** the Anasazi's interactions with the environment, leading to deforestation, soil depletion, and their eventual abandonment of the area.

단락 3
큰 마을로 정착하기 이전의 아나사지의 삶

3 [■] [Q5-B] **Prior to** their settlement, the Anasazi population had been semi-nomadic in the Dolores River basin, farming the reasonably fertile, thin soils of the flat-topped mesas using the swidden, or slash-and-burn, technique for over 1,000 years. [■] Using this method, they **burned down** forests to plant the crops they needed and utilized the new farmland until it became **unsuitable for** producing crops, at which time they **moved on to** an adjacent area and repeated the process, **allowing** the previous area **to lie fallow** and replenish the nutrients necessary **for** its future use. [■] This may **appear to be** a destructive way of growing food that ruins the land, but [Q4-C] with less dense populations and a schedule of movement that allows the land adequate time for replenishment between planting, swidden is a sustainable **means of** acquiring the food that societies need. [■] Kohler's contention was that the permanent settlement of a large, growing population like the Dolores River basin Anasazi relying upon this method would lead to their eventual destruction.

단락 4
인간과 자연 사이의 교류의 변화에 따른 증거

4 Kohler found several types of evidence to show that changes in human-environmental interactions were more **responsible for** the Anasazi disappearance than climatic events. Surprisingly, his first source was the same as the one that had led archeologists astray, trees. Kohler noted a pattern in the types of wood found in charcoal deposits from

Vocabulary

3단락
- fertile [fə́ːrtl] a. 비옥한
- swidden [swídn] n. 화전
- dense [dens] a. 밀집한
- mesa [mèisə] n. 메사 (꼭대기는 평평하고 등성이는 벼랑으로 된 언덕)
- fallow [fǽlou] a. 쉬고 있는
- sustainable [səstéinèibəl] a. 지속 가능한
- replenish [riplèniʃ] v. 다시 충전하다

4단락
- astray [əstréi] ad. 길을 잃고
- shrubbery [ʃrʌ́bəri] n. 관목숲
- charcoal [tʃɑ́ːrkòul] n. 숯
- cottonwood [kátnwùd] n. 미루나무
- deposit [dipázit] n. 침전물
- propagate [prápəgèit] v. 번식하다

different periods. It **seemed that** juniper and pinion pine **were replaced by** faster growing shrubbery and cottonwoods. [Q6-C] He also discovered that the Anasazi **switched from** using pinion pines for construction **to** younger juniper trees, a less desirable wood source, but one that is more fire resistant and easier to propagate in open settings. This, likely, indicated that the pinion became scarcer around the village as the growing population's **demand increased**. This would have also affected their **food supply** as pinion seeds were also gathered as a food source. Additionally, their clearing of the surrounding areas would have had an impact on their hunting **as well. As time progressed**, the Anasazi apparently switched from hunting woodland rabbits and deer to jackrabbits and antelope, species **native to** open environments. Seeds **excavated from** the settlements provided Kohler's final piece of evidence. [Q6-D] During excavation of later settlements, a marked **increase in** pioneer species seeds was found, indicating a disturbance in the natural environment.

단락 5
마을을 세운 이유와 그것이 야기한 문제들이 떠남을 불러일으킨 방법

5   Kohler postulates that the Anasazi aggregated in villages due to the organizational benefits they offered **in the face of** soil depletion during their early periods. [Q7-D] These large settlements allowed them to share food, **invest in** group food processing units and pool their labor for longer distance hunting or trading trips. [Q7-C] Settling in one area, however, **brought about** new problems, like soil depletion and increased distance to usable fields, which led to increased agricultural risk. [Q8-C] This led to agricultural intensification using methods, such as developing mechanisms to better control water flow. These larger villages with more technical agricultural methods produced more food, but were more **susceptible to** a rapid collapse. [Q7-B] The cooperative management of resources for the village meant that they were less flexible in response to environmental changes, so a weak growing season **had** a widespread **impact on** the village. **For this reason**, even a minor, predictable climate change could have **led** the Anasazi **to abandon** their settlements.

Vocabulary

scarce [skɛərz] a. 부족한
excavation [èkskəvéiʃən] n. 발굴

5단락 postulate [pástʃəlèit] v. 상정하다
mechanism [mékənìzəm] n. 기계

jackrabbit [dʒǽkrӕbit] n. 산토끼

aggregate [ǽgrigèit] v. 모이다
susceptible [səséptəbəl] a. 민감한

antelope [ǽntəlòup] n. 영양

process [práses] v. 처리하다

01
What can be inferred from paragraph 2 about Tim Kohler's theory regarding the disappearance of the Anasazi?

(A) He believed that human activity was a more direct cause of the downfall of the Anasazi than weather patterns.
(B) He found it ~~difficult~~ to believe that corn was the main staple of the Anasazi population at the time. ★
(C) He chose to study the Dolores River basin villages because the "Great Drought" had not affected them as ~~much as~~ it had other tribes.
(D) He felt that the environment had nothing to do with the disappearance and that it was ~~entirely~~ caused by human beings.

단락 2에서 아나사지가 사라진 이유에 대한 팀 콜러의 이론에 대해 추론할 수 있는 것은?

(A) 그는 기후 패턴보다 인간의 활동이 아나사지의 몰락의 더 직접적인 원인이라고 믿었다.
(B) 그는 옥수수가 그 당시에 아나사지의 주식 이었다는걸 믿기 ~~힘들어했다~~. ★
(C) 그는 돌로레스 강 유역의 마을들을 조사하기로 한 이유는 great drought이 그들에게 영향을 덜 줬다고 믿었기 때문이다.
(D) 그는 아나사지의 사라짐은 환경과 전혀 관계가 없다고 생각했고 ~~오로지~~ 인간들에 의해 일어난 일이라고 생각했다.

Inference 질문의 키워드인 Tim Kohler's theory가 언급된 부분을 살펴보면 problems that developed due to this growing population's settlement in villages, which caused a pressing need for increased agricultural output, forcing changes in the Anasazi's interactions with the environment, leading to deforestation, soil depletion, and their eventual abandonment of the area. (자라나는 인구의 마을들이 더 많은 농사물을 필요로 해서 아나사지가 환경과 상호작용을 하는 방식을 바꾼 삼림벌채, 토양 고갈, 그리고 결국은 그 지역을 떠나게함을 초래했다 고 믿는다)라고 말한다. 즉, 많은 학자들이 짧아진 재배기간이 아나사지가 그 지역을 떠난 주 원인이라고 믿었던 반면, 콜러는 아나사지가 늘어 나는 인구 수를 수용하기 위해 환경과 상호작용 하는 방법을 바꾸었고 이것이 그들을 결국 떠나게 만들었다라고 주장했다. 따라서 정답은 (A)가 된다. (B)는 콜러는 옥수수가 아나사지의 주식이었다는 사실은 부정하지 않았으므로 오답이고, (C)는 언급된 내용이 아니므로 오답이다. (D)는 오로지 인간들의 책임인 것이 아니라 인간과 자연 사이의 상호작용이 문제였기 때문에 오답이다.

02
Which of the sentences below best expresses the essential information in the highlighted sentence in the passage? Incorrect choices change the meaning in important ways or leave out essential information.

(A) ii) Kohler believed that the radical farming practices the Anasazi employed to increase agricultural output made the land inarable and rather prohibited its population from growing further. ★
(B) ~~Consenting~~ to other archaeologists, he ~~also~~ believed that the need to increase food production led to environmental problems that eventually forced the Anasazi away.
(C) Kohler tried to ~~convince~~ other archeologists that the deforestation and soil depletion caused by the Anasazi settlements was a result of environmental changes that eventually caused the villagers to abandon their homes.
(D) i) Kohler disagreed with other archeologists and thought that the removal of trees, soil nutrients and the fleeing of the Anasazi were brought about by iii) manmade environmental changes caused by the settlement in villages, ii) which increased their need for food.

아래의 문장 중 지문 속의 음영 표시된 문장의 핵심 정보를 가장 잘 표현하고 있는 것은 무엇인가? 오답은 문장의 의미를 현저하게 바꾸거나 핵심 정보를 빠트리고 있다.

(A) ii) 콜러는 농업 출력을 증가시키기 위해 아나사지가 사용했던 급진적인 농업 관행은 땅이 곡식을 경작할 수 없도록 만들었고 인구가 더 이상 증가하지 못하도록 막았다. ★ (중요 정보 빠짐)
(B) 다른 고고학자들과 ~~동의했던~~ 콜러는 음식 재배를 더 증가시켜야 했던 아나사지가 환경적인 문제를 초래했으며 이것이 그들을 떠나게 만들었다~~고도~~ 생각했다.
(C) 콜러는 아나사지 거주지의 삼림벌채와 토양 고갈 등 환경적 변화는 그들이 결국 떠나게된 이유라는 것을 다른 고고학자들에게 ~~설득하려고~~ 했다.
(D) i) 콜러는 다른 고고학자들과 동의하지 않았으며 나무와 토양 영양분의 고갈, 그리고 아나사지의 떠남은 마을에 살게 되면서 iii) 음식에 대한 수요가 증가하여 생긴 ii) 환경에 인간이 준 변화 때문이었다고 생각한다.

Highlight 음영 표시된 문장은 i) Kohler takes exception to this theory, however, and ii) points to problems that developed due to this growing population's settlement in villages, which caused a pressing need for increased agricultural output, iii) forcing changes in the Anasazi's interactions with the environment, leading to deforestation, soil depletion, and their eventual abandonment of the area. (i) 콜러는 이 이론과 동의를 하지 않으며 ii) 마을의 인구 증가가 초래한 문제들을 가리킨다. 이 문제들은 증가된 농사물 재배를 요구했는데, iii) 이것이 아나사지가 자연과 갖는 상호관계를 바꿨으며 이 때문에 삼림 벌채, 토양 고갈, 그리고 그 지역을 버리고 떠나는 것을 야기했다) 이렇게 세 가지 내용으로 나뉜다. 이 내용을 모두 포함한 (D)가 정답이 된다. (A)는 아나사지가 그 지역을 벗어났다는 내용과 콜러가 다른 학자들과 다르게 생각했다는 내용이 없으므로 오답이고, (B)는 콜러는 다른 고고학자들과 동의하지 않았기 때문에 오답이다. (C)는 콜러가 다른 학자들을 설득하려고 했다는 내용은 언급되지 않으므로 오답이다.

03

The term "replenish" in the passage is closest in meaning to

(A) rearrange [rìːəréindʒ]
(B) replace [ripléis]
(C) repair [ripɛ̀ər] ★
(D) refill [riːfíl]

지문의 단어 "보충하다"의 의미와 가장 유사한 것은?

(A) 재정리하다
(B) 대체하다
(C) 고치다 ★
(D) ~을 다시 채우다

Vocabulary 지문의 replenish(보충하다)는 refill(~을 다시 채우다)와 동의어이므로 정답은 (D)이다.

04

According to paragraph 3, which of the following is true about the slash-and-burn technique?

(A) It is rarely a productive way of growing food because it leads to the total depletion of the nutrients in soil.
(B) It is a sustainable means of acquiring the food should the population be dense. ★
(C) If properly conducted, it can fulfill the food production needs of a small civilization.
(D) Although it destroys the environment, it is necessary for civilizations that have settled in one place to produce food.

단락 3에 의하면 베고 태우기 기법에 대한 사실은?

(A) 토양의 영양분을 완전히 고갈시키기 때문에 이것은 음식을 생산하는데 있어서 거의 생산적인 방법이 아니다.
(B) 인구가 밀집되어 있으면 이것은 음식을 얻는 지속 가능한 방법이다. ★
(C) 제대로 사용된다면 작은 문명의 음식 생산 요구를 채울 수 있다.
(D) 환경을 파괴하지만, 정착한 문명들이 음식을 생산하는 데에는 필요한 기법이다.

Fact 질문의 키워드인 slash-and-burn technique이 언급된 부분을 살펴보면 with less dense populations and a schedule of movement that allows the land adequate time for replenishment between planting, swidden is a sustainable means of acquiring the food that societies need ([slash-and-burn technique]은 덜 밀집된 인구와 영양분 재충전에 충분한 시간을 주는 스케줄로 이동을 한다면 화전 방식은 그 지역 사람들이 필요로 하는 음식을 지속적으로 제공할 수 있는 방법이었다)라고 말한다. 즉, 작은 문명에겐 효과적인 기법이었다는걸 알 수 있다. 따라서 정답은 (C)가 된다. (A)는 This may appear to be a destructive way of growing food that ruins the land, but with less dense populations and a schedule of movement that allows the land adequate time for replenishment between planting, swidden is a sustainable means of acquiring the food that societies need. 즉, 이 기법은 덜 밀집된 인구와 영양분이 재충전 할 수 있는 충분한 시간을 주며 사용하면 필요로 하는 음식을 지속적으로 제공해주기 때문에 rarely(거의 ~않는) 생산적이지 않다는 것은 오답이다. (B)는 인구가 밀집되어 있지 않은 전제하에 지속 가능한 기법이기 때문에 오답이다. (D)는 slash-and-burn 기법은 파괴이지 않기 때문에 오답이다.

05

Why does the author mention the Anasazi's use of "swidden, or slash-and-burn, technique." in paragraph 3?

(A) To make the point that humans have known how to convert forestland into arable meadowland for many generations
(B) To introduce one way that early farmers utilized the environment to produce the food they needed

단락 3에서 작가가 아나사지의 "화전 방식"을 언급한 이유는?

(A) 인간들은 숲을 농작이 가능한 벌판으로 만드는 방법을 오랫동안 알고 있었다는 것을 밝히기 위해서
(B) 옛날 농사꾼들이 음식을 재배하기 위해 환경을 사용한 한 가지 예를 소개하기 위해서

(C) To explain how the Anasazi returned nutrients to the soil after they had overused it ★
(D) To show one of the farming methods that works well for a lifestyle after leaving its sedentary settlement

(C) 아나사지가 땅을 너무 많이 쓴 다음에 거기에 영양분이 돌아오도록 어떻게 했는지 설명하기 위해서 ★
(D) 한 곳에 머무는 정착지를 떠난 후에 사용하기 좋은 농사 방법을 보여주기 위해서

Purpose 음영 표시된 부분을 살펴보면 Prior to their settlement, the Anasazi population had been semi-nomadic in the Dolores River basin, farming the reasonably fertile, thin soils of the flat-topped mesas using the swidden, or slash-and-burn, technique for over 1,000 years. (정착 이전의 아나사지는 반유목민의 삶을 돌로레스 강가유역에서 넘게 살고 있었다. 그들은 1000년 넘게 납작한 메사의 적당히 비옥한 얇은 땅을 화전, 혹은 베고 태우기, 방식으로 농사를 지었다)라고 말한다. 즉, 옛날 농사꾼들이 농작물 재배를 통해 어떻게 환경을 변화시켰는지 보여주기 위해 화전방법을 소개한 것이다. 따라서 정답은 (B)가 된다. (C)는 지문에 언급된 내용은 맞지만 질문의 목적과 맞지 않아 오답이고, (A)또한 맞는 말이지만 같은 이유로 오답이다. (D)는 Prior to their settlement. 즉, 정착하기 전에 아나사지들이 사용했던 좋은 기법이기 때문에 오답이다.

06

According to paragraph 4 which of the following is **NOT** one of the pieces of evidence that Kohler used to deduce that human-environmental interaction had caused the Anasazi disappearance?

(A) Changes in the type of wood used in the Anasazi villages over time were discovered.
(B) The Anasazi gathered seeds from the pinion pine trees to use as food.
(C) Anasazi food sources changed to species found on open ranges.
(D) The seeds of first colonizing species were found in excavations of later Anasazi villages. ★

단락 4에 의하면 다음 중 콜러가 인간-자연 상호관계가 아나사지가 사라진 이유라고 유추하게 된 증거가 아닌 것은?

(A) 아나사지 마을에서 사용하던 나무 종류에 변화가 발견 되었다.
(B) 아나사지는 피니언 파인나무의 씨를 음식으로 먹었다.
(C) 아나사지는 넓은 벌판에 사는 종들로 음식을 바꿨다.
(D) 개척자 씨가 나중 아나사지 마을의 발굴에서 발견됐다. ★

Fact 질문의 키워드인 evidence가 언급된 부분을 살펴보면 He also discovered that the Anasazi switched from using pinion pines for construction (그는 아나사지가 피니언 파인을 건축용으로 쓰다가)라고 말한다. 즉, 아나사지는 피니언 파인을 음식으로 먹은 것이 아니라 건축용으로 사용했기 때문에 정답은 (B)가 된다. 이후에 언급되는 This, likely, indicated that the pinion became scarcer around the village as the growing population's demand increased. This would have also affected their food supply as pinion seeds were also gathered as a food source. (이 사실은 아마도 증가된 인구로 인해 증가된 수요 때문에 피니언 나무가 적어지고 있었다는 것을 의미한다. 피니언씨는 또한 음식으로 쓰였기 때문에 이것은 그들의 음식 공급에도 문제를 일으켰을 것이다.)는 콜러가 직접적으로 discover(발견)한 evidence(증거)가 아니라 발견한 증거로부터 유추한 하나의 가설이다. 다시 말해, 그가 직접적으로 발견했던 것은 피니언 나무가 건축물로 사용되었다는 것이었고, 피니언 나무가 음식으로도 사용되었을 수도 있다는 것은 그 사실로부터 유추해낸 추측이다.

07

According to paragraph 5, which of the following was **NOT** true about the Anasazi's settlement in villages?

(A) It was the result of their need to increase the population needed to gather more food.
(B) It made them less able to cope with environmental change because they required constant food sources.
(C) It wreaked havoc on the local farmlands and made them unsuitable for growing crops. ★
(D) It provided benefits to the tribe enabling them to produce more food for the growing population.

단락 5에 의하면 다음 중 아나사지 거주지에 대한 사실이 아닌 것은?

(A) 그것은 그들이 음식을 더 많이 모으기 위해 필요했던 인구를 증가시켜야 되는 필요성에 의해 생긴 결과였다.
(B) 그들이 환경적 변화에 적응 하는데 더 힘들어졌다. 왜냐하면 꾸준한 음식의 근원이 필요했기 때문이다.
(C) 지역의 농사 지을 땅을 파괴했고 그 땅들에 농작물 재배할 수 없게 만들었다. ★
(D) 자라나는 인구를 위해 음식을 더 많이 생산할 수 있게 해준 장점들을 제공했다.

Fact 질문의 키워드인 Anasazi's settlement in villages가 언급된 부분을 살펴보면 Kohler postulates that the Anasazi aggregated in villages due to the organizational benefits they offered in the face of soil depletion during their early periods. (쿨러는 이렇게 가정했다: 아나사지가 모이게 된 이유는 토양의 고갈이 불러일으킨 문제들을 해결하는 데에 대항하기에 마을로 모여 사는 것이 좋기 때문이었다)라고 말한다. 즉, 아나사지가 마을에 정착하게 된 이유는 인구의 증가가 아닌 organizational benefits(조직의 혜택)이었기 때문에 정답은 (A)가 된다.

08

What can be inferred about the settlement of villages from paragraph 5?

(A) Civilizations that settle in villages are much ~~more resistant~~ to environmental changes that affect their ability to produce the food they need to support their populations.
(B) Villages that produce an abundance of food during the main growing season are ~~immune~~ from the effects of environmental changes.
(C) As time goes on, villagers implement novel ways to deal with the agricultural problems that arise due to a large stationary population.
(D) Even predictable climatic fluctuations, ~~other than~~ minor ones, brought about the abandonment of a civilization. ★

단락 5에서 거주지의 마을들에 대해 추론할 수 있는 것은?

(A) 마을에 정착한 문명들은 그들의 인구 유지에 필요한 음식을 생산하는 능력에 영향을 끼치는 환경적 변화들에 ~~더욱 더 저항력~~이 있다.
(B) 주 자라는 계절에 음식을 많이 생산하는 마을은 환경적 변화의 영향을 ~~받지 않는다~~.
(C) 시간이 갈수록 큰 정착된 인구로 인해 생긴 농사 문제를 해결할 새로운 방법들을 개발한다.
(D) 사소한 변화들 ~~빼고는~~ 예측 가능한 기후적 변화들 조차도 문명의 유기를 초래한다. ★

Inference 질문의 키워드인 settlement of villages가 언급된 부분을 살펴보면 This led to agricultural intensification using methods, such as developing mechanisms to better control water flow. (이것은 아나사지 물을 조절하는 새로운 기구를 개발하는 등의 방법으로 농사 강화를 불러일으켰다)라고 말한다. 즉, 시간이 지날수록 늘어나는 인구수를 수용하기 위해 새로운 문제해결 방법을 찾아야 됐었다는 것이니까 정답은 (C)가 된다. (A)는 The cooperative management of resources for the village meant that they were less flexible in response to environmental changes 오히려 저항력이 떨어졌고, (B) 또한 환경적 변화에 영향을 받았기 때문에 오답이다. (D)는 For this reason, even a minor, predictable climate change could have led the Anasazi to abandon their settlements 사소한 기후적 변화도 문명의 유기를 초래할 수 있었기 때문에 오답이다.

09

Look at the four squares [■] that indicate where the following sentence could be added to the passage.

Kohler's contention was that the permanent settlement of a large, growing population like the Dolores River basin Anasazi relying upon (this) method would lead to their eventual destruction.

Where would the sentence best fit? Click on a square [■] to add the sentence to the passage.

4th

네 개의 네모[■]가 다음 문장이 더해질 수 있는 부분을 표시한 거다.

콜러의 문제 제기는 돌로레스 강 유역의 아나사지처럼 큰 정착된 영구적 거주지는 이 방법을 사용하면 망할 수 밖에 없다는 것이었다.

이 문장은 어느 자리에 들어가는 것이 가장 적절한가?

4번째

Insertion 삽입 문장의 키워드는 this method와 contention이다. this method 는 slash-and-burn technique를 지칭하는 것이며 contention 이라는 단어는 앞 문장과 반대의 내용이라는 것을 의미한다. 그러므로 반대의 내용인 This may appear to be a very environmentally destructive way of growing food that would ruin the land, but with less dense populations and a schedule of movement that allows the land adequate time for replenishment between planting, swidden is a sustainable means of acquiring the food that societies need 문장 다음에 오는 네 번째 네모가 정답이다.

10

Directions: An introductory sentence for a brief summary of the passage is provided below. Complete the summary by selecting the THREE answer choices that express the most important ideas in the passage. Some sentences do not belong in the summary because they express ideas that are not presented in the passage or are minor ideas in the passage. **This question is worth 2 points.**

지시: 지문 요약을 위한 도입 문장이 아래에 주어져 있다. 지문의 가장 중요한 내용을 나타내는 보기 3개를 골라 요약을 완성 하시오. 어떤 문장은 지문에 언급되지 않은 내용이나 사소한 정보를 담고 있으므로 요약에 포함되지 않는다. **이 문제는 2점이다.**

Human-environmental interaction led to the eventual abandonment of the Dolores River basin.

(A) Villages with large, or increasing, populations need to undergo agricultural intensification to increase the amount of food they produce for their residents, but these changes can make the village more vulnerable to less extreme climate changes. - paragraph 5

(D) Early Anasazi groups were semi-nomadic farmers who utilized the process of swidden to clear forestland for the use as farmland before they settled in the Dolores River basin around 600 AD. - paragraph 3

(F) Archeological exploration of settlements of different eras has shown that the settlement of the Anasazi in the Dolores River basin led to changes in the type of trees used, food sources and seeds found there. - paragraph 4

인간-자연 상호관계 때문에 돌로레스 강 유역을 아나사지는 버리게 되었다.

(A) 크고 자라나는 인구는 그들이 생산하는 주민들을 위한 음식의 양을 증가시켜야 하므로 농사 강화가 필요하지만, 이러한 농사 강화는 마을이 덜 심한 기후변화에 더 예민해지게 한다.

(D) 이른 아나사지 집단들은 600AD에 돌로레스 강 유역에 머무리기 전에 반 유목민적인 농사꾼들이었으며 그들은 화전 방법을 통해 숲을 사용할 수 있는 농작지로 바꾸었다.

(F) 다양한 시기의 발굴작업을 통해 돌로레스 강 유역의 아나사지의 거주는 다른 종류의 나무 사용, 다른 음식 근원, 그리고 다른 씨가 발견됐다.

(B) When the increase in the Anasazi population in the Dolores River basin outpaced its food production level, it started making changes in its interactions with ~~other villagers~~. - 틀린 정보

(C) ~~In the end~~, archeologists ~~attributed~~ the abandonment of the Anasazi settlements in the Dolores River basin to a catastrophic change in the climate conditions called the "Great Drought." - 틀린 정보

(E) The cooperative management of resources in the Anasazi societies ~~eased~~ the burden with which the people had when ~~they responded to environmental changes~~. - 틀린 정보

(B) 돌로레스 강 유역의 아나사지 인구가 음식 생산량을 뛰어넘었을 때 그들은 다른 ~~마을 사람들과~~ 교류하는 방법에 변화를 주기 시작했다.

(C) ~~결국~~, 고고학자들은 원래 아나사지가 돌로레스 강 유역을 떠난 이유는 Great Drought이라는 극단적 기후 변화 ~~때문이었을 것이라 했다~~.

(E) 아나사지 사회의 자원 공동관리 시스템은 ~~크들아 환경적 변화들에대응할때 겪은 부담을 완화시켰다.~~

Summary 지문의 중심 내용은 아나사지 문명이 사라진 이유에 대한 이론이다. (A)는 다섯 번째 단락의 마을을 세우게 되면서 야기된 문제점들을 요약한 내용과 일치하고, (D)는 세 번째 단락의 중심내용인 큰 마을로 정착하기 이전의 아나사지의 농사 방법과 일치하고, (F)는 네 번째 단락의 중심 내용인 아나사지와 자연 사이 교류의 변화에 따른 결과와 일치한다. 따라서 답은 (A), (D), (F)이다.

TEST 4-2 Global Variations in Species Diversity 세계적으로 다른 종들의 다양성

Introduction	단락 1	양극과 적도 사이에 존재하는 다양성의 변화도
Point	단락 2	온도와 빛의 안정성이 종다양성에 미치는 영향
Point	단락 3	열대지방의 안정적인 식량공급이 종다양성에 미치는 영향
Point	단락 4	북쪽지역 동물들의 생존전략
Point	단락 5	"효과적인 진화 시기" 이론 설명과 수명의 길이가 종다양성에 미치는 영향

문단주제	본문내용	해석
단락 1 양극과 적도 사이에 존재하는 다양성의 변화도	**1** A peculiar aspect of the world today is the presence of a gradient, or gradual **change**, **in** species diversity from the tropics to the polar areas. Species population surveys have shown that regions nearer the equator have the highest species diversity, and as [Q11-A] one **moves to** higher latitudes, the diversity **drops off** dramatically. This gradient can be seen across all species, both flora and fauna, and from higher-level mammals to lower order protozoans.	열대지방에서 극지까지의 점진적인 종들의 다양성의 변화는 세계의 특이한 면이다. 종들의 개체수 조사는 적도 주변의 종들의 다양성이 가장 높고, [Q11-A] 위도가 올라갈수록 다양성은 급격히 떨어진다는 것을 보여준다. 이러한 변화도는 식물과 동물, 상위 포유류부터 하위 원생동물들까지 모든 종들에서 보여진다.
단락 2 온도와 빛의 안정성이 종다양성에 미치는 영향	**2** One of the first explanations for this was that temperature and light stability in tropical regions, **when compared to** the seasonal fluctuations of both in polar regions, **allowed** more species **to develop**; [Q12-A] however, temperature and light do not **seem to fully control** species diversity. This can be seen by **looking at** the seas in polar regions, which remain **at** a nearly constant **temperature** year-round yet still have low species diversity. It may then seem logical that the northern seas' near-freezing temperatures preclude diversity levels as high as **those of** the tropics, but as [Q12-C] one moves deeper to the seafloor, which remains **in** perpetual, frigid **darkness** with **neither** light **nor** warmth from the sun, there is relatively higher species diversity. [Q12-B] Therefore, another important factor, such as the availability	이것에 대한 첫 번째 설명들 중 하나는, 양극지에서의 (온도와 빛) 계절별 변화에 비해서 열대지방 에서의 온도와 빛의 안정성은 더 많은 종의 발달을 가능하게 했다는 것이다. [Q12-A] 하지만 온도와 빛이 종들의 다양성을 완전히 조정하는 것으로 보이지 않는다. 이것은 극지의 바다들을 관찰함으로 인해 알 수 있는데, 이곳들은 연중 거의 일정한 온도를 유지하고 있으면서도 종의 다양성이 낮다. 북쪽 해역의 영하에 가까운 온도가 열대지방에서와 같은 높은 다양성을 저해한다는 것이 논리적으로 보이지 만, [Q12-C] 태양으로부터 받는 온기와 빛이 없는 어둠이 끊임없이 이어지는 해저로 더욱 깊이 들어가면 비교적 다양한 종이 존재한다. 그러므로, 식량을 구할 수 있는 능력과 같은 [Q12-B] 다른 중요한 요소가 종의 다양성의 영향을 끼칠 수밖에 없다.

Vocabulary

1단락
- gradient [gréidiənt] n. 변화도
- latitude [lǽtətjùːd] n. 위도, (위도상으로 본) 지역
- fauna [fɔ́ːnə] n. 동물상
- gradual [grǽdʒuəl] a. 점진적인, 완만한
- flora [flɔ́ːrə] n. 식물군
- protozoan [pròutouzóun] n. 원생동물
- equator [ikwéitər] n. (지구의) 적도

2단락
- stability [stəbíləti] n. 안정성
- logical [ládʒikəl] a. 타당한, 사리에 맞는
- fluctuation [flʌ̀ktʃuéiʃən] n. 변동, 오르내림
- preclude [priklúːd] v. (~로 하여금 ~하지) 못하게 하다
- year-round a. 연중 계속되는

of food, must affect species diversity.

단락 3
열대지방의 안정적인 식량공급이 종 다양성에 미치는 영향

3 One aspect of the food supply that could affect the diversity of species is that [Q14-D] in tropical regions, the food supply remains relatively stable year-round due to the uniform climate. Because of this, species can **specialize in** feeding on one food source without the risk of it not being available **at various times** of year. As they become more **dependent on** their food sources, species adapt more fully and becomes highly specialized. This allows multiple species to **feed on** one food source but only marginally **compete with one another**. This can be seen in the various carrion feeding vultures of the African plains. Although various species of vultures are present on the Serengeti, they have developed different niches. For example, one species has a beak that can tear through leathery hides and a head **devoid of** feathers, which allows them to **stick** their heads **into** the carcass and not **worry about** becoming contaminated because the sun will bake the refuse from their baldheads. Another has **adapted to** feeding on the innards, while still others consume the bones and random scraps. Even though they are all eating from the same carcasses, [Q14-B] they are all ensured a constant supply of food because their niche specializations effectively lower the competition rate.

종들의 다양성에 영향을 끼칠지도 모르는 식량공급의 한 방면으로는 [Q14-D] 열대지방에서는 일관적인 기후에 의해서 식량공급이 일년 내내 안정적 이라는 것이다. 이러한 이유 때문에, 종들은 일년 중 여러 시기에 먹이가 존재하지 않을 위험 없이 한 가지의 먹이를 먹기에 주력할 수 있다는 것이다. 그들이 그들의 음식 자원에 더욱 의존하게 될 때, 종들은 더욱 완전히 적응하고 더욱 전문화 된다. 이것은 다수의 종들이 한 가지 음식 자원을 먹이로 삼을 수 있으면서, 서로와 거의 경쟁하지 않아도 되게 한다. 이것은 여러 종류의 사체를 먹는 아프리카 지역의 독수리들에게서 볼 수 있다. 세렝게티에는 여러 종류의 독수리들이 존재하지만, 그들은 다른 역할을 발전시켰다. 예를 들면, 어떤 종류는 가죽을 찢을 수 있는 부리와 깃털이 없는 머리를 갖고 있고, 이로 인해 사체에 머리를 밀어도 햇빛에 민머리에 묻은 잔여물을 태워버려 머리가 더러워질 걱정을 하지 않아도 된다. 또 다른 종은 내장을 먹는 것에 적응했고, 다른 종들은 뼈와 아무 찌꺼기를 먹는다. 비록 모든 종들은 같은 시체에서 먹이를 먹고 있지만, [Q14-B] 틈새 전문화가 효과적으로 경쟁률을 낮추기 때문에 일정한 먹이 공급을 확실하게 할 수 있다.

단락 4
북쪽지역 동물들의 생존 전략

4 Species that live in higher latitudes, on the other hand, face a constantly changing food supply. During the warmer season, tundra species have a plethora of food sources, such as plant life and newly hatched krill, which are fed on by animals such as caribou, seabirds, fish, and oceanic mammals. However, when the long, frigid winter **sets in**, the area is rather barren, leading many specialized feeders to **migrate to** other areas. There are, however, animals with a more generalist feeding style that remain in the tundra year-round, seasonally adapting their feeding patterns. The gray wolf, for example, **switches from** consuming small mammals and migratory birds during the warmer months **to**

반면에 높은 위도에 사는 종들은 지속 적으로 변화하는 먹이원을 겪는다. 따뜻한 계절에는 툰드라 종들은 카리부, 바닷새, 물고기, 해양 포유류들이 먹는 식물과 갓 부화한 크릴새우와 같은 과다한 먹이원들을 갖고 있다. 하지만, 길고 혹한 겨울이 오면, 그 지역은 더 척박해져서 전문 사냥꾼 들로 하여금 다른 곳으로 이주하게 한다. 그러나, 그곳에서는 더 잡식성 섭식 형태의 동물들이 있는데, 일년내내 툰드라 지역에 머물면서 계절별로 그들의 섭식형태를 맞추어간다. 예로 들면 회색 늑대는, 따뜻한 달들에는 작은 포유류들과 철새들을 먹는 것에서 겨울 동안에는 약해진 카리부들을 사냥하는 것으로 전환한다. 이것은 그 종들이

Vocabulary

perpetual [pərpétʃuəl] a. 끊임없이 계속되는
frigid [frídʒid] a. 몹시 추운

3단락
specialize [spéʃəlàiz] v. ~을 전공하다, ~을 전문적으로 다루다
multiple [mʌ́ltəpəl] a. 많은, 다수의
vulture [vʌ́ltʃər] n. 독수리
carcass [káːrkəs] n. 시체, 죽은 동물

4단락
hatch [hætʃ] v. 어린 새, 동물 등이 부화하다
generalist [dʒénərəlist] n. 다방면에 걸쳐 많이 아는 사람, a. 다방면의
weaken [wíːkən] v. 약화시키다, 약화하다
tundra [tʌ́ndrə] n. 동토대, 툰드라
coexist [kòuigzíst] v. 동시에 공존하다

hunting weakened caribou during the winter. This **assures the species of constant food supplies** throughout the year. These distinct feeding patterns, therefore, do not limit species diversity, since they allow a **variety of** tundra species to coexist despite the lower overall food supply of the region.

5 Since the variability in light, temperature, and food supply does not necessarily reduce species diversity in an area, there must be another explanation for the great latitudinal difference. One new theory is that the evolutionary process itself caused this phenomenon. [Q17-A] The theory of "effective evolutionary time" **draws upon** earlier research that showed that evolution occurs more quickly in smaller species that inhabit warmer temperatures. [■] This likely occurs due to the higher physiological rates of smaller species in tropical regions, which **lead to** shorter lifespans. [■] A rather striking example of this is the freshwater pearl mussel which can inhabit freshwater streams in a variety of latitudes and whose maximum lifespan varies **depending on** latitude, from 29 years at 43°N to nearly 200 at 66°N. [■] This can also be seen in plant species by comparing the relatively shorter lifespans and earlier reproduction rates of plants from tropical regions with those from northern latitudes, such as the giant redwood which has been recorded as living up to 3500 years. While it may seem that the lifespan **differences in** a species would **have little effect on** overall diversity, it can **be shown to** have a great impact. [■] [Q17-C] The shorter lifespans of species in warmer areas **result in** shorter generation lengths, thereby causing a higher mutation rate and speed of selection than **in** higher **latitudes**. This rapid mutation and selection enables distinct species to be produced much more quickly than in the colder northern regions. These new species then **begin filling** unexploited niches in the tropical ecosystem and become even more particularly adapted as more generations are produced.

11 What can be inferred from paragraph 1 about species diversity today?

(A) The north and south poles are home to the lowest species diversity on Earth.
(B) There are more plants in tropical regions, but ~~more animals~~ in northern regions.
(C) The tropics now contain more species than have ever been ~~recorded~~ in history.
(D) ~~Elevation~~ seems to play a large role in the difference in species diversity. ★

단락 1에서 오늘날의 종들의 다양성에 관해서 알 수 있는 것은?

(A) 북극과 남극은 지구에서 가장 낮은 종들의 다양성을 갖고 있다.
(B) 열대 지방에는 더욱 많은 식물들이 살고 있지만, 북쪽 지역에서는 ~~더욱 많은~~ 동물들이 살고 있다.
(C) 열대 지방은 현재 역사에 ~~기록된~~ 어느 때보다도 많은 종들을 갖고 있다.
(D) ~~고도는~~ 종들의 다양성에 큰 역할을 하는 것으로 보인다. ★

Inference 질문의 키워드인 species diversity가 언급된 부분을 살펴보면 as one moves to higher latitudes, the diversity drops off dramatically. (위도가 올라갈수록 다양성은 급격히 떨어진다는 것을 보여준다)라고 말한다. 즉, 위도가 높아지면 (남, 북쪽으로 이동하면) 다양성은 반비례하게 낮아지기 때문에 정답은 (A)가 된다. (B)는 동물과 식물을 나누어 비교한 내용은 언급되지 않으므로 오답이고, (C)는 열대 지방에 많은 종들이 살고 있는건 사실이지만, 역대 최고라는 내용은 언급되지 않으므로 오답이다. (D)는 elevation(고도)가 아닌 latitude(위도)가 맞는 말이기 때문에 오답이다.

12 Select the **TWO** answer choices that are mentioned in paragraph 2 as being the effects of the temperature and light on species diversity. **To receive credit, you must select TWO answers.**

(A) Their stability comes short of explaining the difference in the diversity gradient between areas of different latitude.
(B) Temperature and the stability of light have ~~no effect~~ on the diversity of species in an ecosystem. ★
(C) Freezing temperatures do not appear to be a limiting factor for the diversity of species in an ecosystem.
(D) The polar seafloor ~~does not~~ have a diverse ecosystem because it is excluded from the effects of the sun's light. ★

단락 2에서 종들의 다양성에 온도와 빛이 끼치는 영향에 관한 것인 두 개의 선택지를 선택하시오.

(A) 그들의 안정성은 다른 위도의 지역들에 존재하는 다양성의 변화의 차이를 다 설명하지는 못한다.
(B) 온도와 빛의 안정성은 생태계에서 종들의 다양성에 ~~영향을 끼치지 않는다.~~ ★
(C) 아주 낮은 온도는 생태계에서 종들의 다양성을 제한하는 요인으로는 보이지 않는다.
(D) 극지대의 해저는 태양의 빛에 영향을 받지 못하기 때문에 다양한 생태계를 갖지 ~~않고 있다.~~ ★

Fact 질문의 키워드인 effects of temperature and light이 언급된 부분을 살펴보면 however, temperature and light do not seem to fully control species diversity. (하지만, 온도와 빛은 종들의 다양성을 완전히 설명하는 것으로 보이지 않는다)라고 말한다. 즉, 종들의 다양성에 있어서 온도와 빛이 유일한 원인은 아니었기 때문에 정답은 (A)가 된다. 또, one moves deeper to the seafloor, which remains in perpetual, frigid darkness with neither light nor warmth from the sun, there is relatively higher species diversity. (빛과 온기가 거의 지속적으로 사라지는 바다 깊숙이 들어가보면, 그곳에는 상대적으로 다양한 종들이 살고 있다)라고 말한다. 즉, 아주 낮은 온도에도 종다양성이 존재했기 때문에 정답은 (C)가 된다. (B)는 온도와 빛의 안정성이 only effect는 아니었지만 effect를 가지고는 있었기 때문에 오답이고, (D)는 극지대의 해저는 적절하지 못한 조건을 가지고 있음에도 불구하고 종다양성을 가지고 있기 때문에 오답이다.

13

What does the word "they" refer to in the passage?

(A) feathers [féðər]
(B) carcasses [káːrkəs]
(C) vultures [vʌ́ltʃər]
(D) scraps [skræp] ★

지문에서 "그들" 이 의미하는 것은?

(A) 깃털들
(B) 사체들
(C) 독수리들
(D) 파편들 ★

Reference they가 언급된 부분을 살펴보면 Even though they are all eating from the same carcasses…(비록 그들은 모두 같은 사체에서 먹지만…)라고 말한다. 즉, they가 나타내는 것은 열대지방에서 사는 동물들의 뛰어난 적응력을 보여주기 위해 언급된 독수리 Although various species of vultures are present on the Serengeti, they have developed different niches. (세렝게티에는 여러 종류의 독수리들이 존재하지만, 그들은 다른 역할을 발전시켰다)이다. 따라서 정답은 (C)가 된다.

14

What can be inferred about the food supply in tropical regions from paragraph 3?

(A) Species in tropical regions experience greater food diversity when they specialize on their food sources. ★
(B) Due to the immense competition rate among the species in tropical regions, they have set out to develop niche specializations.
(C) The limited food diversity in the tropical region forces animals to adapt to survive, which creates more species diversity.
(D) The year-round supply of food allows animals that reside in the tropics to be more specialized feeders than those of latitudes that are more northerly.

단락 3에서 열대 지방에서의 식량공급에 관해서 추론할 수 있는 것은?

(A) 열대 지방에 있는 종들은 먹이를 전문화 시킴으로써 다 다양한 먹이를 즐길 수 있다. ★
(B) 열대 지역의 종들 사이의 엄청난 경쟁 때문에 그들의 전문화적인 역할을 개발하였다.
(C) 열대 지방의 제한된 음식의 다양성은 동물들이 살아남기 위해 적응하게 만들고, 이것은 더욱 다양한 종들을 만들어 낸다.
(D) 일 년 내내 공급되는 음식은 열대 지역에 사는 동물들이 더욱 북쪽의 위도에 사는 동물들에 비해서 더욱 전문화되게 한다.

Inference 질문의 키워드인 food supply in tropical regions가 언급된 부분을 살펴보면 in tropical regions the food supply remains relatively stable year-round due to the uniform climate. Because of this, species can specialize in feeding on one food source without the risk of it not being available at various times of year. (열대지방에서는 일관적인 기후에 의해서 식량공급이 일년 내내 안정적이라는 것이다. 이러한 이유 때문에, 종들은 일 중 여러 시기에 먹이가 존재하지 않을 위험 없이 한 가지의 먹이를 먹기 위해서 전문화 할 수 있다는 것 이다)라고 말한다. 즉, 열대지방의 안정적인 식량공급 덕분에 그 지역에 살고 있는 동물들이 더 전문화 될 수 있었던 것이기 때문에 정답은 (D)가 된다. (A)는 종들이 먹이를 전문화(narrow) 시키면 시킬수록 먹이의 다양성은 줄어들 수 밖에 없으므로 오답이고, (B)는 they are all ensured a constant supply of food because their niche specializations effectively lower the competition rate 즉, 경쟁률 때문에 역할을 분담한 것이 아니라 경쟁률이 낮아진 것은 하나의 결과물일 뿐, 직접적인 원인은 constant food supply(지속적인 음식 공급)이기 때문에 오답이다. (C)는 열대지방에는 일관적인 기후에 덕분에 식량공급이 오히려 일년 내내 안정적이기 때문에 오답이다.

15

The term "marginally" in the passage is closest in meaning to

(A) slightly [sláitli]
(B) jointly [dʒɔ́intli]
(C) theoretically [θìːərétikəli]
(D) seasonally [síːzənəlly] ★

지문의 단어 "조금만"의 의미와 가장 유사한 것은?

(A) 약간
(B) 공동으로
(C) 이론상으로
(D) 계절적으로 ★

Vocabulary 지문의 marginally(조금만)와 동의어인 slightly(약간)이 정답이다.

16 Why does the author mention "freshwater pearl mussels"?

(A) To provide an example that shows that lifespans are shorter at lower latitudes ★
(B) To show that small animals tend to have ~~longer~~ lifespans than larger animals
(C) To emphasize the wide latitudinal ranges of some species
(D) To illustrate a species-diversifying factor by using an example of a species with a wide lifespan range.

글쓴이가 "민물 진주 홍합"을 언급하는 이유는?

(A) 더욱 낮은 위도에서의 수명들이 짧다는것에 대한 예시를 주기 위해서 ★
(B) 작은 동물들이 큰 동물들보다 긴 수명을 가지는 경향이 있다는 것을 보이기 위해서
(C) 몇몇 종들의 서식지가 갖는 다양한 위도들을 강조하기 위해서
(D) 폭넓은 생명 범위를 가진 종들의 예를 사용함으로서, 종의 다양성의 한 요소를 실례로 들기위해

Purpose 음영 표시된 부분을 살펴보면 A rather striking example of this is the freshwater pearl mussel which can inhabit freshwater streams in a variety of latitudes and whose maximum lifespan varies depending on latitude, from 29 years at 43°N to nearly 200 at 66°N. (여러 위도의 민물에 살고 최대 수명이 위도에 따라서 43°N일 때29년, 66°N일 때 200년 가까이 사는 민물 진주 홍합은 이것의 놀라운 예시라고 할 수 있다)라고 말한다. (D)는 폭넓은 생명 범위를 가진 예로 mussel을 들어서, 낮은 위도에서 짧은 주기 때문에 더 많은 변이가 생겨서 결국 종의 다양성을 이끌어내는 한 요소로서 위도가 중요하다는 것을 설명하고 있으므로, 정답이다. (A)는 내용으로 틀린 것은 아니지만, 본문에서 예를 넣은 의도를 봤을 때, 저위도일수록 생명 주기가 짧다만을 얘기하고자 하는 게 아니므로 오답이고, (종다양성의 원인으로 언급이 빠짐) (B)는 더 긴(longer)이 아니라 더 짧은(shorter)이 맞는 말이므로 오답이다. (C)는 민물 진주 홍합의 특징에 해당하는 말이지만 본문에서 언급되는 이유와는 맞지 않기 때문에 오답이다.

17 According to paragraph 5, which of the following is true regarding the "effective evolutionary time" theory? **To receive credit, you must select TWO answer choices.**

(A) Proponents of the theory discovered that smaller animals evolve faster in warmer environments than they do in colder climates.
(B) The theory provides that species diversity has enabled species to fill unexploited niches, ~~ultimately leading~~ to their evolution.
(C) The theory suggests that new niches in tropical ecosystems would be filled much quicker than those in polar ecosystems.
(D) Scientists developed the theory ~~after~~ observing that animals such as the freshwater pearl mussel rarely mutated in northern climates. ★

단락 5에 의하면, "효과적인 진화 시기"이론에 관해서 추론할 수 있는 것은?

(A) 이론의 지지자들은 작은 동물들이 추운 환경보다 따뜻한 환경에서 더욱 빨리 진화한다는 것을 발견했다.
(B) 이 이론은 종다양성이 종들을 미개발된 역할들을 채워 나가게 함으로써 그들의 진화를 ~~야기시킨~~다고 한다.
(C) 이 이론은 열대 생태계의 새로운 역할들은 극지대의 생태계들보다 더욱 빨리 채워진다는 것을 말해준다.
(D) 과학자들은 민물 진주 홍합 등이 북쪽의 기후에서는 드물게 돌연변이가 되는 것을 보고난 ~~후에~~ 이론을 개발했다. ★

Inference 질문의 키워드인 effective evolutionary time이 언급된 부분을 살펴보면 The theory of "effective evolutionary time" draws upon earlier research that showed that evolution occurs more quickly in smaller species that inhabit warmer temperatures. (이러한 "효과적인 진화의 시기"이론은 진화가 따뜻한 온도에 사는 작은 종들에게서 더 빨리 일어난다는 연구에서 의거되었다)라고 말한다. 즉, 비교적 따뜻한 지역에서 사는 작은 동물들이 추운 지역에서 사는 동물들보다 더 빠르게 진화한다는 뜻이므로 정답은 (A)가 된다. (C)는 The shorter lifespans of species in warmer areas result in shorter generation lengths, thereby causing a higher mutation rate and speed of selection than in higher latitudes. (따뜻한 지역에 사는 종들의 짧은 수명은 짧은 세대의 길이를 초래하고, 그럼으로써 더 높은 위도에서보다 더욱 빠른 변화와 도태 속도를 가능하게 한다)라고 말한다. 즉, 수명이 짧은 동물들이 수명이 긴 동물들보다 더 짧은 세대의 길이를 초래한다는 것이다. 따라서 정답은 (C)가 된다. (B)는 종다양성은 진화의 결과물이지 진화의 원인은 아니기 때문에 오답이고, (D)또한 과학자들이 민물 진주 홍합의 늦은 진화과정을 관찰 한 후에 이 이론을 만들었다는 내용은 언급되지 않으므로 오답이다.

18 Which of the sentences below best expresses the essential information in the highlighted sentence in the passage? Incorrect choices change the meaning in important ways or leave out essential information.

(A) i) While one may reasonably conclude that species diversity is lower in colder ecosystems, ii) the chilly, lightless depths of the arctic oceans, which receive no solar heat or illumination, display some of the highest species diversity in the arctic region.

(B) Despite lacking light and heat, the ocean's seafloor displays a ~~higher level~~ of species diversity ~~than either~~ the tropical or the northern regions because of the constant temperatures found there. ★

(C) i) One can assume that the extremely cold temperature of the northern seas is what prevents them from having diversity levels as high as those of the tropical regions.

(D) ~~Although~~ there is relatively higher species diversity in the northern seafloors, it ~~may not seem~~ logical that the near-freezing temperatures of the arctic regions discourage the diversity levels from catching up with those of the tropics.

아래의 문장 중 지문 속의 음영 표시된 문장의 핵심 정보를 가장 잘 표현하고 있는 것은 무엇인가? 오답은 문장의 의미를 현저하게 바꾸거나 핵심 정보를 빠트리고 있다.

(A) i) 누군가는 논리적으로 종들의 다양성이 더 추운 생태계에서 줄어든다고 결론지을 수 있지만, ii) 태양열이나 빛을 받지 못하는 춥고 빛이 들지 않는 극지대의 바다 깊숙이는 극지대에서 가장 높은 다양성을 보이는 곳들 중 하나이다.

(B) 비록 빛이나 열은 없지만, 바다의 해저는 일관적인 온도를 갖고 있기 때문에 ~~열대나~~ 북쪽 지역들보다 ~~높은~~ 종들의 다양성을 보인다. ★

(C) i) 우리는 북쪽 해안의 종다양성이 열대 지방의 종다양성만큼 높지 않은 이유는 극도로 낮은 온도라고 추측해 볼 수 있다.

(D) 북쪽 해저에는 상대적으로 높은 종다양성이 ~~있지만~~, 낮은 온도가 극지방의 종다양성이 열대지방의 다양성을 따라잡지 못하게 한다는 것은 ~~비논리적으로~~ 들린다.

Highlight 음영 표시된 문장은 i) It may then seem logical that the northern seas' near-freezing temperatures preclude diversity levels as high as those of the tropics, ii) but as one moves deeper to the seafloor, which remains in perpetual, frigid darkness with neither light nor warmth from the sun, there is relatively higher species diversity. i) 북쪽 바다들의 거의 얼어붙기 직전의 온도가 열대 지방의 높은 다양성을 방지한다고 보는 것이 논리적일 것이지만, ii) 빛과 온기가 거의 지속적으로 사라지는 바다 깊숙이 들어가보면, 그곳에는 상대적으로 다양한 종들이 살고 있다)이렇게 두 가지 내용으로 나뉜다. 이 내용을 모두 포함한 (A)가 정답이 된다. (B)는 i)에 해당하는 내용이 없으므로 오답이고, (C)는 ii)의 내용이 없기 때문에 오답이다. (D)는 음영 표시된 문장은 낮은 온도의 극지방엔 낮은 종다양성이 있다고 생각할 수도 있지만, 사실은 그렇지 않다라고 설명한다. 하지만 (D)는 북쪽 해저에 존재하는 높은 종다양성이 있지만 극지방엔 낮은 종다양성이 존재한다고 믿는 것이 논리적이지 않다라고 설명하기 때문에 오답이다.

19 Look at the four squares [■] that indicate where the following sentence could be added to the passage.

> (This) can (also) be seen in plant species by comparing the relatively shorter lifespans and earlier reproduction rates of plants from tropical regions with those from northern latitudes, such as the giant redwood which has been recorded as living up to 3500 years.

Where would the sentence best fit? Click on a square [■] to add the sentence to the passage.

3rd

네 개의 네모[■]는 다음 문장이 삽입될 수 있는 부분을 나타내고 있다.

> 이것은 또한 열대 지방 식물들이 3500년까지 사는 것으로 기록된 거대한 미국 삼나무와 같은 북쪽 위도의 식물들에 비교해서 상대적으로 짧은 수명과 빠른 번식 속도를 갖는 것에서 찾아볼수 있다.

이 문장은 어느 자리에 들어가는 것이 가장 적절한가?

3번째

Insertion 삽입 문장의 단서는 키워드는 also 이다. 삽입 문장은 미국 삼나무를 예시로 들며 식물들이 열대지방에선 북쪽지역보다 더 짧은 수명과 빠른 번식 속도를 갖고 있다는 것을 나타내려는 것이기 때문에 세 번째 네모 앞에 있는 A rather striking example of this is the freshwater pearl mussel which can inhabit freshwater streams in a variety of latitudes and whose maximum lifespan varies depending on latitude, from 29 years at 43°N to nearly 200 at 66°N. 또 다른 (동물)예시 다음에 오는 것이 가장 적절하다. 따라서 정답은 3 번째 네모이다.

20

Directions: An introductory sentence for a brief summary of the passage is provided below. Complete the summary by selecting the THREE answer choices that express the most important ideas in the passage. Some sentences do not belong in the summary because they express ideas that are not presented in the passage or are minor ideas in the passage. **This question is worth 2 points**

지시: 지문 요약을 위한 도입 문장이 아래에 주어져 있다. 지문의 가장 중요한 내용을 나타내는 보기 3개를 골라 요약을 완성 하시오. 어떤 문장은 지문에 언급되지 않은 내용이나 사소한 정보를 담고 있으므로 요약에 포함되지 않는다. **이 문제는 2점이다.**

A peculiar aspect of the world today is the presence of a gradient, or gradual change, in the diversity of species at different latitudes.

(B) The stable food supply in tropical regions enables species to become highly specialized in feeding on one food source, effectively lowering the competition rate. - paragraph 3

(C) Although there are more stable food supplies in warmer regions, animals in northern climates have developed feeding strategies that allow them to ensure access to food year-round. - paragraph 4

(E) The increased physiological rates of species in warmer climates results in shorter lifespans that lead to more rapid mutations which in turn cause a larger number of species to exist in tropical regions. - paragraph 5

다른 위도에서의 점진적인 종들의 다양성의 변화는 세계의 특이한 면이다.

(B) 열대 지방의 안정적인 식량공급량은 종들이 한 가지의 먹이원을 섭취하는데 더욱 전문화 될 수 있게 함으로써 경쟁률을 효과적으로 낮춘다.

(C) 비록 따뜻한 지역에서는 더욱 안정적인 식량공급원들이 있지만, 북쪽 기후의 동물들은 일 년 내내 음식을 먹을 수 있게 보장하는 사냥 방법을 개발했다.

(E) 따뜻한 기후에서 증가하는 동물들의 생리학적 변화속도는 열대 지방들에서 많은 수의 종들이 존재하게 하는 더욱 빠른 변화를 만들어내는 더욱 짧은 수명을 초래한다.

(A) The higher temperatures and the abundance of light near the equator ~~dehydrate~~ species in tropical areas, ~~shortening~~ their lifespans. - 틀린 정보

(D) When the stability of food supplies in higher latitudes fluctuates, it poses danger to both specialists and ~~generalists~~ inhabiting the regions. - 틀린 정보

(F) The adaptation of the freshwater pearl mussel illustrates the wide spectrum of ecosystems to which marine-animals can adapt. - paragraph 5 detail

(A) 적도 근처의 더 높은 온도와 빛의 풍부함은 열대지방의 종들이 ~~탈수 상태가 되게~~ 만들고 그들의 수명을 줄인다.

(D) 고위도 지역에서 식량공급의 안정성이 변동할 때, 그 지역에서 살고 있는 전문화된 동물과 ~~보편적인 동물~~ 모두에게 위험을 제공한다.

(F) 민물 진주 홍합의 적응능력은 해양 동물들이 광범위한 생태계에 적응할 수 있다는 것을 보여준다.

Summary 지문의 중심 내용은 종다양성 차이점의 원인이다. (B)는 세 번째 단락의 중심내용인 열대지방의 안정적인 식량공급이 종다양성에 미치는 영향과 일치하고, (C)는 네 번째 단락의 중심내용인 북쪽지역 동물들의 생존전략과 일치하고, (E)는 다섯 번째 단락의 중심내용인 "효과적인 진화의 시기" 이론과 일치한다. 따라서 답은 (B), (C), (E)이다.

USHER iBT TOEFL
INTERMEDIATE READING

TEST 5
답안 및 취약 유형 분석표

해석·해설

답안 및 문제 유형 분석표

TEST 5-1

01 (D) Fact
02 (D) Purpose
03 (A) Purpose
04 (C) Inference
05 (C) Purpose
06 (D) Inference
07 (B) Highlight
08 (D) Vocabulary
09 1st ■ Insertion
10 (B), (C), (E) Summary

TEST 5-2

11 (A) Inference
12 (B) Vocabulary
13 (B) Fact
14 (A) Inference
15 (A) Fact
16 (C) Highlight
17 (D) Vocabulary
18 (B) Fact
19 3rd ■ Insertion
20 (A), (E), (F) Summary

각 문제 유형별 맞춘 개수를 아래에 적어 보세요.

유형	맞춘 답의 개수	정답률
단어 (Vocabulary)	/ 3	정답률: %
사실 확인 문제 (Fact)	/ 4	정답률: %
지시어 찾기 (Reference)	/ 0	정답률: %
끼워 넣기 (Insertion)	/ 2	정답률: %
문장 변환문제 (Highlight)	/ 2	정답률: %
목적 (Purpose)	/ 3	정답률: %
추론 (Inference)	/ 4	정답률: %
단락 요약(Summary / Category Chart)	/ 2	정답률: %
전체	/20	정답률: %

※ 자신이 취약한 유형은 READING STRATEGIES를 통해 다시 한번 점검하시기 바랍니다. (p.44)

TEST 5-1　Documenting the Incas 잉카의 기록들

Introduction	단락 1	잉카제국의 붕괴와 함께 초래된 문제점 소개
Point	단락 2	스페인과 잉카의 다른 운영 체계 때문에 초래된 문제점
Point	단락 3	잉카 기록에서 의도적인 문제점들의 형성
Point	단락 4	구전으로 얻은 개인적인 지식에 의존하면서 생긴 오류들
Point	단락 5	오직 한쪽의 이야기에 의존하면서 생긴 오류들
Point	단락 6	지역이름의 불규칙성 때문에 야기된 문제점
Point	단락 7	결론과 리포트를 더 사실적으로 만들 수 있는 해결책

Photo from Geschichte des Kostumsn

문단주제 / 본문내용 / 해석

단락 1 — 잉카제국의 붕괴와 함께 초래된 문제점 소개

1 Beginning with the founding of the capital city of Cusco in the early 1200s, the Inca Empire expanded along the mountainous west coast of South America. [Q22-D] Within 250 years, their conquests of neighboring societies allowed them to control over 3,000 miles of coastline and land covering [Q22-A] parts of present day Peru, Bolivia, Ecuador, Chile and Argentina. [Q21-B] The power of their army and their effective administration of this vast empire made them the greatest of the New World civilizations. This great empire would, however, collapse less than 100 years later when the Spanish conquistador Francisco Pizarro arrived and conquered the area for Spain in the 1530s. [Q21-A,C] Since the Inca language did not have writing system, much of what is currently known about this magnificent civilization was recorded by these Spanish conquerors. This has led to many problems related to the veracity of the historical records of the early Inca Empire.

이른 1200년도에 수도인 쿠스코의 설립으로 시작해 잉카 제국은 남미의 산지가 가득한 서부 해안 으로 확장했다. [Q22-D] 250년 동안에 주변의 사회들을 정복함으로써 [Q22-A] 오늘날의 페루, 볼리비아, 에콰도르, 칠레, 그리고 아르헨티나의 부분을 포함하는 3,000마일의 해안지대와 영토를 지배할 수 있는 힘을 쥐게 되었다. [Q21-B] 군대의 힘과 광대한 제국의 효과적인 관리는 그들을 신세계 문명들 중 가장 위대하게 만들어주었다. 그러나 이 위대한 제국은 100년도 안된 1530년대에 스페인의 정복자 프란시스코 피자로가 스페인을 위해서 그 지역을 정복을 함으로써 무너졌다. [Q21-A,C] 잉카언어는 문자 체계를 가지고 있지 않았기 때문에 현재에 잉카 문명에 대해서 알려진 많은 것은 스페인의 정복자들에 의해서 기록된 것들이다. 이것은 초기 잉카 제국에 대한 역사적 기록들의 정확도에 관한 많은 문제를 많이 일으켰다.

단락 2 — 스페인과 잉카의 다른 운영체계 때문에 초래된 문제점

2 [Q23-A] The first of these is that the ruling system used by the Inca was different from that of the Spanish Empire and may not have been fully understood by the early conquerors. In order to record the historical information, they gleaned from their Inca informants. Then, they simply adapted

[Q23-A] 첫 번째 문제는 잉카에서 사용되었던 지배 시스템이 스페인 제국과 매우 달랐으며 초기의 정복자들이 이해를 하지 못했을 수도 있다는 점이다. 그들은 역사적 정보를 기록하기 위해 잉카 정보원들에게 전수를 받았다. 그리고 수집한 정보를 스페인의 지배 방식에 적용했다. [■]

Vocabulary

1단락
- mountainous [máuntənəs] ad. 산악의
- conquistador [kankwístədɔ́ːr] n. 정복자
- coastline [kóustlàin] n. 해안 지대
- magnificent [mægnífəsənt] a. 웅장한
- administration [ædmìnəstréiʃən] n. 관리직

2단락
- glean [gliːn] v. 얻다
- sequential [sikwénʃəl] a. 순차적인
- flourish [fláːriʃ] v. 번창하다
- adapt [ədǽpt] v. 조정하다
- monarchy [mánərki] n. 군주제
- compile [kəmpáil] v. 편집하다
- concurrently [kənkɔ́ːrəntly] a. 동시에

the information **to** the Spanish style of governance. [■] As time went on, these kinds of inaccuracies would have been compounded since most scholars would have used these recordings as primary sources for their later research. A good example of this is their list of Inca rulers. [■] The Inca **told** the early conquerors **of** thirteen kings who ruled over the empire, and the Spanish recorded them as thirteen sequential rulers, as that was how the monarchy worked in Spain; however, it isn't clear if these recorded names were individuals or titles. [■] [Q24-C] If they were titles, they could have been held concurrently, and there **may have been** fewer than thirteen kings that **ruled over** the empire. [■] Since the empire only flourished under the last four kings, this isn't a major problem in understanding the Inca culture, but it **points to** how cultural bias and inaccuracies **regarding** the Inca could have begun with the earliest recorded histories of them.

단락 3
의도적으로 야기된 문제점

3 [Q25-C] Another problem with the accounts compiled by the Spanish was that they may have been intentionally inaccurate. The Spanish **wanted to downplay** certain aspects of the Inca civilization, such as the extent of their wealth. If the conquistadors accurately recorded Incan gold production, they would have had to **turn** it all **over** to the Spanish Crown. By downplaying the extent of the Inca's wealth, the conquistadors **were able to amass** their own gold caches. The inaccuracies may have also been the fault of the Inca themselves. Since they were helping their new conquerors, the Inca may have **misled them to make** themselves look better or exaggerated their importance in society.

단락 4
구전으로 얻은 개인적인 지식에 의존하면서 생긴 오류들

4 **Relying on** elite members of the Incan society to learn about their history caused another problem. Since they had no written language system, all of their historical information had been passed down through the oral tradition. **Over** time, many of these stories may have developed unintentional inaccuracies. A prime example of this would be the founding of Cusco, which **was said to have happened** after four

Vocabulary

3단락
intentionally [inténʃənəli] a. 의도적으로
extent [ikstént] n. 정도

inaccurate [inǽkjərit] a. 부정확한
amass [əmǽs] v. 모으다

downplay [dáunpléi] v. 경시하다

4단락
elite [ilí:t] n. 엘리트 계층
prime [praim] a. 주된
impressive [imprésiv] adj. 인상적인

oral [ɔ́:rəl] a. 구두의
emerge [imə́:rdʒ] v. 나오다

unintentional [ʌninténʃənəl] a. 고의가 아닌
exploits [éksplɔit] n. 착취한 것들

		brothers and four sisters **emerged from** a cave and led followers they found in another cave to the site of Cusco, where they founded the civilization. The origin of these early leaders and stories of their exploits were likely exaggerated to paint them **in** a more impressive **light**. Because of the nature of the oral tradition, **it is probable that** the more recent Incan stories **were likely to be** more accurate.	나와 다른 동굴에서 찾은 추종자들을 이끌고 현 쿠스코의 위치로 가서 문명을 건설했다고 한다. 초기 지도자들의 유래와 그들의 업적에 대한 이야기들은 그들을 더 인상적이게 묘사하기 위해서 과장되었을 확률이 크다. 구전의 특성상, 더욱 더 최근의 잉카에 관한 이야기들이 더 정확할 확률이 높다.
단락 5 오직 한쪽의 이야기에 의존하면서 생긴 오류	**5**	The Inca may have also whitewashed the accounts of their expansion and conquest of neighboring settlements, such as the Lupaca to their south. Because of their policy of dispersing uncooperative people and repopulating the area with people who they **were able to deal with**, the Incan leaders were the only sources of Spanish knowledge of their empire and were, therefore, able to control the description of their conquests and could **portray** themselves **as** righteous and invincible warriors. This makes it **all but** impossible to establish the accuracy of their narratives.	잉카 문명은 그들의 남쪽에 위치한 루파카와 같은 주변 주거지의 정복과 영토의 확장에 관한 이야기들을 숨겼을 수도 있다. 비협조적인 사람들을 분산시키고 자신들이 다루기 쉬운 사람들로 땅을 채우는 정책 때문에 스페인에게 잉카 지도자들은 그들의 제국에 관한 유일한 정보통이었다. 따라서 잉카 지도자들은 자기의 정복에 관한 이야기를 조작할 수 있었고 자신을 도덕적이고 천하무적인 전사로 표현할 수 있었다. 따라서 그들의 이야기에 정확성을 부여하기는 어렵다.
단락 6 지역이름의 불규칙성 때문에 야기된 문제점	**6**	A final problem that **calls** the truthfulness of the Spanish-written histories **into question** is the incongruent uses of place names. It **seems that** different writers **used** various **names to describe** the areas, such as provinces and towns that they encountered in the Incan Empire. [Q26-D] This, **compounded with** the great **changes in** the locations of settlements over the last five centuries, makes it difficult to verify any of the location information in accounts of the Incan Empire.	잉카에 관한 스페인의 기록의 진실성과 관련된 마지막 문제는 일치하지 않는 장소 이름들이다. 여러 작가들은 자기들이 방문한 잉카제국의 주와 도시들을 설명하기 위해서 다양한 이름들을 사용하였다. [Q26-D] 이 점과 더불어 지난 500년간 있었던 많은 주거지 위치의 변동들 때문에 잉카 제국과 관련된 위치 정보를 확인하기가 어렵다.
단락 7 결론과 리포트를 더 사실적으로 만들 수 있는 해결책	**7**	Despite the possibility of all of these inaccurate accounts creeping into the Spanish-written historical records of the Incan Empire, researchers still **find** them **to be** important source materials. By cross-referencing different accounts of the same events and using archeological research, scientists can verify some of the accounts to form an accurate chronology and picture of what actually **went on** during the Incan Empire.	스페인이 기록한 잉카 제국의 역사에 부정확한 내용들이 있을 수 있음에도 불구하고 연구자들은 그것들을 연구를 위한 중요한 소재로 생각한다. 동일한 사건에 대한 다양한 기록들을 상호 참조하고 고고학적 연구를 참고함으로써 과학자들은 몇몇의 사건들을 입증하여 정확한 연대기를 만들고 실제로 잉카제국 기간 동안 일어난 일을 묘사할 수 있다.

▌ Vocabulary ▌

5단락 expansion [ikspǽnʃən] n. 확대
uncooperative [ʌnkouɑ́pərèitiv] a. 비협조적인
righteous [ráitʃəs] a. 옳은

6단락 truthfulness [trúːθfəlnis] n. 정직함
encounter [inkáuntər] v. 만나다

7단락 creeping [kríːpiŋ] a. 몰래 들어가는
archaeological [ὰːrkiəládʒikəl] a. 고고학의

settlements [sétlmənt] n. 식민지
repopulate [riːpápjəlèit] v. 사람을 다시 살게 하다
invincible [invínzəbəl] a. 천하무적의
incongruent [inkáŋgruənt] a. 맞지 않은
compound [kámpaund kɔ́m-] v. 합성되다

cross-referencing [krɔːs-réfərəns] v. 상호 참조
accounts [əkáunt] n. 이야기

disperse [dispɔ́ːrs] v. 분산하다

province [právins] n. 주

accurate [ǽkjurət] a. 정확한

01 According to paragraph 1, which of the following is **NOT** true about the Inca civilization that existed in South America?

(A) They were unable to record their history until after their civilization had been conquered by outsiders.
(B) They were militarily and organizationally superior to many of the cultures that surrounded their capital city.
(C) They did not have their own record on their conquest of neighboring countries. ★
(D) Their ~~written language~~ was too complex for most people to use, so they used Spanish to record their histories.

단락 1을 참고해서 아래의 어느 것이 남미에 위치한 잉카문명에 대한 거짓된 정보인가?

(A) 그들은 정복되기 전까지 자기의 역사를 기록 할 수 없었다.
(B) 그들은 군사적으로 그리고 구조적으로 수도를 둘러싼 주변의 문화보다 뛰어났다.
(C) 그들은 주변 국가 침략에 대한 자기들만의 기록을 보유하고 있지 않다. ★
(D) 그들의 문자 체계는 대부분의 사람들이 사용하기에 너무 복잡했기에 스페인어를 사용해서 역사를 기록했다.

Fact 질문의 키워드인 Inca civilization이 언급된 부분을 살펴보면 Since the Inca language did not have writing system (잉카는 문자 체계를 가지고 있지 않았기 때문에)라고 말한다. 즉, 잉카 문명의 문자 체계는 복잡했던 것이 아니라 처음부터 존재하지 않았기 때문에 정답은 (D)가 된다.

02 Why does the author mention 3,000 miles of coastline in paragraph 1?

(A) To point out that the Incan Empire eventually overtook the ~~entire~~ western coast of South America ★
(B) To give an example of the great distances that Incan warriors travelled in order to ~~defend~~ their civilization from invasion
(C) To show the reader that the Inca could travel great distances even before the ~~introduction of horses~~ by the Spanish
(D) To show the reader how far the Inca expanded their territory from its beginning in the city of Cusco

작가는 단락 1에 3,000마일의 해안지대를 왜 언급하는가?

(A) 잉카 제국이 결국에는 남미의 모든 서쪽 해안을 점령했다는 점을 얘기하기 위해서 ★
(B) 잉카의 전사들이 자기의 문명을 침략으로부터 지켜내기 위해서 이동한 엄청난 거리의 하나의 예시를 들기 위해서
(C) 잉카는 스페인으로부터 말을 소개받기 이전에 이미 많은 거리를 이동할 수 있었다는 것을 독자들에게 알리기 위해서
(D) 잉카가 처음 시작인 수도의 쿠스코에서부터 정확히 얼마나 영역을 확장했는지 독자들에게 보여주기 위해서

Purpose 음영 표시된 부분을 살펴보면 Within 250 years, their conquests of neighboring societies allowed them to control over 3,000 miles of coastline and land covering parts of present day Peru, Bolivia, Ecuador, Chile and Argentina. (250년 이내에 주변의 사회들을 정복함으로써 오늘날의 페루, 볼리비아, 에콰도르, 칠레, 그리고 아르헨티나의 부분을 포함하는 3,000마일의 해안지대와 땅을 통제할 수 있는 힘을 쥐게 되었다)라고 말한다. 즉, 잉카 문명이 그들의 수도인 쿠스코의 설립으로 시작해 이후에 광범위하게 확장해나갔다는 것을 알려주기 위해 음영 표시된 부분이 언급된 것이므로 정답은 (D)가 된다. (A)는 잉카가 남아메리카의 전체가 아닌 일부를 점령한 것이기 때문에 오답이고, (B)는 보호가 아니라 다른 곳들을 점령해서 영역을 넓혔다 라는 내용을 뒷받침해주기 위해 음영 표시된 부분이 언급된 것이기 때문에 오답이다. (C)는 본문에 언급되는 내용이 아니므로 오답이다.

03 Why does the author mention that the Spanish "simply adapted the information to the Spanish style of governance" in paragraph 2?

(A) To explain how the Spanish dealt with the information they were given about aspects of the Inca civilization that they didn't fully understand
(B) To point out one of the ways that the Spanish directly ~~influenced~~ the way of life in the early Incan society
(C) To reveal that the problems of the Inca ruling system could be ~~solved~~ by the Spanish system ★
(D) To give an example of the Spanish conquistador's feelings of ~~superiority~~ over the Inca they found in Peru

왜 작가는 단락 2에 스페인이 "단순히 정보를 스페인의 지배 방식에 개조했다"라고 얘기를 하는가?

(A) 스페인이 잉카 문명에 대해서 완벽하게 이해하지 못했던 정보들을 어떻게 처리했는지 설명하기 위해서
(B) 스페인이 초기 잉카 사회의 삶에 직접적인 ~~영향을 준~~ 방법 중에 하나를 얘기하기 위해서
(C) 잉카 지배 시스템이 보유한 문제점들은 스페인 지배 시스템에 의해 ~~해결될 수 있다는~~ 것을 보여주기 위해서 ★
(D) 스페인의 지배자들이 잉카에게 느꼈던 ~~우월한 감정들~~의 예시를 들기 위해서

Purpose   음영 표시된 부분을 살펴보면 The first of these is that the ruling system used by the Inca was different from that of the Spanish Empire and may not have been fully understood by the early conquerors. (첫 번째 문제는 잉카에서 사용되었던 지배 시스템이 스페인 제국과 매우 달랐으며 초기의 정복자들이 이해를 하지 못했을 수도 있다는 점이다)라고 말한다. 즉, 스페인 정복자들이 잉카의 운영체계를 제 대로 이해하지 못했을 가능성이 크다는 뜻이고, 그들이 수집한 정보를 자신들의 방식으로만 해석했을 가능성이 크다는 것이니까 정답은 (A)가 된다. (B)는 스페인이 잉카 사회의 삶에 영향을 미쳤다는 내용은 언급되지 않으므로 오답이고, (C)는 스페인 정복자들은 잉카의 운영체계에 대한 정보를 입수만 했을 뿐 문제점을 찾아 고치려고 시도하진 않았기 때문에 오답이다. (D)또한 본문에는 직접적으로 나와있는 내용이 아니기 때문에 오답이다.

---

04   What can be inferred about the rulers of the Inca Empire from the information presented in paragraph 2?

(A) Their names were ~~very similar~~ and this caused confusion for the Spanish writers who were recording their history.
(B) We ~~now know~~ that there were ~~fewer~~ than thirteen of them ruling concurrently over the empire.
(C) It is still unclear how many kings actually ruled over the Incas because of possible inaccuracies in the historical record.
(D) A Spanish cultural bias that placed ~~more importance~~ on the last four successful rulers caused inaccuracy in the accounts of the early rulers. ★

단락 2에서 주어진 정보로 잉카의 지배자들에 관해서 추론 할 수 있는 것은?

(A) 그들의 이름은 ~~매우 비슷했기에~~ 역사를 기록하고서는 스페인 작가들에게 많은 혼란을 주었다.
(B) 13명 보다 ~~적은~~ 잉카 지배자들이 동시에 통치를 했다는 것이 ~~현재 확실해졌다~~.
(C) 역사의 기록에 불명확한 정보의 존재의 가능성 때문에 아직도 정확히 몇 명의 왕들이 잉카를 지배했는지 확실하지 않다.
(D) 마지막 네 명의 성공적인 잉카 지배자들에 더 중요성을 둔 스페인의 문화적 편견이 초창기의 지배자들의 기록에 대한 부정확성을 초래하였다. ★

Inference   질문의 키워드인 rulers of the Inca Empire가 언급된 부분을 살펴보면 If they were titles, they could have been held concurrently, and there may have been fewer than thirteen kings that ruled over the empire. (만약 그것들이 직위였다면 동시에 적용되었을 수도 있으며 잉카 제국을 통치하였던 왕들은 13명보다 적었을 수도 있다)라고 말한다. 즉, if(만약에)라는 것은 아직도 기록의 오류 때문에 어떤 것이 사실인지 확실히 알 수 없다는 것을 뜻하기 때문에 정답은 (C)가 된다. (A)는 이름이 같았던 것이 아니라 사람의 이름인지 직위의 제목인지가 헷갈 렸다는 것이기 때문에 오답이고, (B)는 오류가 있는 기록들 때문에 13명이었는지 13명보다 적었는지 확실하게 알 수 없기 때문에 오답이다. (D)는 스페인의 문화적 편견이 마지막 4명의 지배자들에게 중요성을 두었다고 나와있지 않을뿐더러, 그것 때문에 부정확성이 초래된 것은 더더욱 아니기 때문에 오답이다.

---

05   What role does paragraph 3 play in the passage?

(A) It shows that the conquistadors intentionally falsified the historical records they kept to show their ~~superiority~~ over the Inca.
(B) It is meant to emphasize that the intention of the Spanish conquest was ~~to amass more gold~~. ★
(C) It introduces the possibility that the inaccuracies found in the historical record were not merely caused by misunderstandings.
(D) It helps understand how the conquered Incans lied to the Spanish conquistadors ~~to secure themselves better positions~~.

단락 3은 전체 문장에서 무슨 역할을 가지고 있나?

(A) 스페인의 지배자들은 의도적으로 역사 기록을 거짓화해서 자신의 ~~우월함을~~ 보여주려 했다는 점을 보여주고 있다.
(B) 스페인의 지배자들은 ~~금을 더 모으기 위해서~~ 잉카 제국을 점령했다는 것을 강조하기 위해서이다. ★
(C) 역사 기록의 오류는 서로의 오해만으로 이루어지지 않았을 수도 있다는 가능성을 보여주기 위해서이다.
(D) 점령 당한 잉카들은 ~~자신을 더 좋은 위치에~~ 확정시키기 위해서 스페인 지배자들에게 거짓말을 했다는 점을 독자들에게 이해시키기 위해서이다.

Purpose   단락 3의 첫 부분을 살펴보면 Another problem with the accounts compiled by the Spanish was that they may have been intentionally inaccurate. (또 다른 문제점은 스페인이 수집한 기록들이 의도적으로 부정확했을 수도 있다는 점이다)라고 말한다. 즉, 역사 기록에서 발견된 부정확한 정보는 뜻하지 않게 발생한(단락 2) 것이 아니라 고의적이었을 수도 있다는 것을 3단락에서 설명해주는 것이기 때문에 정답은 (C)가 된다. (A)는 자신의 우월함이 아닌 더 많은 금을 얻기 위해서 의도적으로 정보를 왜곡시킨 것이기 때문에 오답이고, (B)는 금을 얻기 위해서 점령한 것이 아니라 점령한 후 금을 캐내기 시작한 것이기 때문에 오답이다. (D)는 존재감을 과장시켜 자신들의 중요성을 높이기 위해서 거짓말을 한 것이기 때문에 오답이다.

06 What can be inferred from paragraph 6 about place names in the Incan empire?

(A) Scientists have ~~mixed~~ the various names by different Spanish writers ~~up with~~ the changes in the locations of the settlements. ★
(B) The Spanish writers ~~purposefully~~ used inaccurate place names to prevent other writers from knowing where they had been.
(C) In the 500 years since the Spanish invasion, the descendants of the Inca ~~were enforced to change~~ the names of their towns and provinces to confuse the conquerors.
(D) Modern researchers have had difficulty mapping out the areas once inhabited by the ancient Incas.

단락 5를 보고 잉카 제국의 장소 이름들에 대해서 추론할 수 있는 것은?

(A) 과학자들은 스페인에 의해 기록된 다양한 장소 이름들을 주거지 위치 변동으로 ~~혼동하였다~~. ★
(B) 스페인의 작가들은 다른 작가들로부터 자기가 어디에 있었는지 숨기기 위해서 ~~악도적으로~~ 장소들에 거짓된 이름을 주었다.
(C) 스페인의 정복이 일어 난지 500년동안 잉카의 후손들은 통치자들을 헷갈리게 하기 위해서 도시나 주의 이름을 ~~바꾸도록 강요당했다~~.
(D) 현대 연구자들은 고대 잉카들이 살던 곳들을 지도화 하는 A을 무척 어려워한다.

Inference 질문의 키워드인 place names in the Incan empire이 언급된 부분을 살펴보면 This makes it difficult to verify any of the location information in accounts of the Incan Empire. (이것은 잉카 제국과 관련된 위치 정보를 확인하는 것을 어렵게 한다)라고 말한다. 즉, 잉카에 대한 정보를 기록하던 스페인 작가들이 잉카의 장소들의 이름을 바꾸고 다른 종류를 사용했기 때문에 현재 연구자들은 잉카들이 살았던 곳을 정 확하게 표시하기가 힘들다는 것이기 때문에 정답은 (D)가 된다. (A)는 장소 이름을 기록할 때 스페인 사람들이 사용한 incongruent names(일치하지 않는 이름들)과 지난 500년동안 일어난 주거지 변동들이 합쳐져서 과학자들이 연구를 하는데 주었다는 것이 맞는 내용이므로 오답이고, (B)는 작가들이 의도적으로 장소이름들을 통일하지 않은 것은 아니기 때문에 오답이다. (C)는 잉카의 후손들이 장소이름들을 바꾼 것이 아니라 스페인 작가들이 기록하는 과정에서 오류가 있었던 이유 때문에 오답이다.

07 Which of the sentences below best expresses the essential information in the highlighted sentence in the passage? Incorrect choices change the meaning in important ways or leave out essential information.

(A) The Spanish learned the names and titles of the 13 consecutive rulers who reigned over the Incas before they arrived.
(B) iii) The Spanish applied their system of consecutive monarchy when writing about i) the 13 Inca leaders they learned about ii) even though the names they were given may not have been actual people, but rather governmental positions.
(C) The Incas recounted the lives of their 13 sequential leaders using names and titles similar to those in the monarchy system in Spain ~~so that~~ the Spanish could easily understand their history.
(D) The list of Inca leaders may have been inaccurate ~~because~~ the Spanish did not realize that the names they were given were ~~actually the titles~~ of the positions held by the leaders, ~~not~~ their given names. ★

밑의 문장들 중에 하이라이트 된 문장의 제일 중요한 정보만 담긴 것은? 잘못된 답들은 중요한 의미를 바꾸고 핵심적인 정보를 빼놓는다.

(A) 스페인은 잉카의 13명의 연속적인 왕들의 이름과 직위를 잉카에 도착하기 전에 배웠다.
(B) iii) 주어진 이름은 사람의 이름이 아닌 정부에서의 지위였을 수도 있지만 스페인은 i) 13명의 잉카의 지도자들을 기록할 때 ii) 자기들의 지배 방식인 연속적인 왕권으로 적용시켰다.
(C) 잉카는 13명의 순차적인 지도자들의 인생을 이름이랑 지위를 스페인의 왕권 방식이랑 비슷하게 해서 스페인이 자신들의 역사를 ~~더 쉽게 이해할 수 있도록 했다~~.
(D) 스페인은 주어진 이름이 사람의 이름이 아닌 지배자들의 ~~차위와 제목이라는~~ 것을 깨닫지 못해서 잉카 지도자의 명단은 정확하지 않을 수도 있다. ★

Highlight 음영 표시된 문장은 i) The Inca told the early conquerors of thirteen kings who ruled over the empire, and ii) the Spanish recorded them as thirteen sequential rulers, as that is how the monarchy worked in Spain; iii) however, it isn't clear if these recorded names were individuals or titles. (i) 잉카는 초기의 정복자들에게 잉카 제국을 지배하고 있는 13명의 왕들을 얘기했지만 ii) 스페인은 자기들의 왕권이 운영하는 방식인 13명의 순차적인 왕들이라고 기록을 했다. iii) 하지만 기록된 이름들은 개인의 이름인지 아니면 직위인지는 분명하지 않다.) 이렇게 세 가지 내용으로 나뉜다. 이 내용을 모두 포함한 (B)가 정답이 된다. (A)는 ii)와 iii) 의 내용이 없으므로 오답이고, (C)는 만약 잉카인들이 스페인들의 방식으로 바꾸어 이해하기 쉽게 설명해주었다면 오류가 생길 이유도 없었을 것이지만, 두 지역의 차이점을 고려하지 않고 스페인은 자신들만의 방식으로 이해하여 적용하였기 때문에 오류가 있었던 것이다. 따라서 (C)는 오답이고, (D)는 ii)의 내용을 포함하고 있지 않을 뿐만 아니라 iii) 와의 내용과는 달리 이름들이 직책이라는 것을 기정사실화하기 때문에 오답이다.

08

The term "chronology" in the passage is closest in meaning to:

(A) an ordering of past events according to how long they lasted ★
(B) an explanation of why past events happened when they did
(C) a study of past events
(D) a list that pairs events with dates

지문의 단어 "연대순"의 의미와 가장 유사한 것은?

(A) 과거 사건들이 얼마나 오래 지속됐는지에 따른 배열 ★
(B) 과거 사건들이 왜 그 시기에 일어났는지에 대한 설명
(C) 과거 사건들에 대한 연구
(D) 사건을 날짜와 짝지은 목록 (연대기)

Vocabulary 지문의 chronology(연대순)과 유사한 뜻을 가진 a list that pairs events with dates(연대기)가 정답이다.

09

Look at the four squares [■] that indicate where the following sentence could be added to the passage.

As time went on, these kinds of inaccuracies would have been compounded since most scholars would have used these recordings as primary sources for their later research.

Where would the sentence best fit? Click on a square [■] to add the sentence to the passage.

1st

네 개의 네모 [■]는 다음 문장이 삽입될 수 있는 부분을 나타내고 있다.

대부분의 학자들은 이런 종류의 기록들을 나중의 연구를 위한 1차 자료로 사용했기 때문에 시간이 지날수록 이런 불명확함은 혼합되었을 수도 있다.

이 문장은 어느 자리에 들어가는 것이 가장 적절한가?

첫번째

Insertion 삽입 문장의 키워드는 these kind of inaccuracies이다. 첫 번째 네모 앞에 있는 문장을 살펴보면 스페인이 잉카의 역사를 기록하면서 발생한 오류가 언급된다. 즉, 삽입 문장은 이러한 오류들을 이용해 연구를 진행해온 학자들 때문에 초기에 있던 오류들이 더 혼합되고 덜 명확해졌을 가능성이 크다는 뜻이다. 또한, 이것에 대한 예시를 소개해주는 말이 첫 번째 다음 문장에 나타나기 때문에 정답은 첫 번째 네모이다.

10

Directions: An introductory sentence for a brief summary of the passage is provided below. Complete the summary by selecting the THREE answer choices that express the most important ideas in the passage. Some sentences do not belong in the summary because they express ideas that are not presented in the passage or are minor ideas in the passage. **This question is worth 2 points.**

지시: 지문 요약을 위한 도입 문장이 아래에 주어져 있다. 지문의 가장 중요한 내용을 나타내는 보기 3개를 골라 요약을 완성 하시오. 어떤 문장은 지문에 언급되지 않은 내용이나 사소한 정보를 담고 있으므로 요약에 포함되지 않는다. **이 문제는 2점이다.**	

Although it was once the most powerful empire in the New World, it is difficult to get accurate firsthand accounts of the Inca Civilization.

(B) Many of the early records written by the Spanish are inaccurate due to misunderstandings and inherent cultural biases. - paragraph 2, 4

(C) The Spanish and Inca may have both intentionally misrepresented the history of the Empire for their own personal gain and glorification. - paragraph 3, 5

(E) Movements and inaccurate record keeping have made it difficult to locate the settlements that existed during the height of the Inca Empire. - paragraph 6

새로운 세계의 제일 강력한 제국이었지만 잉카 제국과 관련된 1차적인 사실적인 이야기를 얻기에는 힘들다.

(B) 스페인이 기록한 초기의 문서들은 오해와 문화적 편견으로 인해서 오류가 많다.

(C) 스페인과 잉카 둘 다 자기의 이득과 명예를 위해서 의도적으로 잘못 기록 했을 수도 있다.

(E) 움직임과 오류가 있는 기록들 때문에 잉카 제국 정점에 있었던 주거지들을 정확하게 찾는 것이 힘들다.

(A) At the height of their Empire the Incas controlled most of the western coast of South America and their territory extended into five countries. - paragraph 1 detail

(D) Conflicting accounts of the Incan conquests given by the ~~adversaries~~ and themselves further puzzled researchers. - 틀린 정보

(F) Researchers still use ~~firsthand accounts by~~ the Inca Empire despite the inaccuracies they contain. - 틀린 정보

(A) 잉카 제국이 제일 강력했을 때는 남미의 서부 해안을 거의 모두 다스리고 있었으며 다섯 개의 국가로 영역이 넓혀 있었다.

(D) 잉카의 ~~태적과~~ 그들 자신들에 의해 전해진 잉카 정복의 모순되는 이야기들은 연구자들을 헷갈리게 했다.

(F) 연구자들은 오류에도 불구하고 잉카제국이 ~~직접~~ 커록한 자료들을 사용한다. ★

Summary 지문의 중심 내용은 기록된 잉카제국의 역사에서 발견된 오류의 원인이다. (B)는 두 번째와 네 번째 단락의 중심내용인 의도치 않게 발생된 오류들의 내용과 일치하고, (C)는 세 번째와 다섯 번째 단락의 중심내용인 의도적으로 발생된 오류의 내용과 일치하고, (E)는 여섯 번째 단락의 지역의 이름을 통일하지 못해 발생된 오류 때문에 초래된 결과와 일치한다. 따라서 답은 (B), (C), (E) 이다. (F)는 잉카 제국은 문자 체계를 보유하지 않았기 때문에 직접 기록을 남길 수가 없었기 때문에 오답이다.

TEST 5-2 Architectural Change in Eighth Century Japan
8세기 일본의 건축학적 변화

Introduction	단락 1	8세기 일본에게 대륙에 있는 이웃국가들이 미친 영향
Point	단락 2	나라시대의 결혼 풍습이 왕궁의 위치에 미친 영향
Point	단락 3	전통적인 건축 기술과 신토 종교의 믿음
Point	단락 4	관료정치의 확장과 그에 따른 결과
Point	단락 5	당나라의 건축 기술과 불교의 수용이 일본의 건축 스타일에 미친 영향
Point	단락 6	협상을 통한 세력간의 갈등 해결

문단 주제	본문 내용	해 석
단락 1 8세기 일본에게 대륙에 있는 이웃국가들이 미친 영향	**1** Japanese architecture underwent dramatic changes as the Nara period began in the early 8th century. During this period, great political and societal changes, such as the establishment of the capital at Heijō-kyō (modern day Nara), made traditional architectural arrangements and styles less advantageous and necessitated a new system. [Q1-A] On this **quest for** more adequate architectural styles the Japanese were influenced by the architecture of continental Asian powers, such as China's Tang Dynasty.	일본 건축양식은 8세기 초에 나라시대가 시작되며 역동적인 변화를 겪었다. 이 기간 동안, (현재는 나라라고 알려진) 하이죠쿠 수도건설과 같은 커다란 정치적 및 사회적 변화가 전통적인 건축 배열과 스타일을 이익이 덜 되게 만들었으며, 그래서 새로운 시스템을 필요로 하게 되었다. [Q1-A] 더 적합한 건축양식을 찾는 과정에서 일본은 중국의 당나라와 같은 아시아 대륙 나라들의 건축으로부터 많은 영향을 받았다.
단락 2 나라시대의 결혼 풍습이 왕궁의 위치에 미친 영향	**2** One of the most glaring catalysts for the **change in** architectural styles was the **shift in** marriage practices of the Japanese elite. **Prior to** this period, Japanese rulers married members of one of the most powerful clans of the period, the Soga lords' families, in politically motivated alliances, and established palaces at the bride's family home **in addition to that of** their own family headquarters. The royal court generally **resided with** the bride's family **for** the first **years** of their marriage and then moved between their multiple palaces throughout the marriage as children grew older and alliances shifted. This system was workable during this period because of the relatively small royal court and rudimentary architectural style.	건축학 스타일의 변화를 불러일으킨 가장 큰 기폭제 중 하나는 일본 엘리트층의 결혼관습의 변화였다. 이 시기 이전의 일본의 지도자들은 그 당시에 가장 영향력 있던 가문 중 하나인 소가 가문과 정치적 의도를 띈 결혼을 하였고, 자기 가족의 궁전에 추가로 신부의 집에까지 궁전을 지었다. 왕실은 대체로 신부의 가족과 결혼 첫 몇 년을 같이 살다가 아이들이 크거나 동맹들이 변하면서 소유하고 있는 다수의 궁궐들을 옮겨다니면서 살았다. 이 시기에 이 관습이 가능했던 것은 상대적으로 작은 조정과 간단한 건축 스타일 덕분이었다.

Vocabulary

1단락 architecture [á:rkətèktʃər] n. 건축   capital [kǽpitl] n. 수도   establishment [istǽbliʃmənt] n. 설립
adequate [ǽdikwit] a. 충분한   continental [kàntənéntl] a. 대륙의

2단락 glaring [glέriŋ] a. 두드러진   alliance [əláiəns] n. 동맹   reside [ri:sáid] v. 거주하다
rudimentary [rù:dəméntəri] a. 가장 기초적인

3단락 fortress [fɔ́:rtris] n. 요새   shrine [ʃrain] n. 신사   thatched [θætʃt] a. 초가   beam [bi:m] n. 기둥

단락 3 전통적인 건축 기술과 신토 종교의 믿음	**3** Prior to the Nara period, traditional Japanese structures, such as palaces, gate towers, fortresses, and shrines, **were built with** wooden beams, dirt floors, and thatched roofs. [Q3-A] Since these beams were **in** direct **contact with** the moist ground, they often rotted away in less than 20 years. [Q3-C] The simple, temporary nature of these buildings meant that they could be moved or constructed in new areas without great labor or material expenditures and were easily rebuildable when damaged. This was **important to** Shinto adherents because [Q3-D] replacing buildings **allowed for** a spiritual cleansing of the land. This **taboo against** unclean spirits also **led to** the continuous movement of the capital before the Nara period; new emperors moved the court to avoid contamination from the death of their predecessors.	나라 시대 이전에는 궁궐, 문탑, 요새, 신사 등 전통적인 건축은 나무 기둥, 흙 바닥, 그리고 초가 지붕으로 만들어졌다. [Q3-A] 이러한 기둥들이 습기 많은 흙 바닥과 직접 닿고 있었기 때문에 기둥들은 20년 이내에 썩어버렸다. [Q3-C] 건물들이 이렇게 간단하고 일시적이었기 때문에 많은 노동이나 재료 구매 경비 지출 없이 쉽게 이동하거나 새로운 장소에 다시 만들 수 있었고, 손상된 건물들은 쉽게 재건축이 가능했다. 이 점이 신토신봉자들에게 중요했던 이유는 [Q3-D] 건물을 바꾸는 것을 통해 그 땅을 영적으로 정화할 수 있기 때문이었다. 이러한 더러운 영혼에 대한 금기는 나라시대 이전에 수도를 계속 옮겨 다닌 이유이기도 하다; 새 천황들은 그들 이전 천황의 영혼으로부터 나쁜 영향을 받는 것을 피하기 위해 왕궁을 다른 위치로 옮겼다.
단락 4 관료정치의 확장과 그에 따른 결과	**4** Moving the capital became unfeasible during the Nara period **due to the expansion of** the bureaucracy **involved in** the court during the previous two centuries. [Q4-A] **By the time the Nara emperors rose to power**, they were overseeing a staff of 10,000 workers and needed a location that provided adequate housing for them. The need to **keep in contact with** these people and to **provide for** them meant that palaces **needed to be maintained** in areas with abundant resources. Further, moving such a large court and reconstructing **enough** buildings **to house** them effectively killed the mobile capital tradition and led the emperors to **settle in** Heijō-kyō.	이전의 두 세기 동안 왕궁의 관료들이 늘어나면서 나라시대에는 수도를 옮기는 것이 현실적으로 힘들어졌다. [Q4-A] 나라 천황들이 권력을 잡았을 때는 10,000명이 넘는 일꾼들이 있었고 그들의 숙소를 해결할 수 있는 넓은 지역이 필요했다. 이 사람들과 연락을 취하고 먹여 살리기 위해서는 궁궐들은 많은 자원이 있는 곳에 유지되어야만 했다. 또한, 이렇게 큰 정부를 옮기고 그들을 위해 충분한 건물들을 짓는 것은 사실상 이동하는 수도의 관습을 끝냈고, 천황들은 하이죠쿄에 정착하게 되었다.
단락 5 당나라의 건축 기술과 불교의 수용이 일본의 건축 스타일에 미친 영향	**5** To construct this Imperial city, [Q5-D] Japanese architects looked to the urban design and construction techniques of their continental neighbors' geometrically situated capitals with their [Q5-B] bulkier, more permanent buildings constructed using stone foundations, mortise joints, and tiled roofs which allowed them to stand for years. [■] The construction of a large, continental-style capital with these types of buildings required a tremendous amount of manpower and building materials, but it was **attractive to** emperors **looking to legitimize** their reigns **in a manner** directly **comparable to** the powerful Chinese dynasty. [■] The construction of these types of buildings was also heavily influenced by	이 천황의 도시를 짓기 위해서는 [Q5-D] 일본의 건축가들은 그들의 대륙의 이웃들의 지리적으로 위치된 수도의 도시적 디자인과 건축 기술들을 본받았다. 그 대륙의 이웃들의 건물들은 [Q5-B] 돌 기반, 장붓 구멍 연결체, 그리고 기와지붕들을 사용한 더 부피가 크고 영구적인 건물들을 만들어 이 건물들은 오랫동안 버틸 수 있었다. [■] 이런 건물들로 구성된 큰 대륙적 스타일의 수도를 짓는 데는 엄청난 양의 노동과 건축재료를 필요로 했지만, 강력한 중국왕조와 직접적으로 비교하는 방식으로 그들의 군림을 정당화 하려는 천황들에게는 매력적이었다. [■] 또한, 이런

Vocabulary

moist [mɔist] a. 습기가 많은
cleansing [klénziŋ] n. 깨끗이 하는 것

temporary [témpərèri] a. 임시적인
taboo [təbú:] n. 금기

labor [léibər] n. 노동력
contamination [kəntæmənéiʃən] n. 오염

4단락 unfeasible [ʌnfíːzəbəl] a. 실행할 수 없는
abundant [əbʌ́ndənt] a. 풍부한

expansion [ikspǽnʃən] n. 확장
resource [ríːsɔːrs, -zɔːrs, risɔ́ːrs, -zɔ́ːrs] n. 자원

bureaucracy [bjuərάkrəsi] n. 관료
mobile [móubəl, -biːl] a. 유동적인

5단락 Imperial [impíəriəl] a. 제국의

geometric [dʒìːəmétrik] a. 기하학적인

bulky [rèidiéiʃən] a. 부피가 큰

the widespread acceptance of Buddhism, which had **been introduced from** the continental kingdoms two hundred years earlier. [■] After this, the Japanese officially adopted Buddhism, but conflicts with hostile believers in the Shinto Kami prevented them from building lasting Buddhist temples. During the Nara period, the Japanese Buddhists built temple complexes **modeled after** those found in continental nations, such as the Hōryū-ji, one of the oldest surviving wooden structures in the world. [■]

단락 6
협상을 통한 세력간의 갈등

6 This shift in architecture during this period caused a series of conflicts across the Japanese royal court. Rulers **wished to display** their power through the construction of a grand capital rivaling that of the Tang Dynasty, but this was difficult **at the time** and required a great expenditure. [Q7-B] In addition, while the opulent lifestyle of the new building styles **would have been** comfortable for the ruling class, [Q8-D] they **were hesitant to give up** the multiple palaces they enjoyed **under** the mobile court **system**. Conflicts even arose between religions because of the Shinto **belief in** replacing buildings frequently and the Buddhists' **desire for** permanent religious buildings. Eventually these conflicts were solved through a compromise **in** building **methods**. Shinto shrines, with their religious **reliance on** rebuilding and cleansing, and many residential buildings **adhered to** the traditional style that was more economical, mobile, and replaceable. Government buildings, city gates, and Buddhist temples, **on the other hand**, were constructed **in** the more permanent, grandiose continental **style**. Even the issues **related to** the immobility of the court were solved through an architectural compromise. Rulers, who were now **in residence** in the grand capital, constructed smaller palaces in remote areas where they could temporarily reside. This gave the court a bit of mobility and may have **made it easier for them to oversee** the parts of their populations which lived **far away from** the new capital city.

종류의 건물들의 건설은 대륙의 왕조에서 200년 전에 소개된 불교의 넓은 수용의 영향도 크게 받았다. [■] 이 이후에 일본인들은 정식으로 불교를 인정했지만, 신토카미의 공격적인 신자들과의 갈등이 영구적인 불교 절들의 건설을 막았다. 나라시대에 일본 불교인들은 대륙의 나라들에 있는 절들을 본떠 절 건물들을 만들었는데 그 중 하나인 호류지는 세계에서 가장 오래된 남아있는 나무 건물들 중 하나이다. [■]

이 시기의 이런 건축의 변화는 일본의 정부에 일련의 분쟁들을 일으켰다. 통치자들은 당 왕조에 필적하는 거대한 수도건설을 통해 그들의 권력을 과시하길 원했지만, 그 당시에는 어려웠고 엄청난 재정지출이 요구되었다. [Q7-B] 또한, 이런 새 건물들이 보장하는 부유한 삶이 지도층에게 편했겠지만, [Q8-D] 그들은 유동적 왕궁 시스템하에 즐기던 여러 궁궐들을 포기하기 싫어했다. 심지어는 분쟁은 종교들 사이에도 일어났다; 신토 종교의 건물들을 수시로 재건축하고자 하는 신앙와 불교인들의 영구 적인 종교적 건물들을 원하는 욕구 사이에 갈등이 생긴 것이다. 결국 이런 갈등들은 건축 방법의 협상을 통해 해결됐다. 재건축과 정화에 대한 종교적 의존성이 있는 신토 신사와 많은 거주건물들은 경제적이고, 이동이 가능하고, 대체가능한 전통 양식을 고수했다. 반면에 정부 건물, 도시 벽문, 그리고 불교 절들은 더 거대하고 영구적인 대륙적인 스타일로 만들어졌다. 심지어는 유동적이지 못한 왕궁의 문제까지 건축학적 절충으로 해결되었다. 웅장한 수도에 사는 통치자들은 일시적으로 지낼 수 있는 궁궐들을 멀리 떨어진 지역에 지었다. 이 시스템은 대륙의 다른 통치자들에 의해서도 쓰였는데, 이 시스템 을 통해 왕궁은 소량의 유동성을 가질 수 있게 되었고 천황들은 새로운 수도에서 멀리 떨어진 백성들을 다스릴 수 있게 되었다.

Vocabulary

foundation [faundéiʃən] n. 기반
reign [rein] n. 군림

6단락
expenditure [ikspénditʃər] n. 지출
residential [rèzidénʃəl] a. 주택지의

mortise [mɔ́ːrtis] n. 장붓구멍
dynasty [dáinəsti / díː-] n. 왕조

opulent [ápjələnt / ɔ́p-] a. 부유한
remote [rimóut] a. 외딴

legitimize [lidʒítəmàiz] v. 정당화하다

compromise [kámprəmàiz / kɔ́m-] v. 타협하다

11 What can be inferred about architecture in eighth century Japan from paragraph 1?

(A) It lagged behind the far more sophisticated architectural styles that were found in continental Asia.
(B) It only retrogressed due to the new system derived from the great changes in society. ★
(C) Changes in Japanese architecture were brought about by societal and political changes that occurred in Tang China.
(D) The founding of the city of Heijō-kyō was possible because of changes that occurred in the Japanese architectural style.

단락 1에 따르면 8세기 일본의 건축학에 대해 추론할 수 있는 것은?

(A) 대륙에서 찾아볼 수 있었던 더 복잡한 건축학적 스타일의 건축들보다 훨씬 뒤떨어졌다.
(B) 사회에서 일어난 큰 변화들에 의해 만들어진 새로운 시스템 때문에 오히려 쇠퇴하였다. ★
(C) 일본 건축학의 변화는 중국의 당나라와 사회적 정치적 변화에 의해 생겼다.
(D) 도시 하이조쿄의 건설은 일본의 건축학적 스타일의 변화 때문에 가능했다.

> **Inference** 질문의 키워드인 architecture in eighth century Japan이 언급된 부분을 살펴보면 On this quest for more adequate architectural styles the Japanese were influenced by the architecture of continental Asian powers, such as China's Tang Dynasty. (더 적합한 건축학 풍채를 찾는 과정에서 일본은 중국의 당나라와 같은 아시아 대륙 나라들의 건축학에게 많은 영향을 받았다)라고 말한다. 즉, 대륙에서 쓰이는 건축학적 스타일이 큰 도시 설립에 더 적합하였으므로 일본의 건축학 스타일은 대륙의 스타일에 뒤떨어졌을 것이라고 유추할 수 있다. 따라서 정답은 (A)가 된다. (B)는 사회에서 일어난 변화들은 오히려 일본의 건축 스타일 변화에 큰 기폭제 역할을 해주었기 때문에 오답이고, (C)는 당나라가 아닌 일본이기 때문에 오답이다. (D)는 하이조쿄의 설립이 일본의 건축 시스템에 변화를 준 계기가 되었던 것이기 때문에 오답이다.

12 The term "alliances" in the passage is closest in meaning to

(A) Conflicts [kánflikt / kɔ́n-]
(B) Partnerships [páːrtnərʃip]
(C) Transactions [trænsǽkʃən, trænz-]
(D) Communications [kəmjùːnəkéiʃən] ★

지문의 단어 "동맹"의 의미와 가장 유사한 것은?

(A) 갈등
(B) 협력
(C) 거래
(D) 소통 ★

> **Vocabulary** 지문의 alliances(동맹)와 동의어인 partnerships(협력)이 정답이다.

13 According to paragraph 3, all of the following are typical of Japanese construction prior to the Nara period **EXCEPT**:

(A) Early Japanese buildings were constructed using wood and thatching that rotted easily when exposed to the elements.
(B) The easy deterioration of the materials used in early Japanese construction meant that it was difficult to move the buildings without damaging them.
(C) The materials used to build early Japanese buildings allowed them to be built in a multitude of locations with little difficulty or cost. ★
(D) The Shinto religion prescribed that buildings should be constructed using materials and building techniques that made them easily replaceable.

지문의 단락 3에서 나라시대 이전의 일본 건축에 대해 사실이 아닌 것은?

(A) 이른 일본의 건물들은 자연에 접촉하면 쉽게 썩는 나무와 초가로 만들어졌다.
(B) 이른 일본식 건축에 사용된 재료는 쉽게 부패되어서 건물들을 손상시키지 않으면서 옮기기 힘들었다.
(C) 이른 일본식 건물에 사용된 재료들은 건물들이 여러 장소에 조금의 어려움과 조금의 가격으로 만들 수 있게 해주었다. ★
(D) 신토 종교는 건물들이 쉽게 교체될 수 있게 해주는 재료들로 만드는 것을 요구했다.

Fact   지문의 키워드인 Japanese construction이 언급된 부분을 살펴보면 The simple, temporary nature of these buildings meant that they could be moved or constructed in new areas without great labor or material expenditures. (건물들이 이렇게 간단하고 일시적이었기 때문에 많은 노동이나 재료의 구매없이 쉽게 이동하거나 새로운 장소에 다시 만들 수 있었다)라고 말한다. 즉, 쉽게 부패되는 건물재료들 덕분에 건물을 옮기는 것에 대한 부담감이 줄어들었고, 따라서 더 어려워진 것이 아니라 오히려 더 쉬워진 것이기 때문에 정답은 (B)가 된다.

14
According to paragraph 4, which of the following can be inferred regarding the royal court during the Nara period?

(A) The work done by the government workers associated with the court could not proceed without proper housing.
(B) The growth in the size of bureaucracy necessitated a corresponding need to make the court ~~more mobile~~ to find enough housing.
(C) Emperors who ruled during the Nara period ~~overlooked~~ the importance of supervising an immense number of government personnel. ★
(D) The court's settlement in Heijō-kyō was the result of it being the ~~hometown~~ of the largest portion of government workers at the time.

단락 4에 의하면 나라시대의 정부에 대해 추론할 수 있는 것은?

(A) 정부의 직원들이 하는 일은 제대로 주택 없이 진행될 수 없었다.
(B) 관료 제도 크기의 증가는 충분한 주택공급을 제공하기 위해 왕궁을 ~~유동적으로~~ 만들 필요성을 만들었다.
(C) 나라시대의 천황들은 엄청나게 많은 정부직원들을 감독 하는 일의 중요성을 ~~관과하였다~~. ★
(D) 정부가 하이죠쿠에 머물게 된 이유는 하이죠쿠가 그 당시 정부 직원들의 대다수의 ~~고향~~이었기 때문이다.

Inference   질문의 키워드인 royal court during the Nara period가 언급된 부분을 살펴보면 By the time the Nara emperors rose to power, they were overseeing a staff of 10,000 workers and needed a location that provided adequate housing for them. (나라 천황들이 권력을 잡았을 때는 10,000명이 넘는 직원들이 있었고 그들의 숙박을 해결할 수 있는 넓은 땅이 있는 위치가 필요했다)라고 말한다. 즉, 정부의 직원들이 제대로 된 숙박없이는 자신들이 하는 일을 할 수 없었다는 것을 유추할 수 있기 때문에 정답은 (A)가 된다. (B)는 Further, moving such a large court and reconstructing enough buildings to house them effectively killed the mobile capital tradition. 오히려 관료 제도 크기의 증가는 유동적인 왕궁시스템을 한 곳에 정착(덜 유동적으로)시켜야 했기 때문에 오답이고, (C)는 they were overseeing a staff of 10,000 workers. oversee(감독하다)와 overlook(간과하다)는 반의어이고, 오히려 그들은 많은 직원을 수용하기 위해 필요한 방법을 모색하였기 때문에 오답이다. (D)는 본문에 언급되는 내용이 아니므로 오답이다.

15
According to paragraph 5, which of the following is **NOT** true regarding new construction methods used during the Nara period?

(A) Japanese Buddhists built temple styles ~~taken after by~~ the continental neighbors using tiled roofs and mortise joints.
(B) The Japanese built a new capital city using more durable construction materials that allowed its buildings to be more permanent.
(C) The construction techniques utilized during this period allowed the construction of some buildings that have lasted for a long time.
(D) The Japanese borrowed extensively from their neighbors, including both the methods of construction and the basic design aspects of buildings and cities. ★

단락 5에 의하면 다음중 나라시대의 새 건축 방법에 대해 옳지 않은 것은?

(A) ~~대륙의 나라들이~~ 장붓 구멍 연결체와 기와지붕들을 사용함으로써 일본의 건축물 스타일을 ~~빼꼈다~~.
(B) 일본인들은 더 강한 재료로 새로운 수도를 지어서 그 수도의 건물들은 더 영구적이었다.
(C) 이 시기에 사용된 건축 기술들은 오랫동안 남아있는 건물들을 만들게 해줬다.
(D) 일본인들은 그들의 이웃들로부터 건축의 방법과 기본적인 건물과 도시 디자인 등 많은 것을 빌렸다. ★

Fact 지문의 키워드인 new construction methods이 언급된 부분을 살펴보면 To construct this Imperial city, Japanese architects looked to the urban design and construction techniques of their continental neighbors' geometrically situated capitals with their bulkier, more permanent buildings constructed using stone foundations, mortise joints, and tiled roofs which allowed them to stand for years. (이 천황의 도시를 짓기 위해서는 일본의 건축가들은 그들의 대륙의 이웃들의 도시적 디자인과 건축 기술들을 본받았다. 그 대륙의 이웃들의 건물들은 돌 기반, 장붓 구멍 연결체, 그리고 기와지붕들을 사용한 더 부피가 크고 영구적인 건물들을 만들어 이 건물들은 오랫동안 서 있을 수 있었다)라고 말한다. 즉, 일본 불교인들은 다른 대륙 나라들의 건설 스타일을 베낀 것은 맞지만 장붓 구멍 연결체와 기와지붕들을 사용한 것은 아니기 때문에 정답은 (A)가 된다.

16 Which of the sentences below best expresses the essential information in the highlighted sentence in the passage? Incorrect choices change the meaning in important ways or leave out essential information.

(A) Japanese architects adopted building designs and techniques from their neighbors that were durable to make other cities ~~similar~~ to their imperial city. ★
(B) The Japanese new capital city with increased durability and enhanced design was constructed by ~~architects~~ from neighboring countries.
(C) iii)Japanese built more durable buildings with better construction design and techniques ii) derived from their adjacent countries in order to i) establish their capital city.
(D) The new construction techniques used in the Japanese imperial city, namely the stone foundations, mortise joints, and tiles roofs, were a model of urban design and construction techniques ~~for their continental neighbors~~.

다음 문장 중 지문의 하이라이트 된 문장의 중요한 내용을 가장 잘 나타내는 문장은? 오답은 의미를 바꾸거나 중요한 정보를 빼놓는다.

(A) 일본 건축가들은 다른 도시들을 자신들의 제국의 중심 지처럼 만들기 위하여 이웃들의 튼튼한 건물 디자인과 건축 기술을 빌렸다. ★
(B) 더욱 뛰어난 내구성과 향상된 디자인을 가지게 된 일본의 새로운 수도는 주변 국가 ~~건축가들~~로 인해 건설되었다.
(C) iii)일본 건축가들은 수도를 설립하기 위해 ii)인접한 국가들에서 유래된 보다 뛰어난 i)건축 디자인과 기술들을 가지고 더욱 더 튼튼한 건물들을 지었다.
(D) 일본 제국의 도시에서 사용된 돌 기반, 장붓 구멍연결체, 기와지붕 등의 새로운 건축 기술들은 ~~그들의 대륙의 이웃들에게~~ 도시 디자인과 건축 기술의 좋은 모델이 되어주었다.

Highlight 음영 표시된 문장은 i) To construct this new Imperial city, ii) Japanese architects looked to the urban design and construction techniques of their continental neighbors' geometrically situated capitals iii) with their bulkier, more permanent buildings constructed using stone foundations, mortise joints, and tiled roofs which allowed them to stand for years.(i) 이 새로운 천황의 도시를 짓기 위해서는 ii) 일본의 건축가들은 그들의 대륙의 이웃들의 도시적 디자인과 건축 기술들을 본받았다. iii)그 대륙의 이웃들의 건물들은 돌 기반, 장붓 구멍 연결체, 그리고 기와지붕들을 사용한 더 부피가 크고 영구적인 건물들을 만들어 이 건물들은 몇 년씩 서있을 수 있었다) 이렇게 세 부분으로 나뉜다. 이 내용을 모두 포함한 (C)가 정답이 된다. (A)는 일본인들은 자신들의 도시를 다른 도시들처럼 만들고 싶어했기 때문에 오답이고, (B)는 주변 국가의 건축가들이 아니라 국내 건축가들이 지었기 때문에 오답이다. (D)는 내륙 이웃들이 그들에게 좋은 모델이 되어준 것이기 때문에 오답이다.

17

The term "reliance" in the passage is closest in meaning to

(A) limit [límit]
(B) policy [páləsi] ★
(C) disagreement [dìsəgríːmənt]
(D) dependence [dipéndəns]

지문의 단어 "의존성"의 의미와 가장 유사한 것은?

(A) 한계
(B) 제도 ★
(C) 이견
(D) 의존성

Vocabulary 지문의 reliance(의존성)과 동의어인 dependence(의존성)이 정답이다.

18

According to paragraph 6, which of the following is true about the conflicts that arose over construction techniques in Japan during the eighth century?

(A) The construction of a grand new capital to show off the power of the Japanese emperor led to a ~~rivalry~~ with the Tang Chinese.
(B) Japanese emperors were reluctant to give up their multitude of luxurious palaces to settle into the capital city.
(C) The Shinto and Buddhist stuck to a ~~uniform~~ construction style after having a religious conflict. ★
(D) Compromises in society made it possible for the rulers to maintain their ~~grandiose~~ court ~~throughout~~ the country.

단락 6에 의하면 8세기 일본의 건축 기술에 대해 일어난 갈등에 대해 옳은 것은?

(A) 거대한 새 수도의 건축은 일본 천황의 권력을 과시했는데, 이는 중국의 당나라와 ~~라이벌 관계를~~ 불러일으켰다.
(B) 일본의 천황들은 자기의 여러 고급의 궁궐들을 포기하고 수도에 정착하는 것을 주저하였다.
(C) 신토 신자들과 불교 신자들은 종교적 갈등을 겪고 난 후 ~~똑같은~~ 건축 스타일을 고수하였다. ★
(D) 사회에서 일어난 타협은 지도자들이 자신들의 ~~장대한~~ 법정을 ~~전국에~~ 유지할 수 있도록 해주었다.

Fact 질문의 키워드인 conflicts이 언급된 부분을 살펴보면 they were hesitant to give up the multiple palaces they enjoyed under the mobile court system. (그들은 유동적 법정 시스템하에 즐기던 여러 궁궐들을 포기하기 싫어했다.)라고 말한다. 즉, 그들이 즐겼던 여러 개의 호화스러운 궁궐을 포기하고 한 곳에 정착해야 한다는 것을 꺼려하였기 때문에 정답은 (B)가 된다. (A)는 일본과 중국의 당나라 사이에 라이벌 관계가 형성 되었다는 내용이 언급되지 않으므로 오답이고, (D)는 법정을 유지할 수 있었던 것은 사실이나 이것을 전국에 걸쳐 유지한 것이 아니라 전국엔 smaller palaces를 건설하고 유지하였기 때문에 오답이다. (C)는 신토는 유동성이 있는 전통 스타일을 고집했고, 불교는 보다 영구적인 대륙의 스타일로 바꾸었기 때문에 두 세력이 똑같은 건축 스타일을 고수하였다는 건 옳지 않으므로 오답이다.

19

Look at the four squares [■] that indicate where the following sentence could be added to the passage.

> **After this**, the Japanese officially adopted Buddhism, but conflicts with hostile believers in the Shinto Kami prevented them from building lasting Buddhist temples.

Where would the sentence best fit? Click on a square [■] to add the sentence to the passage.

3rd

네 개의 네모 [■]는 다음 문장이 삽입될 수 있는 부분을 나타내고 있다

이 이후에 일본인들은 정식으로 불교를 인정했지만, 신토카미의 공격적인 신자들과의 갈등이 오래 남아 있는 불교 절들의 건설을 막았다.

이 문장은 어느 자리에 들어가는 것이 가장 적절한가?

3번째

Insertion 삽입 문장의 키워드는 After this(this는 불교를 수용한 것임)와 adopted Buddhism이다. 즉, 이 이후에 불교가 인정되었다고 하는 삽입문장은 본문의 불교의 수용에 대한 내용 다음에 삽입 되는 것이 옳다. 그러므로 세 번째 네모 앞의 내용인 The construction of these types of buildings was also heavily influenced by the widespread acceptance of Buddhism, which had been introduced from the continental kingdom. (또한, 이런 종류의 건물들의 건설은 대륙의 왕조에서 소개된 불교의 넓은 수용의 영향도 크게 받았다) 다음에 언급되는 것이 가장 적절함으로 정답은 세 번째 네모이다.

20

Directions: An introductory sentence for a brief summary of the passage is provided below. Complete the summary by selecting the THREE answer choices that express the most important ideas in the passage. Some sentences do not belong in the summary because they express ideas that are not presented in the passage or are minor ideas in the passage. **This question is worth 2 points**.

지시: 지문 요약을 위한 도입 문장이 아래에 주어져 있다. 지문의 가장 중요한 내용을 나타내는 보기 3개를 골라 요약을 완성하시오. 어떤 문장은 지문에 언급되지 않은 내용이나 사소한 정보를 담고 있으므로 요약에 포함되지 않는다. **이 문제는 2점이다.**

> Changes in Japanese society during the 8th Century led to major architectural changes as well.
>
> (A) The construction of more durable buildings attracted Japanese rulers and was further influenced by the acceptance of Buddhism.- paragraph 5
>
> (E) During the Nara period the imperial court expanded to include over 10,000 workers who needed to be adequately housed in locations that made it easy for them to fulfill their obligations. - paragraph 4
>
> (F) A shift in the marriage customs of the Japanese elite during the Nara period made it less likely that the royal court would construct and reside in multiple palaces during their marriage. - paragraph 2

> 8세기 일본 사회의 변화는 큰 건축학적 변화로 이어 졌다.
>
> (A) 더욱 더 튼튼한 건물들의 건축은 일본 지도자들을 매료시켰고 더 나아가 불교의 수용의 영향을 받았다.
>
> (E) 나라시대에는 정부 직원들이 10000명이 넘었는데 이들은 그들의 업무를 이행하기에 편리한 지역에 지낼 수 있도록 집을 지어 줬어야만 했다.
>
> (F) 나라시대에 일본고위층의 결혼 관습의 변화로 인해 왕궁의 직원들이 여러 궁궐을 짓고 거기서 결혼한 동안 지내는 일이 적어졌다.

(B) ~~Lacking~~ enough manpower and building materials to build the continental-style capital, the Japanese rulers ~~adhered to~~ the system of moving across smaller palaces.
　　　　　　　　　　　　　　　　　　　　　　　- 반/반

(C) The expanding bureaucracy of the Nara period increased the need to ~~move around~~ the capital from place to place to oversee their work more efficiently.
　　　　　　　　　　　　　　　　　　　　　　　- 틀린 정보

(D) With their rivalry with the Tang Dynasty, the Japanese strove to show off their architectural mightiness.
　　　　　　　　　　　　　　　　　　　　　　　- paragraph 5 Minor

(B) 큰 대륙적 스타일의 수도를 짓는데 필요한 충분한 양의 노동과 건축재료가 ~~없던~~ 일본의 지도자들은 작은 궁궐들 사이에서 왔다 갔다 하는 시스템을 ~~고수하였다~~.

(C) 나라시대의 확장하던 관료 제도는 그들의 일을 더 효율적으로 감독하기 위해 수도를 이곳저곳 ~~옮겨야~~ 하는 필요성을 증가시켰다.

(D) 당 나라와 라이벌 관계에 있던 일본은 그들의 건축술의 위대함을 과시하려고 노력하였다.

Summary 지문의 중심 내용은 8세기 일본 건축 기술의 변화이다. (A)는 다섯 번째 단락의 중심내용인 당나라의 건축 기술과 불교의 수용이 일본의 건축 스타일에 미친 영향과 일치하고, (E)는 네 번째 단락의 중심내용인 관료정치의 확장과 그에 따른 결과와 일치하고, (F)는 두 번째 단락의 중심 내용인 나라시대의 결혼 풍습이 왕궁의 위치에 미친 영향과 일치한다. 따라서 답은 (A), (E), (F)이다.

USHER iBT TOEFL
INTERMEDIATE READING

TEST 6
답안 및 취약 유형 분석표

해석 · 해설

답안 및 문제 유형 분석표

TEST 6-1

01 (A) Inference

02 (C) Fact

03 (B) Purpose

04 (C) Fact

05 (D) Fact

06 (D) Highlight

07 (B) Inference

08 (B) Vocabulary

09 3rd ■ Insertion

10 (D), (E), (F) Summary

TEST 6-2

11 (A) Fact

12 (C) Purpose

13 (A) Purpose

14 (B) Inference

15 (A) Inference

16 (B) Highlight

17 (D) Purpose

18 (B) Vocabulary

19 2nd ■ Insertion

20 (B), (D), (F) Summary

각 문제 유형별 맞춘 개수를 아래에 적어 보세요.

유형	맞춘 답의 개수	정답률
단어 (Vocabulary)	/ 2	정답률: %
사실 확인 문제 (Fact)	/ 4	정답률: %
지시어 찾기 (Reference)	/ 0	정답률: %
끼워 넣기 (Insertion)	/ 2	정답률: %
문장 변환문제 (Highlight)	/ 2	정답률: %
목적 (Purpose)	/ 4	정답률: %
추론 (Inference)	/ 4	정답률: %
단락 요약 (Summary / Category Chart)	/ 2	정답률: %
전체	/ 20	정답률: %

※ 자신이 취약한 유형은 READING STRATEGIES를 통해 다시 한번 점검하시기 바랍니다. (p.44)

TEST 6-1 How Camels Survive in Arid Environments
어떻게 낙타들은 건조한 환경들에서 살아남나

Introduction	단락 1	사막기후에서도 살아남을 수 있는 낙타 소개
Point	단락 2	낙타의 물없이도 오랜기간 살아남을 수 있는 능력
Point	단락 3	낙타의 많은 양의 물을 잃고도 정상적으로 움직일수 있는 능력
Point	단락 4	낙타의 체내 수분을 보존하는 능력
Point	단락 5	낙타혹의 유용성
Point	단락 6	낙타의 내부온도를 조절할 수 있는 능력
Point	단락 7	낙타의 열을 얻는 것을 감소시키는 신체적 특징

Photo by Mohammed Moussa, available under the Creative Commons Attribution-Share Alike 4.0 International license.

문단주제	본문내용	해석
단락 1 사막기후에서도 살아남을 수 있는 낙타 소개	**1** Their **ability to survive** extreme temperatures and food or water deprivation has made camels invaluable in Asia, Africa and the Middle East. These large animals **come in** two varieties, Central Asia's two-humped Bactrian and the single-humped desert dromedaries of Africa and the Middle East, which were independently domesticated 5,000 years ago. They have since **acted as** beasts of burden, desert transport, and sources of wool, leather, milk and meat [Q11-C] because they, unlike other livestock, have specialized mechanisms for survival in desert environments.	낙타들의 극단적인 온도와 먹이와 물의 결핍으로부터 살아남을 수 있는 능력은 낙타들을 아시아, 아프리카와 중동 지역에서 귀중하게 만들었다. 이런 커다란 동물은 중앙아시아의 쌍봉 백트리안 그리고 아프리카의 중동의 사막 단봉 낙타로 구분되는데, 이것들은 5000년전에 별도로 사육되었다. 그때부터 그들은 짐을 나르는 짐승, 운송수단, 그리고 털, 가축, 우유와 고기의 원천으로까지 쓰였다. [Q11-C]그들은 다른 가축들과 달리 건조한 사막기 후에서의 생존을 위한 전문화된 체계를 갖고 있기 때문이다.
단락 2 낙타의 물없이도 오랜기간 살아남을 수 있는 능력	**2** Their first adaptations is their ability to go **for long periods** without water. Unlike most animals, the camel can go without water for two weeks without negative effects. This is possible because they can drink up to 200 liters of water at once. [Q12-C] When they drink these great amounts, some of the water **is** rapidly **transferred to** their blood streams and carried throughout the body to hydrate the bodily tissues. This is unique because in most animals such a dilution of the bloodstream would cause a fatal rupturing of the red blood	이러한 적응들 중 첫 번째는 물이 없이 오랜 기간을 버틸 수 있다는 것이다. 대부분의 동물들과는 달리 낙타들은 해로운 영향을 받지 않고 이 주 동안 물을 마시지 않고 버틸 수 있다. 이것은 한 번에 200리터에 달하는 엄청난 물의 양을 마실 수 있는 능력에서 나온다. [Q12-C] 낙타들이 이러한 엄청난 양의 물을 마실 때, 일정량은 빠르게 혈류로 옮겨지고 온몸으로 옮겨져 신체 조직들에게 물을 공급한다. 대부분의 동물들의 이런 혈류의 희석은 치명적인 적혈구의 파괴를 일으키기 때문에 이것은 특별하다고 볼 수 있다. 하지만, 낙타들의 특별하게 적응된 적혈구들은 이것을 살아남을 수 있게 하였고 다른 대부분의

Vocabulary

1단락
extreme [ikstríːm] a. 극도의, 극심한
invaluable [invǽljuəbəl] a. 매우 유용한, 귀중한
domesticate [douméstəkèit] v. 길들이다 [사육하다]
deprivation [dèprəvéiʃən] n. 박탈, 부족
independently [ìndipéndəntli] ad. 독립하여, 자주적으로

2단락
transfer [trænsfɔ́ːr] v. 옮기다, 이동하다
ovoid [óuvɔid] a. 난형의, 타원형의
hydrate [háidreit] v. 수화시키다, 물을 채우다
dehydration [dìːhaidréiʃən] n. 탈수, 건조
unique [juːníːk] a. 유일무이한, 독특한

	cells. However, camels' specially adapted red blood cells can survive this and have a unique ovoid shape, compared to the rounder red blood cells of most animals, which **allows** them **to flow** more freely during times of dehydration.	동물들의 동그란 적혈구와 달리 탈수 상태에 더욱 자유롭게 흐를 수 있게 만드는 독특한 타원형을 갖고 있다.
단락 3 낙타의 많은 양의 물을 잃고도 정상적으로 움직일 수 있는 능력	**3** Camels also handle water loss better than most animals. [Q13-B, Q14-A] In humans, **for instance**, a 2% water loss stresses the body and anything more than 12% is fatal, but camels can survive losing 25% of their bodies' water content. This is because of how their bodies lose water. [Q14-B] Unlike most animals, camels metabolize the water between cells and in their guts, rather than the water in their cells. [Q14-D] By protecting the cellular water content, their bodies **are able to function** properly even after dramatic water losses.	낙타들은 또한 다른 대부분의 동물들 보다 물손실을 잘 버틴다. [Q13-B, Q14-A] 사람들을 예로 들자면, 2%의 물손실은 몸에 부담을 주고 12%를 넘으면 치명적인 반면에, 낙타들은 25%의 물손실에서 살아남을 수 있다. 이것은 그들의 몸들이 물을 손실 하는 방법 때문에 가능하다. [Q14-B] 다른 많은 동물 들과는 달리, 낙타들은 세포내의 물 대신에 세포들 사이와 그들의 소화기관에서 찾을 수 있는 물을 대사한다. [Q14-D] 그들의 몸은 세포내의 물을 보호함 으로써 많은 양의 물을 잃은 후에도 제대로 작동할 수 있다.
단락 4 낙타의 체내 수분을 보존하는 능력	**4** **In addition to** being able to **cope with** water loss, camels have special abilities and adaptations which prevent it. [Q15-A] The most obvious of these is the fact that camels sweat very little. [Q15-B] They also have efficient digestive systems which produce very dry, concentrated urine and feces. Camel feces is **so** dry **that** it can be lit and **used as** fuel for fires almost **immediately after** being deposited. [Q15-C] Another way they conserve water is through their respiratory system. In most animals, **a large amount of** water is exhaled during respiration, giving the breath a relative humidity of nearly 100%. Camels, **on the other hand**, breathe relatively slowly, reducing the number of exhaled breaths and have specialized scrolled nasal bones called turbinates, which increase the nasal cavity surface area, to nearly 1000 sq. cm., and capture moisture from the exhaled air, reducing its relative humidity up to 25%, and hydrate the dry desert air which they breathe in. The network of capillaries in their cooler nasal cavities also **keeps the brain cooler** through heat diffusion.	물손실에 대처할 수 있는 것에 더해서, 낙타들은 그것을 방지하는 특별한 능력과 적응력을 갖고 있다. [Q15-A] 이것들 중 가장 명백한 것은 낙타들은 땀을 적게 흘린다는 것이다. [Q15-B] 그들은 또한 건조하고 농축된 오줌과 배설물을 생산하는 효율적인 소화기관계를 갖고 있다. 낙타의 배설물은 배설된 후 즉시 불을 붙여서 연료로 쓰일 수 있을 정도로 건조하다. [Q15-C] 그들이 물을 보존하는 또 다른 방법은 호흡계를 통해서이다. 대부분의 동물들은 거의 100% 습도의 숨을 내뱉으면서 많은 양의 수분도 내뱉는다. 낙타들은, 반면에, 날숨의 횟수를 줄이면서 비교적 천천히 숨을 쉬고, 특별하게 발달된 비갑개라고 불리는 소용돌이 모양의 코뼈를 갖고, 이것은 코뼈의 표면적을 거의 천 제곱 센티미터 가까이 늘리고 상대적인 습기를 25%까지 줄이며 내쉬는 공기에 존재하는 습기를 흡수하고 들이 마시는 사막의 건조한 공기에 습기를 더해준다. 차가운 비강의 모세혈관들은 또한 열 확산을 통해서 뇌를 차갑게 유지시킨다.

Vocabulary

3단락
stress [stres] n. 압박, 긴장 v. 강조하다, 스트레스를 주다
content [kəntént] n. (어떤 것의) 속에 든 것들, 내용물
gut [gʌt] n. 내장, 소화관 a. 직감에 따른
fatal [féitl] a. 죽음을 초래하는, 치명적인
metabolize [mətǽbəlàiz] v. 대사작용을 하다
cellular [séljələr] a. 세포의

4단락
prevent [privént] v. 방지하다
digestive [didʒéstiv] a. (명사앞에만 씀) 소화의 (digestive system n. 소화계통)
conserve [kənsə́ːrv] v. 아끼다, 아껴쓰다
exhale [ekshéil] v. (숨, 연기등을) 내쉬다, 내뿜다
nasal [néizəl] a. 코의
obvious [ábviəs / ɔ́b-] a. 분명한, 명백한
concentrated [kánsəntrèitid] a. 집중적인, 결연한, 농축된
respiratory [réspərətɔ̀ːri] a. 호흡의, 호흡기관의 (respiratory system n. 호흡기계)
humidity [hjuːmídəti] n. 습도
diffusion [difjúːʒən] n. 방산, 발산

단락 5 낙타혹의 유용성	5 There is, perhaps, no better known, or misunderstood, camel adaptation to heat and dehydration than the hump. Commonly **thought to hold** water, these humps are actually fat accumulations. Unlike other animals, which are covered by a layer of fat, camels store theirs in their humps. Fat cells hold in body heat, so by **having most** of their fat **concentrated on** their backs, camels can more easily dissipate heat, reducing their internal temperatures. Water is also produced when this fat is metabolized, but it is all **used up in the process.**
단락 6 낙타의 내부온도를 조절할 수 있는 능력	6 Camels also **deal with** heat rather uniquely. Most mammals maintain a stable internal temperature and utilize physical processes, such as panting, sweating, or **exposing** more skin **to** open air in shaded regions, to **maintain** their **temperatures as close to** the ideal **as possible**. These methods reduce the animal's temperature, but also cause water loss. [Q17-B] Camels, on the other hand, avoid this by having an internal temperature that varies more widely than other mammals. [■] The diurnal variation in a camels' temperature can be as high as 6°C. [■] This wide temperature fluctuation would mean major problems for most other species. [■] In humans, for instance, an internal temperature increase of even half this much can cause brain damage and even death. Scientists believe that this fluctuation reduces the **need for** sweating and panting, which **saves camels** as **much** as 5L of water **per day**. [■]
단락 7 낙타의 열을 얻는것을 감소시키는 신체적 특징	7 Their physical features and actions **not only** dissipate heat, **but also avoid gaining** heat altogether. Their tall, spindly legs keep their cores aloft, where air temperatures are cooler and their uninsulated nearly hairless underbellies dissipate heat quickly. Further, their thin, lightcolored wool doesn't absorb much heat and **protects the skin from** the effects of the sun. The fat in their hump also absorbs heat before it reaches the core, where it would increase their internal temperature. This is compounded by their natural proclivity for standing facing the sun, which reduces the amount of surface area directly exposed to the sun's rays.

Vocabulary

5단락
- misunderstand [mìsʌndərstǽnd] v. 오해하다
- dissipate [dísəpèit] v. 소멸되다, 소멸하다
- accumulation [əkjùːmjəléiʃən] n. 축적, 누적
- store [stɔːr] n. 가게 v. 저장하다

6단락
- uniquely [juːníːkly] ad. 유일하게, 동등하게
- internal [intə́ːrnl] a. (명사앞에서만 씀) 내부의
- diurnal [daiə́ːrnəl] a. 주행성의, 하루동안의
- maintain [meintéin] v. [수준 등을 동일하게] 유지하다
- pant [pænt] v. (숨을) 헐떡이다
- sweat [swet] n. 땀 v. 땀을 흘리다

7단락
- avoid [əvɔ́id] v. 방지하다, 모면하다
- proclivity [prouklívəti] n. (흔히 좋지 못한) 성향
- spindly [spíndli] a. (가늘고 약한) 막대기같은
- expose [ikspóuz] v. (보통때는 가려져 있는 것을) 드러내다
- core [kɔːr] n. 속, 중심부

01

According to paragraph 1, which of the following can be inferred about camels?

(A) The people who domesticated the camels had few other animals which they could attempt to domesticate.
(B) Applications of camels are quite ~~limited~~ because their adaptations are specially adjusted for survival in desert environments. ★
(C) Camels are ~~only~~ raised in arid areas because they cannot survive in areas that get a great deal of rainfall.
(D) The two populations of camels, Bactrian and dromedary, were derived from a ~~common ancestor~~ around 5,000 years ago.

단락 1에 의하면, 다음 중 낙타들에 관해서 추론할 수 있는 것은?

(A) 낙타들을 사육한 사람들은 그들이 사육하려고 시도할 수 있는 소수의 다른 동물들을 갖고 있었다.
(B) 낙타의 쓰임새는 그들의 적응이 사막 환경에서 살아남기 위해 맞춰져 있기 때문에 ~~제한되어 있다~~. ★
(C) 낙타들은 많은 양의 강우량을 갖고 있는 지역에서는 살아남을 수 없기 때문에 건조한 ~~지역들에서만~~ 길러진다.
(D) 쌍봉 낙타와 단봉 낙타의 두 인구들은 5000년 전의 ~~공통적인 조상으로부터~~ 유래 됐다.

Inference 질문의 키워드인 camels가 언급된 부분을 살펴보면 because they, unlike other livestock, have specialized mechanisms for survival in desert environments.(그들은 다른 가축들과 달리 건조한 사막 기후에서의 생존을 위한 전문화된 체계를 갖고 있기 때문이다)라고 말한다. 즉, 다른 가축들과는 달리 사막에서도 살아남을 수 있었다는 것이니까 그 당시에 낙타 외에도 다른 동물들이 사육되었다는 것을 유추할 수 있다. 따라서 정답은 (A)가 된다. (B)는 They have since acted as beasts of burden, desert transport, and sources of wool, leather, milk and meat (그때부터 그들은 짐을 나르는 짐승, 운송수단, 그리고 털, 가축, 우유와 고기의 원천으로까지 쓰였다)에서 그들의 쓰임새는 다양했다는 것을 설명 하기 때문에 오답이고, (C)는 본문에서는 사막 기후에서의 낙타 적응력만 언급할 뿐 강수량이 많은 곳에 대한 내용은 언급되지 않으므로 오답이다. (D)또한 "5,000년 전" 은 낙타가 사육되었던 때를 가리키는 것이지 두 종의 낙타가 같은 조상으로부터 진화한 것은 아니기 때문에 오답이다.

02

According to paragraph 2 and 3, which of the following is true about the role of the blood stream in camel's ability to go for long periods without water?

(A) Camels' red blood cells are a special shape that allows them to ~~withstand~~ the sudden influx of water into their bloodstreams. ★
(B) The water that enters the camels' blood stream after they drink is rapidly brought to ~~hump~~ where it is stored for use later.
(C) Camels can drink and store large amounts of water at once because some of the water is rapidly absorbed into their bloodstreams.
(D) Camels can survive long periods of dehydration because their blood is ~~not as liquid~~ as that of other animals.

단락 2와 3에 의하면, 다음 중 오랜 기간 동안 물없이 버틸 수 있는 낙타의 능력에 혈류가 갖는 역할에 관해서 사실인 것은?

(A) 낙타의 적혈구들은 혈류에 갑작스럽게 밀어닥치는 물들을 ~~버틸 수 있게~~ 하는 특별한 모양으로 만들어져 있다. ★
(B) 낙타들이 물을 마신 이후에 낙타들의 혈류에 들어가는 물은 빠르게 ~~혹에~~ 이후에 쓰여질 수 있게 저장된다.
(C) 낙타들은 일정량의 물이 그들의 혈류에 빠르게 흡수되기 때문에 한 번에 많은 양의 물을 마실수 있다.
(D) 낙타들은 그들의 피가 다른 동물들에 비해서 ~~유동적이지 않기~~ 때문에 물없이 오랫동안 버틸 수 있다.

Fact 질문의 키워드인 role of the blood stream이 언급된 부분을 살펴보면 When they drink these great amounts, some of the water is rapidly transferred to their blood streams and carried throughout the body to hydrate the bodily tissues. (낙타들이 이러한 엄청난 양의 물을 마실때, 일정량은 빠르게 혈류로 옮겨지고 온 몸으로 옮겨져 신체조직들에 물을 공급한다)라고 말한다. 즉, 다른 동물들과는 다르게 낙타는 많은 양의 물을 한번에 마시고 혈류로 옮겨지기 때문에 물 없이 오랜 기간을 버틸 수 있다는 것이다. 따라서 정답은 (C)가 된다. (A)는 낙타의 적혈구는 특별한 모양을 가지고 있는 것은 맞지만 많은 양의 물을 버틸 수 있도록 도와주는 것은 아니므로 오답이고, (B)는 hump(혹)이 아닌 body(몸)이므로 오답이다. (D)는 which allows them to flow more freely during times of dehydration에서 다른 동물들보다 낙타의 피는 more liquid=flow more freely이기 때문에 오답이다.

03

The author provides the information of "a 2% water loss stresses the body" in paragraph 3 in order to

(A) illustrate the point at which water loss becomes severe in ~~human beings~~
(B) emphasize the camels' ability to function properly even in the case of massive water loss
(C) show how susceptible ~~human beings~~ are to dehydration when they are in desert environments.
(D) explain that ~~the way~~ humans lose water is different from that of camels ★

왜 글쓴이는 "2%의 물손실은 몸에 부담을 준다"를 단락 3 에서 언급하는가?

(A) 물 손실이 ~~인간~~에게 심각해지는 시점을 보여주기 위해서
(B) 낙타의 물을 많이 잃고도 정상적으로 생활할 수 있는 능력을 강조하기 위해서
(C) ~~사람들이~~ 사막의 환경에서 탈수에 얼마나 약한지 보여주기 위해서
(D) 사람들이 물을 손실하는 ~~방법은~~ 낙타들의 몸이 물을 손실하는 ~~방법과는~~ 다르다는 것을 설명하기 위해서 ★

Purpose 음영 표시된 부분을 살펴보면 In humans, for instance, a 2% water loss stresses the body and anything more than 12% is considered fatal, but camels can survive losing 25% of their bodies' water content. (사람들을 예로 들자면, 2%의 물손실은 몸에 부담을 주고 12%를 넘으면 치명적인 반면에, 낙타들은 25%의 물손실에서 살아남을 수 있다)라고 말한다. 즉, 사람들에 비해서 낙타가 훨씬 더 많은 양의 물을 잃고도 버틸 수 있다는 것을 설명하기 위해서 쓰였다는 것을 알 수 있다. 따라서 정답은 (B)가 된다. (A)와 (C)는 사람들에 대한 정보에 중점을 두고 있지만 음영 표시된 부분이 언급된 이유는 낙타에 중점을 두고 있기 때문에 오답이고, (D)는 다르다는 것을 보여주기 위해서가 아니기 때문에 오답이다.

04

According to paragraph 2 and 3, all of the following are true of the use and loss of water in camels **EXCEPT**:

(A) Camels can survive after a loss of water that is twice as much as a human could endure.
(B) Camels utilize water from their digestive systems and other areas before drawing water from within their cells. ★
(C) Camels reduce the amount of water ~~in their cells~~ and protect the cellular water content.
(D) Camels' method of water metabolization allows them to consume water much less often than most other animals.

단락 2와 3에 의하면, 낙타들의 물의 사용과 손실에 관해서 사실이 아닌 것은?

(A) 낙타들은 사람들이 버틸 수 있는 양의 두 배나 되는 물을 잃고도 살아 남을 수 있다.
(B) 낙타들은 소화 기관계와 다른 공간의 물을 세포 안의 물들보다 먼저 사용한다. ★
(C) 낙타들은 그들의 세포안에 있는 물의 양을 줄이고 세포 내의 물을 보호한다.
(D) 낙타들이 대사하는 방법은 그들이 다른 동물보다 훨씬 덜 자주 물을 소비하는 것을 가능하게 한다.

Fact 질문의 키워드인 use and loss of water in camels이 언급된 부분을 살펴보면 Unlike most animals, camels metabolize the water between cells and in their guts, rather than the water in their cells. (다른 많은 동물들과는 달리, 낙타들은 세포내의 물 대신에 세포들 사이와 그들의 소화기관에서 찾을 수 있는 물을 대사한다)라고 말한다. 즉, 낙타는 세포 안에 있는 물의 양을 유지시키기 위해서 세포들 사이와 그들의 소화기관에서 찾을 수 있는 물을 대사한다. 따라서 정답은 (C)가 된다.

05

According to paragraph 4, which of the following was **NOT** one of the ways that camels were specially adapted to reduce water loss?

(A) Despite being exposed to extremely high temperatures, camels do not perspire as much as other mammals. ★
(B) The camel digestive system has become very efficient, producing waste products that have very low water contents.

단락 4에 의하면, 낙타들이 물 손실을 줄이기 위해서 특별하게 적응한 방법들 중 하나가 아니었던 것은?

(A) 극단적으로 높은 기온들에 노출됐음에도 불구하고, 낙타들은 다른 동물들만큼 땀을 흘리지 않는다. ★
(B) 낙타들은 아주 적은 양의 물들을 갖고 있는 배설물들은 생산하는 아주 효과적인 소화 기관계를 갖고 있다.

(C) Camel respiration has developed in a way that allows it to be much more efficient in terms of water loss than other animals.
(D) Camels' turbinates increase the inhaling capacity of the nasal cavity and thus enhance their ~~sense of smell~~.

(C) 낙타의 호흡은 다른 동물들에 비해 훨씬 더 효과적이게 하는 방법으로 발달되었다.
(D) 낙타의 비강은, 코의 들이쉬는 능력을 늘려서, 냄새 맡는 감각을 강화 시킨다.

Fact 질문의 키워드인 reduce water loss가 언급된 부분을 살펴보면. Camels, on the other hand, breathe relatively slowly, reducing the number of exhaled breaths and have specialized scrolled nasal bones called turbinates, which increase the nasal cavity surface area to nearly 1000sq. cm (낙타들은, 반면에, 내뿜는 숨의 수를 줄이면서 비교적 천천히 숨을 쉬고, 특별하게 발달된 비갑개라고 불리는 소용돌이 모양의 코뼈를 갖고, 이 것은 코뼈의 표면적을 거의 천 제곱 센티미터 가까이 늘린다)라고 말한다. 즉, (D)는 냄새 얘기가 언급된 적이 없으므로 오답이다.

06
Which of the sentences below best expresses the essential information in the highlighted sentence in the passage? Incorrect choices change the meaning in important ways or leave out essential information.

(A) ii) The nasal cavity of camels has uniquely adapted bones called turbinates that iii) reclaim moisture from the breath as the camel exhales and allow the camel to ~~take it back~~ in when inhaling. ★
(B) ii) Since camels have specialized nasal bones called turbinates that increase the nasal surface area and capture moisture from the air they ~~breathe in~~, i) they are able to breathe more slowly than most large mammals.
(C) i) Camel respiration occurs very slowly ~~because~~ of the ii) specialized bones, called turbinates, in the camels' nasal passages that increase the nasal surface area to iii) capture more moisture from the breaths and iv) add it back to the dry inhaled air.
(D) i) Camels respire slowly ii) through a nasal cavity with specially adapted bones called turbinates that greatly increase the nasal surface area and allow the iii) harvesting of moisture from the breath before expelling it and iv) adding the moisture back into the dry inhaled air.

아래의 문장 중 지문 속의 음영 표시된 문장의 핵심 정보를 가장 잘 표현하고 있는 것은 무엇인가? 오답은 문장의 의미를 현저하게 바꾸거나 핵심정보를 빠트리고 있다.

(A) iii) 낙타들의 비강은 낙타가 숨을 내쉬거나 다시 들이마셔 나오는 ii) 습기를 ~~타서~~ 흡수하게 하는 비갑개라고 불리는 독특하게 발달한 뼈들을 갖고 있다. ★
(B) ii) 낙타들은 비갑개라는 코의 표면적을 증가시키고 ~~들어마시는~~ 공기로부터 수분을 사로잡는 전문화 된 코뼈를 갖고 있기 때문에 i) 대부분의 큰 포유류들보다 더 느리게 숨을 쉴 수 있다.
(C) 낙타의 호흡은 ii) 코의 표면적을 늘려서 iii) 숨을 내쉴 때 더 많은 습기를 흡수하게 하고 iv) 들이마실 때엔 습기를 더해주는 낙타의 비강에 존재하는 비갑개라고 불리는 특별하게 발달된 ~~뼈들 때문에~~ i) 아주 천천히 일어난다.
(D) ii) 낙타들은 코의 표면적을 크게 증가시키고 숨을 내쉬기 전에 숨으로부터 습기를 모으는 것을 허락하고 마실 때에는 건조한 공기에 습기를 더해주는 비갑개라고 불리는 특별하게 발달한 뼈들을 갖고 있는 비강을 통해 i) 아주 천천히 호흡한다.

Highlight 음영 표시된 문장은 i) Camels, on the other hand, breathe relatively slowly, reducing the number of exhaled breaths ii) and have specialized scrolled nasal bones called turbinates which increase the nasal cavity surface area, to nearly 1000 sq. cm., and iii) capture moisture from the exhaled air, reducing its relative humidity up to 25%, and iv) hydrate the dry desert air which they breathe in. (i) 낙타들은, 반면에, 내뿜는 숨의 수를 줄이면서 비교적 천천히 숨을 쉬고, ii) 특별하게 발달된 비갑개라고 불리는 소용돌이 모양의 코뼈를 갖고, 이것은 코뼈의 표면적을 거의 천 제곱센티미터 가까이 늘리고 iii) 상대적인 습기를 25%까지 줄이며 내쉬는 공기에 존재하는 습기를 흡수하고 iv) 들이마시는 사막의 건조한 공기에 습기를 더해준다) 이렇게 네 가지 내용으로 나뉜다. 이 내용을 모두 포함한 (D)가 정답이 된다. (A)는 i)와 iv)의 내용이 없으므로 오답이고, (B)는 들어 마시는 공기에서 수분을 흡수하는 것이 아니라 내쉬는 공기에서 습기를 흡수하는 것이기 때문에 오답이다. (C)는 모든 내용을 다 포함하고 있지만 코뼈가 특수하게 발달된 것은 숨쉬는 속도가 느려진 이유가 아니기 때문에 오답이다.

07

What can be inferred about the changes in camels' internal temperature from paragraph 6?

(A) Camels' internal temperatures vary to ~~match~~ the external temperatures, so they are more active during the daytime when their core temperature is warmer.
(B) Without the ability to bear large fluctuations in their internal temperatures, camels would not be able to refrain from using up their own moisture.
(C) Camels are capable of maintaining a ~~stable~~ internal temperature without using any physical techniques that cause water loss. ★
(D) The changes in camels' body temperature over the course of the day are ~~seldom~~ affected by fluctuations in ambient temperatures.

단락 6에서 낙타들의 체온의 변화에 관해서 추론할 수 있는 것은?

(A) 낙타들의 체온은 외부의 온도에 ~~맞춰서~~ 변화하고, 그렇기에 그들은 그들의 내부 온도가 더 따듯한 낮에 더욱 활발하다.
(B) 광범위한 체온 변화를 견딜 수 있는 능력없이는, 낙타들은 그들의 습기를 사용하는 것을 피하지 못할 것이다.
(C) 낙타들은 물 손실을 일으키는 물리적 기술을 사용하지 않고도 ~~일정한~~ 온도를 유지할 수 있다. ★
(D) 하루 중 변하는 낙타들의 체온은 주위 온도 변동에 ~~거의~~ 영향을 받지 ~~않는다~~.

Inference 질문의 키워드인 changes in camels' internal temperature이 언급된 부분을 살펴보면 Camels, on the other hand, avoid this by having an internal temperature that varies more widely than other mammals. (반면에 낙타들은, 다른 동물들에 비해서 훨씬 더 달라지는 체온을 통해서 이것을 방지한다)라고 말한다. 즉, 다른 동물들보다 낙타들은 광범위한 체온 변동을 버틸 수 있는 능력이 있으므로 다른 동물들이 사용하는 냉각 기술들을 사용하지 않아도 된다는 것이다. 만약 이 능력이 없었으면 그들과 같이 냉각 기술들을 사용했어야 됐을 것이고 그들의 습기를 사용해야만 했을 것이므로 정답은 (B)가 된다. (A)는 체내온도가 바뀌는 것은 사실이지만 이것이 외부온도를 맞추기 위함은 아니므로 오답이고, (C)는 낙타들이 물리적 기술을 사용하지 않는 것은 사실이지만 일정한 체온을 유지할 수 있는 능력은 없기 때문에 오답이다. (D)는 endotherm(온혈 동물)들과는 다르게 낙타 같은 ectotherm(변온 동물)은 주변 온도의 변동에 따라 체온이 바뀐다. 즉, 주변 온도에게 영향을 받는다는 것이기 때문에 오답이다.

08

The term "altogether" in the passage is closest in meaning to

(A) merely [míərli]
(B) fully [fúli]
(C) necessarily [nèsəsérəli] ★
(D) even [íːvən]

지문의 단어 "전적으로"의 의미와 가장 유사한 것은?

(A) 단순히
(B) 완전히
(C) 필연적으로 ★
(D) 더욱

Vocabulary 지문의 altogether(전적으로)와 동의어인 fully(완전히)가 정답이다.

09

Look at the four squares [■] that indicate where the following sentence could be added to the passage.

In humans, for instance, an internal temperature increase of even half this much can cause brain damage and even death.

Where would the sentence best fit? Click on a square [■] to add the sentence to the passage.

3rd

네 개의 네모 [■]는 다음 문장이 삽입될 수 있는 부분을 나타내고 있다.

사람들을 예로 들면, 이것의 반만 되는 체온의 증가는 뇌 손상과 심하면 죽음에 이르게도 할 수 있다.

이 문장은 어느 자리에 들어가는 것이 가장 적절한가?

3번째

Insertion ★세 번째 네모 앞에 other가 답근거이다. 삽입 문장의 키워드는 In humans, for instance, half this much, brain damage and even death이다. 세 번째 네모 앞 문장을 살펴보면 This wide of a temperature fluctuation would mean major problems for most other species. (이러한 광범위한 체온의 변화는 대부분의 다른 종들에게는 심각한 문제를 일으킬 수 있다)라고 말한다. 즉, most other species의 예로 사람의 경우가 언급된 것이고, half this much는 temperature fluctuation을 의미하는 것이며, 결정적으로 brain damage and even death는 major problems의 예시로 쓰인 것이다. 따라서 정답은 세 번째 네모이다.

10

Directions: An introductory sentence for a brief summary of the passage is provided below. Complete the summary by selecting the THREE answer choices that express the most important ideas in the passage. Some sentences do not belong in the summary because they express ideas that are not presented in the passage or are minor ideas in the passage. **This question is worth 2 points.**

지시: 지문 요약을 위한 도입 문장이 아래에 주어져 있다. 지문의 가장 중요한 내용을 나타내는 보기 3개를 골라 요약을 완성하시오. 어떤 문장은 지문에 언급되지 않은 내용이나 사소한 정보를 담고 있으므로 요약에 포함되지 않는다. **이 문제는 2점이다.**

The physiology of the camel makes it uniquely able to survive in desert regions.

(D) The camel's unique ability to withstand swings in its internal temperatures allows them to withstand high temperatures without the need for cooling methods that deplete water from the body. - paragraph 6

(E) The internal systems of camels are very efficient and reduce the amount of water their bodies lose during normal metabolic processes. - paragraph 4

(F) Their ability to cope with and fully function after losing as much as 25% of their bodies' water content and their blood's ability to withstand both sudden inundations of water and near dehydration allow camels to go without water for long spans. - paragraph 2,3

낙타의 생리는 낙타들이 사막 지역들에서 독특하게 살아 남을 수 있게 만들었다.

(D) 체온의 변화를 견딜 수 있는 낙타의 독특한 능력은 그들이 높은 기온에도 몸에서 물을 쓰게 만드는 다른 냉각 기술을 사용하지 않고도 버틸 수 있게 한다.

(E) 낙타의 내부 시스템은 아주 효율적이고 그들의 몸이 평범한 신진 대사 중에 사용하는 물의 양을 줄인다.

(F) 그들 몸 속의 물의 25%까지 잃는 것을 버티고 완벽하게 기능할 수 있는 능력과 급작한 물의 쇄도와 탈수에 가까운 상태를 버틸 수 있는 피의 능력은 낙타들이 물 없이 오랜 시간을 버티는 것을 가능하게 한다.

(A) ~~Because~~ they can tolerate dry desert climates better than other livestock, camels evolved into two species 5,000 years ago and have acted as beasts of burden. - 틀린 정보

(B) The ~~water~~ present in camels' humps acts as an insulation tool and plays a vital role in holding in body heat. - 틀린 정보

(C) The camel's ability to dissipate heat is ~~hardly~~ attributed to its physical characteristics, such as its tall legs and light-colored wool. - 틀린 정보

(A) 낙타들은 사막의 건조한 기후들을 다른 가축들보다 더욱 잘 버틸 수 있었기 ~~때문에~~ 5000년 전에 두 종으로 진화하였고 짐을 나르는 짐승의 역할을 수행해왔다.

(B) 낙타 혹에 있는 ~~물은~~ 절연 도구로서 쓰이고 몸의 열을 보유하는 데에 중요한 역할을 한다.

(C) 낙타가 열을 없애는 능력을 가지고 있는 것은 이것의 긴 다리와 얇고 밝은 색의 털같은 육체적인 조건 때문은 ~~아니다~~.

Summary 지문의 중심 내용은 어떻게 낙타들이 건조한 환경조건에서 살아남냐이다. (D)는 여섯 번째 단락의 중심내용인 낙타의 내부 온도를 조절 할 수 있는 능력과 일치하고, (E)는 네 번째 단락의 중심내용인 낙타의 물을 보존하는 능력과 일치하고, (F)는 두 번째와 세 번째 단락의 중심내용인 낙타의 물없이 오랜 기간 동안 버틸 수 없는 능력과 많은 양의 물을 잃고도 정상적으로 움직일 수 있는 능력과 일치한다. 따라서 정답은 (D), (E), (F)이다.

TEST 6-2 Hunter-gatherers in Southwest Asia
서남 아시아의 수렵 채집인들

Introduction	단락 1	서남 아시아에 위치했던 케바란 사회의 영향력
Point	단락 2	기후 변화에 의한 나투피안 문명의 발달
Point	단락 3	큰 정착지를 바탕으로 한 도구의 발달
Point	단락 4	나투피안 정착지와 주변 환경 조건
Point	단락 5	계급을 바탕으로 한 나투피안 사회
Point	단락 6	기후 변화와 나투피안들의 적응력

Photo by Hanay, available under the Creative Commons Attribution-Share Alike 3.0 Unported license.

단락 1
서남 아시아에 위치했던 케바란 사회의 영향력

1　During the end of the last glacial period, the Kebaran Civilization flourished in the area of Southwest Asia now **known as** the Middle East. [Q21-C] This population was to have a large **influence on** humanity, because of their early consumption of cereals and their tool development. [Q21-B] Being a nomadic civilization, they **moved across a multitude of** climates **over the course of** the year, spending their summers in the cooler highlands and their winters in the rocky waterside caves. [Q21-D] This migration **required** them **to adapt** tools to suit each location. These were likely used to hunt gazelle and harvest wild cereals. [Q22-C] Human consumption of these cereals became **so** important **that** they currently **make up** 50% and 56% of the world's protein and food energy consumption, **respectively**.

마지막 빙하기의 막판에 케바란 문명은 현재 중동으로 불리는 서남 아시아 지역에서 번창했다. [Q21-C] 이 인구는 곡식의 초기 섭취와 도구 개발 때문에 인류에 큰 영향을 미치게 되었다. [Q21-B] 유목 문명이었던 케바란들은 여름에 시원한 고랭지에 지내고 겨울에 물가에 위치한 동굴들에 지내면서 일 년 중 여러 기후로 이동했다. [Q21-D] 이러한 이동은 각각 지역에 적합한 도구를 맞추는 것을 요구했다. 이러한 도구들은 아마 가젤을 사냥하고 야생 곡식들을 수확하는데 사용 되었다. [Q22-C] 인간들의 이러한 곡식들의 섭취는 너무 중요해진 나머지 이들은 현재 세계의 단백질과 식품 열량 섭취를 각각 50%와 56%를 차지한다.

단락 2
기후 변화에 의한 나투피안 문명의 발달

2　Despite the dietary changes they caused, the Kebaran society did not remain forever. [Q23-A] Around 13,000 BC, a warmer, wetter period saw the rise of the Natufian Culture. Their appearance **coincided with** the **shift in** plant life in the area. As temperatures rose, plants that required the warmer temperatures of lower altitudes **spread to** higher altitudes. The production of pistachios, oak, almonds, wild barley and wild emmer wheat flourished as they **moved from**

케바란이 일으킨 식이요법의 변화에도 불구하고 이 사회는 오랫동안 지속되지 않았다. [Q23-A] 약 13,000 BC에 더 따뜻하고 강수량이 많은 시기가 나투피안 문명의 성장을 보게 되었다. 이들의 출현이 이 지역의 식물들의 변화와 일치한다. 기온이 상승하면서 낮은 고도의 따뜻한 온도를 필요로 했던 식물들은 더 높은 고도로 확산되었다. 낮은 고도의 모래 많은 토양에서 높은 고도의 점토 바탕의 영양분이 풍부한 토양으로 이동하면서 피스타치오, 아몬드, 야생 보리 그리고 야생 에머 소맥의 수 확량이 증가하고, [Q23-A] 이것은

Vocabulary

1단락　glacial [gléiʃəl] a. 빙하기의
　　　　consumption [kənsʌ́mpʃən] n. 소비, 섭취
　　　　civilization [sìvəlizéiʃən] n. 문명
　　　　nomadic [noumǽdik] a. 유목의
　　　　humanity [hju:mǽnəti] n. 인류, 인간
　　　　migration [maigréiʃən] n. 이주

2단락　appearance [əpíərəns] n. 출현
　　　　altitude [ǽltətjùːd] n. 고도
　　　　coincide [kòuinsáid] v. 동시에 일어나다, 일치하다
　　　　flourish [flə́ːriʃ] v. 번창하다

the lower altitude's sandy soil **to** the richer, clay-based soil of higher altitudes; [Q23-A] these increased harvests **allowed** the Natufian Culture **to expand as well**. Within 1,500 years, the culture had completely replaced the Kebaran and spread from the mountains to the Mediterranean.

3 This culture **proved to be** more sedentary than its predecessors. [Q24-B] This is an interesting case in history, since they settled before the advent of farming, relying instead on harvesting wild nuts and grains. Their entire society adapted a new hunting and gathering technique **based on** larger settlements that could harvest more of the crops. [■] These new settlements featured semi-subterranean pit-houses and pits where the crops could be stored. [■] These large settlements were also generally located near smaller satellite camps where they could collect and process their finds. Artifacts from these camps show that the Natufians greatly increased the sophistication of their tools and confirmed their dietary **reliance on** grains. [■] They **were even found to have created** processing tools, such as grinding stones, and harvesting tools, like the flint blade sickle. [■] While these tools could be useful on a multitude of plants, their **use for** cereal harvesting has been proven by the presence of "sickle gloss" on their blades. This is when a flint blade becomes shiny due to the build-up of silica particles from cereal grass stalks.

4 The village locations were also affected by the crops they **relied upon**. They were generally located along the boundary between the coastal grasslands and the higher altitudes where nuts and cereals prospered. They also **seemed to settle in places** where they could collect high quality stone for creating new tools. By **settling in** these places, they could harvest the cereal crops as they **came into season** during the spring and harvest nuts in the fall, providing year-round nourishment. **In addition to** using their stored crops in summer and winter, they also hunted the lowland animals. They would even **cooperate with** neighboring communities to

Vocabulary

3단락 advent [ǽdvent] n. 출현　　adapt [ədǽpt] v. 맞추다　　technique [tekníːk] n. 기법, 방법　　artifact [áːrtəfækt] n. 유물
sophistication [səfìstəkèiʃən] n. 정교함　　reliance [riláiəns] n. 의존, 의지

4단락 boundary [báundəri] n. 경계선　　grassland [grǽslænd] n. 초원　　prosper [práspər] v. 번창하다
harvest [háːrvist] n. 수확　　lowland [lóulænd] a. 저지대의　　cooperate [kouápərèit] v. 협력하다

perform massive game drives and ambushes on gazelles and other animals.

단락 5
계급을 바탕으로한 나투피안 사회

5 Year-round food sources **led to** a Natufian population boom. As the population increased, a new, highly complex social structure developed. [Q38-A] This was discovered through excavation of Natufian cemeteries, where evidence was found that indicated **differences in** social standing between tribe members. Certain burial sites contained the symbolic dentalium seashell, while others, even those of children, **were filled with** common furnishings such as stone bowls, showing a clear difference in societal standing of the deceased. These rankings may have been **the result of** the food redistribution and **efforts to maintain** order that would have been required by such a large sedentary community. Some argue that the number of dentalium shells per burial may differ simply because certain cemeteries are located where the shells are more available. However, these cemeteries also contained limestone grave covers and mortar markers, which **are thought to have served as** ritualistic territorial markers for the lands held by the Natufian's highly respected elders after they passed.

단락 6
기후 변화와 나투피안들의 적응력

6 Eventually, as their population expanded, the Natufians faced another dramatic lifestyle upheaval due to climate change. Around 11,000 BC, the climate around the Mediterranean **began to dry out**. This reduced the area in which the wild grains and nuts grew, and increased the society's **need to settle** near a reliable water source. This could have spelled the end of the Natufian society very quickly had they not learned the life cycle of the cereal plants over the previous two millennia of **living off of** and with them. Instead, they **were able to** deliberately **plant and control** the cereal plants. Even the modest scale of this early farming **helped** the society **supplement** their **declining** wild wheat and barley harvests and thus ensured their survival. Within a short time, farming **flourished in** Southwest Asia, and full-scale farming societies appeared, leading to more civilized hunter-gatherer/ farming communities in the area, where the Natufians developed the world's first dedicated form of agriculture.

연중 계속 되는 음식 자원은 나투피안 인구 증가로 이어졌다. 인구가 증가하면서 새로운 복잡한 사회 구조가 생겨났다. [Q27-A] 이것은 이들의 부족원들 사이 차이를 나타내는 증거들이 무덤 발굴을 통해 발견 되었다. 어떤 매장 장소에는 상징적인 뿔조개가 들어있는 반면, 심지어 어린이들이 매장 장소와 같은 다른 이들의 매장 장소는 돌 그릇 같은 일상적인 비품들이 들어 있었는데, 이것은 고인의 사회적 지위의 명확한 차이를 보여준다. 이러한 사회적 계급은 이렇게 큰 정착사회에서 요구되는 식량 재분배와 질서유지를 위한 노력의 결과에 의한 것일 수 있다. 이러한 묘지들은 석회무덤뚜껑과 모르타르 묘석들을 포함하고 있었는데, 이것들은 나투 피안인들의 존경을 받았던 연장자가 사후에 머물게 될 영토를 위한 의례적인 지역 표시로 사용되었다고 여겨진다.

결국 이들의 인구가 증가하자 나투피안들은 기후 변화에 의해 또 다른 생활 대변동을 맞이하게 되었다. 대략 11,000 BC경에 지중해 주변 기후가 건조해지기 시작했다. 이것은 실질적으로 야생 곡식과 견과류들이 자랄 수 있는 지역을 줄이고 수자원이 확실한 곳 주변에 정착해야 한다는 사회의 필요성을 높였다. 이것은 나투피안 사회가 곡식을 바탕으로 2,000년 동안 살면서 이 식물들의 생명 주기를 배우지 못했다면 나투피안 사회의 빠른 멸망을 의미를 초래할 수도 있었다. 대신에 이들은 계획적으로 곡식들을 심고 조절할 수 있었다. 이런 작은 크기의 초기 농업조차도 야생밀과 보리의 감소를 보충하는데 사회를 도와 이들의 생존을 보장했다. 짧은 시간 안에 농업은 서남 아시아에서 번창했고 대규모 농업 사회들이 나타나면서 나투 피안들이 처음으로 지구상에서 계획적인 농업을 시작한 지역에서 더 문명화된 수렵 채집 농업 사회들로 이어졌다.

Vocabulary

5단락
- complex [kəmpléks] a. 복잡한
- redistribution [rìːdistríbjuː(ː)tion] n. 재분배
- excavation [èkskəvéiʃən] n. 발굴
- sedentary [sédəntèri] a. 정착의
- symbolic [simbálik] a. 상징적인

6단락
- upheaval [ʌphíːvəl] n. 대변동
- supplement [sʌ́pləmənt] n. 보충
- reliable [riláiəbəl] a. 확실한
- declining [dekláiniŋ] a. 쇠퇴하는
- millennia [miléniəm] n. 천년
- modest [mádist] a. 작은

11 According to paragraph 1, all of the following are true of the early Kebaran culture that existed in Southwest Asia **EXCEPT**:

(A) They moved across various environments of ~~uniform climate~~ over the course of the year.
(B) They were a hunter-gatherer society that had to move around to follow their food sources. ★
(C) Their apparatus advancement and grain consumption left a significant remark on mankind.
(D) They adapted tools to the each different area in which they lived.

단락 1에 의해 서남 아시아에 존재한 케바란 문명에 대해 사실이 아닌 것은?

(A) 이들은 일 년 동안 ~~같은 기후의~~ 여러 환경들을 걸쳐 생활하였다.
(B) 이들은 식품 근원을 찾기 위해 움직이는 수렵 채집 사회였다. ★
(C) 이들은 이 지역에서 자라는 곡식에 의존하게 되었다.
(D) 이들은 살고 있는 각자 다른 지역에 따라 도구를 맞췄다.

Fact 질문의 키워드인 early Kebaran culture이 언급된 부분을 살펴보면 they moved across a multitude of climates over the course of the year.(그들은 (케바란들은) 일년 중 여러 기후들로 이동했다)라고 말한다. 즉, 여름엔 시원한 고랭지에 지내고 겨울엔 물가 곁에 위치한 동굴들에 지내는 등 여러 기후들을 걸쳐 생활했기 때문에 정답은 (A)가 된다.

12 Why does the author mention that cereal grains "currently make up 50% and 56% of the world's protein and food energy consumption, respectively" in paragraph 1?

(A) To explain ~~why~~ cereal grains remain the staple of most diets in less developed civilizations.
(B) To emphasize that the importance of consuming cereal in the ancient time has yet to ~~surpass~~ that of today's society. ★
(C) To point out that the Kebaran Civilization's utilization of cereal grains was so influential that it still affects our diets today.
(D) To show that cereal grains were an excellent source of nourishment without which the Kebaran probably would not have survived.

단락 1에서 작가는 왜 곡식이 "현재 세계의 단백질과 식품 열량 섭취를 각각 50%와 56%를 차지한다"를 언급하는가?

(A) 발달이 덜 된 문명에서 곡식이 왜 주 식단인지 설명하기 위해서
(B) 고대 시기에서의 곡식 섭취의 중요성은 아직 오늘날 사회에서의 중요성을 ~~뛰어넘지~~ 못한다는 것을 강조하기 위해서 ★
(C) 케바란 문명의 곡식 활용이 너무 영향이 커서 우리의 현재 식단도 영향을 받는다는 것을 가리키기 위해서
(D) 없었다면 케바란들이 생존하지 못했을 곡식이 영양분 공급에 훌륭하다는 것을 보여주기 위해서

Purpose 음영 표시된 부분을 살펴보면 Human consumption of these cereals became so important that they currently make up 50% and 56% of the world's protein and food energy consumption, respectively. (이 곡식들의 섭취는 너무 중요해진 나머지 이들은 현재 세계의 단백질과 식품 열량 섭취를 각각 50%와 56%를 차지한다)라고 말한다. so~that절의 의미를 알면 정답이 (C)라는 것을 확실히 알 수 있다. 이들의 곡식 섭취를 시작으로 오늘 날에도 곡식섭취는 매우 중요하다는 뜻이므로 정답은 (C)가 된다. (A)는 곡식이 저개발 문명 뿐만 아니라 전세계적으로 주 식단인 것은 사실이나 왜 주 식단인지에 대한 설명은 언급되지 않기 때문에 오답이고, (B)는 음영 표시된 부분이 언급되는 이유는 고대 시기와 동등하게 오늘날에도 곡식은 중요하다는 것이지 고대시기 때의 곡식섭취 중요성이 오늘날의 중요성보다 떨어진다는 내용은 언급되지 않으므로 오답이다. (D)는 유추할 수 있는 내용이긴 하지만 음영 표시된 부분이 언급된 이유는 아니므로 오답이다.

13

What is the purpose of paragraph 2 in the passage?

(A) It introduces a new civilization in place of the Kebaran society whose characteristics are important in the rest of the passage.
(B) It shows that after the plants moved to more nutrient rich soil, ~~Kebaran~~ were eventually able to produce farming crops.
(C) It ~~supports~~ the ideas presented in the first paragraph explaining the importance of cereal grains and nuts to the Kebaran Civilization.
(D) It suggests the idea that the Kebaran society did not last forever regardless of the continuation of tools and grain consumption. ★

본문에서 단락 2의 목적은 무엇인가?

(A) 본문 나머지 부분에서 그들의 특성이 중요하게 여겨지는 케바란 대신에 등장한 새로운 문명을 소개해준다.
(B) 식물들이 더 영양분이 많은 토양으로 옮기자 ~~케바란인들은~~ 결국 견과류와 곡식을 생산할 수 있다는 것을 보여준다.
(C) 케바란 문명에게 곡식과 견과류가 중요하다고 제시한 첫 단락의 내용을 ~~지지한다~~.
(D) 케바란 사회가 도구 사용과 곡식 섭취의 지속성에 상관없이 영원히 유지될 수 없었다는 내용을 제시한다. ★

Purpose 2단락의 첫 부분을 살펴보면 Around 13,000 BC, a warmer, wetter period saw the rise of the Natufian Culture. (약 13,000 BC에 더 따뜻하고 강수량이 많은 시대가 나투피안 문명의 성장을 보게 되었다)라고 말한다. 즉, 기후의 변화가 일어났고 이것이 나투피안 문명의 성장과 관계가 있다는걸 알 수 있다. 또, these increased harvests allowed the Natufian Culture to expand as well. (이것은 나투피안 문명도 같이 확산 될 수 있게끔 했다)에서 기후 변화 때문에 더 많은 양의 음식물을 수확할 수 있었고 이것이 나투피안 문명이 확산하는데 큰 공헌을 했다고 한다. 따라서 답은 (A)가 된다. (B)는 케바란인들이 아닌 나투피안인들이기 때문에 오답이고, (C)는 2단락에선 케바란 문명이 나투피안 문명의 성장과 함께 사라졌다는 내용을 담고 있기 때문에 오답이다. (D)는 맞는 말이지만 나투피안의 설립에 중심을 두고 있는 단락의 역할과는 맞지 않기 때문에 오답이다.

14

What can be inferred by the fact that Natufian settlement was considered "an interesting case in history"?

(A) They were the ~~only~~ society that researchers ever found in the area where they lived.
(B) Most civilizations that were not nomadic relied upon domestication of plants and animals to produce the food they needed.
(C) Since the Natufians preferred relying on wild nut and grain crops, they were ~~hesitant~~ to be more sedentary than their predecessors. ★
(D) Althoughthey devised a new hunting and gathering technique, the Natufians were ~~farmers~~.

나투피안 정착지가 "역사적으로 흥미로운 경우"로 여겨지는 사실에 대해 무엇을 유추할 수 있는가?

(A) 이들은 연구가들이 발견한 이 지역에서 거주하고 있는 ~~유일한~~ 사회였다.
(B) 비유목 사회인 대부분의 문명들은 음식을 제공하는데 필요한 식물들의 농업과 동물에 의존했다.
(C) 나투피안 인들은 야생 견과류와 곡식 작물에 의존하는 것을 선호하였기 때문에 그들은 그들의 선조들보다 한 곳에 오래 머무르는 것을 ~~망설였다~~. ★
(D) 그들이 새로운 수렵 채집 방식을 만들었음에도 불구하고 나투피안 인들은 ~~농부들~~이었다.

Inference 음영 표시된 부분을 살펴보면 This is an interesting case in history, since they settled before the advent of farming, relying instead on harvesting wild nuts and grains. (이것은 야생 견과류와 곡식에 의존하면서 농업의 출현 이전에 정착을해 역사적으로 흥미로운 경우이다)라고 말한다. 즉, 이것이 역사적으로 흥미로운 경우인 이유는 이들이 농업이 만들어지기 전에도 정착을 했기 때문이다. 다시 말해 다른 비 유목 사회들 대부분은 농업이 만들어진 이후에 정착을 했다는 것이다. 따라서 정답은 (B)가 된다. (A)는 이들이 유일한 경우였다는 내용은 언급되지 않으므로 오답이고, (C)는 This culture proved to be more sedentary than its predecessors. 이들은 이들의 선조들 보다 더 한 곳에 머물러 살았기 때문에 오답이다. (D)는 이들은 farming(농사)가 만들어지기 전부터 harvest(수확)을 하던 사람이었으므로 오답이다.

15 Which of the following is implied by the settlement of the Natufian society from the excavated artifacts mentioned in paragraph 5?

(A) The Natufians developed new social classes that were more complex than those in nomadic societies.
(B) Although the differing number of grave adornments may reflect societal ranking, it is mainly believed that this is due to the availability of shells. ★
(C) The Natufians felt that if they buried food vessels with their dead relatives they could ensure they would have nourishment in the afterlife.
(D) The dentalium seashells found in the graves were meant to show the great love a family had for its children.

단락 5에 언급된 발굴된 유물을 통해서 알 수 있는 나투피안 사회의 정착에 대한 사실은?

(A) 나투피안은 유목 사회때보다 더 복잡한 새로운 사회 계층을 만들었다.
(B) 비록 다른수의 무덤 장식물들이 사회적 지위를 반영할지라도, 이것은 조개의 이용가능성때문이라고 주로 믿어져 왔다. ★
(C) 나투피안들은 그들의 죽은 친척들과 함께 음식 용기들을 같이 묻으면 사후에 영양이 있을 것을 보장할 수 있다고 믿었다.
(D) 무덤에서 발견된 뿔조개는 가족이 자기 자식들에게 보이는 큰 사랑을 의미했다.

Inference 질문의 키워드인 excavated artifacts가 언급된 부분을 살펴보면 This was discovered through excavation of Natufian cemeteries, where evidence was found that indicated differences in social standing between tribe members. (이것은 이들의 부족원들 사이 차이를 나타내는 증거들이 무덤 발굴을 통해 발견 되었다)라고 말한다. 즉, 나투피안 사회에는 계급을 바탕으로한 사회였다는 것이므로 정답은 (A)가 된다. (B)는 비록 본문에서는, 해안가 지역에서 좀더 조개껍질을 이용 할 수 있으므로, 무덤당 조개 껍질의 숫자가 다른 것이라고 일부가 주장 한다고 하였으나, 이것은, 일부의 주장일 뿐이라는 부수적 설명 일 뿐 사회적 계층분화의 이유로서 언급된 것은 아니므로 오답이고, (C) 또한 사후에 대한 내용은 언급 되지 않으므로 오답이다. (D)는 Certain burial sites contained the symbolic dentalium seashell. 뿔조개가 발견되긴 했지만 무엇을 상징했는지에 대한 내용은 언급되지 않으므로 오답이다.

16 Which of the sentences below best expresses the essential information in the highlighted sentence in the passage? Incorrect choices change the meaning in important ways or leave out essential information.

(A) ii) The burial sites of children contained normal household items which showed that iii) they were seen as less important members of society.
(B) i) The inclusion of decorative items, like seashells, iii) denoted a higher position in the society than did ii) the everyday items buried with other members of society, like children.
(C) The dentalium seashells were symbolically buried with low ranking members of society who did not have elaborate furnishings with which they could be buried.
(D) Seashells and ordinary furnishings were buried with the children of only the most elite members of the society. ★

아래의 문장 중 지문 속의 음영 표시된 문장의 핵심 정보를 가장 잘 표현하고 있는 것은 무엇인가? 오답은 문장의 의미를 현저하게 바꾸거나 핵심 정보를 빠트리고 있다.

(A) ii) 어린이들은 매물 장소들은 일반적인 가정 용품들이 있는 것을 통해 이들은 iii) 사회에서 덜 중요한 인원으로 인식 되었다는 사실을 알수 있다.
(B) i) 조개들과 같은 장식적 용품들의 포함은 ii) 어린이들과 같이 사회의 다른 인원들과 같이 매장된 일상적인 용품에 비해 iii) 사회에서 높은 위치를 의미한다.
(C) 뿔조개는 화려한 장식품들과 같이 매장되지 못한 낮은 계급원들과 상징적으로 매장되었다.
(D) 조개들과 정교한 비품들은 사회의 가장 엘리트 부원들의 어린이들의 무덤들에만 매장되었다. ★

Highlight 음영 표시된 문장은 i) Certain burial sites contained the symbolic dentalium seashell, ii) while others, even those of children, were filled with commonfurnishings such as stone bowls, iii) showing a clear difference in societal standing of the decease(어떠한 매물 장소들은 iii) 고인들의 사회적 위치에 분명한 차이를 보이는 i) 상징적인 뿔조개들이 있었고 ii) 어린이들을 포함한 어떤 이들은 돌 그릇과 같은 흔한 비품들로 가득 찼다) 이렇게 세 가지 부분으로 나뉜다. 이 내용을 모두 포함하는 (B)가 정답이 된다. (A)는 i)의 내용을 포함 하고 있지 않기 때문에 오답이고, (C)는 뿔조개는 high-ranking members들의 무덤에서 발견되었기 때문에 오답이다. (D)는 흔한 비품들은 상대적으로 낮은 계급의 사람들 무덤에서 발견되었기 때문에 오답이다.

17 Why does the author mention the climate change that occurred around 11,000 BC in paragraph 6?

(A) To point out that Natufians ~~failed~~ to learn the life cycle of cereal plants after last two millennia of relying on them ★
(B) To explain why the Natufian society was forced to find ~~new areas~~ to ensure its survival
(C) ~~To call attention~~ to the ~~suitability~~ of the lifestyle the Natufians enjoyed after the climate had changed
(D) To show the reason that the Natufian society moved from being hunter-gatherers to a becoming the first true farming society

단락 6에서 작가는 왜 약 11,000 BC에 일어난 기후 변화를 언급하는가?

(A) 나투피안 인들이 시리얼 곡물에 의존한지 2,000년 후에도 곡물의 생활주기를 파악하는 데에 ~~실패했다는~~ 것을 가리키기 위해서 ★
(B) 나투피안 사회가 생존을 보장하기 위해서 ~~새로운 영역을~~ 찾을 수 밖에 없었던 이유를 설명하기 위해서
(C) 기후가 변화한 후 나투피안들이 즐겼던 생활의 ~~적합성에 주의를 환기시키기 위해서~~
(D) 나투피안 사회가 수렵 채집인들이 첫 실질적 농업 사회로 변화한 이유를 보여주기 위해서

Purpose 질문의 키워드인 climate change가 언급된 부분을 살펴보면 Within a short time, farming flourished in Southwest Asia, and full-scale farming societies appeared, leading to more civilized hunter-gatherer/farming communities in the area, where the Natufians developed the world's first dedicated form of agriculture. (짧은 시간 안에 농업은 서남 아시아에서 번창했고 대규모 농업 사회들이 나타나면서 나투피안들이 처음으로 지구상에서 계획적인 농업을 시작한 지역에서 더 문명화된 수렵 채집 농업 사회들로 이어졌다)라고 말한다. 즉, 갑작스러운 기후변화 때문에 나투피안들은 새로운 환경에 적응했어야 했고 이것은 그들의 생활패턴을 변화시키면서 그들을 농업 사회로 만들었다. 따라서 정답은 (D)가 된다. (A)는 오랜 기간 동안 곡식바탕의 사회에서 살면서 곡물의 생활패턴을 파악했기 때문에 오답이고, (B)는 Instead, they were able to deliberately plant and control the cereal plants에서 기후 변화가 일어난 후에 나투피안들은 새로운 정착지를 찾는 대신 그들이 작물을 수확하던 방법에 변화를 주었기 때문에 오답이다. (C)는 문제가 묻는 기후 변화가 언급된 이유와는 일치하지 않기 때문에 오답이고, 적합성에 주의를 환기시키기 위해서라면 문제가 있었다는 뜻인데, 기후 변화 후에 나투피안들이 받아들인 생활은 매우 적합했고 아무런 문제가 없었기 때문에 오답이다.

18 The term "declining" in the passage is closest in meaning to

(A) first being formed [fəːrst bíːiŋ fɔːrm]
(B) weakening [wíːkən]
(C) at its best [ət its best] ★
(D) rapidly expanding [rǽpidli ikspǽndiŋ]

지문의 단어 "쇠퇴하는"의 의미와 가장 유사한 것은?

(A) 처음으로 형성되는
(B) 약화되는
(C) -의 최고에 있는 ★
(D) 급격히 확대하는

Vocabulary 지문의 declining(쇠퇴하는)과 동의어인 weakening(약화되는)이 정답이다.

19 Look at the four squares [■] that indicate where the following sentence could be added to the passage.

These large settlements were also generally located near smaller satellite camps where they could collect and process their finds.

Where would the sentence best fit? Click on a square [■] to add the sentence to the passage.

2nd

네 개의 네모 [■]는 다음 문장이 삽입될 수 있는 부분을 나타내고 있다.

이 큰 정착지들은 또한 발견물들을 수집하고 가공할 수 있는 작은 위성 캠프 근처에 보통 위치했다.

이 문장은 어느 자리에 들어가는 것이 가장 적절한가?

2번째

Insertion 삽입 문장의 키워드는 these large settlements 와 also이다. 두 번째 네모 앞 문장을 살펴보면 These new settlements featured semi-subterranean pit-houses and pits where the crops could be stored 즉 새로운 정착지들이 가지고 있는 하나의 특징을 설명해 주는데 삽입 문장도 그 정착지들이 가지고 있던 (also)또 하나의 특징을 설명한다. 따라서 삽입 문장은 두 번째 네모 자리에 오는 것이 가장 적절함으로 정답은 두 번째 네모이다.

20

Directions: An introductory sentence for a brief summary of the passage is provided below. Complete the summary by selecting the THREE answer choices that express the most important ideas in the passage. Some sentences do not belong in the summary because they express ideas that are not presented in the passage or are minor ideas in the passage. **This question is worth 2 points.**

지시: 지문 요약을 위한 도입 문장이 아래에 주어져 있다. 지문의 가장 중요한 내용을 나타내는 보기 3개를 골라 요약을 완성하시오. 어떤 문장은 지문에 언급되지 않은 내용이나 사소한 정보를 담고 있으므로 요약에 포함되지 않는다. **이 문제는 2점이다.**

Changes in civilizations in Southwest Asia had major effects on humankind.

(B) Changes in the diets of the Kebaran civilization led to changes in humanity that altered both the way people live and the food they eat that have lasted for over 13,000 years. - paragraph 1

(D) The Natufian Culture derived from the earlier nomadic Kebaran Society and eventually became the first settled society because of the abundance of food sources in the area, even before the development of farming. - paragraph 2,3

(F) After many centuries of living near their food sources the Natufians learned enough about them to understand how they grew and utilized this information to domesticate the crops. - paragraph 6

서남 아시아의 문명들의 변화는 인류에 큰 영향을 미쳤다.

(B) 케바란 문명의 식단 변화는 13,000년 동안 사람들이 살고 음식을 먹는 방식을 모두 인류의 변화로 이어졌다.

(D) 나투피안 문명은 이전 케바란 유목 사회에서 유래되고 결국 이는 농업의 발달 이전에 이 지역의 풍부한 식재료 때문에 첫 정착 사회가 되었다.

(F) 식재료 주변에 몇 백 년 동안 거주한 후 나투피안들은 이들에 대해 충분히 배워 이들이 어떻게 자라는지 이해하게 되어 이 정보를 갖고 작물들을 재배하기 시작했다.

(A) Since the Natufian culture still remained in its primitive state, it had been more or less an ~~egalitarian~~ society.
- 틀린 정보

(C) If it were not for their knowledge on the life cycle of the cereal plants they had obtained over the previous two millennia, the Natufians would have ~~flourished~~ as a farming community. - 틀린 정보

(E) Because of the accumulations of silica particles from cereal stalks, anthropologists have recognized that the Natufians' blades were used for cereal harvesting.
- paragraph 3 detail

(A) 나투피안 문명은 원시 상태로 머물렀기 때문에 ~~평등한~~ 사회였다.

(C) 지난 2,000년을 걸쳐 얻은 곡식의 생활 주기에 대한 정보가 없었다면, 그들은 농업 공동체로 ~~번창했을 것이다~~.

(E) 곡물 줄기에서 나오는 이산화규소 입자들의 축적 때문에, 인류학자들은 나투피안들의 날이 곡식을 수확하는데 사용되었다는 것을 알아보았다.

Summary 지문의 중심 내용은 나투피안 문명의 발달과 특징이다. (B)는 첫 번째 단락의 중심내용인 서남 아시아에 위치했던 케바란 사회가 오늘날의 사회한테까지 미친 영향과 일치하고, (D)는 두 번째와 세 번째 단락의 중심내용인 나투피안 문명이 정착할 수 있었던 계기와 일치하고, (F)는 여섯 번째 단락의 중심내용인 기후 변화에도 그 동안 쌓아온 지식을 바탕으로 계속해서 살아남은 나투피안 문명과 일치한다.

USHER iBT TOEFL
INTERMEDIATE READING

TEST 7
답안 및 취약 유형 분석표

해석·해설

답안 및 문제 유형 분석표

TEST 7-1

01 (B) Purpose

02 (D) Inference

03 (B) Vocabulary

04 (B) Fact

05 (A) Inference

06 (C) Highlight

07 (B) Reference

08 (D) Inference

09 4th ■ Insertion

10 (B), (E), (F) Summary

TEST 7-2

11 (B) Highlight

12 (B) Inference

13 (C), (D) Fact

14 (C) Vocabulary

15 (C) Inference

16 (A) Fact

17 (A) Purpose

18 (D) Inference

19 3rd ■ Insertion

20 (A), (C), (F) Summary

각 문제 유형별 맞춘 개수를 아래에 적어 보세요.

유형	맞춘 답의 개수	정답률	
단어 (Vocabulary)	/ 2	정답률:	%
사실 확인 문제 (Fact)	/ 3	정답률:	%
지시어 찾기 (Reference)	/ 1	정답률:	%
끼워 넣기 (Insertion)	/ 2	정답률:	%
문장 변환문제 (Highlight)	/ 2	정답률:	%
목적 (Purpose)	/ 2	정답률:	%
추론 (Inference)	/ 6	정답률:	%
단락 요약(Summary / Category Chart)	/ 2	정답률:	%
전체	/ 20	정답률:	%

※ 자신이 취약한 유형은 READING STRATEGIES를 통해 다시 한번 점검하시기 바랍니다. (p.44)

TEST 7-1　Life on Mars 화성의 생명체

Introduction	단락 1	다른 행성들, 특히 화성의 생명에 대한 인간의 탐구
Point	단락 2	지구와 화성의 유사점
Point	단락 3	현재의 화성에서의 척박한 대기 환경들
Point	단락 4	한때 화성 표면 위에 존재했지만 지금은 사라진 물
Point	단락 5	생명체들이 화성에서 살아남기 위해 사용할 수 있었던 방법들
Point	단락 6	과거에는 지구와 비슷했지만 현재에는 지구와 다른 화성의 환경
Point	단락 7	바이킹 호의 화성에서의 생명체의 부재 확인과 화성의 토양이 모든 생명 물질들을 파괴하는 사실

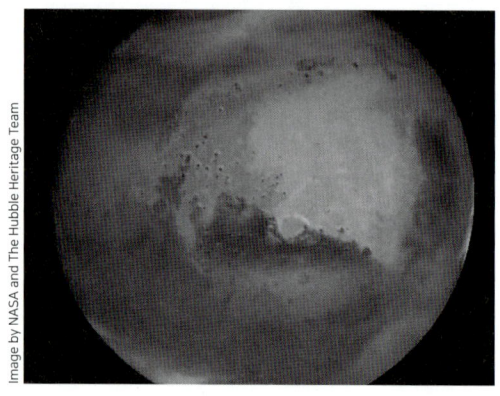
Image by NASA and The Hubble Heritage Team

문단주제	본문내용	해석
단락 1 다른 행성들, 특히 화성의 생명에 대한 인간의 탐구	**1** Since the beginning of time, humans have wondered if they were alone in the universe. In the modern times, cosmologists and astrophysicists, Stephen Hawking and Carl Sagan, have claimed that extraterrestrial life is **not only** possible, **but** probable. They **base** their theories **on** the Mediocrity, or Copernican, Principle which states that because life developed on Earth, **it is likely to develop** or has already developed on planets with similar molecular structures where the laws of physics work similarly. [Q2-D] Astronomers believe that over 40 million Earth-sized planets orbiting Sun-like stars in their habitable zones, the regions where atmospheric pressures allow liquid surface water, may exist in the Milky Way alone. One in particular has **inspired** scientists **to search for** signs of life, Mars.	태초부터 인간들은 그들이 우주에서 혼자인지에 대하여 궁금증을 품어 왔다. 현대 시대에, 우주학자이자 천체물리학자인 Stephen Hawking과 Carl Sagan은 지구 밖의 생명은 가능할 뿐만이 아니라, 그럴듯 하다고 주장했다. 그들은 그들의 이론들을 지구안에서 생명체가 발전했기 때문에 물리 법칙이 비슷하고 비슷한 분자 구조가 존재하는 다른 행성에서도 생명체가 존재할 거라고 주장하는 평범성의 원리(코페르니쿠스 원리)에 근거하였다. [Q2-D] 천문 학자들은 액체상태의 지표수를 가능케 하는 대기압이 있는 지역인 생존가능 지역에서 태양과 같은 행성을 도는 지구크기의 4천만개 이상의 행성이 은하수 하나에만 존재할 수 있다고 믿었다. 특히 과학자들로 하여금 생명체의 흔적을 파악하도록 격려한 것이 바로 화성이다.
단락 2 지구와 화성의 유사점	**2** **Contrary to** popular belief, Mars and Earth are remarkably similar. Although Earth is much larger than Mars, they have nearly identical land surfaces. They also share similar atmospheric chemistry when **compared to** other planets in our solar system. Further, Mars is **subject to** seasonal temperature variations like Earth's due to its 25° axis tilt, which is only 1.5° different than Earth's 23.5° tilt. A more important similarity that could allow life on Mars is the	대중적인 믿음과는 달리, 화성과 지구는 놀라울 정도로 비슷하다. 비록 지구가 화성보다 훨씬 크지라도, 둘은 거의 똑같은 토지 면적을 갖고 있다. 또한 둘은 태양계 안의 다른 행성들과 비교해 보았을 때에 비슷한 대기 화학 성분을 공유한다. 더 나아가서, 화성의 중심축은 지구의 23.5°와 1.5°밖에 차이가 나지 않는 25°기울어져 있기 때문에 지구와 비슷한 계절적인 온도 변화에 노출 되어 있다. 화성에서의 생명체의 존재를 허용하는 더 중요한 유사성은 두 행성이 태양의

Vocabulary

1단락
- wonder [wʌ́ndər] v. 궁금해 하다
- mediocrity [mì:diɑ́krəti] n. 평범
- astrophysicist [æ̀stroufízisist] n. 천체물리학자
- extra-terrestrial [ékstrə-təréstriəl] a. 지구 밖의
- cosmologist [kɑzmoulɑ́dʒist] n. 우주론자
- molecular [moulékjulər] a. 분자의
- era [íərə] n. 시대

2단락
- remarkably [rimɑ́ːrkəbli] ad. 현저하게, 눈에 띄게
- atmospheric [æ̀tməsférik] a. 대기의
- although [ɔːlðóu] c. 비록
- variation [vɛ̀əriéiʃən] n. 변화
- identical [aidéntikəl] a. 동일한
- similarity [sìməlǽrəti] n. 유사점

fact that both planets orbit in the Sun's habitable zone, which could allow Martian surface water **in addition to** the water frozen in its polar ice caps.

3   Despite these similarities, Mars' conditions are currently very inhospitable. [■] The most glaring problem is that the current Martian atmosphere **is deadly for** Earth-based organisms. [■] The thin, carbon dioxide (CO2)-heavy composition of the atmosphere, besides being **toxic to** oxygen-dependent organisms, does not retain solar heat when it is not directly **exposed to** the Sun; therefore, nighttime temperatures drop precipitously and the average surface temperature is a frigid -30°C. [■] In addition, Mars' minimal atmosphere **does little to prevent** deadly ultraviolet solar radiation **from reaching** its surface **in the way that** ozone gases in Earth's atmosphere do. [■] This is compounded by Mars' lack of the type of magnetic field that protects the Earth from the effects of solar flares that further destroy its environment.

4   [Q4-A] Another major problem that prevents life on Mars is the **dearth of** liquid surface water. While the ice caps do contain a tremendous amount of water and CO2, scientists have been **unable to find** liquid water on Mars' surface, but this does not mean it never existed. Scientists believe that Earth's surface water was the result of venting from early volcanoes and have no **reason to believe** that this couldn't have happened on Mars, since there are now extinct volcanoes scattered across its surface. [Q4-C] In addition, if its atmosphere was once thicker, it may have trapped enough solar heat to allow the water locked up in polar ice caps to form the rivers and seas whose effects are currently seen on the Martian landscape. [Q4-D] In fact, craters left by meteoroids that struck the eroded areas of the surface, where it **is assumed** water once ran, show that they must have struck after the water disappeared and have been dated to several hundred million, **if not** a billion, years old.

Vocabulary

3단락
- habitable [hǽbətəbəl] a. 살기에 적합한
- inhospitable [inháspitəbəl] a. 살기에 부적합한
- precipitously [prisípətəsly] ad. 급격하게
- deadly [dédli] ad. 치명적인
- atmosphere [ǽtməsfiər] n. 대기
- dependent [dipéndənt] a. 의존하는

4단락
- major [méidʒər] a. 주요한
- scatter [skǽtər] v. 흩어버리다, 흩어지다
- dearth [dəːrθ] n. 결핍, 부족
- currently [kə́ːrəntli] ad. 현재의
- vent [vent] n. 분출구, v. 분출하다
- meteoroid [míːtiərɔ̀id] n. 유성체

| 단락 5 | 생명체들이 화성에서 살아남기 위해 사용할 수 있었던 방법들 | 5 [Q5-A] These factors, however, do not necessarily prohibit the presence of life on Mars. While most organisms require **protection from** solar forces and **access to** water and oxygen, it is not a universal need. Bacteria that require CO_2 **instead of** oxygen have been discovered, and some organisms may be able to draw enough water from the trace amounts found in surface rocks. Further, protection from solar radiation can occur through a mechanism as simple as developing an outer shell or living under the surface to reduce the effects of solar radiation. | [Q5-A] 하지만 이러한 요인들은 반드시 화성에서 생명체의 존재를 불가능하게 하는 것은 아니다. 대부분의 생명체들은 태양의 힘으로부터의 보호와 물과 공기로의 접근을 필요로 하지만, 이것은 보편적인 필요는 아니다. 산소 대신에 이산화탄소를 필요로 하는 박테리아도 발견되었고 몇몇 생명체들은 돌 표면으로부터의 극소량으로 충분한 물을 얻어내는 것도 가능할 것이다. 더 나아가서, 자외선으로 부터의 보호는 외부 껍질을 발달시키거나 태양 방사의 영향을 줄이기 위해 표면 아래에 사는 것과 같은 간단한 체계를 통해서 이루어질 수 있다. |

| 단락 6 | 과거에는 지구와 비슷했지만 현재에는 지구와 다른 화성의 환경 | 6 Another theory allowing life on Mars is the possibility of Earth-like conditions in the past. Scientists have discovered signs of flowing surface water, but Mars could have been even more Earth-like **at one time**. A change **could have occurred** as CO_2 became **trapped in** rocks. Since Mars lacks the tectonic and volcanic activity that cycles CO_2 in the Earth's atmosphere, the atmosphere could have been **depleted of** gaseous CO_2 over time, which would have reduced the greenhouse effect and destabilized the atmosphere, allowing most of it to dissipate **over time**. This could have allowed a gradual disappearance of water from Mars' surface or its absorption below Mars' crust, where it may still exist, until life became unsustainable. | 화성에서의 생명체의 존재를 허락해 주는 또 다른 이론은 지구와 유사한 과거 화성 환경의 가능성이다. 과학자들은 화성 표면에서 흐르는 물의 흔적 들을 발견했지만 화성은 한때 어쩌면 지구와 더 비슷했었을 수도 있다. 이산화탄소가 돌 안에 갇히면서 변화가 일어났을 수도 있다. 화성에는 지구의 대기에서 이산화탄소를 순환시키는 지각운동이나 화산 활동이 부족하기 때문에, 시간이 지남에 따라 대기의 기체 이산화탄소는 고갈됨으로써 온실효과가 감소되고 대기가 불안정화되면서 이것은 점점 분산되어 갔다. 이것은 화성의 표면으로부터의 물의 점차적인 감소를 일어나게 했거나, 생명체가 존재 할 수 없을 때까지 물이 행성 자체에 흡수 되도록 했을 것이다. |

| 단락 7 | 바이킹 호의 화성에서의 생명체의 부재 확인과 화성의 토양이 모든 생명 물질들을 파괴하는 사실 | 7 [Q8-D] Unfortunately, the two Viking spacecraft found no traces of life, either current or past, on the Martian surface. It was, however, found that the surface soil was self-sterilizing because the harsh solar radiation on the surface reacts with its minerals and destroys all organic matter. Interestingly, though, they did discover elements which would be **necessary to support** life, namely nitrogen and phosphorus. From these tests, the most that can be hypothesized is that even though the current conditions on Mars cannot currently support life, it may have been possible at some point **in the past**. | [Q8-D] 불행하게도, 두 개의 바이킹 우주선은 화성 표면에서의 과거 또는 현재의 생명체의 흔적을 발견하지 못했다. 하지만, 화성 표면에 닿는 자외선은 표면의 광물과 반응하고 모든 생명 물질들을 파괴하기 때문에 화성의 토양이 자체 불모화를 한다는 것을 발견했다. 하지만 흥미롭게도, 바이킹 호들은 질소와 인과 같은 생명체가 사는 데에 필요한 성분들을 발견했다. 이러한 시험으로부터 가장 최선으로 가정될 수 있는 것은 현재에 화성은 생물체가 살 수 없는 환경이지만, 한 때에는 살 수 있었을 것이라는 것이다. |

Vocabulary

5단락
- necessarily [nèsəsérəli] ad. 필연적으로
- trace [treis] n. 흔적, v. 추적하다

6단락
- theory [θíəri] n. 이론
- tectonic [tektánik] a. 지각 운동의

7단락
- unfortunately [ʌnfɔ́ːrtʃənitli] ad. 불행하게도
- mineral [mínərəl] n. 광물

- prohibit [prouhíbit] v. 금지하다
- mechanism [mékənìzəm] n. 체계
- possibility [pàsəbíləti] n. 가능성
- deplete [diplíːt] v. 고갈시키다
- sterilizing [stérəlàiz] a. 불모화 시키는
- interestingly [íntəristiŋly] ad. 흥미롭게도

- presence [prézəns] n. 존재
- reduce [ridjúːs] v. 감소시키다
- harsh [haːrʃ] a. 가혹한
- hypothesize [haipάθəsàiz] v. 가정하다

01

Why does the author mention "over 40 million Earth-sized planets orbiting Sun-like stars in their habitable zones"?

(A) To indicate the number of planets that ~~support some form of life~~ on their surfaces in the Milky Way ★
(B) To illustrate the large number of planets on which life could theoretically exist in just our galaxy
(C) To emphasize the ~~unique characteristics~~ of Mars to be selected as the subject of study among that many planets
(D) To contradict a common ~~misperception~~ of the estimated number of Earth-like planets

왜 작가는 "4000만개가 넘는 지구 크기의 행성이 태양과 같은 별을 살기에 적합한 구역을 돈다"는 것을 언급하는가?

(A) 은하수 안에서 ~~어떠한 형태의 생명체~~를 가지고 있는 행성의 개수에 대해서 나타내기 위해서 ★
(B) 우리의 은하 안에서 이론적으로 생물체가 존재할 수 있는 행성의 개수를 보여주기 위해서
(C) 그 많은 행성들 중에서 연구대상으로 선택된 화성의 ~~고유한 특징들을~~ 강조하기 위해서
(D) 흔히 지구 비슷한 행성의 숫자를 ~~잘못 알고 있는 점을~~ 반박하기 위해서

Purpose 음영 표시된 부분을 살펴보면 Astronomers believe that over 40 million Earth-sized planets orbiting Sun-like stars in their habitable zones may exit in the Milky Way alone. (천문학자들은 살 수 있는 구역에서 태양과 같은 별들의 궤도를 돌고 있는 지구 크기만한 행성들이 은하수 만에도 4천만개가 존재할 것이라고 믿는다)라고 말한다. 단락 1에선 Stephen Hawking과 Carl Sagan의 이름을 거론하며 다른 행성 에서도 생명체가 존재할 것이라고 주장한다. 그 내용을 뒷받침해줄 근거로 음영 표시된 문장이 언급된 것이고, 이론적으로는 수많은 행성에 생명체가 있을 수 있다는 것을 알려주기 위한 것이므로 정답은 (B)가 된다. (A)는 작가는 행성의 개수에 대해서 알려주려던 것이 아니라 이론적인 면을 강조하려던 것이기 때문에 오답이고, (C)는 화성이 연구대상으로 선택된 것은 사실이지만 이것의 고유한 특징을 강조하기 위해 언급된 것은 아니기 때문에 오답이다. (D)는 사람들이 가지고 있는 오해에 대해선 언급된 적이 없기 때문에 오답이다.

02

What can be inferred from paragraph 1 about the existence of life in the universe?

(A) The Milky Way alone contains ~~more~~ Earth-sized planets orbiting Sun-like stars than all other galaxies' combined.
(B) The ~~majority~~ of planets that exist in the universe are concentrated in the hospitable zones. ★
(C) Scientists have concentrated their search for life on Mars because of its ~~unique~~ location in the habitable zone.
(D) The planetary-mass objects outside the habitable zones lack sufficient atmospheric pressure to support liquid water.

단락 1에 따르면 우주 안에서의 생명체의 존재에 관한 내용으로 추론될 수 있는 것은?

(A) 은하계는 다른 태양과 같은 별 주위를 도는 지구 크기의 행성을 다른 모든 은하에서 존재하는 지구 크기의 행성들을 합친 것보다 ~~많아~~ 포함한다
(B) 우주 안에 존재하는 ~~태부분의~~ 행성들은 살기에 적합한 구역에 집중되어 있다 ★
(C) 과학자들은 화성이 ~~독특하게~~ 살기 적합한 구역에 위치해 있기 때문에 그들의 생명체에 대한 탐구를 화성에 집중 했다
(D) 살 수 있는 구역 밖에 있는 행성의 질량 개체들은 물을 존재하게 할 수 있는 충분한 기압인 압력을 가지고 있지 않다

Inference 질문의 키워드인 existence of life in the universe가 언급된 부분을 살펴보면 Astronomers believe that over 40 million Earth-sized planets orbiting Sun-like stars in their habitable zones, the regions where atmospheric pressures allow liquid surface water, may exist in the Milky Way alone. (천문학자들은 기압적인 압력들이 행성의 표면 위에 액체 상태의 물이 존재하게 하는 살 수 있는 구역에서 태양과 같은 별들의 궤도를 돌고 있는 지구 크기만한 행성들이 은하수만에도 4천만개가 존재할 것이라고 믿는다)라고 말한다. 즉, habitable zone(살 수 있는 구역) 밖에 있는 행성들은 물을 존재하게 할 수 있게 하는 충분한 기압적인 압력을 가지고 있지 않다고 유추할 수 있다.따라서 정답은 (D)가 된다. (A)는 본문에서 은하계에서만 4천만개 이상의 지구와 비슷한 행성들이 존재한다고 설명한다. 즉, 다른 은하에는 더 많은 지구와 비슷한 행성들이 존재할 수도 있기 때문에 오답이고, (B)는 살기 적합한 구역에 많은 행성이 존재하는 것은 사실이지만 행성의 대부분이 그 구역에 존재한다는 것은 본문에서 직접적으로 설명되는 부분이 아니기 때문에 오답이다. (C)는 살기 적합한 구역엔 4천만개 이상의 행성들이 존재하므로 화성이 그 구역에 존재하는 것은 특별한 것이 아니라 오히려 일반적이다. 따라서 (C)는 오답이다.

03

The term "inhospitable" in the passage is closest in meaning to

(A) unjust [ʌndʒʌ́st]
(B) unfavorable [ʌnféivərəbəl]
(C) impossible [impásəbəl] ★
(D) unpredictable [ʌnpridíktəbəl]

지문의 단어 "거주하기에 부적당한"의 의미와 가장 유사한 것은?

(A) 부당한
(B) 알맞지 않은
(C) 불가능한 ★
(D) 예측할 수 없는

Vocabulary 지문의 inhospitable(거주하기에 부적당한)와 동의어인 unfavorable(알맞지 않은)이 정답이다. (C)는 거주할 수 있는 여지를 아예 배제하기 때문에 오답이다.

04

According to paragraph 4, which of the following is **NOT** true about the existence of water on the Martian surface?

(A) At the current time, there is no liquid water flowing across the surface of Mars.
(B) Prior to the disappearance of water, meteoroids whose presence is noted in today's craters struck Mars.
(C) Scientists believe that liquid water could have existed on Mars in the past if the atmosphere were able to hold in heat from the Sun.
(D) The effects of running water, such as the presence of eroded rocks in some places, have been noted on the surface of Mars.

단락 4에 따르면, 화성 표면의 물의 존재에 대한 내용으로 옳지 않은 것은?

(A) 현재에는 화성 위로 흐르고 있는 액체 물은 없다.
(B) 물이 사라지기 전에, 오늘의 침식된 표면에 흔적이 남아 있는 유성들이 화성에 타격을 가했다.
(C) 과학자들은 과거에 화성의 대기가 태양으로부터의 열을 보관할 수 있었다면 화성에 물이 존재할 수도 있었다고 믿는다.
(D) 몇몇 장소 안에서의 침식된 돌들의 존재같은 흐르는 물의 영향들은 화성의 표면에서 발견되었다.

Fact 질문의 키워드인 existence of water이 언급된 부분을 살펴보면 In fact, craters left by meteoroids that struck the eroded areas of the surface, where it is assumed water once ran, show that they must have struck after the water disappeared (실제로, 한때에는 물이 흘렀다고 예상되는, 침식된 화성의 표면들에 타격을 가했던 유성들에 의해 남겨진 구덩이들은, 유성들이 물이 사라진 후에 타격을 가했다는 것을 보여준다)라고 말한다. 즉, 물이 사라지기 전이 아니라 사라진 후에 유성이 화성을 타격한 것이기 때문에 정답은 (B)가 된다.

05

What can be inferred about life on Mars from paragraph 5?

(A) Given an ideal set of adaptations, life could exist on Mars today even with the inhospitable conditions that exist there.
(B) There are organisms found on Mars to have lived under the surface to reduce the effects of solar radiation.
(C) Rocks on the Martian surface have been found to contain a lot of liquid water.
(D) Microorganisms often found on Mars have developed an outer shell to avoid solar forces. ★

단락 5로부터 화성의 생명체에 대해서 추론될 수 있는 내용은?

(A) 주어진 일련의 적응에 따르면, 생명체는 오늘날의 화성의 상태가 살기에는 부적합 해도 존재할 수 있었을 것이다.
(B) 태양 방사의 영향을 줄이기 위해 표면 아래에 사는 생물체들이 화성에서 존재한다.
(C) 화성 표면의 돌들은 많은 양의 물을 포함하고 있다고 발견되었다.
(D) 화성에서 종종 발견되는 미생물은 태양 방사를 피하기 위해 외부 껍질을 발달시켰다. ★

Inference   질문의 키워드인 life on Mars가 언급된 부분을 살펴보면 These factors, however, do not necessarily prohibit the presence of life on Mars. (하지만 이러한 요인들은 반드시 화성에서 생명체의 존재를 금지하지는 않는다)라고 말한다. 즉, 단락 5에서 설명하듯 화성의 표면 아래에 사는 것과 같은 여러 가지 방법을 통해 화성 생물체들이 살아 남을 수도 있기 때문에 정답은 (A)가 된다. (B)는 본문에 태양 방사의 영향을 줄이기 위한 방법으로 표면 밑에 사는 것이 제시되긴 하지만 아직 실제로 이 방법을 직접적으로 사용하고 있는 생물체는 발견되지 않았기 때문에 오답이고, (C)는 화성 표면의 돌들은 trace amounts(아주 작은 양의 물)을 포함하고 있기 때문에 오답이다. (D)는 본문에선 자외선으로부터 보호하는 방법의 예로 껍질이 제시되는 것일 뿐, 언급된 미생물(박테리아)은 외부 껍질이 아닌 산소 대신 이산화탄소를 사용해 숨을 쉬며 화성에서 서식하고 있기 때문에 오답이다.

---

06   Which of the sentences below best expresses the essential information in the highlighted sentence in the passage? Incorrect choices change the meaning in important ways or leave out essential information.

(A) On Earth, plate movement and volcanic eruptions recycle CO2 back into its gaseous form in the atmosphere where it causes the greenhouse effect that ~~destabilizes~~ the atmosphere and is responsible for the hole in the Ozone layer.
(B) In absence of the ability to ii) recycle CO2 from the air to the ground, iii) Mars lacks the greenhouse effect and has an unstable atmosphere iv) that gets easily dispersed over time. ★
(C) i) ii) As it lacks the Earth's geological features that recycle CO2 back into its gaseous form in the atmosphere, iii) iv) Mars has an unstable atmosphere that is easily blown away due to the lack of the CO2's insulating greenhouse effect.
(D) Volcanic and tectonic changes on the Earth caused a cycling of CO2 that resulted in the ~~disappearance~~ of gaseous CO2 from Mars and led to a reduction in the greenhouse effect, bringing about even further environmental destabilization.

아래의 문장 중 지문 속의 음영 표시된 문장의 핵심 정보를 가장 잘 표현하고 있는 것은 무엇인가? 오답은 문장의 의미를 현저하게 바꾸거나 핵심 정보를 빠트리고 있다.

(A) 지구에서는 지각 운동과 화산 폭발은 이산화탄소를 대기를 ~~불안정화시키는~~ 온실효과를 초래하는 기체 상태로 대기로 돌려 보내고 이것은 오존층의 구멍의 원인이다.
(B) ii)이산화탄소를 대기로부터 지면으로 순환시킬 수 있는 능력이 없는 iii) 화성은 온실효과가 없고 iv) 쉽게 날라가는 불안정한 대기를 가지고 있다. ★
(C) i) ii) 화성이 지구의 이산화탄소를 재활용해서 대기로 기체 상태로 되돌려 보내는 지질적인 특징이 없기 때문에, iii) iv) 화성은 이산화탄소의 잡아두는 온실효과의 결핍때문에 쉽게 날라가는 불안정한 대기를 가지고 있다.
(D) 지구의 화산과 지각운동의 변화는 화성으로부터 이산화탄소의 ~~사라짐~~을 초래하는 이산화탄소의 순환을 유발시켰고 온실효과의 감소를 초래 하였으며, 더 심한 환경적인 불안정을 유발시켰다.

Highlight   음영 표시된 문장은 i) Since Mars lacks the tectonic and volcanic activity that cycles CO2 into Earth's atmosphere, ii) over time the atmosphere could have been depleted of gaseous CO2, iii) which would have reduced the greenhouse effect and destabilized the atmosphere, iv) allowing most of it to dissipate over time. i) 화성에는 지구의 대기에서 이산화탄소를 순환시키는 지각운동 이나 화산 활동이 부족하기 때문에, ii) 시간이 지남에 따라 대기의 기체 이산화탄소는 고갈됨으로써 iii) 온실효과가 감소되고 대기가 불안정화되면서 iv) 대기는 점점 분산되어 갔다.) 이렇게 네 가지 내용으로 나뉜다. 이 내용을 모두 포함한 (C)가 정답이 된다. (A)는 대기를 불안정하게 하는 원인은 온실효과가 아니라 이산화탄소의 depletion(소모)이기 때문에 오답이고, (B)는 (C)와 비교되게 화산과 지각변동에 대한 내용을 직접적으로 언급하지 않기 때문에 오답이고, (D)는 지구의 지각운동이나 화산운동이 화산에게 직접적인 영향을 주지는 않기 때문에 오답이다.

---

07   What does the word "It" refer to in the passage?

(A) tectonic and volcanic activity
(B) atmosphere
(C) carbon Dioxide ★
(D) greenhouse effect

지문에서 "it"이 의미하는 것은?

(A) 지질 운동과 화산 운동
(B) 대기
(C) 이산화탄소 ★
(D) 온실효과

Reference Since Mars lacks the tectonic and volcanic activity that cycles CO2 into Earth's atmosphere, over time the atmosphere could have been depleted of gaseous CO2, which would have reduced the greenhouse effect and destabilized the atmosphere, allowing most of it to dissipate over time 에서 화산은 이산화탄소를 순환시킬 수 없고, 이것이 온실효과를 감소시키고 대기를 불안정하게 만들었고 결국 대기를 분산시켰다는 것이다. 만약 안정적이었다면 분산시키는 것이 불가능했을 것이며, 불안정해진 상태에선 분산시키는 것이 가능했을 것이다. 따라서 정답은 (B)가 된다.

08

According to paragraph 7, which of the following can be inferred regarding the findings made by the Viking Spacecraft?

(A) They could not determine the ~~state~~ of the soil because of the harsh solar radiation's interaction with minerals. ★
(B) They ~~proved~~ that despite the lack of life currently observable on Mars, organisms once populated the planet.
(C) The discovery of nitrogen and phosphorus is a ~~tell-tale indication~~ of organic matter on Mars.
(D) The detection of any signs of previous life on the surface of Mars is unlikely due to the harsh conditions that destroy organic materials there.

단락 7에 따르면, 바이킹 호에 의한 발견에 대해서 추론될 수 있는 내용은?

(A) 그들은 태양열과 광물의 상호 작용 때문에 땅의 ~~상태~~를 알아낼 수가 없었다. ★
(B) 그들은 현재에는 화성에서 관찰될 수 있는 생명체가 없지만 한때에는 화성에 살았다는 것을 ~~증명했다~~.
(C) 질소와 인의 발견은 화성에 생명 물질이 존재한다는 것을 ~~나타낸다~~.
(D) 화성표면에서의 생명체의 흔적 발견은 생명 물질을 파괴시키는 가혹한 환경때문에 가능성이 없을 것이다.

Inference 질문의 키워드인 findings made by the Viking Spacecraft가 언급된 부분을 살펴보면 It was, however, found that the surface soil was self-sterilizing because the harsh solar radiation on the surface reacts with its minerals and destroys all organic matter. (하지만, 화성 표면에 닿는 자외선은 표면의 광물과 반응하고 모든 생명 물질들을 파괴하기 때문에 화성의 토양이 자체 불모화를 한다는 것을 발견했다) 라고 말한다. 즉, 생명체가 사는 데에 필요한 성분들은 발견되었지만 생명체의 흔적 존재는 발견할 수 없었기 때문에 정답은 (D)가 된다. (A)는 땅이 self-sterilizing하다는 것을 발견했기 때문에 오답이고, (B)는 the harsh solar radiation on the surface reacts with its minerals and destroys all organic matter.(화성 표면에 닿는 자외선은 표면의 광물과 반응하고 모든 생명 물질들을 파괴한다)에서 화성에는 현재 아무런 생명체가 존재하지 않기 때문에 오답이다. (C)는 질소와 인은 대기에 있는 요소이기 때문에 오답이다.

09

Look at the four squares [■] that indicate where the following sentence could be added to the passage.

This is compounded by Mars' lack of the type of magnetic field that protects the Earth from the effects of solar flares that further destroy its environment.

Where would the sentence best fit? Click on a square [■] to add the sentence to the passage.

4th

네 개의 네모 [■]는 다음 문장이 삽입될 수 있는 부분을 나타내고 있다.

이것은 지구를 태양의 불꽃으로부터 이것의 환경을 더 파괴하는 것을 막아주는 종류의 자기장의 결핍으로 인해 악화된다.

이 문장은 어느 자리에 들어가는 것이 가장 적절한가?

네 번째

Insertion 삽입 문장의 키워드는 compounded by와 destroy이다. 네 번째 네모 앞의 문장을 살펴보면 화성의 대기는 지구의 대기처럼 태양의 자외선이 들어오는 것을 막지 못한다고 말한다. 즉, 화성에서 생명체가 존재할 수 없는 요인을 언급해 준다는 것이다. 이 문제점이 compounded by (더 복잡해지다) Mars' lack of the type of magnetic field that protects the Earth From the effects of solar flares that further destroy its environment또 다른 문제점을 언급해주는 것이 옳다. 따라서 정답은 네 번째 네모이다. solar flares 때문에 세 번째 박스는 성립하지 않는다.

10 **Directions:** An introductory sentence for a brief summary of the passage is provided below. Complete the summary by selecting the THREE answer choices that express the most important ideas in the passage. Some sentences do not belong in the summary because they express ideas that are not presented in the passage or are minor ideas in the passage. **This question is worth 2 points.**

| 지시: 지문 요약을 위한 도입 문장이 아래에 주어져 있다. 지문의 가장 중요한 내용을 나타내는 보기 3개를 골라 요약을 완성하시오. 어떤 문장은 지문에 언급되지 않은 내용이나 사소한 정보를 담고 있으므로 요약에 포함되지 않는다. **이 문제는 2점이다.**

The current conditions on Mars do not allow it to support life, but it may have at one time.

(B) Presently, the lack of a suitable atmosphere that regulates solar energy and the lack of liquid water on the Martian surface make it all but impossible for living organisms to be present on Mars.
　　　　　　　　　　　　　　　- paragraph 3,4

(E) Mars' location in the sun's hospitable zone and the possibility of past conditions that more closely resembled those on Earth could have allowed it to support life before it underwent great atmospheric changes.
　　　　　　　　　　　　　　　- paragraph 2,6

(F) The Viking spacecraft found nothing that pointed to the existence of life on the Martian surface, but also noted that current reactions between the soil and solar radiation would have effectively destroyed any organic matter that may have been present.
　　　　　　　　　　　　　　　- paragraph 7

현재의 화성의 상태는 생명체가 살 수 없다, 하지만 한때에는 생명체가 화성에 살았을 수도 있다.

(B) 현재에는, 화성에서의 태양 에너지를 통제하는 살기 적합한 대기의 결핍과 화성 표면의 물의 결핍은 모든 생물체들이 화성에 거의 살 수 없게 만든다.

(E) 화성의 살기 적합한 구역 안의 위치와 지구의 환경과 비슷할 수 있었던 과거 화성의 가능성은 화성이 극심한 대기의 변화를 겪기 전에는 생명체가 화성에 살도록 했을지도 모른다.

(F) 바이킹 우주선은 현재 화성 표면에서의 생명체의 흔적은 발견하지 못했다. 하지만 현재의 토양과 자외선의 반응은 존재하는 모든 생명 물질을 효과적으로 파괴했을 것이라는 것을 발견했다.

(A) Since the beginning of recorded human history, scientists such as Copernicus, Stephen Hawking, and Carl Sagan have been on a quest to find extraterrestrial life on Mars. - paragraph 1 detail

(C) ~~Due to the lack of ozone~~ gases in the atmosphere, Mars experiences more severe fluctuations in ~~seasonal temperature~~ than Earth does. - 틀린 정보

(D) Scientists have noted that Mars' atmosphere is unstable because it is ~~rich~~ in carbon dioxide and ~~sufficient~~ in greenhouse gases. - 반/반

(A) 기록된 인간 역사의 시초 이후로부터, 코페르니쿠스, 스테판 호킹, 카를 세곤과 같은 사람들은 화성에서의 지구 밖의 생명체를 찾는 탐사에 열중했다.

(C) 화성 대기 안의 온실효과의 ~~결핍~~ 때문에 화성은 지구보다 더 심한 ~~계절온도의~~ 변동을 겪는다.

(D) 과학자들은 화성의 대기가 이산화탄소가 ~~풍부하고~~ 충분한 온실 가스를 가지고 있기 때문에 불안정하다는 것을 나타냈다.

Summary　지문의 중심 내용은 화성에서의 생명체 존재 여부이다. (B)는 세 번째와 네 번째 단락의 중심내용인 현재의 화성에서의 척박한 대기 환경들과 지금은 사라진 물과 일치하고, (E)는 두 번째와 여섯 번째 단락의 중심내용인 지구와 화성의 유사점과 과거에 지구와 비슷했던 화성의 환경들과 일치하고, (F)는 일곱 번째 단락의 중심내용인 바이킹 호의 화성에서의 생명체의 부재 확인과 일치한다. 따라서 정답은 (B), (E), (F) 이다.

TEST 7-2 Agriculture and Settlement around the Nile River
농업과 나일강 부근의 정착

Introduction	단락 1	사하라의 사막화가 초래한 나일 강의 정착지
Point	단락 2	식량 생산의 진정한 기원
Point	단락 3	강이 거쳐간 위대한 변화와 이것이 정착민들에게 미친 영향
Point	단락 4	나일 강에서의 정착이 중동 작물 생산에 미친 영향
Point	단락 5	나일 강에서의 다른 식품 근원
Point	단락 6	농업 개발을 기반으로 한 제국 설립

Photo by Rod Waddington available under the Creative Commons Attribution-Share Alike 2.0 Generic license.

문단주제	본문내용	해석
단락 1 사하라 사막화가 초래한 나일 강의 정착지	**1** The lush vegetation of the Nile River valley stands **in marked contrast to** the barren white sands of the nearby Sahara. Surprisingly, this contrast was the **impetus for** the development of settlements and domesticated agriculture across Africa. Researchers have **concluded that** the Sahara previously had ample water supplies and attracted inhabitants from the surrounding areas; [Q12-B] however, as conditions declined and the region became more arid, these people **were** driven out and **forced to find** new, fertile places to settle. [Q12-B] The Nile valley filled this role and **allowed** these people **to support** themselves while they **waited for** the Saharan conditions to improve again.	나일 강 유역의 무성한 식물은 인근 사하라 사막의 황량한 하얀 모래 사장과 현저한 대조를 이룬다. 놀랍게도 이 대조는 거주지의 개발과 아프리카에 걸친 재배 농업 위한 자극제였다. 연구진은 사하라 사막은 이전에 충분한 물 공급이 있었고 인근 주민 들을 끌어들였다고 결론을 내렸지만, [Q12-B] 이 조건이 감소하기 시작하고 그 지역이 더 건조해지자, 이 사람들은 분산되었고 정착할 수 있는 새로운, 비옥한 장소를 찾을 것을 강요당했다. [Q12-B] 나일강 유역은 이 역할을 해냈고 그들이 사하라 사막에서의 조건들이 다시 개선되기를 기다리는 동안 그들이 자급자족 할 수 있도록 했다.
단락 2 식량 생산의 진정한 기원	**2** These changes reveal one surprising aspect of the **shift to** agriculture and **dependence on** food production in Egypt; it did not begin in the Nile valley **as** is commonly assumed. [Q13-A] The process of **moving from** a nomadic culture **into** one with established villages using technology to domesticate and produce the livestock and plants required for such a lifestyle actually began further west in what is **now** the arid Sahara. [■] **Prior to** the last glacial period, the Sahara was **conducive to** inhabitation due to its abundant vegetation, grasslands and woodlands, [Q13-B] all of which encouraged nomadic groups	이러한 변화들은 농업으로의 변화와 이집트에서 식량 생산의 의존도에 대해 하나의 놀라운 측면을 드러냈다. 흔히 생각되는 것과는 달리 그것은 나일강 유역에서 시작되지 않았다. [Q13-A] 유목문화로부터 기술을 사용하여 가축을 사육하고 농작물을 생산하는 정착마을로 넘어가는 과정은 현재는 건조한 사하라인, 실제로 더 서쪽지역에서 시작되었다. [■] 마지막 빙하기 전에, 사하라에서의 거주에 도움이 되었다. 현지 유목민 그룹이 호수와 그 주변에서 사냥과 모임을 지속하면서 [Q13-B] 충분한 물과 식량 공급을 보장받을 수 있도록 호수 주변에 따라 남아있게끔 장려한 풍부한 식물, 초원, 그리고 숲이 있었기

Vocabulary

1단락
- lush [lʌʃ] a. 무성한, 우거진
- ample [ǽmpl] a. 충분한
- fertile [fə́ːrtl] a. 비옥한, 기름진
- impetus [ímpətəs] n. (일의 추진에 필요한) 자극(제)
- decline [dikláin] v. 감소하다 n. 감소
- valley [vǽli] n. 계곡, 골짜기
- barren [bǽrən] a. 척박한, 황량한
- arid [ǽrid] a. (땅이나 기후가) 매우 건조한

2단락
- nomadic [noumǽdik] a. 유목의, 방랑의
- glacial [gléiʃəl] a. 빙하의
- domesticate [douméstəkèit] v. 길들이다, 사육하다
- abundant [əbʌ́ndənt] a. 풍부한
- livestock [láivstàk] n. 가축
- floodplain [flʌ́dplèin] n. (홍수의) 범람원

to remain along its lakes, where they were guaranteed sufficient water and food from the lake and its surrounding areas as they hunted and gathered. [■] The area's eventual desertification forced these people and nearly all of the local wildlife to flee to a more suitable area, such as the fertile Nile River valley. [■] Once they arrived in the river valley they had little choice but to settle in one place. [Q13-D] Here, they **were boxed in** on the narrow floodplain by the hostile deserts, the river, and settlers that were living around them, [Q13-C] all of which restricted their ability to wander and gather food. [■]

때문이다. [■] 그 지역의 최종적 사막화는 사람들과 거의 모든 현지 야생동물을 기름진 나일 강 유역과 같은 더 적합한 지역으로 도망치게 만들었다. [■] 그들이 한번 강 유역에 도착하면 그들은 한 장소에 정착하는 것 밖에 선택의 여지가 없었다. [Q13-D] 그곳에서, 그들은 [Q13-C] 그들이 돌아다니고 식량을 구하는 능력을 제한한 거친 사막과 강, 그리고 주위에 거주하고 있던 정착민 그룹에 의해 좁은 범람원에 갇혀 꼼짝 못하게 되었다. [■]

단락 3
강이 거쳐간 위대한 변화와 이것이 정착민들에게 미친 영향

3 Another aspect of the Nile Valley's settlement was the tremendous change that the river **went through**. Today, most people know that the Nile is the longest river in the world, but **at the time** it was much smaller and slower, running through a series interconnected riverbeds across the floodplain, **instead of** today's massive river. Eventually the sediment and silt carried through these channels aggregated and **built up** the floodplain, raising the river's level considerably. [Q15-C] This allowed lush vegetation to grow along the floodplain and **turned** the Nile valley **into** an oasis sandwiched between the inhospitable Sahara and Eastern deserts, stretching 800 km from the present day Sudan to Cairo. **As time wore on**, settlers in this area became **dependent upon** the river and **separated** their year **into** three sections based upon its actions: the inundation when the overflowing river **spread** silt **across** the floodplain, the growing season when they tended their crops in the sediment-filled fields, and harvest time when they collected the bounty provided by the nutrients the river had **brought them**.

나일 강 유역의 정착에 대한 또 다른 측면은 강이 경험한 엄청난 변화였다. 오늘날 대부분의 사람들은 나일 강이 세계에서 가장 긴 강이라는 것을 알지만, 정착했을 그 당시에는 오늘날의 거대한 강 대신 범람원에 걸쳐 연속되고 서로 연결되어 있는 강바닥을 통해 흘러가는 나일 강은 훨씬 작고 느렸다. 결국 이러한 통로를 통해 운반된 침전물과 토사물이 모여 범람원을 지었고 강 수면을 상당히 높였다. [Q15-C] 이것은 무성한 식물이 이 좁은 범람원을 따라 자라도록 만들고, 나일 강 유역을 거주할 수 없는 사하라 사막과 오늘날 수단에서부터 카이로까지의 800km로 뻗은 동부 사막 사이에 끼어있는 오아시스로 바꾸었다. 시간이 지나자, 이 지역의 정착 민들은 강에 의존하였고 강의 활동에 따라 일년을 세 부분으로 나누었다. 그 세 부분은 강이 넘쳐나고 범람원을 걸쳐 토사물을 퍼뜨린 범람 시기, 퇴적물로 가득찬 들판에서 그들의 농작물을 손질하는 성장 시기, 그리고 강이 가져온 영양소가 제공하는 풍 부함을 사용하는 수확 시기였다.

단락 4
나일 강에서의 정착이 중동 작물 생산에 미친 영향

4 In this valley, early settlers cultivated food crops that had been previously domesticated in Southwest Asia, namely wheat, barley, peas, and lentils. [Q16-B] These crops' **ability to flourish** in the Nile valley sustained these early civilizations for generations, and [Q16-C] they remain important components of the Egyptian diet **to this day**. As time went by, these

이 골짜기에서 초기 정착민들은 이전 서남 아시아에서 재배된 식량 작물, 즉 밀, 볼, 완두콩, 그리고 렌틸콩을 경작하였다. [Q16-B] 나일 강 유역에서 번성할 수 있는 이러한 작물들의 능력은 여러 세대 동안 초기 문명을 지속시켰고, [Q16-C] 그것들은 현재까지 아직도 이집트 인들의 식단에 중요한 요소로 남아있다. 시간이 지나자 정착지는 성장했고,

Vocabulary

3단락
tremendous [triméndəs] a. 엄청난
aggregate [ǽgrigèit] v. 종합하다
inundation [ínəndèiʃən] n. 범람, 침수

interconnect [ìntərkənékt] v. 서로 연결하다
sediment [sédəmənt] n. 침전물
bounty [báunti] n. 너그러움, 풍부함

riverbed [rívərbèd] n. 강바닥
inhospitable [ìnháspitəbəl] a. 사람이 살기 힘든

4단락
cultivate [kʌ́ltəvèit] v. 경작하다, 일구다
barley [báːrli] n. 보리
lentils [lèntil] n. 렌틸콩, 편두

	settlements grew and **used** the river **for** transportation. [Q16-D] This allowed them to introduce these crops to settlements farther south, where people had **relied upon** the cultivation of plants **native to** the African environment.	강은 교통 수단으로 사용되었다. [Q16-D] 이것은 사람들이 이전에 아프리카 환경에 고유한 작물 재배에 의존했던 먼 남쪽 정착지에 이러한 작물을 소개할 수 있게 하였다.
단락 5 나일 강에서의 다른 식품 근원	**5** This verdant area also **provided for** the settlers' other dietary needs. Since the strip of land was narrow, **the number of** large mammals that could establish territories in this area was limited. In fact, the remains of only three large species have been found, the Dorcas gazelle, aurochs-a type of wild cattle, and the hartebeest. Settlers, therefore, relied on other protein sources such as birds and fish. While migratory birds, like ducks and geese, were regularly taken, fish were the primary protein source, especially catfish. **In addition**, the seasonal **variety of** plant in the area gave them **access to an abundance of** carbohydrate-rich foods. More than twenty varieties of edible plants, seeds, fruit, and vegetables have **been excavated from** the ruins of these early settlements.	이 풀로 뒤덮인 지역은 또한 정착자들의 기타 식이요법상의 필요성을 공급해 주었다. 좁고 긴 지대이었기 때문에 이 지역에 정착할 수 있는 포유동물의 수는 제한적이었다. 실은, 오직 세 개의 큰 종들의 화석이 발견되었는데, 그 종들은 도르카스 가젤, 야생 가축의 종류인 오록스, 그리고 하테비스트였다. 그러므로, 정착민들은 새나 생선 같은 다른 단백질원에 의존했다. 오리와 기러기와 같은 철새들은 정기적으로 섭취되었지만, 특히 메기와 같은 생선이 주요 단백질이었다. 이 외에도, 이 지역에 있는 계절별 식물들은 그들에게 탄수화물이 풍부한 음식의 풍요로움을 선사했다. 20여개의 품종이 넘는 식용 식물, 씨앗, 과일, 그리고 채소가 초기 정착지의 유적에서 출토되었다.
단락 6 농업 개발을 기반으로 한 제국 설립	**6** Eventually, the fertile soils and predictable flooding of the river allowed the settlers to develop an empire whose wealth **was based on** the great agricultural bounty it was able to reap. [Q18-D] Today, Ancient Egyptians are **regarded as** one of the first civilizations to practice widespread agriculture. They developed advanced farming techniques such as basin irrigation, which **put them in control of** the river level and allowed them to utilize it **in a way** that best suited their needs. [Q18-C] These new developments allowed them to grow **not only** food crops, **but also** industrial and fabric crops **for use in** cooking, medicine, and construction. The most well-known of these was papyrus, parts of which were **used as** food, as a material for construction and as a medium for writing. These developments spread **outside of** the Nile valley and changed African and world civilizations forever.	결국, 비옥한 토지와 예측 가능한 강의 홍수는 정착민들이 왕국을 건설할 수 있게 하였으며, 그 왕국의 부는 왕국이 수확할 수 있었던 엄청난 농업의 풍요로움에 기반을 두고 있다. [Q18-D] 오늘날 이집트인들은 농업을 널리 실행한 초기 문명 중에 하나라고 여겨진다. 그들은 강의 수면을 조절할 수 있고 자신들의 필요성에 가장 적합하게 사용할 수 있게 만들어준 수반관계(basin irrigation)와 같은 고급농업 기술을 개발했다. [Q18-C] 이러한 새로운 개발은 식량 작물뿐만 아니라 요리, 의학, 건설에 사용되는 산업 및 섬유 작물을 기를 수 있도록 도와주었다. 이들 중에서 가장 잘 알려진 것은 부분적으로 음식이나 건축에 사용되는 재료로, 혹은 서면 도구로 사용된 파피루스였다. 이러한 발전은 나일 계곡 외부로 확산되었고 아프리카와 세계 문명을 영원히 바꾸었다.

▌ Vocabulary ▌

5단락   verdant [vɔ́ːrdənt] a. 파릇파릇한   catfish [kǽtfiʃ] n. 메기   carbohydrate [kàːrbouháidreit] n. 탄수화물
           edible [édəbəl] a. 먹을 수 있는

6단락   reap [riːp] v. 거두다   basin [béisən] (큰 강의) n. 유역   irrigation [ìrəgéiʃən] n. 관개, 물을 끌어들임

11 Which of the sentences below best expresses the essential information in the highlighted sentence in the passage? Incorrect choices change the meaning in important ways or leave out essential information.

(A) Scientists now believe that iii) the inhabitants of the regions around the Sahara left for more hospitable places ii) when the vegetation began to die and their water supplies dwindled.

(B) i) Research suggests that long ago people from neighboring areas moved to the Sahara region but iii) they were forced to seek out new, more productive, habitats ii) when the water supply dried up.

(C) People believe that the Sahara desert was ~~repopulated~~ by a large human settlement that had abandoned the region ii) when the climate became less suitable for human habitation. ★

(D) Researchers hypothesize that i) nomadic people dwelling in arid areas were attracted to the Sahara with an ample amount of water supplies.

아래의 문장 중 지문 속의 음영 표시된 문장의 핵심 정보를 가장 잘 표현하고 있는 것은 무엇인가? 오답은 문장의 의미를 현저하게 바꾸거나 핵심 정보를 빠트리고 있다.

(A) 이제 과학자들은 그 지역 사하라 사막의 인근 거주자들은 ii) 식물들이 죽어가고 물 자원이 감소하기 시작했을 때 iii) 좀더 살기 좋은 지역으로 떠났다고 믿는다.

(B) i) 연구는 오래 전에 인근 지역에서 온 사람들은 사하라 지역으로 이동했다고 제안했지만 그들은 ii) 물 자원이 바닥나 iii) 새롭고, 더 생산성 있는 서식지를 억지로 찾아야만 했었다.

(C) 사람들은 기후가 사람이 살기에 부적합해 졌을 때 이동 했던 거대한 인구가 사하라에서 ~~타서살게~~ 되었다고 믿는다. ★

(D) i) 건조한 지역에 살았던 유목민들은 풍부한 물 공급량을 가진 사하라에 매혹되었다고 연구자들은 가정한다.

> **Highlight** 음영 표시된 문장은 i) Researchers have concluded that the Sahara previously had ample water supplies and attracted inhabitants from the surrounding areas; ii) however, as conditions declined and the region became more arid, iii) these people were driven out and forced to find new, fertile places to settle.(i) 연구진은 사하라 사막은 이전에 충분한 물 공급이 있었고 인근 주민들을 끌어들였다고 결론을 내렸지만, ii) 이 조건이 감소하기 시작하고 그 지역이 더 건조되자, iii) 이 사람들은 분산되었고 정착할 수 있는 새로운, 비옥한 장소를 찾을 것을 강요 당했다) 이렇게 세가지 내용으로 나뉜다. 이 내용을 모두 포함한 (B)가 정답이 된다. (A)는 i)의 내용을 포함하고 있지 않기 때문에 오답이고, (C)는 기후가 사람살기에 부적합해졌을 때 사람들이 사하라를 버리고 다른 더 좋은 곳으로 이동한 것이기 때문에 오답이다. (D)는 ii)와 iii)의 내용을 포함하고 있지 않기 때문에 오답이다.

12 What can be inferred from paragraph 1 about the inhabitation of the Nile River valley and the Sahara region?

(A) Before the desertification of the Sahara region, the land in the Nile River valley was ~~uninhabitable~~.

(B) The movement of the settlers in the Nile River valley was caused by an increase in the infertility of the Sahara region.

(C) At one time, settlement was not concentrated in the Nile River valley ~~because~~ it was ~~smaller~~ in size compared to today.

(D) The roaming tribes that inhabited the Sahara came ~~from the Nile River valley~~ when the influx of new settlers caused the land to become infertile. ★

단락 1에서 사하라 지역과 나일강 유역의 거주에 대해서 추론할 수 있는 것은?

(A) 사하라 지역의 사막화 전에는 나일 강 유역에는 ~~아무도 살 수 없었다~~.

(B) 정착민들의 나일강 유역으로의 이동은 사하라 지역의 비옥함의 감소 때문에 일어났다.

(C) 한때, 정착은 오늘날과 비교했을 때 사이즈가 작았기 때문에, 나일강 주변에 밀집되지 않았다.

(D) 사하라 지역에 거주했던 부랑 부족들은 새로운 정착민들의 밀어닥침이 땅이 척박하게 만들어 졌을 때 ~~나일 강 유역에서~~ 왔다. ★

> **Inference** However, as conditions declined and the region became more arid… The Nile valley filled this role (이 조건이 감소하기 시작하고 그 지역이 더 건조되자… 나일강 유역은 이 역할을 해냈다)라고 말한다. 즉, 사하라 지역의 조건이 나빠지자 사람들이 나일강 지역으로 옮겨갔다는 것이기 때문에 정답은 (B)가 된다. (C)오늘날보다 작다는 내용 없이, 나일 뿐만 아니라 사하라 지역에도 살 수 있었기 때문이라고 본문에 언급 되어있으므로, 오답이고, (D)는 나일 강에서 사하라로 옮겨갔다는 내용은 언급되지 않고, 그 반대가 언급되기 때문에 오답이다.

13

According to paragraph 2, which of the following is **NOT** true regarding the shift to agriculture and dependence on food production in early Egypt? **To receive credit, you must select TWO answers.**

(A) The process of shifting from a nomadic lifestyle to a more settled existence began in the Sahara region. ★
(B) Early nomadic groups became more settled along lakes because they provided both the food and water required to support the population.
(C) The major change in the Sahara region forced the inhabitants to move to an area where widespread hunting and gathering was possible.
(D) When the semi-settled groups moved to the Nile region they joined the populations that were already cultivating food in the area.

단락 2에 따르면, 농업으로의 변동과 초기 이집트에서 식량 생산에 대한 의존도에 대해 사실이 아닌 것은?

(A) 유목인의 삶의 방식에서 더 정착된 정체성으로 바뀌게 된 과정은 사하라 지역에서 시작되었다. ★
(B) 초기 유목인 그룹은 강가를 따라 인구를 지원하기 위해 요구되는 식량과 물의 자원을 공급이 되었기에 그곳에 더 정착하게 되었다.
(C) 사하라 지역의 주요한 변화는 거주민들을 광범위한 수렵채집이 가능했던 지역으로 강제적으로 이동하게끔 만들었다.
(D) 반 정착한 그룹이 나일 지역으로 이동했을 때, 그들은 그 지역에서 벌써 식량을 경작하고 있었던 사람들에 가담했다.

Fact 질문의 키워드인 shift to agriculture가 언급된 부분을 살펴보면 Here, they were boxed in on the narrow floodplain by the hostile deserts, the river, and settlers that were living around them, all of which restricted their ability to wander and gather food. (그곳에서, 그들은 그들이 돌아다니고 식량을 구하는 능력을 제한한 거친 사막과 강, 그리고 주위에 거주하고 있던 정착민 그룹에 의해 좁은 범람원에서 둘러싸였 다)라고 말한다. 즉, 나일 강으로 이주한 뒤엔 hunting and gathering(수렵채집)이 불가능했다는 것이기 때문에 정답은 (C)가 된다. (D)또한 그들이 새로운 장소로 이동했을 때 그들의 돌아다니고 식량을 구하는 능력을 제한시킨 요인 중 settlers that were living around them은 그 곳에서 이미 식량을 경작하고 있었던 사람들이 아니라 정착지 주변에 살고 있었던 사람들을 뜻하는 것이기 때문에 오답이다.

14

The term "conducive to" in the passage is closest in meaning to

(A) expanded to [expanded tuː]
(B) a result of [ei rizʌ́lt of]
(C) favorable to [féivərəbəl tuː]
(D) able to handle [éibəl tuː hǽndl] ★

지문의 단어 "-에 도움이 되는"의 의미와 가장 유사한 것은?

(A) 확장되다
(B) -의 결과
(C) -에 호의적인
(D) 처리할 수 있는 ★

Vocabulary 지문의 conducive to(-에 도움이 되는)와 동의어인 favorable to(-에 호의적인)이 정답이다.

15

What can be inferred about the major changes that occurred in the Nile River from paragraph 3?

(A) In ancient Egyptian times the Nile was a much smaller but longer river that constantly changed directions across the interconnected riverbeds.
(B) Over time, the once elongated Nile River has been curtailed to today's limited size due to the excessive accumulation of sediment. ★
(C) Without the buildup of the fertile sediment that the river carried, the region would have been much less habitable.
(D) The yearly floods that occurred during the inundation spread silt across the floodplain and drained it of its nutrients.

단락 3에서 나일강에서 발생한 주된 변화에 대해 추론할 수 있는 것은?

(A) 고대 이집트 시대에서 나일강은 훨씬 작았지만 서로 연결된 강바닥을 걸쳐 지속적으로 방향을 바꾸는, 길이가 타컨 강이었다.
(B) 시간이 지나면서 한때 길었던 나일강은 과도한 퇴적물의 축적 때문에 오늘날의 작은 사이즈로 줄여졌다. ★
(C) 강이 운반했던 비옥한 퇴적물의 축적이 없었다면, 그 지역은 훨씬 덜 살기 좋은 곳이었을 것이다.
(D) 범람 중에 발생한 연간 홍수는 범람원을 걸쳐 토사물을 퍼뜨렸고 이것의 영양분을 빼냈다.

Inference 질문의 키워드인 major changes가 언급된 부분을 살펴보면 This allowed lush vegetation to grow along the floodplain and turned the Nile valley into an oasis (이것은 무성한 식물이 이 좁은 범람원을 따라 자라도록 만들고, 나일강 유역을 오아시스로 바꾸었다)라고 말한다. 즉, 강에 의해 운반된 침전물과 토사물은 강의 수면을 높였고, 이것이 무성한 식물을 자라게 해주었다. 따라서, 만약 이것이 없었으면 나일 강 지역은 그 당시에 실제로 그랬던 것만큼 살기 좋은 곳은 아니었을 거라는 것이기 때문에 정답은 (C)가 된다. (A)는 본문에선 smaller and slower이라고 언급하기 때문에 오답이고, (D)는 본문에 언급되지 않기 때문에 오답이다. (B)는 나일 강은 시간이 지나면서 크기가 커졌고 오히려 오늘날의 나일 강은 세계에서 가장 긴 강이라고 알려져 있기 때문에 오답이고, (D)는 범람 시기는 오히려 영양분을 가져다 주는 시기이기 때문에 오답이다.

16 According to paragraph 4, all of the following are true of the crops that the early settlers grew in the Nile River valley EXCEPT:

(A) The crops had ~~originally~~ been domesticated in the region but were ~~sent to~~ areas of Southwest Asia where they flourished.
(B) The wheat, barley, peas and lentils that they grew became the main source of sustenance for the population for generations.
(C) These crops were such an important part of their diet that they continue to be an important part of the local diet even today.
(D) The cultivating methods of relatively new crops native to Southwest Asia were introduced farther south. ★

단락 4에서 나일강 유역에서 초기 정착민들이 기른 농작물에 대해 사실이 아닌 것은?

(A) 농작물은 ~~원래~~ 그 지역에서 재배되었으나, 그것들이 번창할 수 있었던 서남 아시아 지역으로 ~~보내졌다~~.
(B) 그들이 기른 밀, 보리, 완두콩, 렌틸콩은 몇 세대에 걸쳐 인간들에게 생계의 주요 원천이 되었다.
(C) 그 농작물들은 오늘날까지도 지역 식단의 중요한 부분으로 지속될 정도로 그들의 식단에 중요한 부분이었다.
(D) 새로운 작물들의 재배 방법은 더욱 남쪽으로 도입되었고 아프리카 환경의 토착 식물들의 재배 방법을 대체하였다. ★

Fact 질문의 키워드인 crops that the early settlers grew in the Nile River가 언급된 부분을 살펴보면 In this valley, early settlers cultivated food crops that had been previously domesticated in Southwest Asia, namely wheat, barley, peas, and lentils.(이 골짜기에서 초기 정착민들은 이전 서남 아시아에서 재배된 식량 작물, 즉 밀, 볼, 완두콩, 그리고 렌틸콩을 경작하였다)라고 말한다. 즉, 농작물들은 원래 서남 아시아 지역에서 자랐으므로 정답은 (A)가 된다.

17 Why does the author mention that the crops from Southwest Asia "remain important components of the Egyptian diet even to this day"?

(A) To help understand the long lasting importance of these crops
(B) To illustrate an idea of the ~~changes~~ that have occurred in the Egyptian diet over time
(C) To make the point that these crops have grown in Egypt for ~~so long that~~ they're now considered Egyptian ~~foods~~
(D) To stress the ~~ability~~ of the crops to flourish in the Nile valley and to sustain early civilizations ★

글쓴이가 서남 아시아로부터 온 농작물이 "현재까지 아직도 이집트 인들의 식단에 중요한 요소로 남아있다"를 언급한 의도는?

(A) 그 작물의 장기적인 중요성에 대한 이해를 돕기 위해서
(B) 시간에 걸쳐 이집트 인들의 식단에 일어난 ~~변화~~에 대한 개념을 보여주기 위해서
(C) 그 농작물이 이집트 ~~음식이라 생각될 정도로~~ 이집트에서 오랫동안 재배되었다는 점을 주장하기 위해서
(D) 그 작물들의 나일 유역에서 번창하고 초기 문명들을 유지시킬 수 있는 ~~능력~~을 강조하기 위해서 ★

Purpose 음영 표시된 부분을 살펴보면 These crops' ability to flourish in the Nile valley sustained these early civilizations for generations, and they remain important components of the Egyptian diet to this day.(나일 강 유역에서 번성할 수 있는 이러한 작물들의 능력은 여러 세대 동안 초기 문명을 지속시켰고, 그것들은 현재까지 아직도 이집트 인들의 식단에 중요한 요소로 남아있다.)라고 말한다. 키워드는 to this day이다. "오늘날까지" 라고 언급해주며 이 농작물들이 오늘날까지 식용되고 있고, 이것은 이집트 인들의 식단에 매우 중요한 부분을 차지하고 있다는 것이기 때문에 정답은 (A)가 된다. (B)는 변화가 아니라 지속성을 나타내기 위해서이기 때문에 오답이고, (C)는 본문의 흐름과 연관성이 없는 선택지이기 때문에 오답이다. (D)는 옳은 말이지만 작가가 음영 표시된 부분을 언급한 이유는 능력을 강조하기 위해서가 아니라 농작물들의 지속성과 중요성을 강조하기 위해서 이기 때문에 오답이다.

18 According to paragraph 6, which of the following can be inferred regarding the system of agriculture that the settlers developed in the Nile River valley?

(A) In ~~little regard~~ to the predictable patterns of flooding of the Nile River valley, the farming techniques enabled the settlers to build an empire.
(B) The ancient Egyptians began to domesticate crops to use for nourishment when hunting ~~did not~~ provide enough food.
(C) The novel techniques used by the ancient Egyptians enabled the production ~~not~~ of food crops but of industrial and fabric crops, such as papyrus as a writing medium. ★
(D) Without the advanced farming and water control techniques developed by the settlers, ancient Egypt would not have become the first civilization to practice widespread agriculture.

단락 6에 따르면 정착민들이 나일강 유역에서 만들어낸 농업 시스템에 대해 추론할 수 있는 것은?

(A) 나일 강 유역 범람의 예상 가능한 패턴들과는 ~~별개로~~, 농업 기술들은 정착민들이 제국을 건설할 수 있도록 해주었다.
(B) 이집트 인들은 사냥이 충분한 식량을 ~~공급하지 못했을~~ 때 영양 공급을 위해 농작물 재배를 실행했다.
(C) 고대 이집트인들에 의해 사용된 기발한 기술은 식품 작물들이 ~~아닌~~ 파피루스와 같은 산업과 직물 관련 작물들의 생산이 가능하게 하였다. ★
(D) 나일강 유역의 정착민들에 의해 발전된 농업 기술과 과수량 조절 기술없이는 고대 이집트는 농업을 널리 실행한 초기 문명이 될 수 없었을 것이다.

> **Inference** 질문의 키워드인 system of agriculture가 언급된 부분을 살펴보면 Today, Ancient Egyptians are regarded as one of the first civilizations to practice widespread agriculture. They developed advanced farming techniques such as basin irrigation, which put them in control of the river level and allowed them to utilize it in a way that best suited their needs. (오늘날 이집트인들은 농업을 널리 실행한 초기 문명중에 하나라고 여겨진다. 그들은 강의 수면을 조절할 수 있고 자신들의 필요성에 가장 적합하게 사용할 수 있게 만들어준 수반관계 (basin irrigation)와 같은 고급 농업기술을 개발했다)라고 말한다. 즉, 이러한 발전된 기술이 없었으면 고대 이집트는 농업을 널리 알릴 수 없었을 것이기 때문에 정답은 (D)가 된다. (A)는 Eventually, the fertile soils and predictable flooding of the river allowed the settlers to develop an empire(결국, 비옥한 토지와 예측 가능한 홍수는 정착민들이 제국을 만들 수 있도록 도와주었다)에서 예측 가능했던 홍수 또한 제국 설립에 중요한 역할을 했기 때문에 오답이고, (B)는 전 단락에서 사냥을 통해서도 중요한 공급원을 얻었다고 설명하기 때문에 오답이다. (C)는 식품 작물과 산업과 직물 관련 작물을 모두 생산하였기 때문에 오답이다.

19 Look at the four squares [■] that indicate where the following sentence could be added to the passage.

Once they arrived in the river valley they had little choice but to settle in one place.

Where would the sentence best fit? Click on a square [■] to add the sentence to the passage.

3rd

네 개의 네모 [■]는 다음 문장이 삽입될 수 있는 부분을 나타내고 있다.

그들이 한번 강 유역에 도착하자 그들은 한 장소에 정착하는 것 밖에 선택의 여지가 없었다.

이 문장은 어느 자리에 들어가는 것이 가장 적절한가?

세 번째

> **Insertion** 삽입 문장의 키워드는 once they arrived와 little choice but to settle이다. 세 번째 네모 전 문장에선 사하라의 최종적 사막화는 사람들이 나일 강으로 이주하게 만들었다고 한다. 그리고 세 번째 네모 다음 문장에선 이들이 왜 더이상 광범위한 수렵채집을 하지 못하였는지에 대한 이유를 설명한다. 따라서 자세한 이유들이 설명되기 전에 세 번째 네모에 삽입 문장이 들어가 나일 강에 도착했다는 정보와 한 장소에 정착해야 했다는 내용을 언급해 주는 것이 가장 적절하므로 정답은 세 번째 네모이다.

20

Directions: An introductory sentence for a brief summary of the passage is provided below. Complete the summary by selecting the THREE answer choices that express the most important ideas in the passage. Some sentences do not belong in the summary because they express ideas that are not presented in the passage or are minor ideas in the passage. **This question is worth 2 points.**

지시: 지문 요약을 위한 도입 문장이 아래에 주어져 있다. 지문의 가장 중요한 내용을 나타내는 보기 3개를 골라 요약을 완성하시오. 어떤 문장은 지문에 언급되지 않은 내용이나 사소한 정보를 담고 있으므로 요약에 포함되지 않는다. **이 문제는 2점이다.**

The Sahara and Nile River valley shaped the development of human settlement and agriculture.

(A) The desertification of the Sahara region forced its human and animal inhabitants to move to areas like the Nile valley where they had little choice but to settle and cultivate food. - paragraph 1,2

(C) Changes in the Nile valley due to the aggregation of sediment made it a more fruitful region than the surrounding areas and provided food sources for humans. - paragraph 3

(F) New techniques developed by the ancient Egyptians allowed them to form a wealthy empire that pioneered agricultural methods that were adopted by societies around the world. - paragraph 6

사하라 사막과 나일 강 유역은 인간의 정착과 농업의 발전을 형성했다.

(A) 사하라 지역의 사막화는 인간과 동물 거주자들이 선택의 여지가 없었지만, 정착하고 식량을 경작할 수 있었던 강 유역과 같은 곳으로 강제로 이동하게끔 했다.

(C) 침전물의 쌓임으로 인한 나일 강 유역의 변화는 주위 지역보다 더 비옥한 지역으로 만들었고 인간들에게 식량을 제공했다.

(F) 고대 이집트인들에 의하여 개발된 새로운 기술들은 세계의 사회에 의해 채택된 농법을 개척했던 풍요로운 제국을 형성할 수 있게 도와주었다.

(B) ~~After~~ the last glacial period, the Sahara region turned into an ~~inhabitable~~ area open to a large human population with its ample food sources. - 틀린 정보

(D) As people began using the Nile River for transportation, they started ~~trading with~~ settlers farther south, from whom they ~~imported~~ crops native to the African environment. - 틀린 정보

(E) The ~~large~~ mammals that inhabited the narrow fertile strip or land alongside the Nile River provided settlers with the ~~constant, ample~~ supply of the protein necessary for human survival. - 반/반

(B) 마지막 빙하기 ~~이후에~~ 사하라 지역은 풍부한 식량 자원으로 거대한 인구에게 오픈되어 있는 ~~살기 좋은~~ 지역으로 변했다.

(D) 사람들이 나일 강을 교통수단으로 사용하면서, 그들은 남쪽 멀리 있는 거주자들과 ~~교류를 하기 시작하였고~~ 그들에게서 아프리카 환경에 고유한 작물을 ~~수입하였다.~~

(E) 나일강의 좁고 비옥한 작은 땅 옆에 거주하는 ~~큰~~ 포유류 동물은 인간의 생계를 위해 필요한 ~~지속적이고 풍부한~~ 양의 단백질을 정착민들에게 제공하였다.

Summary 지문의 중심 내용은 나일 강에서의 정착과 이에 따른 이점이다. (A)는 첫 번째와 두 번째 단락의 중심내용인 사람들이 사하라를 뒤로하고 나일 강으로 이주하게 된 계기와 일치하고, (C)는 세번째 단락의 중심내용인 나일 강이 거쳐간 위대한 변화와 이것이 정착민들에게 미친 영향과 일치하고, (F)는 여섯 번째 단락의 중심내용인 농업 개발을 기반으로 한 제국 설립과 일치한다. 따라서 답은 (A), (C), (F)이다.

USHER iBT TOEFL
INTERMEDIATE READING

TEST 0.5
답안 및 취약 유형 분석표

해석·해설

답안 및 문제 유형 분석표

TEST 부록

01 (A) Fact

02 (D) Purpose

03 (B) Purpose

04 (D) Fact

05 (A) Vocabulary

06 (A) Highlight

07 (C) Inference

08 (A) Fact

09 1st ■ Insertion

10 (A), (E), (F) Summary

각 문제 유형별 맞춘 개수를 아래에 적어 보세요.

유형	맞춘 답의 개수	정답률
단어 (Vocabulary)	/ 1	정답률: %
사실 확인 문제 (Fact)	/ 3	정답률: %
지시어 찾기 (Reference)	/ 0	정답률: %
끼워 넣기 (Insertion)	/ 1	정답률: %
문장 변환문제 (Highlight)	/ 1	정답률: %
목적 (Purpose)	/ 2	정답률: %
추론 (Inference)	/ 1	정답률: %
단락 요약(Summary / Category Chart)	/ 1	정답률: %
전체	/ 10	정답률: %

※ 자신이 취약한 유형은 READING STRATEGIES를 통해 다시 한번 점검하시기 바랍니다. (p.44)

TEST 부록 — Sea Turtle Navigation 바다 거북이의 길 찾기

Introduction	단락 1	바다 거북이의 능력에 대한 다양한 추측
Point	단락 2	과학자들이 설명하는 자철석의 역할
Point	단락 3	자철석 이론에 대한 결점
Point	단락 4	새로운 빛과 관련된 이론의 발견
Point	단락 5	소리와 냄새가 바다 거북이에 미치는 영향
Point	단락 6	유전적인 유사성과 바다 거북이 항해의 연관성

문단주제	본문내용	해석
단락 1 바다 거북이의 능력에 대한 다양한 추측	**1** For centuries, oceanic navigation has been one of the biggest **challenges to** seafarers around the world because navigation on the high seas is more difficult than on land. Yet, since the early cretaceous period, the sea turtle has successfully **travelled across** vast oceans moving between foraging sites and nesting areas. This amazing ability has justifiably intrigued scientists for years. Celestial navigation, **based on** observing the positions of the Sun, Moon, and stars, has not been **accepted as** a method employable by sea turtles **due to** their poor eyesight. Another theory suggests that dissolved traces of unique odors from the turtles' destinations guide them, but this has also not **gained** much **support** because dispersal of the odors in the ocean would create a convoluted path and could, therefore, not explain how sea turtles migrate **in** a more-or-less straight **line** to their destination. Furthermore, **depending on** ocean currents, [Q21-A] the odor trails may be travelling **in the same direction** as the turtles, thus never reaching them.	수 세기 동안, 해양 항해술은 세계의 선원들에게 가장 큰 난관들 중 하나였다. 외양에서의 길 찾기는 육지에서 보다 더 어려웠기 때문이다. 그럼에도 불구하고, 백악기 초반부터 바다 거북이는 사냥터부터 둥지 사이를 오가며 광대한 바다들을 가로질러 성공적으로 여행해 왔다. 이러한 바다 거북이들의 놀라운 능력은 당연하게도 수년간 과학자들의 흥미를 끌었다. 해와 달, 그리고 별들의 위치를 관찰하여 기반으로 삼는 천문 항법은 바다거북의 좋지 않은 시력 때문에 바다거북에 의해 사용되어질 수 있는 방법으로 받아들여지지 않았다. 다른 이론은 거북이들의 목적지에서 나오는 고유의 냄새가 거북이들을 이끈다는 것이지만, 이것도 역시 바다에서는 냄새의 확산으로 인해 흐트러진 길을 만들어 낸다는 이유로 많은 지지를 얻지 못했다; 이것은 바다 거북이들이 거의 직선으로 그들의 목적지까지 움직이는 것을 설명하지 못한다. 더욱이, [Q21-A] 해류에 따라서 냄새의 자취는 거북이들과 같은 방향으로 흐를 수 있고, 그래서 거북이들에게 닿을 수 없을 수도 있다.
단락 2 과학자들이 설명하는 자철석의 역할	**2** [Q22-D] One theory, however, has **gained support** from the scientific community. Studies have found small **amounts of** a magnetic compound called magnetite in the brains of **a few species of** sea turtles. This compound, which is also	[Q22-D] 하지만 한 이론은 과학계에서 지지를 얻고 있다. 연구조사들은 몇몇 종의 바다 거북이들의 뇌에서 자철석이라고 불리는 자기성질의 성분을 찾아 내었다. 비둘기, 꿀벌, 다른 많은 종류의 동물들에게서도 찾을 수 있는 이

Vocabulary

1단락
- navigation [nævəgéiʃən] n. 항해술 navigate v. 길을 찾다.
- cretaceous [kritéiʃəs] n. 백악기
- employable [emplɔ́iəibəl] a. 고용자격을 갖춘, 쓸모있는
- convoluted [kánvəlù:tid] a. 대단히 난해한, 나선형의
- challenge [tʃælindʒ] n. (사람의 능력, 기술을 시험하는) 도전
- intrigue [intrí:g] v. 강한 흥미를 불러 일으키다
- dispersal [dispə́:rsəl] n. 해산, 확산

2단락
- magnetite [mǽgnətàit] n. 자철석
- chamber [tʃéimbər] n. (공공건물의) 회의실, (특수한 목적을 갖고 있는) 방
- crucial [krú:ʃəl] a. 중대한, 결정적인
- hatchling [hǽtʃliŋ] n. 갓 부화한 새끼
- alter [ɔ́:ltər] v. 변하다, 달라지다, 바꾸다

found in pigeons, honeybees, and **a variety of** other animals, is known to **play** a crucial **role in** navigation. [Q22-D, Q23-B] It was shown that, sea turtle hatchlings, when placed inside a pool within a magnetic chamber, altered their course **in response to changes in** the chamber's magnetic field. What makes sea turtles' utilization of magnetite interesting is the fact that it is **so** precise **that** sea turtles in the vast ocean can measure **not only** the intensity of the magnetic pull **but also** the **difference in** the angle of the magnetic poles. Previously, scientists thought that magnetite could only **be used as** a compass, providing directional information, but this ability **allows** turtles **to orient** themselves within a more detailed magnetic map of Earth.

단락 3 — 자철석 이론에 대한 결점

3 To study the role of magnetite in sea turtle navigation further, Floriano Papi and a team of biologists designed an experiment in the late 1990s, in which green sea turtles **travelling from** Ascension Island back **to** Brazil **were fitted with** strong magnets on their heads. [■] Papi believed that the magnet would inhibit the turtles' ability to calculate their position on Earth. [Q24-D] Surprisingly, however, the magnets made no difference to the migratory performance of the turtles. [■] The findings demonstrated that the magnetite theory is not **devoid of** shortcomings. [■] Substantial evidence both for and against magnetic navigation **led to** the theory that while magnetic positioning plays a vital role in the open sea, **far away from** the destination, sea turtles use several other **methods to complement** it when they are young or when they are **close to** land. [■]

단락 4 — 새로운 빛과 관련된 이론의 발견

4 When sea turtles are born, they must immediately **make their way into** deep waters to escape predators on land and in coastal waters. Scientists hypothesize that the hatchlings calculate the direction towards water by using light intensity as a cue. [Q27-C] The juveniles are thought to instinctively head towards light because moonlight reflecting against the water means that the ocean is brighter than land. Unfortunately,

Vocabulary

intensity [inténsəti] n. 강렬함, 강함, (빛 등의) 강도
utilization [jútəlizèiʃən] n. 이용, 활용

3단락
migratory [máigrətɔ̀ːri] a. 이주하는
performance [pərfɔ́ːməns] n. 공연, 실적, 성과
demonstrate [démənstrèit] v. 보여주다, 입증하다
substantial [səbstǽnʃəl] a. (양, 가치 중요성이) 상당한

4단락
immediately [imíːdiitli] ad. 즉각, 즉시
coastal [kóustəl] a. 해안의
hypothesize [haipáθəsàiz] v. 가설을 세우다
cue [kjuː] n. (무엇을 하라는) 신호
juvenile [dʒúːvənəl] a. 청소년의
instinctive [instíŋktiv] a. 본능적인, 직관적인 (instinctively ad. 본능적으로, 무의식적으로)
occupy [ákjəpài] v. (공간, 지역, 시간을) 차지하다

hatchlings have **been reported to be disoriented** by artificial light **coming from** human-occupied islands, severely decreasing their **chances for** survival. In the shallow coastal waters, the juvenile turtles detect the direction, in which the waves push them, to calculate which direction they must swim to get to deep waters.

단락 5
소리와 냄새가 바다 거북이에 미치는 영향

5   When the turtle is making its way to land either to forage or to lay eggs, it uses the magnetite **along with** auditory and olfactory cues. It is hypothesized that turtles use both the low-frequency sounds of waves hitting the beach and the smell coming from land to pinpoint the location of their destination.

단락 6
유전적인 유사성과 바다 거북이 항해의 연관성

6   The mysteries of sea turtle navigation **end with** their navigation methods, but also **extend to** navigation patterns, **as** can be seen in the mitochondrial DNA (mtDNA- genetic material that is **inherited** solely **from** the maternal parent and is, therefore, identical in close relatives) of hawksbill turtles in the Persian Gulf. [Q28-A] Each hawksbill turtle tested in the nesting site had the same mtDNA, with only minimal variability, **leading to the conclusion** that most of the hawksbill turtles in the nesting site have **emerged from** the same nest. This explains why areas around the world that appear **ideal for** sea turtle foraging and nesting are not recolonized after human interference wipes out the native populations. For example, Grand Cayman Island was once **home to** one of the largest green sea turtle populations in the world, but after the turtles **were driven off** by humans, wildlife protection laws and habitat reconstruction have proven **unsuccessful in bringing** back the turtles.

Vocabulary

5단락   auditory [ɔ́ːditɔ̀ːri] a. 청각의   olfactory [alfǽktəri] a. 후각의   pinpoint [pínpɔ̀int] v. (위치, 시간을) 정확히 찾아내다
destination [dèstənéiʃən] n. 목적지, 도착지

6단락   extends to   phr. ~로 늘리다, ~까지 미치다
identical [aidéntikəl] a. 동일한, 똑같은   minimal [mínəməl] a. 아주 적은, 최소의   variability [vèəriəbíləti] n. 가변성, 변동성
recolonize [riːkálənàiz] v. 다시 식민하다

01

Why hasn't the idea that sea turtles navigate by using odor trails gained much support from scientists?

(A) The odor trails may not drift into the direction of the sea turtles.
(B) Some feeding and breeding locations do ~~not~~ give off odors that can be identified by sea turtles.
(C) Odors from the sea turtles' destinations may be ~~too finely dissolved~~ to be detectable. ★
(D) Odor trails form in a relatively ~~straight path~~ across the ocean, making it difficult for sea turtles to come across them.

바다 거북이들이 냄새를 이용해서 방향을 잡는다는 개념이 과학자들로부터 많은 지지를 얻지 못한 이유는 무엇인가?

(A) 냄새의 자취가 바다 거북이들을 향해서 흐르지 않을 수도 있다.
(B) 몇몇 사냥터와 새끼를 낳는 장소들은 바다 거북이들이 감지할 수 있는 냄새를 풍기지 ~~않는~~다.
(C) 바다 거북이들의 목적지에서 나오는 냄새는 감지하기에 ~~너무 많이 용해될~~ 수도 있다. ★
(D) 냄새의 자취는 바다를 가로지르는 비교적 ~~직선의~~ 길을 만들고, 바다 거북이들이 그들을 지나가기에 힘들게 한다.

Fact 질문의 키워드인 odor trails가 언급된 부분을 살펴보면 the odor trails may be travelling in the same direction as the turtles, thus never reaching them. (해류에 따라서 냄새의 자취는 거북이들과 같은 방향으로 흐를 수 있다)라고 말한다. 즉, 냄새가 거북이들과 같은 방향으로 흐를 때, 다시 말해 냄새가 거북이들을 향해 흐르지 않는 경우도 있기 때문에 정답은 (A)가 된다. (B)는 냄새의 방향이 문제의 원인이고 거북이들의 몇몇 목적지들은 냄새를 풍기지 않는다는 내용은 언급되지 않으므로 오답이고, (C) 또한 냄새가 용해되어 거북이들이 감지할 수 있다는 내용은 언급되나 이것이 너무 많이 용해되어 거북이들이 더 이상 감지할 수 없다는 내용은 언급되지 않으므로 오답이다. (D)는 냄새의 자취는 straight path가 아닌 convoluted path(흐트러진 길)을 따라가기 때문에 오답이다.

02

What is the purpose of paragraph 2 in the passage?

(A) An experiment is conducted ~~to find~~ a similarity between navigating animals.
(B) A hypothesis is suggested but then partially ~~rejected~~ by evidence. ★
(C) A problem is introduced and then its ~~solution~~ is described.
(D) A specific example is used to support a proposed theory.

글에서 단락 2의 목적은?

(A) 항해하는 동물들간의 공통점을 ~~찾기위해~~ 실험이 진행되었다.
(B) 가설이 제시되지만 증거에 의해 부분적으로 ~~거각당한다~~. ★
(C) 문제점이 소개되고 ~~해결책~~이 설명돼 있다.
(D) 제안된 이론을 지지하기 위해 특정한 예시가 쓰인다.

Purpose 두 번째 단락의 주요 내용은 거북이의 자철석을 이용한 항해 방법이다. 즉, 첫 번째 단락에서 설명된 별들의 위치를 이용한 항해 방법과 냄새를 이용한 항해 방법의 결점에 대한 내용에 이어 두 번째 단락에선 거북이들이 이 두 가지의 방법없이도 성공적으로 항해할 수 있는 것에 대한 또 다른 이론으로 자철석이 언급된다. It was shown that, sea turtle hatchlings, when placed inside a pool within a magnetic chamber, altered their course in response to changes in the chamber's magnetic field.(바다거북이 새끼들은 자기장이 존재하는 방안의 물 속에 놓아 졌을때, 자기장의 변화에 따라서 수영하는 방향을 바꾸었다는 것이 보여졌다)와 같은 예를 제시하며 자철석 이론을 지지하기 때문에 정답은 (D)가 된 다. (A)는 This compound, which is also found in pigeons, honeybees, and a variety of other animals, is known to play a crucial role in navigation. (비둘기, 꿀벌, 다른 많은 종류의 동물들에게서도 찾을 수 있는 이 성분은 방향을 잡는 것에 아주 중요한 역할을 한다고 알려져 있다) 에서 항해하는 동물들간의 공통점이 존재하는 것은 맞지만 두 번째 단락의 목표와는 일치하지 않기 때문에 오답이고, (B)는 가설이 제시된 것은 맞지만 부분적으로 기각당하는 건 세 번째 단락의 내용이므로 오답이다. (C)는 두 번째 단락에선 문제에 대한 해결책이 제시되는 것이 아니라 또 다른 이론이 소개되는 것이기 때문에 오답이다.

03

Why does the author mention the experiment performed on sea turtle hatchlings in paragraph 2?

(A) To illustrate how ~~poorly~~ sea turtles measure Earth's magnetic pull
(B) To provide evidence that sea turtles use Earth's magnetic field to guide themselves
(C) To explain that the sea turtles' ability to use magnetite ~~increases with age~~
(D) To ~~prove~~ that even baby sea turtles can use the magnetite to navigate through the sea ★

왜 글쓴이가 바다 거북이 새끼들을 단락 2에서 언급하는가?

(A) 바다 거북이들이 지구의 자기 흡인력을 얼마나 ~~형편없어~~ 측정하는지 보여주기 위해서
(B) 바다 거북이들이 길을 찾는데 지구의 자기장을 이용한다는 것에 대한 증거를 제공하기 위해서
(C) 바다 거북이들의 자철석을 이용하는 능력이 ~~나아가 들며 증가한다~~는 것을 설명하기 위해서
(D) 심지어 새끼 바다 거북이도 자철석을 이용해 바다를 항해할 수 있다는 것을 ~~증명하기~~ 위해서 ★

Purpose 음영 표시된 문장을 살펴보면 It was shown that, sea turtle hatchlings, when placed inside a pool within a magnetic chamber, altered their course in response to changes in the chamber's magnetic field.(바다 거북이 새끼들은 자기장이 존재하는 방안의 물 속에 놓아졌을 때, 자기장의 변화에 따라서 수영하는 방향을 바꾸었다는 것이 보여졌다)라고 말한다. 즉, 거북이들이 자철석을 이용해 항해한다는 것을 예시와 함께 증명하기 위해 바다 거북이 새끼들이 자철석을 이용해 항해한다는 내용을 언급한 것이다. 따라서 정답은 (B)가 된다. (C)는 바다 거북이 새끼들을 이용한 실험이기 때문에 자철석을 이용하는 능력이 나이와 함께 증가한다고 생각할 수도 있지만 본문에는 언급되는 내용이 아니므로 오답이고, (D)는 새끼 바다 거북이가 실험에 사용된 것은 사실이지만 새끼들도 자철석을 이용할 수 있다는 것을 증명하기 위해 실험이 이루어진 것은 아니기 때문에 오답이다. (A)는 이 실험은 거북이들이 자철석을 이용해 정확하게 항해한다는 것을 증명하기 위함이므로 오답이다.

04

According to paragraph 3, scientists believe that sea turtles must combine magnetic mapping with other navigation methods because

(A) The ~~poor eyesight~~ prevents the sea turtles from reaching their destination successfully. ★
(B) The function of the turtles' magnetite is ~~devoid~~ of drawbacks.
(C) The turtles ~~had difficulty~~ finding their ultimate destinations far away from their current location.
(D) The sea turtles successfully arrived at their destination even when their magnetic field was disturbed.

단락 3에 의하면, 왜 과학자들은 바다 거북이들이 자기장을 이용한 지도와 다른 길 찾기 방법을 사용한다고 믿었는가?

(A) ~~좋지 않은 시력~~은 바다 거북이들이 그들의 목적지에 성공적으로 도착하지 못하게 한다. ★
(B) 바다 거북이들의 자철석 기능에는 결점이 ~~없다~~.
(C) 거북이들은 자신들의 현 위치와 너무 멀리 떨어져 있는 최종 목적지들을 찾는데 ~~어려워했다~~.
(D) 바다 거북이들은 그들의 자기장이 방해받았을 때에도 성공적으로 그들의 목적지에 도착했다.

Fact 질문의 키워드인 magnetic mapping이 언급된 부분을 살펴보면 Surprisingly, however, the magnets made no difference to the migratory performance of the turtles.(하지만 놀랍게도, 자석들은 본질적으로 거북이들의 이동하는 능력에 영향을 끼치지 않았다)라고 말한다. 플로리아노 파피와 다른 생물학자들이 그들의 실험에서 거북이들의 자철석의 역할을 더욱더 확실히 알기 위해 실험에 사용된 거북이들의 자철석을 강한 자석으로 방해하였으나, 실험 결과는 놀랍게도 이런 방해에도 불구하고 거북이들이 성공적으로 목적지에 도달했다. 즉, 거북이들은 자기장 말고도 다른 길 찾기 방법을 이용한다는 결론을 낼 수 있었다는 것이기 때문에 정답은 (D)가 된다. (A)는 바다 거북이들의 시력이 좋지 않아 그들이 태양과 별들의 위치를 이용해 항해하는 것이 불가능한 것은 사실이지만, 좋지않은 시력 때문에 자철석 외에 다른 항해 방법을 사용하는 것은 아니기 때문에 오답이고, (B)는 The findings demonstrated that the magnetite theory is not devoid of shortcomings. 본문에선 결점이 분명히 있다고 설명하기 때문에 오답이다. (C)는 거북이가 목적지에서 멀리 있을 경우엔 오히려 자철석이 중요한 역할을 하기 때문에 다른 길 찾는 방법이 필요없고, 거북이들이 어리거나 육지와 가까울 때는 다른 여러 방법을 사용해 보완할 필요가 있다고 본문에서 설명하기 때문에 오답이다.

05

The word "substantial" in the passage is closest in meaning to

(A) significant [signífikənt]
(B) gradual [grǽdʒuəl]
(C) appropriate [əpróuprièit]
(D) apparent [əpǽrənt] ★

지문의 단어 "상당한"의 의미와 가장 유사한 것은?

(A) 중요한
(B) 점진적인
(C) 합당한
(D) 명백한 ★

Vocabulary 지문의 substantial(상당한)와 동의어인 significant(중요한)이 정답이다.

06

Which of the sentences below best expresses the essential information in the highlighted sentence in the passage? Incorrect choices change the meaning in important ways or leave out essential information.

(A) iii)In order to avoid their predators, i), ii)sea turtle hatchlings must travel into the depths of the ocean.
(B) Juvenile sea turtles swim to the deep waters as soon as they are born to elude predators ~~not on land~~ but in coastal waters.
(C) Sea turtles move towards the deep ocean ~~so that~~ their predators do ~~not~~ prey on them while on land or in coastal waters. ★
(D) Sea turtle hatchlings ~~learn to~~ elude their predators on land and in coastal waters ~~as soon as~~ they reach the deep waters.

아래의 문장 중 지문 속의 음영 표시된 문장의 핵심 정보를 가장 잘 표현하고 있는 것은 무엇인가? 오답은 문장의 의미를 현저하게 바꾸거나 핵심 정보를 빠뜨리고 있다.

(A) iii)천적들을 피하기 위해서 i), ii)바다 거북이 새끼들은 바다 깊숙이 이동해야 한다.
(B) 바다 거북이 새끼들은 ~~육지에 있는~~ 천적들이 아닌 연안 해안가에 있는 천적들을 피하기 위해 태어나자 마자 깊은 물 속으로 헤엄친다.
(C) 바다 거북이들은 깊은 바다를 향해서 움직이는데 ~~그럼으로써~~ 그들의 천적들은 그들이 육지나 연안 해안가에 있을 때 그들을 사냥하지 ~~않는다~~. ★
(D) 바다 거북이 새끼들은 깊은 물에 ~~도착하자마자~~ 육지나 연안수의 천적들로부터 도망가는 법을 ~~배운다~~.

Highlight 음영 표시된 문장은 i) When sea turtles are born, ii) they must immediately make their way into deep waters iii) to escape predators on land and in coastal waters. i) 바다 거북이들이 태어나면, iii) 지상과 연안 해안가의 천적들로부터 도망쳐 ii) 그들은 즉시 깊숙한 물쪽으로 도망가야 한다) 이렇게 세 가지 내용으로 나뉜다. 이 내용을 모두 포함한 (A)가 정답이 된다. (B)는 육지와 연안 해안가 모두에 천적들이 있기 때문에 오답이고, (C)는 중요정보가 빠졌기 때문에 오답이다. (D)는 바다 깊숙이 도망치는 것은 배우는 것(learn)이 아니라 본능적(instinct)인 것이기 때문에 오답이다.

07

According to paragraph 4, what can be inferred about navigation in sea turtle hatchlings?

(A) Sea turtles do ~~not~~ use magnetic navigation until they mature into adults. ★
(B) Hatchlings can ~~distinguish~~ moonlight from artificial light.
(C) Sea turtles that hatch at night have higher chances of reaching the water compared to turtles that hatch during the day.
(D) Hatchlings ~~learn~~ to calculate the direction towards water by using light intensity as a cue.

단락 4에 의하면, 바다 거북이들의 방향잡기에 대해 추론할 수 있는 것은?

(A) 바다 거북이들은 그들이 성년기에 들 때까지 자기장을 이용한 길 찾기를 사용하지 ~~않는다~~. ★
(B) 새끼들은 달빛과 인공적인 빛을 ~~구분할 수 있다~~.
(C) 밤에 부화하는 바다 거북이들은 낮에 부화하는 거북이들에 비해서 물에 도착할 확률이 더 높다.
(D) 새끼들은 빛의 강도를 신호로 사용함으로써 물을 향한 방향을 계산하는 것을 ~~배운다~~.

Inference 지문의 키워드인 navigation in sea turtle hatchlings가 언급된 부분을 살펴보면 The juveniles are thought to instinctively head towards light because moonlight reflecting against the water means that the ocean is brighter than land.(밤에는 달빛이 물에 반사되기 때문에 바다가 육지보다 더 밝다는 것을 뜻하기 때문에 이 어린 새끼들이 본능적으로 불빛을 향해 나아간다고 생각되었다)라고 말한다. 즉, 빛에 반응 하는 바다 거북이 새끼들은 바다와 육지 모두 밝은 낮보다 달빛이 바다에 반사되는 저녁에 생존 가능성이 더 크다는 것이다. 따라서 정답은 (C)가 된다. (A)는 세 번째 단락에서 설명했듯이 바다 거북이들이 어릴 땐 자기장도 사용하지만 다른 방법들도 동원하기 때문에 오답이고, (B)는 달빛과 인공적인 빛들을 구별할 수 없기 때문에 사람들 때문에 만들어지는 인공적인 빛들에 의해 영향을 받는 것이므로 오답이다. (D)는 새끼들이 계산하는 것을 배운다는 내용은 언급된 적이 없기 때문에 오답이다.

08

According to paragraph 6, how do scientists know that turtles return to the breeding locations in which they were born?

(A) Sea turtles of the same breeding site had genetic markers that were identical to each other.
(B) They discovered that sea turtles inherit mtDNA from not their biological ~~but~~ foster mother.
(C) It was found that hawksbill turtles were the ~~sole~~ sea turtle inhabitants of several islands in the Persian Gulf.
(D) Despite efforts, islands that have ideal conditions for green sea turtle breeding have not been recolonized. ★

단락 6에 의하면, 과학자들은 어떻게 바다거북이들이 그들이 태어나고 부화했던 장소로 돌아간다는 것을 알 수 있었나?

(A) 같은 곳에서 태어난 바다 거북이들은 서로가 같은 유전적 표시를 갖고 있었다.
(B) 그들은 바다 거북이들이 ~~생모가 아닌~~ 양모한테서 mtDNA를 물려 받는다는 것을 발견했다.
(C) 대모 거북이들은 페르시아 만의 여러 섬들 중에서 ~~유일한~~ 거북이 주민이었다는 것이 발견 되었다.
(D) 노력에도 불구하고, 초록 바다 거북이의 번식에 최적의 환경을 갖고 있는 섬들은 아직 거북이들에 의해서 서식되지 않고 있다. ★

Fact 질문의 키워드인 return to breeding locations in which they were born이 언급된 부분을 살펴보면 Each hawksbill turtle tested in the nesting site had the same mtDNA, with only minimal variability, leading to the conclusion that most of the hawksbill turtles in the nesting site have emerged from the same nest. (각각의 대모 거북이들의 둥지는 다수의 동일한 mtDNA 샘플들을 갖고 있었고, mtDNA 샘플들은 아주 약간의 차이만을 갖고 있었기 때문에 특정한 둥지의 대도 거북이들의 대부분은 같은 둥지에서 태어났다는 결론을 도출한다)라고 말한다. 즉, 시험결과가 말해주듯이 같은 곳에서 태어난 바다거북이들은 유전적인 유사성을 가지고 있고, 이것은 그 실험장소에서 발견된 바다거북이들은 자신들이 태어나고 부화했던 장소로 돌아와서 서식하고 있다는 것을 나타낸다. (C)는 페르시아 만의 여러 섬에서 서식하는 거북이들은 오직 대모 거북이 종이라는 내용은 언급되지 않기 때문에 오답이고, (B)는 양모에 대한 내용이 언급되지 않을뿐더러 생모한테서 유전자를 물려받는 것이기 때문에 오답이다. (D)또한 본문에서 설명되는 부분이지만 결정적으로 유전적인 유사성에 대한 내용을 담고 있지 않기 때문에 오답이다.

09

Look at the four squares [■] that indicate where the following sentence could be added to the passage.

Papi believed that the magnet would inhibit the turtles' ability to calculate their position on Earth.

Where would the sentence best fit? Click on a square [■] to add the sentence to the passage.

1st

네 개의 네모 [■]는 다음 문장이 삽입될 수 있는 부분을 나타내고 있다.

파피는 자석이 거북이들이 지구에서 그들의 위치를 계산하는 능력을 방해할거라고 믿었다.

이 문장은 어느 자리에 들어가는 것이 가장 적절한가?

첫 번째

Insertion 삽입 문장의 키워드는 Papi와 inhibit the turtles' ability이다. 첫 번째 네모 앞 문장을 살펴보면 플로리아노 파피와 다른 학자들이 모여 거북이들의 자철석을 이용한 해항 방법을 실험하기 위해 그들의 머리에 강한 자석을 부착했다. 그리고 첫 번째 네모 다음 문장을 살펴보면 놀랍게도 자석을 부착했음에도 불구하고 거북이들이 무리없이 목적지에 도착했다는 것을 알 수 있다. 그러면 그 중간에 첫 번째 네모 다음 문장의 내용과 상반 되는 내용이 들어가야 하며, 삽입 문장에서 설명하듯 부착된 자석이 거북이들이 그들의 목적지에 도착하는데 방해를 줄 것이라고 생각했다가 들어가는 것이 가장 적합하다. 따라서 정답은 첫 번째 네모이다.

10

Directions: An introductory sentence for a brief summary of the passage is provided below. Complete the summary by selecting the THREE answer choices that express the most important ideas in the passage. Some sentences do not belong in the summary because they express ideas that are not presented in the passage or are minor ideas in the passage. **This question is worth 2 points.**

지시: 지문 요약을 위한 도입 문장이 아래에 주어져 있다. 지문의 가장 중요한 내용을 나타내는 보기 3개를 골라 요약을 완성하시오. 어떤 문장은 지문에 언급되지 않은 내용이나 사소한 정보를 담고 있으므로 요약에 포함되지 않는다. **이 문제는 2점이다.**

The navigational skills of the sea turtles have intrigued scientists for years.

(A) Although not fully understood, the most widely accepted method believed to be used by turtles is magnetic positioning through magnetite.
  - paragraph 2,3
(E) Studying the mtDNA of sea turtles has shown that sea turtles usually return to the nesting area in which they were born. - paragraph 6
(F) Using scents, light, and sounds as cues, sea turtles augment their navigation as juveniles or when near land. - paragraph 4,5

바다 거북이들의 길을 찾는 능력은 수 년간 과학자들의 흥미를 끌었다.

(A) 비록 완벽히 이해 되지는 않았지만, 거북이들이 사용하는 방법 중에 가장 널리 받아들여진 것은 자철석을 이용한 위치추적이다.
(E) 바다 거북이들의 mtDNA를 공부함으로써 바다 거북이들은 대게 그들이 태어났던 둥지로 돌아 온다는 것이 밝혀졌다.
(F) 바다 거북이들은 유아기 때나 육지에 가까이 있을 때에 냄새, 빛, 소리를 신호로 이용해서 그들의 길 찾는 능력을 보강한다.

(B) Despite continuous efforts, such as wildlife protection and habitat reconstruction, Grand Cayman has yet retrieved the green sea turtle population it used to have. - paragraph 6 detail
(C) ~~Depending on~~ the age, the species, and the presence of predator in the vicinity, sea turtles use ~~different~~ methods of navigation. - paragraph 3 minor
(D) It is now believed that sea turtles use neither the position of the stars ~~nor the smell~~ of their destination as cues for directional navigation. - 반/반

(B) 야생 보호법과 주거지 재건과 같은 지속적인 노력에도 불구하고, 그랜드 케이맨 섬은 예전만큼의 초록 바다 거북이 개체 수를 되찾아 오지 못했다.
(C) 나이, 종들, 부근의 천적들의 존재에 ~~따라서~~ 바다 거북이들은 길을 찾는데 ~~다른~~ 방법들을 사용한다.
(D) 이제 바다 거북이들은 별들의 위치나 그들의 목적지의 ~~냄새~~를 길의 방향을 잡는 신호로 사용하지 않는다고 믿어진다.

Summary 지문의 중심 내용은 바다 거북이의 항해방법이다. (A)는 두 번째와 세 번째 단락의 중심내용인 과학자들이 설명하는 자철석의 역할 및 결점과 일치하고, (E)는 여섯 번째 단락의 중심내용인 유전적인 유사성과 바다 거북이 항해의 연관성과 일치하고, (F)는 네 번째와 다섯 번째 단락의 중심내용인 빛, 소리, 냄새가 바다 거북이에 미치는 영향과 일치한다. 따라서 답은 (A), (E), (F)이다.

USHER iBT TOEFL
INTERMEDIATE READING
부록
해석·해설

TEST 1 - 1
Comets

01 The term 'roughly' in the passage is closest in meaning to

(A) clearly [klíərli]
(B) typically [típikəli] ★
(C) frequently [frí:kwəntli]
(D) approximately [əpráksəmitli]

지문의 단어 "대략"의 의미와 가장 유사한 것은?

(A) 분명하게
(B) 일반적으로 ★
(C) 자주
(D) 약

Vocabulary 지문의 roughly(대략)은 approximately(약)와 동의어이므로 (D)가 정답이다.

02 The term "undergo" in the passage is closest in meaning to

(A) allow [əláu]
(B) experience [ikspíəriəns]
(C) prevent [privént]
(D) cause [kɔːz] ★

지문의 단어 "겪다"의 의미와 가장 유사한 것은?

(A) 허용하다
(B) 경험하다
(C) 방지하다
(D) 일으키다 ★

Vocabulary 지문의 undergo(겪다)는 experience(경험하다)와 동의어이므로 (B)가 정답이다.

03 What does the word "its" refer to in the passage?

(A) comet's ★
(B) orbit's
(C) inactive mass's
(D) sun's

지문에서 "그것의" 이 의미하는 것은?

(A) 혜성의 ★
(B) 궤도의
(C) 비활성된 질량의
(D) 태양의

Reference its가 언급된 문장을 살펴보면 They complete most of their orbit as frozen and relatively inactive masses that are difficult to discern, but as they come closer to the sun, the effects of its massive energy sublimate the frozen materials within this nucleus to form a glowing ball of dust and gases known as the coma 에서 태양과 가까워질수록 이것의 거대한 에너지가 얼어붙은 물질들을 기체화한다. 즉 태양과 가까워 짐으로써 얻게 되는 태양의 거대한 에너지를 말한다. 따라서 정답은 (D)가 된다.

04 According to paragraph 4, all of the following is true about the coma that develops around the comet as it orbits the sun EXECPT:

(A) The coma is formed as volatile frozen material becomes gaseous and expands around the comet's nucleus.
(B) The coma of some comets can expand so much that they are larger than the diameter of the sun.
(C) The presence of a coma is used to easily distinguish comets from other celestial bodies such as asteroids.
(D) When a comet approaches close enough to the sun, the coma becomes the long tail.

단락 4에 따르면, 혜성이 태양 주위를 돌 때 생기는 코마에 관해서 사실이 아닌 것은?

(A) 코마는 휘발성의 얼어있는 물질들이 기체화 되고 혜성의 중심부에서 팽창할 때 일어난다.
(B) 몇 몇 혜성의 코마는 태양의 지름보다 커질 수 있을 만큼 늘어날 수 있다.
(C) 코마의 존재는 소행성들과 같은 다른 천체들로부터 혜성들을 쉽게 구별하는데 쓰인다.
(D) 혜성이 태양에 충분히 가까이 접근 하면, 코마는 긴 꼬리로 바뀐다.

Fact 질문의 키워드인 coma that develops around the comet as it orbits the sun이 언급된 부분을 살펴보면 When they reach approximately 1.5 AU from the sun, solar energy's effects become more extreme and parts of the coma are blown into a tail. (이것들이 태양과 대략 1.5 AU만큼 가까워질 때면, 태양 에너지의 영향은 더욱 극대화되고 코마의 어느 부분은 꼬리로 날라간다)라고 말한다. 즉, coma 자체는 소멸되지 않기 때문에 정답은 (D)가 된다.

부록 (해석·해설) 409

TEST 1 - 2
Darwin and Evolution Theory

01 The term "segregation" in the passage is closest in meaning to

(A) separation [sèpərèiʃən]
(B) uniqueness [ju:ní:knes] ★
(C) harshness [há:rʃnis]
(D) unity [jú:nəti]

"분리"가 글에서 뜻하는 가장 가까운 의미는?

(A) 분리
(B) 독특함 ★
(C) 척박함
(D) 통일

Vocabulary 지문의 segregation(분리)는 separation(분리)와 동의어이므로 (A)가 정답이다.

---

02 The word "it" in the passage refers to?

(A) common use ★
(B) similarity
(C) common ancestry
(D) adaptive evolution

글에서 "이것"이 뜻하는 것은?

(A) 흔한 용도 ★
(B) 유사성
(C) 공통된 조상
(D) 적응진화

Reference it이 언급된 부분을 살펴보면 This cannot be attributed to common use, so it must indicate common ancestry and adaptive evolution to fit the organisms' functions. (이것은 공통된 쓰임새로 설명될 수 없기에 이것은 공통된 조상과 생물들의 기능을 만족하기 위한 적응진화를 나타낸다)에서 오웬이 찾은 유사성들이 동물의 진화를 나타낸다는 것을 의미하기 때문에 정답은 (B)가 된다.

---

03 According to paragraph 3, which of the following is NOT true about the homology and vestigial structures?

(A) Richard Owen found similarities between the structures in vertebrates which served different purposes.
(B) Vestigial structures, like the non-used leg bones in whales and snakes, indicate that at one time their ancestors had working legs.
(C) The presence of homology and vestigial structures in modern organisms helped proved Darwin's idea that species change over time. ★
(D) Homology occurs because animals use body parts in the same way, so they evolve in a similar manner.

단락 3에 의하면, 상동과 잔여 구조들에 관해서 사실이 아닌 것은?

(A) 리차드 오웬은 다른 목적을 가진 척추동물들의 구조에서 유사성을 찾았다.
(B) 고래들과 뱀의 쓰이지 않는 다리 뼈와 같은 잔여 구조 들은 한 때 그들의 조상이 다리를 사용했다는 것을 나타낸다.
(C) 현대 생물들에게 있는 상동과 잔여 구조들은 다윈의 생물들이 시간이 흐름에 따라 변화한다는 개념을 증명하는데 도움을 줬다. ★
(D) 상동은 동물들의 신체 구조가 같은 방법으로 쓰였기 때문에 일어났고, 그렇기 때문에 같은 방법으로 진화했다.

Fact 질문의 키워드인 homology and vestigial structures가 언급된 부분을 살펴보면 Owen found homology, or anatomical similarity, in the body parts of different animals which served different purposes. (오웬은 상동 혹은 해부학적 유사성을 다른 목적을 가진 여러 동물의 신체 부위에서 찾아 내었다)라고 말한다. 즉, 동물들은 자신들의 신체 부위를 다른 방법으로 쓴다는 것이기 때문에 정답은 (D)가 된다.

---

04 The term "jointly" in the passage is closest in meaning to

(A) simply [símpli]
(B) rightfully [ráitfəli] ★
(C) together [təgéðər]
(D) therefore [ðéərfɔ:r]

"공동으로"라는 단어가 이 글에서 뜻하는 가장 가까운 바는?

(A) 단순히
(B) 정당하게 ★
(C) 함께
(D) 그러므로

Vocabulary 지문의 jointly(공동으로)는 together(함께)와 동의어이므로 (C)가 정답이다.

TEST 2 - 1
Determining the Ages of the Planets and the Universe

01 The term "vast" in the passage is closest in meaning to

(A) powerful [páuərfəl] ★
(B) extensive [iksténsiv]
(C) wealthy [wélθi]
(D) ancient [éinʃənt]

지문의 단어 "거대한"의 의미와 가장 유사한 것은?

(A) 강력한 ★
(B) 막대한
(C) 부유한
(D) 고대의

Vocabulary 지문의 vast(거대한)와 비슷한 뜻을 가지는 extensive(막대한)이 정답이다.

02 According to paragraph 1, which of the following is true of the planets and the non-planetary objects in the solar system?

(A) The planets orbit the sun at the ~~same speed~~ because the gas cloud that collapsed to form them exerted a uniform force on them all.
(B) The collapse of a gas cloud, ~~long after~~ forming planets, created the majority of other non-planetary objects. ★
(C) The extreme gravitational force exerted by the sun ~~caused~~ the collapse of the dust cloud which formed most of the objects found in the solar system.
(D) The orbits of some non-planetary bodies in the solar system follow a path that is dissimilar to those of the planets.

단락 1에 의하면 태양계 안의 행성들과 비 행성 물체에 대해서 옳은 것은?

(A) 붕괴된 후 행성들을 만든 가스 구름이 일정한 힘을 그들에게 가했기 때문에 그 행성들은 태양을 같은 ~~속도로~~ 돈다.
(B) 가스 구름의 붕괴는 행성들을 만든 ~~한참 후에~~ 비 행성들의 대부분을 만들었다. ★
(C) 태양에 의해 발산된 그 극한의 중력은 태양계 안에서 발견되는 거의 모든 물체를 형성한 먼지 구름의 붕괴를 ~~야기시켰다~~.
(D) 태양계 안의 몇몇의 비 행성 물체의 궤도는 행성의 궤도와는 다른 경로를 따라 간다.

Inference 단락 1을 살펴보면 The orbits of planets and the majority of non-planetary objects in our solar system have a very interesting characteristic; despite their vast differences, they have astounding similarities. (행성들의 궤도와 태양계 안의 대부분의 비 행성 물체들은 아주 흥미로운 특징을 가지고 있다; 그들의 다양한 차이점에도 불구하고 그것들은 믿기 어려운 유사성을 가지고 있다)라고 말한다. 즉, majority(대부분)에 속하지 않은 몇몇의 비 행성들은 같은 궤도를 가지고 있지 않다. 따라서 답은 (D)가 된다. (A)는 같은 속도가 아닌 같은 궤도로 도는 것이기 때문에 오답이고, (B)는 행성들과 비 행성들이 동시에 만들어졌기 때문에 오답이다. (C)는 먼지 구름을 붕괴시킨 원인은 본문에 언급 되지않기 때문에 오답이다.

03 The term "dense" in the passage is closest in meaning to

(A) new [njuː]
(B) thick [θik]
(C) mature [mətjúər] ★
(D) seasonal [síːzənəl]

지문의 단어 "밀집한"의 의미와 가장 유사한 것은?

(A) 새로운
(B) 굵은
(C) 성숙한 ★
(D) 계절적인

Vocabulary 지문의 dense(밀집한)와 동의어인 thick(굵은)이 정답이다.

04

According to paragraph 5, which of the following is true regarding the expansion of the universe?

(A) Collecting physical materials on which to conduct the universe's age testing is complicated but ~~not impossible~~.
(B) Scientists who studied the Big Bang theorized that it is the reason for the drifting apart of the galaxies.
(C) Scientists ~~proved~~ the existence of the Big Bang through empirical analysis. ★
(D) Scientists have been able to determine the timing of the Big Bang, but ~~cannot~~ correlate it to the age of the universe.

단락 5에 따르면 우주의 팽창에 대해서 맞는 내용은?

(A) 우주의 나이 연구를 위해 필요한 물리적 물질을 모으는 것은 복잡하지만 ~~불가능하지는 않다~~.
(B) 빅뱅을 연구한 과학자들은 빅뱅이 은하 팽창의 이유라고 이론화했다.
(C) 과학자들은 실증적 분석을 통해서 빅뱅의 존재를 ~~증명하였다~~. ★
(D) 과학자들은 빅뱅의 발생시기를 파악할 수는 있었지만 이것을 우주의 나이에 연관시키지는 ~~못했다~~.

Fact 질문의 키워드인 expansion of the universe가 언급된 부분을 살펴보면 Scientists conjecture that this occurs because the universe began with an explosion, known as the Big Bang, which sent all of the dense matter concentrated at the center of the explosion hurtling across space. (과학자들은 이 현상은 밀도가 높은 물체들을 폭발의 중심에 집중시켜 놓고 우주에 걸쳐서 던져 버린 빅뱅이라고 알려진 폭발 때문에 일어난다고 추측한다)라고 말한다. 즉, 빅뱅의 여파때문에 은하가 계속해서 팽창하고 있다는 것이다. 따라서 답은 (B)가 된다. (A)는 물리적 물질을 모을 수 있는 방법은 없기 때문에 오답이고, (C)는 빅뱅이 일어났다는 추론을 한것이지, 빅뱅의 존재를 증명한건 아니기 때문에 오답이다. (D)는 빅뱅의 발생시기를 파악했다는 내용은 언급되지 않으므로 오답이다. (D)는 과학자들이 빅뱅의 타이밍을 알아내 우주의 나이를 추측할 수 있었던 것이기 때문에 오답이다.

TEST 2 - 2
Early Research in Organic Chemistry

01 The term "eventually" in the passage is closest in meaning to

(A) finally [fáinəli]
(B) certainly [sə́:rtənli] ★
(C) quickly [kwíkli]
(D) easily [íːzəli]

지문의 단어 "최종적으로"의 의미와 가장 유사한 것은?

(A) 마침내
(B) 분명히 ★
(C) 빨리
(D) 쉽게

Vocabulary 지문의 eventually(최종적으로)는 finally(마침내)와 동의어이므로 정답은 (A)이다.

02 Which of the following is true of the theory of Vitalism from paragraph 2?

(A) The "vital spark" or "force" that early scientists studying organic compounds were looking for ~~turned out to be~~ the element ~~carbon~~.
(B) Antoine Lavoisier was an early ~~supporter~~ of the theory of Vitalism until he was persuaded to believe that the "vital spark" was not found in plants.
(C) Scientists opposed to the theory of Vitalism felt that all living creatures were created by a ~~natural process~~ that gave them life, not a "vital spark." ★(not mentioned)
(D) The ability of a scientist to produce organic materials in the laboratory convinced scientists that there was no "vital spark" that gave organisms life.

단락 2에서 생기론에 대해 추론할 수 있는 것은?

(A) 유기화합물을 연구하던 초기 과학자들이 찾던 '생기'나 '힘'은 원소 ~~탄소로 밝혀졌다~~.
(B) 앙투안 라부아지에는 식물에서 '생기'가 발견되지 않 았다고 믿도록 흔들리기 이전에는 생기론의 초기 차 ~~지자였다~~.
(C) 생기론을 반대하던 과학자들은 모든 생물에게 생명을 준건 '생기'가 아니라 ~~자연적인 과정~~이라 믿었다. ★
(D) 실험실에서 유기물을 생산할 수 있는 과학자들의 능력 이 유기체들에게 삶을 주는 '생기'가 없노라고 과학자들을 설득했다.

Inference 문제의 키워드인 theory of Vitalism이 언급된 부분을 살펴보면 Despite the eventual invalidation of the vitalist theory, German chemist Friedrich Wohler's accidental synthesis of organic material in his laboratory.(독일 화학자인 프레드릭 뵐러의 실험실에서의 우발적인 유기물 합성 덕에 일어난 생기론 자들의 이론이 결국 무효로 됐음에도 불구하고)라고 말한다. 즉, 프레드릭 뵐러의 실험이 결과적으로 '생기'가 없노라고 다른 과학자들을 설득했다는걸 알 수 있기 때문에 (D)가 답이 된다. (A)는 '생기'의 힘은 탄소였다고 하는 내용은 없기 때문에 오답이고, 앙투안 라부아지에는 생기론을 믿지 않았기 때문에 (B)는 오답이다.

03 The term "component" in the passage is closest in meaning to

(A) special [spéʃəl]
(B) developmental [divéləpməntəl] ★
(C) constituent [kənstítʃuənt]
(D) eventual [ivéntʃuəl]

지문의 단어 "구성요소의"의 의미와 가장 유사한 것은?

(A) 특별한
(B) 발전의 ★
(C) 구성하는
(D) 도구

Vocabulary 지문의 component(구성요소의)는 constituent(구성하는)과 동의어이므로 정답은 (C)이다.

04 The term "attain" in the passage is closest in meaning to

(A) achieve [ətʃíːv]
(B) employ [emplɔ́i]
(C) expect [ikspékt] ★
(D) seek [siːk]

지문의 단어 "얻다"의 의미와 가장 유사한 것은?

(A) 획득하다
(B) 사용하다
(C) 예상하다 ★
(D) 모색하다

Vocabulary 지문의 attain(얻다)는 achieve(획득하다)와 동의어이므로 정답은 (A)이다.

TEST 3 - 1
El Niño

01 The term "affects" in the passage is closest in meaning to

(A) influences [ínfluəns]
(B) explains [ikspléin] ★
(C) improves [imprú:v]
(D) depends on [dipénd an]

지문의 단어 "영향을 끼치다"의 의미와 가장 유사한 것은?

(A) 영향을 미치다
(B) 설명하다 ★
(C) 개선하다
(D) ~에 의존하다

Vocabulary 지문의 affects(영향을 끼치다)는 influences(영향을 미치다)와 동의어므로 (A)가 정답이다.

02 What can be inferred about the Southern Oscillation from paragraph 3?

(A) It has been found to ~~better function~~ in the eastern Pacific Ocean than in its western portions.
(B) It ~~first occurred~~ in the early 20th century when it was discovered by British physicist and statistician Gilbert Walker.
(C) It functions ~~only~~ as a cause of the El Niño across the vast Pacific waters. ★
(D) The atmospheric pressures in the two horizontal ends of the Pacific had an asymmetrical relationship.

단락 3에서 남방 진동에 대해 어떤 것이 추론될 수 있는가?

(A) 이는 태평양의 서쪽보다 동쪽에서 ~~더 강한 것으로~~ 들어났다.
(B) 이는 영국 물리학자이자 통계학자 길버트워커에 의해 처음 발견되었을 때 ~~처음으로 일어났다.~~
(C) 이는 광대한 태평양 바다에서 일어나는 엘니뇨의 ~~원인으로만~~ 작용한다. ★
(D) 태평양 양극단에 대기압은 비대칭적인 관계이다.

Inference Southern Oscillation가 언급된 부분을 3단락에서 찾으면 영국의 물리학자 Gilbert Walker가 an inverse correlation between atmospheric pressure at weather stations in the eastern and western Pacific (동태평양 기상관측소의 기압과 서태평양 기상관측소의 기압이 비대칭 관계를 가지고 있다)라는 점을 발견했다는 걸 알 수 있다. 따라서 (D)가 답이다. (A)는 서쪽보다 동쪽에서 더 강하다는 언급이 없으므로 오답이고, (B)는 길버트 워커가 발견했을 때 처음 발생한 현상이다 라는 언급이 없어 오답이다. (C)는 남방진동과 엘리뇨가 상관관계를 가지고 있다고 해서 남방진동이 엘니뇨의 원인으로만 작용한다는 건 억지이므로 오답이다.

03 The term "accumulation" in the passage is closest in meaning to

(A) acceptance [ækséptəns]
(B) creation [kri:éiʃən]
(C) fine detail [fain dí:teil] ★
(D) growing collection [gróuiŋ kəlékʃən]

지문의 단어 "축적"의 의미와 가장 유사한 것은?

(A) 수용
(B) 창조
(C) 정교한 세부사항 ★
(D) 늘어나는 수집물

Vocabulary 지문의 accumulation(축적)과 비슷한 뜻을 가지는 growing collection(늘어나는 수집물)이 정답이다.

04

According to paragraph 5, which of the following is true regarding the historical incidence of El Niño?

(A) Researchers have been able to prove that the effects of El Niño now last three times ~~longer~~ than they did in the 1600s.
(B) Spanish colonists kept detailed records of the surface temperature of the Pacific Ocean that allowed modern researchers to determine the ~~length~~ of previous El Niño periods. ★
(C) It appears that the temperature of the ocean's surface increases more dramatically during modern El Niño periods than it did in the past.
(D) Scientists have noticed that El Niño's warming has done the ~~most severe~~ damage to the United States of America.

단락 5에 따르면, 엘니뇨의 역사적 발생에 대해 사실인 것은?

(A) 연구자들은 1600년도보다 엘니뇨의 영향이 3배나 ~~오래 지속된다는~~ 것을 증명했다.
(B) 현대 연구자들이 스페인 식민지 주민들을 태평양의 수면 온도에 관한 상세한 기록들을 통해 이전 엘니뇨 기간들의 ~~길이를~~ 알 수 있게끔 했다. ★
(C) 과거에 비해 현대 엘니뇨 기간에 바다의 수면 온도의 증가가 더 급격한 것으로 보인다.
(D) 과학자들은 엘니뇨의 따뜻해지는 현상이 미국에게 ~~가장 심한~~ 피해를 줬다는 걸 발견했다.

Fact 문제의 키워드인 historical incidence를 5단락에서 살펴보면 An even more alarming finding is that temperature increase's severity is rising. (이보다 더 걱정스러운 발견은 온도 상승의 정도의 증가하고 있다는 것이다)라고 주장한다. 즉, 현대 엘니뇨 기간에 수온의 증가가 과거에 비해 더 급격하다는 것을 알 수 있다. 따라서 답은 (C)이다. (A)와 (B)는 각각 영향과 길이가 아니라 지문에선 빈도를 의미하고 있으므로 오답이고, (D)는 1990년대 말부터라는 언급이 없으므로 오답이다.

TEST 3 - 2
England's Sixteenth Century Economy

01 What can be inferred from paragraph 1 about the population of England during the Late Tudor Period?

(A) Population rates ~~decreased~~ from their all-time high because of the numerous deaths that occurred during the spread of the "Black Death."
(B) The population increase that occurred during this time made England the ~~most populous~~ country in the European region at the time. ★
(C) England's population and economic conditions increased more rapidly than those of continental countries because it was not as affected by disease and war as they were.
(D) Improvements in England's economy ~~led to~~ decreases in the mortality rate and increases in the fertility rate, causing the population to nearly double in 100 years.

늦은 Tudor 시대에 영국의 인구에 대해 단락 1에서 추론할 수 있는 것은?

(A) 흑사병의 확산으로 일어난 수 많은 죽음 때문에 인구 비율은 불변의 최대치에서 감소하였다.
(B) 이 시대의 인구 증가는 영국이 동시대의 유럽 지역에서 가장 인구가 많게끔 만들었다. ★
(C) 영국의 인구와 경제적 상황은 대륙의 다른 나라들보다 빨리 증가했는데 이것은 질병과 전쟁으로 덜 영향을 받아서 그런 것이다.
(D) 영국의 경제의 발전은 사망률의 감소와 출산율의 증가를 커져왔고 이것은 100년 사이에 인구가 거의 두 배로 증가하게끔 하였다.

Inference 문제의 키워드인 population of England가 언급된 부분을 살펴보면 This dramatic increase, along with other factors, led to vast changes in England's economy and allowed it to become Europe's largest, far surpassing those of the war and plague ravaged continent. (이런 극적인 증가는 다른 요소들과 함께 영국 경제에 큰 변화를 일으켰고, 영국 경제는 전염병과 전쟁으로 황폐화된 다른 지역 들의 경제를 능가할 정도로 유럽에서 가장 커졌다)라고 했다. 즉, 상대적으로 전쟁과 질병의 영향을 덜 받아서 발전할 수 있었다고 유추할 수 있다. 따라서 (C)가 답이 된다. (A)는 흑사병으로 인한 인구 감소는 late Tudor Period 전이다. 즉, Late Tudor Period에는 감소하였던 인구가 흑사병이 돌기 전 인구만큼 증가하였기 때문에 오답이다. (B)는 영국이 유럽에서 가장 인구가 많았다는 내용은 언급되지 않으므로 오답이고, (D)는 인구가 증가해서 경제가 발전한 것이기 때문에 오답이다.

02 According to paragraph 4, all of the following were ways that landowners attempted to maximize the profits from their property **EXCEPT**:

(A) Entry Fees were paid to ~~tenants~~ to allow them to maximize their profits.
(B) Landowners shortened the contracts as they pleased.
(C) They planted crops that were the most favorable for the market. ★
(D) They advocated for more efficient farm practices, like crop rotation, to be utilized on their properties.

단락 4에 의하면, 수익을 최대화하기 위해 지주들이 시도하지 않은 것은 무엇인가?

(A) 소작농에게 부과된 입장료가 그들의 이익을 극대화 시켰다.
(B) 지주들은 그들이 원하는 대로 연속적 계약을 줄였다.
(C) 지주들이 시장에서 가장 수요가 높은 곡물들을 길렀다. ★
(D) 지주들은 그들이 소유하고 있는 땅에서 윤작과 같은 더욱 효율적인 농사 방법이 사용되길 주장했다.

Fact 문제의 키워드인 ways landowners attempted to maximize the profits from their property가 언급된 부분을 살펴보면 Another way they maximized their profits was to charge potential tenants an "entry fee" before they would even consent to renting to them(지주들이 그들의 수익을 증가하기 위한 또 다른 방법으로 잠재적인 임차인들에게 그들이 임차에 대해 동의가 떨어지기 전에 "입지세"를 청구하였다)라고 한다. 즉, 지주들이 임차인들에게 입지세를 요구한 거지, 임차인들이 입지세를 받은 건 아니기 때문에 오답이다. 따라서 답은 (A)가 된다.

03

The term "potential" in the passage is closest in meaning to

(A) serious [síəriəs]
(B) possible [pásəbəl]
(C) related [riléitid]
(D) common [kámən] ★

지문의 단어 "잠재적인"의 의미와 가장 유사한 것은?

(A) 진지한
(B) 가능성 있는
(C) 관련된
(D) 흔한 ★

Vocabulary 지문의 potential(잠재적인)은 possible(가능성 있는)과 동의어이므로 정답은 (B)이다.

04

The term "operate" in the passage is closest in meaning to

(A) dominate [dámənèit] ★
(B) function [fʌ́ŋkʃən]
(C) originate [ərídʒənéit]
(D) fail [feil]

지문의 단어 "운영하다"의 의미와 가장 유사한 것은?

(A) 지배하다 ★
(B) 작동하다
(C) 유래하다
(D) 실패하다

Vocabulary 지문의 operate(운영하다)는 function(작동하다)과 동의어이므로 정답은 (B)이다.

TEST 4 - 1
Environmental Impact of the Anasazi

01 According to paragraph 1, which of the following is true of the theories related to the disappearance of the Anasazi?

(A) The tree ring studies ~~by~~ the Anasazi indicate that these ancient people had been driven from their villages due to the "Great Drought."
(B) Although the Anasazi were able to survive other droughts, they started evacuating ~~after~~ the "Great Drought."
(C) The indication of drought conditions by the tree rings studied was not sufficient to explain the civilizations abandonment of the area.
(D) Tim Kohler's theory that human-nature interaction caused the Anasazi to flee resulted in the ~~revelation~~ of the "Great Drought." ★

단락 1에 의하면 다음 중 아나사지의 사라짐에 대해 추론 할 수 있는 것은?

(A) 나이테에 대한 ~~아나사지와~~ 연구는 이 고대인들이 great drought때문에 그들의 마을로부터 쫓겨났다는 것을 나타낸다.
(B) 아나사지는 다른 가뭄들을 견딜 수 있었음에도 불구하고 great drought ~~이후에~~ 피난하기 시작했다.
(C) 나이테에 난 가뭄 자국은 그 지역의 문명들이 떠나간 이유를 설명하기엔 불충분했다.
(D) 인간-자연상호관계가 아나사지를 도망치게 했다는 팀 콜러의 이론은 great drought의 존재를 ~~발견되도록~~ 만들었다. ★

Inference 질문의 키워드인 disappearance of Anasazi가 언급된 부분을 살펴보면 This, however, began to be called into question recently. (하지만 최근에는 이것에 대하여 문제가 제기되고 있다)라고 한다. 즉, Great Drought만으론 그 지역의 문명이 사라졌다고 단정지을 수 없다는 것이기 때문에 정답은 (C)가 된다. (A)는 아나사지가 한 연구가 아니라 고고학자들이 연구를한 것이기 때문에 오답이고, (B)는 Great Drought 때문에 아자사지가 이동했다는 근거가 불충분하다고 언급하기 때문에 오답이다. (D)는 팀 콜러의 이론은 Great Drought 이론의 결점을 보완하고자 제안되었고, Great Drought의 존재를 발견되도록 하지는 않았기 때문에 오답이다.

02 The word "it" in the passage refers to?

(A) question [kwéstʃən]
(B) ongoing event [ángòuiŋ ivént]
(C) Great Drought [greit draut]
(D) evacuation [ivækjuéiʃən] ★

지문에서 "it"이 의미하는 것은?

(A) 질문
(B) 진행되고 있는 사건
(C) 거대한 가뭄
(D) 피난 ★

Reference it이 언급된 부분을 살펴보면 Today, historians believe that the Anasazi evacuation had been occurring before the "Great Drought" and that the drought was not an unprecedented event; villagers had likely survived others before it에서 Great Drought이 전무한 사건은 아니며, Great Drought 이전에도 다른 비슷한 가뭄들도 견뎌냈다고 하는 것이니 정답은 (C)가 된다.

03 The term "adjacent" in the passage is closest in meaning to

(A) cool [kuːl]
(B) deep [diːp]
(C) large [laːrdʒ] ★
(D) nearby [níərbài]

지문의 단어 "인접한"의 의미와 가장 유사한 것은?

(A) 차가운
(B) 깊은
(C) 거대한 ★
(D) 인근의

Vocabulary 지문의 adjacent(인접한)는 nearby(인근의)와 동의어이므로 정답은 (D)이다.

The term "susceptible to" in the passage is closest in meaning to

(A) well-known for
(B) slow to replace losses from ★
(C) likely to be affected by
(D) unable to benefit from

지문의 단어 "~의 영향을 받기 쉬운"의 의미와 가장 유사한 것은?

(A) ~로 잘 알려져 있는
(B) ~로부터의 손실을 느리게 대체하는 ★
(C) ~로 인해 영향을 받기 쉬운
(D) ~로부터 이익을 받을 수 없는

Vocabulary 지문의 susceptible to(~의 영향을 받기 쉬운)는 likely to be affected by(~로 인해 영향을 받기 쉬운)와 동의어이므로 정답은 (C)이다.

TEST 4 - 2
Global Variations in Species Diversity

01 The term "ensured" in the passage is closest in meaning to

(A) contributed to [kəntríbjut tuː]
(B) predicted [pridíkt] ★
(C) resulted in [rizʌ́lt in]
(D) guaranteed [gæ̀rəntíː]

지문의 단어 "보장받다"의 의미와 가장 유사한 것은?

(A) 기여되다
(B) 예측되다 ★
(C) 결과적으로 ~이 되다
(D) 보장되다

Vocabularly 지문의 ensured(보장받다)와 동의어인 guaranteed(보장되다)가 정답이다.

02 According to paragraph 4, all of the followings are true of the food supply in higher latitudes **EXCEPT**:

(A) Regions with higher latitude have less steady food supplies than regions near the equator.
(B) The seasonal nature of the food supply forces many animals to move towards different regions in search of food supplies.
(C) When the colder winter season begins the food supplies decrease and animals must either hibernate or migrate.
(D) The relatively lower overall food supply does not necessarily limit species diversity. ★

단락 4에 의하면, 더욱 높은 위도에서 식량공급에 관해서 사실이 아닌 것은?

(A) 더욱 높은 위도를 갖고 있는 지역들은 적도 부분의 지역들 보다 불안정한 식량공급을 갖고 있다.
(B) 식량공급이 계절에 의해서 받는 영향은 동물들이 식량 공급원을 찾아서 낮은 위도로 움직이게 만든다.
(C) 추운 겨울이 시작되면, 식량공급원은 줄어들고 동물들은 동면을 하거나 남쪽으로 이주해야 한다.
(D) 상대적으로 낮은 전반적인 식량공급량은 종다양성을 제한하지 않는다. ★

Fact 질문의 키워드인 food supply in higher latitudes가 언급된 부분을 살펴보면 However, when the long, frigid winter sets in, the area is rather barren, leading many specialized feeders to migrate to other areas. (하지만, 상당히 척박한 지역에서의 길고 추운 겨울이 올 때면 많은 전문화된 사냥꾼들이 다른 지역으로 이주를 가게 한다)라고 말한다. 즉, 추운 겨울이 시작되면 동물들이 더 많은 식량공급원을 찾기 위해 이주를 하는 것은 맞지만 동면한다는 내용은 언급되지 않으므로 정답은 (C)가 된다.

03 The term "frigid" in the passage is closest in meaning to

(A) cold [kould]
(B) original [ərídʒənəl]
(C) giant [dʒáiənt] ★
(D) moving [múːviŋ]

지문의 단어 "몹시 추운"의 의미와 가장 유사한 것은?

(A) 추운
(B) 원본의
(C) 거대한 ★
(D) 움직이는

Vocabularly 지문의 frigid(몹시 추운)와 동의어인 cold(추운)가 정답이다.

04

According to paragraph 5, which of the following is true regarding evolution and longevity in tropical regions?

(A) Species that exist in the tropics tend to be smaller than those found in northern latitudes ~~because~~ their lifespans are significantly shorter. ★
(B) Tropical species reproduce and die more quickly than species from other regions, therefore successive generations, with mutations, are produced more rapidly.
(C) Animals in tropical regions experience a higher mutation rate than those in higher latitudes, thereby increasing their ~~longevity~~.
(D) The shorter generation lengths of smaller species living in tropical regions ~~hinder~~ their maturation and therefore reproduction.

단락 5에 의하면, 열대 지방에서의 수명과 진화에 관해서 사실인 것은?

(A) 열대 지방에 존재하는 종들은 북쪽 위도에서 발견되는 종들에 비해서 수명이 현저하게 짧기 ~~때문에~~ 더욱 작다. ★
(B) 열대의 종들은 다른 지역들의 종들보다 더욱 빠르게 번식하고 죽고, 그러므로 변화를 갖고 있는 잇따른 세대들은 더욱 빨리 만들어진다.
(C) 열대지방의 동물들은 고위도의 동물들보다 더 빠른 변화 속도를 겪고, 이것이 그들을 ~~장수~~할 수 있도록 한다.
(D) 열대지방에 살고 있는 작은 종의 짧은 세대길이는 그들이 성숙하지 못하게 하고 따라서 번식하지 ~~못하게 한다~~.

Fact 질문의 키워드인 evolution and longevity in tropical regions가 언급된 부분을 살펴보면 This rapid mutation and selection enables distinct species to be produced much more quickly than in the colder northern regions. (이러한 빠른 변화와 도태는 다른 종들이 추운 북쪽 지역에서보다 훨씬 더 빨리 만들어지게 한다)라고 말한다. 즉, 열대지역 동물들의 수명이 추운 지역의 동물들보다 더 짧기 때문에 더 빠르게 도태하고 진화한다는 것이다. 따라서 정답은 (B)가 된다. (A)는 수명이 짧기 때문에 사이즈가 작은 것이 아니라, 사이즈가 작기 때문에 수명이 짧은 것이기 때문에 오답이고, (C)는 열대지방의 동물들은 오히려 수명이 짧고 그것이 더 빠른 변화 속도를 가능케 하는 것이기 때문에 오답이다. (D)는 종들의 짧은 세대길이가 그들의 성숙과 번식을 막는다는 내용은 언급되지 않으므로 오답이다.

TEST 5 - 1
Documenting the Incas

01 What can be inferred about stories passed down through the oral tradition from paragraph 4?

(A) Because people are ~~still alive~~ to verify the events that occurred in them, recent stories are more accurate than ancient ones.
(B) Inaccuracies develop in the stories over time as they are passed down from one generation to the next.
(C) Most early stories, like the one about the founding of Cusco, are meant to explain ~~how civilizations came to be~~.
(D) ~~Spanish elites~~ passed down inaccurate stories ~~orally~~ to the next generation in order to make themselves seem more impressive. ★

단락 4에서 구전으로 전수받은 이야기들에 대해서 추론할 수 있는 것은?

(A) 있었던 일들에 대해서 사실성을 확인해줄 사람들이 ~~아직 살아있기 때문에~~ 최근 이야기들이 옛날 이야기들에 비해 더 정확하다.
(B) 시간이 지나고 이야기들이 다음 세대에게 전수될수록 이야기들에 부정확한 요소들이 발달했다.
(C) 쿠스코의 설립과 같은 초기의 이야기들은 ~~문명들이 어떻게 만들어졌는지~~ 설명을 하기 위한 것들이다.
(D) ~~스페인 엘리트들은~~ 자신들을 더 위대하게 만들기 위해서 정확하지 않은 이야기들을 ~~구전으로~~ 다음 세대에 전수하는 경우가 많다. ★

Inference 질문의 키워드인 stories passed down through the oral tradition이 언급된 부분을 살펴보면 Over time, many of these stories may have developed unintentional inaccuracies. (시간이 지나면서, 많은 이야기들은 의도하지 않은 부정확한 내용을 얻게 되었을 수 있다)라고 말한다. 즉, 구전은 시간이 지나고 세대를 거칠수록 말이 달라지기 때문에 문자 체계가 없었던 잉카는 갈수록 이야기의 오류가 많이 생성되었다는 것이기 때문에 정답은 (B)가 된다. (A)는 아직까지 살아 있다는 내용은 언급되지 않으므로 오답이고, (C)는 문명이 어떻게 만들어졌는지를 보여주기 위함이 아니라 초창기 지도자들의 위엄을 설립하기 위해서이기 때문에 오답이다. (D)는 스페인 엘리트들이 아닌 잉카제국의 사람들이 다음 세대에게 전달했기 때문에 오답이다.

02 The term "prime" in the passage is closest in meaning to

(A) high quality [hai kwáləti]
(B) unused [ʌ̀njú:zd]
(C) easily accessible [í:zəli-æksésəbəl] ★
(D) low-lying [lou-láiiŋ]

지문의 단어 "주요한"의 의미와 가장 유사한 것은?

(A) 높은 수준의
(B) 사용되지 않은
(C) 쉽게 접근할 수 있는 ★
(D) 저지의

Vocabulary 지문의 prime(주요한)과 비슷한 의미를 가지고 있는 high quality(높은 수준의)가 정답이다.

03 The term "accurate" in the passage is closest in meaning to

(A) popular [pápjələr]
(B) correct [kərékt]
(C) understandable [ʌ̀ndərstǽndəbəl] ★
(D) academic [æ̀kədémik]

지문의 단어 "정확한"의 의미와 가장 유사한 것은?

(A) 인기있는
(B) 올바른
(C) 이해할 수 있는 ★
(D) 학문적인

Vocabulary 지문의 accurate(정확한)과 동의어인 correct(올바른)이 정답이다.

04 According to paragraph 5, which of the following is true about the Incan conquests over other tribes?

(A) The Incan leaders generally only ~~took~~ over areas where the people were the friendliest to them. ★
(B) No one really knows what truly happened in them because of the lack of verifiable sources outside of the Incan community.
(C) They were misrepresented in the histories recorded by the ~~Spanish~~ in order to further weaken the Incan Empire.
(D) The vast expanse of the Inca empire was the result of its leaders' ~~righteousness and strength~~.

단락 5에서 잉카의 정복에 대해서 옳은 것은?

(A) 잉카의 지배자들은 대체적으로 자기한테 제일 친절하게 대해주는 사람들이 있는 ~~곳만~~ 정복했다. ★
(B) 잉카의 지역사회 밖에 사실성을 증명해줄 정보통이 부족했기에 정말 어떤 일들이 일어났는지 확실하게 알 수 있는 사람은 없다.
(C) 그들은 잉카 제국을 더 약화시키기 위해서 ~~스패인은~~ 역사에 헛되게 기록을 했다.
(D) 잉카 제국의 광대한 영토는 지배자들의 ~~정의와 강인함이~~ 이루어낸 결과였다.

Fact 질문의 키워드인 conquests of the Incan Civilization이 언급된 부분을 살펴보면 the Incan leaders were the only sources of Spanish knowledge of their empire (스페인에게 잉카 지도자들은 그들의 제국에 관한 유일한 정보통이었다)라고 말한다. 즉, 잉카에게는 자신이 더 친숙한 사람들을 모으고 나머지는 다른 곳으로 분포 시키는 경우가 많아서 잉카 사회 말고는 그 사실을 증명해 줄 수 있는 사람이나 증거가 부족했기 때문에 정답은 (B)가 된다. (A)는 자기한테 친숙한 사람들이 사는 지역만을 지배한 것이 아니라, 친숙하지 않은 사람들을 그들로 대체시킨 것이기 때문에 오답이고, (C)는 잉카인들이 자기자신들의 역사를 왜곡시킨 것이기 때문에 오답이다. (D)는 잉카 지배자들이 진짜 정의롭고 강인했던 것이 아니라, 자기 자신들이 그렇게 보이게 기록을 조작했기 때문에 오답이다.

TEST 5 - 2
Architectural Change in Eighth Century Japan

01 The term "dramatic" in the passage is closest in meaning to

(A) Remarkable [rimá:rkəbəl]
(B) Apparent [əpǽrənt, əpéər-] ★
(C) Interesting [íntəristiŋ, -trəst, -tərést-]
(D) Gradual [grǽdʒuəl]

지문의 단어 "급격한"의 의미와 가장 유사한 것은?

(A) 놀랄 만한
(B) 명백한 ★
(C) 흥미로운
(D) 점진적인

Vocabulary 지문의 dramatic(급격한)과 동의어인 remarkable(놀랄 만한)이 정답이다.

02 What can be inferred from paragraph 2 about early Japanese marriage customs?

(A) Living with the bride's family allowed the imperial in-laws a greater influence over the royal court.
(B) They, needing more rudimentary architectural styles, provided a ~~catalyst~~ for changes in architectural structures. ★
(C) They were feasible in the contemporary period because they were needed to make the ~~already big~~ royal court system even bigger.
(D) The imperial family married into families with large landholdings so they could gain the property needed to ~~build more palaces~~.

단락 2에 따르면 옛날 일본의 결혼 관습에 대하여 추론할 수 있는 것은?

(A) 왕의 처가들은 신부의 가족과 함께 삶으로써 왕궁에 더 많은 영향력을 행사할 수 있었다.
(B) 더 간단한 건축 스타일을 필요했던 그들은 건축구조의 변화에 카폭제를 제공해 주었다. ★
(C) 그들은 ~~아마 컸던~~ 왕궁시스템을 더 크게 만들게하기 위해 필요했기 때문에 당시에 가능했다.
(D) ~~더 많은 궁궐들을 짓기~~ 위한 땅을 얻기 위해서 왕의 가족들은 땅이 많은 가족들과 결혼했다.`

Inference 질문의 키워드인 early Japanese marriage customs이 언급된 부분을 살펴보면 문제의 내용이 포함된 단락 2를 보면 Prior to this period, Japanese rulers married members of one of the most powerful clans of the period, the Soga lords' families, in politically motivated alliances, and established palaces at the bride's family home in addition to that of their own family headquarters. (이 시기 이전의 일본의 지도자들은 그 당시에 가장 영향있던 가문 중 하나인 소가 가문과 정치적 의도를 띤 결혼을 하였고, 자기 가족의 궁전에 추가로 신부의 집에까지 궁전을 지었다)라고 말한다. 즉, 왕의 처가들이 결혼을 정치적인 연합을 위해 했기 때문에 신부의 가족과 같이 살면서 왕궁에 더 많은 영향력을 가할 수 있었을 것이라고 유추할 수 있다. 따라서 답은 (A)가 된다. (C)는 그 당시의 왕궁시스템은 작았다고 본문에 언급되기 때문에 오답이고, (D)는 결혼은 정치적인 이유에서 나왔지 땅을 얻기 위해 나온 것은 아니기 때문에 오답이다. (B)는 This system was workable during this period because of the relatively small royal court and rudimentary architectural styles. 옛날 일본의 결혼 관습이 가능했던 이유는 간단한 건축 구조 덕분이었다. 하지만, 이런 관습에 변화가 생기면서 더욱더 복잡한 구조가 요구되었고 이것이 건축 스타일 변화에 큰 기폭제 역할을 한 것이기 때문에 오답이다.

03

What does the word "them" refer to in the passage?

(A) stone foundations ★
(B) mortise joints
(C) roofs
(D) buildings

지문에서 "them"이 의미하는 것은?

(A) 돌 기반 ★
(B) 장부 이음들
(C) 지붕들
(D) 건물들

Reference them이 언급된 부분을 살펴보면 Japanese architects looked to the urban design and construction techniques of their continental neighbors' geometrically situated capitals with their bulkier, more permanent buildings constructed using stone foundations, mortise joints, and tiled roofs which allowed them to stand for years.(일본의 건축가들은 그들의 대륙의 이웃들의 도시적 디자인과 건축 기술들을 본받았다. 그 대륙의 이웃들의 건물들은 돌 기반, 장붓 구멍 연결체, 그리고 기와지붕들을 사용한 더 부피가 크고 영구적인 건물들을 만들어 이 건물들은 몇 년씩 서 있을 수 있었다)라고 말한다. 즉, permanent buildings(영구적인 건물들)을 만들기 위해 다양한 건축 기술이 도입 되었고, 이것들이 모여 them을 오랫동안 서 있을 수 있도록 가능케 한 것이니까 정답은 (D)가 된다.

04

Why does the author mention that Hōryū-ji the "one of the oldest surviving wooden structures in the world" in paragraph 5?

(A) To show that structures built in Japan during the Nara period were the ~~most~~ durable buildings that had ever been created
(B) To contrast the great permanence of a Buddhist structure from the Nara period with the short period of usefulness of previous Japanese construction projects
(C) To give an idea of the ~~new type~~ of building materials used to construct Buddhist temples in Japan during the Nara period ★
(D) To introduce the idea that even though the Buddhist structures were more durable, they were ~~similar to~~ earlier buildings constructed of wood

단락 5에서 작가는 왜 호려지가 "세계에서 가장 오래 남아있는 건물 중의 하나"라는 말을 하는 것인가?

(A) 나라시대에 일본에 만들어진 건물들이 역사상 가장 튼튼한 건물이라는 것을 보이기 위해서
(B) 나라시대의 불교 건물들의 엄청난 영구성을 그 전 일본의 건축물들의 짧은 생명과 대조하기 위해서
(C) 나라시대의 일본 절을 만들 때 쓰인 새로운 종류의 건축재료가 무엇이었는지 알려주기 위해서 ★
(D) 불교 건물들이 더 튼튼했지만 나무로 만들었기 때문에 그 이전의 건물들과 ~~비슷했다는~~ 아이디어를 소개하기 위해서

Purpose 음영 표시된 부분을 살펴보면 During the Nara period, the Japanese Buddhists built temple complexes modeled after those found in continental nations, such as the Hōryū-ji, one of the oldest surviving wooden structures in the world.(나라시대에 일본 불교인들은 대륙의 나라들에 있는 절들을 본떠 절 건물들을 만들었는데 그 중 하나인 호려지는 세계에서 가장 오래된 남아있는 나무 건물들 중 하나이다) 라고 말한다. 즉, 음영 표시된 문장은 호려지와 나라시대의 새로운 건물들의 영구성을 강조하기 위한 문장이기 때문에 정답은 (B)가 된다(답근거는 끼워넣기 문장이다. 실제 토플에서 어려운 유형 참고할 것). (A)는 가장 튼튼한 건물이라는 내용은 언급되지 않으므로 오답이고, (C)는 호려지를 건설하 는데 사용된 재료는 나무, 즉, 전에도 사용하던 재료이기 때문에 오답이다. (D)는 불교 건물들이 나무로 만들어졌기 때문에 그 이전의 똑같이 나무로 만든 건물들과 비슷했던 것은 사실이지만, 그 비슷함을 강조하기 위해 음영 표시된 문장이 언급된 것은 아니기 때문에 오답이다.

TEST 6 - 1
How Camels Survive in Arid Environments

01 The term "mechanisms for" in the passage is closest in meaning to

(A) benefits of [bénəfit əv]
(B) need for [ni:d fər] ★
(C) means of [mi:nz əv]
(D) importance [impɔ́ːrtəns]

지문의 단어 "-을 위한 체계"의 의미와 가장 유사한 것은?

(A) -의 장점
(B) -의 필요성 ★
(C) 수단
(D) 중요성

Vocabulary 지문의 mechanisms for(-을 위한 체계)와 동의어인 means of(수단)가 정답이다.

---

02 The term "diffusion" in the passage is closest in meaning to

(A) learning [lə́ːrniŋ]
(B) spread [spred]
(C) adoption [ədápʃən] ★
(D) teaching [tíːtʃiŋ]

지문의 단어 "확산"의 의미와 가장 유사한 것은?

(A) 배움
(B) 전파
(C) 채용 ★
(D) 가르침

Vocabulary 지문의 diffusion(확산)과 동의어인 spread(전파)가 정답이다.

---

03 What can be inferred from paragraph 5 about the importance of the hump for camels living in desert regions?

(A) The storage of fat in the hump effectively reduces the temperature of the camel in hot environments.
(B) The hump stores fat that the camel can metabolize to ~~form water~~ when it hasn't been able to find water for a long time. ★
(C) The hump assists in keeping the whole body ~~warm at night~~ with the heat retained during the day.
(D) Camels' humps are ~~confirmed~~ to ~~hold water~~ and misunderstood to dissipate heat more easily.

단락 5에서 사막 지역에 사는 낙타들의 혹의 중요성에 관해서 추론할 수 있는 것은?

(A) 혹에 지방을 저장하는 것은 뜨거운 환경에 있는 낙타의 온도를 감소시킨다.
(B) 혹은 낙타가 오랜 시간 동안 물을 찾을 수 없었을 때 ~~물을 만들기~~ 위해서 낙타가 대사할 수 있는 지방을 저장한다. ★
(C) 혹은 낮에 유지한 ~~열을 저녁에~~ 사용함으로써 몸 전체를 따뜻하게 해준다.
(D) 낙타의 혹은 물을 ~~저장한다고~~ 확인되었고 열을 더 쉽게 소멸시킨다고 잘못 이해되었다.

Inference 질문의 키워드인 importance of the hump가 언급된 부분을 살펴보면 Fat cells hold in body heat, so by having most of their fat concentrated on their backs, camels can more easily dissipate heat, reducing their internal temperatures.(지방 세포들은 몸의 체온을 유지하기 때문에, 대부분의 지방을 혹에 집중함으로써 낙타들은 열을 더욱 쉽게 없앨 수 있으며 내부 체온을 낮출 수 있다)라고 말한다. 혹에 지방을 저장해 둠으로써 낙타들은 열을 더욱 쉽게 없앨 수 있었다는 것이니까 정답은 (A)가 된다. (B)는 지방이 대사될 때 물이 생산되는 것은 맞지만 그 과정에서 다 소멸됨으로 오답이고, (C)는 본문에 언급되는 내용이 아니므로 오답이다. (D)는 Commonly thought to hold water, these humps are actually fat accumulations. 즉, 낙타의 혹이 처음엔 물을 저장한다고 믿어졌으나, 사실 지방을 축적시킨다고 밝혀졌기 때문에 오답이다.

04

According to paragraph 7, which of the following is true of camels' way of avoiding dehydration and overheating?

(A) The camel is not only able to deal with high internal temperatures, but its body is also adapted to reduce the absorption of heat from its surroundings.
(B) Unlike heat gaining, the camels' physical attributes have relatively ~~little~~ relation to heat dissipation. ★
(C) Camels utilize ~~not~~ behavioral patterns ~~but~~ physiological and physical characteristics to avoid gaining heat.
(D) Despite the thin, light-colored wool's ~~lack~~ of skin protection from the harmful effects of the sun, it doesn't absorb much heat.

단락 7에 의하여 낙타가 탈수와 과열을 피하는 방법에 대하여 맞는 것은?

(A) 낙타는 높은 체온을 견딜 수 있을 뿐만이 아니라, 낙타의 몸은 주변으로부터 열을 흡수하는 것을 줄이게 적응되어 있다.
(B) 열을 얻는 것과는 다르게 낙타의 물리적 특성들은 열 분산과는 상대적으로 낮은 관계를 가지고 있다. ★
(C) 낙타들은 행동 패턴을 사용하는 ~~태신~~ 생리학적이고 육체적인 특성을 사용해 열을 얻는 것을 피한다.
(D) 태양의 해로운 영향들로부터 피부를 보호하는 능력이 ~~떨어짐에도~~ 불구하고 얇고 옅은 색의 털은 많은 양의 열을 흡수하지 않는다.

Purpose   질문의 키워드인 dehydration and overheating이 언급된 부분을 살펴보면 Their physical features and actions not only dissipate heat, but also avoid gaining heat altogether.(그들의 물리적인 특징들과 행동들은 열을 없앨 뿐만 아니라 얻는 것을 아예 방지한다)라고 말한다. 즉, 낙타는 높은 체온을 견딜 수 있는 육체적인 조건을 가지고 있을 뿐만 아니라 흡수되는 열의 양 또한 줄일 수 있는 능력을 가지고 있다. 따라서 정답은 (A)가 된다. (B)는 낙타의 물리적 특성은 두 영역 모두와 관련성이 깊기 때문에 오답이고, (C)는 본문에서 This is compounded by their natural proclivity for standing facing the sun, which reduces the amount of surface area directly exposed to the sun's ray.라고 설명한다. 즉, 낙타들은 태양을 바라보는 특정한 행동 패턴을 사용함으로써 열을 얻는 것을 피하기 때문에 (C)는 오답이다. (D)는 낙타의 털은 태양으로부터 피부를 보호할 수 있는 능력을 갖추고 있기 때문에 오답이다.

TEST 6 - 2
Hunter-gatherers in Southwest Asia

01 According to paragraph 2, which of the following is true of the effects of climate change in the Southwest Asian region?

(A) It caused the introduction of new forms of plant life that had not previously existed to ~~low lying~~ areas. ★
(B) It ~~depleted~~ the soil in the higher grounds that had been previously rich in nutrients.
(C) It allowed plants to spread out and produce more edible food products that the inhabitants could rely upon for sustenance.
(D) It caused the ~~demise~~ of the Kebaran society which could ~~no longer~~ migrate across the area due to the wetter weather.

단락 2에 따르면, 서남 아시아 지역의 기후 변화에 대한 사실이 아닌 것은?

(A) 이전까지 ~~저지대~~ 지역에 존재하지 않던 새로운 식물들의 출현을 일으켰다. ★
(B) 이전에 영양소가 풍부했던 높은 고도의 토양을 ~~고갈시켰다.~~
(C) 식물들이 확산하고 거주자들이 생존을 위해 의존하는 음식 제품들을 더 많이 제공할 수 있게끔 했다.
(D) 강수량이 많은 기후에 의해 ~~더 이상~~ 이주하지 못한 케바란 사회의 ~~종말을~~ 일으켰다.

> **Fact** 질문의 키워드인 effects of climate change가 언급된 부분을 살펴보면 As temperatures rose, plants that required the warmer temperatures of lower altitudes spread to higher altitudes. (기온이 상승하면서 낮은 고도의 따뜻한 온도를 필요로 했던 식물들은 더 높은 고도로 확산되었다)라고 말한다. 즉, 기존에 저지대에서만 발견되었던 식물들이 고지대로 확산되면서 사람들에게 더 많은 식량을 제공해주었다는 것이다. 따라서 정답은 (C)가 된다. (A)는 저지대에 새로운 식물들이 생긴것이 아니라 고지대이므로 오답이고, (B)는 they moved from the lower altitude's sandy soil to the richer, clay-based soil of higher altitudes 에서 기후의 변화와 함께 높은 고도의 토양이 전보다 더 영양분이 풍부해졌다는 것이기 때문에 오답이다. (D)는 케바란 문명은 많은 강수량 때문에 이주를 못해서 무너진 것이 아니라 기후 변화 덕분에 수확량을 증가시킬 수 있었던 나투피안 문명이 성장하면서 무너진 것이기 때문에 오답이다.

02 According to paragraph 4, which of the following is true about the settlements of the Natufian Civilization?

(A) They had a great ~~impact~~ on the types of crops that grew near them.
(B) They even performed massive game drives to complement their ~~deficient~~ nourishment. ★
(C) They were situated in places that would allow their inhabitants the best access to the supplies they needed to feed themselves.
(D) They were generally found in the ~~higher altitudes~~ because of the abundant nuts and grains that grew there.

단락 4에 따르면, 나투피안 문명의 정착지들에 대해 사실인 것은?

(A) 이들은 주변에 자라는 작물들의 종류에 큰 ~~영향을~~ 미쳤다.
(B) 이들은 ~~부족한~~ 영양분을 보충하기 위해 심지어 거대한 동물 사냥을 실시하였다. ★
(C) 이들은 거주자들이 자신들이 섭취하는데 필요한 재료들의 접근이 가장 좋은 장소에 정착했다.
(D) 이들은 풍부한 견과류와 곡식들이 자라는 ~~높은 고도에~~ 보통 발견 되었다.

> **Fact** 질문의 키워드인 settlements of the Natufian Civilization이 언급된 부분을 살펴보면 By settling in these places, they could harvest the cereal crops as they came into season during the spring and harvest nuts in the fall, providing year-round nourishment. (이런 장소에 정착하면서 이들은 봄에 제철이 되면서 곡식 작물들을 수확하고 가을에 견과류를 수확함으로써 일년 내내 영양분을 제공할 수 있었다)라고 말한다. 즉, 그들은 그들이 먹던 곡식들을 일년 내내 구할 수 있는 곳에 정착하였고, 또 이곳은 새로운 도구를 만들기에도 좋은 조건을 가지고 있었으므로 정답은 (C)가 된다. (A)는 The village locations were also affected by the crops they relied upon. 작물종이 정착지 위치에 영향을 미친 것이기 때문에 오답이고 (B)는 나투피안들은 자신들이 살고 있는 곳에서 봄에는 곡식 작물들을 수확하고, 가을엔 견과류를 수확하고, 여름과 겨울에는 저장된 작물들을 섭취하면서 이미 일년 내내 충분한 영양분을 섭취할 수 있었다. 거기에 더해, 주변 사람들과 협력하여 거대한 동물 사냥도 실시하였는데, They would even cooperate with neighboring communities to perform massive game drives 여기서의 "심지어"는 부족한 영양분을 보충하기 위해서가 아니라 이미 충분한 영양분을 더 확실하게 확보하기 위해서 이므로 오답이다. (D)는 They were generally located along the boundary between the coastal grasslands and the higher altitudes where nuts and cereals prosper 초원과 높은 고도 사이에 위치해 있었기 때문에 오답이다.

03

The term "relied upon" in the passage is closest in meaning to

(A) depended on [dipénd ɔn]
(B) predicted [pridíkt] ★
(C) developed from [divéləpt frəm]
(D) shaped by [ʃeip bait]

지문의 단어 "-에 의존하다"의 의미와 가장 유사한 것은?

(A) -에 의지하다
(B) 예상하다 ★
(C) -로부터 발전하다
(D) -에 의해서 형태가 잡히다

Vocabulary 지문의 relied upon(-에 의존하다)와 동의어인 depended on(-에 의지하다)가 정답이다.

04

The term "scale" in the passage is closest in meaning to

(A) duties [djúːti]
(B) importance [impɔ́ːrtəns] ★
(C) size [saiz]
(D) needs [niːdz]

지문의 단어 "규모"의 의미와 가장 유사한 것은?

(A) 의무
(B) 중요성 ★
(C) 크기
(D) 필요

Vocabulary 지문의 scale(규모)와 동의어인 size(크기)가 정답이다.

TEST 7 - 1
Life on Mars

01 According to paragraph 2, which of the following is NOT true regarding comparisons between the Earth and Mars?

(A) Mars and Earth are nearly the ~~identical size~~, but Earth has slightly ~~more land mass~~.
(B) Due to the slight margin between Earth's and Mars' axis, the two planets share similar climate patterns. ★
(C) The atmospheric composition of the planets is more similar to one another than it is to the other planets in the solar system.
(D) Mars revolves around the sun in the same habitable zone that allows the Earth to support life.

단락 2에 따르면, 아래 내용 중에서 지구와 화성 비교 내용 중에 틀린 것은?

(A) 화성과 지구는 거의 동일한 크기이지만, 지구가 화성보다는 약간 더 많은 육지 덩어리를 가지고 있다.
(B) 지구와 화성의 회전축 사이의 작은 차이 때문에 두 행성은 비슷한 기후 패턴들을 공유한다. ★
(C) 화성과 지구의 대기의 구성은 태양계 안의 다른 행성에 비해서는 더 유사하다.
(D) 지구로 하여금 생명체를 가지게 해준 것과 같은 살기 적합한 구역에서 화성은 돈다.

Fact 질문의 키워드인 Although Earth is much larger than Mars, they have nearly identical land surfaces. (비록 지구가 화성보다 훨씬 클지라도, 둘은 거의 똑같은 토지 면적을 갖고 있다.)라고 말한다. 즉, 지구는 화성보다 더 크기 때문에 정답은 (A)가 된다.

02 The term "remarkably" in the passage is closest in meaning to

(A) very closely [véri klóusli] ★
(B) surprisingly [sərpráiziŋli]
(C) usually [júːʒuəli]
(D) predictably [pridíktéibli]

지문의 단어 "두드러지게"의 의미와 가장 유사한 것은?

(A) 매우 가까이 ★
(B) 놀랍게
(C) 일반적으로
(D) 예상대로

Vocabulary 지문의 remarkably(두드러지게)와 동의어인 surprisingly(놀랍게)가 정답이다.

03 According to paragraph 3, which of the following is true regarding the possibility of life existing on Mars?

(A) The atmosphere of Mars is unable to support any life forms because ~~all~~ living organisms require oxygen to survive.
(B) Nighttime temperatures drop precipitously ~~due to~~ the planet's minimal atmosphere ~~doing little to prevent~~ deadly ultraviolet solar radiation from reaching its surface. ★
(C) Mars' thin atmosphere allows more solar radiation to reach the planet's surface than most currently known life forms can handle.
(D) The thin composition of Mars' atmosphere is toxic to every type ~~of organism but~~ oxygen-dependent organisms.

단락 3에 따르면, 화성에서의 생물체 존재의 가능성에 대한 내용으로 옳은 것은?

(A) 화성의 대기는 모든 살아있는 생명체는 살기 위해 산소를 요구하기 때문에 어떠한 생물체도 살 수 없다.
(B) 화성의 최저 대기가 치명적인 자외선이 표면에 닿는 것을 막지 못해서 밤 기온은 급격하게 떨어진다. ★
(C) 화성의 얇은 대기는 현재에 알려진 생명체들이 견뎌내기에는 더 많은 자외선이 들어오도록 허락한다.
(D) 화성의 얇은 대기는 산소에 의존하는 생물체 빼고 모든 종류의 생물체에게 해롭다.

Fact 질문의 키워드인 possibility of life existing on Mars가 언급된 부분을 살펴보면 In addition, Mars' minimal atmosphere does little to prevent deadly ultraviolet solar radiation from reaching its surface in the way that ozone gases in Earth's atmosphere do. 더군다나, 그 최저의 대기는 지구 대기 안의 오존 가스들이 자외선이 행성에 침투하는 것을 막아주는것 만큼 치명적인 자외선이 화성으로 들어오는 것을 막아 주지 못한다)라고 말한다. 즉, 화성은 지구의 오존 가스들과 같이 자외선을 차단하는 요소를 갖고 있지 않기 때문에 더 많은 자외선의 영향을 받을 수 밖에 없다. 따라서 정답은 (C)가 된다. (A)는 화성의 대기는 주로 이산화탄소로 구성되어 있지만 박테리아같이 이산화탄소만으로도 살아갈 수 있는 생명체들이 존재하기 때문에 오답이고, (B)는 밤온도가 급격하게 떨어지는 이유는 화성이 열을 유지하지 못하기 때문에 오답이다. (D)는 본문에선 산소에 의존하는 생물체들에게 특히나 해롭다고 설명하기 때문에 오답이다.

04 The term "tremendous" in the passage is closest in meaning to

(A) calm [kaːm]
(B) huge [hjuːdʒ]
(C) actual [ǽktʃuəl] ★
(D) beautiful [bjúːtəfəl]

지문의 단어 "엄청난"의 의미와 가장 유사한 것은?

(A) 차분한
(B) 거대한
(C) 실제의 ★
(D) 아름다운

Vocabulary 지문의 tremendous(엄청난)와 동의어인 huge(거대한)이 정답이다.

TEST 7 - 2
Agriculture and Settlement around the Nile River

01 The term "considerably" in the passage is closest in meaning to

(A) gradually [grǽdʒuəli]
(B) surprisingly [sərpráiziŋli] ★
(C) predictably [pridíktéibli]
(D) significantly [sɪgnífɪkəntli]

지문의 단어 "많이"의 의미와 가장 유사한 것은?

(A) 점차적으로
(B) 놀랍게 ★
(C) 예상 가능하게
(D) 상당히

Vocabulary 지문의 considerably(많이)와 동의어인 significantly(상당히)가 정답이다.

---

02 According to paragraph 5, which of the following is true regarding the food sources found in the Nile River valley?

(A) The ~~large~~ mammals found in the area provided the settlers with ~~most~~ of the protein they needed in their diets.
(B) Settlers were able to find most of the nourishment they needed in the valley due to a wealth of carbohydrate-rich foods.
(C) Despite a large number of ~~resident~~ bird species, the settlers preferred to catch fish to provide themselves with nourishment. ★
(D) The plants, seeds, fruit, and vegetables found in the region were ~~not nutritious~~, so the settlers ~~replaced~~ them with their imported crops.

단락 5에 의하면, 나일강 유역에서 발견된 식량 자원에 관해 사실인 것은?

(A) 그 지역에서 발견된 큰 포유 동물들은 정착민들이 ~~가장~~ 필요로 했던 단백질을 제공하였다.
(B) 정착민은 그들이 필요한 영양분의 대부분을 나일강 유역에서 많은 탄수화물이 풍부한 음식들 덕분에 찾을 수 있었다.
(C) ~~거주하는~~ 많은 수의 조류에도 불구하고, 정착민들은 영양분을 공급받기 위해 생선 잡기를 선호하였다. ★
(D) 그 지역에서 발견된 식물, 씨앗, 과일, 그리고 채소들은 ~~영양분이 없어서~~ 정착민들은 그들을 ~~수입된 농작물로 대체하였다.~~

Fact 질문의 키워드인 food sources found in the Nile River valley가 언급된 부분을 살펴보면 fish were the primary protein source, especially catfish. In addition, the seasonal variety of plant in the area gave them access to an abundance of carbohydrate-rich foods. (특히 메기와 같이 생선이 주요 단백질원이었다. 이외에도, 이 지역에 있는 계절별 식물들은 그들에게 탄수화물이 풍부한 음식의 풍요로움을 선사했다)라고 말한다. 즉, 나일 강 정착민들은 그 지역에 존재했던 영양가 많은 식물과 동물들에 의지하며 살아갔다는 것이기 때문에 정답은 (B)가 된다. (A)는 큰 포유동물들은 거의 존재하지 않았기 때문에 오답이고, (C)는 본문에서 resident가 아닌 migratory라고 설명하기 때문에 오답이다. (D)는 오히려 영양가가 많았기 때문에 정착민들에게 주요 공급원이었다고 본문에서 설명되기 때문에 오답이다.

---

03 What does the word "it" refer to in the passage?

(A) flooding [flʌ́dɪŋ]
(B) empire [émpaɪər]
(C) river [rívər]
(D) wealth [welθ] ★

지문에서 "it"이 의미하는 것은?

(A) 홍수
(B) 제국
(C) 강
(D) 재산 ★

Reference it이 언급된 부분을 살펴보면 Eventually, the fertile soils and predictable flooding of the river allowed the settlers to develop an empire whose wealth was based on the great agricultural bounty it was able to reap 에서 제국의 재산을 설명할 때 이것이 재배할 수 있었던 농업적 풍요로움이라고 설명한다. 즉, 제국이 재배할 수 있었던 농업적 풍요로움이 그 제국의 재산에 기반이 되었다는 것이기 때문에 정답은 (B)가 된다.

04

The term "widespread" in the passage is closest in meaning to

(A) important [impɔ́ːrtənt]
(B) advantageous [æ̀dvəntéiʒəs]
(C) common [kámən]
(D) complex [kəmpléks] ★

지문의 단어 "널리 퍼진"의 의미와 가장 유사한 것은?

(A) 중요한
(B) 유리한
(C) 흔한
(D) 복잡한 ★

Vocabulary 지문의 widespread(널리 퍼진)와 동의어인 common(흔한)이 정답이다.

TEST 부록
Sea Turtle Navigation

01 The word "Furthermore" in the passage is closest in meaning to

(A) similarly [símələrli] ★
(B) however [hauévər]
(C) in addition [in ədíʃən]
(D) in general [in dʒénərəl]

지문의 단어 "더욱이"의 의미와 가장 유사한 것은

(A) 비슷하게 ★
(B) 하지만
(C) 게다가
(D) 전반적으로

Vocabulary 지문의 furthermore(더욱이)와 동의어인 in addition(게다가)가 정답이다.

02 The word "precise" in the passage is closest in meaning to

(A) repeated [ripí:tid]
(B) fast [fǽst] ★
(C) unusual [ʌnjú:ʒəl]
(D) exact [igzǽkt]

지문의 단어 "정밀한"의 의미와 가장 유사한 것은?

(A) 반복되는
(B) 빠른 ★
(C) 특이한
(D) 정확한

Vocabulary 지문의 precise(정확한)와 동의어인 exact(정확한)이 정답이다.

03 The word "it" in the passage refers to

(A) evidence
(B) magnetic positioning
(C) sea turtle
(D) land

지문에서 "이것"이 의미하는 것은?

(A) 증거
(B) 자기장을 이용한 위치 확인
(C) 바다 거북이
(D) 땅

Reference it 이 언급된 부분을 살펴보면 Substantial evidence both for and against magnetic navigation led to the theory that while magnetic positioning plays a vital role in the open sea, far away from the destination, sea turtles use several other methods to complement it when they are young or when they are close to land 에서 거북이들이 목적지에서 멀리 있을 경우엔 자철석이 중요한 역할을 하기 때문에 다른 길 찾는 방법이 필요없다고 하나, 그들이 어리거나 육지와 가까이 있을 때는 다른 방법들을 동원해 이것을 보완할 필요가 있다고 설명한다. 즉, 목적지에서 멀리 떨어져 있을 때 중요한 역할을 하는 자기장의 효율성이 거북이들이 어리거나 육지와 가까이 있을 때는 떨어진다는 것을 알 수 있으며, 자기장을 이용한 위치확인을 보완하기 위해 다른 여러 방법을 사용할 필요가 있다는 것이기 때문에 정답은 (B)가 된다.

According to paragraph 6, which of the following statements is a characteristic of Grand Cayman Island?

(A) Hawksbill turtles from Grand Cayman Island have ~~migrated~~ to the Persian Gulf. ★
(B) The green sea turtle population of the island is yet to be recovered.
(C) It is now difficult for sea turtles to reach the island because of the ~~ongoing~~ habitat reconstruction.
(D) Grand Cayman Island is ~~still~~ home to the largest green sea turtle population due to a global decline in green sea turtle populations.

단락 6에 의하면, 다음의 문장들 중 그랜드 케이맨 섬의 특징인 것은?

(A) 그랜드 케이맨 섬의 대모 거북이들은 페르시안 만으로 ~~이주했다~~. ★
(B) 이 섬의 초록 바다 거북이 인구는 아직 회복되지 않았다.
(C) ~~계속 진행중인~~ 주거지 재건때문에 바다 거북이들이 이 섬으로 가는 것은 현재 어렵다.
(D) 그랜드 케이맨 섬은 세계적인 초록 바다 거북이 인구의 하락 때문에 ~~아직도~~ 가장 많은 수의 초록 바다 거북이 인구가 사는 곳이다.

Fact 질문의 키워드인 characteristic of Grand Cayman Island가 언급된 부분을 살펴보면 but after the turtles were driven off by humans, wildlife protection laws and habitat reconstruction have proven unsuccessful in bringing back the turtles. (하지만 사람들에 의해서 이 섬의 거북이들이 몰아내진 후에는, 야생 보호법과 주거지 재건은 바다 거북이들을 다시 데려오는 것에 효과가 없다는 것이 증명되었다)라고 말한다. 즉, 바다 거북이들은 자신들이 태어난 장소로 돌아가 서식하게 되어 있기 때문에 인간에 의해 한번 파괴된 바다 거북이 생태계는 다시 복구되기 힘든데, 그랜드 케이맨도 그런 서식지 중에 하나이고, 따라서 그곳에 서식하는 바다 거북이 인구는 아직 회복되지 않았다. 따라서 정답은 (B)가 된다. (A) 는 본문에 언급되는 내용이 아니고, 바다 거북이들은 대부분 자신들이 태어난 장소에서 서식하기 때문에 현재 페르시아 만에 거주하고 있는 바다 거북이들은 처음부터 페르시아 만에 거주했을 가능성이 높다. 따라서 (A)는 오답이고, (C)는 본문에서는 주거지 재건이 있었음에도 한번 파괴된 바다 거북이 생태계가 복구되는 것이 힘들다고 설명하기 때문에 오답이다. (D)는 그랜드 케이맨 섬엔 소수의 초록 바다 거북이만이 서식하고 있기 때문에 오답이다.

별도 구매 서비스 소개

usherin.usher.co.kr

1. USHER **단어암기** 프로그램 소개
2. **첨삭권** 소개
3. **인강**
4. **모의토플**
5. 토플 Reading 공부방법
6. 토플 Listening 공부방법
7. 수강 후기

USHER 단어암기 프로그램 소개

usherin.usher.co.kr

1. 듣고 - 아직도 눈으로만 외우나요?
어셔단어 프로그램에서는 듣고, 쓰고, 품사외우고, 동의어까지 한번에 진행합니다.

2. 말하고 - 아직도 발음을 못하나요?
발음 연습을 정확하게 프로그램이 읽어, 단어 외우면서 발음까지 한번에 준비할 수 있습니다.

3. 집중 암기하고 - 천천히 성장 VS 고성장
90일 동안 외울 단어를 13일 안에 끝내므로 반복효과 및 고성장을 이루어 낼수있습니다.

4. internet based test - 즉시채점+틀린것만 계속 테스트
틀린 단어들만 다시 시험보기가 가능합니다.

5. 기분좋은 성취 확인 - 향상 기록 personal trainer
본인이 본 시험 기록 내용이 누적 확인되어 본인에 성취를 확인 할수있습니다.

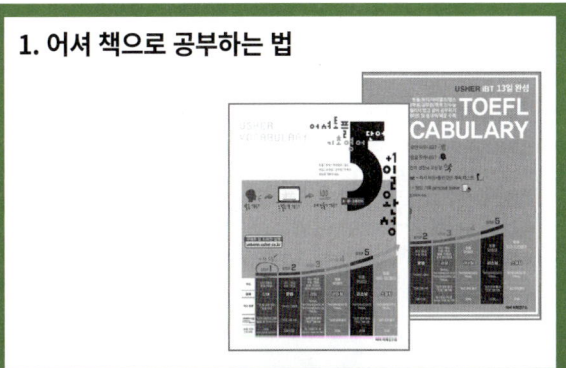

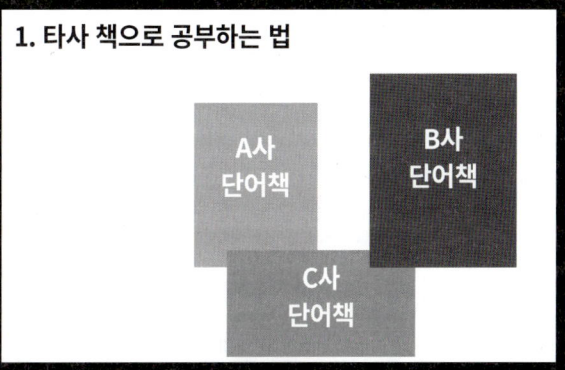

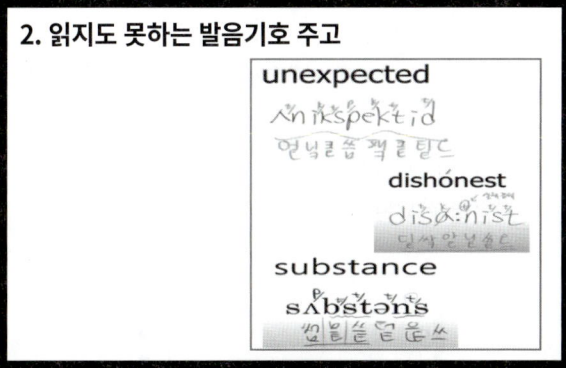

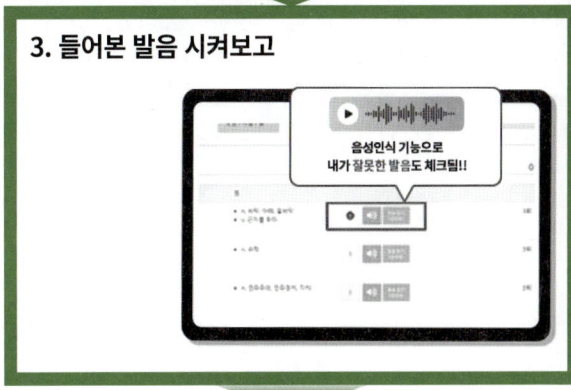

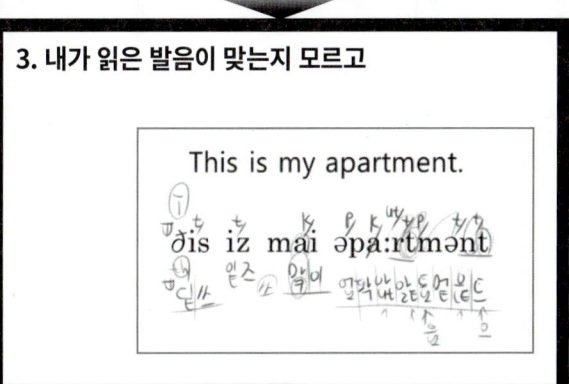

4. 인터벌

4. 빽빽이 써가면서 단어 외워야하는데

5. 분량을 나눠서 모의시험

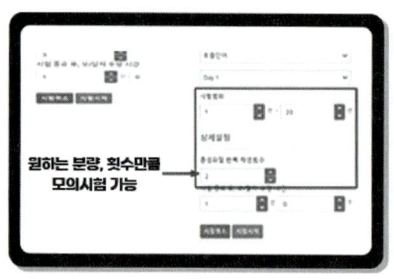

5. 빽빽이 써가면서 단어 외워야하는데

6. 준비되면 시전시험!
듣고 → 스펠링 → 품사 → 뜻 순으로 적기

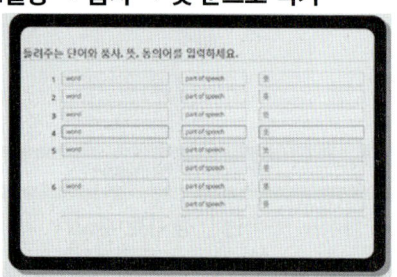

6. 학교 or 학원가서 종이에
한글 또는 스펠링 중 하나만 시험

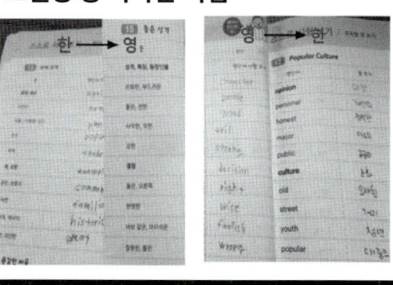

7. 하나라도 틀리면 오답처리
시험결과 자동체크

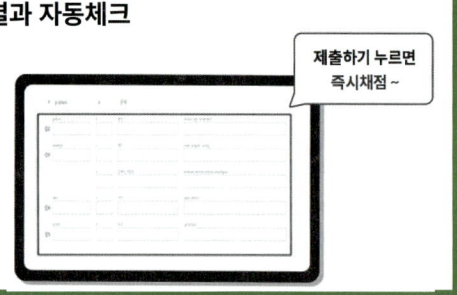

7. 채점을 내가 하면 잘못 외운 스펠링체크 못해주고
친구가 해주면 우정으로 틀린 것도 맞다고 해주고

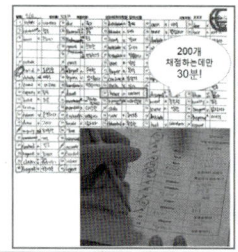

8. 틀린 단어 묶음으로 즉시 **오답노트** 만들어줌

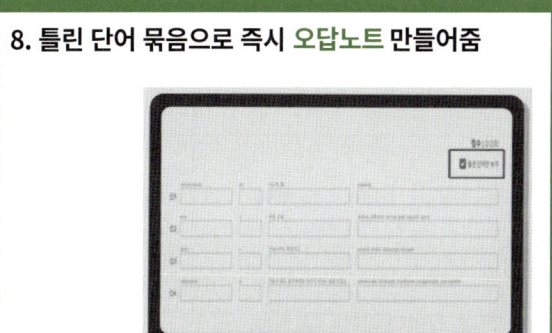

8. 내가 뭘 틀렸는지 일일히 추려내야 하지만… 보통은 보지도 않고 그냥 버리게 됨

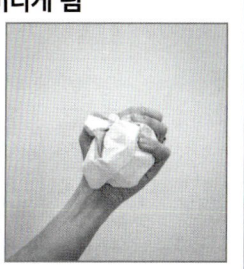

9. 틀린 개수 0으로 만들기 틀린 단어만 **재시험**

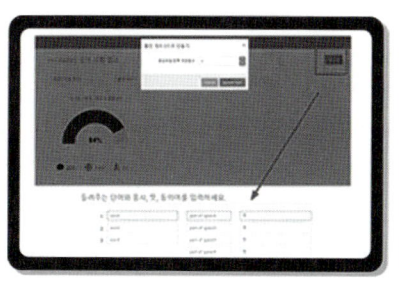

9. 틀린 단어가 뭔지 보지도 않고

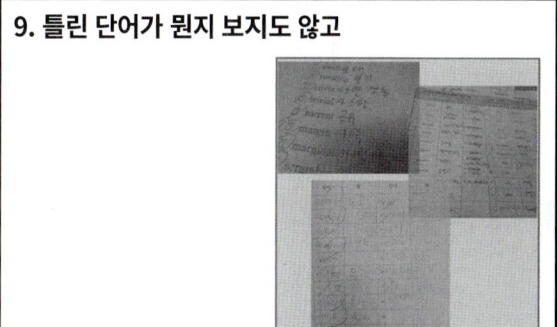

10. 한달 동안 시험 본 모든 기록 체크해주며 자극주는 시스템

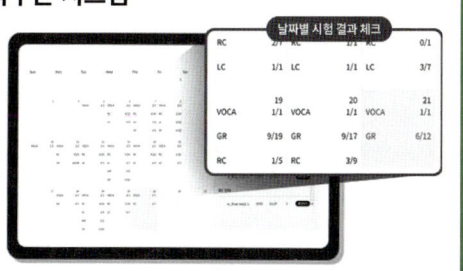

10. 종이가 너덜너덜해지면 그냥 버림

단어 프로그램 가격 소개

💬 카카오톡으로 문의하기

	1개월 사용	3개월 사용	6개월 사용
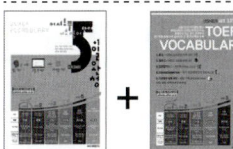 기초영단어	25,000원	~~75,000원~~ 60,000원 (1개월당 20,000원 20% DC)	~~150,000원~~ 84,000원 (1개월당 7,000원 44% DC)
토플단어	25,000원	~~75,000원~~ 60,000원 (1개월당 20,000원 20% DC)	~~150,000원~~ 84,000원 (1개월당 7,000원 44% DC)
기초영단어 + 토플단어	40,000원	~~120,000원~~ 90,000원 (1개월당 30,000원 25% DC)	~~240,000원~~ 108,000원 (1개월당 9,000원 55% DC)

2 첨삭권 소개
usherin.usher.co.kr

01 스피킹/라이팅 첨삭이 필요한 이유?

대체로 독학을 할 수 있다고 생각하는 리딩, 리스닝과는 달리 스피킹 라이팅은 독학이 힘듭니다.

이유는? "내가 뭘 틀렸는지 모르니까!!!"

대안은?? 독학이라고 했으니, 과외나, 학원은 빼고, 남는 건 첨삭이나, 그냥 혼자 틀린 걸 계속 보거나….

그런데, 첨삭을 받으러 검색을 해보면 가격이 라이팅 한편 당 23,000…원…?

한편만 첨삭 받으면 끝날 것 같진 않은 내 실력을 봐서는…

비용 감당 안됨. 어쩌지?

02 학원까지 다니고 싶진 않은데 스피킹/라이팅 첨삭만 받을 순 없나요?

▼라이팅 첨삭 *10회권은 어셔수강생에게만 제공됩니다*
(2024.08. 현재)

1회권	어셔	1회 첨삭권 25,000원	최저가 1회당 25,000원
	해**	1회권 없음 2회 첨삭권 54,000원	1회당 27,000원
	영**	1회 첨삭(1일 소요)권 28,000원	1회당(1일 소요) 28,000원
5회권	어셔	5회 첨삭권 100,000원	최저가 1회당 20,000원
	해**	5회권 없음	5회권 없음
	영**	5회 첨삭(1일 소요)권 119,000원	1회당(1일 소요) 23,800원
10회권 *어셔 수강생 한정	어셔	10회 첨삭권 150,000원	최저가 1회당 15,000원
	해**	10회권 없음	10회권 없음
	영**	10회권 없음	10회권 없음

▼스피킹 첨삭
(2024.08. 현재)

1회권	어셔	1회 첨삭권 15,000원	최저가 1회당 15,000원
	해**	1회권 없음 2회 첨삭권 54,000원	1회당 27,000원
	영**	1회 첨삭(1일 소요)권 16,000원	1회당(1일 소요) 16,000원
5회권	어셔	5회 첨삭권 60,000원	최저가 1회당 12,000원
	해**	5회권 없음	5회권 없음
	영**	5회 첨삭(1일 소요)권 68,000원	1회당(1일소요) 13,600원
10회권 *어셔 수강생 한정	어셔	10회 첨삭권 110,000원	최저가 1회당 11,000원
	해**	10회권 없음	10회권 없음
	영**	10회권 없음	10회권 없음

구매처 및 자세한 설명 usherin.usher.co.kr

03 첨삭 구성은 어떻게 되나요?

▼ 스피킹 첨삭

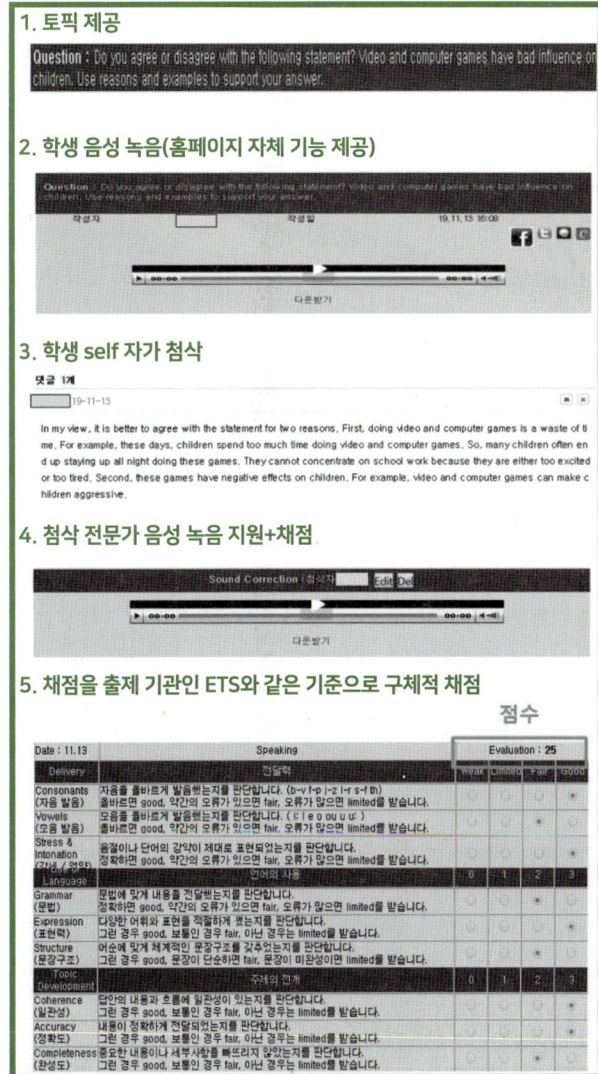

▼ 라이팅 첨삭

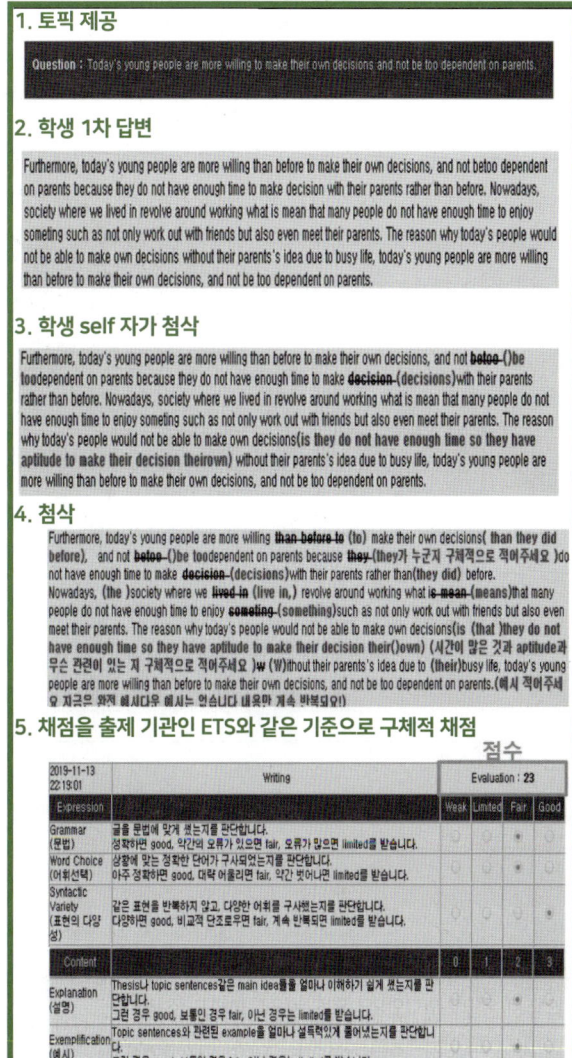

04 첨삭 신청하기

라이팅 첨삭권

10회권은 어셔수강생에게만 제공됩니다

1회 첨삭권	5회 첨삭권	10회 첨삭권
사용기간 15일	사용기간 30일	사용기간 60일
25,000원	~~125,000원~~ → 100,000원	~~250,000원~~ → 150,000원

스피킹 첨삭권

10회권은 어셔수강생에게만 제공됩니다

1회 첨삭권	5회 첨삭권	10회 첨삭권
사용기간 15일	사용기간 30일	사용기간 60일
15,000원	~~75,000원~~ → 60,000원	~~150,000원~~ → 110,000원

첨삭은 근무일 기준(평일)으로 진행되며, 주말 또는 휴일은 익일 평일에 진행됩니다.

3. 인강-리딩
usherin.usher.co.kr

목표	STEP 1 내신 1등급 수능 1등급	STEP 2 내신 1등급 수능 1등급	STEP 3 (이 책 수준) 내신 1등급 수능 1등급 토플 70점대 토익 800점대	STEP 4 토플 80점대	STEP 5 토플 90점대	STEP 6 토플 100~120점대
과목	단어	문법	리딩	라이팅	리스닝	스피킹
책의 종류	①초·중·고등 단어 ②토플 단어	①어셔인 그래머	①BASIC ②INTERMEDIATE 01 ③INTERMEDIATE 02 ④FINAL	①INTERMEDIATE ②FINAL	①INTERMEDIATE ②FINAL	①INTERMEDIATE ②FINAL
USHER어플 Study Tool	①단어시험프로그램 ②발음 체크(모든 단어)	①프로그램 4종	①실전 문제 풀이, 프로그램 3종	①실전 문제 풀이	①실전 문제 풀이, 프로그램 2종	①실전 문제 풀이
소요 시간 (1회 독해)	13일 (하루 200개 단어관리)	5일+10일	15~18일/각 권 (BASIC 1지문/1일 기준)	20일	20일	20일

나의 성격 PERSONALITY
INTP 미래 지향, 긍정

핵심 가치 CORE VALUE
성장 # 자조(스스로 돕는다) # 착함 # 긍정 # 정확함 # 결과 # 책임감 # 도전

나의 강점 STRENGTH
관리력 # 집중력 # 기획력 # 체계적 개발능력 # 집요함 # 속도

"할 얘기 많은" "멋진" 삶!!

수업 특징
- 단순화
- 긴장감
- 바뀔때까지

USHER
이덕호

나의 성격 PERSONALITY
ENTP
저는 유연성과 적응력을 가진 사람입니다. 성공의 길과 개인적 성장은 순식간에 이루어지는 것이 아닙니다. 하지만 저는 작은 발전의 단계를 거듭하면서 성장하고자 합니다. 저는 변화하는 세상에 꾸준히 적응하고, 그것을 통해 계속해서 성장하려고 합니다.

핵심 가치 CORE VALUE
저의 주된 가치는 꾸준함입니다. 어떤 일이든지 지속성이 있으면 결국 목표를 달성할 수 있다고 믿습니다.

나의 강점 STRENGTH
저는 변화하는 환경에 잘 적응하고, 다양한 상황에서 필요한 해결책을 발견하는 것을 잘합니다.

This Too Shall Pass
이 또한 지나가리라

VISION BIG5
건강한 삶 저는 몸과 마음이 건강한 삶을 추구합니다.
항상 배우기 저는 세상이 계속 변하고 발전하는 것처럼, 자신도 항상 새로운 것을 배우며 성장하고자 합니다.
긍정적인 삶 저는 긍정의 힘을 믿습니다. 긍정적인 태도를 가지고 삶을 대하고자 합니다.
인내심 저는 어려움을 겪을 때에도 인내심을 잃지 않고 목표를 향해 나아갑니다.
감사함 저는 삶의 모든 것에 감사의 마음을 가지고 그 감사의 마음을 통해 더 많은 긍정적인 에너지를 발산하고자 합니다.

USHER
김채운 부원장

USHER
김석균

나의 성격 PERSONALITY
ISTJ 현실주의자. 모든 일을 꾸준히 체계적으로

핵심 가치 CORE VALUE
#희망 #긍정 #재미

나의 강점 STRENGTH
#성실함 #솔직함 #원칙적 #긍정적 #체계적

하루아침에 되는것은 없다

VISION BIG5
1. 발전하는 하루 2. 건강한 신체 3. 활기찬 분위기
4. 겸손한 마음 5. 간결한 수업

4 모의토플
usherin.usher.co.kr

01 모의토플? 왜 봐야 하지?

Q1. 토플 시험 초보자
난 토플이 뭔지, 이름도 겨우 들었거나,
토플 공부를 해야한다는걸 겨우 알았는데,
일단, 내 실력이나 좀 보고,
대충 시험 구성부터 잡아 보고 싶다면?

A. 27만원짜리 진짜 토플 덜컥 잡고,
돈 날리지 말고,
일단 5만원짜리 모의 토플로,
어찌 생겼는지 파악하는 기회로 사용
바랍니다.

Q2. 영어 실력 충분히 있는 분?

A. 나는 영어 실력은 충분히 있는데,
그냥 시험 유형정도나 파악하고,
바로 시험 보면 되지 않을까?
라는 자신감이 있을 때,
실제 시험 전 몸풀기로 활용
바랍니다.

**Q3. 토플 공부를 하면서,
본인의 실력 향상이 궁금하신 분**

A. 이제 한달 공부 했는데,
내 공부 한 것이 얼마나 나아졌을지
궁금하다면, 실력 점검용으로
활용 바랍니다.

**Q4. 실제 시험전에 최종 확인을
원하시는 분**

A. 실제 시험장을 가야 하는데,
계속 종이로만 공부해서,
실제 토플시험장에서 모니터 적응과,
라이팅에서의 타이핑 적응등이
부족하다는걸 안다면,
미리 시험장 분위기를 확인용이 활용
바랍니다.

02 왜 모의토플? 을 봐야 하는가?

▼상세설명

📖 Reading
가. 종이로 보는것과 컴퓨터로 보는 것 만으로도 심한경우 리딩 점수 30점 만점중, 5점 차이까지 나므로, 별도로 준비 해야합니다.
나. 밑줄치면 시험 보거나, 연필로 위치를 가리키며 시험을 보는것과, 마우스를 움직여 가며 보는 것을 다르게 느끼는 경우, 시험장 환경에 적응하기 위해
다. 시험장의 엄격한 시간 관리를 미리 준비해야 하므로
라. 내가 많이 틀린 문제 분석을 통해 어느 유형이 약한지 파악하기 위해
마. (선택: 내가 어느유형이 약한지 파악후, 추가 관련 문제의 인강을 통해 미진한 부분에 대한 설명을 듣기 위해)

🎧 Listening
가. 스피커를 통해 시험을 보는게 아닌, 헤드셋을 통해 나오는 소리에서의 차이를 어색해 하는 경우가 있다.
나. 시험장 화면에서, 가장 조심 해야 하는 것은, 리딩은 한번 본 화면도 다시 되돌아 와서 체크 할수있지만, 리스닝의 경우, 한번 진행한 문제는 되돌아 가서 수정이 안되는데, 연습 없는 학생들이 가장 어이없게 많이 하는 실수이므로, 실수를 방지하기 위해
다. 시험장의 엄격한 시간 관리를 미리 준비해야 하므로
라. 내가 많이 틀린 문제 분석을 통해 어느 유형이 약한지 파악하기 위해
마. (선택: 내가 어느유형이 약한지 파악후, 추가 관련 문제의 인강을 통해 미진한 부분에 대한 설명을 듣기 위해)

🎤 Speaking
가. 시험장에서 마이크에 대고 말하는 것은, 무조건 소리를 크게 내야하는데, 학생들의 경우, 옆에 잘 하는 학생들이 있을경우, 기가 죽어 목소리를 작게 내서, 본인 실력보다 낮은 점수를 받는 경우가 있으므로, 미리 연습해서 본인의 목소리가 얼마나 작게 녹음 되는지 확인 해볼 기회
나. 1번부터 4번까지 네 개의 문제 순서에 적응하여, 실제 시험당일 문제 순서에 당황할일 없게 하기 위해
다. 내가 어느 유형이 약한지 파악하기 위해
라. (선택: 시험 본 것을 "**첨삭**"으로 이어져, 내 실력의 문제를 점검하기 위해) - **별도서비스**
마. (선택: 내가 어느유형이 약한지 파악후, 추가 관련 문제의 인강을 통해 미진한 부분에 대한 설명을 듣기 위해)

✏️ Writing
가. 시험장에서 라이팅 시험은 모두 타이핑 시험인데, 시험장 갈때까지도 독수리 타자를 쳐야 할만큼 준비 없는 것을 막기 위해
나. (선택: 시험 본 것을 "**첨삭**"으로 이어져, 내 실력의 문제를 점검하기 위해) - **별도서비스**
다. (선택: 내가 어느유형이 약한지 파악후, 추가 관련 문제의 인강을 통해 미진한 부분에 대한 설명을 듣기 위해)

03 토플의 평가 영역(리딩, 리스닝, 스피킹, 라이팅) 및 어셔 모의토플 소개

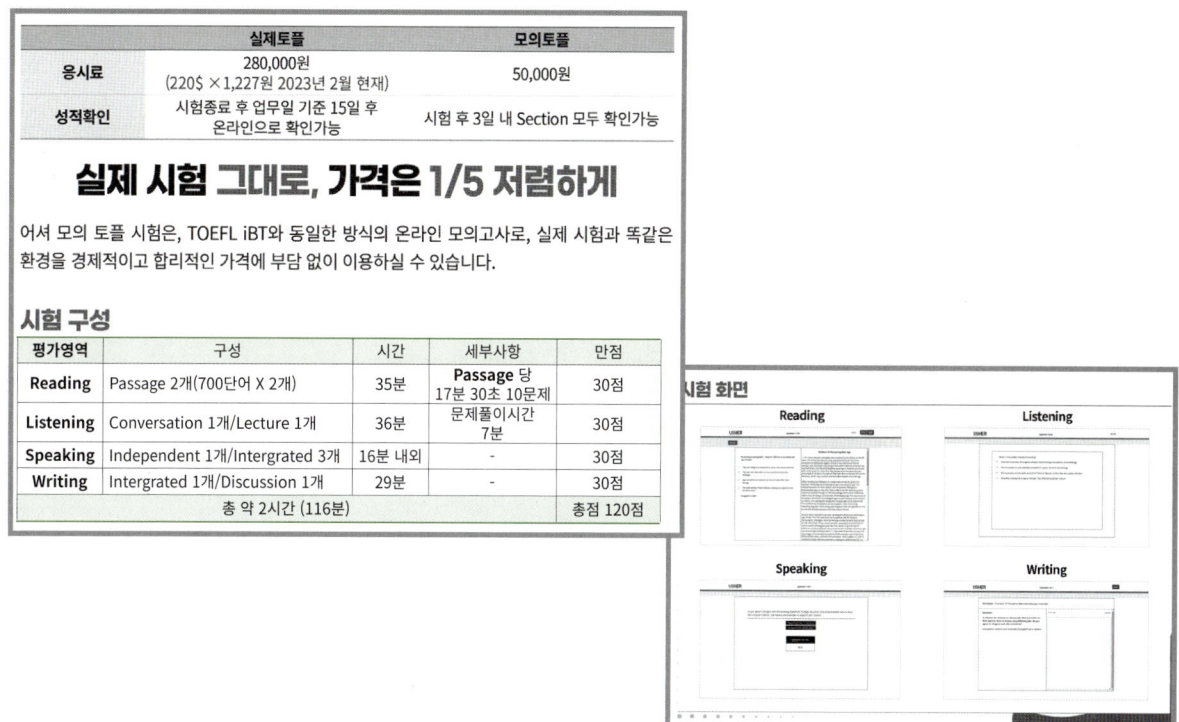

	실제토플	모의토플
응시료	280,000원 (220$ ×1,227원 2023년 2월 현재)	50,000원
성적확인	시험종료 후 업무일 기준 15일 후 온라인으로 확인가능	시험 후 3일 내 Section 모두 확인가능

실제 시험 그대로, 가격은 1/5 저렴하게

어셔 모의 토플 시험은, TOEFL iBT와 동일한 방식의 온라인 모의고사로, 실제 시험과 똑같은 환경을 경제적이고 합리적인 가격에 부담 없이 이용하실 수 있습니다.

시험 구성

평가영역	구성	시간	세부사항	만점
Reading	Passage 2개(700단어 X 2개)	35분	Passage 당 17분 30초 10문제	30점
Listening	Conversation 1개/Lecture 1개	36분	문제풀이시간 7분	30점
Speaking	Independent 1개/Intergrated 3개	16분 내외	-	30점
Writing	Intergrated 1개/Discussion 1개	29분	-	30점
총 약 2시간 (116분)				총점 120점

04 구매하기 (개별 과목 별도)

시험명	사용기간	가격
USHER 공식 토플모의고사 Full TEST	1년	50,000원
USHER 공식 토플모의고사 Half(R/L) TEST	1년	27,000원
USHER 공식 토플모의고사 Half(S/W) TEST	1년	27,000원
개별 과목	1년	15,000원

5 토플 Reading 공부방법
usherin.usher.co.kr

리딩 점수에 따라서

- 20점 미만이라면, 리스닝에는 너무 많은 힘을 쓰지 말고, 단어와 리딩에 집중 바랍니다.
  둘 다 하려다 하나도 못 할 수 있습니다.
- 20점 이상이라면, 1. 단어 2. 구문 3. 묶기 4. 열번읽기 까지 꼼꼼히 처리 바랍니다.
- 25점 이상이면, 단어, 구문은 거의 알 겁니다.
  대략 틀린 것 정도 간단히 마무리 하고 **묶기 및 오답 패턴 확인**에 집중하면 됩니다.

각각의 과정을 적으면 다음과 같습니다.

Step 1. 문제풀이
Step 2. TAGGING
Step 3. 구문 / 단어시험
Step 4. 묶기
Step 5. 타이핑
Step 6. 별지
Step 7. 접속사 암기

과정 순서대로 공부를 해야하는 구체적인 이유와 방법을 적어보겠습니다.

Step 1. 문제 풀이

- 문제 풀이는 실전 화면처럼 컴퓨터로 직접 풀면서 익숙해지는게 좋습니다.

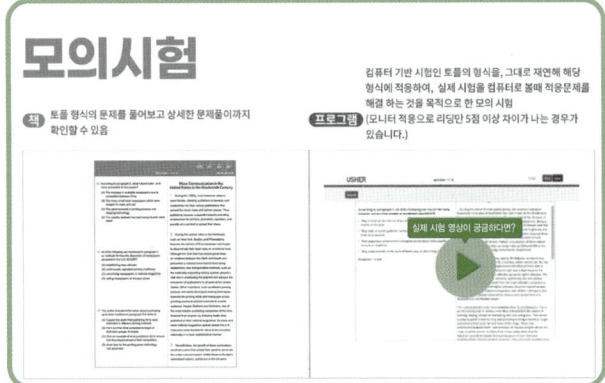

Step 2. TAGGING

- 문제 풀이 직후, 잊기 전에, 문제 풀면서 가장 짜증 났던 부분 = 즉, 이해하기 힘들었던 부분을 체크해 둬야 합니다.

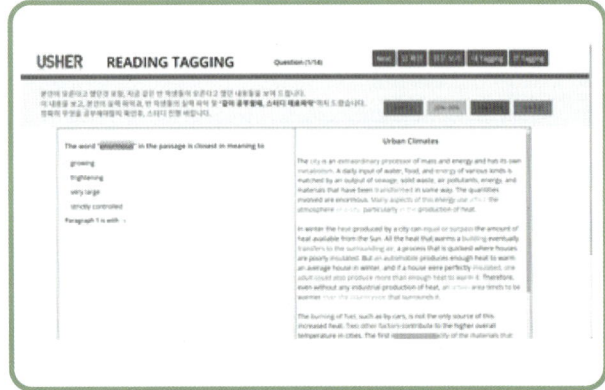

Step 3. 구문 / 단어 시험

- 귀찮은 거 압니다. 그래도 해두시기 바랍니다. 리딩 20점 미만은 실력 없어서 하기 싫어도 해야 하고, 리딩 25점 넘는 분들은 별로 할 것도 없겠지만, 그래도 다 챙겨 두시기 바랍니다.

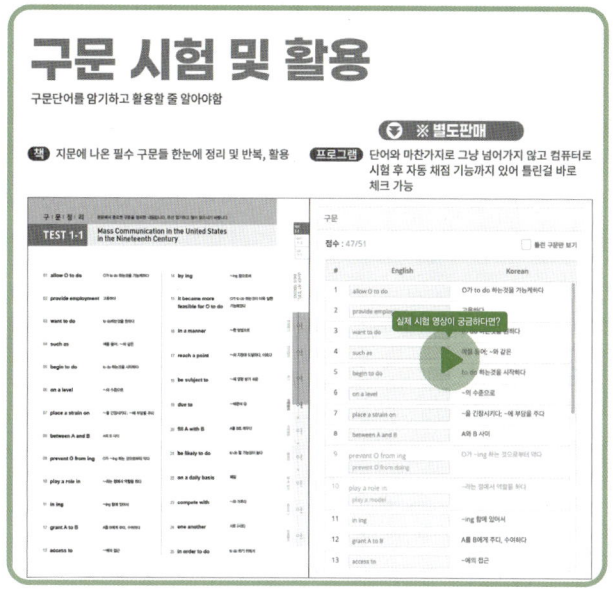
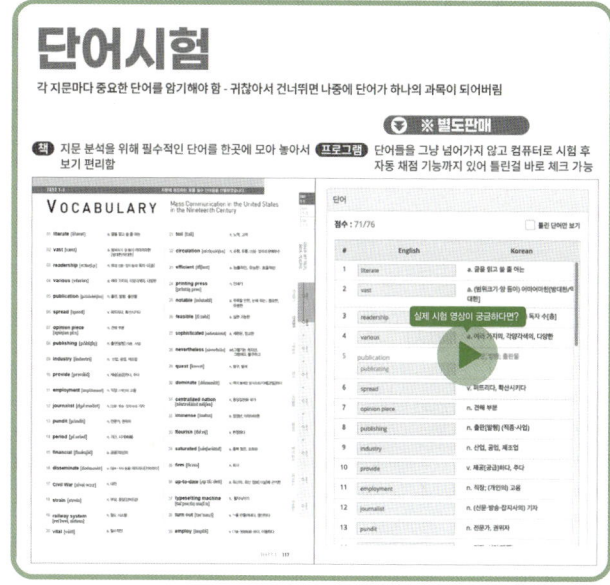

Step 4. 묶기

- 리딩 20점 미만은 실력이 없으니, 파악+ 실력 자체를 늘리기 위해 필요합니다.
- 리딩 25점 이상은 만점 받기 위해서, 본인이 어느 부분이 약한지 "샅샅이 훑어야 할 때", 가장 강력한 툴입니다.
  "30점의 절박함과 귀찮음 중", 더 강한 것이 여러분의 행동을 바꿀겁니다.

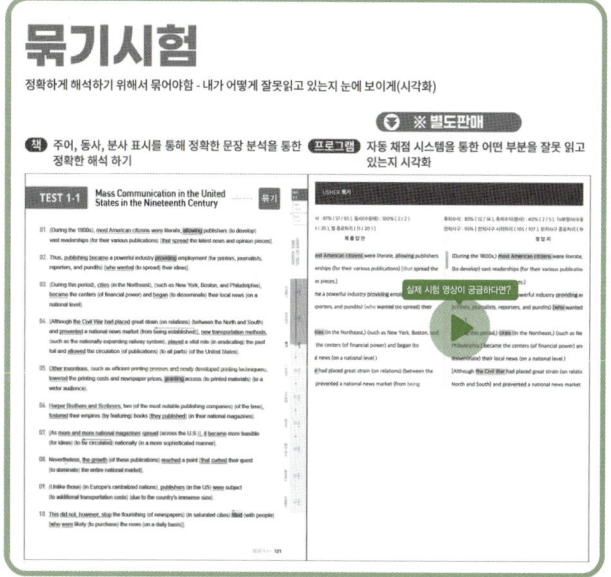

Step 5. 열번읽기(내 발음 체크 = 말 할 수 있으면 들린다)

- 리딩 20점 미만의 학생들에게 가장 중요한 점은 "말 할 수 없으면, 들을 수 없다!!!" 입니다.
- 본인만 아는 이상한 발음으로 기억하면, 절대 못듣습니다.
  이그제그래이션? Exaggeration을 이렇게 읽는 학생. 답 없습니다.
- 말 할 수 있는지는, 학원 프로그램이 모두 파악해 줍니다. 채점까지.
  여러분은 성실함만 있으면 됩니다.

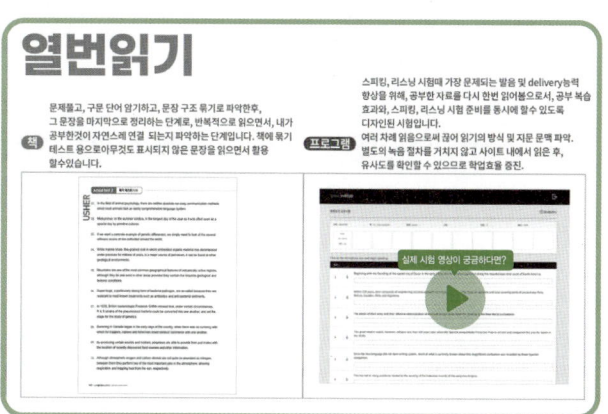

Step 6. 타이핑

- 라이팅 시험은 영타가 기본인데, 이를 따로 준비하는것이 아닌, 공부한 자료를 반복 연습함서, 영타와 복습을 동시에 진행 가능케 하는 시험
- 주어진 문장을 따라 써 보며 정확도와 속도를 올려, 문맥 파악과 더불어 컴퓨터 기반 시험인 토플에서 고득점 하기 위한 필수 역량을 증진

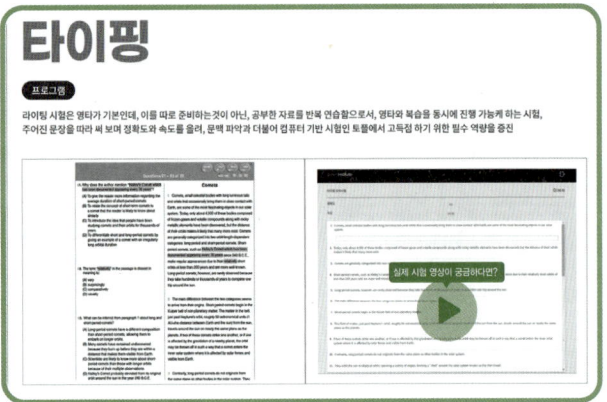

Step 7. 별지

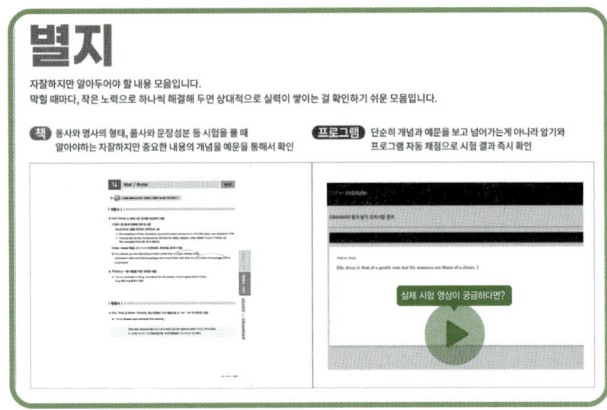

Step 8. 접속사 암기

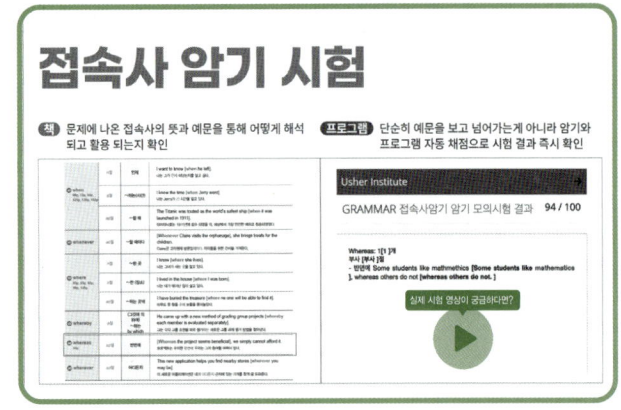

어셔어학원을 다니면,

어셔어학원을 다니면, 이 과정을 모두 스터디 시간에 **무료**로 합니다.
하지만, 사정이 있어서 **인강을 듣거나 프로그램만 구매하시는 분들은**
반드시, 위 내용들을 기억하고, 실행하면, 실력 향상에 큰 도움 되실겁니다.

6. 토플 Listening 공부방법

usherin.usher.co.kr

리스닝 점수에 따라서

- 20점 미만이라면, 리스닝에는 너무 많은 힘을 쓰지 말고, 단어와 리딩에 집중 바랍니다.
  둘 다 하려다 하나도 못 할 수 있습니다.
- 20점 이상이라면, 1. 단어 2. 구문 3. 딕테이션 4. 열번읽기 까지 꼼꼼히 처리 바랍니다.
- 25점 이상이면, 단어, 구문은 거의 알 겁니다.
  대략 틀린 것 정도 간단히 마무리 하고 **딕테이션 및 오답 패턴 확인**에 집중하면 됩니다.

각각의 과정을 적으면 다음과 같습니다.

Step 1. 문제풀이
Step 2. TAGGING
Step 3. 구문 / 단어시험
Step 4. 딕테이션
Step 5. 열번읽기 (내 발음 체크 = 말 할 수 있으면 들린다)
Step 6. 타이핑

과정 순서대로 공부를 해야하는 구체적인 이유와 방법을 적어보겠습니다.

Step 1. 문제 풀이
- 문제 풀이는 실전 화면처럼 컴퓨터로 직접 풀면서 익숙해지는게 좋습니다.

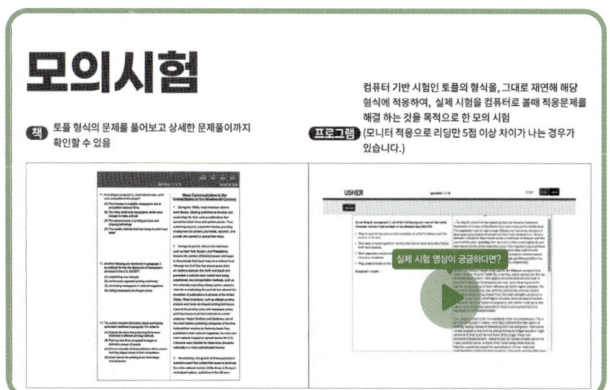

Step 2. TAGGING
- 문제 풀이 직후, 잊기 전에, 문제 풀면서 가장 짜증 났던 부분 = 즉, 이해하기 힘들었던 부분을 체크해 둬야 합니다.

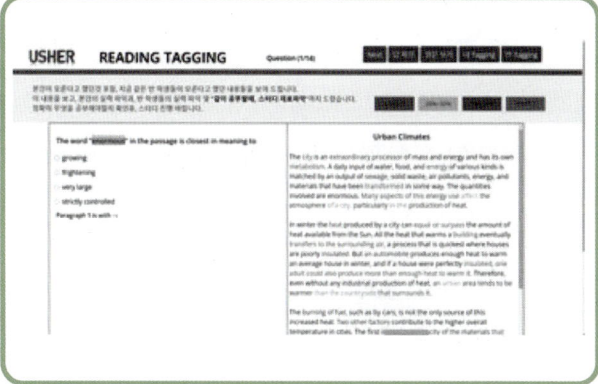

Step 3. 구문 / 단어 시험

- 귀찮은 거 압니다. 그래도 해두시기 바랍니다.

Step 4. 딕테이션

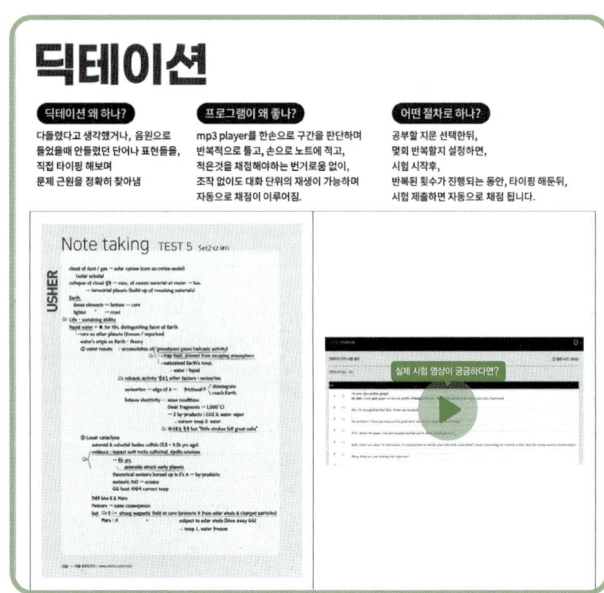

Step 5. 열번읽기(내 발음 체크 = 말 할 수 있으면 들린다)

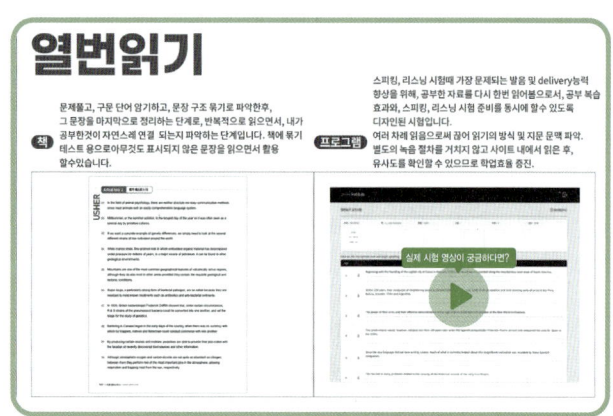

Step 6. 타이핑

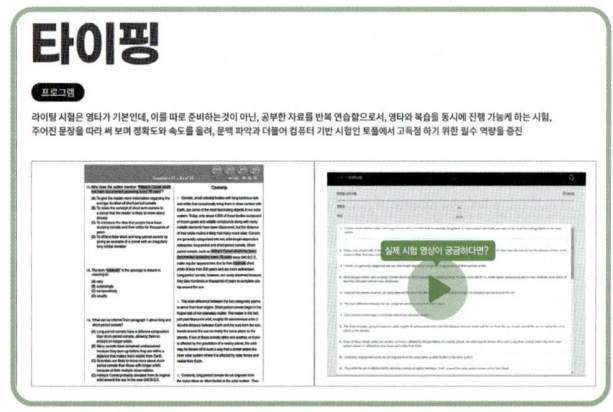

7 수강 후기
usherin.usher.co.kr

김유석
97점 두달간 토플 시험에서의 승리: 훌륭한 교사진, 함께 노력한 학원 동료들에게 감사를

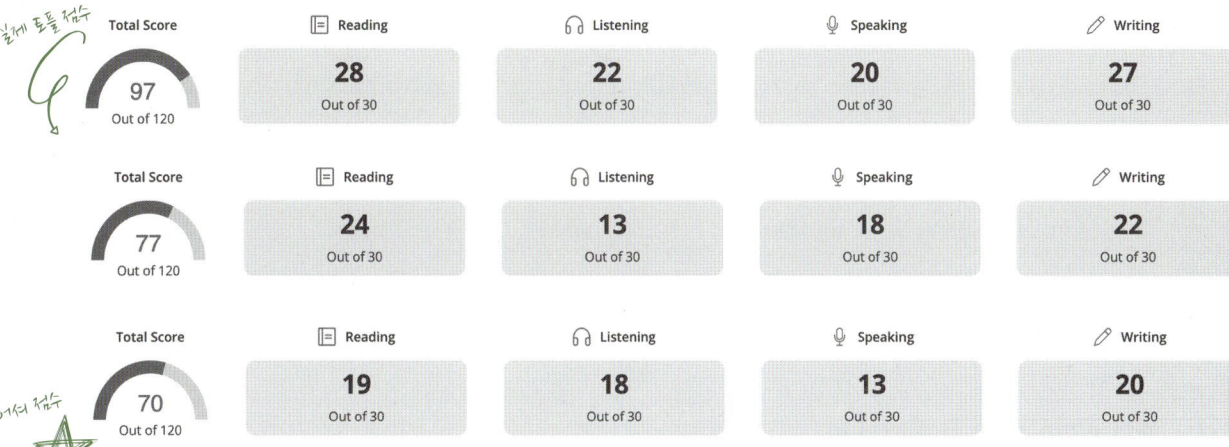

반배치고사		GR			RC	LC
일자	반	SW1	SW2	SW1+SW2		
2024-03-29	성인 정규 Intermediate반	10	18	28	32	23
2024-02-29	성인 정규 Intermediate반	11	11	22	28	22
2024-01-23	신규	9	13	22	25	

모의토플					
일자	RC	LC	SP	WR	합계
2024-03-15	17	25	19	20	81
2024-02-16	22	19	0	0	41

2024.03 성인교육중급반 김유석 성취표

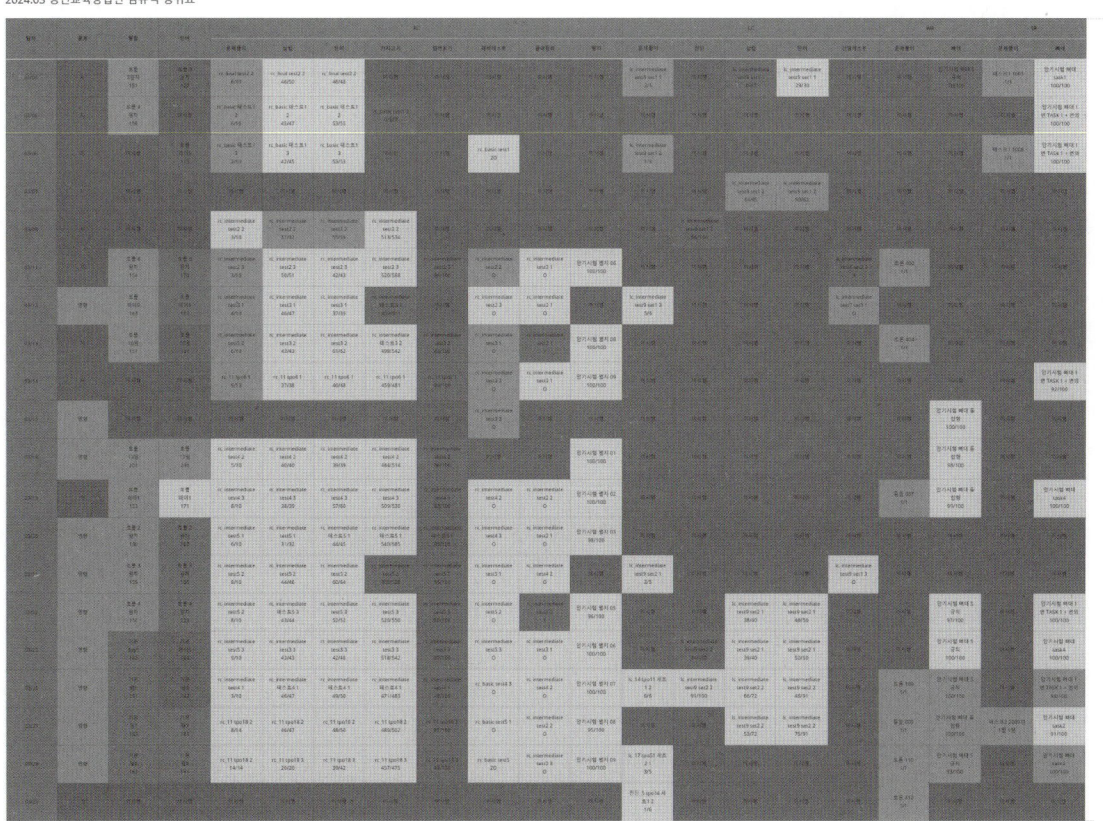

마이페이지 MYPAGE

배치고사 신청/결과확인	예습공지 게시판	수강증 확인	교재 확인하기	증명서 발급
사물함 안내	무료교재 mp3/부록	토익특강 성적표	쿠폰함	사물함 신청

김유석님 반갑습니다 회원정보수정

온라인클래스 강의창 테스트

수강중인 강의 / 반별게시판	결제 진행중인 강의	결제내역	장바구니	교재확인 / 배송조회
0건	0건	20건	0건	0건
자세히 보기	자세히 보기	자세히 보기	자세히 보기	자세히 보기

▍처음 학원에 들어올 때 시작 했던 반
2024년 02월 성인 정규 Intermediate반

▍수강 했던반 / 총 개월수
2024년 02월 성인 정규 Intermediate반
2024년 03월 성인 정규 Intermediate반
2024년 04월 성인 정규 K1반

▍학원에 오기전에 가지고 있었던 점수 (파트별)
- 토익점수_ 합계 : 0 RC : 0 LC : 0
- 토플점수_ 합계 : 70 RC : 19 LC : 18 SP : 13 WR : 20

▍목표했던 토플 점수
100점

▍취득한 토플 점수
RC: 28 LC: 22 SP: 20 WR: 27

▍최초/중간/ 최종
- 최초_ 합계 : 70 RC : 19 LC : 18 SP : 13 WR : 20
- 중간_ 2024-01-23 배치고사 SW:22, RC:25, LC:0
  2024-02-16 모의고사 RC:22, LC:19, SP:0, WR:0
  2024-02-29 배치고사 SW:22, RC:28, LC:22
  2024-03-15 모의고사 RC:17, LC:25, SP:19, WR:20
  2024-03-29 배치고사 SW:28, RC:32, LC:23
- 최종_ RC: 0 LC: 0 SP: 0 WR: 0

▍토플 공부한 이유(학업 이유)
일본유학(EJU)

▌파트별 상세 설명

• Reading

제가 가장 나댈수 있는 영역입니다.

저는 한 달동안 삼지문 -> 인터 -> K반 까지 승반했었던 유일한 사람이기에, 현재 인터반 학생들이 주의깊게 봤으면 합니다. 다만 한가지 전제조건은, 저는 원래 문해력으로 승부보는 사람이었다는 점입니다. 즉 지문 이해력은 높으나, 영어해석능력이 부족해서 RC영역에서 고생했다는 점을 말해두고 싶습니다.

우선 첫 달은, 영어를 읽고 푸는데에 대한 '자신감', 그리고 긴 문장을 만났을때 '익숙함' 에 중요성에 대해서 배웠습니다. 혜성쌤 께서 강조하신 '오늘 푼 지문 10번 읽기' 과제를 다 하진 못했었으나, 세번씩이라도 읽다보니, 모르는 단어가 나오거나, 긴 문장을 봤을때 느끼는 자신감이 상당히 올라갔고, 정답률 또한 올라갔습니다. 그러나, 아직 이 시기에서는, 문장 직독직해의 수준이 낮은상태였으며, 주어진 시간안에 한 지문을 읽는것이 불안했습니다.

두 번째 달에는, 사실상 제 RC영역에 가장 큰 영향을 주신 김석균 선생님의 수업을 들었습니다.

선생님의 가르침 하에서 선생님이 강조하시는, 그리고 제가 느끼는 중요성의 순서는 다음과 같습니다.

1. 수업시간에 선생님께서 워드에 정리하고, 수업 후에 올려주시는 메모를 빠르게 기억하고 넘어가기 입니다.

>> 각 지문 테마 별, 자주 나오는 단어나 표현들이 익숙해지기 때문에, 다음 번, 비슷한 지문을 만났을 때, 읽는 속도와 정확성, 자신감이 매우 다릅니다.

2. 묶기 빠르게 할 것***

묶기를 연구해가며 하지마세요. 묶기는 하나의 시험입니다. 문장 내에서, 본인이 약한 문법의 영역을 파악할 수 있는 부분이기 때문에, 빠르게 풀 되, 묶기의 결과를 잘 살펴보고, 메모를 남겨둡시다. 특히 토플 RC에서 등위접속사 and, or 과 같은 문법을 다르게 읽는다면, 해석이 전혀 다른 내용이 되기 때문에 지문 이해에 큰 방해가 될 것 입니다.

3. 해석테스트

토플의 RC는 사실 이해를 하지 못한다고 해도, 70프로의 정답률을 보장할 수 있는 시험이라고 생각합니다.

그 이유로는, 어차피 문제에서 물어보는것은 지문의 특정 부분에 관해서 이고, 지문을 한번 읽었을때 기억을 살려, 빠르게 문제에서 요구하는 부분을 지문에서 찾기만 한다면, 정답률 또한 상당히 올라갈 것 입니다.

다만, 지문을 읽고 기억하는데에 있어서, 중요한 능력이 직독직해라고 생각합니다. 토플은 영어단어 바꿔넣기의 시험. 즉 영어를 잘한다는 느낌보다, 유의어 단어나 표현을 얼마나 알고있는지를 묻기에, 기계적인 암기능력을 요구한다고 생각합니다.

그렇기 때문에, 직독직해가 된다면, 유의어가 페러프라이징 된 선지를 고를수 있기때문에, 정답률이 올라갑니다.

또한, 결정적으로 직독직해를 잘 하게 된다면, 영어문장을 빠르게 읽게 되기 때문에, 시간안에 문제를 다 읽고 푸는것이 가능해 진다고 생각합니다. 이런 직독직해능력을 기를 수 있고, 내 상태를 점검할 수 있는 해석테스트를 열심히 준비합시다.

4. 네 번째로 제가 생각하는 석균쌤의 RC포인트 + 어셔에서 가장 중요하게 강요하는 부분인 단어 입니다.

어셔를 다니면서 단어시험은 가장 큰 스트레스중 하나라고 생각합니다. 우선 학원측에서 단어암기를 하라고 과제를 내주면, 암기조차 안하는 학생들이 있기 때문에, 인터반 기준 200개중 180개의 빡센 목표를 요구하는 것 같습니다.

다만 제 생각으론, 단어를 암기하는데에 있어 가장 중요한것은 200개중 180개로 통과해서 초록불을 띄우는 것이 아니라, 내가 한번 본 단어의 뉘양스를 얼마나 파악했는지 입니다.

아마 저와 수업을 들어보신 분들은 공감하시겠지만, 석균쌤이 수업중에 나온 단어에 대해 동의어를 물어보실 때, 가장 대답을 잘하는 학생이 저 였을 것입니다. 하지만, 반면에 3월달 VOCA 성취율이 가장 낮은 학생도 저라고 생각합니다. 매번 160~170개로 180개를 통과하지 못한이 허다했거든요.

하지만 그렇다고해서 저는 단어공부의 시간을 줄인적이 없습니다. 대신 낯선 단어가 갖고있는 의미, 그리고 동의어, 이 단어가 어떤 주제의 지문에서 나오는가 에 초점을 맞췄습니다.

그와 반대로, 단어시험 통과율이 엄청 높으신 분들 혹은, 학원을 오랫동안 다니신 분들에게 있어, RC의 점수를 큰 폭으로 향상시키는 대에 방해되는것이 바로 180개 제한 통과방식인것 같습니다. 160개에서 180개로 단어시험 정답률을 높이기 위해선, 한글뜻에 초점을 맞추게 되고, 그러다보면, RC지문에서 만난 낯선 단어를 빠르게 의미를 떠올리는데에 딜레이가 생길 것 입니다. 물론 우선 단어의 익숙함을 줄이고, RC지문에서 만났을 때, 자신감 있게 한글로 해석할 수 있다면, RC의 한 지문을 읽는데에 유의미한 정답률 상승이 있다고 생각합니다. 그렇기 때문에, 단어를 열심히 외우시고, 통과를 잘하는 분들이라면, 지문에서 모르는 단어가 나왔을때는, 남들도 모르는 단어라고 생각하고 일단 자신감 있게 읽고 넘어가셔야 한 지문을 넘어 RC, RC를 넘어 LC, SPK, WRT까지,, 나머지 영역에도 전반적인 영향을 주는 자신감을 잃지 않을 수 있습니다. 그렇기에 본인의 자신감을 유지하는데에 가장 중요한 단어를 소홀히 하시지 마시길 바랍니다.

마지막으로 제 어셔에서의 토플 기간동안 가장 중요했던 3월달 첫 주 "삼지문 반" 입니다.

삼지문반을 수강함으로써, RC에서의 제 단점을 확실히 파악하는것이 가능했습니다.

수강후기 Reading 영역 첫 문두 에서도 말했다시피, 저는 상대적으로 감각적인 문해력을 가진 반면에, 영어를 한국말로 옮기는 부분에 대해서 많이 부족했었습니다. 그러다보니 제가 이해를 할 수 있는 지문들에 대해서는 70% 까지의 정답률을 보장했으나, 이해가 되지않는 주제에 관해서는 그야말로 처참했었죠..

그러다 원장님이 삼지문반 승반테스트를 진행하시고, RC영역에 대해서 설명해주실때, 그야말로 광명을 찾았습니다.

RC = R+C, 즉, Reading +comprehension 이라는 말, Reading 이 7, Comprehension이 3의 비율을 갖는다는 것을 듣고 나서야 비로소, 그때서야 제 단점이 Reading (직독직해) 라는 점에 대해 확신할 수 있었습니다.

그 이후로는, 인터반 -> 삼지문반으로 하반당했다는 압박을 머금고 친한 동료들 경선이와 건우형과 함께 세가지 지문 부수기에 목숨 걸었습니다. 저의 지문 이해력과 설명 + 경선, 건우의 직독직해 설명이 서로에게 큰 시너지를 주었습니다. 3월의 첫 주에 삼지문 반을 경험한 것이, 지속적인 제 RC점수의 상승에 포문을 열었다고 생각합니다.

그렇게 터프하게 학원 불 꺼져도 11시 반까지 공부하다가 보니 한 가지 재미있는 일화도 남겼던것이 기억에 남네요 ㅋㅋㅋ
원장님이 퇴근하시다가 어둠속에서 공부하던 저와 소연, 경선의 공부하는 동영상을 찍어가신것, 채운쌤께서도 퇴근 하시다가 저희를 발견하시고 기분좋아하셨던 그런것들이 저희에게도 큰 원동력이 되었던 것 같습니다.

다시 궤도로 돌아와서 정리하자면, 삼지문 반을 거쳐, 3월 모의토플 이전까지 문제풀이및 석균쌤의 수업에 익숙해졌고, 3월 셋째 주부터 RC점수가 팍 뛰더니 변동기에 들어오기 시작한 것 같습니다. 그리고 3월 이후 어셔에서의 생활을 마무리 하려던 찰나, 석균쌤과 채운쌤의 설득과 조언에 못이겨 4/2, 4/3의 수업도 듣게 되었고, 이 기간에 RC 고득점 평탄화가 이뤄져, 저를 하여금 어셔에서 졸업을 하도록 만들어 준 것 같습니다.

마무리로, 쌤들 말 안듣는 친구들에게도 한마디 하자면, 자기 멋대로 공부를 하려면 우선 쌤들이 시킨것부터 끝내고 하는것은 어떨까요? 석균쌤의 말씀대로, 제 RC점수가 상승하고 안정된 시기는, 어셔의 syllabus를 다 채우는데 성공한 시점부터라는 점을 알아주셨음 합니다.

- Listening

저에게 있어서, 시험 한번한번의 변동이 가장 큰 과목입니다.
모의토플 에서는 25점도 맞아보았고, 수업시간에 풀었던 문제는 컨버 렉쳐 렉쳐 다 맞은 적도 있었던것을 비추어 볼 때,
듣기의 고점 자체를 한번 끌어올리는데에는 성공했다고 생각됩니다.
먼저 그렇게 끌어올리는데 성공했던 이유를 생각해 보면

첫째. 채운쌤의 세뇌.
질문과 답변 위주로 들어라, 고유명사 연도 는 꼭 적어라, 동사위주로 들어라, 예시는 예시가 나온이유, 그것에 대한 결과를 들어야 한다,, 노트테이킹은 왼쪽에서 오른쪽으로 해라.
사실 더 많은데,, 신입분들은 수업료 내고 들으시라고 여기까지만 !! / 기존 학생들은 본인들이 메모했던 내용들을 한번 정리한다음, WRT통합형의 파이브룰즈 처럼 달달 외우는 것을 추천합니다.

둘째. 디스커버리 유튜브채널의 영상 "마지막 알레스카인" 반복 청취.
1시간 46분짜리 몰아보기 영상을 매 대중교통에서, 집안일 할때, 밥먹을때 반복해서 들었을 시기가 LC점수가 가장 잘 나왔던 시기입니다. 저는 시골출신에, 서바이벌에 관심이 많아 재밌게 봤던 영상인데, 토플 bio지문에 나오는 단어들을 귀로 반복해서 들었던것이 상당히 고무적 이었습니다. 시각을 이용해서 공부하지 않는 시간에는 꼭 귀라도 영어로 채워두길 바랍니다.

셋째. 딕테이션을 단어 단어 단어 적고, 중간에 비었던 부분을 다시 매꾸는 것이 아니라, 영어를 한 뭉탱이 단위로 듣고 적었을 때, 내용이 가장 잘 들렸고, 그러다 보니 노트 위에도 적어야 하는 내용만 적을 수 있어서, 정답률이 높았던 것 같습니다. 채운쌤이 말하시는 딕테이션의 방식 1단계 2단계 3단계를 잘 수행하시길 바랍니다.

다만, 더 높은 점수를 내지 못한 이유에는

첫째. 어셔에 있는 도중, 리스닝 자습에 시간을 많이 쓰지 못한것.
RC와 LC는 몇번 고점을 찍는것이 가능하다면, 그 이후에는 점수의 변동을 잡아주는것이 중요하다고 생각하는데, 이 변동을 잡는것에 시간을 투자하지 못한것 같아서 아쉽습니다.

둘째. 노트테이킹을 점점 많이 적게 된 것.
노트테이킹의 양에 대해서도, 선생님들마다 다르지만, 저는 적게 적었을때가 오히려 더 정답률이 높았습니다.
단순하게 내용을 많이 적은것은, 디테일을 놓칠 확률이 큽니다.

셋째. 단기기억 기르는 연습을 게을리 함.
영어는 한국말처럼 단어만 투욱 툭 던져서는 의미가 만들어지지 않는다고 선생님들이 많이 말씀하십니다.
그렇다면 영어를 잘 듣기위해선, 언어 하나의 덩어리가 어디부터 어디까지인지 인식을 하고, 기억을 하고있어야 합니다.
청취테스트 연습을 부지런히 한다면, 본인이 들은 한 덩어리 덩어리가, 잘 기억에 남고, LC정답률 상향에 크게 기여할 것 같습니다.
LC영역에서 저의 결론은 "문제풀이 방식에 시간을 쏟지 맙시다" 라는 것입니다. 토플 리스닝 특성 상, 내용이 잘 들리고, 디테일을 기억하거나 노트에 옮겨적는다면 문제는 어지간히 다 맞을 것 이라 생각합니다.

- Speaking

4과목 중 가장 낮은 점수를 맞아서 가장 할말이 적습니다. 뼈대 잘 외우고, 12간지 잘 외우고, 리스닝영역 문장단위로 적고!! 이 삼박자가 맞지 않고서는 의미있는 점수를 낼 수 없다고 생각합니다. 토플이 단과시험이 아니고, 여러 영역을 요구하는 만큼, 전체의 성적을 끌어올리기 위해선, 무리를 해서라도 하루에 스피킹 하나정도 녹음하는것을 추천드립니다.

두번째로 스피킹 1번과 같은경우 암기가 끝이 아니고, 주어진 주제문에 대해 뼈대와 12간지를 변형시키는 유연함 도 길러야한다는 점 잊지 말아주세요.

저 같은 경우, 솔직히 유연하게 대처하는 연습이 소홀했기 때문에, 걍 논리 안맞는 문장나와도 자신있게 어거지로 밀고 들어갔습니다. 그래서 20점이라도 나오지 않았나 싶어요..
자신있게 어거지로 밀고가서 20점이라도 확보하려면 뼈대 + 12간지를 반드시 외워야 할 것입니다.

- Writing

4과목중 가장 의외인 점수를 가져다준 고마운 과목입니다. 사실 WRT이 고맙기보단 당연히 채운쌤께 너무 감사드립니다..
스피킹과 더불어 공부량이 적었던 과목인데, 왜 27점이 나왔을까요??...
바로 제 WRT점수가 12간지와 파이브룰스에 위대함을 다시금 증명했다고 생각합니다.
물론 저도 작전을 세우긴 했는데,, 그게 12간지의 위대함과 더불어 잘 들어맞았네요.
제 작전은, 제가 많은 내용을 생산할 수록, 문법과 스펠링 미스가 많아져서, WRT의 총점을 깎을것이라 예상해서, 안전빵 문장들만 가져다 적었습니다. 절때 어렵게 쓰려고 하지 마시고, 본인만의 예시 뼈대를 만들고, 12간지에 기대어 최대한 문장을 간단하게 쓰는것을 추천드립니다.

- 어셔의 관리 프로그램 (asap프로그램) 관련 사용 팁

점수 취득 후 얻게된 결과
1) 한번 실패를 맛 보았던 토플에서 성공을 거둔것.
매번 꿈에 나오던 학창시절 담당일진을 길에서 만나 뚜드려 팬것과 동일한 기분이지 않을까요??
2) 자신감
내 인생에 있어서 가장 높았던 벽 '토플'을 넘었기 때문에,, 앞으로 못할건 하나도 없을것 같다는 근자감

저는 ○○스에서 1년 이상의 시간과 돈을 써가며 영어의 5형식부터 공부했었습니다. ○○스의 기본문법 교실은 to부정사가 뭔지 모르는 저에게는 꽤나 재미있고 이해가 잘 갔던 수업이었죠.
그러나 문제는 ○○스 토플 커리큘럼에 들어가면서 시작입니다. 제가 생각한 ○○스 토플의 문제를 순서대로 나열하자면,
1) 영어 기초반에서 토플 기초반으로 넘어갈 때, 간극이 꽤 크다.
>> 단어 요구량이 너무 차이나기 때문에, 영어 기초반에서 공부한 뒤 바로 토플 기초반수업 못따라갑니다.
2) 영어실력의 "근본"을 경시한다.
>> 이게 가장 큰 문제라고 생각합니다. 특히, 만약 이글을 보는 본인의 목표가 80점 이상이라면.
제 생각으론, ○○스의 '입문+인터미디엇' 반의 수준이, 어셔의 '완초 1~2반' 이랑 비슷합니다.
근데 차이점이 있다면, ○○스에서는 딱 그정도의 영어수준을 지닌 학생들이 그 상태에서 점수를 잘 내도록 교과과정이 맞춰져 있습니다. 그말은 즉, 더 높은 점수대로 도전하는 "근본"을 쌓는데에 아 무 런 도움이 되지 않는 다는 점입니다.
본인이 영어가 안읽히고, 안들려도.. 그 상태에서 점수를 내게 알려주는 방법이 ○○스식 입니다.
이 방식으로는 저같이 영어의 "근본"이 없는 학생들에게 있어서 90점대의 아성에 도전할수가 없습니다.
3)각 과목 선생님들이 다르고, 같은 과목의 선생님들도 너무 많다.
>> 템플릿 다 난리납니다. 같은 과목의 선생님들 마다 말이 아 다르고 어 다릅니다.
각 과목의 선생님들의 목소리가 너무 큽니다. 수업시간 40~50분의 짧은 시간에 수업을 듣기 위해서, 하루 과목당 4~5시간 정도의 자습량을 요구합니다. 즉, 토플 4과목의 과제를 마치지 않는다면, 수업을 듣는 의미가 없습니다.
○○스 다녀보신 분들 수업 1주차 부터 같은 교실에 사람들이 적어지는것을 경험했거나, 혹은 본인이 점점 수업에 참여를 못하게 되는 학생이셨죠?
그~러~니, 어셔를 토플 학원에 안중을 넣고 계신 분이라면, 혹은 지금 다니고 계신 분이라면 영어의 "근본"을 쌓기위해서 어떻게 해야하나 열심히 고민해보세요. 공부법에 최첨단 방식은 없습니다.
암기, 반복, 직독직해 이런 무식 하다고 여겨지는 공부가 아직도 사용 되는 이유는 '전통적' 이기 때문입니다. 전통이 전통으로 이어져 온 것에는 그것이 최선책 이어왔기 때문입니다.
학생분들의 뇌는 그저, 때려 넣는것만 생각하시고, 학원에서 시키는것에 대해 의문을 가지지좀 마세요.
그렇게 본인이 학원보다 좋은방법을 알고 있었다면, 지금 이 후기를 볼 일도 없을 테니까요.
뇌의 사용량을 다른데 투자할 것 없이, 내용을 집어넣는 것에만 집중한다는것이 얼마나 효율적입니까?
대신, 학원이 이걸 왜 시키는걸까? 에 대해서만 '고민' 수준에서 머물도록 하는것을 추천합니다..
어셔 어학원에서의 시간들을 돌이켜보며...
어셔에서의 두 달은 제 수명 1~2년을 끌어쓴다는 느낌으로 지냈습니다.
1) 수면은 두달동안 평균 5시간 안넘을거라 생각하구요,,
2) 점심또한 편의점 삼각김밥만 먹어서 소화장애 심각했었죠..
같이 공부했던 친구들은 알겠지만 제 말버릇 중 하나가 소화안되서 죽을것같다..
위생천/까스활명수 마셔야겠다 아마 지겹도록 들었을 것입니다

근데 할만했습니다.. 어셔에서 토플은 공부라기 보단, 하나의 팀 스포츠라고 생각합니다. 매일같이 남아서 동료들과 훈련을 하고, 스스로의 한계를 극복하고, 결과로써 증명한다. 이렇게 생각했기 때문에 어셔에서 상당히 즐거운 시간을 보낼 수 있었습니다.
인생에서 무언가를 위해 몰두하는 경험을 쌓기위해 최적의 환경을 잘 조성해주신 원장님, 그리고 채운쌤과 석균쌤, 해성쌤과 같이 교사진들의 엄청난 하드워킹.. 어셔에서의 두 달은 진정한 낙수효과에 대해서도 느끼게 해준 것 같습니다.
저는 두 달하고 빠질생각으로 다녔기 때문에 제가 열심히 해야하는건 당연했구요..
그런데도 불구하고 나를 가르치는 선생님들은 몇년씩 이 생활을 반복하고 있다는 사실을 생각해 본다면,, 적어도 본인이 어셔에 있는 동안은 그들보다 열심히 해야한다는걸 잊지마세요.

■ 어셔생활백서

[1] 밥집:
1) 먹고싶은것 없으면 "감미옥" - 시간은 금입니다. 가장 가까운 복합 한식 분식집이며, 맛 또한 일대에서 상위권입니다. 만약 사장님께 아양을 잘 떤다면, 공짜 밥 무한리필도 가능합니다.
2) 먹고싶은것 없고, 감미옥이 질린다면 "KFC" (도보 왕복 약 8분)
3) 학원 MZ세대들이 아마,, 제일 좋아할 김치볶음밥&돈까스 "하트타임" (KFC 근처)
4) 든든한 국밥 "장터순대국" (KFC 아랫층)
5) "뉴코아 킴스클럽" 푸드코드: 가지마세요 시간 다 뺏깁니다. (도보 왕복 약 16분)
>> 참고로 점심은 빠르게 편의점에서 드시고 구문/단어, 묶기 하세요.. 시간은 금입니다.

[2] 자습실 (=학원 오픈시간)
1) 평일: 매일 아침 7시 30분 안에 열리고, 오후 11시 ~ 11시 30분에 닫힙니다.
2) 주말: 주 마다 쌤들께 여쭤보세요. 열릴때도, 안 열릴때도 있습니다.
>> 토플 학원의 학원비는 결코 싸지 않습니다. 최대한 학원의 전기, 수도, 난방 비용을 털어간다는 생각으로 남으세요.

[3] 대인관계:
제 생각으로 어셔에서 공부 다음으로 중요한 영역같습니다. 얼굴을 본 기억이 있는 사람과 마주친다면 정중히 인사부터 나눕시다. 특히, 열심히 하는 학생이 있다면, 혹은 점수를 잘 내는 친구가 있다면 잘 보고 배웁시다.

■ Thanks to

1) 경선.. 어셔가 나에게 선물한 가장 친한 친구.. 덕분에 어셔 너무 재미있게 다녔다... 나도 가끔 너무힘들고 맨탈 흔들릴때 있었는데, 그때마다 경선이의 활기랑 에너지가 나아갈 힘을 계속해서 준것같아.. 진짜 너 없었으면 쉽게 졸업하기 힘들었을것같아 너무고맙다 경선아. 빠르게 졸업하고 서로 남은 한국에서의 목표한 바를 완수한 다음에 또 신나게 놀아보자

2) 소연.. 아마 본인은 모르실 것 같은데, 소연님이 제 점수가 오르는데 1등 공신이십니다.. 소연님 분석을 꽤 했거든요 ㅋㅋㅋ 소연님 같은 분이랑 수업을 들을수 있었던것이 진짜 엄청난 행운이었습니다. 그리고 왜 또 공부는 그렇게 열심히 하시는지.. 서로 각자의 위치로 돌아간다음에도 잊지말고 자주 연락해요. (콩고물 얻어먹을라니까)

3) 환준.. 같은 일유생의 키즈나.. 인터에서 K반으로 넘어간 동료이자 산책 나카마... 뭐 우리는 일본에서 끈덕지게 볼것같으니 짧게 씀

4) 건우.. 건우햄 행동력 하나는 진짜 끝내줍니다.. 사실 저도 제 친구들 사이에서 미친행동력으로 비난과 감탄 둘다 받는데 형은 그 이상인 것 같아요.. F-k ng 트래블러 건우형. 저도 여행 좋아하니까 아프리카 정도 아니면 한번 같이 가는것도 좋을지도 ..?

5) 혜성.. 경선, 건우와 더불어 삼지문 -> 인터반의 동료.. 혜성님 힘들어 하시다가 저랑 경선이가 혜성님 웃게 만들었을때 상당히 성취감 있었습니다. 그리고 제가 생각하는 가장 빨리 졸업할 것 같은 맴버 3명중 한 분이십니다. 자신감 잃지마시고 토플 부수기 기원합니다.

6) 인터반 친구들
졸업하고 하느라 교실의 분위기도 많이 달라졌지만,, 다들 함께 할 수 있었기 때문에 토플이라는 거대한 압박 안에서 나름 즐겁게 보냈던것 같습니다.. 2월달에 인터반의 화목하고 재미난 분위기를 만들어두고 가신 하륜이형, 동훈이형도 너무 감사드리고,, 수업시간에 저랑 경선이가 어떻게보면 수업을 방해할 수도 있을 수준에 헛소리를 해도 다들 웃고 넘어가주셔서 감사합니다. 모두 목표한 바를 이루시길 기원합니다.

김유석 어셔졸업 일등공신 채운쌤:
처음에 상담할 시기부터 제 토플공부에 가장 크게 기여해주셨다는 점 알아주셨음 합니다 ㅋㅋㅋ
선생님만 믿고 다른생각 안한 덕에, 기대하지 않은 좋은 점수를 만들 수 있었던 것 같아요.. 비록 처음 반 배치가 완초 2반으로 떨어졌지만, 쌤 께서 2달안에 졸업하려면, 힘들더라도 인터반이 좋을수 있다고 조언해주신 덕에, 인터반에서 기분좋은 시작을 할 수 있었습니다. 그리고 또 가끔 제 기강이 해이해질 타이밍에 완벽히, 교실 전체에 기강 다져주신것도 큰 도움이 되었습니다 ㅋㅋㅋㅋㅋ
12간지야 뭐 말하는거 입아프구요.. 저는 선생님께서 단순히 '선생님'이라는 직책을 빼고도 '김채운'이라는 훌륭한 사람을 만난것에 대해 좋은 경험한 것 같습니다. 하지만 건강도 잘 챙기셔서 롱런하셨음 좋겠어요 ㅋㅋ 채운쌤 너무 감사합니다 !!

석균쌤:
가끔 편한길 찾고싶어서 쌤한테 시도할때마다 본전도 못찾고 깨진 기억들이 떠오르네요.. 덕분에 정신차리고 공부했습니다 쌤.ㅋㅋㅋ
어셔 한달 더 다니고 싶었던 가장 큰 이유가 바로 석균쌤의 수업이었는데,, 다행히도 금방 졸업을 했네요...
그리고 리딩 테마별로 지문 별 문제풀이 순서를 직접 고안하셨는지는 모르겠지만,, 테마별 리딩 문제풀이 순서가 너무 도움됐습니다.. 딱 우주에 대해 잊어먹었을 즈음에 복습시키고,, 슬슬 적응되던 테마에서 벗어나서 낯선거 풀게시키고.. 그 외에도 쌤께 고마운거 많지만 이만 줄이겠습니다. 쌤은 쿨하시니까요 ~

조교쌤들도 너무 감사했습니다 !! 특히 예림쌤, 유하쌤, 명준쌤,, 매번 해태할때마다 답답하셨을텐데,, 저였으면 좀 화났을수도 있엇을 것 같은데, 친절하게 질문받아주시고 너무 감사했습니다 !!!